FORD | ASPIRE
1994-97 REPAIR MANUAL

D1085561

CHILTON™

President	Dean F. Morgantini, S.A.E.
Vice President–Finance	Barry L. Beck
Vice President–Sales	Glenn D. Potere
Executive Editor	Kevin M. G. Maher
Production Manager	Ben Greisler, S.A.E.
Production Assistant	Melinda Possinger
Project Managers	George B. Heinrich III, S.A.E., Will Kessler, A.S.E., S.A.E., James R. Marotta, S.T.S., Richard Schwartz, Todd W. Stidham
Schematics Editor	Christopher G. Ritchie
Editor	Thomas A. Mellon, S.A.E.

CHILTON™ *Automotive Books*

PUBLISHED BY **W. G. NICHOLS, INC.**

Manufactured in USA
© 1998 W. G. Nichols
1020 Andrew Drive
West Chester, PA 19380
ISBN 0-8019-8972-8
Library of Congress Catalog Card No. 98-71351
1234567890 7654321098

629
C538
ASPIRE
cop.1

Contents

22.95
9/30/98
RJJ

Contents

DRIVE TRAIN   **7**

SUSPENSION AND STEERING   **8**

BRAKES   **9**

BODY AND TRIM   **10**

GLOSSARY

MASTER INDEX

SAFETY NOTICE

Proper service and repair procedures are vital to the safe, reliable operation of all motor vehicles, as well as the personal safety of those performing repairs. This manual outlines procedures for servicing and repairing vehicles using safe, effective methods. The procedures contain many NOTES, CAUTIONS and WARNINGS which should be followed, along with standard procedures to eliminate the possibility of personal injury or improper service which could damage the vehicle or compromise its safety.

It is important to note that repair procedures and techniques, tools and parts for servicing motor vehicles, as well as the skill and experience of the individual performing the work vary widely. It is not possible to anticipate all of the conceivable ways or conditions under which vehicles may be serviced, or to provide cautions as to all possible hazards that may result. Standard and accepted safety precautions and equipment should be used when handling toxic or flammable fluids, and safety goggles or other protection should be used during cutting, grinding, chiseling, prying, or any other process that can cause material removal or projectiles.

Some procedures require the use of tools specially designed for a specific purpose. Before substituting another tool or procedure, you must be completely satisfied that neither your personal safety, nor the performance of the vehicle will be endangered.

Although information in this manual is based on industry sources and is complete as possible at the time of publication, the possibility exists that some car manufacturers made later changes which could not be included here. While striving for total accuracy, NP/Chilton cannot assume responsibility for any errors, changes or omissions that may occur in the compilation of this data.

PART NUMBERS

Part numbers listed in this reference are not recommendations by Chilton for any product brand name. They are references that can be used with interchange manuals and aftermarket supplier catalogs to locate each brand supplier's discrete part number.

SPECIAL TOOLS

Special tools are recommended by the vehicle manufacturer to perform their specific job. Use has been kept to a minimum, but where absolutely necessary, they are referred to in the text by the part number of the tool manufacturer. These tools can be purchased, under the appropriate part number, from your local dealer or regional distributor, or an equivalent tool can be purchased locally from a tool supplier or parts outlet. Before substituting any tool for the one recommended, read the SAFETY NOTICE at the top of this page.

ACKNOWLEDGMENTS

NP/Chilton expresses appreciation to Ford Motor Company for their generous assistance.

A special thanks to the fine companies who supported the production of this book. Hand tools, supplied by Craftsman, were used during all phases of vehicle teardown and photography. A Rotary lift, the largest automobile lift manufacturer in the world offering the biggest variety of surface and inground lifts available, was also used.

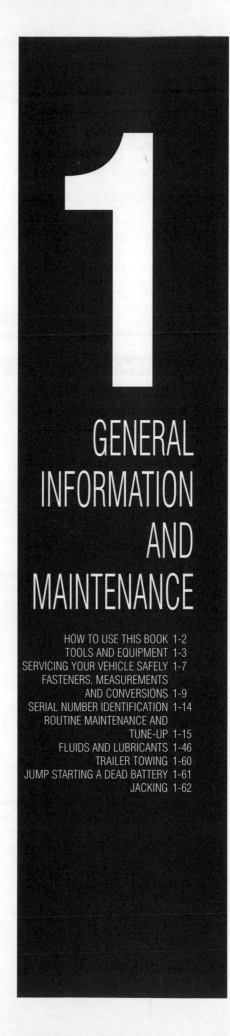

1
GENERAL INFORMATION AND MAINTENANCE

HOW TO USE THIS BOOK

Chilton's Total Car Care manual for the Aspire is intended to help you learn more about the inner workings of your vehicle while saving you money on its upkeep and operation.

The beginning of the book will likely be referred to the most, since that is where you will find information for maintenance and tune-up. The other sections deal with the more complex systems of your vehicle. Operating systems from engine through brakes are covered to the extent that the average do-it-yourselfer becomes mechanically involved. This book will not explain such things as rebuilding a differential for the simple reason that the expertise required and the investment in special tools make this task uneconomical. It will, however, give you detailed instructions to help you change your own brake pads and shoes, replace spark plugs, and perform many more jobs that can save you money, give you personal satisfaction and help you avoid expensive problems.

A secondary purpose of this book is a reference for owners who want to understand their vehicle and/or their mechanics better. In this case, no tools at all are required.

Where to Begin

Before removing any bolts, read through the entire procedure. This will give you the overall view of what tools and supplies will be required. There is nothing more frustrating than having to walk to the bus stop on Monday morning because you were short one bolt on Sunday afternoon. So read ahead and plan ahead. Each operation should be approached logically and all procedures thoroughly understood before attempting any work.

All sections contain adjustments, maintenance, removal & installation procedures and, in some cases, repair or overhaul procedures. When repair is not considered practical, we tell you how to remove the part and then how to install the new or rebuilt replacement. In this way, you at least save the labor costs. Backyard repair of some components is just not practical.

Avoiding Trouble

Many procedures in this book require you to "label and disconnect . . ." a group of lines, hoses or wires. Don't be lulled into thinking you can remember where everything goes—you won't. If you hook up vacuum or fuel lines incorrectly, the vehicle will run poorly, if at all. If you hook up electrical wiring incorrectly, you may instantly learn a very expensive lesson.

You don't need to know the official or engineering name for each hose or line. A piece of masking tape on the hose and a piece on its fitting will allow you to assign your own label such as the letter A or a short name. As long as you remember your own code, the lines can be reconnected by matching similar letters or names. Do remember that tape will dissolve in gasoline or other fluids; if a component is to be washed or cleaned, use another method of identification. A permanent felt-tipped marker can be very handy for marking metal parts. Remove any tape or paper labels after assembly.

Maintenance or Repair?

It's necessary to mention the difference between maintenance and repair. Maintenance includes routine inspections, adjustments, and replacement of parts which show signs of normal wear. Maintenance compensates for wear or deterioration. Repair implies that something has broken or is not working. A need for repair is often caused by lack of maintenance. Example: draining and refilling the automatic transmission fluid is maintenance recommended by the manufacturer at specific mileage intervals. Failure to do this can ruin the transmission/transaxle, requiring very expensive repairs. While no maintenance program can prevent items from breaking or wearing out, a general rule can be stated: MAINTENANCE IS CHEAPER THAN REPAIR.

Two basic mechanic's rules should be mentioned here. First, whenever the left side of the vehicle or engine is referred to, it is meant to specify the driver's side. Conversely, the right side of the vehicle means the passenger's side. Second, most screws and bolts are removed by turning counterclockwise, and tightened by turning clockwise.

Safety is always the most important rule. Constantly be aware of the dangers involved in working on an automobile and take the proper precautions. See the information in this section regarding SERVICING YOUR VEHICLE SAFELY and the SAFETY NOTICE on the acknowledgment page.

Avoiding the Most Common Mistakes

Pay attention to the instructions provided. There are 3 common mistakes in mechanical work:

1. Incorrect order of assembly, disassembly or adjustment. When taking something apart or putting it together, performing steps in the wrong order usually just costs you extra time; however, it CAN break something. Read the entire procedure before beginning disassembly. Perform everything in the order in which the instructions say you should, even if you can't immediately see a reason for it. When you're taking apart something that is very intricate, you might want to draw a picture of how it looks when assembled at one point in order to make sure you get everything back in its proper position. We will supply exploded views whenever possible. When making adjustments, perform them in the proper order; often, one adjustment affects another, and you cannot expect even satisfactory results unless each adjustment is made only when it cannot be changed by any other.

2. Overtorquing (or undertorquing). While it is more common for overtorquing to cause damage, undertorquing may allow a fastener to vibrate loose causing serious damage. Especially when dealing with aluminum parts, pay attention to torque specifications and utilize a torque wrench in assembly. If a torque figure is not available, remember that if you are using the right tool to perform the job, you will probably not have to strain yourself to get a fastener tight enough. The pitch of most threads is so slight that the tension you put on the wrench will be multiplied many times in actual force on what you are tightening. A good example of how critical torque is can be seen in the case of spark plug installation, especially where you are putting the plug into an aluminum cylinder head. Too little torque can fail to crush the gasket, causing leakage of combustion gases and consequent overheating of the plug and engine parts. Too much torque can damage the threads or distort the plug, changing the spark gap.

There are many commercial products available for ensuring that fasteners won't come loose, even if they are not torqued just right (a very common brand is Loctite®). If you're worried about getting something together tight enough to hold, but loose enough to avoid mechanical damage during assembly, one of these products might offer substantial insurance. Before choosing a threadlocking compound, read the label on the package and make sure the product is compatible with the materials, fluids, etc. involved.

3. Crossthreading. This occurs when a part such as a bolt is screwed into a nut or casting at the wrong angle and forced. Crossthreading is more likely to occur if access is difficult. It helps to clean and lubricate fasteners, then to start threading with the part to be installed positioned straight in. Then, start the bolt, spark plug, etc. with your fingers. If you encounter resistance, unscrew the part and start over again at a different angle until it can be inserted and turned several times without much effort. Keep in mind that many parts, especially spark plugs, have tapered threads, so that gentle turning will automatically bring the part you're threading to the proper angle, but only if you don't force it or resist a change in angle. Don't put a wrench on the part until it's been tightened a couple of turns by hand. If you suddenly encounter resistance, and the part has not seated fully, don't force it. Pull it back out to make sure it's clean and threading properly.

Always take your time and be patient; once you have some experience, working on your vehicle may well become an enjoyable hobby.

TOOLS AND EQUIPMENT

▶ **See Figures 1 thru 15**

Naturally, without the proper tools and equipment it is impossible to properly service your vehicle. It would also be virtually impossible to catalog every tool that you would need to perform all of the operations in this book. Of course, It would be unwise for the amateur to rush out and buy an expensive set of tools on the theory that he/she may need one or more of them at some time.

The best approach is to proceed slowly, gathering a good quality set of those tools that are used most frequently. Don't be misled by the low cost of bargain tools. It is far better to spend a little more for better quality. Forged wrenches, 6 or 12-point sockets and fine tooth ratchets are by far preferable to their less expensive counterparts. As any good mechanic can tell you, there are few worse experiences than trying to work on a vehicle with bad tools. Your monetary savings will be far outweighed by frustration and mangled knuckles.

Begin accumulating those tools that are used most frequently: those associated with routine maintenance and tune-up. In addition to the normal assortment of screwdrivers and pliers, you should have the following tools:

- Wrenches/sockets and combination open end/box end wrenches in sizes from ⅛–¾ in. or 3–19mm (depending on whether your vehicle uses standard or metric fasteners) and a ¹³⁄₁₆ in. or ⅝ in. spark plug socket (depending on plug type).

➡**If possible, buy various length socket drive extensions. Universal-joint and wobble extensions can be extremely useful, but be careful when using them, as they can change the amount of torque applied to the socket.**

- Jackstands for support.
- Oil filter wrench.
- Spout or funnel for pouring fluids.
- Grease gun for chassis lubrication (unless your vehicle is not equipped with any grease fittings—for details, please refer to information on Fluids and Lubricants found later in this section).
- Hydrometer for checking the battery (unless equipped with a sealed, maintenance-free battery).
- A container for draining oil and other fluids.
- Rags for wiping up the inevitable mess.

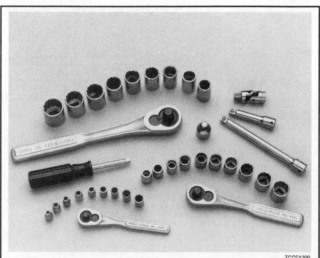

TCCS1200

Fig. 1 All but the most basic procedures will require an assortment of ratchets and sockets

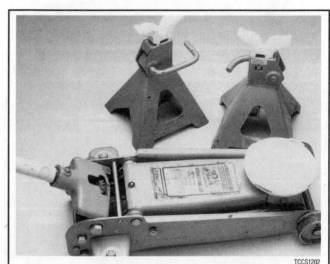

TCCS1202

Fig. 3 A hydraulic floor jack and a set of jackstands are essential for lifting and supporting the vehicle

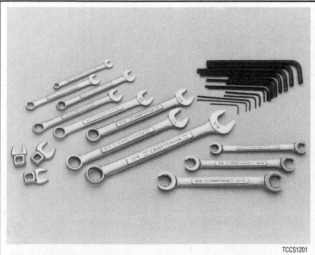

TCCS1201

Fig. 2 In addition to ratchets, a good set of wrenches and hex keys will be necessary

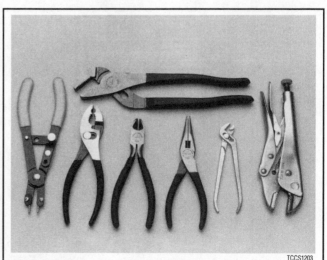

TCCS1203

Fig. 4 An assortment of pliers, grippers and cutters will be handy for old rusted parts and stripped bolt heads

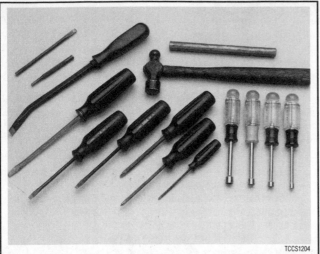

Fig. 5 Various drivers, chisels and prybars are great tools to have in your toolbox

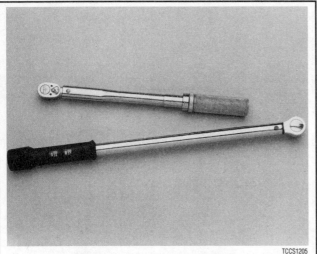

Fig. 6 Many repairs will require the use of a torque wrench to assure the components are properly fastened

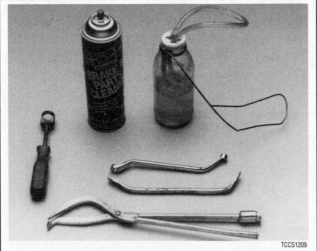

Fig. 7 Although not always necessary, using specialized brake tools will save time

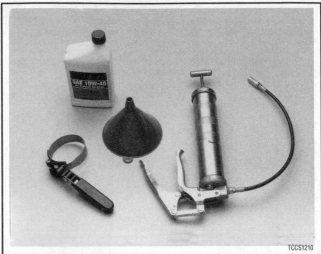

Fig. 8 A few inexpensive lubrication tools will make maintenance easier

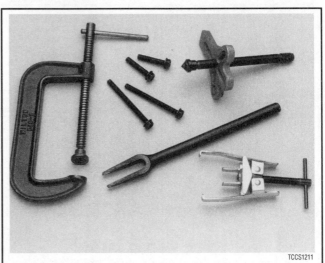

Fig. 9 Various pullers, clamps and separator tools are needed for many larger, more complicated repairs

Fig. 10 A variety of tools and gauges should be used for spark plug gapping and installation

In addition to the above items there are several others that are not absolutely necessary, but handy to have around. These include Oil Dry® (or an equivalent oil absorbent gravel—such as cat litter) and the usual supply of lubricants, antifreeze and fluids, although these can be purchased as needed. This is a basic list for routine maintenance, but only your personal needs and desire can accurately determine your list of tools.

After performing a few projects on the vehicle, you'll be amazed at the other tools and non-tools on your workbench. Some useful household items are: a large turkey baster or siphon, empty coffee cans and ice trays (to store parts), ball of twine, electrical tape for wiring, small rolls of colored tape for tagging lines or hoses, markers and pens, a note pad, golf

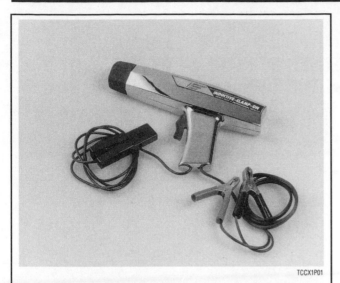

Fig. 11 Inductive type timing light

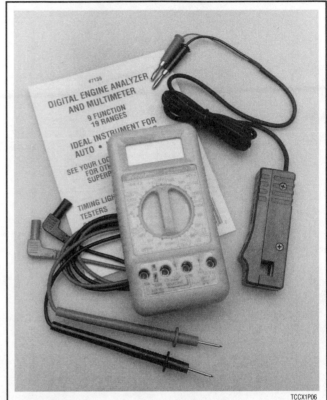

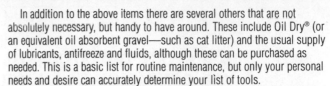

Fig. 14 Most modern automotive multimeters incorporate many helpful features

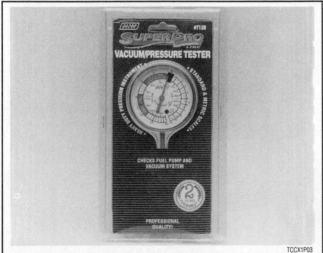

Fig. 12 A screw-in type compression gauge is recommended for compression testing

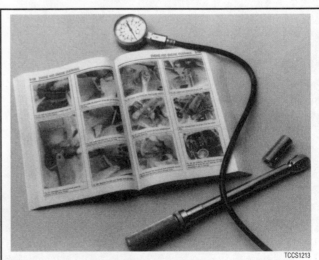

Fig. 13 A vacuum/pressure tester is necessary for many testing procedures

Fig. 15 Proper information is vital, so always have a Chilton Total Car Care manual handy

tees (for plugging vacuum lines), metal coat hangers or a roll of mechanics's wire (to hold things out of the way), dental pick or similar long, pointed probe, a strong magnet, and a small mirror (to see into recesses and under manifolds).

A more advanced set of tools, suitable for tune-up work, can be drawn up easily. While the tools are slightly more sophisticated, they need not be outrageously expensive. There are several inexpensive tach/dwell meters on the market that are every bit as good for the average mechanic as a professional model. Just be sure that it goes to a least 1200–1500 rpm on the tach scale and that it works on 4, 6 and 8-cylinder engines. (If you have one or more vehicles with a diesel engine, a special tachometer is required since diesels don't use spark plug ignition systems). The key to these purchases is to make them with an eye towards adaptability and wide range. A basic list of tune-up tools could include:

- Tach/dwell meter.
- Spark plug wrench and gapping tool.
- Feeler gauges for valve or point adjustment. (Even if your vehicle does not use points or require valve adjustments, a feeler gauge is helpful for many repair/overhaul procedures).

A tachometer/dwell meter will ensure accurate tune-up work on vehicles without electronic ignition. The choice of a timing light should be made carefully. A light which works on the DC current supplied by the vehicle's battery is the best choice; it should have a xenon tube for brightness. On any vehicle with an electronic ignition system, a timing light with an inductive pickup that clamps around the No. 1 spark plug cable is preferred.

In addition to these basic tools, there are several other tools and gauges you may find useful. These include:

- Compression gauge. The screw-in type is slower to use, but eliminates the possibility of a faulty reading due to escaping pressure.
- Manifold vacuum gauge.
- 12V test light.
- A combination volt/ohmmeter
- Induction Ammeter. This is used for determining whether or not there is current in a wire. These are handy for use if a wire is broken somewhere in a wiring harness.

As a final note, you will probably find a torque wrench necessary for all but the most basic work. The beam type models are perfectly adequate, although the newer click types (breakaway) are easier to use. The click type torque wrenches tend to be more expensive. Also keep in mind that all types of torque wrenches should be periodically checked and/or recalibrated. You will have to decide for yourself which better fits your purpose.

Special Tools

Normally, the use of special factory tools is avoided for repair procedures, since these are not readily available for the do-it-yourself mechanic. When it is possible to perform the job with more commonly available tools, it will be pointed out, but occasionally, a special tool was designed to perform a specific function and should be used. Before substituting another tool, you should be convinced that neither your safety nor the performance of the vehicle will be compromised.

Special tools can usually be purchased from an automotive parts store or from your dealer. In some cases special tools may be available directly from the tool manufacturer.

SERVICING YOUR VEHICLE SAFELY

▸ **See Figures 16, 17, 18 and 19**

It is virtually impossible to anticipate all of the hazards involved with automotive maintenance and service, but care and common sense will prevent most accidents.

The rules of safety for mechanics range from "don't smoke around gasoline," to "use the proper tool(s) for the job." The trick to avoiding injuries is to develop safe work habits and to take every possible precaution.

Do's

- Do keep a fire extinguisher and first aid kit handy.
- Do wear safety glasses or goggles when cutting, drilling, grinding or prying, even if you have 20–20 vision. If you wear glasses for the sake of vision, wear safety goggles over your regular glasses.

- Do shield your eyes whenever you work around the battery. Batteries contain sulfuric acid. In case of contact with the eyes or skin, flush the area with water or a mixture of water and baking soda, then seek immediate medical attention.
- Do use safety stands (jackstands) for any undervehicle service. Jacks are for raising vehicles; jackstands are for making sure the vehicle stays raised until you want it to come down. Whenever the vehicle is raised, block the wheels remaining on the ground and set the parking brake.
- Do use adequate ventilation when working with any chemicals or hazardous materials. Like carbon monoxide, the asbestos dust resulting from some brake lining wear can be hazardous in sufficient quantities.
- Do disconnect the negative battery cable when working on the electrical system. The secondary ignition system contains EXTREMELY HIGH VOLTAGE. In some cases it can even exceed 50,000 volts.

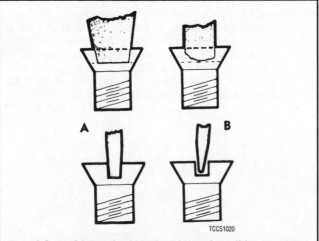

TCCS1020

Fig. 16 Screwdrivers should be kept in good condition to prevent injury or damage which could result if the blade slips from the screw

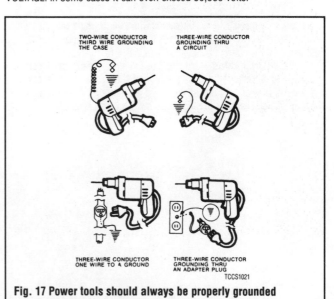

TCCS1021

Fig. 17 Power tools should always be properly grounded

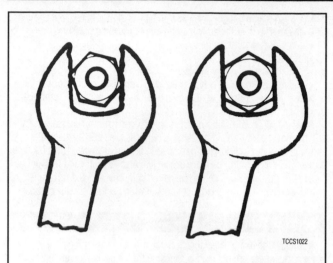

TCCS1022

Fig. 18 Using the correct size wrench will help prevent the possibility of rounding off a nut

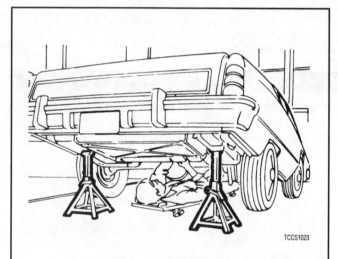

TCCS1023

Fig. 19 NEVER work under a vehicle unless it is supported using safety stands (jackstands)

• Do follow manufacturer's directions whenever working with potentially hazardous materials. Most chemicals and fluids are poisonous if taken internally.

• Do properly maintain your tools. Loose hammerheads, mushroomed punches and chisels, frayed or poorly grounded electrical cords, excessively worn screwdrivers, spread wrenches (open end), cracked sockets, slipping ratchets, or faulty droplight sockets can cause accidents.

• Likewise, keep your tools clean; a greasy wrench can slip off a bolt head, ruining the bolt and often harming your knuckles in the process.

• Do use the proper size and type of tool for the job at hand. Do select a wrench or socket that fits the nut or bolt. The wrench or socket should sit straight, not cocked.

• Do, when possible, pull on a wrench handle rather than push on it, and adjust your stance to prevent a fall.

• Do be sure that adjustable wrenches are tightly closed on the nut or bolt and pulled so that the force is on the side of the fixed jaw.

• Do strike squarely with a hammer; avoid glancing blows.

• Do set the parking brake and block the drive wheels if the work requires a running engine.

Don'ts

• Don't run the engine in a garage or anywhere else without proper ventilation—EVER! Carbon monoxide is poisonous; it takes a long time to leave the human body and you can build up a deadly supply of it in your system by simply breathing in a little every day. You may not realize you are slowly poisoning yourself. Always use power vents, windows, fans and/or open the garage door.

• Don't work around moving parts while wearing loose clothing. Short sleeves are much safer than long, loose sleeves. Hard-toed shoes with neoprene soles protect your toes and give a better grip on slippery surfaces. Jewelry such as watches, fancy belt buckles, beads or body adornment of any kind is not safe working around a vehicle. Long hair should be tied back under a hat or cap.

• Don't use pockets for toolboxes. A fall or bump can drive a screwdriver deep into your body. Even a rag hanging from your back pocket can wrap around a spinning shaft or fan.

• Don't smoke when working around gasoline, cleaning solvent or other flammable material.

• Don't smoke when working around the battery. When the battery is being charged, it gives off explosive hydrogen gas.

• Don't use gasoline to wash your hands; there are excellent soaps available. Gasoline contains dangerous additives which can enter the body through a cut or through your pores. Gasoline also removes all the natural oils from the skin so that bone dry hands will suck up oil and grease.

• Don't service the air conditioning system unless you are equipped with the necessary tools and training. When liquid or compressed gas refrigerant is released to atmospheric pressure it will absorb heat from whatever it contacts. This will chill or freeze anything it touches. Although refrigerant is normally non-toxic, R-12 becomes a deadly poisonous gas in the presence of an open flame. One good whiff of the vapors from burning refrigerant can be fatal.

• Don't use screwdrivers for anything other than driving screws! A screwdriver used as an prying tool can snap when you least expect it, causing injuries. At the very least, you'll ruin a good screwdriver.

• Don't use a bumper or emergency jack (that little ratchet, scissors, or pantograph jack supplied with the vehicle) for anything other than changing a flat! These jacks are only intended for emergency use out on the road; they are NOT designed as a maintenance tool. If you are serious about maintaining your vehicle yourself, invest in a hydraulic floor jack of at least a 1½ ton capacity, and at least two sturdy jackstands.

FASTENERS, MEASUREMENTS AND CONVERSIONS

Bolts, Nuts and Other Threaded Retainers

▶ See Figures 20, 21, 22 and 23

Although there are a great variety of fasteners found in the modern car or truck, the most commonly used retainer is the threaded fastener (nuts, bolts, screws, studs, etc). Most threaded retainers may be reused, provided that they are not damaged in use or during the repair. Some retainers (such as stretch bolts or torque prevailing nuts) are designed to deform when tightened or in use and should not be reinstalled.

Whenever possible, we will note any special retainers which should be replaced during a procedure. But you should always inspect the condition of a retainer when it is removed and replace any that show signs of damage. Check all threads for rust or corrosion which can increase the torque necessary to achieve the desired clamp load for which that fastener was originally selected. Additionally, be sure that the driver surface of the fastener has not been compromised by rounding or other damage. In some cases a driver surface may become only partially rounded, allowing the driver to catch in only one direction. In many of these occurrences, a fastener may be installed and tightened, but the driver would not be able to

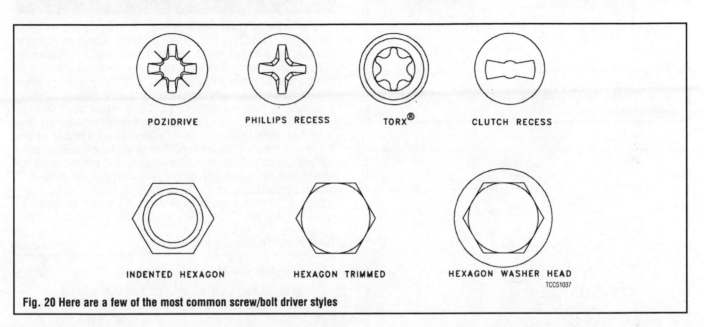

POZIDRIVE PHILLIPS RECESS TORX® CLUTCH RECESS

INDENTED HEXAGON HEXAGON TRIMMED HEXAGON WASHER HEAD

TCCS1037

Fig. 20 Here are a few of the most common screw/bolt driver styles

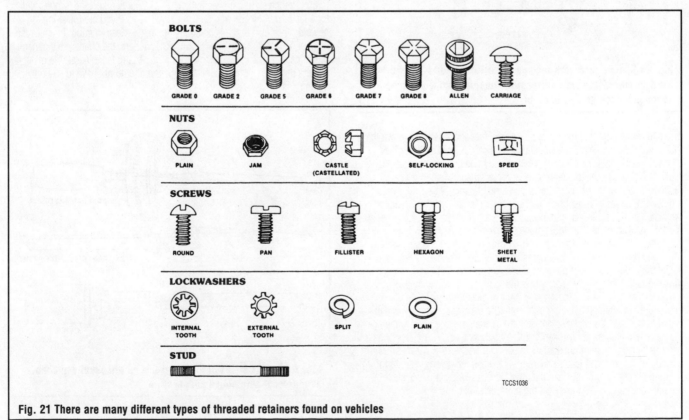

BOLTS
GRADE 0 GRADE 2 GRADE 5 GRADE 6 GRADE 7 GRADE 8 ALLEN CARRIAGE

NUTS
PLAIN JAM CASTLE (CASTELLATED) SELF-LOCKING SPEED

SCREWS
ROUND PAN FILLISTER HEXAGON SHEET METAL

LOCKWASHERS
INTERNAL TOOTH EXTERNAL TOOTH SPLIT PLAIN

STUD

TCCS1036

Fig. 21 There are many different types of threaded retainers found on vehicles

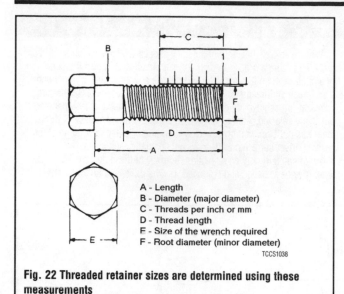

A - Length
B - Diameter (major diameter)
C - Threads per inch or mm
D - Thread length
F - Size of the wrench required
F - Root diameter (minor diameter)

TCCS1038

Fig. 22 Threaded retainer sizes are determined using these measurements

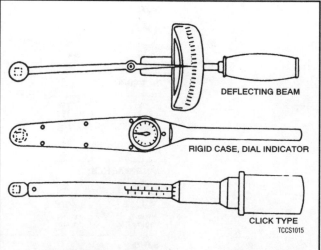

T - INTERNAL DRIVE
E - EXTERNAL

TCCS1016

Fig. 23 Special fasteners such as these Torx® head bolts are used by manufacturers to discourage people from working on vehicles without the proper tools

grip and loosen the fastener again. (This could lead to frustration down the line should that component ever need to be disassembled again).

If you must replace a fastener, whether due to design or damage, you must ALWAYS be sure to use the proper replacement. In all cases, a retainer of the same design, material and strength should be used. Markings on the heads of most bolts will help determine the proper strength of the fastener. The same material, thread and pitch must be selected to assure proper installation and safe operation of the vehicle afterwards.

Thread gauges are available to help measure a bolt or stud's thread. Most automotive and hardware stores keep gauges available to help you select the proper size. In a pinch, you can use another nut or bolt for a thread gauge. If the bolt you are replacing is not too badly damaged, you can select a match by finding another bolt which will thread in its place. If you find a nut which threads properly onto the damaged bolt, then use that nut to help select the replacement bolt. If however, the bolt you are replacing is so badly damaged (broken or drilled out) that its threads cannot be used as a gauge, you might start by looking for another bolt (from the same assembly or a similar location on your vehicle) which will thread into the damaged bolt's mounting. If so, the other bolt can be used to select a nut; the nut can then be used to select the replacement bolt.

In all cases, be absolutely sure you have selected the proper replacement. Don't be shy, you can always ask the store clerk for help.

✴ WARNING

Be aware that when you find a bolt with damaged threads, you may also find the nut or drilled hole it was threaded into has also been damaged. If this is the case, you may have to drill and tap the hole, replace the nut or otherwise repair the threads. NEVER try to force a replacement bolt to fit into the damaged threads.

Torque

Torque is defined as the measurement of resistance to turning or rotating. It tends to twist a body about an axis of rotation. A common example of this would be tightening a threaded retainer such as a nut, bolt or screw. Measuring torque is one of the most common ways to help assure that a threaded retainer has been properly fastened.

When tightening a threaded fastener, torque is applied in three distinct areas, the head, the bearing surface and the clamp load. About 50 percent of the measured torque is used in overcoming bearing friction. This is the friction between the bearing surface of the bolt head, screw head or nut face and the base material or washer (the surface on which the fastener is rotating). Approximately 40 percent of the applied torque is used in overcoming thread friction. This leaves only about 10 percent of the applied torque to develop a useful clamp load (the force which holds a joint together). This means that friction can account for as much as 90 percent of the applied torque on a fastener.

TORQUE WRENCHES

▶ **See Figures 24 and 25**

In most applications, a torque wrench can be used to assure proper installation of a fastener. Torque wrenches come in various designs and most automotive supply stores will carry a variety to suit your needs. A torque wrench should be used any time we supply a specific torque value for a fastener. A torque wrench can also be used if you are following the general guidelines in the accompanying charts. Keep in mind that because there is no worldwide standardization of fasteners, the charts are a general guideline and should be used with caution. Again, the general rule of "if you are using the right tool for the job, you should not have to strain to tighten a fastener" applies here.

DEFLECTING BEAM

RIGID CASE, DIAL INDICATOR

CLICK TYPE

TCCS1015

Fig. 24 Various styles of torque wrenches are usually available at your local automotive supply store

Standard Torque Specifications and Fastener Markings

In the absence of specific torques, the following chart can be used as a guide to the maximum safe torque of a particular size/grade of fastener.
- There is no torque difference for fine or coarse threads.
- Torque values are based on clean, dry threads. Reduce the value by 10% if threads are oiled prior to assembly.
- The torque required for aluminum components or fasteners is considerably less.

U.S. Bolts

SAE Grade Number	1 or 2			5			6 or 7		
Number of lines always 2 less than the grade number.									
Bolt Size (Inches)—(Thread)	Maximum Torque			Maximum Torque			Maximum Torque		
	Ft./Lbs.	Kgm	Nm	Ft./Lbs.	Kgm	Nm	Ft./Lbs.	Kgm	Nm
¼ — 20	5	0.7	6.8	8	1.1	10.8	10	1.4	13.5
— 28	6	0.8	8.1	10	1.4	13.6			
5/16 — 18	11	1.5	14.9	17	2.3	23.0	19	2.6	25.8
— 24	13	1.8	17.6	19	2.6	25.7			
3/8 — 16	18	2.5	24.4	31	4.3	42.0	34	4.7	46.0
— 24	20	2.75	27.1	35	4.8	47.5			
7/16 — 14	28	3.8	37.0	49	6.8	66.4	55	7.6	74.5
— 20	30	4.2	40.7	55	7.6	74.5			
½ — 13	39	5.4	52.8	75	10.4	101.7	85	11.75	115.2
— 20	41	5.7	55.6	85	11.7	115.2			
9/16 — 12	51	7.0	69.2	110	15.2	149.1	120	16.6	162.7
— 18	55	7.6	74.5	120	16.6	162.7			
5/8 — 11	83	11.5	112.5	150	20.7	203.3	167	23.0	226.5
— 18	95	13.1	128.8	170	23.5	230.5			
¾ — 10	105	14.5	142.3	270	37.3	366.0	280	38.7	379.6
— 16	115	15.9	155.9	295	40.8	400.0			
7/8 — 9	160	22.1	216.9	395	54.6	535.5	440	60.9	596.5
— 14	175	24.2	237.2	435	60.1	589.7			
1 — 8	236	32.5	318.6	590	81.6	799.9	660	91.3	894.8
— 14	250	34.6	338.9	660	91.3	849.8			

Metric Bolts

Relative Strength Marking	4.6, 4.8			8.8		
Bolt Markings						
Bolt Size Thread Size x Pitch (mm)	Maximum Torque			Maximum Torque		
	Ft./Lbs.	Kgm	Nm	Ft./Lbs.	Kgm	Nm
6 x 1.0	2–3	.2–.4	3–4	3–6	4–.8	5–8
8 x 1.25	6–8	.8–1	8–12	9–14	1.2–1.9	13–19
10 x 1.25	12–17	1.5–2.3	16–23	20–29	2.7–4.0	27–39
12 x 1.25	21–32	2.9–4.4	29–43	35–53	4.8–7.3	47–72
14 x 1.5	35–52	4.8–7.1	48–70	57–85	7.8–11.7	77–110
16 x 1.5	51–77	7.0–10.6	67–100	90–120	12.4–16.5	130–160
18 x 1.5	74–110	10.2–15.1	100–150	130–170	17.9–23.4	180–230
20 x 1.5	110–140	15.1–19.3	150–190	190–240	26.2–46.9	160–320
22 x 1.5	150–190	22.0–26.2	200–260	250–320	34.5–44.1	340–430
24 x 1.5	190–240	26.2–46.9	260–320	310–410	42.7–56.5	420–550

TCCS1098

Fig. 25 Standard and metric bolt torque specifications based on bolt strengths—WARNING: use only as a guide

Beam Type

▶ See Figure 26

The beam type torque wrench is one of the most popular types. It consists of a pointer attached to the head that runs the length of the flexible beam (shaft) to a scale located near the handle. As the wrench is pulled, the beam bends and the pointer indicates the torque using the scale.

Click (Breakaway) Type

▶ See Figure 27

Another popular design of torque wrench is the click type. To use the click type wrench you pre-adjust it to a torque setting. Once the torque is reached, the wrench has a reflex signaling feature that causes a momentary breakaway of the torque wrench body, sending an impulse to the operator's hand.

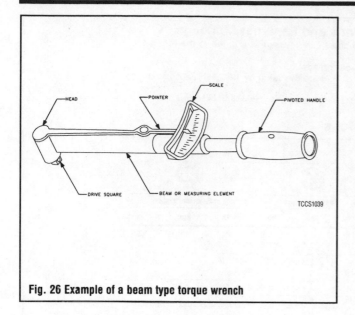

Fig. 26 Example of a beam type torque wrench

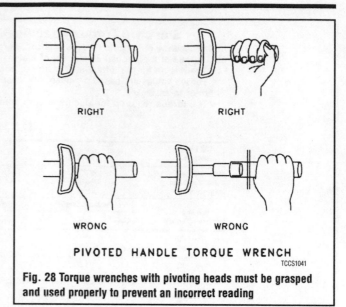

PIVOTED HANDLE TORQUE WRENCH

Fig. 28 Torque wrenches with pivoting heads must be grasped and used properly to prevent an incorrect reading

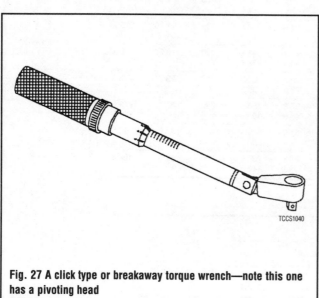

Fig. 27 A click type or breakaway torque wrench—note this one has a pivoting head

Pivot Head Type

◆ See Figures 27 and 28

Some torque wrenches (usually of the click type) may be equipped with a pivot head which can allow it to be used in areas of limited access. BUT, it must be used properly. To hold a pivot head wrench, grasp the handle lightly, and as you pull on the handle, it should be floated on the pivot point. If the handle comes in contact with the yoke extension during the process of pulling, there is a very good chance the torque readings will be inaccurate because this could alter the wrench loading point. The design of the handle is usually such as to make it inconvenient to deliberately misuse the wrench.

➡ It should be mentioned that the use of any U-joint, wobble or extension will have an effect on the torque readings, no matter what type of wrench you are using. For the most accurate readings, install the socket directly on the wrench driver. If necessary, straight extensions (which hold a socket directly under the wrench driver) will have the least effect on the torque reading. Avoid any extension that alters the length of the wrench from the handle to the head/driving point (such as a crow's foot). U-joint or wobble extensions can greatly affect the readings; avoid their use at all times.

Rigid Case (Direct Reading)

◆ See Figure 29

A rigid case or direct reading torque wrench is equipped with a dial indicator to show torque values. One advantage of these wrenches is that they can be held at any position on the wrench without affecting accuracy. These wrenches are often preferred because they tend to be compact, easy to read and have a great degree of accuracy.

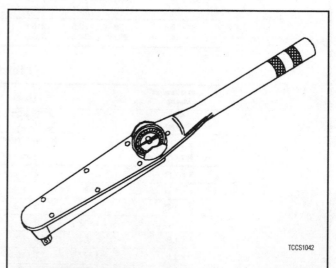

Fig. 29 The rigid case (direct reading) torque wrench uses a dial indicator to show torque

TORQUE ANGLE METERS

◆ See Figure 30

Because the frictional characteristics of each fastener or threaded hole will vary, clamp loads which are based strictly on torque will vary as well. In most applications, this variance is not significant enough to cause worry. But, in certain applications, a manufacturer's engineers may determine that more precise clamp loads are necessary (such is the case with many aluminum cylinder heads). In these cases, a torque angle method of installation would be specified. When installing fasteners which are torque angle tightened, a predetermined seating torque and standard torque wrench are

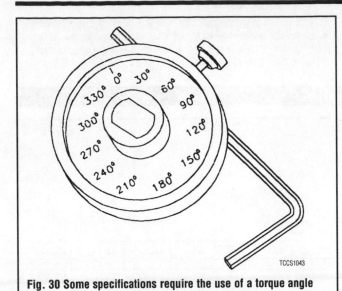

Fig. 30 Some specifications require the use of a torque angle meter (mechanical protractor)

TCCS1043

usually used first to remove any compliance from the joint. The fastener is then tightened the specified additional portion of a turn measured in degrees. A torque angle gauge (mechanical protractor) is used for these applications.

Standard and Metric Measurements

♦ See Figure 31

Throughout this manual, specifications are given to help you determine the condition of various components on your vehicle, or to assist you in their installation. Some of the most common measurements include length (in. or cm/mm), torque (ft. lbs., inch lbs. or Nm) and pressure (psi, in. Hg, kPa or mm Hg). In most cases, we strive to provide the proper measurement as determined by the manufacturer's engineers.

Though, in some cases, that value may not be conveniently measured with what is available in your toolbox. Luckily, many of the measuring devices which are available today will have two scales so the Standard or Metric measurements may easily be taken. If any of the various measuring tools which are available to you do not contain the same scale as listed in the specifications, use the accompanying conversion factors to determine the proper value.

CONVERSION FACTORS

LENGTH–DISTANCE

Inches (in.)	x 25.4	= Millimeters (mm)	x .0394	= Inches
Feet (ft.)	x .305	= Meters (m)	x 3.281	= Feet
Miles	x 1.609	= Kilometers (km)	x .0621	= Miles

VOLUME

Cubic Inches (in3)	x 16.387	= Cubic Centimeters	x .061	= in3
IMP Pints (IMP pt.)	x .568	= Liters (L)	x 1.76	= IMP pt.
IMP Quarts (IMP qt.)	x 1.137	= Liters (L)	x .88	= IMP qt.
IMP Gallons (IMP gal.)	x 4.546	= Liters (L)	x .22	= IMP gal.
IMP Quarts (IMP qt.)	x 1.201	= US Quarts (US qt.)	x .833	= IMP qt.
IMP Gallons (IMP gal.)	x 1.201	= US Gallons (US gal.)	x .833	= IMP gal.
Fl. Ounces	x 29.573	= Milliliters	x .034	= Ounces
US Pints (US pt.)	x .473	= Liters (L)	x 2.113	= Pints
US Quarts (US qt.)	x .946	= Liters (L)	x 1.057	= Quarts
US Gallons (US gal.)	x 3.785	= Liters (L)	x .264	= Gallons

MASS–WEIGHT

Ounces (oz.)	x 28.35	= Grams (g)	x .035	= Ounces
Pounds (lb.)	x .454	= Kilograms (kg)	x 2.205	= Pounds

PRESSURE

Pounds Per Sq. In. (psi)	x 6.895	= Kilopascals (kPa)	x .145	= psi
Inches of Mercury (Hg)	x .4912	= psi	x 2.036	= Hg
Inches of Mercury (Hg)	x 3.377	= Kilopascals (kPa)	x .2961	= Hg
Inches of Water (H_2O)	x .07355	= Inches of Mercury	x 13.783	= H_2O
Inches of Water (H_2O)	x .03613	= psi	x 27.684	= H_2O
Inches of Water (H_2O)	x .248	= Kilopascals (kPa)	x 4.026	= H_2O

TORQUE

Pounds–Force Inches (in–lb)	x .113	= Newton Meters (N·m)	x 8.85	= in–lb
Pounds–Force Feet (ft–lb)	x 1.356	= Newton Meters (N·m)	x .738	= ft–lb

VELOCITY

Miles Per Hour (MPH)	x 1.609	= Kilometers Per Hour (KPH)	x .621	= MPH

POWER

Horsepower (Hp)	x .745	= Kilowatts	x 1.34	= Horsepower

FUEL CONSUMPTION*

Miles Per Gallon IMP (MPG)	x .354	= Kilometers Per Liter (Km/L)
Kilometers Per Liter (Km/L)	x 2.352	= IMP MPG
Miles Per Gallon US (MPG)	x .425	= Kilometers Per Liter (Km/L)
Kilometers Per Liter (Km/L)	x 2.352	= US MPG

*It is common to covert from miles per gallon (mpg) to liters/100 kilometers (1/100 km), where mpg (IMP) x 1/100 km = 282 and mpg (US) x 1/100 km = 235.

TEMPERATURE

Degree Fahrenheit (°F)	= (°C x 1.8) + 32
Degree Celsius (°C)	= (°F – 32) x .56

TCCS1044

Fig. 31 Standard and metric conversion factors chart

The conversion factor chart is used by taking the given specification and multiplying it by the necessary conversion factor. For instance, looking at the first line, if you have a measurement in inches such as "free-play should be 2 in." but your ruler reads only in millimeters, multiply 2 in. by the conversion factor of 25.4 to get the metric equivalent of 50.8mm. Likewise, if the specification was given only in a Metric measurement, for example in Newton Meters (Nm), then look at the center column first. If the measurement is 100 Nm, multiply it by the conversion factor of 0.738 to get 73.8 ft. lbs.

SERIAL NUMBER IDENTIFICATION

Vehicle

♦ **See Figures 32 and 33**

The Vehicle Identification Number (VIN) is located on the left side of the dash panel, behind the windshield.

A seventeen-digit combination of numbers and letters forms the VIN. Refer to the illustration for VIN details.

The code can be deciphered as follows:

- Nos. 1, 2 and 3: Vehicle manufacturer
- No. 4: Type of restraint system
- No. 5: Designation
- Nos. 6 and 7: Body type

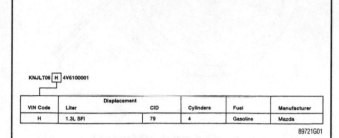

Fig. 33 The 17-digit VIN number contains information on engine and body type, as well as model year

- No. 8: Engine type
- No. 9: Check digit
- No. 10: Model year
- No. 11: Assembly plant
- Nos. 12–17: Production sequence number

Engine

The Aspire is equipped with a 1.3L SFI engine.

Transaxle

The Aspire is equipped with either a 5-speed manual transaxle or a 3-speed automatic transaxle.

Fig. 32 The Vehicle Identification Number (VIN) on the dash panel is visible through the driver's side of the windshield

VEHICLE IDENTIFICATION CHART

Engine Code						Model Year	
Code	Liters	Cu. In. (cc)	Cyl.	Fuel Sys.	Eng. Mfg.	Code	Year
H	1.3L	79	4	SFI	Mazda	R	1994
H	1.3L	79	4	SFI	Mazda	S	1995
H	1.3L	79	4	SFI	Mazda	T	1996
H	1.3L	79	4	SFI	Mazda	V	1997

SFI - Sequential Fuel Injection

89721C01

GENERAL ENGINE SPECIFICATIONS

Year	Engine ID/VIN	Engine Displacement Liters (cc)	No. of Cyl.	Fuel System Type	Net Horsepower @ rpm	Net Torque @ rpm (ft. lbs.)	Compression Ratio	Oil Pressure (lbs. @ rpm)
1994	H	1.3L (1300)	4	SFI	63.5@5000	73@3000	9.7:1	50-64@3000
1995	H	1.3L (1300)	4	SFI	63.5@5000	73@3000	9.7:1	50-64@3000
1996	H	1.3L (1300)	4	SFI	63.5@5000	73@3000	9.7:1	50-64@3000
1997	H	1.3L (1300)	4	SFI	63.5@5000	73@3000	9.7:1	50-64@3000

SFI - Sequential Fuel Injection

89721C02

ROUTINE MAINTENANCE AND TUNE-UP

UNDERHOOD MAINTENANCE COMPONENT LOCATIONS

1. Air filter element (in housing)
2. Engine oil dipstick
3. Spark plug wire and plug
4. Radiator cap
5. Coolant recovery tank
6. Windshield washer fluid reservoir
7. Battery
8. Fuel filter
9. Brake master cylinder reservoir
10. Automatic transaxle dipstick
11. Distributor cap and rotor
12. Oil filler cap
13. PCV valve
14. Evaporative canister

89721P05

Proper maintenance and tune-up is the key to long and trouble-free vehicle life, and the work can yield its own rewards. Studies have shown that a properly tuned and maintained vehicle can achieve better gas mileage than an out-of-tune vehicle. As a conscientious owner and driver, set aside a Saturday morning, say once a month, to check or replace items which could cause major problems later. Keep your own personal log to jot down which services you performed, how much the parts cost you, the date, and the exact odometer reading at the time. Keep all receipts for such items as engine oil and filters, so that they may be referred to in case of related problems or to determine operating expenses. As a do-it-yourselfer, these receipts are the only proof you have that the required maintenance was performed. In the event of a warranty problem, these receipts will be invaluable.

The literature provided with your vehicle when it was originally delivered includes the factory recommended maintenance schedule. If you no longer have this literature, replacement copies are usually available from the dealer. A maintenance schedule is provided later in this section, in case you do not have the factory literature.

Air Cleaner (Element)

REMOVAL & INSTALLATION

▶ See Figures 34, 35, 36, 37 and 38

1. If necessary, loosen the intake air duct retainer and disconnect any hoses that would interfere with the filter element removal.
2. Disconnect the housing clamps.
3. Lift the upper half of the housing up enough to gain access to the filter element.
4. Grasp the element and remove it from the housing.

To install:

5. Place a new filter element in the bottom half of the housing.
6. Install the top half of the housing cover and engage the retaining clamps.
7. If applicable, fasten the intake air duct retainer and connect any hoses which were previously removed.

Fig. 34 If necessary for access, loosen the air duct retainer

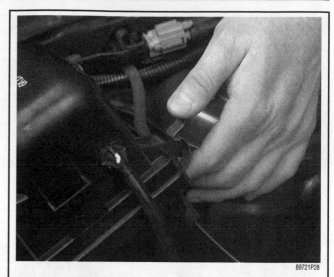

Fig. 35 Disengage the air filter housing retaining clamps

Fig. 36 Disconnect any hoses that would interfere with removal of the filter element

Fuel Filter

REMOVAL & INSTALLATION

▶ See Figures 39 thru 44

✳ CAUTION

Observe all applicable safety precautions when working around fuel. Whenever servicing the fuel system, always work in a well ventilated area. Do not allow fuel spray or vapors to come in contact with a spark or open flame. Keep a dry chemical fire extinguisher near the work area. Always keep fuel in a con-

Fig. 37 Lift the lid up to access the filter and remove the element

tainer specifically designed for fuel storage; also, always properly seal fuel containers to avoid the possibility of fire or explosion.

➡The direction of flow of the fuel filter is marked OUT on the top of the filter. Be sure to replace the new filter in the same direction of flow as the old one.

The fuel filter is located in the engine compartment, in-line between the fuel line and injection supply manifold.

1. Relieve the fuel system pressure. Refer to Section 5 for this procedure.

2. Loosen the hose clamp and disconnect the top fuel line from the filter. Cap the line to prevent contamination or fuel spillage.

3. Loosen the filter bracket nuts, then remove the filter and bracket.

4. Loosen the bracket bolt and separate the filter from the bracket.

5. Loosen the lower hose retaining clamp and remove the filter. Cap the line to prevent contamination or fuel spillage.

To install:

6. Connect the lower hose to the filter and engage its retaining clamp.

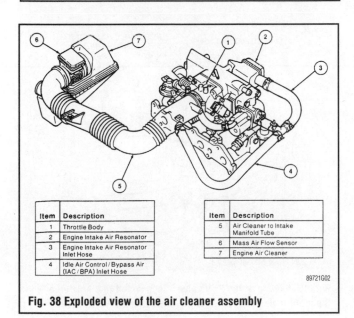

Item	Description
1	Throttle Body
2	Engine Intake Air Resonator
3	Engine Intake Air Resonator Inlet Hose
4	Idle Air Control / Bypass Air (IAC / BPA) Inlet Hose

Item	Description
5	Air Cleaner to Intake Manifold Tube
6	Mass Air Flow Sensor
7	Engine Air Cleaner

Fig. 38 Exploded view of the air cleaner assembly

Fig. 40 Use pliers to compress and remove the top hose retaining clamp, then disconnect the hose

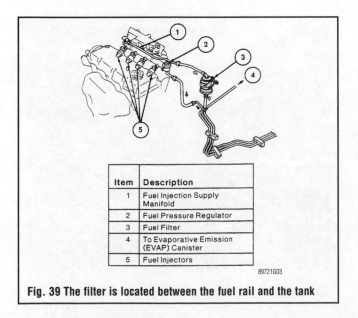

Item	Description
1	Fuel Injection Supply Manifold
2	Fuel Pressure Regulator
3	Fuel Filter
4	To Evaporative Emission (EVAP) Canister
5	Fuel Injectors

Fig. 39 The filter is located between the fuel rail and the tank

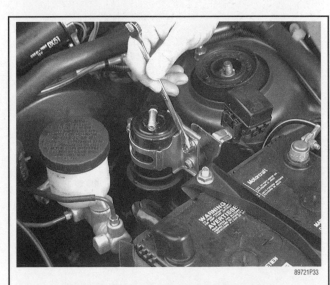

Fig. 41 Loosen the filter bracket retaining nuts and bolt . . .

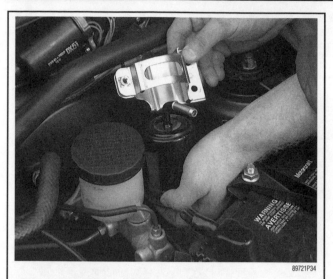

Fig. 42 . . . and separate the filter from the bracket

Fig. 43 Disconnect the lower hose in the same manner as the upper hose

Fig. 44 Make sure the direction of flow mark (OUT) is facing up

7. Install the filter into the bracket, making sure the direction of flow is correct (the word OUT is facing up).
8. Install and tighten the bracket bolt to 6–8 ft. lbs. (8–11 Nm).
9. Install the nuts and tighten them snugly.
10. Connect the top fuel line to the filter and engage the fuel line hose clamp.

PCV Valve

REMOVAL & INSTALLATION

◆ **See Figures 45, 46 and 47**

1. Grasp the PCV valve and pull it from the grommet in the valve cover.
2. Disconnect the valve from the oil separator hose.
3. Inspect the valve, grommet and hose for damage or deterioration, and replace any of the components if necessary.
   To install:
4. Connect the valve to the oil separator hose.
5. Push the valve into the grommet until it is fully seated.

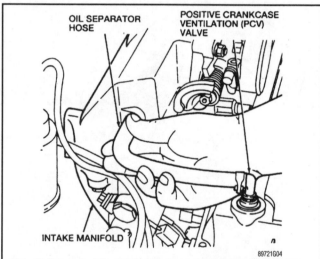

Fig. 45 One end of the PCV valve is connected to a hose, while the other end is inserted into a grommet in the valve cover

Fig. 46 Grasp the PCV valve and pull it from the grommet

Fig. 47 Pull the valve from the oil separator hose

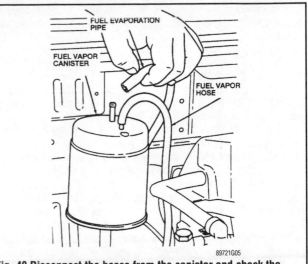

Fig. 49 Disconnect the hoses from the canister and check the ends for damage or wear

Evaporative Canister

SERVICING

▶ **See Figures 48 and 49**

The fuel evaporative emission control canister should be inspected for damage or leaks at the hose fittings. Repair or replace any old or cracked hoses. Replace the canister if it is damaged in any way. The canister is located under the hood, to the right of the engine.

For more detailed canister service, refer to Section 4.

Battery

PRECAUTIONS

Always use caution when working on or near the battery. Never allow a tool to bridge the gap between the negative and positive battery terminals. Also, be careful not to allow a tool to provide a ground between the positive cable/terminal and any metal component on the vehicle. Either of these conditions will cause a short circuit, leading to sparks and possible personal injury.

Do not smoke, have an open flame or create sparks near a battery; the gases contained in the battery are very explosive and, if ignited, could cause severe injury or death.

All batteries, regardless of type, should be carefully secured by a battery hold-down device. If this is not done, the battery terminals or casing may crack from stress applied to the battery during vehicle operation. A battery which is not secured may allow acid to leak out, making it discharge faster; such leaking corrosive acid can also eat away at components under the hood.

Always visually inspect the battery case for cracks, leakage and corrosion. A white corrosive substance on the battery case or on nearby components would indicate a leaking or cracked battery. If the battery is cracked, it should be replaced immediately.

GENERAL MAINTENANCE

▶ **See Figure 50**

A battery that is not sealed must be checked periodically for electrolyte level. You cannot add water to a sealed maintenance-free battery (though

Fig. 48 The evaporative canister is located on the right (passenger) side of the engine, against the firewall

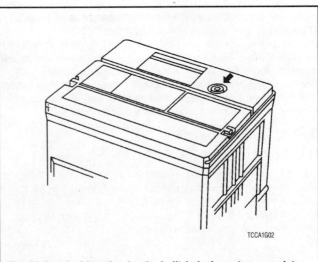

Fig. 50 A typical location for the built-in hydrometer on maintenance-free batteries

not all maintenance-free batteries are sealed); however, a sealed battery must also be checked for proper electrolyte level, as indicated by the color of the built-in hydrometer "eye."

Always keep the battery cables and terminals free of corrosion. Check these components about once a year. Refer to the removal, installation and cleaning procedures outlined in this section.

Keep the top of the battery clean, as a film of dirt can help completely discharge a battery that is not used for long periods. A solution of baking soda and water may be used for cleaning, but be careful to flush this off with clear water. DO NOT let any of the solution into the filler holes. Baking soda neutralizes battery acid and will de-activate a battery cell.

Batteries in vehicles which are not operated on a regular basis can fall victim to parasitic loads (small current drains which are constantly drawing current from the battery). Normal parasitic loads may drain a battery on a vehicle that is in storage and not used for 6–8 weeks. Vehicles that have additional accessories such as a cellular phone, an alarm system or other devices that increase parasitic load may discharge a battery sooner. If the vehicle is to be stored for 6–8 weeks in a secure area and the alarm system, if present, is not necessary, the negative battery cable should be disconnected at the onset of storage to protect the battery charge.

Remember that constantly discharging and recharging will shorten battery life. Take care not to allow a battery to be needlessly discharged.

BATTERY FLUID

Check the battery electrolyte level at least once a month, or more often in hot weather or during periods of extended vehicle operation. On non-sealed batteries, the level can be checked either through the case on translucent batteries or by removing the cell caps on opaque-cased types. The electrolyte level in each cell should be kept filled to the split ring inside each cell, or the line marked on the outside of the case.

If the level is low, add only distilled water through the opening until the level is correct. Each cell is separate from the others, so each must be checked and filled individually. Distilled water should be used, because the chemicals and minerals found in most drinking water are harmful to the battery and could significantly shorten its life.

If water is added in freezing weather, the vehicle should be driven several miles to allow the water to mix with the electrolyte. Otherwise, the battery could freeze.

Although some maintenance-free batteries have removable cell caps for access to the electrolyte, the electrolyte condition and level on all sealed maintenance-free batteries must be checked using the built-in hydrometer "eye." The exact type of eye varies between battery manufacturers, but most apply a sticker to the battery itself explaining the possible readings. When in doubt, refer to the battery manufacturer's instructions to interpret battery condition using the built-in hydrometer.

➡**Although the readings from built-in hydrometers found in sealed batteries may vary, a green eye usually indicates a properly charged battery with sufficient fluid level. A dark eye is normally an indicator of a battery with sufficient fluid, but one which may be low in charge. And a light or yellow eye is usually an indication that electrolyte supply has dropped below the necessary level for battery (and hydrometer) operation. In this last case, sealed batteries with an insufficient electrolyte level must usually be discarded.**

Checking the Specific Gravity

▶ **See Figures 51, 52 and 53**

A hydrometer is required to check the specific gravity on all batteries that are not maintenance-free. On batteries that are maintenance-free, the specific gravity is checked by observing the built-in hydrometer "eye" on the top of the battery case. Check with your battery's manufacturer for proper interpretation of its built-in hydrometer readings.

Battery electrolyte contains sulfuric acid. If you should splash any on your skin or in your eyes, flush the affected area with plenty of clear water. If it lands in your eyes, get medical help immediately.

The fluid (sulfuric acid solution) contained in the battery cells will tell you many things about the condition of the battery. Because the cell plates must be kept submerged below the fluid level in order to operate, maintaining the fluid level is extremely important. And, because the specific gravity of the acid is an indication of electrical charge, testing the fluid can be an aid in determining if the battery must be replaced. A battery in a vehicle with a properly operating charging system should require little maintenance, but careful, periodic inspection should reveal problems before they leave you stranded.

As stated earlier, the specific gravity of a battery's electrolyte level can be used as an indication of battery charge. At least once a year, check the spe-

Fig. 51 On non-maintenance-free batteries, the fluid level can be checked through the case on translucent models; the cell caps must be removed on other models

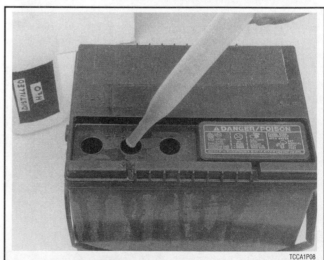

Fig. 52 If the fluid level is low, add only distilled water through the opening until the level is correct

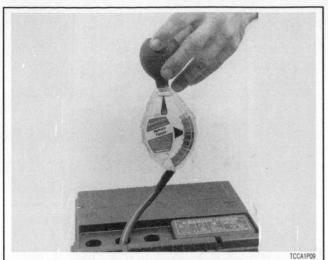

Fig. 53 Check the specific gravity of the battery's electrolyte with a hydrometer

Fig. 55 The underside of this special battery tool has a wire brush to clean post terminals

cific gravity of the battery. It should be between 1.20 and 1.26 on the gravity scale. Most auto supply stores carry a variety of inexpensive battery testing hydrometers. These can be used on any non-sealed battery to test the specific gravity in each cell.

The battery testing hydrometer has a squeeze bulb at one end and a nozzle at the other. Battery electrolyte is sucked into the hydrometer until the float is lifted from its seat. The specific gravity is then read by noting the position of the float. If gravity is low in one or more cells, the battery should be slowly charged and checked again to see if the gravity has come up. Generally, if after charging, the specific gravity between any two cells varies more than 50 points (0.50), the battery should be replaced, as it can no longer produce sufficient voltage to guarantee proper operation.

CABLES

▶ **See Figures 54, 55, 56, 57 and 58**

Once a year (or as necessary), the battery terminals and the cable clamps should be cleaned. Loosen the clamps and remove the cables, negative cable first. On batteries with posts on top, the use of a puller specially made for this purpose is recommended. These are inexpensive and available in most auto parts stores. Side terminal battery cables are secured with a small bolt.

Fig. 56 Place the tool over the battery posts and twist to clean until the metal is shiny

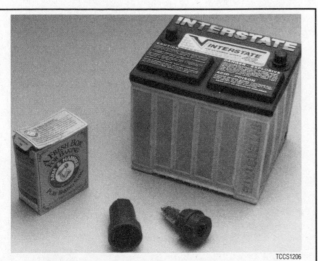

Fig. 54 Maintenance is performed with household items and with special tools like this post cleaner

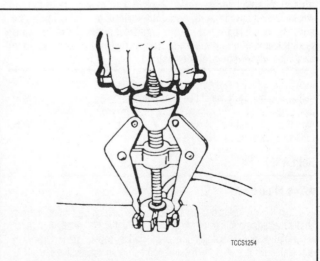

Fig. 57 A special tool is available to pull the clamp from the post

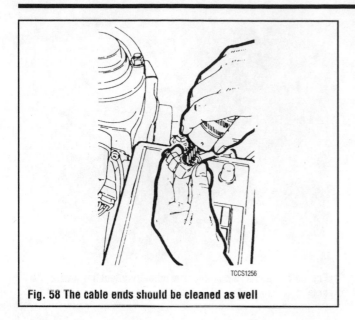

Fig. 58 The cable ends should be cleaned as well

Clean the cable clamps and the battery terminal with a wire brush, until all corrosion, grease, etc., is removed and the metal is shiny. It is especially important to clean the inside of the clamp thoroughly (an old knife is useful here), since a small deposit of foreign material or oxidation there will prevent a sound electrical connection and inhibit either starting or charging. Special tools are available for cleaning these parts, one type for conventional top post batteries and another type for side terminal batteries. It is also a good idea to apply some dielectric grease to the terminal, as this will aid in the prevention of corrosion.

After the clamps and terminals are clean, reinstall the cables, negative cable last; DO NOT hammer the clamps onto battery posts. Tighten the clamps securely, but do not distort them. Give the clamps and terminals a thin external coating of grease after installation, to retard corrosion.

Check the cables at the same time that the terminals are cleaned. If the cable insulation is cracked or broken, or if the ends are frayed, the cable should be replaced with a new cable of the same length and gauge.

CHARGING

✳✳ CAUTION

The chemical reaction which takes place in all batteries generates explosive hydrogen gas. A spark can cause the battery to explode and splash acid. To avoid serious personal injury, be sure there is proper ventilation and take appropriate fire safety precautions when connecting, disconnecting, or charging a battery and when using jumper cables.

A battery should be charged at a slow rate to keep the plates inside from getting too hot. However, if some maintenance-free batteries are allowed to discharge until they are almost "dead," they may have to be charged at a high rate to bring them back to "life." Always follow the charger manufacturer's instructions on charging the battery.

REPLACEMENT

▶ See Figure 59

When it becomes necessary to replace the battery, select one with an amperage rating equal to or greater than the battery originally installed. Deterioration and just plain aging of the battery cables, starter motor, and associated wires makes the battery's job harder in successive years. The slow increase in electrical resistance over time makes it prudent to install a new battery with a greater capacity than the old.

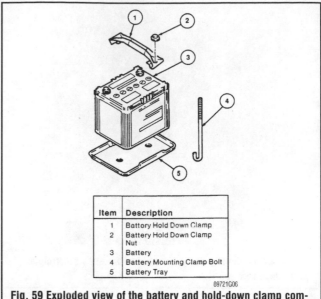

Item	Description
1	Battery Hold Down Clamp
2	Battery Hold Down Clamp Nut
3	Battery
4	Battery Mounting Clamp Bolt
5	Battery Tray

Fig. 59 Exploded view of the battery and hold-down clamp components

Belts

▶ See Figure 60

INSPECTION

▶ See Figures 61, 62, 63, 64 and 65

Inspect the belts for signs of glazing or cracking. A glazed belt will be perfectly smooth from slippage, while a good belt will have a slight texture of fabric visible. Cracks will usually start at the inner edge of the belt and run outward. All worn or damaged drive belts should be replaced immediately. It is best to replace all drive belts at one time, as a preventive maintenance measure, during this service operation.

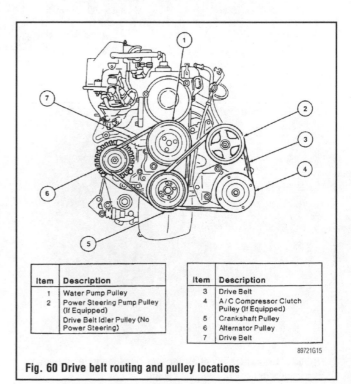

Item	Description
1	Water Pump Pulley
2	Power Steering Pump Pulley (If Equipped) Drive Belt Idler Pulley (No Power Steering)

Item	Description
3	Drive Belt
4	A/C Compressor Clutch Pulley (If Equipped)
5	Crankshaft Pulley
6	Alternator Pulley
7	Drive Belt

Fig. 60 Drive belt routing and pulley locations

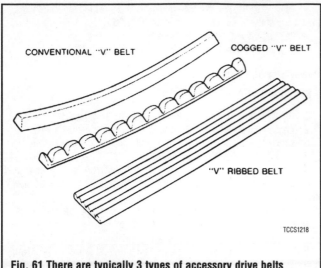

Fig. 61 There are typically 3 types of accessory drive belts found on vehicles today

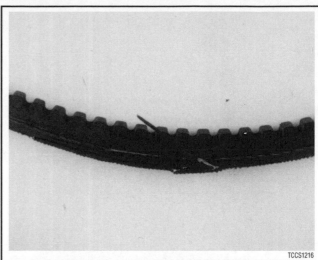

Fig. 64 The cover of this belt is worn, exposing the critical reinforcing cords to excessive wear

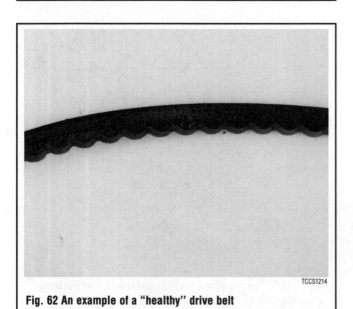

Fig. 62 An example of a "healthy" drive belt

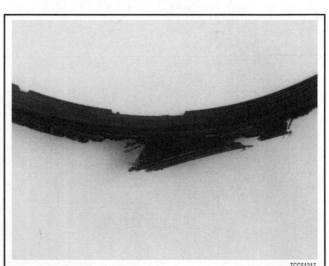

Fig. 65 Installing too wide a belt can result in serious belt wear and/or breakage

ADJUSTMENT

A/C Compressor

♦ See Figures 66, 67 and 68

This procedure applies to vehicles with A/C that are not equipped with power steering. For adjustment on models with A/C and power steering, refer to the power steering pump belt adjustment procedure in this section.

➡️**Always check the belt deflection when the vehicle is cold; if the vehicle is operating, turn it off and allow it to cool for at least 30 minutes.**

1. Inspect the belt for damage or wear.
2. Loosen the drive belt idler pulley nut.

➡️**Turn the fan belt idler pulley bolt clockwise to tighten the A/C compressor belt and counterclockwise to loosen it. Make sure the belt is properly seated on the pulley before adjustment.**

3. Use Rotunda offset belt tension gauge 021-0028A, or equivalent, and following the tool manufacturer's instructions, adjust the belt to the following specifications:

Fig. 63 Deep cracks in this belt will cause flex, building up heat that will eventually lead to belt failure

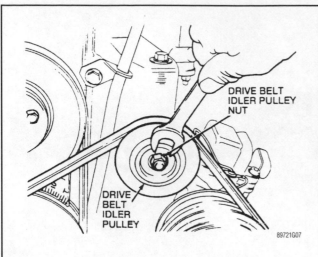

Fig. 66 Use an open end wrench to loosen the drive belt idler pulley nut

- New belt: 110–132 lbs. (50–60 kg). Run the engine for 10 minutes, then readjust the tension to 110–132 lbs. (50–60 kg).
- Used belt: 95–110 lbs. (43–50 kg).
4. Tighten the idler pulley bolt to 27–38 ft. lbs. (37–52 Nm).

Power Steering Pump

◗ **See Figures 68, 69, 70 and 71**

1. Remove the air cleaner intake tube and air cleaner assembly.
2. Loosen the power steering pump bolt and the adjustment locknut. Make sure the belt is properly seated on the pulley before adjustment.
3. Turn the adjustment bolt to set the belt tension.
4. Use Rotunda offset belt tension gauge 021-0028A, or equivalent, and following the tool manufacturer's instructions, adjust the belt to the following specifications:
- New belt: 110–132 lbs. (50–60 kg). Run the engine for 10 minutes, then readjust the tension to 110–132 lbs. (50–60 kg).
- Used belt: 95–110 lbs. (43–50 kg).
5. Tighten the power steering pump bolt to 27–38 ft. lbs. (37–52 Nm).
6. Tighten the adjustment locknut to 14–19 ft. lbs. (19–25 Nm).
7. Install the air cleaner and intake tube.

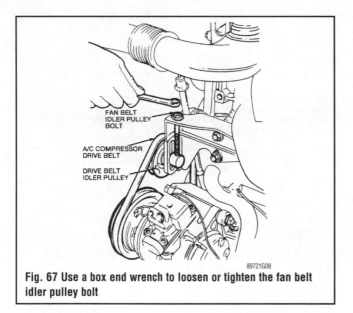

Fig. 67 Use a box end wrench to loosen or tighten the fan belt idler pulley bolt

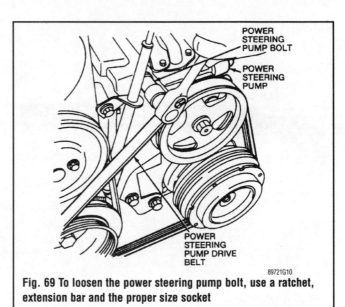

Fig. 69 To loosen the power steering pump bolt, use a ratchet, extension bar and the proper size socket

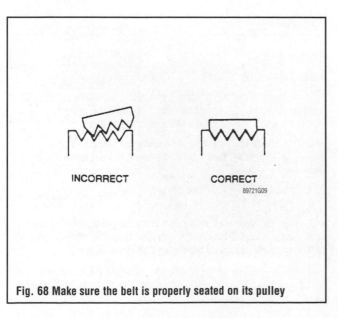

Fig. 68 Make sure the belt is properly seated on its pulley

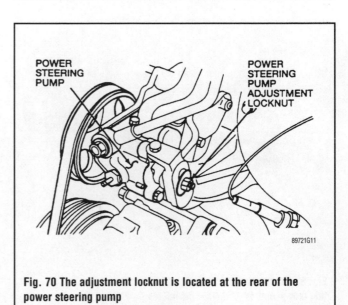

Fig. 70 The adjustment locknut is located at the rear of the power steering pump

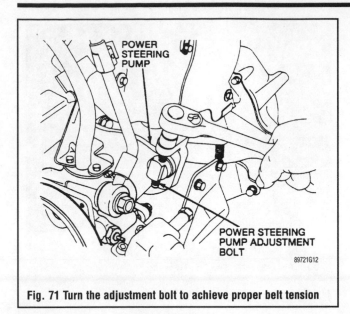

Fig. 71 Turn the adjustment bolt to achieve proper belt tension

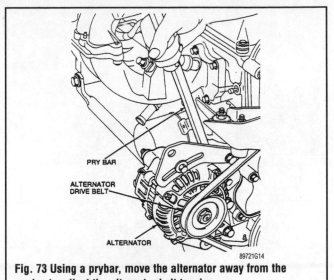

Fig. 73 Using a prybar, move the alternator away from the engine to adjust the alternator belt tension

Alternator

◆ See Figures 68, 72 and 73

1. Loosen the alternator adjustment bolt.
2. Raise the car and support it with safety stands.
3. Loosen the lower alternator bolt, then lower the car.
4. Make sure the belt is properly seated on the pulley.
5. Use Rotunda offset belt tension gauge 021-0028A, or equivalent, and follow the tool manufacturer's instructions to adjust the tension.

✳✳ WARNING

Never pry the alternator rear housing and bearing.

6. Adjust the belt to the proper tension by positioning a prybar on the area around a case bolt, then pry the alternator until the proper tension is reached.
7. The tension specifications are:
   • New belt: 86–103 lbs. (39–47 kg). Run the engine for 10 minutes, then readjust tension to 86–103 lbs. (39–47 kg).
   • Used belt: 68–86 lbs. (31–39 kg).
8. Tighten the alternator adjustment bolt to 14–19 ft. lbs. (19–25 Nm).
9. Raise the car and support it with safety stands.

10. Tighten the lower alternator bolt to 27–38 ft. lbs. (37–52 Nm).
11. Lower the car.

REMOVAL & INSTALLATION

A/C Compressor

◆ See Figures 66, 67, 74 and 75

This procedure applies to vehicles with A/C that are not equipped with power steering. For removal and installation on models with A/C and power steering, refer to the power steering pump belt procedure in this section.

1. Loosen the drive belt idler pulley nut.
2. Loosen the fan belt idler pulley bolt until the belt is slack enough to remove it.
3. Remove the belt from the idler, clutch and crankshaft pulleys.
4. Remove the belt from the engine compartment.

To install:

5. Route the belt around the idler, clutch and crankshaft pulleys. Make sure the belt is properly seated on each pulley.
6. Adjust the belt to the proper tension.
7. Tighten the drive belt idler pulley nut to 27–38 ft. lbs. (37–52 Nm).

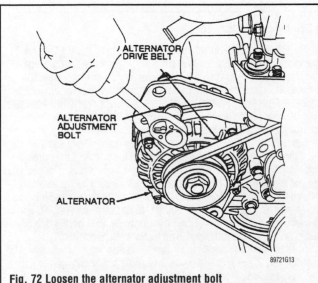

Fig. 72 Loosen the alternator adjustment bolt

Fig. 74 Loosen the idler pulley bolt and rotate the pulley to release belt tension

Fig. 75 Removing the A/C compressor's drive belt

Power Steering Pump

▶ **See Figures 68, 69 and 71**

1. Remove the air cleaner intake tube and air cleaner.
2. Loosen the power steering pump bolt.
3. Loosen the adjustment locknut until there is enough slack to remove the belt.
4. Remove the belt from the power steering, crankshaft and A/C compressor pulleys.
5. Remove the belt from the engine compartment.

To install:

6. Route the belt around the power steering , A/C compressor and crankshaft pulleys. Make sure the belt is properly seated on each pulley.
7. Adjust the belt to the proper tension.
8. Tighten the power steering pump bolt to 27–38 ft. lbs. (37–52 Nm).
9. Tighten the adjustment locknut to 14–19 ft. lbs. (19–25 Nm).
10. Install the air cleaner and intake tube.

Alternator

▶ **See Figures 68, 76 and 77**

1. Loosen the alternator adjustment bolt until there is enough slack to remove the belt.

Fig. 76 Location of the alternator adjustment bolt

2. Raise the car and support it with safety stands.
3. Loosen the lower alternator bolt and lower the car.
4. Remove the belt from the water pump, crankshaft and alternator pulleys.
5. Remove the belt from the engine compartment.

To install:

6. Route the belt around the alternator, water pump and crankshaft pulleys. Make sure the belt is properly seated on each pulley.

✸✸ CAUTION

Never pry the alternator rear housing and bearing

7. Adjust the belt to the proper tension by positioning a prybar on the area around a case bolt, then pry the alternator until the proper tension is reached.
8. Tighten the alternator adjustment bolt to 14–19 ft. lbs. (19–25 Nm).
9. Raise the car and support it with safety stands.
10. Tighten the lower alternator bolt to 27–38 ft. lbs. (37–52 Nm).
11. Lower the car.

Fig. 77 Removing the alternator belt

Timing Belts

INSPECTION

▶ **See Figures 78 thru 85**

The 1.3L engine utilizes a timing belt to drive the camshaft from the crankshaft's turning motion and to maintain proper valve timing. Some manufacturers schedule periodic timing belt replacement to assure optimum engine performance, to make sure the motorist is never stranded should the belt break (as the engine will stop instantly) and, in some cases (vehicles with interference engines), to prevent the possibility of severe internal engine damage should the belt break.

Although the 1.3L engine is not listed by its manufacturer as an interference engine (one whose valves might contact the pistons if the camshaft was rotated separately from the crankshaft), the first 2 reasons for periodic replacement still apply. Ford does not publish a timing belt replacement interval for this engine, but most belt manufacturers recommend intervals anywhere from 45,000 miles (72,500 km) to 90,000 miles (145,000 km). You will have to decide for yourself if the peace of mind offered by a new belt is worth the time and expense on higher mileage engines.

Whether or not you decide to replace the timing belt, you would be wise to check it periodically to make sure it has not become damaged or worn. Generally speaking, a severely worn belt may cause engine performance to

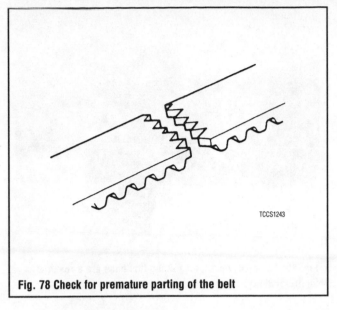

Fig. 78 Check for premature parting of the belt

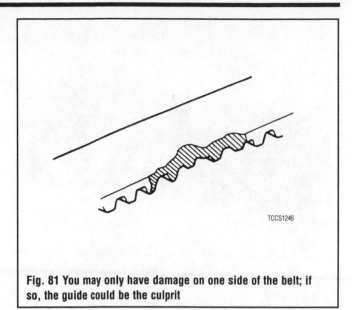

Fig. 81 You may only have damage on one side of the belt; if so, the guide could be the culprit

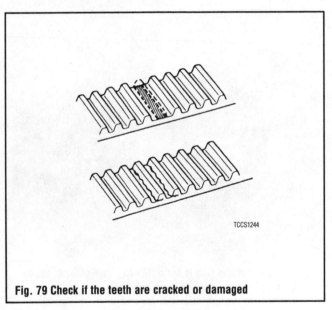

Fig. 79 Check if the teeth are cracked or damaged

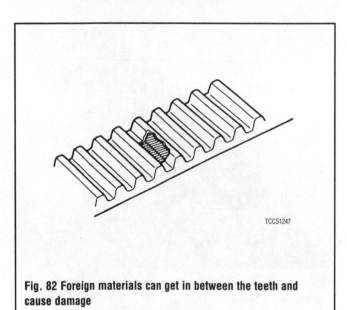

Fig. 82 Foreign materials can get in between the teeth and cause damage

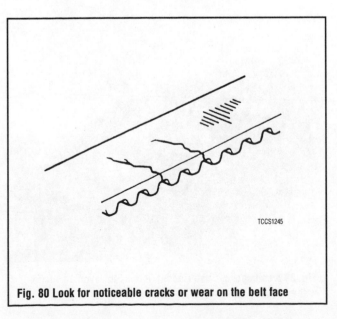

Fig. 80 Look for noticeable cracks or wear on the belt face

Fig. 83 Inspect the timing belt for cracks, fraying, glazing or damage of any kind

Fig. 84 Damage on only one side of the timing belt may indicate a faulty guide

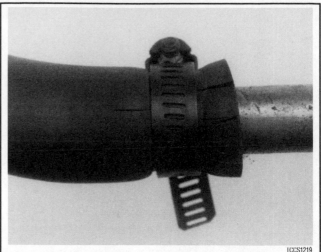

Fig. 86 The cracks developing along this hose are a result of age-related hardening

Fig. 85 ALWAYS replace the timing belt at the interval specified by the manufacturer

Fig. 87 A hose clamp that is too tight can cause older hoses to separate and tear on either side of the clamp

drop dramatically, but a damaged belt (which could give out suddenly) may not give as much warning. In general, any time the engine timing cover(s) is (are) removed, you should inspect the belt for premature parting, severe cracks or missing teeth. Also, an access plug is provided in the upper portion of the timing cover so that camshaft timing can be checked without cover removal. If the timing is found to be off, cover removal and further belt inspection or replacement is necessary.

Hoses

INSPECTION

▶ See Figures 86, 87, 88 and 89

Upper and lower radiator hoses, along with the heater hoses, should be checked for deterioration, leaks and loose hose clamps at least every 15,000 miles (24,000 km). It is also wise to check the hoses periodically in early spring and at the beginning of the fall or winter when you are performing other maintenance. A quick visual inspection could discover a weakened hose which might have left you stranded if it had remained unrepaired.

Fig. 88 A soft spongy hose (identifiable by the swollen section) will eventually burst and should be replaced

Fig. 89 Hoses are likely to deteriorate from the inside if the cooling system is not periodically flushed

Whenever you are checking the hoses, make sure the engine and cooling system are cold. Visually inspect for cracking, rotting or collapsed hoses, and replace as necessary. Run your hand along the length of the hose. If a weak or swollen spot is noted when squeezing the hose wall, the hose should be replaced.

REMOVAL & INSTALLATION

1. Remove the radiator pressure cap.

✳✳ CAUTION

Never remove the pressure cap while the engine is running, or personal injury from scalding hot coolant or steam may result. If possible, wait until the engine has cooled to remove the pressure cap. If this is not possible, wrap a thick cloth around the pressure cap and turn it slowly to the stop. Step back while the pressure is released from the cooling system. When you are sure all the pressure has been released, use the cloth to turn and remove the cap.

2. Position a clean container under the radiator and/or engine drain-cock or plug, then open the drain and allow the cooling system to drain to an appropriate level. For some upper hoses, only a little coolant must be drained. To remove hoses positioned lower on the engine, such as a lower radiator hose, the entire cooling system must be emptied.

✳✳ CAUTION

When draining coolant, keep in mind that cats and dogs are attracted by ethylene glycol antifreeze, and are quite likely to drink any that is left in an uncovered container or in puddles on the ground. This will prove fatal in sufficient quantity. Always drain coolant into a sealable container. Coolant may be reused unless it is contaminated or several years old.

3. Loosen the hose clamps at each end of the hose requiring replacement. Clamps are usually either of the spring tension type (which require pliers to squeeze the tabs and loosen) or of the screw tension type (which require screw or hex drivers to loosen). Pull the clamps back on the hose away from the connection.

4. Twist, pull and slide the hose off the fitting, taking care not to damage the neck of the component from which the hose is being removed.

➡If the hose is stuck at the connection, do not try to insert a screwdriver or other sharp tool under the hose end in an effort to free it,

as the connection and/or hose may become damaged. Heater connections especially may be easily damaged by such a procedure. If the hose is to be replaced, use a single-edged razor blade to make a slice along the portion of the hose which is stuck on the connection, perpendicular to the end of the hose. Do not cut deep, to prevent damaging the connection. The hose can then be peeled from the connection and discarded.

5. Clean both hose mounting connections. Inspect the condition of the hose clamps and replace them, if necessary.

To install:

6. Dip the ends of the new hose into clean engine coolant to ease installation.

7. Slide the clamps over the replacement hose, then slide the hose ends over the connections into position.

8. Position and secure the clamps at least ¼ in. (6.35mm) from the ends of the hose. Make sure they are located beyond the raised bead of the connector.

9. Close the radiator or engine drains and properly refill the cooling system with the clean drained engine coolant or a suitable mixture of ethylene glycol coolant and water.

10. If available, install a pressure tester and check for leaks. If a pressure tester is not available, run the engine until normal operating temperature is reached (allowing the system to naturally pressurize), then check for leaks.

✳✳ CAUTION

If you are checking for leaks with the system at normal operating temperature, BE EXTREMELY CAREFUL not to touch any moving or hot engine parts. Once temperature has been reached, shut the engine OFF, and check for leaks around the hose fittings and connections which were removed earlier.

CV-Boots

INSPECTION

▶ **See Figures 90 and 91**

The CV (Constant Velocity) boots should be checked for damage each time the oil is changed and any other time the vehicle is raised for service. These boots keep water, grime, dirt and other damaging matter from entering the CV-joints. Any of these could cause early CV-joint failure which can be expensive to repair. Heavy grease thrown around the inside of the front

Fig. 90 CV-boots must be inspected periodically for damage

Fig. 91 A torn boot should be replaced immediately

wheel(s) and on the brake caliper/drum can be an indication of a torn boot. Thoroughly check the boots for missing clamps and tears. If the boot is damaged, it should be replaced immediately. Please refer to Section 7 for procedures.

Spark Plugs

▶ See Figure 92

A typical spark plug consists of a metal shell surrounding a ceramic insulator. A metal electrode extends downward through the center of the insulator and protrudes a small distance. Located at the end of the plug and attached to the side of the outer metal shell is the side electrode. The side electrode bends in at a 90° angle so that its tip is just past and parallel to the tip of the center electrode. The distance between these two electrodes (measured in thousandths of an inch or hundredths of a millimeter) is called the spark plug gap.

The spark plug does not produce a spark but instead provides a gap across which the current can arc. The coil produces anywhere from 20,000 to 50,000 volts (depending on the type and application) which travels through the wires to the spark plugs. The current passes along the center electrode and jumps the gap to the side electrode, and in doing so, ignites the air/fuel mixture in the combustion chamber.

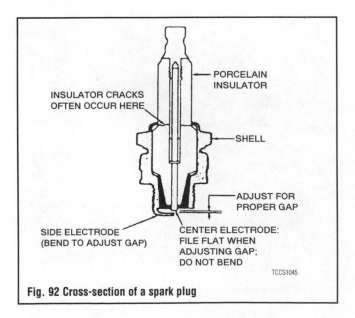

Fig. 92 Cross-section of a spark plug

SPARK PLUG HEAT RANGE

▶ See Figure 93

Spark plug heat range is the ability of the plug to dissipate heat. The longer the insulator (or the farther it extends into the engine), the hotter the plug will operate; the shorter the insulator (the closer the electrode is to the block's cooling passages) the cooler it will operate. A plug that absorbs little heat and remains too cool will quickly accumulate deposits of oil and carbon since it is not hot enough to burn them off. This leads to plug fouling and consequently to misfiring. A plug that absorbs too much heat will have no deposits but, due to the excessive heat, the electrodes will burn away quickly and might possibly lead to preignition or other ignition problems. Preignition takes place when plug tips get so hot that they glow sufficiently to ignite the air/fuel mixture before the actual spark occurs. This early ignition will usually cause a pinging during low speeds and heavy loads.

The general rule of thumb for choosing the correct heat range when picking a spark plug is: if most of your driving is long distance, high speed travel, use a colder plug; if most of your driving is stop and go, use a hotter plug. Original equipment plugs are generally a good compromise between the 2 styles and most people never have the need to change their plugs from the factory-recommended heat range.

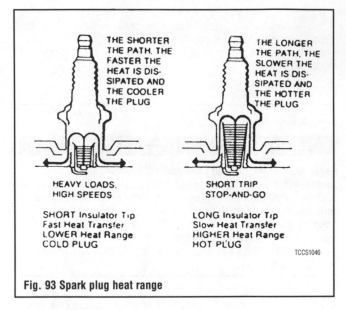

Fig. 93 Spark plug heat range

REMOVAL & INSTALLATION

▶ See Figures 94, 95, 96 and 97

A set of spark plugs usually requires replacement after about 20,000–30,000 miles (32,000–48,000 km), depending on your style of driving. In normal operation, plug gap increases about 0.001 in. (0.025mm) for every 2500 miles (4000 km). As the gap increases, the plug's voltage requirement also increases. It requires a greater voltage to jump the wider gap and about two to three times as much voltage to fire the plug at high speeds than at idle. The improved air/fuel ratio control of modern fuel injection, combined with the higher voltage output of modern ignition systems, will often allow an engine to run significantly longer on a set of standard spark plugs, but keep in mind that efficiency will drop as the gap widens (along with fuel economy and power).

When you're removing spark plugs, work on one at a time. Don't start by removing the plug wires all at once, because, unless you number them, they may become mixed up. Take a minute before you begin and number the wires with tape.

1. Disconnect the negative battery cable, and if the vehicle has been run recently, allow the engine to thoroughly cool.

2. Carefully twist the spark plug wire boot to loosen it, then pull upward and remove the boot from the plug. Be sure to pull on the boot and not on the wire, otherwise the connector located inside the boot may become separated.

3. Using compressed air, blow any water or debris from the spark plug well to assure that no harmful contaminants are allowed to enter the combustion chamber when the spark plug is removed. If compressed air is not available, use a rag or a brush to clean the area.

➡**Remove the spark plugs when the engine is cold, if possible, to prevent damage to the threads. If removal of the plugs is difficult, apply a few drops of penetrating oil or silicone spray to the area around the base of the plug, and allow it a few minutes to work.**

4. Using a spark plug socket that is equipped with a rubber insert to properly hold the plug, turn the spark plug counterclockwise to loosen and remove the spark plug from the bore.

❊❊ WARNING

Be sure not to use a flexible extension on the socket. Use of a flexible extension may allow a shear force to be applied to the plug. A shear force could break the plug off in the cylinder head, leading to costly and frustrating repairs.

Fig. 96 Remove the spark plug and check the electrodes for damage, wear and gap

Fig. 94 Grasp the spark plug wire by the boot and disconnect it from the plug by pulling with a slight twisting motion

Fig. 97 Coat the threads of the plug with an anti-seize compound before installation

To install:

5. Inspect the spark plug boot for tears or damage. If a damaged boot is found, the spark plug wire must be replaced.

6. Using a wire feeler gauge, check and adjust the spark plug gap. When using a gauge, the proper size should pass between the electrodes with a slight drag. The next larger size should not be able to pass while the next smaller size should pass freely.

7. Carefully thread the plug into the bore by hand. If resistance is felt before the plug is almost completely threaded, back the plug out and begin threading again. In small, hard to reach areas, an old spark plug wire and boot could be used as a threading tool. The boot will hold the plug while you twist the end of the wire and the wire is supple enough to twist before it would allow the plug to crossthread.

❊❊ WARNING

Do not use the spark plug socket to thread the plugs. Always carefully thread the plug by hand or using an old plug wire to prevent the possibility of crossthreading and damaging the cylinder head bore.

Fig. 95 Using a spark plug socket with a rubber insert to grip the plug, turn the spark plug counterclockwise to loosen

8. Carefully tighten the spark plug. If the plug you are installing is equipped with a crush washer, seat the plug, then tighten about ¼ turn to crush the washer. If you are installing a tapered seat plug, tighten the plug to specifications provided by the vehicle or plug manufacturer.

9. Apply a small amount of silicone dielectric compound to the end of the spark plug lead or inside the spark plug boot to prevent sticking, then install the boot to the spark plug and push until it clicks into place. The click may be felt or heard, then gently pull back on the boot to assure proper contact.

INSPECTION & GAPPING

▶ **See Figures 98 thru 108**

Check the plugs for deposits and wear. If they are not going to be replaced, clean the plugs thoroughly. Remember that any kind of deposit will decrease the efficiency of the plug. Plugs can be cleaned on a spark plug cleaning machine, which can sometimes be found in service stations, or you can do an acceptable job of cleaning with a stiff brush. If the plugs are cleaned, the electrodes must be filed flat. Use an ignition points file, not an emery board or the like, which will leave deposits. The electrodes must be filed perfectly flat with sharp edges; rounded edges reduce the spark plug voltage by as much as 50%.

Fig. 99 A carbon fouled plug, identified by soft, sooty, black deposits, may indicate an improperly tuned vehicle. Check the air cleaner, ignition components and engine control system

Fig. 98 A normally worn spark plug should have light tan or gray deposits on the firing tip

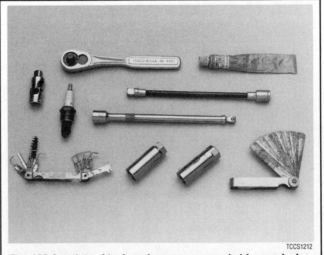

Fig. 100 A variety of tools and gauges are needed for spark plug service

TCCS2137

Fig. 101 A physically damaged spark plug may be evidence of severe detonation in that cylinder. Watch that cylinder carefully between services, as a continued detonation will not only damage the plug, but could also damage the engine

TCCS2138

Fig. 103 An oil fouled spark plug indicates an engine with worn piston rings and/or bad valve seals allowing excessive oil to enter the chamber

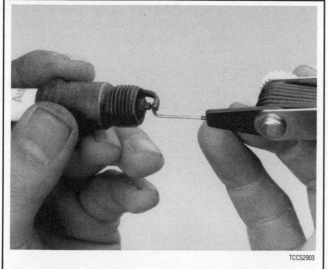

TCCS2903

Fig. 102 Checking the spark plug gap with a feeler gauge

TCCS2904

Fig. 104 Adjusting the spark plug gap

Fig. 105 This spark plug has been left in the engine too long, as evidenced by the extreme gap—Plugs with such an extreme gap can cause misfiring and stumbling accompanied by a noticeable lack of power

Fig. 107 A bridged or almost bridged spark plug, identified by a build-up between the electrodes caused by excessive carbon or oil build-up on the plug

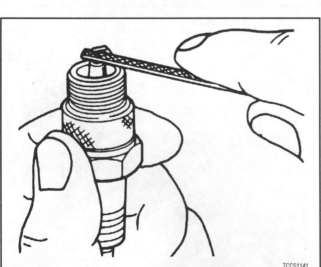

Fig. 106 If the standard plug is in good condition, the electrode may be filed flat—CAUTION: do not file platinum plugs

Check spark plug gap before installation. The ground electrode (the L-shaped one connected to the body of the plug) must be parallel to the center electrode and the specified size wire gauge (please refer to the Tune-Up Specifications chart for details) must pass between the electrodes with a slight drag.

➡**NEVER adjust the gap on a used platinum type spark plug.**

Always check the gap on new plugs as they are not always set correctly at the factory. Do not use a flat feeler gauge when measuring the gap on a used plug, because the reading may be inaccurate. A round-wire type gapping tool is the best way to check the gap. The correct gauge should pass through the electrode gap with a slight drag. If you're in doubt, try one size smaller and one larger. The smaller gauge should go through easily, while the larger one shouldn't go through at all. Wire gapping tools usually have a bending tool attached. Use that to adjust the side electrode until the proper distance is obtained. Absolutely never attempt to bend the center electrode. Also, be careful not to bend the side electrode too far or too often, as it may weaken and break off within the engine, requiring removal of the cylinder head to retrieve it.

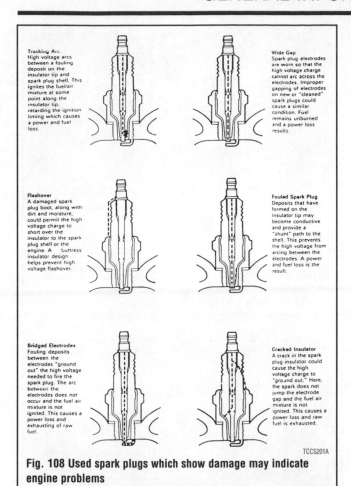

Fig. 108 Used spark plugs which show damage may indicate engine problems

Spark Plug Wires

TESTING

▶ See Figure 109

At every tune-up/inspection, visually check the spark plug wires for burns, cuts, or breaks in the insulation. Check the boots and the nipples on the distributor cap and/or coil. Replace any damaged wiring.

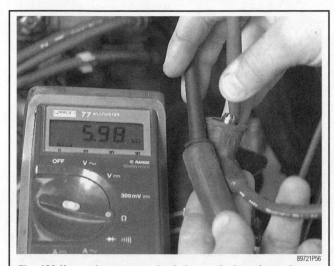

Fig. 109 Use a ohmmeter to check the spark plug wire resistance

Every 50,000 miles (80,000 km) or 60 months, the resistance of the wires should be checked with an ohmmeter. Wires with excessive resistance will cause misfiring, and may make the engine difficult to start in damp weather.

To check resistance, an ohmmeter should be used on each wire to test resistance between the end connectors. Remove and install/replace the wires in order, one-by-one.

Resistance on these wires must not exceed 7,000 ohms per foot. To properly measure this, remove the wires from the plugs, and remove the distributor cap. Do not remove the wires from the cap. Measure the resistance through the terminal in the distributor cap. Do not pierce any ignition wire for any reason. Measure only from the two ends.

➡ **Whenever the high tension wires are removed from the plugs, coil, or distributor, silicone grease must be applied to the boot before reconnection. Coat the entire interior surface with Ford silicone grease D7AZ-19A331-A or its equivalent.**

REMOVAL & INSTALLATION

▶ See Figures 110 and 111

1. If the wires are to be re-used, matchmark or label all the wires prior to removal.

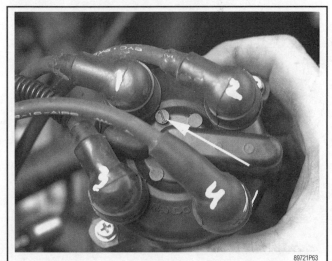

Fig. 110 The location of the number one spark plug tower (arrow) may be marked on the cap

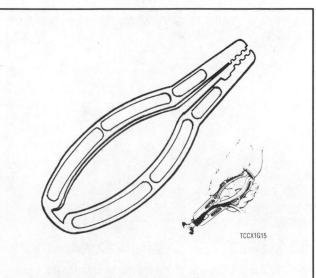

Fig. 111 Example of a spark plug wire puller

2. If the wires are being replaced, remove and replace them one-by-one.

3. In all cases, use a spark plug removal tool to grasp the protective boot at the connector. Do not pull on the wires. Grasp and twist the boot to remove the wire.

➡Whenever the high tension wires are removed from the plugs, coil, or distributor, silicone grease must be applied to the boot before reconnection. Coat the entire interior surface with Ford silicone grease D7AZ-19A331-A or its equivalent.

Distributor Cap and Rotor

REMOVAL & INSTALLATION

▸ **See Figures 110, 112, 113, 114, 115 and 116**

1. Disconnect the negative battery cable.
2. Matchmark the spark plug wires to their respective towers on the distributor cap.
3. Disconnect the spark plug wires from the cap.
4. Loosen the distributor cap's hold-down screws.

Fig. 114 . . . then remove the distributor cap

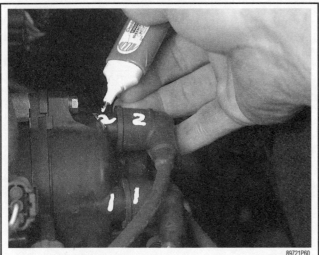

Fig. 112 Matchmark the spark plug wires to their respective towers on the distributor cap

Fig. 115 Remove the wire from the cap by grasping the boot and pulling up with a slight twisting motion

Fig. 113 Use a Phillips head screwdriver to unfasten the distributor cap hold-down screws . . .

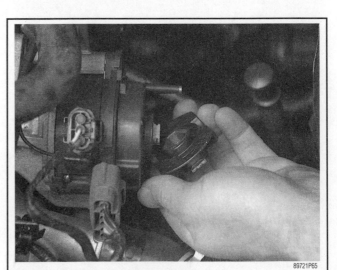

Fig. 116 The rotor is removed by pulling it straight from the shaft

5. Remove the distributor cap.
6. Grasp the rotor and pull it from the shaft.

To install:

7. Position the rotor on the shaft and press it firmly, but gently, until firmly seated.
8. Position the cap on the distributor and fasten the hold-down screws.
9. Install the spark plug wires.
10. Start the vehicle and check for proper operation.

INSPECTION

1. Remove the distributor cap and rotor.
2. Wash the inside and outside of the cap, as well as the rotor, with soap and water, then dry them thoroughly with compressed air or a lint-free cloth.
3. Look closely at the distributor cap, inspecting it for signs of deterioration such as cracks, a broken carbon button or carbon tracks.
4. Inspect the terminals for dirt or corrosion.
5. Inspect the rotor for carbon build-up, cracks or damage to the blade or spring.
6. If damage is found, replace the distributor cap and/or rotor.

Ignition Timing

GENERAL INFORMATION

▶ **See Figure 117**

Ignition timing is the measurement, in degrees of crankshaft rotation, of the point at which the spark plugs fire in each of the cylinders. It is measured in degrees before or after Top Dead Center (TDC) of the compression stroke.

Ideally, the air/fuel mixture in the cylinder will be ignited by the spark plug just as the piston passes TDC of the compression stroke. If this happens, the piston will be beginning the power stroke just as the compressed and ignited air/fuel mixture starts to expand. The expansion of the air/fuel mixture then forces the piston down on the power stroke and turns the crankshaft.

Because it takes a fraction of a second for the spark plug to ignite the mixture in the cylinder, the spark plug must fire a little before the piston reaches TDC. Otherwise, the mixture will not be completely ignited as the piston passes TDC and the full power of the explosion will not be used by the engine.

The timing measurement is given in degrees of crankshaft rotation before the piston reaches TDC (Before Top Dead Center or BTDC). If the setting for the ignition timing is 5°BTDC, each spark plug must fire 5° before each piston reaches TDC. This only holds true, however, when the engine is at idle speed.

As the engine speed increases, the piston goes faster. The spark plugs have to ignite the fuel even sooner if it is to be completely ignited when the piston reaches TDC.

If the ignition is set too far advanced (BTDC), the ignition and expansion of the fuel in the cylinder will occur too soon and tend to force the piston down while it is still traveling up. This causes engine ping. If the ignition spark is set too far retarded after TDC (ATDC), the piston will have already passed TDC and started on its way down when the fuel is ignited. This will cause the piston to be forced down for only a portion of its travel. This will result in poor engine performance and lack of power.

Timing marks consist of O marks or scales and can be found on the rim of the crankshaft pulley and the timing cover. The mark(s) on the pulley correspond(s) to the position of the piston in the No. 1 cylinder. A strobo-scopic (dynamic) timing light hooked into the circuit of the No. 1 cylinder spark plug can be used to indicate ignition timing as follows:

Every time the spark plug fires, the timing light flashes. By aiming the timing light at the timing marks while the engine is running, the exact position of the piston within the cylinder can be easily read, since the strobo-scopic flash makes the pulley appear to be standing still. Proper timing is indicated when the mark and scale are in proper alignment.

Because these vehicles utilize high voltage, electronic ignition systems, only a timing light with an inductive pickup should be used. The pickup simply clamps to the No. 1 spark plug wire, eliminating the adapter. It is not susceptible to cross-firing or false triggering, which may occur with a conventional light, due to the greater voltages produced by electronic ignition.

INSPECTION & ADJUSTMENT

▶ **See Figures 118, 119 and 120**

1. Start the car and let it reach operating temperature.
2. Turn all accessories **OFF**.
3. Connect a timing light according to the tool manufacturer's instructions.
4. Check the timing by aiming the light at the pointer on the timing belt cover. The yellow timing mark on the crankshaft pulley should line up with the pointer and should read 10 ° BTDC.
5. If the timing is incorrect, loosen the distributor hold-down bolts.
6. Rotate the distributor until the desired timing is achieved.
7. Tighten the distributor hold-down bolts to 14–19 ft. lbs. (19–25 Nm).
8. Recheck the timing and, if it is still correct, remove the light.
9. If the timing is still incorrect, repeat Steps 5 through 8.

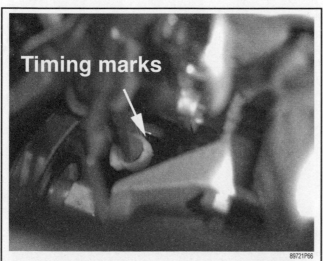

Fig. 117 The timing marks are located on a scale attached to the timing belt cover

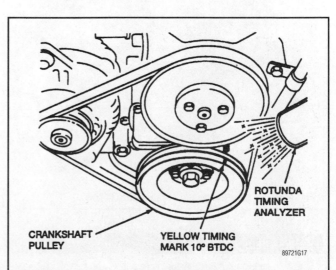

Fig. 118 Aim the timing light at the pointer on the timing scale located on the timing cover

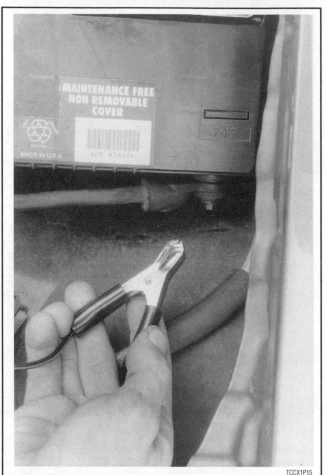

Fig. 119 Most timing lights have leads which attach to the battery

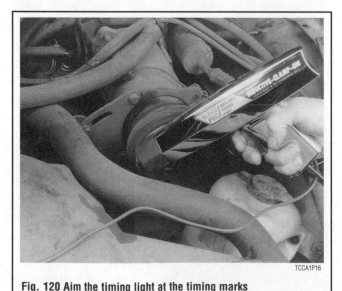

Fig. 120 Aim the timing light at the timing marks

Valve Lash

The 1.3L engine used in the Aspire is equipped with hydraulic lifters. No adjustment is necessary or possible.

Idle Speed and Mixture Adjustments

IDLE SPEED

▶ See Figures 121, 122 and 123

➡ Before adjusting the idle speed, make sure the ignition timing is correct and that all electrical loads, such as the cooling fan and lamps, are OFF.

1. Connect a digital multimeter with an inductive pickup to the No. 1 spark plug wire.
2. Ground the PCM STI (TEN) pin at the Data Link Connector (DLC). Refer to the accompanying illustration.
3. Start the engine and let it reach normal operating temperature, then note the idle speed.
4. The idle should be 650–750 rpm on a manual transaxle in **NEUTRAL** or 700–800 rpm on an automatic transaxle in **PARK**.
5. If the idle is not as specified, turn the idle speed adjustment screw (refer to the accompanying illustration) until the correct idle speed is reached.

Fig. 121 The idle speed adjustment screw is located in a recessed bore on the throttle body assembly

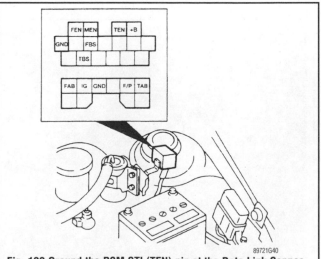

Fig. 122 Ground the PCM STI (TEN) pin at the Data Link Connector (DLC)

TUNE-UP SPECIFICATIONS

Year	Engine ID/VIN	Engine Displacement Liters (cc)	Spark Plugs Gap (in.)	Ignition Timing (deg.) MT	AT	Fuel Pump (psi)	Idle Speed (rpm) MT	AT	Valve Clearance In.	Ex.
1994	H	1.3L (1300)	0.039-0.043	10° BTDC	10° BTDC	30-38	650-750	650-750	HYD	HYD
1995	H	1.3L (1300)	0.039-0.043	10° BTDC	10° BTDC	30-38	650-750	650-750	HYD	HYD
1996	H	1.3L (1300)	0.039-0.043	10° BTDC	10° BTDC	30-38	650-750	650-750	HYD	HYD
1997	H	1.3L (1300)	0.039-0.043	10° BTDC	10° BTDC	30-38	650-750	650-750	HYD	HYD

NOTE: The Vehicle Emission Control Information label often reflects specification changes made during production. The label figures must be used if they differ from those in this chart.
BTDC - Before Top Dead Center
HYD - Hydraulic

89721C03

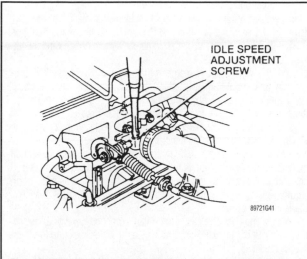

Fig. 123 Turn the idle speed adjustment screw until the proper idle is reached

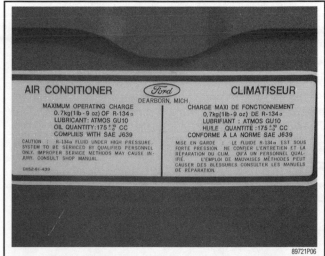

Fig. 124 The A/C label under the hood includes information on the refrigerant type and capacity

6. Turn the engine **OFF** and let it cool.
7. Remove the ground from the DLC.
8. After the engine has cooled, start the engine, let it reach normal operating temperature and check the idle speed.

IDLE MIXTURE

The mixture adjustments are controlled by the Powertrain Control Module (PCM). No adjustment is necessary or possible.

Air Conditioning System

SYSTEM SERVICE & REPAIR

▶ See Figure 124

➡It is recommended that the A/C system be serviced by an EPA Section 609 certified automotive technician utilizing a refrigerant recovery/recycling machine.

The do-it-yourselfer should not service his/her own vehicle's A/C system for many reasons, including legal concerns, personal injury, environmental damage and cost. The following are some of the reasons why you may decide not to service your own vehicle's A/C system.

According to the U.S. Clean Air Act, it is a federal crime to service or repair (involving the refrigerant) a Motor Vehicle Air Conditioning (MVAC) system for money without being EPA certified. It is also illegal to vent R-134a refrigerant into the atmosphere.

State and/or local laws may be more strict than the federal regulations, so be sure to check with your state and/or local authorities for further information. For further federal information on the legality of servicing your A/C system, call the EPA Stratospheric Ozone Hotline.

➡Federal law dictates that a fine of up to $25,000 may be levied on people convicted of venting refrigerant into the atmosphere. Additionally, the EPA may pay up to $10,000 for information or services leading to a criminal conviction of the violation of these laws.

When servicing an A/C system you run the risk of handling or coming in contact with refrigerant, which may result in skin or eye irritation or frostbite. Although low in toxicity (due to chemical stability), inhalation of concentrated refrigerant fumes is dangerous and can result in death; cases of fatal cardiac arrhythmia have been reported in people accidentally subjected to high levels of refrigerant. Some early symptoms include loss of concentration and drowsiness.

Also, refrigerants can decompose at high temperatures (near gas heaters or open flame), which may result in hydrofluoric acid, hydrochloric acid and phosgene (a fatal nerve gas).

R-134a refrigerant is a greenhouse gas which, if allowed to vent into the atmosphere, will contribute to global warming (the Greenhouse Effect).

It is usually more economically feasible to have a certified MVAC automotive technician perform A/C system service to your vehicle. While it is illegal to service an A/C system without the proper equipment, the home mechanic would have to purchase an expensive refrigerant recovery/recycling machine to service his/her own vehicle.

PREVENTIVE MAINTENANCE

Although the A/C system should not be serviced by the do-it-yourselfer, preventive maintenance can be practiced and A/C system inspections can be performed to help maintain the efficiency of the vehicle's A/C system. For preventive maintenance, perform the following:

• The easiest and most important preventive maintenance for your A/C system is to be sure that it is used on a regular basis. Running the system for five minutes each month (no matter what the season) will help ensure that the seals and all internal components remain lubricated.

➡Some newer vehicles automatically operate the A/C system compressor whenever the windshield defroster is activated. When running, the compressor lubricates the A/C system components; therefore, the A/C system would not need to be operated each month.

• In order to prevent heater core freeze-up during A/C operation, It is necessary to maintain a proper antifreeze protection. Use a hand-held coolant tester (hydrometer) to periodically check the condition of the antifreeze in your engine's cooling system.

➡Antifreeze should not be used longer than the manufacturer specifies.

• For efficient operation of an air conditioned vehicle's cooling system, the radiator cap should have a holding pressure which meets manufacturer's specifications. A cap which fails to hold these pressures should be replaced.

• Any obstruction of or damage to the condenser configuration will restrict air flow which is essential to its efficient operation. It is, therefore, a good rule to keep this unit clean and in proper physical shape.

➡Bug screens which are mounted in front of the condenser (unless they are original equipment) are regarded as obstructions.

• The condensation drain tube expels any water, which accumulates on the bottom of the evaporator housing, into the engine compartment. If this tube is obstructed, the air conditioning performance can be restricted and condensation buildup can spill over onto the vehicle's floor.

SYSTEM INSPECTION

Although the A/C system should not be serviced by the do-it-yourselfer, preventive maintenance can be practiced and A/C system inspections can be performed to help maintain the efficiency of the vehicle's A/C system. For A/C system inspection, perform the following:

The easiest and often most important check for the air conditioning system consists of a visual inspection of the system components. Visually inspect the air conditioning system for refrigerant leaks, damaged compressor clutch, abnormal compressor drive belt tension and/or condition, plugged evaporator drain tube, blocked condenser fins, disconnected or broken wires, blown fuses, corroded connections and poor insulation.

A refrigerant leak will usually appear as an oily residue at the leakage point in the system. The oily residue soon picks up dust or dirt particles from the surrounding air and appears greasy. Through time, this will build up and appear to be a heavy dirt impregnated grease.

For a thorough visual and operational inspection, check the following:
• Check the surface of the radiator and condenser for dirt, leaves or other material which might block air flow.
• Check for kinks in hoses and lines. Check the system for leaks.
• Make sure the drive belt is properly tensioned. When the air conditioning is operating, make sure the drive belt is free of noise or slippage.
• Make sure the blower motor operates at all appropriate positions, then check for distribution of the air from all outlets with the blower on **HIGH** or **MAX**.

➡Keep in mind that under conditions of high humidity, air discharged from the A/C vents may not feel as cold as expected, even if the system is working properly. This is because vaporized moisture in humid air retains heat more effectively than dry air, thereby making humid air more difficult to cool.

• Make sure the air passage selection lever is operating correctly. Start the engine and warm it to normal operating temperature, then make sure the temperature selection lever is operating correctly.

Windshield Wipers

ELEMENT (REFILL) CARE & REPLACEMENT

▶ **See Figures 125 thru 134**

For maximum effectiveness and longest element life, the windshield and wiper blades should be kept clean. Dirt, tree sap, road tar and so on will cause streaking, smearing and blade deterioration if left on the glass. It is advisable to wash the windshield carefully with a commercial glass cleaner at least once a month. Wipe off the rubber blades with the wet rag afterwards. Do not attempt to move wipers across the windshield by hand; damage to the motor and drive mechanism will result.

To inspect and/or replace the wiper blade elements, place the wiper switch in the **LOW** speed position and the ignition switch in the **ACC** position. When the wiper blades are approximately vertical on the windshield, turn the ignition switch to **OFF**.

Examine the wiper blade elements. If they are found to be cracked, broken or torn, they should be replaced immediately. Replacement intervals will vary with usage, although ozone deterioration usually limits element life to about one year. If the wiper pattern is smeared or streaked, or if the blade chatters across the glass, the elements should be replaced. It is easiest and most sensible to replace the elements in pairs.

If your vehicle is equipped with aftermarket blades, there are several different types of refills and your vehicle might have any kind. Aftermarket blades and arms rarely use the exact same type blade or refill as the original equipment. Here are some typical aftermarket blades; not all may be available for your vehicle:

The Anco® type uses a release button that is pushed down to allow the refill to slide out of the yoke jaws. The new refill slides back into the frame and locks in place.

Some Trico® refills are removed by locating where the metal backing strip or the refill is wider. Insert a small screwdriver blade between the frame and metal backing strip. Press down to release the refill from the retaining tab.

Other types of Trico® refills have two metal tabs which are unlocked by squeezing them together. The rubber filler can then be withdrawn from the frame jaws. A new refill is installed by inserting the refill into the front frame jaws and sliding it rearward to engage the remaining frame jaws. There are usually four jaws; be certain when installing that the refill is

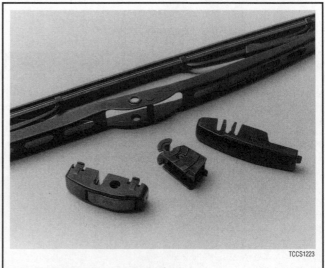

Fig. 125 Bosch® wiper blade and fit kit

TCCS1223

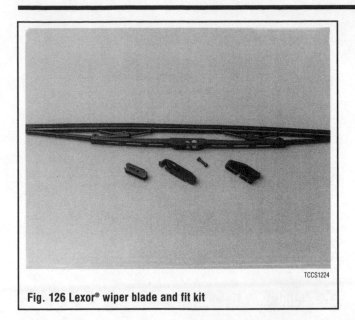

TCCS1224

Fig. 126 Lexor® wiper blade and fit kit

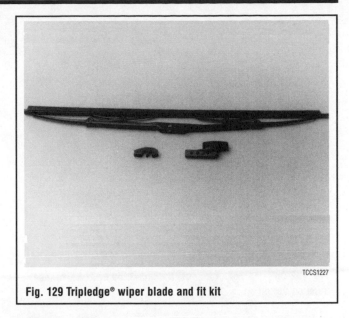

TCCS1227

Fig. 129 Tripledge® wiper blade and fit kit

TCCS1225

Fig. 127 Pylon® wiper blade and adapter

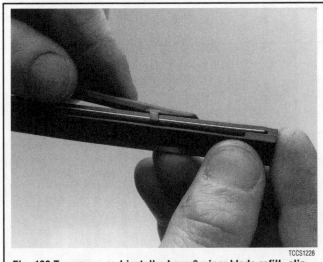

TCCS1228

Fig. 130 To remove and install a Lexor® wiper blade refill, slip out the old insert and slide in a new one

TCCS1226

Fig. 128 Trico® wiper blade and fit kit

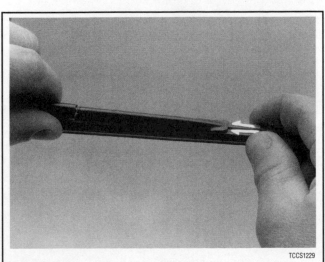

TCCS1229

Fig. 131 On Pylon® inserts, the clip at the end has to be removed prior to sliding the insert off

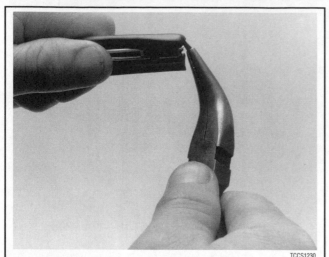

Fig. 132 On Trico® wiper blades, the tab at the end of the blade must be turned up . . .

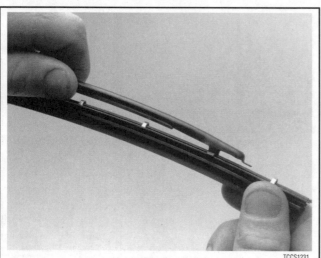

Fig. 133 . . . then the insert can be removed. After installing the replacement insert, bend the tab back

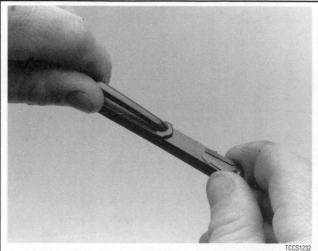

Fig. 134 The Tripledge® wiper blade insert is removed and installed using a securing clip

engaged in all of them. At the end of its travel, the tabs will lock into place on the front jaws of the wiper blade frame.

Another type of refill is made from polycarbonate. The refill has a simple locking device at one end which flexes downward out of the groove into which the jaws of the holder fit, allowing easy release. By sliding the new refill through all the jaws and pushing through the slight resistance when it reaches the end of its travel, the refill will lock into position.

To replace the Tridon® refill, it is necessary to remove the wiper blade. This refill has a plastic backing strip with a notch about 1 in. (25mm) from the end. Hold the blade (frame) on a hard surface so that the frame is tightly bowed. Grip the tip of the backing strip and pull up while twisting counter-clockwise. The backing strip will snap out of the retaining tab. Do this for the remaining tabs until the refill is free of the blade. The length of these refills is molded into the end and they should be replaced with identical types.

Regardless of the type of refill used, be sure to follow the part manufac-turer's instructions closely. Make sure that all of the frame jaws are engaged as the refill is pushed into place and locked. If the metal blade holder and frame are allowed to touch the glass during wiper operation, the glass will be scratched.

Tires and Wheels

Common sense and good driving habits will afford maximum tire life. Fast starts, sudden stops and hard cornering are hard on tires and will shorten their useful life span. Make sure that you don't overload the vehicle or run with incorrect pressure in the tires. Both of these practices will increase tread wear.

➡**For optimum tire life, keep the tires properly inflated, rotate them often and have the wheel alignment checked periodically.**

Inspect your tires frequently. Be especially careful to watch for bubbles in the tread or sidewall, deep cuts or underinflation. Replace any tires with bubbles in the sidewall. If cuts are so deep that they penetrate to the cords, discard the tire. Any cut in the sidewall of a radial tire renders it unsafe. Also look for uneven tread wear patterns that may indicate the front end is out of alignment or that the tires are out of balance.

TIRE ROTATION

▶ **See Figures 135 and 136**

Tires must be rotated periodically to equalize wear patterns that vary with a tire's position on the vehicle. Tires will also wear in an uneven way as the front steering/suspension system wears to the point where the alignment should be reset.

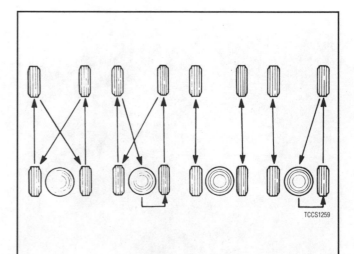

Fig. 135 Common tire rotation patterns for 4 and 5-wheel rota-tions

TCCS1234

Fig. 136 Unidirectional tires are identifiable by sidewall arrows and/or the word "rotation"

Rotating the tires will ensure maximum life for the tires as a set, so you will not have to discard a tire early due to wear on only part of the tread. Regular rotation is required to equalize wear.

When rotating "unidirectional tires," make sure that they always roll in the same direction. This means that a tire used on the left side of the vehicle must not be switched to the right side and vice-versa. Such tires should only be rotated front-to-rear or rear-to-front, while always remaining on the same side of the vehicle. These tires are marked on the sidewall as to the direction of rotation; observe the marks when reinstalling the tire(s).

Some styled or "mag" wheels may have different offsets front to rear. In these cases, the rear wheels must not be used up front and vice-versa. Furthermore, if these wheels are equipped with unidirectional tires, they cannot be rotated unless the tire is remounted for the proper direction of rotation.

➡**The compact or space-saver spare is strictly for emergency use. It must never be included in the tire rotation or placed on the vehicle for everyday use.**

TIRE DESIGN

▶ **See Figure 137**

For maximum satisfaction, tires should be used in sets of four. Mixing of different types (radial, bias-belted, fiberglass belted) must be avoided. In most cases, the vehicle manufacturer has designated a type of tire on which the vehicle will perform best. Your first choice when replacing tires should be to use the same type of tire that the manufacturer recommends.

When radial tires are used, tire sizes and wheel diamcters should be selected to maintain ground clearance and tire load capacity equivalent to the original specified tire. Radial tires should always be used in sets of four.

✷✷ CAUTION

Radial tires should never be used on only the front axle.

When selecting tires, pay attention to the original size as marked on the tire. Most tires are described using an industry size code sometimes referred to as P-Metric. This allows the exact identification of the tire specifications, regardless of the manufacturer. If selecting a different tire size or brand, remember to check the installed tire for any sign of interference with the body or suspension while the vehicle is stopping, turning sharply or heavily loaded.

Snow Tires

Good radial tires can produce a big advantage in slippery weather, but in snow, a street radial tire does not have sufficient tread to provide traction and control. The small grooves of a street tire quickly pack with snow and the tire behaves like a billiard ball on a marble floor. The more open, chunky tread of a snow tire will self-clean as the tire turns, providing much better grip on snowy surfaces.

To satisfy municipalities requiring snow tires during weather emergencies, most snow tires carry either an M + S designation after the tire size stamped on the sidewall, or the designation "all-season." In general, no change in tire size is necessary when buying snow tires.

Most manufacturers strongly recommend the use of 4 snow tires on their vehicles for reasons of stability. If snow tires are fitted only to the drive wheels, the opposite end of the vehicle may become very unstable when braking or turning on slippery surfaces. This instability can lead to unpleasant endings if the driver can't counteract the slide in time.

Note that snow tires, whether 2 or 4, will affect vehicle handling in all non-snow situations. The stiffer, heavier snow tires will noticeably change the turning and braking characteristics of the vehicle. Once the snow tires are installed, you must re-learn the behavior of the vehicle and drive accordingly.

➡**Consider buying extra wheels on which to mount the snow tires. Once done, the "snow wheels" can be installed and removed as needed. This eliminates the potential damage to tires or wheels from seasonal REMOVAL & INSTALLATION. Even if your vehicle has styled wheels, see if inexpensive steel wheels are available. Although the look of the vehicle will change, the expensive wheels will be protected from salt, curb hits and pothole damage.**

TIRE STORAGE

If they are mounted on wheels, store the tires at proper inflation pressure. All tires should be kept in a cool, dry place. If they are stored in the garage or basement, do not let them stand on a concrete floor; set them on strips of wood, a mat or a large stack of newspaper. Keeping them away from direct moisture is of paramount importance. Tires should not be stored upright, but in a flat position.

INFLATION & INSPECTION

▶ **See Figures 138 thru 145**

The importance of proper tire inflation cannot be overemphasized. A tire employs air as part of its structure. It is designed around the supporting strength of the air at a specified pressure. For this reason, improper inflation drastically reduces the tire's ability to perform as intended. A tire will lose some air in day-to-day use; having to add a few pounds of air periodically is not necessarily a sign of a leaking tire.

Two items should be a permanent fixture in every glove compartment: an accurate tire pressure gauge and a tread depth gauge. Check the tire pressure

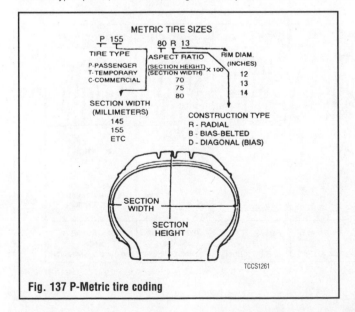

TCCS1261

Fig. 137 P-Metric tire coding

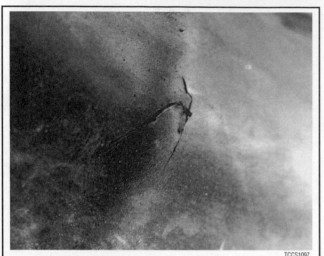

Fig. 138 Tires should be checked frequently for any sign of puncture or damage

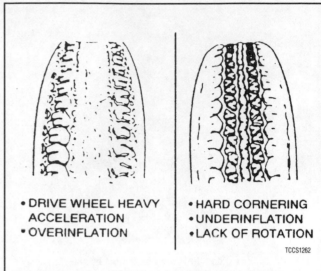

- DRIVE WHEEL HEAVY ACCELERATION
- OVERINFLATION

- HARD CORNERING
- UNDERINFLATION
- LACK OF ROTATION

Fig. 140 Examples of inflation-related tire wear patterns

Fig. 139 Tires with deep cuts, or cuts which show bulging, should be replaced immediately

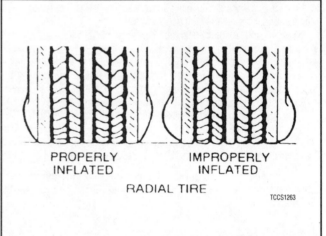

PROPERLY INFLATED   IMPROPERLY INFLATED

RADIAL TIRE

Fig. 141 Radial tires have a characteristic sidewall bulge; don't try to measure pressure by looking at the tire. Use a quality air pressure gauge

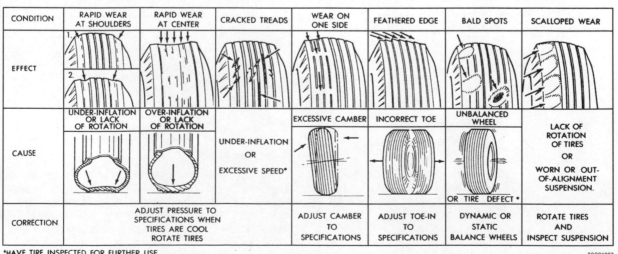

CONDITION	RAPID WEAR AT SHOULDERS	RAPID WEAR AT CENTER	CRACKED TREADS	WEAR ON ONE SIDE	FEATHERED EDGE	BALD SPOTS	SCALLOPED WEAR
EFFECT							
CAUSE	UNDER-INFLATION OR LACK OF ROTATION	OVER-INFLATION OR LACK OF ROTATION	UNDER-INFLATION OR EXCESSIVE SPEED*	EXCESSIVE CAMBER	INCORRECT TOE	UNBALANCED WHEEL OR TIRE DEFECT *	LACK OF ROTATION OF TIRES OR WORN OR OUT-OF-ALIGNMENT SUSPENSION.
CORRECTION	ADJUST PRESSURE TO SPECIFICATIONS WHEN TIRES ARE COOL ROTATE TIRES			ADJUST CAMBER TO SPECIFICATIONS	ADJUST TOE-IN TO SPECIFICATIONS	DYNAMIC OR STATIC BALANCE WHEELS	ROTATE TIRES AND INSPECT SUSPENSION

*HAVE TIRE INSPECTED FOR FURTHER USE.

Fig. 142 Common tire wear patterns and causes

(including the spare) regularly with a pocket type gauge. Too often, the gauge on the end of the air hose at your corner garage is not accurate because it suffers too much abuse. Always check tire pressure when the tires are cold, as pressure increases with temperature. If you must move the vehicle to check the tire inflation, do not drive more than a mile before checking. A cold tire is generally one that has not been driven for more than three hours.

A plate or sticker is normally provided somewhere in the vehicle (door post, hood, tailgate or trunk lid) which shows the proper pressure for the tires. Never counteract excessive pressure build-up by bleeding off air pressure (letting some air out). This will cause the tire to run hotter and wear quicker.

✳✳ CAUTION

Never exceed the maximum tire pressure embossed on the tire! This is the pressure to be used when the tire is at maximum loading, but it is rarely the correct pressure for everyday driving. Consult the owner's manual or the tire pressure sticker for the correct tire pressure.

Once you've maintained the correct tire pressures for several weeks, you'll be familiar with the vehicle's braking and handling personality. Slight

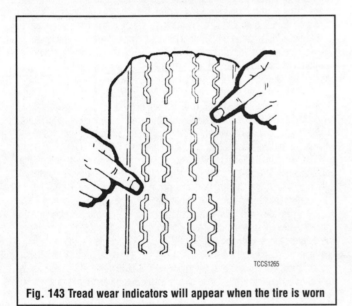

Fig. 143 Tread wear indicators will appear when the tire is worn

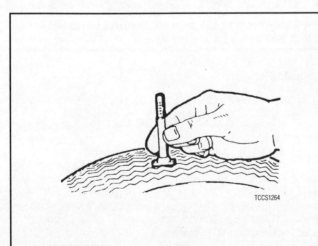

Fig. 144 Accurate tread depth indicators are inexpensive and handy

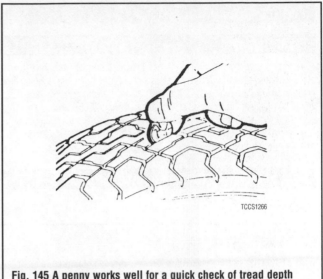

Fig. 145 A penny works well for a quick check of tread depth

adjustments in tire pressures can fine-tune these characteristics, but never change the cold pressure specification by more than 2 psi. A slightly softer tire pressure will give a softer ride but also yield lower fuel mileage. A slightly harder tire will give crisper dry road handling but can cause skidding on wet surfaces. Unless you're fully attuned to the vehicle, stick to the recommended inflation pressures.

All tires made since 1968 have built-in tread wear indicator bars that show up as ½ in. (13mm) wide smooth bands across the tire when 1/16 in. (1.5mm) of tread remains. The appearance of tread wear indicators means that the tires should be replaced. In fact, many states have laws prohibiting the use of tires with less than this amount of tread.

You can check your own tread depth with an inexpensive gauge or by using a Lincoln head penny. Slip the Lincoln penny (with Lincoln's head upside-down) into several tread grooves. If you can see the top of Lincoln's head in 2 adjacent grooves, the tire has less than 1/16 in. (1.5mm) tread left and should be replaced. You can measure snow tires in the same manner by using the "tails" side of the Lincoln penny. If you can see the top of the Lincoln memorial, it's time to replace the snow tire(s).

CARE OF SPECIAL WHEELS

If you have invested money in magnesium, aluminum alloy or sport wheels, special precautions should be taken to make sure your investment is not wasted and that your special wheels look good for the life of the vehicle.

Special wheels are easily damaged and/or scratched. Occasionally check the rims for cracking, impact damage or air leaks. If any of these are found, replace the wheel. But in order to prevent this type of damage and the costly replacement of a special wheel, observe the following precautions:

• Use extra care not to damage the wheels during removal, installation, balancing, etc. After removal of the wheels from the vehicle, place them on a mat or other protective surface. If they are to be stored for any length of time, support them on strips of wood. Never store tires and wheels upright; the tread may develop flat spots.

• When driving, watch for hazards; it doesn't take much to crack a wheel.

• When washing, use a mild soap or non-abrasive dish detergent (keeping in mind that detergent tends to remove wax). Avoid cleansers with abrasives or the use of hard brushes. There are many cleaners and polishes for special wheels.

• If possible, remove the wheels during the winter. Salt and sand used for snow removal can severely damage the finish of a wheel.

• Make certain the recommended lug nut torque is never exceeded or the wheel may crack. Never use snow chains on special wheels; severe scratching will occur.

FLUIDS AND LUBRICANTS

Fluid Disposal

Used fluids such as engine oil, transaxle fluid, antifreeze and brake fluid are hazardous wastes and must be disposed of properly. Before draining any fluids, consult with your local authorities; in many areas, waste oil, antifreeze, etc. is being accepted as a part of recycling programs. A number of service stations and auto parts stores are also accepting waste fluids for recycling.

Be sure of the recycling center's policies before draining any fluids, as many will not accept different fluids that have been mixed together.

Fuel and Engine Oil Recommendations

ENGINE OIL

◆ **See Figures 146 and 147**

The recommended oil viscosity's for sustained temperatures ranging from below 0°F (-18°C) to above 32°F (0°C) are listed in this section. They

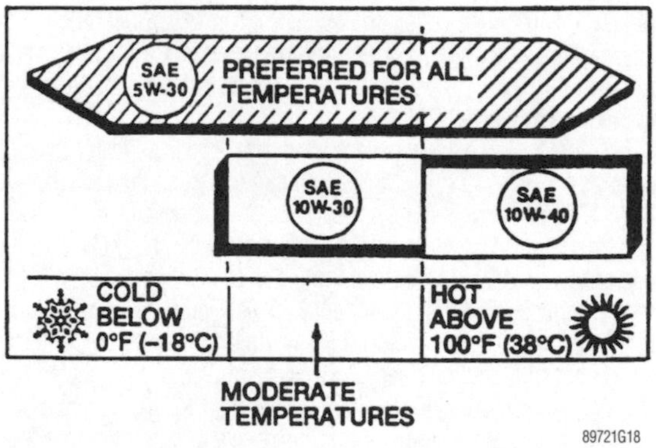

Fig. 146 Typical Aspire engine oil viscosity chart

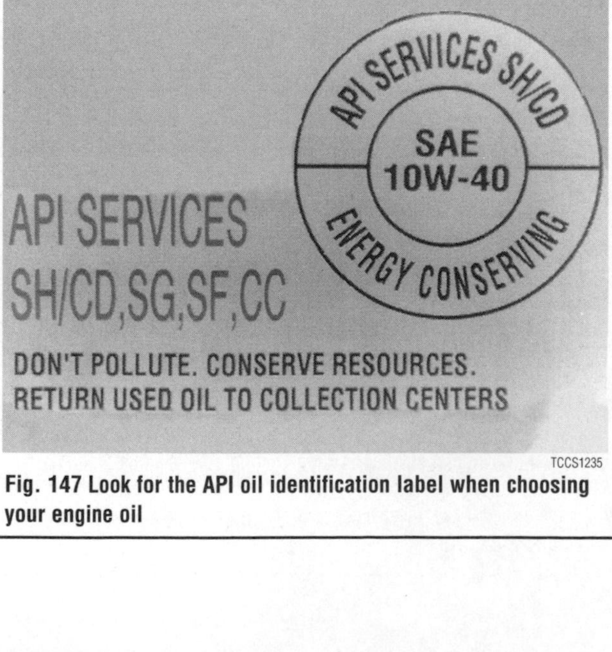

Fig. 147 Look for the API oil identification label when choosing your engine oil

are broken down into multi-viscosity and single viscosities. Multi-viscosity oils are recommended because of their wider range of acceptable temperatures and driving conditions.

➡**Ford recommends that SAE 5W-30 viscosity engine oil should be used for all climate conditions, however, SAE 10W-30 is acceptable for vehicles operated in moderate climates and SAE 10W-40 may be used in hot climates.**

When adding oil to the crankcase or changing the oil or filter, it is important that oil of an equal quality to original equipment be used in your car. The use of inferior oils may void the warranty, damage your engine, or both.

The Society of Automotive Engineers (SAE) grade number of oil indicates the viscosity of the oil (its ability to lubricate at a given temperature). The lower the SAF number, the lighter the oil; the lower the viscosity, the easier it is to crank the engine in cold weather, but the less the oil will lubricate and protect the engine in high temperatures. This number is marked on every oil container.

Oil viscosities should be chosen from those oils recommended for the lowest anticipated temperatures during the oil change interval. Due to the need for an oil that embodies both good lubrication at high temperatures and easy cranking in cold weather, multi-grade oils have been developed. Basically, a multi-grade oil is thinner at low temperatures and thicker at high temperatures. For example, a 10W-40 oil (the W stands for winter) exhibits the characteristics of a 10 weight (SAE 10) oil when the car is first started and the oil is cold. Its lighter weight allows it to travel to the lubricating surfaces quicker and offer less resistance to starter motor cranking than, say, a straight 30 weight (SAE 30) oil. But after the engine reaches operating temperature, the 10W-40 oil begins acting like straight 40 weight (SAE 40) oil, its heavier weight providing greater lubrication with less chance of foaming than a straight 30 weight oil.

The API (American Petroleum Institute) designations, also found on the oil container, indicates the classification of engine oil used under certain given operating conditions. Only oils designated for use Service SG heavy duty detergent should be used in your car. Oils of the SG type perform may functions inside the engine besides their basic lubrication. Through a balanced system of metallic detergents and polymeric dispersants, the oil prevents high and low temperature deposits and also keeps sludge and dirt particles in suspension. Acids, particularly sulfuric acid, as well as other by-products of engine combustion are neutralized by the oil. If these acids are allowed to concentrate, they can cause corrosion and rapid wear of the internal engine parts.

✳✳ CAUTION

Non-detergent motor oils or straight mineral oils should not be used in your Ford gasoline engine.

Synthetic Oil

There are many excellent synthetic and fuel-efficient oils currently available that can provide better gas mileage, longer service life and, in some cases, better engine protection. These benefits do not come without a few hitches, however; the main one being the price of synthetic oils, which is three or four times the price per quart of conventional oil.

Synthetic oil is not for every car and every type of driving, so you should consider your engine's condition and your type of driving. Also, check your car's warranty conditions regarding the use of synthetic oils.

High mileage engines are the wrong candidates for synthetic oil. Older engines with wear have a problem with synthetics: they "use" (consume during operation) more oil as they age. Slippery synthetic oils get past these worn parts easily. If your engine is "using" conventional oil, it will use synthetics much faster. Also, if your car is leaking oil past old seals, you'll have a much greater leak problem with synthetics.

FUEL

Your vehicle is designed to operate using regular unleaded fuel with an 87 octane. Ford recommends that using gasoline with an octane rating lower than 87 can cause persistent and heavy knocking, and may cause internal engine damage.

If your vehicle is having problems with rough idle or hesitation when the engine is cold, it may be caused by low volatility fuel. If this occurs try a different grade or brand of fuel.

OPERATION IN FOREIGN COUNTRIES

If you plan to drive your car outside the United States or Canada, there is a possibility that fuels will be too low in anti-knock quality and could produce engine damage. It is wise to consult with local authorities upon arrival in a foreign country to determine the best fuels available.

Engine

OIL LEVEL CHECK

▶ **See Figures 148, 149, 150 and 151**

> ☀ **CAUTION**
>
> **The EPA warns that prolonged contact with used engine oil may cause a number of skin disorders, including cancer! You should make every effort to minimize your exposure to used engine oil. Protective gloves should be worn when changing the oil. Wash your hands and any other exposed skin areas as soon as possible after exposure to used engine oil. Soap and water, or waterless hand cleaner should be used.**

> ☀ **WARNING**
>
> **Operating the engine without the proper amount and type of engine oil will result in severe engine damage.**

Check the engine oil level every time you fill the gas tank. The car should be on level ground when checking the oil.
1. Turn the car off and wait several minutes.
2. Locate the engine oil dipstick and withdraw it from the tube.
3. Wipe the dipstick with a clean rag and reinsert it in the dipstick tube.

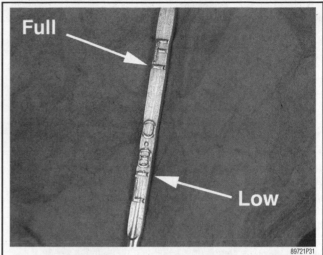

Fig. 149 Observe the oil level on the dipstick and add oil if it is low

Fig. 150 Clean the area around the oil filler cap to prevent dirt from entering the opening when the cap is removed

Fig. 148 Grasp the engine oil dipstick and withdraw it from the tube

Fig. 151 Use a funnel when adding engine oil to prevent spilling it on the engine

4. Remove the dipstick again, hold the dipstick horizontally and observe the level of the oil.

5. The oil level should be at the **FULL** mark on the dipstick.

6. If the level is at or near the **LOW** mark, replace the dipstick and add fresh oil to bring the level up to the **FULL** mark. Do not overfill.

7. Recheck the oil level and close the hood.

➡**Use a multi-grade oil with API classification SG.**

OIL & FILTER CHANGE

◗ **See Figures 152 thru 158**

➡**The engine oil and oil filter should be changed at the recommended intervals on the Maintenance Intervals chart. Although some manufacturers have at times recommended changing the filter only at every other oil change, we recommend that you always change the filter with the oil. The benefit of fresh oil is quickly lost if the old filter is clogged and unable to do its job. Also, leaving the old filter in place leaves a significant amount of dirty oil in the system.**

The oil should be changed more frequently if the vehicle is being operated in a very dusty area. Before draining the oil, make sure that the engine is at operating temperature. Hot oil will hold more impurities in suspension and will flow better, allowing the removal of more oil and dirt.

➡**It is usually a good idea to place your ignition key in the box or bag with the bottles of fresh engine oil. In this way, it will be VERY HARD to forget to refill the engine crankcase before you go to start the engine.**

1. Raise and support the vehicle safely on jackstands.

2. Before you crawl under the car, take a look at where you will be working and gather all the necessary tools such as: a few wrenches or a ratchet and strip of sockets, a drain pan and clean rags. If the oil filter is more accessible from underneath the vehicle, you will also want to grab a bottle of oil, the new filter and a filter wrench at this time.

✳✳ CAUTION

The EPA warns that prolonged contact with used engine oil may cause a number of skin disorders, including cancer! You should make every effort to minimize your exposure to used engine oil. Protective gloves should be worn when changing the oil. Wash your hands and any other exposed skin areas as soon as possible after exposure to used engine oil. Soap and water, or waterless hand cleaner, should be used.

✳✳ WARNING

Operating the engine without the proper amount and type of engine oil will result in severe engine damage.

3. Position the drain pan beneath the oil pan drain plug. Keep in mind that the fast flowing oil, which will spill out as you pull the plug from the pan, will flow with enough force that it could miss the pan. Position the drain pan accordingly and be ready to move the pan more directly beneath the plug as the oil flow lessens to a trickle.

4. Loosen the drain plug with a wrench (or socket and driver), then carefully unscrew the plug with your fingers. Use a rag to shield your fingers from the heat. Push in on the plug as you unscrew it so you can feel when all of the screw threads are out of the hole (and so you will keep the oil from seeping past the threads until you are ready to remove the plug). You can then remove the plug quickly to avoid having hot oil run down your arm. This will also help assure that have the plug in your hand, not in the bottom of a pan of hot oil.

✳✳ CAUTION

Be careful of the oil; when at operating temperature, it is hot enough to cause a severe burn.

Fig. 152 Loosen, but do not remove, the oil pan drain plug

Fig. 153 Push in on the plug as you unscrew it, to keep oil from seeping past the threads until you are ready to remove the plug

Fig. 154 When you are ready, quickly remove the plug and let the oil drain completely

5. Allow the oil to drain until nothing but a few drops come out of the drain hole. Check the drain plug to make sure the threads and sealing surface are not damaged. Clean the plug and install a new seal if it is missing or damaged.

6. Carefully thread the plug into position and tighten it with a torque wrench to 22–30 ft. lbs. (29–41 Nm). If a torque wrench is not available, snug the drain plug and give a slight additional turn. You don't want the plug to fall out (as you would quickly become stranded), but the pan threads are EASILY stripped from overtightening (and this can be time consuming and/or costly to fix).

7. Position the drain pan beneath the filter. To remove the filter, you may need an oil filter wrench, since the filter may have been fitted too tightly and/or the heat from the engine may have made it even tighter. A filter wrench can be obtained at any auto parts store and is well worth the investment. Loosen the filter with the filter wrench. With a rag wrapped around the filter, unscrew the filter from the boss on the engine. Be careful of hot oil that will run down the side of the filter. Make sure that your drain pan is under the filter before you start to remove it from the engine; should some of the hot oil happen to get on you, there will be a place to dump the filter in a hurry, and the filter will usually spill a good bit of dirty oil as it is removed.

8. Wipe the base of the mounting boss with a clean, dry cloth. When you install the new filter, smear a small amount of fresh oil on the gasket with your finger, just enough to coat the entire contact surface. When you tighten the filter, rotate it about a half turn after it contacts the mounting boss (or follow any instructions which are provided on the filter or parts box).

✳✳ WARNING

Never operate the engine without engine oil, otherwise SEVERE engine damage will be the result.

9. Remove the jackstands and carefully lower the vehicle, then IMMEDIATELY refill the engine crankcase with the proper amount of oil. DO NOT WAIT TO DO THIS, because if you forget and someone tries to start the car, severe engine damage will occur.

10. Refill the engine crankcase slowly, checking the level often. You may notice that it usually takes less than the amount of oil listed in the Capacities Chart to refill the crankcase. But, that is only until the engine is run and the oil filter is filled with oil. To make sure the proper level is obtained, run the engine to normal operating temperature. While the engine is warming, look under the vehicle for any oil leakage; if any leakage is found, shut the engine **OFF** immediately, then fix the leak.

11. Shut the engine **OFF**, allow the oil to drain back into the oil pan, and recheck the level. Top off the oil at this time to the FULL mark.

Fig. 155 Check the condition of the oil pan drain plug seal and replace it if it is damaged

Fig. 157 Wipe the filter mounting boss and make sure it is free of dirt

Fig. 156 Use an oil filter wrench to loosen the oil filter

Fig. 158 Before installing a new oil filter, lightly coat the rubber gasket with clean engine oil

→If the vehicle is not resting on level ground, the oil level reading on the dipstick may be slightly off. Be sure to check the level only when the car is sitting level.

12. Drain your used oil into a suitable container for recycling and clean up your tools, as you will be needing them again in a few thousand more miles (kilometers).

Manual Transaxle

FLUID RECOMMENDATIONS

Ford recommends that you use Mercon® automatic transaxle fluid in your manual transaxle.

LEVEL CHECK

♦ **See Figure 159**

The speedometer cable sleeve is also used as a dipstick on models equipped with a manual transaxle.
1. Raise the vehicle and support it with safety stands.
2. Locate the speedometer cable assembly where it enters the transaxle.
3. Wipe the area around the speedometer cable and the cable itself with a clean rag to prevent any chance of dirt or contamination.
4. Remove the speedometer cable boot from the sleeve and slide it up the cable.

→**It may be necessary to use pliers to loosen the cable nut.**

5. Disconnect the speedometer cable from the cable sleeve.
6. Remove the speedometer cable sleeve bolt.
7. Remove the speedometer cable sleeve and gear assembly.
8. Clean the transaxle fluid from the speedometer gear and sleeve.
9. Reinsert the cable sleeve into its bore until it is fully seated.
10. Remove the cable sleeve again and observe the level of the transaxle fluid against the indicator marks on the speedometer cable sleeve.
11. If additional fluid is necessary, add it through the filler hole using a siphon pump or squeeze bottle.
12. Inspect the speedometer O-ring seal located on the sleeve, and replace it if necessary.
13. Install the speedometer gear and sleeve assembly.
14. Install the sleeve bolt.
15. Engage the speedometer cable and install the protective boot over the sleeve.
16. Remove the jackstands and lower the car.

DRAIN & REFILL

1. Raise the vehicle and support it with safety stands.
2. Place a suitable drain pan under the transaxle.
3. Remove the transaxle drain plug and allow the fluid to completely drain into the pan.
4. Install the drain plug with a new washer and tighten it to 29–43 ft. lbs. (40–58 Nm).
5. Remove the speedometer cable sleeve and gear. Refer to the preceding manual transaxle fluid level checking procedure.
6. Fill the transaxle as outlined in the same level checking procedure.
7. Replace the speedometer gear and cable, remove the jackstands and lower the car.
8. Road test the car and check for proper transaxle operation.

Automatic Transaxle

FLUID RECOMMENDATIONS

Ford recommends that you use Mercon® automatic transaxle fluid in your transaxle.

LEVEL CHECK

♦ **See Figures 160, 161, 162 and 163**

It is very important to maintain the proper fluid level in an automatic transaxle. If the level is either too high or too low, poor shifting operation and internal damage are likely to occur. For this reason, a regular check of the fluid level is essential.

It is best to check the fluid at normal operating temperature.
1. Drive the vehicle for 15–20 minutes or idle it at a fast idle speed (about 1200 rpm), allowing the transaxle to reach operating temperature. When the fluid is warm, allow the engine to idle normally.
2. Park the car on a level surface, apply the parking brake and leave the engine idling. Make sure the parking brake is FIRMLY ENGAGED. Shift the transaxle and engage each gear, then place the selector in **P** (PARK).
3. Keep the engine running and open the hood. Locate the transaxle dipstick. Wipe away any dirt in the area of the dipstick to prevent it from falling into the filler tube. Withdraw the dipstick, wipe it with a clean, lint-free rag and reinsert it until it fully seats.
4. Withdraw the dipstick and hold it horizontally while noting the fluid level; it should be between the **L** and **F** marks.

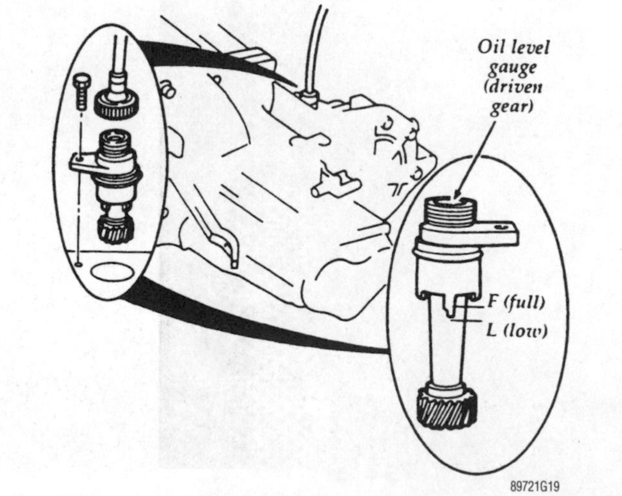

Fig. 159 The speedometer cable and gear, which is mounted on the transaxle, has the fluid level lines marked on the sleeve

Oil level gauge (driven gear)

F (full)
L (low)

89721G19

Fig. 160 The automatic transaxle dipstick is located on the driver's side of the engine compartment

89721P12

Fig. 161 Withdraw the dipstick from the tube . . .

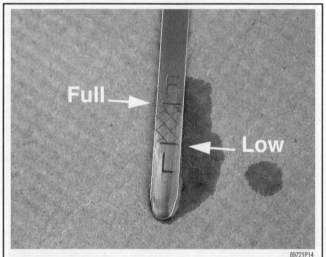

Full →

← Low

Fig. 162 . . . and note the fluid level, which should be between the L and F marks

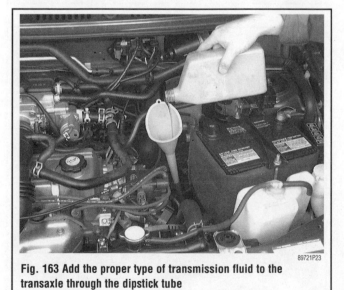

Fig. 163 Add the proper type of transmission fluid to the transaxle through the dipstick tube

5. If the level is below the lower mark, use a funnel and add fluid in small quantities through the dipstick filler neck. Keep the engine running while adding fluid and check the level after each small amount. DO NOT overfill, as this could lead to foaming and transaxle damage or seal leaks.

➡Since the transaxle fluid is added through the dipstick tube, if you check the fluid too soon after adding fluid, an incorrect reading may occur. After adding fluid, wait a few minutes to allow it to fully drain into the transaxle.

DRAIN & REFILL

▶ **See Figures 164 thru 175**

Under normal service (moderate highway driving, excluding excessively hot or cold conditions), the manufacturer feels that automatic transaxle fluid should not need periodic changing. However, if major service is performed to the transaxle, if the transaxle fluid becomes burnt or discolored through severe usage, if the vehicle is subjected to constant stop-and-go driving in hot weather, trailer towing, or long periods of highway use at high speeds, the fluid should be changed to prevent transaxle damage. A severe usage

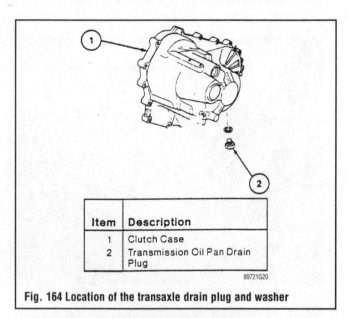

Item	Description
1	Clutch Case
2	Transmission Oil Pan Drain Plug

Fig. 164 Location of the transaxle drain plug and washer

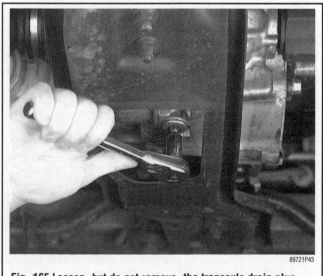

Fig. 165 Loosen, but do not remove, the transaxle drain plug

preventive maintenance change is, therefore, recommended for most vehicles at least every 90,000 miles (145,000 km).

➡Although not a required service, transaxle fluid changing can help assure a trouble-free transaxle. Likewise, changing the transaxle filter at this time is also added insurance.

1. Raise the car and support it securely on jackstands.
2. Place a large drain pan under the transaxle.
3. Remove the transaxle drain plug from the differential housing (accessible through the opening in the crossmember) and allow the fluid to drain completely. Reinstall the drain plug and tighten it to 29–40 ft. lbs. (39–54 Nm).
4. Loosen all of the pan attaching bolts to within a few turns of complete removal, then carefully break the gasket seal and allow what is left of the fluid to drain over the edge of the pan.

✳✳ WARNING

DO NOT force the pan while breaking the gasket seal. DO NOT allow the pan flange to become bent or otherwise damaged.

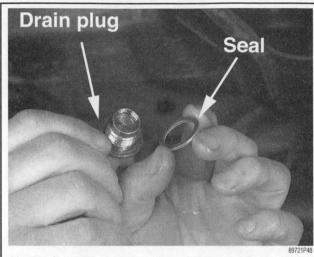
Fig. 168 Check the condition of the transaxle drain plug seal and replace it if damaged

Fig. 166 Unscrew the drain plug by hand . . .

Fig. 169 Loosen the transaxle oil pan retaining bolts . . .

Fig. 167 . . . then, when you are ready, remove the plug and allow the fluid to completely drain

Fig. 170 . . . and remove the pan from the car

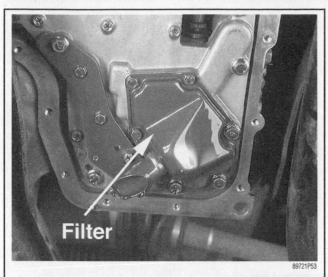

Fig. 171 The filter is attached to the transaxle valve body

Fig. 172 Loosen the filter retaining bolts . . .

Fig. 173 . . . and separate the filter from the valve body

Fig. 174 Use a gasket scraper to remove the gasket material from the pan and its mounting surface

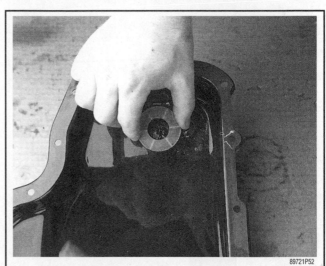

Fig. 175 A small amount of metal shavings on the pan magnet is normal

5. When fluid has drained, remove the pan bolts and carefully lower the pan, doing your best to drain the rest of the fluid into the drain pan.

6. Remove the gasket using a scraper.

7. Remove the magnet from the bottom of the pan and clean the small metal shavings from it (this is normal).

8. If necessary, loosen the transaxle fluid filter mounting bolts, then remove the filter by pulling it down and off of the valve body.

9. Install the new oil filter screen and secure it using the retaining fasteners.

10. Place a new gasket on the fluid pan, then install the pan to the transaxle. Tighten the attaching bolts to 43–69 inch lbs. (5–8 Nm).

11. Remove the jackstands and lower the vehicle.

12. Add three quarts (2.8L) of fluid through the dipstick tube.

➡**The level should always just be below the F mark.**

13. Start the engine and move the gear selector through all gears in the shift pattern. Allow the engine to reach normal operating temperature.

14. Check the transaxle fluid level. Add fluid, as necessary, to obtain the correct level.

Cooling System

♦ See Figure 176

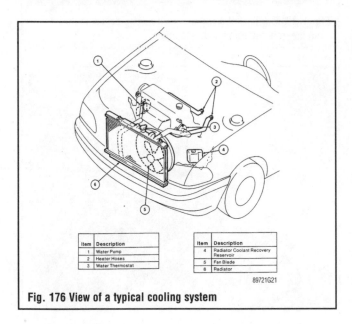

Item	Description
1	Water Pump
2	Heater Hoses
3	Water Thermostat

Item	Description
4	Radiator Coolant Recovery Reservoir
5	Fan Blade
6	Radiator

89721G21

Fig. 176 View of a typical cooling system

FLUID RECOMMENDATIONS

The recommended coolant for all vehicles covered by this manual is a 50/50 mixture of ethylene glycol and water for year-round use. Choose an aluminum compatible, good quality antifreeze with water pump lubricants, rust inhibitors and other corrosion inhibitors, along with acid neutralizers.

INSPECTION

♦ See Figures 177, 178, 179 and 180

Any time you have the hood open, glance at the coolant recovery tank to make sure it is properly filled. Top off the cooling system using the recovery tank and its markings as a guideline. If you top off the system, make a note of it to check again soon. A coolant level that consistently drops is usually a sign of a small, hard to detect leak, although in the worst case it could be a sign of an internal engine leak (blown head gasket/cracked block? . . . check the engine oil for coolant contamination). In most cases, you will be able to trace the leak to a loose fitting or damaged hose (and you might solve a problem before it leaves you stranded). Evaporating ethylene glycol antifreeze will leave small, white (salt-like) deposits, which can be helpful in tracing a leak.

At least annually or every 12,000 miles (19,000 km), all hoses, fittings and cooling system connections should be inspected for damage, wear or leaks. Hose clamps should be checked for tightness, and soft or cracked

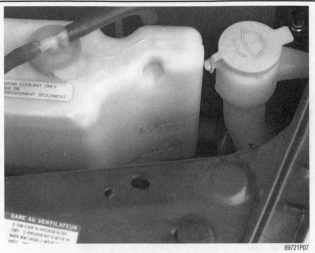

89721P07

Fig. 177 Check the coolant recovery tank to make sure it is properly filled. The coolant should be at the FULL mark

89721P15

Fig. 178 If coolant is to be added, remove the coolant recovery tank cap and set it aside

89721P16

Fig. 179 Using a funnel, add coolant to the recovery tank until it reaches the FULL mark

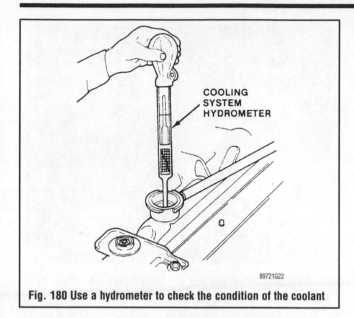

Fig. 180 Use a hydrometer to check the condition of the coolant

hoses should be replaced. Damp spots, or accumulations of rust or dye near hoses or fittings indicate possible leakage. These must be corrected before filling the system with fresh coolant. The pressure cap should be examined for signs of deterioration and aging. The water pump drive belt(s) should be inspected and adjusted to the proper tension. Refer to the information on drive belts found earlier in this section. Finally, if everything looks good, obtain an antifreeze/coolant testing hydrometer in order to check the freeze and boil-over protection capabilities of the coolant currently in your engine. Old or improperly mixed coolant should be replaced.

✳✳ CAUTION

Never open, service or drain the radiator or cooling system when hot; serious burns can occur from the steam and hot coolant. Also, when draining engine coolant, keep in mind that cats and dogs are attracted to ethylene glycol antifreeze and could drink any that is left in an uncovered container or in puddles on the ground. This will prove fatal in sufficient quantities. Always drain coolant into a sealable container. Coolant should be reused unless it is contaminated or is several years old.

At least once every 3 years or 36,000 miles (48,000 km), the engine cooling system should be inspected, flushed and refilled with fresh coolant. If the coolant is left in the system too long, it loses its ability to prevent rust and corrosion. If the coolant has too much water, it won't protect against freezing.

If you experience problems with your cooling system, such as overheating or boiling over, check for a simple cause before expecting the complicated. Make sure the system can fully pressurize (are all the connections tight/is the radiator cap on properly, is the cap seal intact?). Ideally, a pressure tester should be connected to the radiator opening and the system should be pressurized and inspected for leaks. If no obvious problems are found, use a hydrometer antifreeze/coolant tester (available at most automotive supply stores) to check the condition and concentration of the antifreeze in your cooling system. Excessively old coolant or the wrong proportions of water and coolant will adversely affect the coolant's boiling and freezing points.

Check the Radiator Cap
▶ See Figure 181

While you are checking the coolant level, check the radiator cap for a worn or cracked gasket. If the cap doesn't seal properly, fluid will be lost and the engine will overheat. A worn cap should be replaced with a new one.

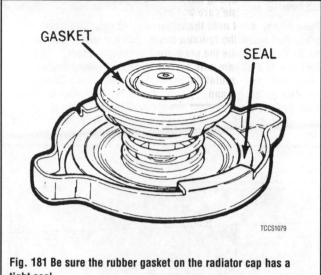

Fig. 181 Be sure the rubber gasket on the radiator cap has a tight seal

Clean Radiator of Debris
▶ See Figure 182

Periodically, clean any debris—leaves, paper, insects, etc.—from the radiator fins. Pick the large pieces off by hand. The smaller pieces can be washed away with water pressure from a hose.

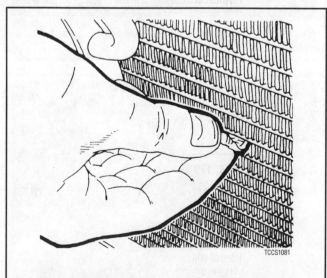

Fig. 182 Periodically remove all debris from the radiator fins

Carefully straighten any bent radiator fins with a pair of needle-nosed pliers. Be careful; the fins are very soft. Don't wiggle the fins back and forth too much. Straighten them once and try not to move them again.

DRAINING, FLUSHING & REFILLING

♦ See Figures 183, 184, 185, 186 and 187

✳✳ CAUTION

Never open, service or drain the radiator or cooling system when hot; serious burns can occur from the steam and hot coolant. Also, when draining engine coolant, keep in mind that cats and dogs are attracted to ethylene glycol antifreeze and could drink any that is left in an uncovered container or in puddles on the ground. This will prove fatal in sufficient quantities. Always drain coolant into a sealable container. Coolant should be reused unless it is contaminated or is several years old.

Fig. 185 Use a 10mm box end wrench to loosen the radiator petcock

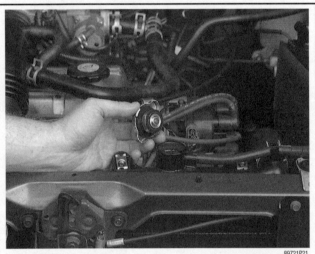
Fig. 183 After the engine has sufficiently cooled, remove the radiator cap

Fig. 186 Let the coolant completely drain through the small piece of hose into a suitable container

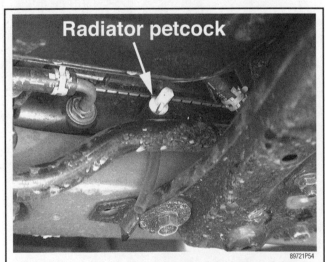
Fig. 184 The radiator petcock is located at the bottom of the radiator on the driver's side

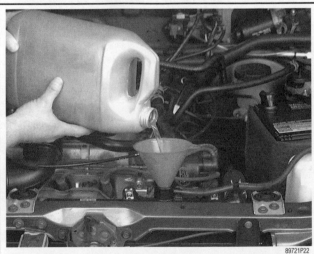
Fig. 187 Using a funnel to avoid spillage, add the correct mixture and amount of coolant to the radiator

A complete drain and refill of the cooling system at least every 30,000 miles (48,000 km) or 3 years will remove the accumulated rust, scale and other deposits. The recommended coolant is a 50/50 mixture of ethylene glycol and water for year-round use. Choose a good quality antifreeze with water pump lubricants, rust inhibitors and other corrosion inhibitors, along with acid neutralizers.

➡Before opening the radiator petcock, spray it with some penetrating lubricant.

1. Place a suitable container under the petcock.
2. Remove the radiator cap.
3. Drain the existing coolant by opening the radiator petcock.
4. Close the petcock, then fill the system with water.
5. Add a can of quality radiator flush.
6. Idle the engine until the upper radiator hose gets hot.
7. Drain the system again.
8. Repeat this process until the drained water is clear and free of scale.
9. Close all petcocks and connect any loose hoses.
10. If equipped with a coolant recovery system, flush the reservoir with water and leave empty.
11. Determine the capacity of the cooling system, then properly refill the system with a 50/50 mixture of fresh coolant and water, as follows:

    a. Fill the radiator with coolant until it reaches the radiator filler neck seat.

    b. Start the engine and allow it to idle until the thermostat opens (the upper radiator hose will become hot).

    c. Turn the engine **OFF** and refill the radiator until the coolant level is at the filler neck seat.

    d. Fill the engine coolant overflow tank with coolant to the FULL HOT mark, then install the radiator cap.

12. If available, install a pressure tester and check for leaks. If a pressure tester is not available, run the engine until normal operating temperature is reached (allowing the system to naturally pressurize), then check for leaks.

❈❈ CAUTION

If you are checking for leaks with the system at normal operating temperature, BE EXTREMELY CAREFUL not to touch any moving or hot engine parts. Once the temperature has been reached, shut the engine OFF, and check for leaks around the hose fittings and connections which were removed earlier.

13. Check the level of protection with an antifreeze/coolant hydrometer.

Brake Master Cylinder

▶ See Figure 188

The master cylinder reservoir is located under the hood, attached to the firewall on the driver's side of the engine compartment.

FLUID RECOMMENDATIONS

❈❈ WARNING

BRAKE FLUID EATS PAINT. Take great care not to splash or spill brake fluid on painted surfaces. Should you spill a small amount on the car's finish, don't panic, just flush the area with plenty of water.

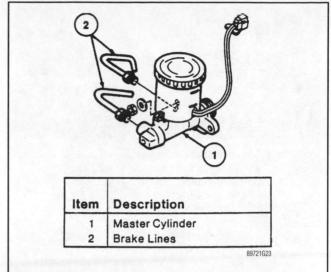

Item	Description
1	Master Cylinder
2	Brake Lines

89721G23

Fig. 188 Typical brake master cylinder used on the Aspire

When adding fluid to the system, ONLY use fresh DOT 3 brake fluid from a sealed container. DOT 3 brake fluid will absorb moisture when it is exposed to the atmosphere, which will lower its boiling point. A container that has been opened once, closed and placed on a shelf will allow enough moisture to enter over time to contaminate the fluid within. If your brake fluid is contaminated with water, you could boil the brake fluid under hard braking conditions and lose all or some braking ability. Don't take the risk, buy fresh brake fluid whenever you must add to the system.

LEVEL CHECK

▶ See Figures 189, 190, 191 and 192

Observe the brake fluid level through the master cylinder reservoir; the fluid level should be between the MIN and MAX lines.

89721P08

Fig. 189 The brake fluid level should be between the MAX and MIN marks

Fig. 190 If fluid has to be added, clean all dirt away from the top of the master cylinder

Fig. 191 Unscrew and remove the cap

Fig. 192 Add brake fluid until the level is correct

Before removing the master cylinder reservoir cap, make sure the vehicle is resting on level ground and clean all dirt away from the top of the master cylinder. Unscrew the cap and fill the master cylinder until the level is between the MIN and MAX lines.

If the level of the brake fluid is less than half the volume of the reservoir, it is advised that you check the brake system for leaks. Leaks in a hydraulic brake system most commonly occur at a wheel cylinder.

Power Steering Pump

FLUID RECOMMENDATIONS

Fill the power steering pump reservoir with a good quality power steering fluid or Automatic Transmission Fluid (ATF) Type **F**.

LEVEL CHECK

Position the vehicle on level ground. Run the engine until the fluid is at normal operating temperature. Turn the steering wheel all the way to the left and right several times. Position the wheels in the straight ahead position, then shut off the engine. Check the fluid level in the reservoir; it should be at the **FULL** mark. If fluid is required, remove the cap and add fluid until it reaches the **FULL** mark.

Steering Gear

The steering gear is factory-filled with steering gear grease. This lubricant should not be changed and the housing should not be drained; periodic lubrication is not required for the steering gear.

Chassis Greasing

▶ See Figures 193, 194 and 195

The chassis should be lubricated at least once a year or more, depending on the conditions under which the vehicle is operated.

Refer to the illustrations for the lubrication points on the components that require this service.

The components that require lubrication and their recommended lubricants are as follows:

- Wheel bearings: premium long-life grease
- Clutch assembly: premium long-life grease
- Parking brake cables: multi-purpose grease

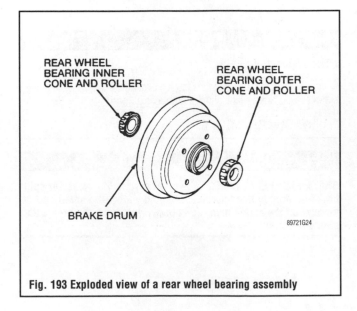

Fig. 193 Exploded view of a rear wheel bearing assembly

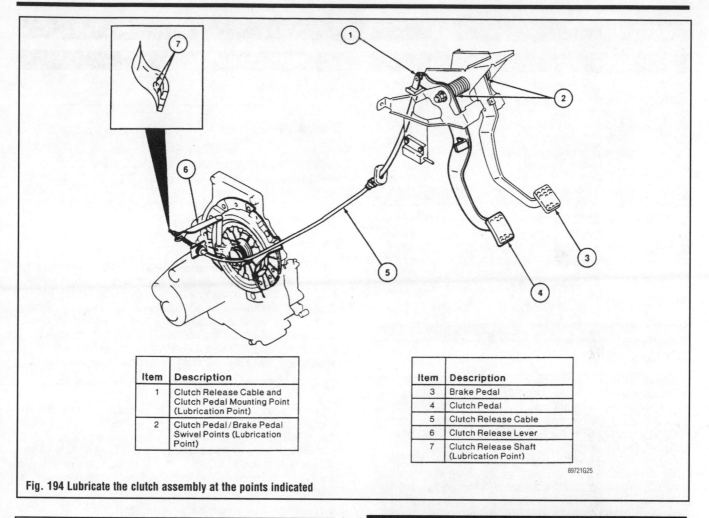

Item	Description
1	Clutch Release Cable and Clutch Pedal Mounting Point (Lubrication Point)
2	Clutch Pedal / Brake Pedal Swivel Points (Lubrication Point)

Item	Description
3	Brake Pedal
4	Clutch Pedal
5	Clutch Release Cable
6	Clutch Release Lever
7	Clutch Release Shaft (Lubrication Point)

89721G25

Fig. 194 Lubricate the clutch assembly at the points indicated

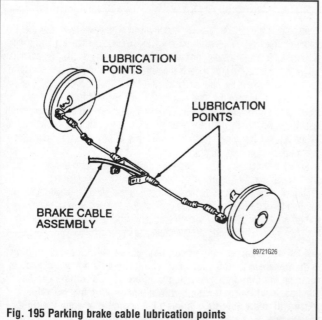

Fig. 195 Parking brake cable lubrication points

Body Lubrication

Whenever you take care of chassis greasing, it is also advised that you walk around the vehicle and give attention to a number of other surfaces which require a variety of lubrication/protection.

Lubricate the door and tailgate hinges, door locks, door latches, and the hood latch when they become noisy or difficult to operate. A high quality polyethylene grease should be used as a lubricant.

HOOD/DOOR LATCH & HINGES

Wipe clean any exposed surfaces of the door hatches and hinges, hood latch, liftgate hinges and latches. Then, treat the surfaces using a multi-purpose grease spray that meets Ford's ESB-M1C193-A specification.

LOCK CYLINDERS

These should be treated with Ford Lock Lubricant, part no. D0AZ-19587-AA or equivalent. Consult your local parts supplier for equivalent lubricants.

DOOR WEATHERSTRIPPING

Spray the door weatherstripping using a silicone lubricant to help preserve the rubber.

TRAILER TOWING

General Recommendations

Your vehicle was primarily designed to carry passengers and cargo. It is important to remember that towing a trailer will place additional loads on your vehicle's engine, drive train, steering, braking and other systems. However, if you decide to tow a trailer, using the prior equipment is a must.

Local laws may require specific equipment such as trailer brakes or fender mounted mirrors. Check your local laws.

Trailer Weight

The weight of the trailer is the most important factor. A good weight-to-horsepower ratio is about 35:1, 35 lbs. of Gross Combined Weight (GCW) for every horsepower your engine develops. Multiply the engine's rated horsepower by 35 and subtract the weight of the vehicle, passengers and luggage. The number remaining is the approximate ideal maximum weight you should tow, although a numerically higher axle ratio can help compensate for heavier weight.

Hitch (Tongue) Weight

♦ **See Figure 196**

Calculate the hitch weight in order to select a proper hitch. The weight of the hitch is usually 9–11% of the trailer gross weight and should be measured with the trailer loaded. Hitches fall into various categories: those that mount on the frame and rear bumper, the bolt-on type, or the weld-on distribution type used for larger trailers. Axle mounted or clamp-on bumper hitches should never be used.

Check the gross weight rating of your trailer. Tongue weight is usually figured as 10% of gross trailer weight. Therefore, a trailer with a maximum gross weight of 2000 lbs. will have a maximum tongue weight of 200 lbs. Class I trailers fall into this category. Class II trailers are those with a gross weight rating of 2000–3000 lbs., while Class III trailers fall into the 3500–6000 lbs. category. Class IV trailers are those over 6000 lbs. and are for use with fifth wheel trucks, only.

When you've determined the hitch that you'll need, follow the manufacturer's installation instructions, exactly, especially when it comes to fastener torques. The hitch will be subjected to a lot of stress and good hitches come with hardened bolts. Never substitute an inferior bolt for a hardened bolt.

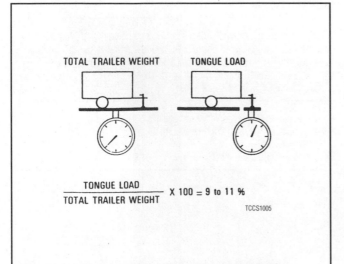

Fig. 196 Calculating proper tongue weight for your trailer

Cooling

ENGINE

Overflow Tank

One of the most common, if not THE most common, problems associated with trailer towing is engine overheating. If you have a cooling system without an expansion tank, you'll definitely need to get an aftermarket expansion tank kit, preferably one with at least a 2 quart capacity. These kits are easily installed on the radiator's overflow hose, and come with a pressure cap designed for expansion tanks.

Flex Fan

Another helpful accessory for vehicles using a belt-driven radiator fan is a flex fan. These fans are large diameter units designed to provide more airflow at low speeds, by using fan blades that have deeply cupped surfaces. The blades then flex, or flatten out, at high speed, when less cooling air is needed. These fans are far lighter in weight than stock fans, requiring less horsepower to drive them. Also, they are far quieter than stock fans. If you do decide to replace your stock fan with a flex fan, note that if your vehicle has a fan clutch, a spacer will be needed between the flex fan and water pump hub.

Oil Cooler

Aftermarket engine oil coolers are helpful for prolonging engine oil life and reducing overall engine temperatures. Both of these factors increase engine life. While not absolutely necessary in towing Class I and some Class II trailers, they are recommended for heavier Class II and all Class III towing. Engine oil cooler systems usually consist of an adapter, screwed on in place of the oil filter, a remote filter mounting and a multi-tube, finned heat exchanger, which is mounted in front of the radiator or air conditioning condenser.

TRANSAXLE

An automatic transaxle is usually recommended for trailer towing. Modern automatics have proven reliable and, of course, easy to operate, in trailer towing. The increased load of a trailer, however, causes an increase in the temperature of the automatic transaxle fluid. Heat is the worst enemy of an automatic transaxle. As the temperature of the fluid increases, the life of the fluid decreases.

It is essential, therefore, that you install an automatic transaxle cooler. The cooler, which consists of a multi-tube, finned heat exchanger, is usually installed in front of the radiator or air conditioning compressor, and hooked in-line with the transaxle cooler tank inlet line. Follow the cooler manufacturer's installation instructions.

Select a cooler of at least adequate capacity, based upon the combined gross weights of the vehicle and trailer.

Cooler manufacturers recommend that you use an aftermarket cooler in addition to, and not instead of, the present cooling tank in your radiator. If you do want to use it in place of the radiator cooling tank, get a cooler at least two sizes larger than normally necessary.

➡**A transaxle cooler can, sometimes, cause slow or harsh shifting in the transaxle during cold weather, until the fluid has a chance to come up to normal operating temperature. Some coolers can be purchased with, or retrofitted with, a temperature bypass valve which will allow fluid flow through the cooler only when the fluid has reached a certain operating temperature.**

Handling A Trailer

Towing a trailer with ease and safety requires a certain amount of experience. It's a good idea to learn the feel of a trailer by practicing turning, stopping and backing in an open area such as an empty parking lot.

JUMP STARTING A DEAD BATTERY

♦ See Figure 197

Whenever a vehicle is jump started, precautions must be followed in order to prevent the possibility of personal injury. Remember that batteries contain a small amount of explosive hydrogen gas which is a by-product of battery charging. Sparks should always be avoided when working around batteries, especially when attaching jumper cables. To minimize the possibility of accidental sparks, follow the procedure carefully.

✳✳ CAUTION

NEVER hook the batteries up in a series circuit or the entire electrical system will go up in smoke, including the starter!

Vehicles equipped with a diesel engine may utilize two 12 volt batteries. If so, the batteries are connected in a parallel circuit (positive terminal to positive terminal, negative terminal to negative terminal). Hooking the batteries up in parallel circuit increases battery cranking power without increasing total battery voltage output. Output remains at 12 volts. On the other hand, hooking two 12 volt batteries up in a series circuit (positive terminal to negative terminal, positive terminal to negative terminal) increases total battery output to 24 volts (12 volts plus 12 volts).

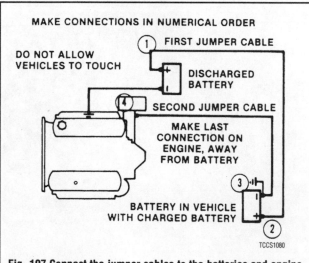

Fig. 197 Connect the jumper cables to the batteries and engine in the order shown

Jump Starting Precautions

- Be sure that both batteries are of the same voltage. Vehicles covered by this manual and most vehicles on the road today utilize a 12 volt charging system.
- Be sure that both batteries are of the same polarity (have the same terminal, in most cases NEGATIVE grounded).
- Be sure that the vehicles are not touching or a short could occur.
- On serviceable batteries, be sure the vent cap holes are not obstructed.
- Do not smoke or allow sparks anywhere near the batteries.
- In cold weather, make sure the battery electrolyte is not frozen. This can occur more readily in a battery that has been in a state of discharge.
- Do not allow electrolyte to contact your skin or clothing.

Jump Starting Procedure

1. Make sure that the voltages of the 2 batteries are the same. Most batteries and charging systems are of the 12 volt variety.
2. Pull the jumping vehicle (with the good battery) into a position so the jumper cables can reach the dead battery and that vehicle's engine. Make sure that the vehicles do NOT touch.
3. Place the transmissions/transaxles of both vehicles in **Neutral** (MT) or **P** (AT), as applicable, then firmly set their parking brakes.

➡If necessary for safety reasons, the hazard lights on both vehicles may be operated throughout the entire procedure without significantly increasing the difficulty of jumping the dead battery.

4. Turn all lights and accessories OFF on both vehicles. Make sure the ignition switches on both vehicles are turned to the **OFF** position.
5. Cover the battery cell caps with a rag, but do not cover the terminals.
6. Make sure the terminals on both batteries are clean and free of corrosion or proper electrical connection will be impeded. If necessary, clean the battery terminals before proceeding.
7. Identify the positive (+) and negative (-) terminals on both batteries.
8. Connect the first jumper cable to the positive (+) terminal of the dead battery, then connect the other end of that cable to the positive (+) terminal of the booster (good) battery.
9. Connect one end of the other jumper cable to the negative (-) terminal on the booster battery and the final cable clamp to an engine bolt head, alternator bracket or other solid, metallic point on the engine with the dead battery. Try to pick a ground on the engine that is positioned away from the battery in order to minimize the possibility of the 2 clamps touching should one loosen during the procedure. DO NOT connect this clamp to the negative (-) terminal of the bad battery.

✳✳ CAUTION

Be very careful to keep the jumper cables away from moving parts (cooling fan, belts, etc.) on both engines.

10. Check to make sure that the cables are routed away from any moving parts, then start the donor vehicle's engine. Run the engine at moderate speed for several minutes to allow the dead battery a chance to receive some initial charge.
11. With the donor vehicle's engine still running slightly above idle, try to start the vehicle with the dead battery. Crank the engine for no more than 10 seconds at a time and let the starter cool for at least 20 seconds between tries. If the vehicle does not start in 3 tries, it is likely that something else is also wrong or that the battery needs additional time to charge.
12. Once the vehicle is started, allow it to run at idle for a few seconds to make sure that it is operating properly.
13. Turn ON the headlights, heater blower and, if equipped, the rear defroster of both vehicles in order to reduce the severity of voltage spikes and subsequent risk of damage to the vehicles' electrical systems when the cables are disconnected. This step is especially important to any vehicle equipped with computer control modules.
14. Carefully disconnect the cables in the reverse order of connection. Start with the negative cable that is attached to the engine ground, then the negative cable on the donor battery. Disconnect the positive cable from the donor battery and finally, disconnect the positive cable from the formerly dead battery. Be careful when disconnecting the cables from the positive terminals not to allow the alligator clips to touch any metal on either vehicle or a short and sparks will occur.

JACKING

▶ See Figures 198, 199, 200 and 201

Your vehicle was supplied with a jack for emergency road repairs. This jack is fine for changing a flat tire or other short term procedures not requiring you to go beneath the vehicle. If it is used in an emergency situation, carefully follow the instructions provided either with the jack or in your owner's manual. Do not attempt to use the jack on any portions of the vehicle other than those specified by the vehicle manufacturer. Always block the diagonally opposite wheel when using a jack.

A more convenient way of jacking is the use of a garage or floor jack. You may use the floor jack to raise the car in the positions indicated in the accompanying photographs.

Never place the jack under the radiator, engine or transaxle components. Severe and expensive damage will result when the jack is raised. Additionally, never jack under the floor pan or bodywork; the metal will deform.

Whenever you plan to work under the vehicle, you must support it on jackstands or ramps. Never use cinder blocks or stacks of wood to support the vehicle, even if you're only going to be under it for a few minutes. Never crawl under the vehicle when it is supported only by the tire changing jack or other floor jack.

Fig. 200 To raise the front of the car, place the hydraulic jack under the front crossmember . . .

Fig. 198 To raise the rear of the car, place the hydraulic jack under the rear crossmember

Fig. 201 . . . then place the jackstands under the frame rails and SLOWLY lower the car onto the stands

➡Always position a block of wood or small rubber pad on top of the jack or jackstand to protect the lifting point's finish when lifting or supporting the vehicle.

Small hydraulic, screw, or scissors jacks are satisfactory for raising the vehicle. Drive-on trestles or ramps are also a handy and safe way to both raise and support the vehicle. Be careful though, some ramps may be too steep to drive your vehicle onto without scraping the front bottom panels. Never support the vehicle on any suspension member (unless specifically instructed to do so by a repair manual) or by an underbody panel.

Jacking Precautions

The following safety points cannot be overemphasized:
• Always block the opposite wheel or wheels to keep the vehicle from rolling off the jack.
• When raising the front of the vehicle, firmly apply the parking brake.
• When the drive wheels are to remain on the ground, leave the vehicle in gear to help prevent it from rolling.

Fig. 199 Place the jackstands under the frame rail and lower the car SLOWLY onto the jackstands

• Always use jackstands to support the vehicle when you are working underneath. Place the stands beneath the vehicle's jacking brackets. Before climbing underneath, rock the vehicle a bit to make sure it is firmly supported.

MANUFACTURER RECOMMENDED NORMAL MAINTENANCE INTERVALS

Component	Type of Service	Miles (x1000) 5.0 / km 8.0	10 / 16	15 / 24	20 / 32	25 / 40	30 / 48	35 / 56	40 / 64	45 / 72	50 / 80	55 / 88	60 / 96	65 / 104	70 / 112	75 / 120	80 / 128
Accessory drive belts	Inspect						✓						✓				
Air cleaner filter	Replace						✓						✓				
Automatic transmission Fluid	Inspect	✓	✓	✓	✓	✓	✓	✓	✓	✓	✓	✓	✓	✓	✓	✓	✓
	Replace						✓						✓				
Brake fluid	Inspect	✓	✓	✓	✓	✓	✓	✓	✓	✓	✓	✓	✓	✓	✓	✓	✓
Brake hoses and pipes	Inspect				✓				✓				✓				✓
Brake pads or shoes, and drums or rotors	Inspect						✓						✓				
Exhaust heat shields	Inspect						✓						✓				
Clutch pedal operation	Inspect						✓						✓				
Cooling system hoses and connections	Inspect						✓						✓				
Timing belt	Replace												✓				
Steering operation and linkage	Inspect						✓						✓				
Engine coolant	Replace						✓						✓				
Engine oil and filter	Replace	✓	✓	✓	✓	✓	✓	✓	✓	✓	✓	✓	✓	✓	✓	✓	✓
Exhaust system	Inspect						✓						✓				
Fuel filter	Replace												✓				
Fuel lines and connections	Inspect						✓						✓				
Idle speed	Inspect						✓						✓				
Ignition timing	Inspect												✓				
Spark plugs	Replace						✓						✓				
Chassis/body nuts and bolts	Inspect/tighten												✓				
Ball joints	Inspect						✓						✓				
Tires	Rotate	✓		✓		✓		✓		✓		✓		✓		✓	
Vacuum hoses	Inspect						✓						✓				
Wheel bearings	Repack												✓				

CAPACITIES

Year	Model	Engine ID/VIN	Engine Displacement Liters (cc)	Oil with Filter (qts.)	Transaxle (pts.) Man	Transaxle (pts.) Auto	Fuel Tank (gal.)	Cooling System (qts.)
1994	Aspire	H	1.3L (1300)	①	5.2	6.0	10	②
1995	Aspire	H	1.3L (1300)	①	5.2	6.0	10	②
1996	Aspire	H	1.3L (1300)	①	5.2	6.0	10	②
1997	Aspire	H	1.3L (1300)	①	5.2	6.0	10	②

① With Filter: 3.6 qts.
Without Filter: 3.3 qts.

② With A/C: 6.3 qts.
Without A/C: 5.8 qts.

89721C06

MANUFACTURER RECOMMENDED SEVERE MAINTENANCE INTERVALS

Component	Type of Service	Miles (x1000) 3.0 / km 5.0	6.0 / 10	9.0 / 15	12 / 20	15 / 25	18 / 30	21 / 35	24 / 40	27 / 45	30 / 50	33 / 55	36 / 60	39 / 65	42 / 70	45 / 75	48 / 80
Accessory drive belts	Inspect										✓						
Air cleaner filter	Inspect			✓												✓	
	Replace										✓						
Automatic transmission Fluid	Inspect	✓	✓	✓	✓	✓	✓	✓	✓	✓	✓	✓	✓	✓	✓	✓	✓
	Replace							✓									
Brake fluid	Inspect	✓	✓	✓	✓	✓	✓	✓	✓	✓	✓	✓	✓	✓	✓	✓	✓
Brake hoses and pipes	Inspect										✓						
Front brake pads and rotors	Inspect					✓					✓					✓	
Rear brake shoes and drums	Inspect										✓						
Exhaust heat shields	Inspect										✓						
Clutch pedal operation	Inspect										✓						
Cooling system hoses and connections	Inspect										✓						
Timing belt	Replace ①																
Steering operation and linkage	Inspect										✓						
Engine coolant	Replace										✓						
Engine oil and filter	Replace	✓	✓	✓	✓	✓	✓	✓	✓	✓	✓	✓	✓	✓	✓	✓	✓
Exhaust system	Inspect										✓						
Fuel filter	Replace ②																
Fuel lines and connections	Inspect										✓						
Idle speed	Inspect										✓						
Ignition timing	Inspect ③																
Spark plugs	Replace										✓						
Chassis/body nuts and bolts	Inspect/tighten					✓					✓					✓	
Ball joints	Inspect						✓						✓				
Tires	Rotate										✓						
Vacuum hoses	Inspect										✓						
Wheel bearings	Repack ④																

① Change timing belt every 60,000 miles (100,000 km)

② Change fuel filter every 60,000 miles (100,000 km)

③ Inspect ignition timing every 60,000 miles (100,000 km)

④ Repack wheel bearings every 60,000 miles (100,000 km)

ENGLISH TO METRIC CONVERSION: LENGTH

To convert inches (ins.) to millimeters (mm): multiply number of inches by 25.4

To convert millimeters (mm) to inches (ins.): multiply number of millimeters by .04

Inches	Decimals	Milli-meters	Inches to millimeters (inches)	Inches to millimeters (mm)	Inches	Decimals	Milli-meters	Inches to millimeters (inches)	Inches to millimeters (mm)
1/64	0.051625	0.3969	0.0001	0.00254	33/64	0.515625	13.0969	0.6	15.24
1/32	0.03125	0.7937	0.0002	0.00508	17/32	0.53125	13.4937	0.7	17.78
3/64	0.046875	1.1906	0.0003	0.00762	35/64	0.546875	13.8906	0.8	20.32
1/16	0.0625	1.5875	0.0004	0.01016	9/16	0.5625	14.2875	0.9	22.86
5/64	0.078125	1.9844	0.0005	0.01270	37/64	0.578125	14.6844	1	25.4
3/32	0.09375	2.3812	0.0006	0.01524	19/32	0.59375	15.0812	2	50.8
7/64	0.109375	2.7781	0.0007	0.01778	39/64	0.609375	15.4781	3	76.2
1/8	0.125	3.1750	0.0008	0.02032	5/8	0.625	15.8750	4	101.6
9/64	0.140625	3.5719	0.0009	0.02286	41/64	0.640625	16.2719	5	127.0
5/32	0.15625	3.9687	0.001	0.0254	21/32	0.65625	16.6687	6	152.4
11/64	0.171875	4.3656	0.002	0.0508	43/64	0.671875	17.0656	7	177.8
3/16	0.1875	4.7625	0.003	0.0762	11/16	0.6875	17.4625	8	203.2
13/64	0.203125	5.1594	0.004	0.1016	45/64	0.703125	17.8594	9	228.6
7/32	0.21875	5.5562	0.005	0.1270	23/32	0.71875	18.2562	10	254.0
15/64	0.234375	5.9531	0.006	0.1524	47/64	0.734375	18.6531	11	279.4
1/4	0.25	6.3500	0.007	0.1778	3/4	0.75	19.0500	12	304.8
17/64	0.265625	6.7469	0.008	0.2032	49/64	0.765625	19.4469	13	330.2
9/32	0.28125	7.1437	0.009	0.2286	25/32	0.78125	19.8437	14	355.6
19/64	0.296875	7.5406	0.01	0.254	51/64	0.796875	20.2406	15	381.0
5/16	0.3125	7.9375	0.02	0.508	13/16	0.8125	20.6375	16	406.4
21/64	0.328125	8.3344	0.03	0.762	53/64	0.828125	21.0344	17	431.8
11/32	0.34375	8.7312	0.04	1.016	27/32	0.84375	21.4312	18	457.2
23/64	0.359375	9.1281	0.05	1.270	55/64	0.859375	21.8281	19	482.6
3/8	0.375	9.5250	0.06	1.524	7/8	0.875	22.2250	20	508.0
25/64	0.390625	9.9219	0.07	1.778	57/64	0.890625	22.6219	21	533.4
13/32	0.40625	10.3187	0.08	2.032	29/32	0.90625	23.0187	22	558.8
27/64	0.421875	10.7156	0.09	2.286	59/64	0.921875	23.4156	23	584.2
7/16	0.4375	11.1125	0.1	2.54	15/16	0.9375	23.8125	24	609.6
29/64	0.453125	11.5094	0.2	5.08	61/64	0.953125	24.2094	25	635.0
15/32	0.46875	11.9062	0.3	7.62	31/32	0.96875	24.6062	26	660.4
31/64	0.484375	12.3031	0.4	10.16	63/64	0.984375	25.0031	27	690.6
1/2	0.5	12.7000	0.5	12.70					

ENGLISH TO METRIC CONVERSION: TORQUE

To convert foot-pounds (ft. lbs.) to Newton-meters: multiply the number of ft. lbs. by 1.3

To convert inch-pounds (in. lbs.) to Newton-meters: multiply the number of in. lbs. by .11

in lbs	N-m	in lbs	N-m	in lbs	N-m	in lbs	N-m	in lbs	N-m
0.1	0.01	1	0.11	10	1.13	19	2.15	28	3.16
0.2	0.02	2	0.23	11	1.24	20	2.26	29	3.28
0.3	0.03	3	0.34	12	1.36	21	2.37	30	3.39
0.4	0.04	4	0.45	13	1.47	22	2.49	31	3.50
0.5	0.06	5	0.56	14	1.58	23	2.60	32	3.62
0.6	0.07	6	0.68	15	1.70	24	2.71	33	3.73
0.7	0.08	7	0.78	16	1.81	25	2.82	34	3.84
0.8	0.09	8	0.90	17	1.92	26	2.94	35	3.95
0.9	0.10	9	1.02	18	2.03	27	3.05	36	4.0

TCCS1C02

ENGLISH TO METRIC CONVERSION: TORQUE

Torque is now expressed as either foot-pounds (ft./lbs.) or inch-pounds (in./lbs.). The metric measurement unit for torque is the Newton-meter (Nm). This unit—the Nm—will be used for all SI metric torque references, both the present ft./lbs. and in./lbs.

ft lbs	N-m	ft lbs	N-m	ft lbs	N-m	ft lbs	N-m
0.1	0.1	33	44.7	74	100.3	115	155.9
0.2	0.3	34	46.1	75	101.7	116	157.3
0.3	0.4	35	47.4	76	103.0	117	158.6
0.4	0.5	36	48.8	77	104.4	118	160.0
0.5	0.7	37	50.7	78	105.8	119	161.3
0.6	0.8	38	51.5	79	107.1	120	162.7
0.7	1.0	39	52.9	80	108.5	121	164.0
0.8	1.1	40	54.2	81	109.8	122	165.4
0.9	1.2	41	55.6	82	111.2	123	166.8
1	1.3	42	56.9	83	112.5	124	168.1
2	2.7	43	58.3	84	113.9	125	169.5
3	4.1	44	59.7	85	115.2	126	170.8
4	5.4	45	61.0	86	116.6	127	172.2
5	6.8	46	62.4	87	118.0	128	173.5
6	8.1	47	63.7	88	119.3	129	174.9
7	9.5	48	65.1	89	120.7	130	176.2
8	10.8	49	66.4	90	122.0	131	177.6
9	12.2	50	67.8	91	123.4	132	179.0
10	13.6	51	69.2	92	124.7	133	180.3
11	14.9	52	70.5	93	126.1	134	181.7
12	16.3	53	71.9	94	127.4	135	183.0
13	17.6	54	73.2	95	128.8	136	184.4
14	18.9	55	74.6	96	130.2	137	185.7
15	20.3	56	75.9	97	131.5	138	187.1
16	21.7	57	77.3	98	132.9	139	188.5
17	23.0	58	78.6	99	134.2	140	189.8
18	24.4	59	80.0	100	135.6	141	191.2
19	25.8	60	81.4	101	136.9	142	192.5
20	27.1	61	82.7	102	138.3	143	193.9
21	28.5	62	84.1	103	139.6	144	195.2
22	29.8	63	85.4	104	141.0	145	196.6
23	31.2	64	86.8	105	142.4	146	198.0
24	32.5	65	88.1	106	143.7	147	199.3
25	33.9	66	89.5	107	145.1	148	200.7
26	35.2	67	90.8	108	146.4	149	202.0
27	36.6	68	92.2	109	147.8	150	203.4
28	38.0	69	93.6	110	149.1	151	204.7
29	39.3	70	94.9	111	150.5	152	206.1
30	40.7	71	96.3	112	151.8	153	207.4
31	42.0	72	97.6	113	153.2	154	208.8
32	43.4	73	99.0	114	154.6	155	210.2

TCCS1C03

ENGLISH TO METRIC CONVERSION: FORCE

Force is presently measured in pounds (lbs.). This type of measurement is used to measure spring pressure, specifically how many pounds it takes to compress a spring. Our present force unit (the pound) will be replaced in SI metric measurements by the Newton (N). This term will eventually see use in specifications for electric motor brush spring pressures, valve spring pressures, etc.

To convert pounds (lbs.) to Newton (N): multiply the number of lbs. by 4.45

lbs	N	lbs	N	lbs	N	oz	N
0.01	0.04	21	93.4	59	262.4	1	0.3
0.02	0.09	22	97.9	60	266.9	2	0.6
0.03	0.13	23	102.3	61	271.3	3	0.8
0.04	0.18	24	106.8	62	275.8	4	1.1
0.05	0.22	25	111.2	63	280.2	5	1.4
0.06	0.27	26	115.6	64	284.6	6	1.7
0.07	0.31	27	120.1	65	289.1	7	2.0
0.08	0.36	28	124.6	66	293.6	8	2.2
0.09	0.40	29	129.0	67	298.0	9	2.5
0.1	0.4	30	133.4	68	302.5	10	2.8
0.2	0.9	31	137.9	69	306.9	11	3.1
0.3	1.3	32	142.3	70	311.4	12	3.3
0.4	1.8	33	146.8	71	315.8	13	3.6
0.5	2.2	34	151.2	72	320.3	14	3.9
0.6	2.7	35	155.7	73	324.7	15	4.2
0.7	3.1	36	160.1	74	329.2	16	4.4
0.8	3.6	37	164.6	75	333.6	17	4.7
0.9	4.0	38	169.0	76	338.1	18	5.0
1	4.4	39	173.5	77	342.5	19	5.3
2	8.9	40	177.9	78	347.0	20	5.6
3	13.4	41	182.4	79	351.4	21	5.8
4	17.8	42	186.8	80	355.9	22	6.1
5	22.2	43	191.3	81	360.3	23	6.4
6	26.7	44	195.7	82	364.8	24	6.7
7	31.1	45	200.2	83	369.2	25	7.0
8	35.6	46	204.6	84	373.6	26	7.2
9	40.0	47	209.1	85	378.1	27	7.5
10	44.5	48	213.5	86	382.6	28	7.8
11	48.9	49	218.0	87	387.0	29	8.1
12	53.4	50	224.4	88	391.4	30	8.3
13	57.8	51	226.9	89	395.9	31	8.6
14	62.3	52	231.3	90	400.3	32	8.9
15	66.7	53	235.8	91	404.8	33	9.2
16	71.2	54	240.2	92	409.2	34	9.4
17	75.6	55	244.6	93	413.7	35	9.7
18	80.1	56	249.1	94	418.1	36	10.0
19	84.5	57	253.6	95	422.6	37	10.3
20	89.0	58	258.0	96	427.0	38	10.6

TCCS1C04

ENGLISH TO METRIC CONVERSION: LIQUID CAPACITY

Liquid or fluid capacity is presently expressed as pints, quarts or gallons, or a combination of all of these. In the metric system the liter (l) will become the basic unit. Fractions of a liter would be expressed as deciliters, centiliters, or most frequently (and commonly) as milliliters.

To convert pints (pts.) to liters (l): multiply the number of pints by .47
To convert liters (l) to pints (pts.): multiply the number of liters by 2.1
To convert quarts (qts.) to liters (l): multiply the number of quarts by .95

To convert liters (l) to quarts (qts.): multiply the number of liters by 1.06
To convert gallons (gals.) to liters (l): multiply the number of gallons by 3.8
To convert liters (l) to gallons (gals.): multiply the number of liters by .26

gals	liters	qts	liters	pts	liters
0.1	0.38	0.1	0.10	0.1	0.05
0.2	0.76	0.2	0.19	0.2	0.10
0.3	1.1	0.3	0.28	0.3	0.14
0.4	1.5	0.4	0.38	0.4	0.19
0.5	1.9	0.5	0.47	0.5	0.24
0.6	2.3	0.6	0.57	0.6	0.28
0.7	2.6	0.7	0.66	0.7	0.33
0.8	3.0	0.8	0.76	0.8	0.38
0.9	3.4	0.9	0.85	0.9	0.43
1	3.8	1	1.0	1	0.5
2	7.6	2	1.9	2	1.0
3	11.4	3	2.8	3	1.4
4	15.1	4	3.8	4	1.9
5	18.9	5	4.7	5	2.4
6	22.7	6	5.7	6	2.8
7	26.5	7	6.6	7	3.3
8	30.3	8	7.6	8	3.8
9	34.1	9	8.5	9	4.3
10	37.8	10	9.5	10	4.7
11	41.6	11	10.4	11	5.2
12	45.4	12	11.4	12	5.7
13	49.2	13	12.3	13	6.2
14	53.0	14	13.2	14	6.6
15	56.8	15	14.2	15	7.1
16	60.6	16	15.1	16	7.6
17	64.3	17	16.1	17	8.0
18	68.1	18	17.0	18	8.5
19	71.9	19	18.0	19	9.0
20	75.7	20	18.9	20	9.5
21	79.5	21	19.9	21	9.9
22	83.2	22	20.8	22	10.4
23	87.0	23	21.8	23	10.9
24	90.8	24	22.7	24	11.4
25	94.6	25	23.6	25	11.8
26	98.4	26	24.6	26	12.3
27	102.2	27	25.5	27	12.8
28	106.0	28	26.5	28	13.2
29	110.0	29	27.4	29	13.7
30	113.5	30	28.4	30	14.2

TCCS1C05

ENGLISH TO METRIC CONVERSION: PRESSURE

The basic unit of pressure measurement used today is expressed as pounds per square inch (psi). The metric unit for psi will be the kilopascal (kPa). This will apply to either fluid pressure or air pressure, and will be frequently seen in tire pressure readings, oil pressure specifications, fuel pump pressure, etc.

To convert pounds per square inch (psi) to kilopascals (kPa): multiply the number of psi by 6.89

Psi	kPa	Psi	kPa	Psi	kPa	Psi	kPa
0.1	0.7	37	255.1	82	565.4	127	875.6
0.2	1.4	38	262.0	83	572.3	128	882.5
0.3	2.1	39	268.9	84	579.2	129	889.4
0.4	2.8	40	275.8	85	586.0	130	896.3
0.5	3.4	41	282.7	86	592.9	131	903.2
0.6	4.1	42	289.6	87	599.8	132	910.1
0.7	4.8	43	296.5	88	606.7	133	917.0
0.8	5.5	44	303.4	89	613.6	134	923.9
0.9	6.2	45	310.3	90	620.5	135	930.8
1	6.9	46	317.2	91	627.4	136	937.7
2	13.8	47	324.0	92	634.3	137	944.6
3	20.7	48	331.0	93	641.2	138	951.5
4	27.6	49	337.8	94	648.1	139	958.4
5	34.5	50	344.7	95	655.0	140	965.2
6	41.4	51	351.6	96	661.9	141	972.2
7	48.3	52	358.5	97	668.8	142	979.0
8	55.2	53	365.4	98	675.7	143	985.9
9	62.1	54	372.3	99	682.6	144	992.8
10	69.0	55	379.2	100	689.5	145	999.7
11	75.8	56	386.1	101	696.4	146	1006.6
12	82.7	57	393.0	102	703.3	147	1013.5
13	89.6	58	399.9	103	710.2	148	1020.4
14	96.5	59	406.8	104	717.0	149	1027.3
15	103.4	60	413.7	105	723.9	150	1034.2
16	110.3	61	420.6	106	730.8	151	1041.1
17	117.2	62	427.5	107	737.7	152	1048.0
18	124.1	63	434.4	108	744.6	153	1054.9
19	131.0	64	441.3	109	751.5	154	1061.8
20	137.9	65	448.2	110	758.4	155	1068.7
21	144.8	66	455.0	111	765.3	156	1075.6
22	151.7	67	461.9	112	772.2	157	1082.5
23	158.6	68	468.8	113	779.1	158	1089.4
24	165.5	69	475.7	114	786.0	159	1096.3
25	172.4	70	482.6	115	792.9	160	1103.2
26	179.3	71	489.5	116	799.8	161	1110.0
27	186.2	72	496.4	117	806.7	162	1116.9
28	193.0	73	503.3	118	813.6	163	1123.8
29	200.0	74	510.2	119	820.5	164	1130.7
30	206.8	75	517.1	120	827.4	165	1137.6
31	213.7	76	524.0	121	834.3	166	1144.5
32	220.6	77	530.9	122	841.2	167	1151.4
33	227.5	78	537.8	123	848.0	168	1158.3
34	234.4	79	544.7	124	854.9	169	1165.2
35	241.3	80	551.6	125	861.8	170	1172.1
36	248.2	81	558.5	126	868.7	171	1179.0

ENGLISH TO METRIC CONVERSION: PRESSURE

The basic unit of pressure measurement used today is expressed as pounds per square inch (psi). The metric unit for psi will be the kilopascal (kPa). This will apply to either fluid pressure or air pressure, and will be frequently seen in tire pressure readings, oil pressure specifications, fuel pump pressure, etc.

To convert pounds per square inch (psi) to kilopascals (kPa): multiply the number of psi by 6.89

Psi	kPa	Psi	kPa	Psi	kPa	Psi	kPa
172	1185.9	216	1489.3	260	1792.6	304	2096.0
173	1192.8	217	1496.2	261	1799.5	305	2102.9
174	1199.7	218	1503.1	262	1806.4	306	2109.8
175	1206.6	219	1510.0	263	1813.3	307	2116.7
176	1213.5	220	1516.8	264	1820.2	308	2123.6
177	1220.4	221	1523.7	265	1827.1	309	2130.5
178	1227.3	222	1530.6	266	1834.0	310	2137.4
179	1234.2	223	1537.5	267	1840.9	311	2144.3
180	1241.0	224	1544.4	268	1847.8	312	2151.2
181	1247.9	225	1551.3	269	1854.7	313	2158.1
182	1254.8	226	1558.2	270	1861.6	314	2164.9
183	1261.7	227	1565.1	271	1868.5	315	2171.8
184	1268.6	228	1572.0	272	1875.4	316	2178.7
185	1275.5	229	1578.9	273	1882.3	317	2185.6
186	1282.4	230	1585.8	274	1889.2	318	2192.5
187	1289.3	231	1592.7	275	1896.1	319	2199.4
188	1296.2	232	1599.6	276	1903.0	320	2206.3
189	1303.1	233	1606.5	277	1909.8	321	2213.2
190	1310.0	234	1613.4	278	1916.7	322	2220.1
191	1316.9	235	1620.3	279	1923.6	323	2227.0
192	1323.8	236	1627.2	280	1930.5	324	2233.9
193	1330.7	237	1634.1	281	1937.4	325	2240.8
194	1337.6	238	1641.0	282	1944.3	326	2247.7
195	1344.5	239	1647.8	283	1951.2	327	2254.6
196	1351.4	240	1654.7	284	1958.1	328	2261.5
197	1358.3	241	1661.6	285	1965.0	329	2268.4
198	1365.2	242	1668.5	286	1971.9	330	2275.3
199	1372.0	243	1675.4	287	1978.8	331	2282.2
200	1378.9	244	1682.3	288	1985.7	332	2289.1
201	1385.8	245	1689.2	289	1992.6	333	2295.9
202	1392.7	246	1696.1	290	1999.5	334	2302.8
203	1399.6	247	1703.0	291	2006.4	335	2309.7
204	1406.5	248	1709.9	292	2013.3	336	2316.6
205	1413.4	249	1716.8	293	2020.2	337	2323.5
206	1420.3	250	1723.7	294	2027.1	338	2330.4
207	1427.2	251	1730.6	295	2034.0	339	2337.3
208	1434.1	252	1737.5	296	2040.8	240	2344.2
209	1441.0	253	1744.4	297	2047.7	341	2351.1
210	1447.9	254	1751.3	298	2054.6	342	2358.0
211	1454.8	255	1758.2	299	2061.5	343	2364.9
212	1461.7	256	1765.1	300	2068.4	344	2371.8
213	1468.7	257	1772.0	301	2075.3	345	2378.7
214	1475.5	258	1778.8	302	2082.2	346	2385.6
215	1482.4	259	1785.7	303	2089.1	347	2392.5

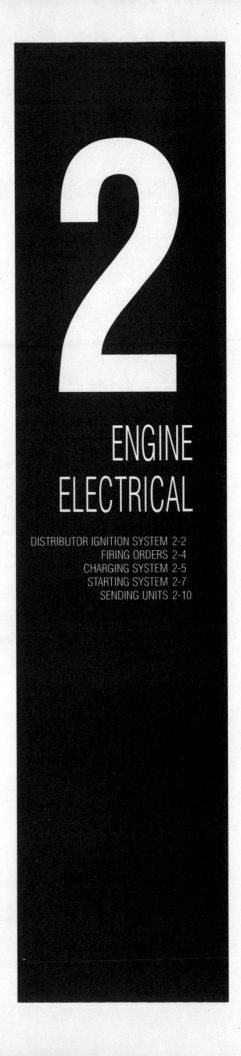

2

ENGINE
ELECTRICAL

DISTRIBUTOR IGNITION SYSTEM

➡**For information on understanding electricity and troubleshooting electrical circuits, please refer to Section 6 of this manual.**

General Information

▶ **See Figure 1**

The distributor ignition system uses a diecast distributor which is driven by the camshaft. A Hall effect stator assembly is incorporated in the distributor housing. Timing adjustments are not required, unless the distributor has been removed from the engine or the distributor has been moved, causing a change in the timing. The ignition system consists of the following components:

- Camshaft position (CMP) sensor
- Crankshaft position (CKP) sensor
- Ignition coil
- Ignition Control Module (ICM)
- Distributor
- Distributor cap and rotor
- Spark plugs and wires

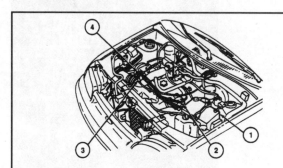

Item	Description
1	Battery
2	Distributor (Integrated Ignition Control Module and Ignition Coil)
3	Spark Plug Wire
4	Spark Plug

89722G01

Fig. 1 Location of the ignition system components

Crankshaft position and engine rpm are read by the Crankshaft Position Sensor (CKP). This information is processed by the Powertrain Control Module (PCM), which then signals the Ignition Control Module (ICM) to fire the ignition coil. The ICM controls the current through the ignition coil primary windings. The ICM turns the current **ON** between the firing points to build up a magnetic field around the coil windings. When the ICM receives the proper signal from the PCM, it turns the coil current **OFF**; this causes the field to collapse and a high voltage pulse of 28,000 volts is induced in the coil secondary winding. This pulse is then transmitted to the central terminal in the distributor cap, through the distributor rotor to the cap terminal, and through the spark plug wire to the spark plug. The voltage then arcs to ground across the plug electrodes and ignites the air/fuel mixture in the combustion chamber.

Diagnosis and Testing

Before performing any component testing, check for and, if necessary, repair the following:

- Damaged, corroded, contaminated, carbon tracked or worn distributor cap and rotor
- Damaged, fouled, improperly seated or gapped spark plug(s)

- Damaged or improperly engaged electrical connections, spark plug wires, etc.
- Discharged battery
- Blown fuses

SECONDARY SPARK TEST

The best way to perform this procedure is to use a spark tester (available at most automotive parts stores). Two types of spark testers are commonly available. The Neon Bulb type is connected to the spark plug wire and flashes with each ignition pulse. The Air Gap type must be adjusted to the individual spark plug gap specified for the engine. This type of tester allows the user to not only detect the presence of spark, but also the intensity (orange/yellow is weak, blue is strong).

1. Disconnect a spark plug wire at the spark plug end.
2. Connect the plug wire to the spark tester and ground the tester to an appropriate location on the engine.
3. Crank the engine and check for spark at the tester.
4. If spark exists at the tester, the ignition system is functioning properly.
5. If spark does not exist at the spark plug wire, remove the distributor cap and ensure that the rotor is turning when the engine is cranked.
6. If the rotor is turning, perform the spark test again using the ignition coil wire.
7. If spark does not exist at the ignition coil wire, test the ignition coil, and other distributor related components or wiring. Repair or replace components as necessary.

Adjustments

Ignition system functions are controlled by the PCM, so no adjustment is necessary. To check or adjust the ignition timing, refer to Section 1 of this manual.

Ignition Coil

TESTING

▶ **See Figure 2**

The ignition coil is mounted in the distributor.
1. Disengage the wire(s) from the coil.

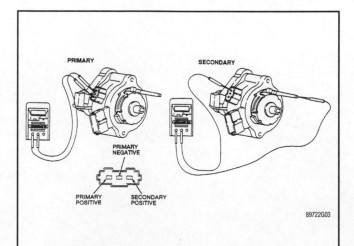

89722G03

Fig. 2 Use an ohmmeter to test the ignition coil resistance—probe the terminals as illustrated

2. Use an ohmmeter, connected as illustrated, to measure the resistance on the primary side of the coil; the resistance should be 0.5–0.7 ohms.

3. Use an ohmmeter, connected as illustrated, to measure the resistance on the secondary side of the coil; as illustrated. the resistance should be 20–31 kilohms.

4. If the resistance readings are not within specifications, the coil is defective and the distributor assembly must be replaced.

5. If resistance readings are within specifications, there may be a larger problem with the EEC system. It may be necessary to have the system further tested (because of the extensive knowledge, experience and equipment necessary to perform this testing) by a professional automotive technician.

REMOVAL & INSTALLATION

♦ See Figure 3

The ignition coil is an integral part of the distributor assembly. If the coil is defective, the whole distributor assembly must be replaced.

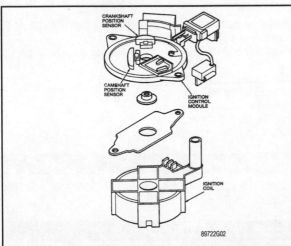

Fig. 3 The ignition coil, module, camshaft position sensor and, on earlier models, crankshaft position sensor, are located in the distributor housing

Ignition Control Module (ICM)

REMOVAL & INSTALLATION

♦ See Figure 3

The Ignition Control Module (ICM) is an integral part of the distributor assembly. If the module is defective, the whole distributor assembly must be replaced.

Distributor

REMOVAL & INSTALLATION

♦ See Figures 4, 5, 6 and 7

1. Disconnect the negative battery cable.
2. Loosen the distributor cap screws and position the cap to one side.
3. Make matchmarks with a scribe or marker on the distributor base flange and cylinder head.
4. Mark the position of the rotor on the distributor housing.
5. Disengage the distributor electrical connections.

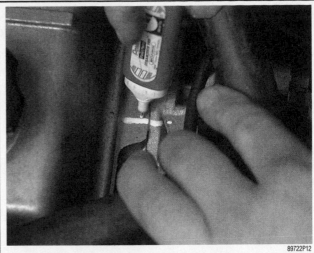

Fig. 4 Matchmark the distributor base flange-to-cylinder head position. This will help during installation

6. Loosen the distributor hold-down bolts.
7. Remove the distributor from the engine.
8. Inspect the distributor O-ring and, if damaged or worn, replace it with a new one.

To Install:

Engine Undisturbed

➡**When installing the distributor, make sure the offset drive tangs engage the camshaft slots.**

1. Make sure that the engine is still with the No. 1 piston up on TDC of its compression stroke.
2. Install the distributor and align the matchmarks on the distributor base flange and cylinder head. Also be sure that the rotor points toward the mark on the distributor housing made previously. Make certain the rotor is pointing to the No. 1 mark on the distributor base.
3. When all the marks are aligned, install the distributor hold-down bolts and tighten them to 14–19 ft. lbs. (19–25 Nm).
4. Install the cap and tighten the screws.
5. Connect the negative battery cable.
6. Engage the electrical connections.
7. Install the No. 1 spark plug, if removed.
8. Recheck the initial timing, and adjust if necessary.

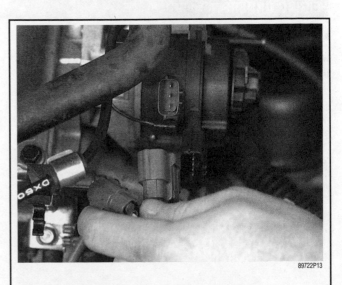

Fig. 5 Unplug the distributor electrical connections

Fig. 6 Loosen the distributor hold-down bolts . . .

Fig. 7 . . . and remove the distributor from the engine compartment

Engine Disturbed

➡When installing the distributor, make sure the offset drive tangs engage the camshaft slots.

1. Make sure that the engine is still with the No. 1 piston up on TDC of its compression stroke.

➡If the engine was disturbed while the distributor was removed, it will be necessary to remove the No. 1 spark plug and rotate the engine clockwise until the No. 1 piston is on the compression stroke. Align the timing marks.

2. If installing the old distributor:
   a. Install the distributor and align the matchmarks on the distributor base flange and cylinder head. Also be sure that the rotor points toward the mark on the distributor housing made previously. Make certain the rotor is pointing to the No. 1 mark on the distributor base.
3. If installing a new distributor:
   a. Install the rotor and cap (with wires still attached) on the distributor, then follow the No. 1 spark plug wire from the plug to the cap; this will be the No. 1 tower on the cap. Mark the location of the tower on the distributor housing, then remove the cap.

   b. Install the distributor and make sure the rotor aligns with the No.1 tower mark made on the distributor.
4. When all the marks are aligned, install the distributor hold-down bolts and tighten them to 14–19 ft. lbs. (19–25 Nm).
5. Install the cap and tighten the screws.
6. Connect the negative battery cable.
7. Engage the electrical connections.
8. Install the No. 1 spark plug, if removed.
9. Recheck the initial timing, and adjust if necessary.

Camshaft Position (CMP) Sensor

For Camshaft Position (CMP) sensor procedures, please refer to Section 4 of this manual.

Crankshaft Position (CKP) Sensor

For Crankshaft Position (CKP) sensor procedures, please refer to Section 4 of this manual.

FIRING ORDERS

◗ See Figure 8

➡To avoid confusion, remove and tag the spark plug wires one at a time, for replacement.

If a distributor is not keyed for installation with only one orientation, it could have been removed previously and rewired. The resultant wiring would hold the correct firing order, but could change the relative placement of the plug towers in relation to the engine. For this reason, it is imperative that you label all wires before disconnecting any of them. Also, before removal, compare the current wiring with the accompanying illustrations. If the current wiring does not match, make notes in your book to reflect how your engine is wired.

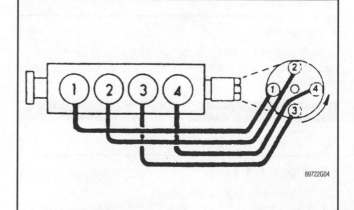

Fig. 8 1.3L Engine
Firing Order: 1–3–4–2
Distributor Rotation: Counterclockwise

CHARGING SYSTEM

General Information

The charging system is a negative (-) ground system which consists of an alternator, regulator, charge indicator lamp, storage battery, circuit protection and wiring connecting the components.

The alternator is belt-driven from the engine. Energy is supplied from the alternator (with integral regulator) to the rotating field through brushes to slip-rings. The slip-rings are mounted on the rotor shaft and are connected to the field coil. This energy supplied to the rotating field from the battery is called excitation current and is used to initially energize the field to begin the generation of electricity. Once the alternator starts to generate electricity, the excitation current comes from its own output, rather than from the battery.

The alternator produces power in the form of alternating current. The alternating current is rectified by diodes into direct current. This direct current is used to charge the battery and power the rest of the electrical system. When the ignition key is turned **ON**, current flows from the battery, through the charging system indicator light on the instrument panel, to the voltage regulator, and to the alternator. Since the alternator is not producing any current, the alternator warning light comes on. When the engine is started, the alternator begins to produce current and turns the alternator light off.

As the alternator turns and produces current, the current is divided in two ways: charging the battery and powering the electrical components of the vehicle. Part of the current is returned to the alternator to enable it to increase its output. In this situation, the alternator is receiving current from the battery and from itself. A voltage regulator is wired into the current supply to the alternator to prevent it from receiving too much current, which would cause it to overproduce current. Conversely, if the voltage regulator does not allow the alternator to receive enough current, the battery will not be fully charged and will eventually go dead.

The battery is connected to the alternator at all times, whether the ignition key is turned on or off. If the battery were shorted to ground, the alternator would also be shorted. This would damage the alternator. To prevent this, circuit protection (usually in the form of a fuse link) is installed in the wiring between the battery and the alternator. If the battery is shorted, such circuit protection will protect the alternator.

PRECAUTIONS

- NEVER ground or short out the alternator or regulator terminals.
- NEVER operate the alternator with any of its or the battery's lead wires disconnected.
- NEVER use a fast battery charger to jump start a dead battery.
- NEVER attempt to polarize an alternator.
- NEVER subject the alternator to excessive heat or dampness (for instance, steam cleaning the engine).
- NEVER use arc welding equipment on the car with the alternator connected.
- ALWAYS observe proper polarity of the battery connections; be especially careful when jump starting the car.
- ALWAYS remove the battery or at least disconnect the ground cable while charging.
- ALWAYS disconnect the battery ground cable while repairing or replacing electrical components.

Alternator

TESTING

▶ **See Figure 9**

The easiest way to test the performance of the alternator is to perform a regulated voltage test.

1. Check the drive belt tension and ensure that it is properly adjusted.
2. Check the battery terminals and make sure they are clean and tight.
3. Check all the charging system wires for insulation damage or corrosion at the connections, and make sure they are properly engaged.
4. Start the engine and allow it to reach operating temperature.
5. Connect a voltmeter between the positive and negative terminals of the battery. Voltage should be 14.1–14.7 volts.
6. If the voltage is higher or lower than specification, connect a voltmeter between the battery positive (B+) voltage output terminal of the alternator and a good engine ground. Voltage should be 14.1–14.7 volts.
7. If voltage is still out of specification, a problem exists in the alternator or voltage regulator. If voltage is now within specification, a problem exists in the wiring to the battery or in the battery itself.

➡ **Many automotive parts stores have alternator bench testers available for use by customers. An alternator bench test is the most definitive way to determine the condition of your alternator.**

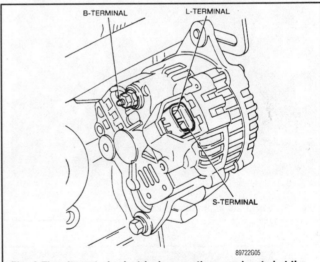

Fig. 9 The alternator's electrical connections are located at the side and rear of the assembly

REMOVAL & INSTALLATION

▶ **See Figures 10 thru 16**

1. Tag and disconnect any wires, hoses or component(s) that will interfere with alternator removal.
2. Disconnect the negative battery cable.
3. Remove the alternator adjustment bolt.
4. Remove the alternator/water pump drive belt from the alternator pulley.
5. Raise the car and support it with safety stands.

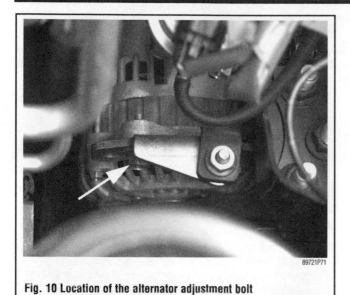

Fig. 10 Location of the alternator adjustment bolt

Fig. 11 Loosen the alternator adjustment bolt . . .

Fig. 12 . . . then loosen the alternator's lower mounting bolt . . .

Fig. 13 . . . and pivot the alternator so that its drive belt can be removed

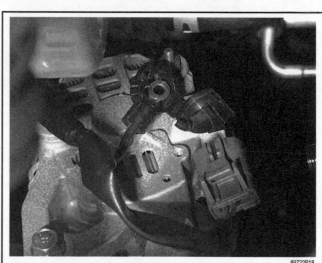

Fig. 14 Disengage the electrical connections from the rear of the alternator . . .

Fig. 15 . . . then remove the bolts and lower the alternator from the car

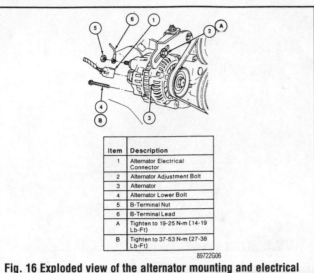

Item	Description
1	Alternator Electrical Connector
2	Alternator Adjustment Bolt
3	Alternator
4	Alternator Lower Bolt
5	B-Terminal Nut
6	B-Terminal Lead
A	Tighten to 19-25 N·m (14-19 Lb-Ft)
B	Tighten to 37-53 N·m (27-38 Lb-Ft)

89722G06

Fig. 16 Exploded view of the alternator mounting and electrical components

6. Loosen the **B** terminal nut and disengage the electrical connection.
7. Unplug the alternator electrical connection.
8. Remove the alternator lower bolt.
9. Remove the alternator from the mounting brackets from the engine compartment.

To install:

10. Install the alternator and finger-tighten the adjustment bolt.
11. Install the alternator lower bolt and tighten until snug.
12. Install the drive belt and adjust the belt to the proper tension. Refer to Section 1 for this procedure.
13. Engage the alternator electrical connections and tighten the **B** terminal nut.
14. Tighten the alternator lower bolt to 27–38 ft. lbs. (37–52 Nm). Lower the car.
15. Tighten the alternator adjustment bolt to 14–19 ft. lbs. (19–25 Nm).
16. Connect the negative battery cable.
17. Start the car and check for proper operation.

STARTING SYSTEM

General Information

The starting system includes the battery, starter motor, solenoid, ignition switch, circuit protection and wiring connecting the components. An inhibitor switch is included in the starting system to prevent the vehicle from being started with the vehicle in gear.

When the ignition key is turned to the **START** position, current flows and energizes the starter's solenoid coil. The iron plunger core is drawn into the solenoid coil. The lever and pin which are connected to the drive assembly engage the starter drive to the ring gear on the flywheel. When the iron core is completely in the coil, its contact disc closes the circuit between the battery and starter motor terminals. The current travels to the starter, which cranks the engine until it starts or the ignition switch is released from the **START** position.

To prevent damage caused by excessive starter armature rotation when the engine starts, the starter incorporates an over-running clutch in the pinion gear.

Starter

TESTING

Voltage Drop Test

♦ See Figure 17

➡The battery must be in good condition and fully charged prior to performing these tests.

1. Make sure the battery terminals are clean and tight.
2. Check the starter motor electrical wires for insulation damage; make sure that the connections are properly engaged and have no dirt or corrosion.
3. Disengage the electrical connections from the distributor to prevent the engine from starting.
4. Using a Digital Volt Ohmmeter (DVOM) set on the voltage scale, connect the DVOM positive lead to the battery positive terminal and the negative lead to the starter solenoid **M** terminal.
5. Use a remote starter or, with the help of an assistant, crank the engine and observe the voltage reading.
6. If the voltage at the **M** terminal is higher than 0.5 volts, move the DVOM negative lead to the solenoid **B** terminal and repeat the test.
7. If the voltage reading is higher than 0.5 volts, there may be a problem with the solenoid or the wires.

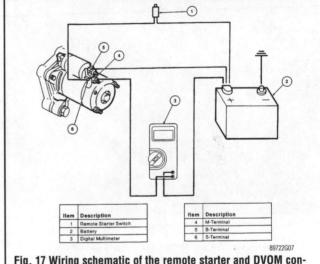

Item	Description		Item	Description
1	Remote Starter Switch		4	M-Terminal
2	Battery		5	B-Terminal
3	Digital Multimeter		6	S-Terminal

89722G07

Fig. 17 Wiring schematic of the remote starter and DVOM connections required when performing a voltage drop test

8. Disengage, clean and reinstall the **B**, **S** and **M** terminals. Repeat Steps 4–6.
9. If the voltage readings are still the same, the solenoid is defective and must be replaced.

REMOVAL & INSTALLATION

Models With Automatic Transaxle

♦ See Figures 18 thru 26

1. Disconnect the negative battery cable.
2. Remove the two upper starter motor retaining bolts.
3. Raise and support the vehicle using safety stands.
4. Loosen the two intake manifold support bolts and remove the support.
5. Loosen the support bracket bolts and remove the bracket.
6. Loosen the starter motor support nuts and washers, then remove the support.

➡When removing the hard shell connector at terminal S, grasp the plastic shell. Do not pull on the wire.

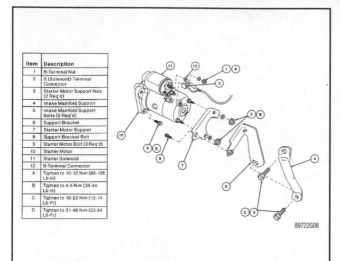

Item	Description
1	B-Terminal Nut
2	S (Solenoid)-Terminal Connector
3	Starter Motor Support Nuts (2 Req'd)
4	Intake Manifold Support
5	Intake Manifold Support Bolts (2 Req'd)
6	Support Bracket
7	Starter Motor Support
8	Support Bracket Bolt
9	Starter Motor Bolt (3 Req'd)
10	Starter Motor
11	Starter Solenoid
12	B-Terminal Connector
A	Tighten to 10-12 N-m (89-106 Lb-In)
B	Tighten to 4-5 N-m (35-44 Lb-In)
C	Tighten to 16-22 N-m (12-14 Lb-Ft)
D	Tighten to 31-46 N-m (23-34 Lb-Ft)

Fig. 18 Starter motor mounting and electrical connections—models with automatic transaxles

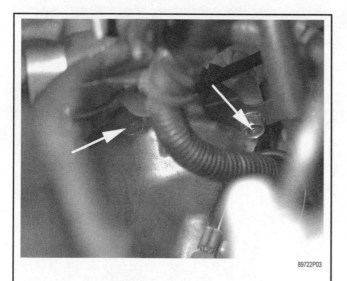

Fig. 19 Loosen the two starter mounting bolts (arrows)

Fig. 20 Loosen the two intake manifold support bolts and remove the support (arrow)

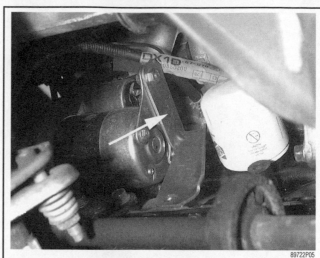

Fig. 21 Loosen the support bracket bolts and remove the bracket (arrow)

Fig. 22 Loosen the starter support bracket bolts and remove the support (arrow)

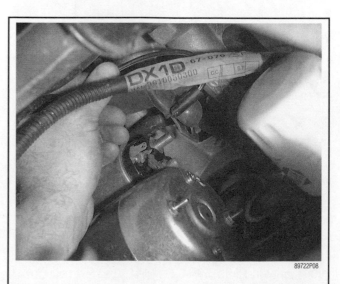

Fig. 23 Disengage the electrical connections from the solenoid

Fig. 24 Loosen the starter mounting bolts . . .

Fig. 25 . . . and remove the starter from the engine

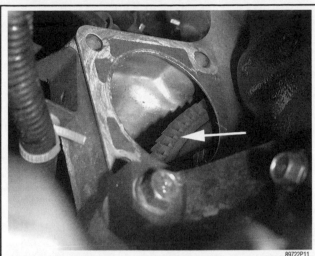

Fig. 26 With the starter off, check the flywheel ring gear teeth for damage or wear

14. Install the support bracket and tighten the retaining bolts.

15. Install the intake manifold support bracket and tighten the retainers to 12–14 ft. lbs. (16–22 Nm).

16. Lower the vehicle.

17. Install the starter motor upper retaining bolts and tighten them to 23–34 ft. lbs. (31–46 Nm).

18. Connect the negative battery cable.

Models With Manual Transaxle

◆ **See Figure 27**

1. Disconnect the negative battery cable.

2. Loosen the **B** terminal washer and nut, then disengage the electrical connection from the solenoid.

➡**When removing the hard shell connector at terminal S, grasp the plastic shell. Do not pull on the wire.**

7. Disengage the **S** terminal connection from the solenoid.

8. Loosen the **B** terminal washer and nut, then disengage the electrical connection from the solenoid.

9. Loosen the lower starter motor bolt and remove the starter motor from the vehicle.

To install:

10. Position the starter in the vehicle.

11. Install the lower starter motor bolt and tighten to 23–34 ft. lbs. (31–46 Nm).

12. Engage the **S** and **B** terminal electrical connections.

➡**When installing the hard shell connector, be careful to push it straight on and make sure it locks in position with a notable click or detent.**

13. Install the starter motor support and tighten the retainers to 35–44 inch lbs. (4–5 Nm).

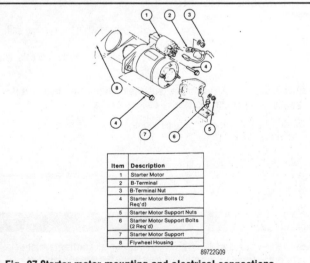

Item	Description
1	Starter Motor
2	B-Terminal
3	B-Terminal Nut
4	Starter Motor Bolts (2 Req'd)
5	Starter Motor Support Nuts
6	Starter Motor Support Bolts (2 Req'd)
7	Starter Motor Support
8	Flywheel Housing

Fig. 27 Starter motor mounting and electrical connections—models with manual transaxles

3. Disengage the **S** terminal connection from the solenoid.
4. Remove the two starter support bolts.
5. Loosen the starter motor support nuts and washers, then remove the support.
6. Loosen the starter motor bolts and remove the starter motor from the vehicle.

To install:

7. Position the starter in the vehicle.
8. Install the starter motor bolts and tighten to 23–34 ft. lbs. (31–46 Nm).

9. Engage the **S** and **B** terminal electrical connections.

➥**When installing the hard shell connector, be careful to push it straight on and make sure it locks in position with a notable click or detent.**

10. Install the starter motor support and tighten the nuts to 35–44 inch lbs. (4–5 Nm).
11. Install the starter motor support bolts and tighten them to 14–18 ft. lbs. (19–25 Nm).
12. Connect the negative battery cable.

SENDING UNITS

➥**This section describes the operating principles of sending units, warning lights and gauges. Sensors which provide information to the Electronic Control Module (ECM) are covered in Section 4 of this manual.**

Instrument panels contain a number of indicating devices (gauges and warning lights). These devices are composed of two separate components. One is the sending unit, mounted on the engine or other remote part of the vehicle, and the other is the actual gauge or light in the instrument panel.

Several types of sending units exist, however, most can be characterized as being either a pressure type or a resistance type. Pressure type sending units convert liquid pressure into an electrical signal which is sent to the gauge. Resistance type sending units are most often used to measure temperature and use variable resistance to control the current flow back to the indicating device. Both types of sending units are connected in series by a wire to the battery (through the ignition switch). When the ignition is turned **ON**, current flows from the battery, through the indicating device, and on to the sending unit.

Coolant Temperature Sender

The coolant temperature sender is threaded into the front side of the cylinder block.

TESTING

1. Disconnect the sending unit electrical harness.
2. Remove the radiator cap and place a mechanic's thermometer in the coolant.
3. Using an ohmmeter, check the resistance between the sending unit terminals.
4. Resistance should be high (375 ohms) with engine coolant cold, and low (180 ohms) with engine coolant hot.

➥**It is best to check resistance with the engine cool, then start the engine and watch the resistance change as the engine warms.**

5. If resistance does not drop as engine temperature rises, the sending unit is faulty.

REMOVAL & INSTALLATION

♦ **See Figures 28 and 29**

✳ CAUTION

Never open, service or drain the radiator or cooling system when hot; serious burns can occur from the steam and hot coolant. Also, when draining engine coolant, keep in mind that cats and dogs are attracted to ethylene glycol antifreeze and could drink any that is left in an uncovered container or in puddles on the ground. This will prove fatal in sufficient quantities. Always drain coolant into a sealable container. Coolant should be reused unless it is contaminated or is several years old.

1. Locate the coolant temperature sending unit on the engine.
2. Disconnect the sending unit electrical harness.
3. Drain the engine coolant below the level of the sending unit.
4. Unfasten and remove the sending unit from the engine.
5. If the same sender is to be reused, remove and discard the O-ring.

Fig. 28 The coolant temperature sending unit is located at the front of the engine, on the driver's side, near the exhaust manifold

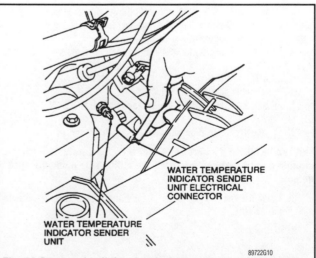

Fig. 29 Grasp and pull the electrical connection to disengage it from the sender

To install:

6. If reusing the old sender, install a new O-ring.

7. Coat the new sending unit with Teflon® tape or electrically conductive sealer.

8. Install the sending unit and tighten to 18–22 ft. lbs. (25–29 Nm).

9. Attach the sending unit's electrical connector.

10. Fill the engine with coolant.

11. Start the engine, allow it to reach operating temperature and check for leaks.

12. Check for proper sending unit operation.

Oil Pressure Sender

The oil pressure sender is located at the rear of the engine, near the oil filter.

TESTING

1. Disconnect the sending unit electrical harness.

2. Using an ohmmeter, check continuity between the sending unit terminals. With the engine stopped, continuity should exist.

→**The switch inside the oil pressure sending unit closes at 6 psi or less of pressure.**

3. Start the engine. With the engine running, continuity should not exist. Shut off the engine.

4. If continuity (or lack thereof) does not exist as stated, the sending unit is faulty.

REMOVAL & INSTALLATION

♦ **See Figure 30**

1. Raise the car and support it with safety stands.

2. Locate the oil pressure sending unit on the engine.

3. Disconnect the sending unit electrical harness.

4. Unfasten and remove the sending unit from the engine.

To install:

5. Coat the new sending unit with Teflon® tape or electrically conductive sealer.

6. Install the sending unit and tighten to 9–13 ft. lbs. (12–18 Nm).

7. Attach the sending unit's electrical connector.

8. Remove the safety stands and lower the car.

9. Start the engine, allow it to reach operating temperature and check for leaks.

10. Check for proper sending unit operation.

Oil pressure sender

89722P07

Fig. 30 The oil pressure sending unit is threaded into the engine block, near the oil filter

Troubleshooting Basic Charging System Problems

Problem	Cause	Solution
Noisy alternator	• Loose mountings • Loose drive pulley • Worn bearings • Brush noise • Internal circuits shorted (High pitched whine)	• Tighten mounting bolts • Tighten pulley • Replace alternator • Replace alternator • Replace alternator
Squeal when starting engine or accelerating	• Glazed or loose belt	• Replace or adjust belt
Indicator light remains on or ammeter indicates discharge (engine running)	• Broken belt • Broken or disconnected wires • Internal alternator problems • Defective voltage regulator	• Install belt • Repair or connect wiring • Replace alternator • Replace voltage regulator/alternator
Car light bulbs continually burn out—battery needs water continually	• Alternator/regulator overcharging	• Replace voltage regulator/alternator
Car lights flare on acceleration	• Battery low • Internal alternator/regulator problems	• Charge or replace battery • Replace alternator/regulator
Low voltage output (alternator light flickers continually or ammeter needle wanders)	• Loose or worn belt • Dirty or corroded connections • Internal alternator/regulator problems	• Replace or adjust belt • Clean or replace connections • Replace alternator/regulator

TCCS2C02

Troubleshooting Basic Starting System Problems

Problem	Cause	Solution
Starter motor rotates engine slowly	• Battery charge low or battery defective	• Charge or replace battery
	• Defective circuit between battery and starter motor	• Clean and tighten, or replace cables
	• Low load current	• Bench-test starter motor. Inspect for worn brushes and weak brush springs.
	• High load current	• Bench-test starter motor. Check engine for friction, drag or coolant in cylinders. Check ring gear-to-pinion gear clearance.
Starter motor will not rotate engine	• Battery charge low or battery defective	• Charge or replace battery
	• Faulty solenoid	• Check solenoid ground. Repair or replace as necessary.
	• Damaged drive pinion gear or ring gear	• Replace damaged gear(s)
	• Starter motor engagement weak	• Bench-test starter motor
	• Starter motor rotates slowly with high load current	• Inspect drive yoke pull-down and point gap, check for worn end bushings, check ring gear clearance
	• Engine seized	• Repair engine
Starter motor drive will not engage (solenoid known to be good)	• Defective contact point assembly	• Repair or replace contact point assembly
	• Inadequate contact point assembly ground	• Repair connection at ground screw
	• Defective hold-in coil	• Replace field winding assembly
Starter motor drive will not disengage	• Starter motor loose on flywheel housing	• Tighten mounting bolts
	• Worn drive end busing	• Replace bushing
	• Damaged ring gear teeth	• Replace ring gear or driveplate
	• Drive yoke return spring broken or missing	• Replace spring
Starter motor drive disengages prematurely	• Weak drive assembly thrust spring	• Replace drive mechanism
	• Hold-in coil defective	• Replace field winding assembly
Low load current	• Worn brushes	• Replace brushes
	• Weak brush springs	• Replace springs

TCCS2C01

3

ENGINE AND ENGINE OVERHAUL

1.3L ENGINE SPECIFICATIONS

Description	English	Metric
Type	Inline-Single Overhead Cam (SOHC)	
Displacement	80.8 cu. in.	1.3L (1300cc)
Number of Cylinders	4	
Bore	2.78 in.	71mm
Stroke	3.29 in.	83.6mm
Firing order	1-3-4-2	
Oil Pressure (hot @ 3000 rpm)	50-64 psi	393-411 kPa
Cylinder Head and Valve Train		
Compression ratio	9.7:1	
Valve guide bore diameter	0.2760-0.2768 in.	7.01-7.03mm
Valve guide height	0.5520-0.5430 in. ①	13.2-13.8mm ①
Valve seat width		
Intake	0.043-0.067 in.	1.1-1.7mm
Exhaust	0.043-0.067 in.	1.1-1.7mm
Valve angle	45°	
Stem-to-valve clearance		
Intake	0.0010-0.0024 in.	0.025-0.060mm
Exhaust	0.0012-0.0026 in.	0.030-0.065mm
Valve stem-to-guide service limit	0.008 in.	0.2mm
Valve face run-out limit	0.0016 in.	0.0406mm
Valve face angle limit	45°	
Valve stem diameter (standard)		
Intake	0.2744-0.2750 in.	6.970-6.985mm
Exhaust	0.2742-0.2748 in.	6.965-6.980mm
Valve springs		
Free length (approx.)	1.717 in.	43.6mm
Out-of-square service limit	0.059 in.	1.5mm
Camshaft		
Lobe height		
Intake	1.4222 in.	36.124mm
Intake minimum	1.4025 in.	35.624mm
Exhaust	1.4332 in.	36.404mm
Exhaust minimum	1.4135 in.	35.904mm
Wear limit	1.4272 in.	36.253mm
End-play	0.002-0.007 in. ②	0.05-0.18mm ②
Journal diameter		
Nos. 1 and 3	1.7103-1.7112 in.	43.440-43.465mm
No. 2	1.7091-1.7100 in.	43.410-43.435mm
Front oil seal		
Contact surface	1.1796-1.811 in.	29.961-30.000mm
Run-out limit (max.) TIR	0.0012 in.	0.03mm
Out-of-round limit (journal wear limit)	0.02 in.	0.05mm
Cylinder Block		
Head gasket suface overall flatness	0.006 in.	0.15mm
Cylinder bore		
Diameter	2.7953-2.7960 in.	71.00-71.019mm
Limit	2.8020 in.	71.17mm
Out-of-round service limit (max.)	0.0007 in.	0.019mm
Taper service limit	0.0007 in.	0.019mm

89723C03

1.3L ENGINE SPECIFICATIONS

Description	English	Metric
Crankshaft		
Crankshaft main bearing		
Journal	1.9661-1.9688 in.	49.938-49.956mm
Out-of-round limit (max.)	0.0020 in.	0.05mm
Run-out service limit	0.0016 in.	0.04mm
Connecting rod journal		
Diameter	1.5724-1.5731 in.	39.940-39.956mm
Out-of-round limit	0.0020 in.	0.05mm
Crankshaft-to-journal		
Clearance	0.0007-0.0014 in,	0.018-0.036mm
Limit	0.0039 in.	0.10mm
Crankshaft free		
End-play limit	0.0031-0.0111 in.	0.08-0.282mm
Service limit	0.012 in.	0.30mm
Connecting rod		
Connecting rod bearings		
Clearance crankshaft		
Desired	0.0009-0.0017 in.	0.024-0.042mm
Allowable	0.0039 in.	0.10mm
Connecting rod		
Piston pin bore diameter	1.8897-1.8904 in.	19.948-19.961mm
Crankshaft bearing bore diameter	1.8897-1.8904 in.	48.00-48.016mm
Out-of-round limit	0.0020 in.	0.05mm
Taper limit	0.0020 in.	0.05mm
Length (center-to-center)	5.230-5.234 in.	132.85-132.95mm
Alignment (bore-to-clearance max. difference)	③	③
Twist/3.94in. (100mm)	0.0016 in.	0.04mm
Bend/3.94 in. (100mm)	0.0016 in.	0.04mm
Side clearance (assembled to crankshaft)		
Service limit	0.012 in.	0.30mm
Pistons		
Piston diameter	2.793-2.794 in. ④	70.964-70.974mm ④
Piston-to-bore limit (select fit)	0.006 in.	0.15mm
Ring groove width		
Compression (top)	0.0602-0.0608 in.	1.530-1.545mm
Compression (second)	0.0598-0.0604 in.	1.520-1.535mm
Oil	0.1583-0.1591 in.	4.020-4.040mm
Piston pin		
Diameter	0.7864-0.7866 in.	19.974-19.980mm
Piston-to-pin interference	0.0-0.00102 in.	0.0-0.026mm
Installing pressure	1,100-3,300 lb.	500-1500 kg
Piston rings		
Ring width		
Compression (top)	0.0579-0.0587 in.	1.47-1.49mm
Compression (second)	0.0579-0.0587 in.	1.47-1.49mm
Side clearance		
No. 1 compression (top)	0.001-0.003 in.	0.03-0.065mm
No. 2 compression (second)	0.001-0.003 in.	0.03-0.065mm
Oil ring	snug fit	

89723C04

1.3L ENGINE SPECIFICATIONS

Description	English	Metric
Pistons		
Ring gap		
Compression (top)	0.006-0.012 in.	0.15-0.30mm
Compression (second)	0.006-0.012 in.	0.15-0.30mm
Oil (steel rail)	0.008-0.028 in.	0.20-0.070mm
Limit	0.39 in.	1.0mm
Lubrication system		
Oil pump		
Rotor assembly and clearance max. (assembled)	0.005 in.	0.14mm
Outer race-to-housing clearance	0.0087 in.	0.22mm
Oil capacity		
Without oil filter	3.0L	3.2 qts.
With oil filter	3.4L	3.6qts.

TIR: Total Indicated Run-out
① Limit is 0.5118-0.5512 in. (13-14mm)
② Service limit: 0.008 in. 0.20mm
③ Pin bore and crank bearing bore must be parallel and in the same vertical plane as the specified total difference when measured at the ends
    of an 8 inch bar—4 inch on the rod centerline
④ Measured 0.65 in. (16.5mm below the oil ring groove)

89723C05

Engine

REMOVAL & INSTALLATION

In the process of removing the engine, you will come across a number of steps which call for the removal of a separate component or system, such as "disconnect the exhaust system" or "remove the radiator." In most instances, a detailed removal procedure can be found elsewhere in this manual.

Removal and installation of the engine can be made easier if you follow these basic points:

• If you have to drain any of the fluids, use a suitable container.

• Always tag any wires or hoses and, if possible, the components they came from before disconnecting them.

• Because there are so many bolts and fasteners involved, store and label the retainers from components separately in muffin pans, jars or coffee cans. This will prevent confusion during installation.

• After unbolting the transaxle, always make sure it is properly supported.

• If it is necessary to disconnect the air conditioning system, have this service performed by a qualified technician using a recovery/recycling station. If the system does not have to be disconnected, unbolt the compressor and set it aside.

• When unbolting the engine mounts, always make sure the engine is properly supported. When removing the engine, make sure that any lifting devices are properly attached to the engine. It is recommended that if your engine is supplied with lifting hooks, your lifting apparatus be attached to them.

• Lift the engine from its compartment slowly, checking that no hoses, wires or other components are still connected.

• After the engine is clear of the compartment, place it on an engine stand or workbench.

• After the engine has been removed, you can perform a partial or full teardown of the engine using the procedures outlined in this manual.

Models With Manual Transaxle

♦ **See Figures 1, 2, 3 and 4**

1. Disconnect the battery cables (negative cable first).
2. Relieve the fuel system pressure. Refer to Section 5.
3. Remove the battery and tray.
4. Remove the hood.
5. Remove the air cleaner assembly and hoses.
6. Remove the electric cooling fan and the radiator.
7. Disconnect the accelerator cable from the throttle body.
8. Loosen the accelerator shaft bracket bolts and remove the bracket.

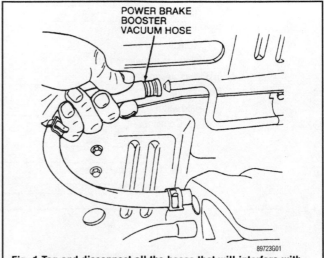

Fig. 1 Tag and disconnect all the hoses that will interfere with engine removal, such as the power brake booster hose

9. Disconnect the speedometer cable from the transaxle.

10. Disconnect the fuel tube hose and tube from the injection supply manifold.

11. Disconnect the hoses from the heater core.

12. Disconnect the power brake booster hose.

13. Tag and disengage all the engine harness electrical connections and grounds.

14. Tag and disengage the Park/Neutral safety switch electrical connection and the transaxle ground.

15. Remove the starter motor and disconnect the clutch cable.

16. Remove all the drive belts and, if applicable, tag and disconnect the lines from the power steering pump.

17. Raise the car and support it with safety stands.

✳✳ CAUTION

The EPA warns that prolonged contact with used engine oil may cause a number of skin disorders, including cancer! You should make every effort to minimize your exposure to used engine oil. Protective gloves should be worn when changing the oil. Wash your hands and any other exposed skin areas as soon as possible after exposure to used engine oil. Soap and water, or waterless hand cleaner, should be used.

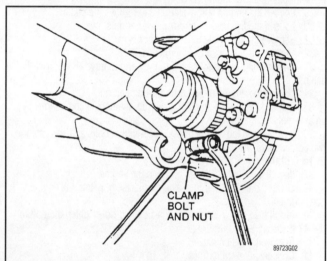

Fig. 2 Use two wrenches (one as a back-up) to loosen the front suspension lower arm clamp bolts and nuts

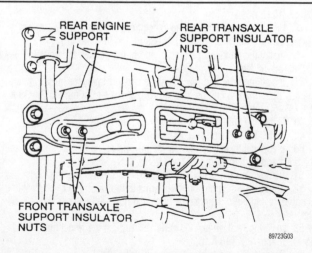

Fig. 3 Location of the front and rear transaxle support insulator nuts

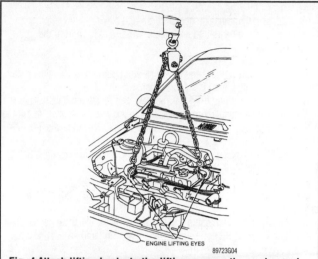

Fig. 4 Attach lifting hooks to the lifting eyes on the engine and take all the slack from the chain

18. Drain the engine oil and transaxle fluid into suitable containers.

19. Remove the front wheels and splash shields.

20. Loosen the front suspension lower arm clamp bolts and nuts. Pull the arms downward, separating the arms from the wheel knuckles.

21. Remove the halfshafts from each side and install plugs in the transaxle to avoid leakage or contamination.

22. Loosen the power steering pump bolts and separate the pump from the engine.

➡**If your vehicle is equipped with air conditioning, refer to Section 1 for information regarding the implications of servicing your A/C system yourself. Only a MVAC-trained, EPA-certified, automotive technician should service the A/C system or its components.**

23. Remove the A/C compressor.

24. Disconnect the transaxle gearshift rod and clevis.

25. Disconnect the gearshift lever stabilizer bar and support it from the transaxle.

26. Detach the exhaust inlet pipe.

27. Loosen the front and rear transaxle support insulator nuts.

28. Tag and disconnect all vacuum lines.

29. Attach lifting hooks to the lifting eyes and remove all the slack in the chain.

30. Loosen the engine mount through-bolt and nut.

31. Loosen the muffler pipe bracket bolts and remove the bracket.

32. Remove the engine and transaxle from the engine compartment as an assembly.

33. Loosen the transaxle case-to-cylinder block front bracket and case rear bracket bolts. Remove the brackets.

34. If necessary, loosen the transaxle-to-engine bolts and separate the two components.

To install:

35. If applicable, attach the transaxle to the engine. Install the starter motor.

36. Install the transaxle case-to-cylinder block front bracket and case rear bracket. Tighten the bracket bolts to 27–38 ft. lbs. (37–52 Nm).

37. Install the muffler pipe bracket and bolts. Tighten the bolts to 28–41 ft. lbs. (38–56 Nm).

38. Lower the engine and transaxle assembly into the vehicle.

39. Install the engine mount through-bolt and nut. Tighten the bolt to 39–47 ft. lbs. (53–64 Nm).

40. Remove the lifting cables.

41. Connect all vacuum lines.

42. Raise the car and support it with safety stands.

43. Install the front and rear transaxle support insulator nuts. Tighten the rear nuts to 21–34 ft. lbs. (28–46 Nm) and the front nuts to 27–38 ft. lbs. (37–52 Nm).

44. Install the exhaust inlet pipe.
45. Connect the transaxle gearshift rod and clevis.
46. Connect the gearshift lever stabilizer bar and support to the transaxle.
47. Install the A/C compressor.
48. If applicable, engage the power steering pump to the engine, install the bolts and tighten them to 27–40 ft. lbs. (36–54 Nm).
49. Remove the plugs from the transaxle and install the halfshafts.
50. Engage the suspension lower arms to the wheel knuckles. Install the clamp nuts and bolts. Tighten the bolts and nuts to 32–40 ft. lbs. (43–54 Nm).
51. Install the splash shields and wheels. Tighten the wheel hub bolt to 65–87 ft. lbs. (88–118 Nm).
52. Remove the safety stands and lower the car.
53. Connect the power steering lines (if so equipped) and install the drive belts.
54. Engage the clutch cable and the starter motor electrical connections.
55. Engage Park/Neutral safety switch, back-up lamp switch and the transaxle ground.
56. Engage all the engine harness electrical connections and grounds.
57. Connect the power brake booster hose.
58. Connect the hoses to the heater core.
59. Connect the fuel tube and hose to the injection supply manifold.
60. Connect the speedometer cable to the transaxle.
61. Install the accelerator shaft bracket and tighten the bolts.
62. Connect the accelerator cable to the throttle body.
63. Install the radiator and electric cooling fan.
64. Install the air cleaner assembly and connect the hoses.
65. Install the hood.
66. Install the battery and tray.
67. Fill the cooling system and transaxle with the proper types and quantities of fluid. Refer to Section 1 for further information.
68. Fill the crankcase with clean engine oil.
69. Connect the battery cables and check for proper engine operation.

Models With Automatic Transaxle

▶ See Figures 1, 2, 3 and 4

1. Disconnect the battery cables (negative cable first).
2. Relieve the fuel system pressure. Refer to Section 5.
3. Remove the battery and tray.
4. Remove the hood.
5. Remove the air cleaner assembly and hoses.
6. Remove the electric cooling fan and the radiator.
7. Disconnect the accelerator cable from the throttle body.
8. Loosen the accelerator shaft bracket bolts and remove the bracket.
9. Disconnect the speedometer cable from the transaxle.
10. Disconnect the fuel tube hose and tube from the injection supply manifold.
11. Disconnect the hoses from the heater core.
12. Disconnect the power brake booster hose, vacuum modulator hose and governor hose.
13. Tag and disengage all the engine harness electrical connections and grounds.
14. Tag and disengage the Park/Neutral safety switch and kickdown solenoid electrical connections, as well as the transaxle ground.
15. Remove the shift-to-manual shaft boot, then disconnect the shift cable and bracket from the transaxle.
16. Remove all the drive belts and, if applicable, tag and disconnect the lines from the power steering pump.
17. Raise the car and support it with safety stands.

✷✷ CAUTION

The EPA warns that prolonged contact with used engine oil may cause a number of skin disorders, including cancer! You should make every effort to minimize your exposure to used engine oil. Protective gloves should be worn when changing the oil. Wash your hands and any other exposed skin areas as soon as possible after exposure to used engine oil. Soap and water, or waterless hand cleaner should be used.

18. Drain the engine oil and transaxle fluid into suitable containers.
19. Remove the front wheels and splash shields.
20. Loosen the front suspension lower arm clamp bolts and nuts. Pull the arms downward, separating the arms from the wheel knuckles.
21. Remove the halfshafts from each side and install plugs in the transaxle to avoid leakage or contamination.
22. If applicable, loosen the power steering pump bolts and separate the pump from the engine.

➡If your vehicle is equipped with air conditioning, refer to Section 1 for information regarding the implications of servicing your A/C system yourself. Only a MVAC-trained, EPA-certified, automotive technician should service the A/C system or its components.

23. Remove the A/C compressor.
24. Disconnect the exhaust inlet pipe.
25. Remove the starter motor.
26. Loosen the front and rear transaxle support insulator nuts.
27. Loosen the muffler pipe bracket bolts and remove the bracket.
28. Loosen the transaxle case-to-block front bracket and case rear bracket bolts. Remove the brackets.
29. Loosen the engine rear plate bolt and remove the plate.
30. Loosen the flywheel-to-torque converter nuts.
31. Remove the safety stands and lower the car.
32. Tag and disconnect all vacuum lines.
33. Attach lifting hooks to the lifting eyes and remove all the slack in the chain.
34. Loosen the engine mount through-bolt and nut.
35. Remove the engine and transaxle from the engine compartment as an assembly.
36. If necessary, loosen the transaxle-to-engine bolts and separate the two components.

To install:

37. If applicable, attach the transaxle to the engine.
38. Lower the engine and transaxle as an assembly into the engine compartment.
39. Install the engine mount through-bolt and nut. Tighten the bolt to 39–47 ft. lbs. (53–64 Nm).
40. Remove the lifting cables.
41. Connect all vacuum lines.
42. Raise the car and support it with safety stands.
43. Install the flywheel-to-torque converter nuts. Tighten the nuts to 25–36 ft. lbs. (34–49 Nm).
44. Install the engine rear plate and bolt. Tighten the bolt to 61–87 inch lbs. (7–10 Nm).
45. Install the transaxle case-to-block front bracket and case rear bracket bolts. Tighten the bolts to 27–38 ft. lbs. (37–52 Nm).
46. Install the muffler pipe bracket and bolts. Tighten the bolts to 28–41 ft. lbs. (38–56 Nm).
47. Install the front and rear transaxle support insulator nuts. Tighten the rear nuts to 21–34 ft. lbs. (28–46 Nm) and the front nuts to 27–38 ft. lbs. (37–52 Nm).
48. Install the starter motor and exhaust inlet pipe.
49. Install the A/C compressor.
50. If applicable, engage the power steering pump to the engine, install the bolts and tighten them to 27–40 ft. lbs. (36–54 Nm).
51. Remove the plugs from the transaxle and install the halfshafts.
52. Engage the suspension lower arms to the wheel knuckles. Install the clamp nuts and bolts. Tighten the bolts and nuts to 32–40 ft. lbs. (43–54 Nm).
53. Install the splash shields and tires. Tighten the wheel hub bolt to 65–87 ft. lbs. (88–118 Nm).
54. Remove the safety stands and lower the car.
55. Connect the power steering lines (if so equipped) and install the drive belts.

56. Connect the shift cable and bracket.
57. Engage Park/Neutral safety switch and kickdown solenoid electrical connections, as well as the transaxle ground.
58. Engage all the engine harness electrical connections and grounds.
59. Connect the power brake booster hose, vacuum modulator hose and governor hose.
60. Connect the hoses to the heater core.
61. Connect the fuel tube and hose to the injection supply manifold.
62. Connect the speedometer cable to the transaxle.
63. Install the accelerator shaft bracket and tighten the bolts.
64. Connect the accelerator cable to the throttle body.
65. Install the radiator and electric cooling fan.
66. Install the air cleaner assembly and connect the hoses.
67. Install the hood.
68. Install the battery and tray.
69. Fill the cooling system and transaxle with the proper types and quantities of fluid. Refer to Section 1 for further information.
70. Fill the crankcase with clean engine oil.
71. Connect the battery cables and check for proper engine operation.

Rocker Arm (Valve) Cover

REMOVAL & INSTALLATION

▶ **See Figures 5 thru 14**

1. Disconnect the Positive Crankcase Ventilation (PCV) valve hose.
2. Disconnect the accelerator cable from the throttle control lever.
3. Remove the throttle cable bracket.
4. Disconnect the air cleaner-to-intake manifold tube.
5. Remove the PCV valve from the valve cover.
6. Disconnect the oil separator hose from the valve cover.
7. Tag and disconnect the spark plug wires from the spark plugs.
8. Remove the upper engine front cover.
9. Loosen the valve cover retaining bolts and remove the cover.
10. Remove the old valve cover gasket and use a scraper to clean any residue from both mating surfaces.

To install:

11. Apply a bead of trim adhesive D7AZ-19B508 or equivalent to the valve cover, then position a new gasket on the cover.
12. Install the cover and tighten the retainers to 44–80 inch lbs. (5–9 Nm).
13. Install the upper engine front cover.
14. Connect the spark plug wires to the plugs.

Fig. 6 Disconnect the accelerator cable from the throttle control lever

Fig. 7 Unfasten the throttle cable bracket-to-valve cover bolts and remove the bracket

Fig. 5 Pull the PCV valve from the grommet in the valve cover

Fig. 8 Unplug all electrical connections, wires and hoses that would interfere with valve cover removal and set them aside

Fig. 9 Disconnect the oil separator hose from the valve cover

Fig. 12 Remove the gasket from the valve cover

Fig. 10 Unfasten the valve cover retaining bolts . . .

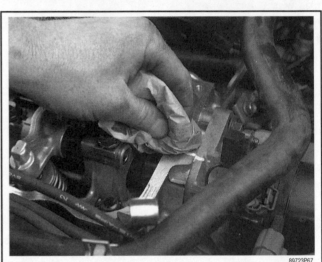

Fig. 13 Use a clean shop towel to remove any dirt or gasket residue from the valve cover mating surfaces

Fig. 11 . . . and remove the valve cover

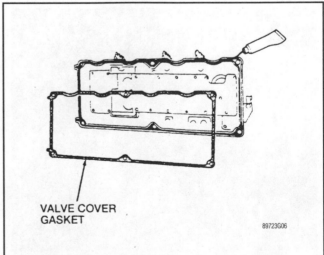

VALVE COVER GASKET

Fig. 14 Apply gasket adhesive to the valve cover to hold the gasket in place during installation

15. Connect the oil separator hose to the valve cover.
16. Install the throttle cable bracket.
17. Connect the PCV valve to the cover.
18. Attach the accelerator cable to the cable bracket and throttle control lever.
19. Connect the air cleaner-to-intake manifold tube.
20. Connect the Positive Crankcase Ventilation (PCV) valve hose.

Rocker Arms/Shafts

REMOVAL & INSTALLATION

▶ **See Figures 15 thru 20**

1. Remove the valve cover.
2. Remove the rocker arm bolts and seats in the sequence illustrated.
3. Remove the rocker arm and shaft assemblies from the cylinder head.
4. Matchmark the rocker and spacers so that they can be re-installed in their original locations.
5. Remove the rocker arms and spacers from the shafts.

Fig. 17 Remove the rocker arm shaft assembly from the cylinder head

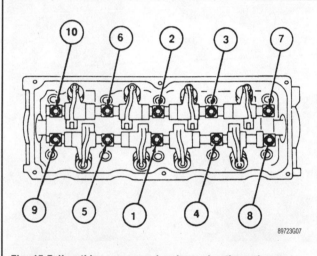
Fig. 15 Follow this sequence when loosening the rocker arm retaining bolts

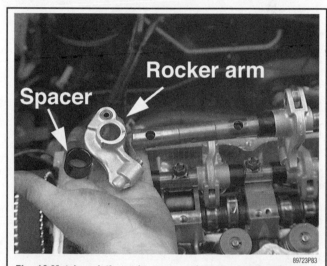
Fig. 18 Matchmark the rocker arms and spacers so that they can be re-installed in their original locations, then remove them

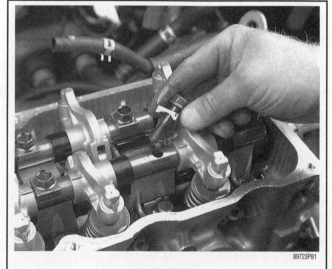
Fig. 16 Remove the rocker arm shaft bolts

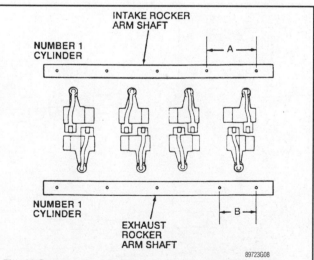
Fig. 19 Compare the lengths of dimensions A and B to determine which is the intake shaft and which is the exhaust shaft

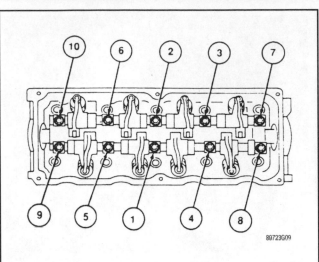

Fig. 20 Tighten the rocker arm bolts in this sequence to the correct torque specification

To install:

➡The intake and exhaust rocker arm shafts can be identified by comparing the lengths of dimensions A and B, as shown in the accompanying illustration. The longer dimension (A) is on the intake rocker arm shaft.

6. Assemble the rocker arm spacers and arms making sure they are in the positions that were marked before disassembly.

7. Install the rocker arm bolts and seats. Tighten the bolts in the sequence illustrated to 16–21 ft. lbs. (22–28 Nm) using a torque wrench.

8. Install the valve cover.

Thermostat

REMOVAL & INSTALLATION

▶ **See Figures 21 thru 30**

1. Disconnect the negative battery cable.
2. If equipped, disconnect the rubber retainer that engages the wiring harness to the radiator hose.

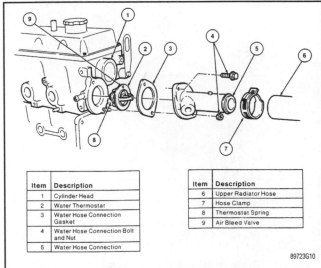

Item	Description
1	Cylinder Head
2	Water Thermostat
3	Water Hose Connection Gasket
4	Water Hose Connection Bolt and Nut
5	Water Hose Connection

Item	Description
6	Upper Radiator Hose
7	Hose Clamp
8	Thermostat Spring
9	Air Bleed Valve

89723G10

Fig. 21 Exploded view of the thermostat assembly and mounting

3. Tag and disengage all electrical connections that would interfere with thermostat removal.

✳✳ **CAUTION**

Never open, service or drain the radiator or cooling system when hot; serious burns can occur from the steam and hot coolant. Also, when draining engine coolant, keep in mind that cats and dogs are attracted to ethylene glycol antifreeze and could drink any that is left in an uncovered container or in puddles on the ground. This will prove fatal in sufficient quantities. Always drain coolant into a sealable container. Coolant should be reused unless it is contaminated or is several years old.

4. Remove the radiator cap.

5. Place a suitable container under the radiator petcock, open the petcock and drain the coolant until it is at a level below the upper radiator hose, then close the petcock.

6. Loosen the upper radiator hose-to-thermostat housing (water hose connection) clamp, then disconnect the hose from the housing.

7. Loosen the housing retaining nut and bolt, and remove the housing.

8. Remove the thermostat and the old gasket.

Fig. 22 If equipped, disconnect the rubber retainer that engages the wiring harness to the radiator hose

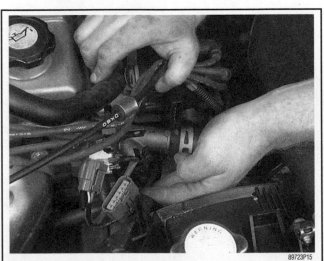

Fig. 23 Tag and disengage any electrical connections that would interfere with thermostat removal

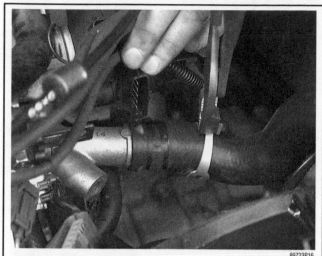

Fig. 24 Compress the upper radiator hose-to-thermostat housing hose clamp tabs with pliers . . .

Fig. 25 . . . and disconnect the hose from the thermostat housing

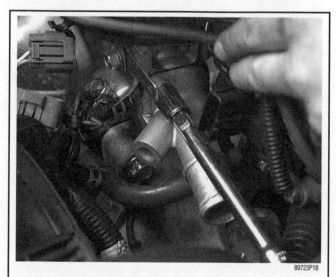

Fig. 26 Loosen the thermostat housing retainers . . .

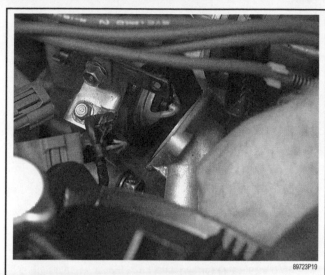

Fig. 27 . . . then remove the housing from the engine

Fig. 28 Remove the old thermostat housing gasket

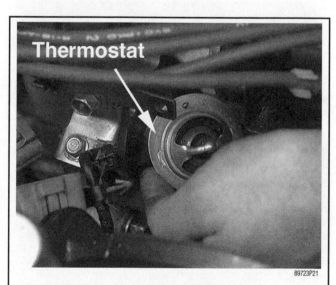

Fig. 29 Pull the thermostat from the cylinder head

Fig. 30 The subvalve (arrow) must be at the top when installing the thermostat

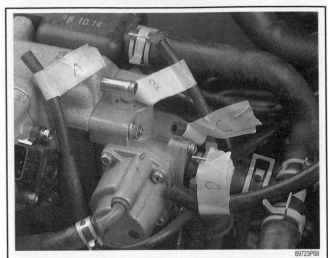

Fig. 31 Tag and disconnect all the hoses and wires on top of the upper intake manifold that would interfere with removal

9. Use a scraper to clean any old gasket material residue from the housing and the cylinder head mating surfaces.

To install:

10. Install the thermostat in the cylinder head, valve end first and the subvalve at the top.

11. Coat the new gasket with a sealing compound such as B5A-19554-A, F2AZ-19554-AA or their equivalents, and install the gasket on the cylinder head, making sure the holes are properly aligned in relation to the bolt hole and stud.

12. Install the thermostat housing carefully so that the gasket will remain in position.

➡ **Make sure the thermostat flange is seated properly into the recess in the housing before tightening the retainers.**

13. Install the nut and bolt. Tighten them to 14–19 ft. lbs. (19–26 Nm).

14. Connect the upper radiator hose to the thermostat housing and tighten the hose clamp.

15. Fill the cooling system to the proper level and install the radiator cap.

16. Connect the negative battery cable and start the car.

17. Let the engine reach normal operating temperature, then check for leaks and proper thermostat operation.

Fig. 32 Unfasten the vacuum line bracket retainers from the rear of the manifold

Intake Manifold

REMOVAL & INSTALLATION

Upper Manifold

▸ **See Figures 31 thru 37**

1. Disconnect the negative battery cable.
2. Relieve the fuel system pressure. Refer to Section 5.

❉❉ CAUTION

Never open, service or drain the radiator or cooling system when hot; serious burns can occur from the steam and hot coolant. Also, when draining engine coolant, keep in mind that cats and dogs are attracted to ethylene glycol antifreeze and could drink any that is left in an uncovered container or in puddles on the ground. This will prove fatal in sufficient quantities. Always drain coolant into a sealable container. Coolant should be reused unless it is contaminated or is several years old.

Fig. 33 Unbolt the upper intake manifold retainers

Fig. 34 After all the bolts are unfastened, slide the upper intake manifold past the hoses

Fig. 35 Tag and disengage the lower hoses (arrows) from the upper manifold

Fig. 36 After everything has been disconnected and moved aside, remove the upper intake manifold

Fig. 37 Remove the upper intake-to-lower intake manifold gasket

3. Remove the radiator cap.

4. Place a suitable container under the radiator petcock, open the petcock and drain the cooling system.

5. Loosen the upper intake manifold support bolts, then remove the support.

6. Disconnect the accelerator cable from the throttle lever.

7. Disconnect the air cleaner-to-intake manifold tube.

8. Tag and disconnect the coolant hoses from the upper manifold.

9. Tag and disconnect all wiring and hoses that will interfere with manifold removal.

10. Loosen the upper intake manifold-to-lower intake manifold bolts.

11. Remove the upper intake manifold and gasket.

To install:

12. Use a scraper to clean any old gasket material residue from the upper and lower manifold mating surfaces.

13. Install a new gasket and place the upper intake manifold in position.

14. Install the upper intake manifold-to-lower intake manifold bolts. Tighten the bolts to 14–20 ft. lbs. (19–26 Nm).

15. Connect the coolant hoses to the upper manifold.

16. Engage all wiring and hoses that were tagged and disconnected during removal.

17. Connect the air cleaner-to-intake manifold tube.

18. Connect the accelerator cable to the throttle lever.

19. Install the upper intake manifold support, then tighten the bolts to 22–34 ft. lbs. (31–46 Nm).

20. Fill the cooling system and connect the negative battery cable.

21. Start the vehicle and check for proper engine operation.

Lower Manifold

◢ **See Figures 38 thru 44**

1. Disconnect the negative battery cable.
2. Relieve the fuel system pressure. Refer to Section 5.

❋❋ CAUTION

Never open, service or drain the radiator or cooling system when hot; serious burns can occur from the steam and hot coolant. Also, when draining engine coolant, keep in mind that cats and dogs are attracted to ethylene glycol antifreeze and could drink any that is left in an uncovered container or in puddles on the ground. This will prove fatal in sufficient quantities. Always drain coolant into a sealable container. Coolant should be reused unless it is contaminated or is several years old.

3. Remove the radiator cap.

4. Place a suitable container under the radiator petcock, open the petcock and drain the cooling system.

5. Loosen the intake manifold support bolts, then remove the support.

6. Disconnect the accelerator cable from the throttle lever.

7. Disconnect the air cleaner-to-intake manifold tube.

8. Tag and disconnect the coolant hoses from the manifold.

9. Tag and disconnect all wiring and hoses that will interfere with manifold removal.

10. Loosen the intake manifold-to-cylinder head bolts.

➡ **You may have to raise the car and support it with jackstands to unfasten the lower nut on the passenger's side of the manifold.**

11. Remove the intake manifold and gasket.

To install:

12. Use a scraper to clean any old gasket material residue from the cylinder head and intake manifold mating surfaces.

13. Install a new gasket and place the intake manifold in position.

14. Install the intake manifold-to-cylinder head bolts. Tighten the bolts to 14–20 ft. lbs. (19–26 Nm).

15. Connect the coolant hoses to the upper manifold.

16. Engage all wiring and hoses that were tagged and disconnected during removal.

17. Connect the air cleaner-to-intake manifold tube.

18. Connect the accelerator cable to the throttle lever.

19. Install the intake manifold support, then tighten the bolts to 22–34 ft. lbs. (31–46 Nm).

20. Fill the cooling system and connect the negative battery cable.

21. Start the vehicle and check for proper engine operation.

Fig. 40 Remove all wiring, hoses and brackets that will interfere with lower manifold removal

Fig. 38 Remove the fuel rail and injectors as an assembly

Fig. 41 Unfasten the lower intake manifold retainers

Fig. 39 Move the fuel injector wiring harness aside

Fig. 42 Make sure to disconnect the lower hoses at the base of the manifold

Fig. 43 Remove the lower intake manifold . . .

Fig. 44 . . . and its gasket from the engine compartment

Exhaust Manifold

REMOVAL & INSTALLATION

▶ **See Figures 45 thru 58**

1. Raise the car and support it with safety stands.
2. Loosen the exhaust inlet pipe nuts and remove the washers.
3. Loosen the muffler pipe bracket bolts, then remove the safety stands and lower the car.
4. Disconnect the air cleaner-to-intake manifold tube.
5. Loosen the exhaust manifold shield bolts and remove the shield.
6. Disengage the oxygen sensor (O2S) electrical connector from the routing bracket and unplug the sensor.
7. Loosen the water pipe clamp located under the distributor.

➡**The water pipe clamp has to be pulled forward to allow clearance for manifold removal.**

8. Remove the exhaust manifold nut that retains the water pipe bracket beneath the manifold.

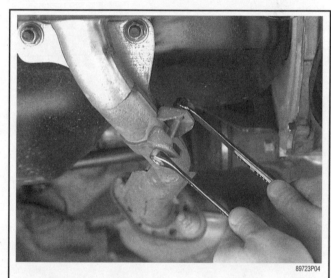

Fig. 45 Loosen the muffler pipe bracket bolts . . .

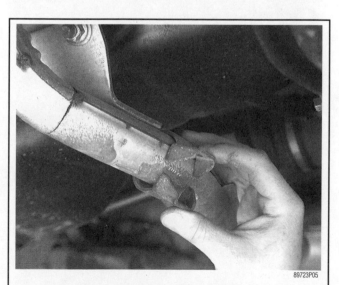

Fig. 46 . . . then separate the bracket from the exhaust pipe

Fig. 47 Loosen the exhaust pipe-to-exhaust manifold flange bolts . . .

Fig. 48 . . . and separate the exhaust pipe from the manifold

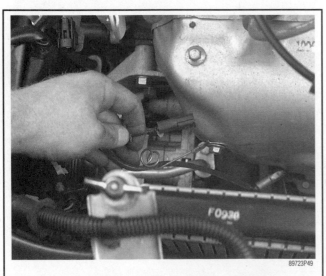

Fig. 49 Unplug the oxygen sensor electrical connection

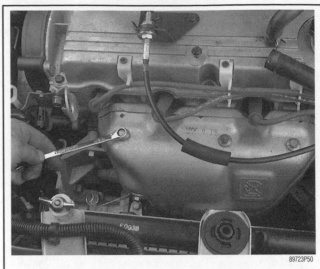

Fig. 50 Loosen the exhaust manifold shield bolts . . .

Fig. 51 . . . then remove the shield from the engine compartment

Fig. 52 Loosen the water pipe clamp located under the distributor

Fig. 53 Remove the exhaust manifold nut that retains the water pipe bracket below the manifold

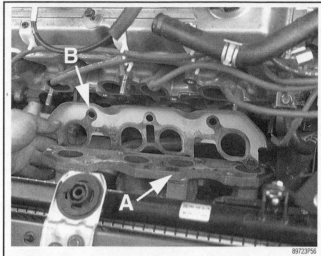

Fig. 56 Remove the exhaust manifold (A) and gasket (B) from the engine compartment

Fig. 54 Location of the exhaust manifold retaining nuts and bolts

Fig. 57 Use a scraper to clean gasket residue from the exhaust manifold-to-cylinder head mating surface . . .

Fig. 55 Loosen the exhaust manifold retaining nuts and bolts

Fig. 58 . . . and the manifold's mating surface

9. Pull the pipe off the stud and slide the assembly towards the driver's side to separate it from the water pump inlet connector.

10. Loosen the bolts and nuts which retain the exhaust manifold.

11. Remove the exhaust manifold from the engine.

12. Remove the exhaust manifold gasket from the cylinder head.

13. Use a scraper to clean any old gasket material residue from the cylinder head and exhaust manifold mating surfaces.

To install:

14. Install a new manifold gasket over the cylinder head studs.

15. Install the exhaust manifold, nuts and bolts. Using a torque wrench, tighten the manifold bolts and nuts to 12–17 ft. lbs. (16–23 Nm).

16. Install the manifold shield and bolts. Tighten the bolts to 12–17 ft. lbs. (16–23 Nm).

17. Connect the water pipe to the pump inlet connector and slide the bracket onto the stud.

18. Tighten the exhaust manifold nut that retains the water bracket below the manifold.

19. Attach the water pipe clamp located under the distributor and tighten the retainer.

20. Engage the O2S sensor electrical connection and secure it to the routing bracket.

21. Connect the air cleaner-to-intake manifold tube.

22. Raise the car and support it with safety stands.

23. Install the muffler inlet pipe gasket on the manifold studs.

24. Push the inlet pipe up until it engages the manifold studs, then install the washers and nuts. Tighten the nuts to 23–34 ft. lbs. (31–46 Nm).

25. Engage the muffler pipe bracket and install the bolts.

26. Remove the safety stands and lower the car.

27. Start the car and check for exhaust leaks.

Radiator

REMOVAL & INSTALLATION

▶ See Figures 59 thru 67

✳✳ CAUTION

Never open, service or drain the radiator or cooling system when hot; serious burns can occur from the steam and hot coolant. Also, when draining engine coolant, keep in mind that cats and dogs are attracted to ethylene glycol antifreeze and could drink any that is left in an uncovered container or in pud-

dles on the ground. This will prove fatal in sufficient quantities. Always drain coolant into a sealable container. Coolant should be reused unless it is contaminated or is several years old.

1. Disconnect the negative battery cable.

2. Unplug the cooling fan motor's electrical connection.

3. Remove the radiator cap.

4. Place a suitable container under the radiator petcock. Open the petcock and drain the cooling system, then close the petcock.

5. Disconnect the overflow hose.

6. Use a pair of pliers to compress the upper radiator hose clamp and slide it away from the radiator. Disconnect the upper radiator hose from the radiator.

7. Disconnect the wiring harness from the routing clamps on the fan shroud.

8. Use a pair of pliers to compress the lower radiator hose clamp, then disconnect the hose from the radiator.

9. On models equipped with an automatic transaxle, disconnect the fluid cooler hoses, then remove the lower bolt and cooler hose bracket.

10. Loosen the radiator support upper bracket bolts (4) that attach the brackets to the body, then remove the brackets.

Fig. 60 Compress the upper hose clamp tabs with pliers, then slide the clamp away from the radiator

Fig. 59 Unplug the cooling fan electrical connection

Fig. 61 Gently twist and pull the radiator hose away from the radiator to disengage it; also detach the overflow hose

Fig. 62 Loosen the radiator support upper bracket bolts . . .

Fig. 63 . . . and remove the brackets

Fig. 64 Lift the radiator up and out of the engine compartment, being careful not to damage the fins

Fig. 65 Use pliers to compress the lower hose clamp, then slide it away from the radiator

Fig. 66 Once the clamp is disengaged, pull the hose away from the radiator to separate it

Fig. 67 Location of the transaxle fluid cooler lines

11. Remove the radiator and fan shroud from the engine compartment, as necessary.

12. If necessary, separate the fan/shroud assembly from the radiator by loosening the bolts. On models with an automatic transaxle there are 3 bolts, and on models with a manual transaxle there are 4 bolts.

To install:

13. If necessary, engage the fan/shroud to the radiator and tighten the bolts.

➡When installing the radiator, make sure the upper brackets are fully engaged on the radiator and that the mounting pins, located on the lower tank of the radiator, are in their proper slots in the core support crossmember. Also be sure that the radiator mounting insulators (2) are in the correct place.

14. Install the radiator/shroud assembly.

15. Place the radiator support brackets in position and tighten the bolts to 71–89 inch lbs. (8–10 Nm).

16. Connect the overflow hose.

17. Connect the upper and lower radiator hoses and engage their clamps.

18. On models equipped with an automatic transaxle, connect the oil cooler hoses, then install the cooler hose bracket and lower bolt.

19. Make sure the radiator petcock is closed and fasten the cooling fan motor's electrical connection.

20. Position the wiring harness in the routing clamps.

21. Fill the cooling system and install the radiator cap.

22. Connect the negative battery cable and start the car.

23. When the engine is warmed up, check for leaks.

Engine Fan

REMOVAL & INSTALLATION

❋❋ CAUTION

Never open, service or drain the radiator or cooling system when hot; serious burns can occur from the steam and hot coolant. Also, when draining engine coolant, keep in mind that cats and dogs are attracted to ethylene glycol antifreeze and could drink any that is left in an uncovered container or in puddles on the ground. This will prove fatal in sufficient quantities. Always drain coolant into a sealable container. Coolant should be reused unless it is contaminated or is several years old.

1. Disconnect the negative battery cable.

2. Unplug the cooling fan motor's electrical connection.

3. Remove the radiator cap.

4. Place a suitable container under the radiator petcock. Open the petcock and drain the cooling system, then close the petcock.

5. Use a pair of pliers to compress the upper radiator hose clamp and slide it away from the radiator. Disconnect the upper radiator hose from the radiator.

6. Disconnect the wiring harness from the routing clamps on the fan shroud.

7. Remove the bolts located at the top of the shroud that attach the shroud to the radiator.

8. Loosen, but do not remove, the bolts located at the bottom of the shroud that attach the shroud to the radiator.

9. Remove the fan shroud, motor and blade assembly from the engine compartment.

To install:

➡When installing the cooling fan assembly, make sure the bottom of the fan shroud engages the lower shroud bolts.

10. Install the fan assembly and tighten the upper and lower bolts to 71–97 inch lbs. (8–11 Nm).

11. Connect the upper radiator hose and engage the clamp.

12. Make sure the radiator petcock is closed and fasten the cooling fan motor's electrical connection.

13. Position the wiring harness in the routing clamps.

14. Fill the cooling system and install the radiator cap.

15. Connect the negative battery cable and start the car.

16. When the engine is warmed up, check for leaks.

Engine Fan Motor

REMOVAL & INSTALLATION

♦ **See Figures 68 and 69**

1. Remove the cooling fan and shroud assembly.

2. Loosen the fan blade nut, then remove the blade from the motor shaft.

3. Remove the wiring harness routing strap and the fan motor retaining screws (3).

4. Remove the motor from the shroud.

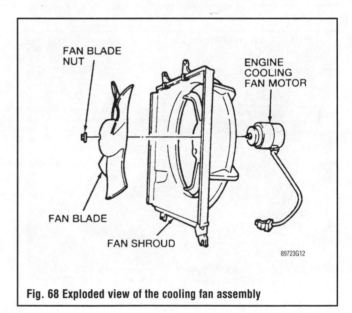

Fig. 68 Exploded view of the cooling fan assembly

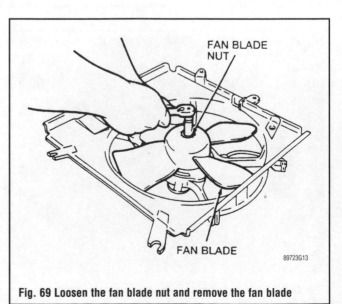

Fig. 69 Loosen the fan blade nut and remove the fan blade

To install:

5. Install the motor on the shroud.

6. Install the motor retaining screws and tighten them to 0.08–0.17 inch lbs. (0.01–0.02 Nm).

7. Install the wiring harness routing clip.

8. Install the fan blade and nut. Tighten the nut to 0.35–0.53 inch lbs. (0.04–0.06 Nm).

9. Install the cooling fan and shroud assembly in the engine compartment.

Water Pump

REMOVAL & INSTALLATION

▶ **See Figures 70 thru 76**

1. Remove the timing belt, as described later in this section.

2. Remove the radiator cap.

3. Place a suitable container under the radiator petcock. Open the petcock and drain the cooling system, then close the petcock.

4. If necessary for access, remove the A/C compressor tensioner pulley bracket.

Fig. 72 If necessary for access, loosen the A/C compressor tensioner pulley bracket bolts . . .

Fig. 70 Remove the water pump pulley (A) from the water pump (B)

Fig. 73 . . . and remove the bracket assembly

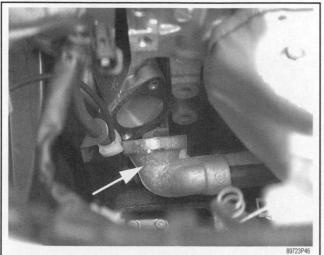

Fig. 71 Loosen the water pump inlet connector-to-water pump bolts and remove the connector (arrow)

Fig. 74 Location of the four water pump mounting bolts

Fig. 75 Loosen the water pump mounting bolts and remove the pump

Fig. 76 Use a scraper to clean any old gasket material residue from the water pump mounting surface (arrow)

5. Loosen the water pump pulley bolts and remove the pulley.

6. Loosen the water pump inlet connector-to-water pump bolts (2). Remove the inlet connector and discard the gasket.

7. Loosen the water pump retaining bolts (4), then remove the water pump from the engine compartment. Discard the old water pump gasket.

8. Use a scraper to clean any old gasket material residue from the water pump and engine block mating surfaces.

To install:

9. Coat the new water pump gasket with a sealing compound such as B5A-19554-A or equivalent.

10. Position the water pump gasket on the cylinder block and a new gasket on the inlet connector.

11. Install the water pump on the engine block, being careful not to move the gasket while aligning the bolt holes.

12. Install the water pump bolts and tighten them to 14–19 ft. lbs. (19–26 Nm).

13. If removed for access, install the A/C compressor tensioner pulley bracket.

14. Install the water pump inlet connector and its retaining bolts. Tighten the bolts to 14–22 ft. lbs. (19–30 Nm).

15. Install the water pump pulley and tighten the bolts.

16. Install the timing belt.

17. Fill the cooling system and install the radiator cap.

18. Start the engine and check for leaks, especially after it reaches operating temperature.

Cylinder Head

REMOVAL & INSTALLATION

◆ See Figures 77 thru 87

1. Disconnect the negative battery cable.

✳✳ CAUTION

Never open, service or drain the radiator or cooling system when hot; serious burns can occur from the steam and hot coolant. Also, when draining engine coolant, keep in mind that cats and dogs are attracted to ethylene glycol antifreeze and could drink any that is left in an uncovered container or in puddles on the ground. This will prove fatal in sufficient quantities. Always drain coolant into a sealable container. Coolant should be reused unless it is contaminated or is several years old.

Fig. 77 Remove the front engine lift hangers . . .

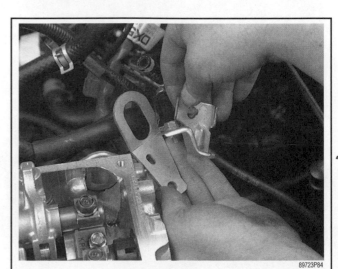

Fig. 78 . . . and the rear engine lift hangers from the cylinder head

2. Remove the radiator cap.

3. Place a suitable container under the radiator petcock, then open the petcock and drain the cooling system.

4. Tag and disconnect the spark plug wires from the plugs.

5. Remove the distributor, as described in Section 2.

6. Remove the timing belt and valve cover, as described elsewhere in this section.

7. Remove the exhaust and intake manifolds, as described earlier in this section.

8. Remove the front and rear engine lift hangers. Disengage the engine ground wire.

9. Tag and disengage all wire harness connectors.

10. Use a pair of pliers to compress the upper radiator hose clamp and slide it away from the radiator. Disconnect the upper radiator hose from the radiator.

11. Remove the water bypass tube or hose and bracket.

➡**It is advisable to loosen the cylinder head bolts in the opposite order of their tightening sequence.**

12. Remove the cylinder head bolts (10).

13. Remove the cylinder head and gasket from the engine.

Fig. 79 Unfasten the engine ground strap bolt and separate the strap from the cylinder head

Fig. 80 Unfasten the cylinder head bolts

Fig. 81 Remove the cylinder head from the engine compartment

Fig. 82 Remove the old cylinder head gasket and discard it

Fig. 83 Place rags or paper towels in the cylinder bores before scraping old gasket material from the block

Fig. 84 Use the gasket scraper to clean all dirt and gasket residue from the cylinder head

To install:

➡The cylinder head must be cleaned and inspected before installation. Please refer to the ENGINE RECONDITIONING procedures later in this section.

14. Use a scraper to clean any old gasket material residue from the cylinder head gasket mating surfaces.

➡The cylinder head gasket has marks on one of its edges that match the shape of the cylinder head; when the gasket is installed, these marks must align properly before cylinder head installation.

15. Install a new gasket and place the cylinder head in position.
16. Install NEW cylinder head bolts and tighten them with a torque wrench in the sequence illustrated and also in the following order:
- First pass: 35–40 ft. lbs. (50–60 Nm)
- Second pass: 56–60 ft. lbs. (75–81 Nm).
17. Install the water bypass tube or hose and bracket.
18. Connect the upper radiator hose and engage the clamp.
19. Fasten all wire harness connectors.
20. Attach the engine ground wire, then install the front and rear engine lift hangers.
21. Install the distributor.
22. Install the intake and exhaust manifolds.

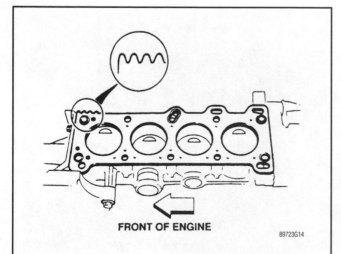

Fig. 85 The cylinder head gasket must match exactly with the shape of the cylinder head

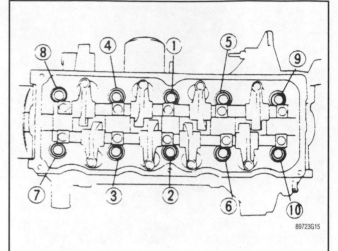

Fig. 86 Tighten the cylinder head bolts in the order shown to the proper specification

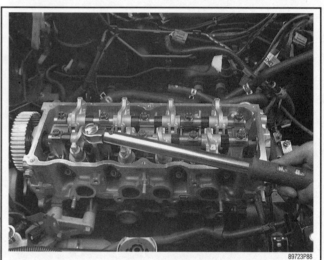

Fig. 87 Use a torque wrench when tightening the cylinder head bolts

23. Install the timing belt.
24. Install the valve cover.
25. Connect the spark plug wires to the plugs.
26. Fill the cooling system and install the radiator cap.
27. Connect the negative battery cable.
28. Start the engine and check for leaks, especially when it reaches operating temperature.

Oil Pan

REMOVAL & INSTALLATION

▸ **See Figures 88 and 89**

1. Disconnect the negative battery cable.
2. Raise the car and support it on safety stands.
3. Drain the engine oil into a suitable container.

✳✳ CAUTION

The EPA warns that prolonged contact with used engine oil may cause a number of skin disorders, including cancer! You should make every effort to minimize your exposure to used engine oil. Protective gloves should be worn when changing the oil. Wash your hands and any other exposed skin areas as soon as possible after exposure to used engine oil. Soap and water, or waterless hand cleaner should be used.

4. Remove the exhaust pipe.
5. Loosen the oil pan nuts and bolts, then remove the oil pan.
6. Remove and discard the oil pan gasket.
7. Use a scraper to clean any old gasket material residue from the oil pan gasket mating surfaces.

To install:
8. Apply oil resistant sealer across the joint line of the block, oil pump and crankshaft rear oil seal retainer.
9. Install the oil pan gasket, then place the pan in position.
10. Install the nuts and bolts. Tighten them to 69–78 inch lbs. (8–9 Nm).
11. Install the oil pan drain plug and tighten it to 22–30 ft. lbs. (29–41 Nm).
12. Add the correct type and amount of engine oil.
13. Install the exhaust inlet pipe.
14. Connect the negative battery cable, start the car and check for leaks.

Oil Pump

REMOVAL & INSTALLATION

▶ See Figures 90, 91, 92 and 93

1. Remove the crankshaft sprockets. Refer to the timing belt sprockets and seals procedure in this section.
2. Unfasten and remove the oil pan.
3. Loosen the oil pump bolts (6), then remove the oil pump and gasket.
4. If necessary, loosen the oil pump screen cover and tube bolts, then remove the screen cover, screen cover gasket and tube.

To install:
5. Clean the oil pump gasket mating surface with a scraper and the screen cover gasket mating surfaces with a single edge razor blade.

✳✳ WARNING

Do not allow the sealing compound to squeeze into the oil pump outlet hole in the pump or cylinder block.

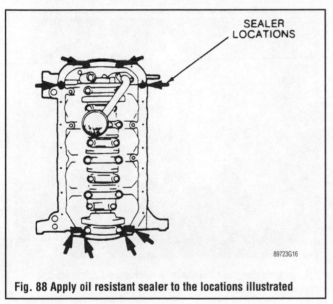

Fig. 88 Apply oil resistant sealer to the locations illustrated

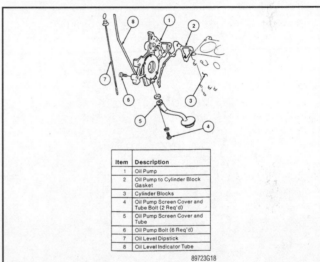

Item	Description
1	Oil Pump
2	Oil Pump to Cylinder Block Gasket
3	Cylinder Blocks
4	Oil Pump Screen Cover and Tube Bolt (2 Req'd)
5	Oil Pump Screen Cover and Tube
6	Oil Pump Bolt (6 Req'd)
7	Oil Level Dipstick
8	Oil Level Indicator Tube

Fig. 90 Exploded view of the oil pump assembly and related components

Fig. 89 Install a new gasket any time the oil pan is removed

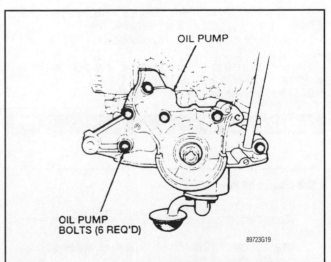

Fig. 91 Loosen the six oil pump bolts before you remove the pump

Fig. 92 A single edge razor blade can be used to clean the screen cover gasket mating surfaces

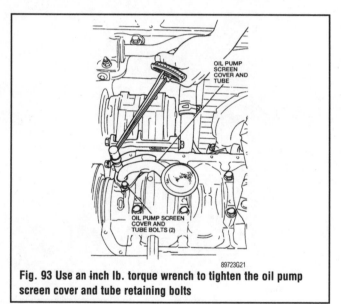

Fig. 93 Use an inch lb. torque wrench to tighten the oil pump screen cover and tube retaining bolts

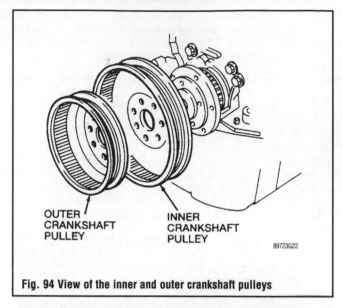

Fig. 94 View of the inner and outer crankshaft pulleys

Fig. 95 Unfasten the front fender splash shield retainers and remove the shield

Fig. 96 The crankshaft pulley retaining washer is secured by four bolts

6. Apply sealing compound B5A-19554-A or its equivalent to each side of the new oil pump gasket, then install the gasket.

7. Install the oil pump and bolts. Tighten the bolts to 14–19 ft. lbs. (19–25 Nm).

8. If removed, install the screen cover gasket, cover and tube. Tighten the retainers to 71–97 inch lbs. (8–11 Nm).

9. Install the oil pan and crankshaft sprockets.

Crankshaft Pulley

REMOVAL & INSTALLATION

▶ See Figures 94 thru 103

1. Remove the drive belts.

2. Loosen the front fender splash shield retainers (3) and remove the shield.

3. Install strap wrench D8L-6000-A or equivalent on the outer crankshaft pulley, and loosen the crankshaft pulley bolt.

4. Loosen the four crankshaft pulley washer retaining bolts, then remove the washer.

Fig. 97 A drive belt may be used to hold the crankshaft pulley while you loosen the washer retaining bolts

Fig. 100 Remove the outer crankshaft pulley . . .

Fig. 98 Remove the crankshaft pulley washer

Fig. 101 . . . and the inner pulley from the crankshaft

Fig. 99 Remove the crankshaft pulley bolt

Fig. 102 If necessary, remove the crankshaft position sensor trigger wheel . . .

Fig. 103 . . . and the alignment pulley from the crankshaft

Fig. 104 Timing belt routing

5. Remove the crankshaft pulley bolt and the strap wrench.
6. Remove the outer and inner crankshaft pulleys.

To install:

7. Install the inner and outer pulleys.

➡Before installing the crankshaft pulley bolt, apply a coating of black silicone rubber D6AZ-19562-BA or equivalent.

8. Finger-tighten the crankshaft pulley bolt.
9. Install the pulley washer and finger-tighten the four retaining bolts.
10. Install strap wrench D8L-6000-A or equivalent on the outer crankshaft pulley, and tighten the crankshaft pulley bolt to 80–85 ft. lbs. (108–118 Nm).
11. Tighten the four retaining washer bolts to 109–152 inch lbs. (12–17 Nm).
12. Remove the strap wrench, then install the splash shield and its retainers.
13. Install the drive belts.

Timing Belt and Cover

REMOVAL & INSTALLATION

◆ **See Figures 104 thru 115**

1. Remove the drive belts.
2. Remove the water pump and crankshaft pulleys.
3. Unfasten the four upper engine front cover bolts, then remove the cover.
4. Unfasten the three lower engine front cover bolts, then remove the cover.
5. Remove the timing belt tensioner spring and spring cover, then remove the tensioner bolt.
6. Mark the direction of rotation of the timing belt.
7. Remove the timing belt by sliding it off the sprockets.

To install:

8. Align the camshaft and crankshaft sprockets with the marks on the cylinder head.
9. Install the timing belt.
10. Install the timing belt tensioner spring and spring cover on the belt tensioner.
11. Install the tensioner and spring assembly on the engine, then finger-tighten the tensioner bolt.
12. Connect the timing belt spring to the anchor.

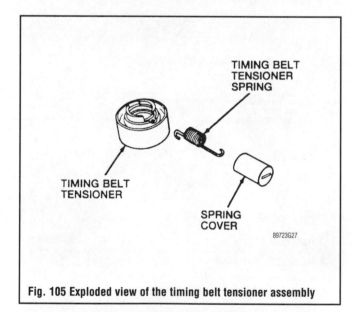

Fig. 105 Exploded view of the timing belt tensioner assembly

TIMING BELT TENSIONER SPRING

TIMING BELT TENSIONER

SPRING COVER

Fig. 106 If installing the old belt, mark the direction of rotation of the timing belt

Fig. 107 Loosen the three water pump pulley retainers

Fig. 110 Make sure the timing marks on both the camshaft . . .

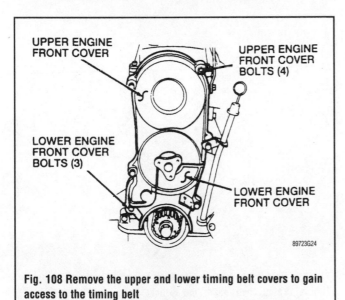

Fig. 108 Remove the upper and lower timing belt covers to gain access to the timing belt

Fig. 111 . . . and crankshaft sprockets are aligned

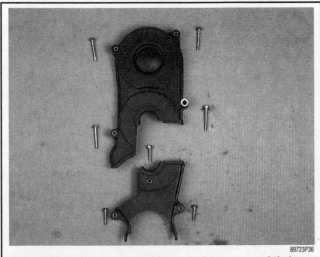

Fig. 109 View of the upper and lower timing covers and their retainers

Fig. 112 Loosen the timing belt tensioner bolt . . .

Fig. 113 . . . then remove the tensioner spring and spring cover

Fig. 114 Slide the timing belt off the sprockets to remove it

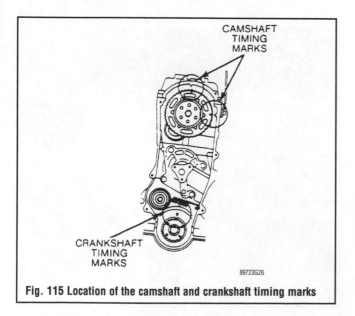

Fig. 115 Location of the camshaft and crankshaft timing marks

13. Rotate the crankshaft two turns in the proper direction of rotation and align the timing marks. Make sure all the timing marks are properly aligned.

14. Tighten the tensioner bolt to 14–19 ft. lbs. (19–26 Nm).

15. Install the lower and upper front covers. Tighten the bolts to 71–97 inch lbs. (8–11 Nm).

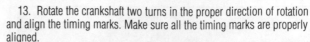

Timing Belt Sprockets and Seals

REMOVAL & INSTALLATION

Camshaft Sprocket and Seal

▶ **See Figures 116, 117, 118 and 119**

1. Remove the timing belt and valve cover.

2. Hold the camshaft with an open end wrench to prevent it from turning, then remove the sprocket bolt, sprocket and dowel pin.

3. Use a suitable size punch and a hammer to drive the seal through the cylinder head, then use side cutters to cut the seal and remove the seal from the head.

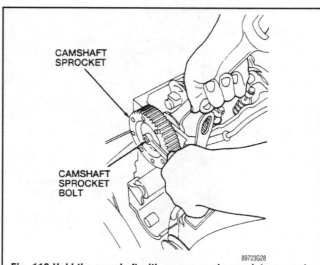

Fig. 116 Hold the camshaft with an open end wrench to prevent it from turning, then loosen the sprocket bolt

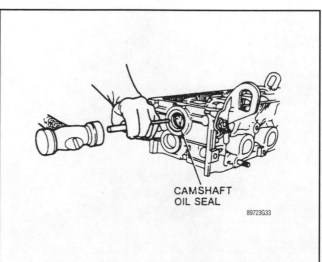

Fig. 117 Drive the camshaft oil seal into the cylinder head using a hammer and punch . . .

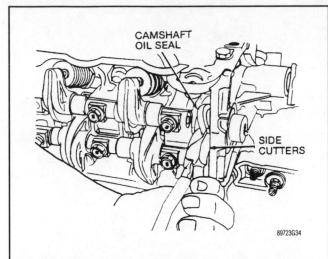

Fig. 118 . . . then use side cutters to cut the seal and remove the seal from the head

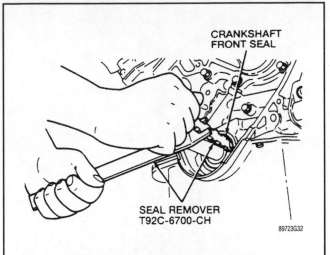

Fig. 120 Seal removal tool T92C-6700-CH or equivalent can be used to remove the crankshaft front seal

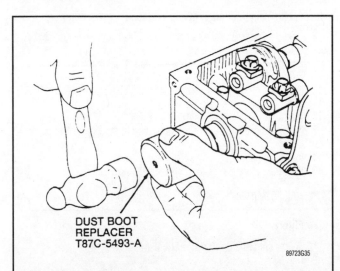

Fig. 119 Use dust boot replacer tool T87C-5493-A or equivalent and a hammer to drive the seal into its bore

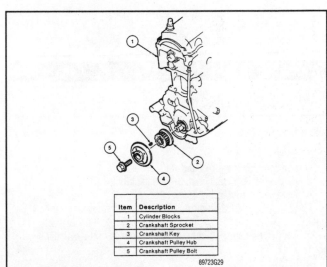

Item	Description
1	Cylinder Blocks
2	Crankshaft Sprocket
3	Crankshaft Key
4	Crankshaft Pulley Hub
5	Crankshaft Pulley Bolt

Fig. 121 Exploded view of the crankshaft sprocket assembly and related components

To install:

4. Lubricate the lip of the new camshaft oil seal and seal surface on the cylinder head with clean engine oil.

5. Use dust boot replacer tool T87C-5493-A or equivalent and a hammer to drive the seal into its bore in the head.

6. Install the camshaft sprocket, dowel pin and bolt.

7. Hold the camshaft with an open end wrench to prevent it from turning, then tighten the sprocket bolt to 36–45 ft. lbs. (49–61 Nm).

8. Install the timing belt and valve cover.

9. Start the engine and check for leaks.

Crankshaft Sprocket and Seal

▶ **See Figures 120, 121, 122 and 123**

1. Remove the timing belt and the crankshaft pulleys.

2. Remove the crankshaft sprocket, pulley hub and key.

3. Use seal removal tool T92C-6700-CH or equivalent to remove the seal.

To install:

4. Lubricate the lip of the new crankshaft oil seal with clean engine oil.

5. Use front seal replacer tool T87C-6019-A to install the seal in its bore.

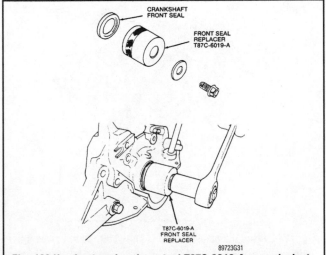

Fig. 122 Use front seal replacer tool T87C-6019-A or equivalent to install the seal in its bore

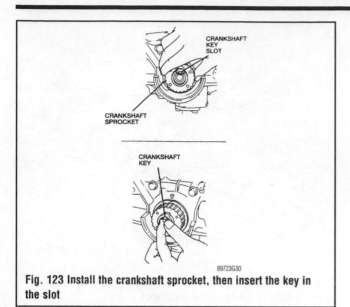

Fig. 123 Install the crankshaft sprocket, then insert the key in the slot

6. Install the crankshaft sprocket, key and pulleys.
7. Install the timing belt.
8. Start the engine and check for leaks.

Camshaft

REMOVAL & INSTALLATION

♦ **See Figures 124 and 125**

1. Remove the battery.
2. Remove the timing belt and valve cover.
3. Remove the camshaft sprocket and distributor.
4. Remove the rocker arm assemblies.
5. Loosen the camshaft thrust plate bolt and remove the thrust plate.
6. Gently pull camshaft from the left-hand side of the cylinder head.

To install:

7. Clean the camshaft and cylinder head surface.

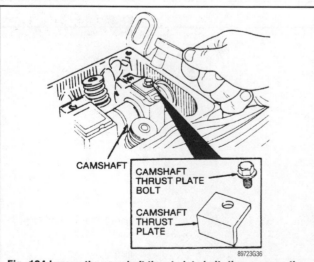

Fig. 124 Loosen the camshaft thrust plate bolt, then remove the plate

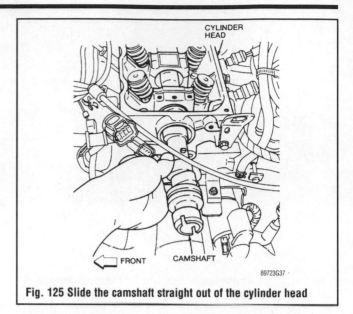

Fig. 125 Slide the camshaft straight out of the cylinder head

➡ **Inspect the camshaft oil seal and replace it if necessary.**

8. Coat the surfaces of the camshaft with clean engine oil and gently install the camshaft in the left-hand side of the cylinder head.
9. Install the camshaft thrust plate and bolt. Tighten the bolt to 71–88 inch lbs. (8–10 Nm).
10. Install the rocker arm assemblies and the distributor.
11. Install the camshaft sprocket.
12. Install the valve cover and the timing belt.
13. Adjust the camshaft timing, as described in the Timing Belt procedure.
14. Install the battery.
15. Start the car and check for proper engine operation.

CAMSHAFT TIMING

♦ **See Figure 115**

1. Set the crankshaft at Top Dead Center (TDC).
2. Unplug the Mass Air Flow (MAF) sensor.
3. Remove the MAF sensor and air cleaner-to-intake manifold tube.
4. Remove the drive belts.
5. Remove the water pump pulley by holding the pulley with strap wrench D85L-6000-A or equivalent and loosen the bolts.
6. Remove the upper timing cover.
7. Make sure the timing mark on the camshaft sprocket is aligned with the pointer on the cylinder head.
8. If the camshaft mark is not in sight, turn the camshaft one complete turn and check the timing mark alignment.
9. If the marks are aligned, the camshaft is properly timed.
10. If the marks are not aligned, continue with the adjustment procedure.
11. Remove the timing belt and the spark plugs.
12. Turn the crankshaft until the timing marks on the crankshaft sprocket and the oil pump housing align.
13. Turn the camshaft until the timing marks on the camshaft sprocket and cylinder head are aligned.
14. Install the timing belt and the spark plugs.
15. Install the upper engine front cover.
16. Install the water pump pulley and tighten the bolts to 36–45 ft. lbs. (49–61 Nm).
17. Install the drive belts.
18. Install the MAF sensor and air cleaner-to-intake manifold tube.
19. Engage the Mass Air Flow (MAF) sensor electrical connector.

Lifters

REMOVAL & INSTALLATION

▶ **See Figure 126**

1. Remove the valve cover and rocker arm shaft assemblies.
2. Pull the lash adjuster from the rocker arm.

To install:

3. Pour clean engine oil into the oil reservoir in the rocker arm and apply engine oil to the lash adjuster.

✳✳ WARNING

Be careful not to damage the O-ring when installing the adjuster.

4. Install the adjuster into the rocker arm.
5. Install the rocker arm and shaft assemblies.
6. Install the valve cover.

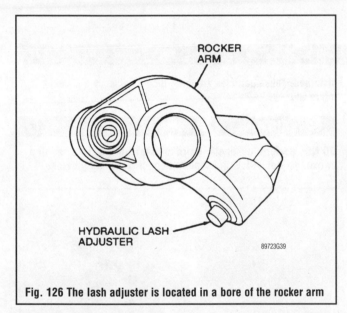

Fig. 126 The lash adjuster is located in a bore of the rocker arm

Crankshaft Rear Cover and Oil Seal

REMOVAL & INSTALLATION

▶ **See Figures 127 and 128**

1. Remove the flywheel.
2. Loosen the flywheel reinforcing plate bolt and remove the plate.
3. Use seal removal tool T92C-6700-CH or equivalent to remove the crankshaft rear oil seal.

To install:

4. Clean the sealing surface on the rear oil seal retainer.
5. Coat the inside and outside of a new seal with clean engine oil.

➡**The flywheel-to-crankshaft bolts can be used in conjunction with seal installation tool T87C-6701-A or equivalent to draw the seal into its bore.**

6. Position the new seal, then place the seal installation tool on top of it, and tighten the flywheel-to-crankshaft bolts until the seal bottoms out.
7. Remove the seal installation tool and install the flywheel reinforcing plate. Tighten the plate to 71–97 inch lbs. (8–11 Nm).
8. Install the flywheel.

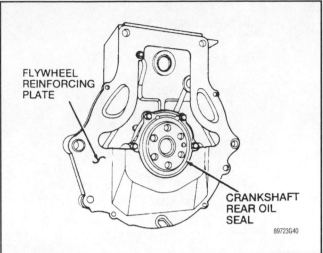

Fig. 127 Remove the flywheel reinforcing plate to gain access to the crankshaft rear oil seal

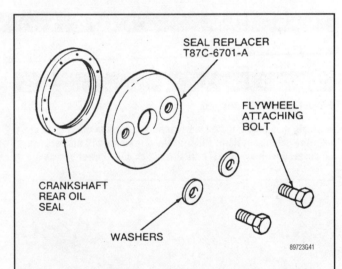

Fig. 128 After positioning the rear oil seal and installation tool, tighten the flywheel bolts until the seal is pressed into place

Flywheel

REMOVAL & INSTALLATION

Models With Manual Transaxle

▶ **See Figure 129**

1. Remove the transaxle, clutch pressure plate and clutch disc.
2. Use flywheel holding tool T74P-6375-A or equivalent to prevent the flywheel from turning, then loosen the flywheel retaining bolts.
3. Remove the flywheel from its mounting.

To install:

4. Clean any old sealant from the bolt holes and bolts.

➡**Coat the bolts threads with Stud and Bearing Mount E0AZ-19554-BA or an equivalent threadlocking compound.**

5. Install the flywheel and finger-tighten the bolts.
6. Use flywheel holding tool T74P-6375-A or equivalent to prevent the flywheel from turning, then tighten the flywheel retaining bolts to 71–76 ft. lbs. (96–103 Nm).
7. Install the clutch disc, pressure plate and transaxle.

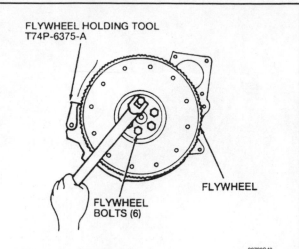

Fig. 129 Use the flywheel holding tool to prevent the flywheel from turning while loosening the bolts

Models With Automatic Transaxle

▶ **See Figure 129**

1. Remove the transaxle.
2. Use flywheel holding tool T74P-6375-A or equivalent to prevent the flywheel from turning, then loosen the retaining bolts.
3. Remove the flywheel from its mounting.
To install:
4. Clean any old sealant from the bolt holes and bolts.

➡**Coat the bolts threads with Stud and Bearing Mount E0AZ-19554-BA or an equivalent threadlocking compound.**

5. Install the flywheel and finger-tighten the bolts.
6. Use flywheel holding tool T74P-6375-A or equivalent to prevent the flywheel from turning, then tighten the retaining bolts to 71–76 ft. lbs. (96–103 Nm).
7. Install the transaxle.

EXHAUST SYSTEM

▶ **See Figures 130 and 131**

Inspection

▶ **See Figures 132 thru 138**

➡Safety glasses should be worn at all times when working on or near the exhaust system. Older exhaust systems will almost always be covered with loose rust particles which will shower you when disturbed. These particles are more than a nuisance and could injure your eye.

✳✳ CAUTION

DO NOT perform exhaust repairs or inspection with the engine or exhaust hot. Allow the system to cool completely before

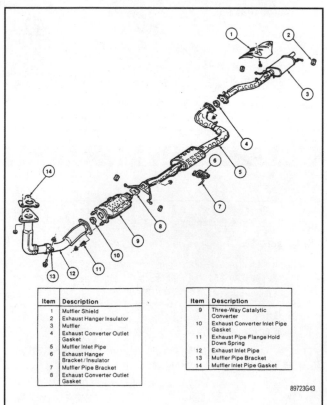

Item	Description
1	Muffler Shield
2	Exhaust Hanger Insulator
3	Muffler
4	Exhaust Converter Outlet Gasket
5	Muffler Inlet Pipe
6	Exhaust Hanger Bracket / Insulator
7	Muffler Pipe Bracket
8	Exhaust Converter Outlet Gasket

Item	Description
9	Three-Way Catalytic Converter
10	Exhaust Converter Inlet Pipe Gasket
11	Exhaust Pipe Flange Hold Down Spring
12	Exhaust Inlet Pipe
13	Muffler Pipe Bracket
14	Muffler Inlet Pipe Gasket

Fig. 130 Exploded view of the exhaust system components—early model Aspire

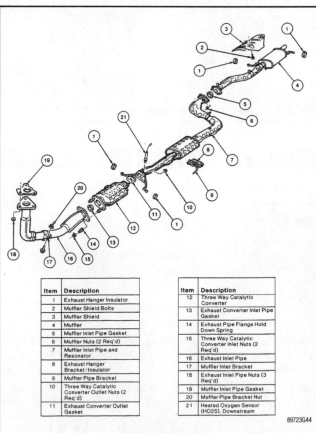

Item	Description
1	Exhaust Hanger Insulator
2	Muffler Shield Bolts
3	Muffler Shield
4	Muffler
5	Muffler Inlet Pipe Gasket
6	Muffler Nuts (2 Req'd)
7	Muffler Inlet Pipe and Resonator
8	Exhaust Hanger Bracket / Insulator
9	Muffler Pipe Bracket
10	Three Way Catalytic Converter Outlet Nuts (2 Req'd)
11	Exhaust Converter Outlet Gasket

Item	Description
12	Three Way Catalytic Converter
13	Exhaust Converter Inlet Pipe Gasket
14	Exhaust Pipe Flange Hold Down Spring
15	Three Way Catalytic Converter Inlet Nuts (2 Req'd)
16	Exhaust Inlet Pipe
17	Muffler Inlet Bracket
18	Exhaust Inlet Pipe Nuts (3 Req'd)
19	Muffler Inlet Pipe Gasket
20	Muffler Pipe Bracket Nut
21	Heated Oxygen Sensor (HO2S), Downstream

Fig. 131 Exploded view of the exhaust system components—late model Aspire

attempting any work. Exhaust systems are noted for sharp edges, flaking metal and rusted bolts. Gloves and eye protection are required. A healthy supply of penetrating oil and rags is highly recommended.

Your vehicle must be raised and supported safely to inspect the exhaust system properly. By placing 4 safety stands under the vehicle for support

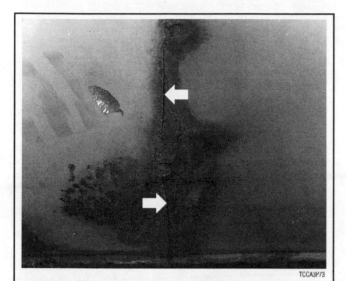

Fig. 132 Cracks in the muffler are a guaranteed leak

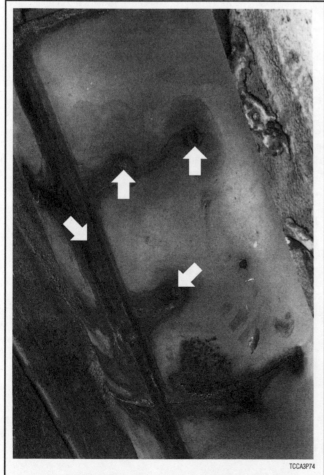

Fig. 133 Check the muffler for rotted spot welds and seams

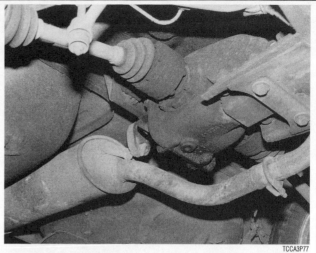

Fig. 134 Make sure the exhaust components are not contacting the body or suspension

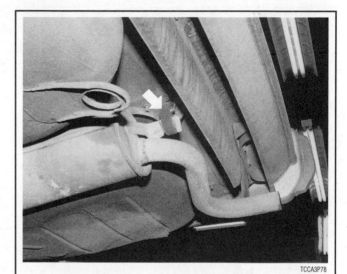

Fig. 135 Check for overstretched or torn exhaust hangers

Fig. 136 Example of a badly deteriorated exhaust pipe

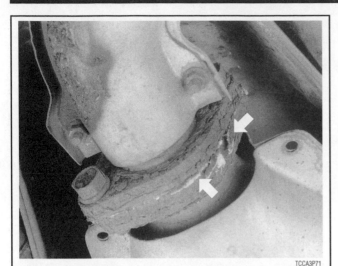

Fig. 137 Inspect flanges for gaskets that have deteriorated and need replacement

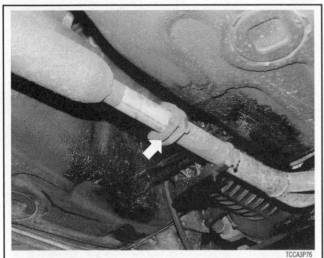

Fig. 138 Some systems, like this one, use large O-rings (donuts) in between the flanges

should provide enough room for you to slide under the vehicle and inspect the system completely. Start the inspection at the exhaust manifold or turbocharger pipe where the header pipe is attached and work your way to the back of the vehicle. On dual exhaust systems, remember to inspect both sides of the vehicle. Check the complete exhaust system for open seams, holes loose connections, or other deterioration which could permit exhaust fumes to seep into the passenger compartment. Inspect all mounting brackets and hangers for deterioration, some models may have rubber O-rings that can be overstretched and non-supportive. These components will need to be replaced if found. It has always been a practice to use a pointed tool to poke up into the exhaust system where the deterioration spots are to see whether or not they crumble. Some models may have heat shield covering certain parts of the exhaust system, it will be necessary to remove these shields to have the exhaust visible for inspection also.

REPLACEMENT

▶ See Figure 139

There are basically two types of exhaust systems. One is the flange type where the component ends are attached with bolts and a gasket in-between. The other exhaust system is the slip joint type. These components slip into one another using clamps to retain them together.

⁂ **CAUTION**

Allow the exhaust system to cool sufficiently before spraying a solvent exhaust fasteners. Some solvents are highly flammable and could ignite when sprayed on hot exhaust components.

Before removing any component of the exhaust system, ALWAYS squirt a liquid rust dissolving agent onto the fasteners for ease of removal. A lot of knuckle skin will be saved by following this rule. It may even be wise to spray the fasteners and allow them to sit overnight.

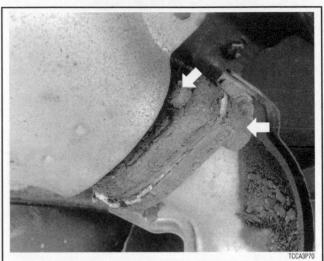

Fig. 139 Nuts and bolts will be extremely difficult to remove when deteriorated with rust

Flange Type

▶ See Figure 140

⁂ **CAUTION**

Do NOT perform exhaust repairs or inspection with the engine or exhaust hot. Allow the system to cool completely before attempting any work. Exhaust systems are noted for sharp edges, flaking metal and rusted bolts. Gloves and eye protec-

Fig. 140 Example of a flange type exhaust system joint

tion are required. A healthy supply of penetrating oil and rags is highly recommended. Never spray liquid rust dissolving agent onto a hot exhaust component.

Before removing any component on a flange type system, ALWAYS squirt a liquid rust dissolving agent onto the fasteners for ease of removal. Start by unbolting the exhaust piece at both ends (if required). When unbolting the headpipe from the manifold, make sure that the bolts are free before trying to remove them. if you snap a stud in the exhaust manifold, the stud will have to be removed with a bolt extractor, which often means removal of the manifold itself. Next, disconnect the component from the mounting; slight twisting and turning may be required to remove the component completely from the vehicle. You may need to tap on the component with a rubber mallet to loosen the component. If all else fails, use a hacksaw to separate the parts. An oxy-acetylene cutting torch may be faster but the sparks are DANGEROUS near the fuel tank, and at the very least, accidents could happen, resulting in damage to the under-car parts, not to mention yourself.

Slip Joint Type

♦ See Figure 141

Before removing any component on the slip joint type exhaust system, ALWAYS squirt a liquid rust dissolving agent onto the fasteners for ease of removal. Start by unbolting the exhaust piece at both ends (if required). When unbolting the headpipe from the manifold, make sure that the bolts are free before trying to remove them. if you snap a stud in the exhaust manifold, the stud will have to be removed with a bolt extractor, which often

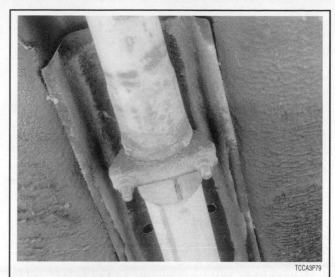

TCCA3P79

Fig. 141 Example of a common slip joint type system

means removal of the manifold itself. Next, remove the mounting U-bolts from around the exhaust pipe you are extracting from the vehicle. Don't be surprised if the U-bolts break while removing the nuts. Loosen the exhaust pipe from any mounting brackets retaining it to the floor pan and separate the components.

ENGINE RECONDITIONING

Determining Engine Condition

Anything that generates heat and/or friction will eventually burn or wear out (ie. a light bulb generates heat, therefore its life span is limited). With this in mind, a running engine generates tremendous amounts of both; friction is encountered by the moving and rotating parts inside the engine and heat is created by friction and combustion of the fuel. However, the engine has systems designed to help reduce the effects of heat and friction and provide added longevity. The oiling system reduces the amount of friction encountered by the moving parts inside the engine, while the cooling system reduces heat created by friction and combustion. If either system is not maintained, a break-down will be inevitable. Therefore, you can see how regular maintenance can affect the service life of your vehicle. If you do not drain, flush and refill your cooling system at the proper intervals, deposits will begin to accumulate in the radiator, thereby reducing the amount of heat it can extract from the coolant. The same applies to your oil and filter; if it is not changed often enough it becomes laden with contaminates and is unable to properly lubricate the engine. This increases friction and wear.

There are a number of methods for evaluating the condition of your engine. A compression test can reveal the condition of your pistons, piston rings, cylinder bores, head gasket(s), valves and valve seats. An oil pressure test can warn you of possible engine bearing, or oil pump failures. Excessive oil consumption, evidence of oil in the engine air intake area and/or bluish smoke from the tail pipe may indicate worn piston rings, worn valve guides and/or valve seals. As a general rule, an engine that uses no more than one quart of oil every 1000 miles is in good condition. Engines that use one quart of oil or more in less than 1000 miles should first be checked for oil leaks. If any oil leaks are present, have them fixed before determining how much oil is consumed by the engine, especially if blue smoke is not visible at the tail pipe.

COMPRESSION TEST

♦ See Figure 142

A noticeable lack of engine power, excessive oil consumption and/or poor fuel mileage measured over an extended period are all indicators of

internal engine wear. Worn piston rings, scored or worn cylinder bores, blown head gaskets, sticking or burnt valves, and worn valve seats are all possible culprits. A check of each cylinder's compression will help locate the problem.

➡A screw-in type compression gauge is more accurate than the type you simply hold against the spark plug hole. Although it takes slightly longer to use, it's worth the effort to obtain a more accurate reading.

1. Make sure that the proper amount and viscosity of engine oil is in the crankcase, then ensure the battery is fully charged.
2. Warm-up the engine to normal operating temperature, then shut the engine OFF.

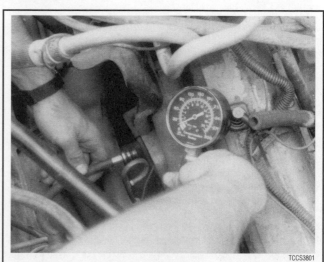

TCCS3801

Fig. 142 A screw-in type compression gauge is more accurate and easier to use without an assistant

3. Disable the ignition system.

4. Label and disconnect all of the spark plug wires from the plugs.

5. Thoroughly clean the cylinder head area around the spark plug ports, then remove the spark plugs.

6. Set the throttle plate to the fully open (wide-open throttle) position. You can block the accelerator linkage open for this, or you can have an assistant fully depress the accelerator pedal.

7. Install a screw-in type compression gauge into the No. 1 spark plug hole until the fitting is snug.

✳✳ WARNING

Be careful not to crossthread the spark plug hole.

8. According to the tool manufacturer's instructions, connect a remote starting switch to the starting circuit.

9. With the ignition switch in the **OFF** position, use the remote starting switch to crank the engine through at least five compression strokes (approximately 5 seconds of cranking) and record the highest reading on the gauge.

10. Repeat the test on each cylinder, cranking the engine approximately the same number of compression strokes and/or time as the first.

11. Compare the highest readings from each cylinder to that of the others. The indicated compression pressures are considered within specifications if the lowest reading cylinder is within 75 percent of the pressure recorded for the highest reading cylinder. For example, if your highest reading cylinder pressure was 150 psi (1034 kPa), then 75 percent of that would be 113 psi (779 kPa). So, the lowest reading cylinder should be no less than 113 psi (779 kPa).

12. If a cylinder exhibits an unusually low compression reading, pour a tablespoon of clean engine oil into the cylinder through the spark plug hole and repeat the compression test. If the compression rises after adding oil, it means that the cylinder's piston rings and/or cylinder bore are damaged or worn. If the pressure remains low, the valves may not be seating properly (a valve job is needed), or the head gasket may be blown near that cylinder. If compression in any two adjacent cylinders is low, and if the addition of oil doesn't help raise compression, there is leakage past the head gasket. Oil and coolant in the combustion chamber, combined with blue or constant white smoke from the tail pipe, are symptoms of this problem. However, don't be alarmed by the normal white smoke emitted from the tail pipe during engine warm-up or from cold weather driving. There may be evidence of water droplets on the engine dipstick and/or oil droplets in the cooling system if a head gasket is blown.

OIL PRESSURE TEST

Check for proper oil pressure at the sending unit passage with an externally mounted mechanical oil pressure gauge (as opposed to relying on a factory installed dash-mounted gauge). A tachometer may also be needed, as some specifications may require running the engine at a specific rpm.

1. With the engine cold, locate and remove the oil pressure sending unit.

2. Following the manufacturer's instructions, connect a mechanical oil pressure gauge and, if necessary, a tachometer to the engine.

3. Start the engine and allow it to idle.

4. Check the oil pressure reading when cold and record the number. You may need to run the engine at a specified rpm, so check the specifications chart located earlier in this section.

5. Run the engine until normal operating temperature is reached (upper radiator hose will feel warm).

6. Check the oil pressure reading again with the engine hot and record the number. Turn the engine **OFF**.

7. Compare your hot oil pressure reading to that given in the chart. If the reading is low, check the cold pressure reading against the chart. If the cold pressure is well above the specification, and the hot reading was lower than the specification, you may have the wrong viscosity oil in the engine. Change the oil, making sure to use the proper grade and quantity, then repeat the test.

Low oil pressure readings could be attributed to internal component wear, pump related problems, a low oil level, or oil viscosity that is too low. High oil pressure readings could be caused by an overfilled crankcase, too high of an oil viscosity or a faulty pressure relief valve.

Buy or Rebuild?

Now that you have determined that your engine is worn out, you must make some decisions. The question of whether or not an engine is worth rebuilding is largely a subjective matter and one of personal worth. Is the engine a popular one, or is it an obsolete model? Are parts available? Will it get acceptable gas mileage once it is rebuilt? Is the car it's being put into worth keeping? Would it be less expensive to buy a new engine, have your engine rebuilt by a pro, rebuild it yourself or buy a used engine from a salvage yard? Or would it be simpler and less expensive to buy another car? If you have considered all these matters and more, and have still decided to rebuild the engine, then it is time to decide how you will rebuild it.

➡ **The editors at Chilton feel that most engine machining should be performed by a professional machine shop. Don't think of it as wasting money, rather, as an assurance that the job has been done right the first time. There are many expensive and specialized tools required to perform such tasks as boring and honing an engine block or having a valve job done on a cylinder head. Even inspecting the parts requires expensive micrometers and gauges to properly measure wear and clearances. Also, a machine shop can deliver to you clean, and ready to assemble parts, saving you time and aggravation. Your maximum savings will come from performing the removal, disassembly, assembly and installation of the engine and purchasing or renting only the tools required to perform the above tasks. Depending on the particular circumstances, you may save 40 to 60 percent of the cost doing these yourself.**

A complete rebuild or overhaul of an engine involves replacing all of the moving parts (pistons, rods, crankshaft, camshaft, etc.) with new ones and machining the non-moving wearing surfaces of the block and heads. Unfortunately, this may not be cost effective. For instance, your crankshaft may have been damaged or worn, but it can be machined undersize for a minimal fee.

So, as you can see, you can replace everything inside the engine, but, it is wiser to replace only those parts which are really needed, and, if possible, repair the more expensive ones. Later in this section, we will break the engine down into its two main components: the cylinder head and the engine block. We will discuss each component, and the recommended parts to replace during a rebuild on each.

Engine Overhaul Tips

Most engine overhaul procedures are fairly standard. In addition to specific parts replacement procedures and specifications for your individual engine, this section is also a guide to acceptable rebuilding procedures. Examples of standard rebuilding practice are given and should be used along with specific details concerning your particular engine.

Competent and accurate machine shop services will ensure maximum performance, reliability and engine life. In most instances it is more profitable for the do-it-yourself mechanic to remove, clean and inspect the component, buy the necessary parts and deliver these to a shop for actual machine work.

Much of the assembly work (crankshaft, bearings, piston rods, and other components) is well within the scope of the do-it-yourself mechanic's tools and abilities. You will have to decide for yourself the depth of involvement you desire in an engine repair or rebuild.

TOOLS

The tools required for an engine overhaul or parts replacement will depend on the depth of your involvement. With a few exceptions, they will be the tools found in a mechanic's tool kit (see Section 1 of this manual). More in-depth work will require some or all of the following:

- A dial indicator (reading in thousandths) mounted on a universal base
- Micrometers and telescope gauges
- Jaw and screw-type pullers
- Scraper
- Valve spring compressor
- Ring groove cleaner
- Piston ring expander and compressor
- Ridge reamer
- Cylinder hone or glaze breaker
- Plastigage®
- Engine stand

The use of most of these tools is illustrated in this section. Many can be rented for a one-time use from a local parts jobber or tool supply house specializing in automotive work.

Occasionally, the use of special tools is called for. See the information on Special Tools and the Safety Notice in the front of this book before substituting another tool.

OVERHAUL TIPS

Aluminum has become extremely popular for use in engines, due to its low weight. Observe the following precautions when handling aluminum parts:

- Never hot tank aluminum parts (the caustic hot tank solution will eat the aluminum.
- Remove all aluminum parts (identification tag, etc.) from engine parts prior to the tanking.
- Always coat threads lightly with engine oil or anti-seize compounds before installation, to prevent seizure.
- Never overtighten bolts or spark plugs especially in aluminum threads.

When assembling the engine, any parts that will be exposed to frictional contact must be prelubed to provide lubrication at initial start-up. Any product specifically formulated for this purpose can be used, but engine oil is not recommended as a prelube in most cases.

When semi-permanent (locked, but removable) installation of bolts or nuts is desired, threads should be cleaned and coated with Loctite® or another similar, commercial non-hardening sealant.

CLEANING

▶ **See Figures 143, 144, 145 and 146**

Before the engine and its components are inspected, they must be thoroughly cleaned. You will need to remove any engine varnish, oil sludge and/or carbon deposits from all of the components to insure an accurate inspection. A crack in the engine block or cylinder head can easily become overlooked if hidden by a layer of sludge or carbon.

Most of the cleaning process can be carried out with common hand tools and readily available solvents or solutions. Carbon deposits can be chipped away using a hammer and a hard wooden chisel. Old gasket material and varnish or sludge can usually be removed using a scraper and/or cleaning solvent. Extremely stubborn deposits may require the use of a power drill with a wire brush. If using a wire brush, use extreme care around any critical machined surfaces (such as the gasket surfaces, bearing saddles, cylinder bores, etc.). USE OF A WIRE BRUSH IS NOT RECOMMENDED ON ANY ALUMINUM COMPONENTS. Always follow any safety recommendations given by the manufacturer of the tool and/or solvent. You should always wear eye protection during any cleaning process involving scraping, chipping or spraying of solvents.

An alternative to the mess and hassle of cleaning the parts yourself is to drop them off at a local garage or machine shop. They will, more than likely, have the necessary equipment to properly clean all of the parts for a nominal fee.

✳✳ CAUTION

Always wear eye protection during any cleaning process involving scraping, chipping or spraying of solvents.

Fig. 144 Use a ring expander tool to remove the piston rings

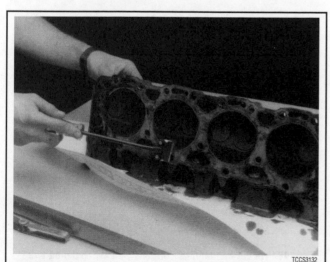

Fig. 143 Use a gasket scraper to remove the old gasket material from the mating surfaces

Fig. 145 Clean the piston ring grooves using a ring groove cleaner tool, or . . .

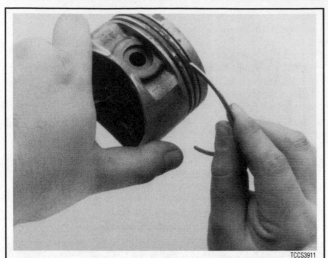

Fig. 146 . . . use a piece of an old ring to clean the grooves. Be careful, the ring can be quite sharp

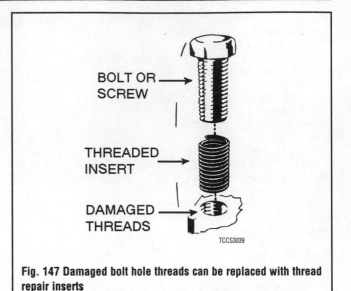

Fig. 147 Damaged bolt hole threads can be replaced with thread repair inserts

Remove any oil galley plugs, freeze plugs and/or pressed-in bearings and carefully wash and degrease all of the engine components including the fasteners and bolts. Small parts such as the valves, springs, etc., should be placed in a metal basket and allowed to soak. Use pipe cleaner type brushes, and clean all passageways in the components. Use a ring expander and remove the rings from the pistons. Clean the piston ring grooves with a special tool or a piece of broken ring. Scrape the carbon off of the top of the piston. You should never use a wire brush on the pistons. After preparing all of the piston assemblies in this manner, wash and degrease them again.

✵✵ WARNING

Use extreme care when cleaning around the cylinder head valve seats. A mistake or slip may cost you a new seat.

When cleaning the cylinder head, remove carbon from the combustion chamber with the valves installed. This will avoid damaging the valve seats.

REPAIRING DAMAGED THREADS

▶ **See Figures 147, 148, 149, 150 and 151**

Several methods of repairing damaged threads are available. Heli-Coil® (shown here), Keenserts® and Microdot® are among the most widely used. All involve basically the same principle—drilling out stripped threads, tapping the hole and installing a prewound insert—making welding, plugging and oversize fasteners unnecessary.

Two types of thread repair inserts are usually supplied: a standard type for most inch coarse, inch fine, metric course and metric fine thread sizes and a spark lug type to fit most spark plug port sizes. Consult the individual tool manufacturer's catalog to determine exact applications. Typical thread repair kits will contain a selection of prewound threaded inserts, a tap (corresponding to the outside diameter threads of the insert) and an installation tool. Spark plug inserts usually differ because they require a tap equipped with pilot threads and a combined reamer/tap section. Most manufacturers also supply blister-packed thread repair inserts separately in addition to a master kit containing a variety of taps and inserts plus installation tools.

Before attempting to repair a threaded hole, remove any snapped, broken or damaged bolts or studs. Penetrating oil can be used to free frozen threads. The offending item can usually be removed with locking pliers or using a screw/stud extractor. After the hole is clear, the thread can be repaired, as shown in the series of accompanying illustrations and in the kit manufacturer's instructions.

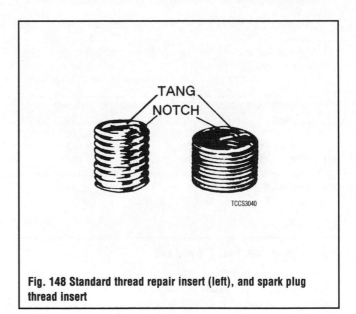

Fig. 148 Standard thread repair insert (left), and spark plug thread insert

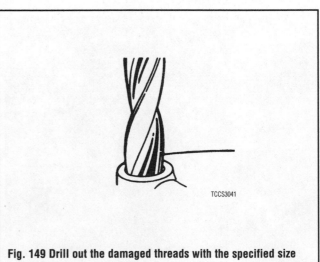

Fig. 149 Drill out the damaged threads with the specified size bit. Be sure to drill completely through the hole or to the bottom of a blind hole

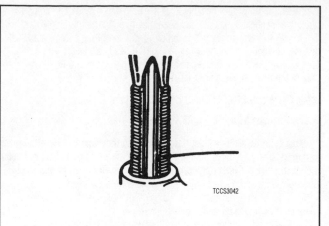

Fig. 150 Using the kit, tap the hole in order to receive the thread insert. Keep the tap well oiled and back it out frequently to avoid clogging the threads

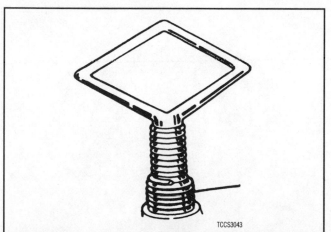

Fig. 151 Screw the insert onto the installer tool until the tang engages the slot. Thread the insert into the hole until it is ¼–½ turn below the top surface, then remove the tool and break off the tang using a punch

Engine Preparation

To properly rebuild an engine, you must first remove it from the vehicle, then disassemble and diagnose it. Ideally you should place your engine on an engine stand. This affords you the best access to the engine components. Follow the manufacturer's directions for using the stand with your particular engine. Remove the flywheel or flexplate before installing the engine to the stand.

Now that you have the engine on a stand, and assuming that you have drained the oil and coolant from the engine, it's time to strip it of all but the necessary components. Before you start disassembling the engine, you may want to take a moment to draw some pictures, or fabricate some labels or containers to mark the locations of various components and the bolts and/or studs which fasten them. Modern day engines use a lot of little brackets and clips which hold wiring harnesses and such, and these holders are often mounted on studs and/or bolts that can be easily mixed up. The manufacturer spent a lot of time and money designing your vehicle, and they wouldn't have wasted any of it by haphazardly placing brackets, clips or fasteners on the vehicle. If it's present when you disassemble it, put it back when you assemble, you will regret not remembering that little bracket which holds a wire harness out of the path of a rotating part.

You should begin by unbolting any accessories still attached to the engine, such as the water pump, power steering pump, alternator, etc. Then, unfasten

any manifolds (intake or exhaust) which were not removed during the engine removal procedure. Finally, remove any covers remaining on the engine such as the rocker arm, front or timing cover and oil pan. Some front covers may require the vibration damper and/or crank pulley to be removed beforehand. The idea is to reduce the engine to the bare necessities (cylinder head(s), valve train, engine block, crankshaft, pistons and connecting rods), plus any other `in block' components such as oil pumps, balance shafts and auxiliary shafts.

Finally, remove the cylinder head(s) from the engine block and carefully place on a bench. Disassembly instructions for each component follow later in this section.

Cylinder Head

There are two basic types of cylinder heads used on today's automobiles: the Overhead Valve (OHV) and the Overhead Camshaft (OHC). The latter can also be broken down into two subgroups: the Single Overhead Camshaft (SOHC) and the Dual Overhead Camshaft (DOHC). Generally, if there is only a single camshaft on a head, it is just referred to as an OHC head. Also, an engine with a OHV cylinder head is also known as a pushrod engine.

Most cylinder heads these days are made of an aluminum alloy due to its light weight, durability and heat transfer qualities. However, cast iron was the material of choice in the past, and is still used on many vehicles today. Whether made from aluminum or iron, all cylinder heads have valves and seats. Some use two valves per cylinder, while the more hi-tech engines will utilize a multi-valve configuration using 3, 4 and even 5 valves per cylinder. When the valve contacts the seat, it does so on precision machined surfaces, which seals the combustion chamber. All cylinder heads have a valve guide for each valve. The guide centers the valve to the seat and allows it to move up and down within it. The clearance between the valve and guide can be critical. Too much clearance and the engine may consume oil, lose vacuum and/or damage the seat. Too little, and the valve can stick in the guide causing the engine to run poorly if at all, and possibly causing severe damage. The last component all cylinder heads have are valve springs. The spring holds the valve against its seat. It also returns the valve to this position when the valve has been opened by the valve train or camshaft. The spring is fastened to the valve by a retainer and valve locks (sometimes called keepers). Aluminum heads will also have a valve spring shim to keep the spring from wearing away the aluminum.

An ideal method of rebuilding the cylinder head would involve replacing all of the valves, guides, seats, springs, etc. with new ones. However, depending on how the engine was maintained, often this is not necessary. A major cause of valve, guide and seat wear is an improperly tuned engine. An engine that is running too rich, will often wash the lubricating oil out of the guide with gasoline, causing it to wear rapidly. Conversely, an engine which is running too lean will place higher combustion temperatures on the valves and seats allowing them to wear or even burn. Springs fall victim to the driving habits of the individual. A driver who often runs the engine rpm to the redline will wear out or break the springs faster then one that stays well below it. Unfortunately, mileage takes it toll on all of the parts. Generally, the valves, guides, springs and seats in a cylinder head can be machined and re-used, saving you money. However, if a valve is burnt, it may be wise to replace all of the valves, since they were all operating in the same environment. The same goes for any other component on the cylinder head. Think of it as an insurance policy against future problems related to that component.

Unfortunately, the only way to find out which components need replacing, is to disassemble and carefully check each piece. After the cylinder head(s) are disassembled, thoroughly clean all of the components.

DISASSEMBLY

OHC Engines

▶ **See Figures 152 and 153**

Whether it is a single or dual overhead camshaft cylinder head, the disassembly procedure is relatively unchanged. One aspect to pay attention to is careful labeling of the parts on the dual camshaft cylinder head. There will be an intake camshaft and followers as well as an exhaust camshaft and

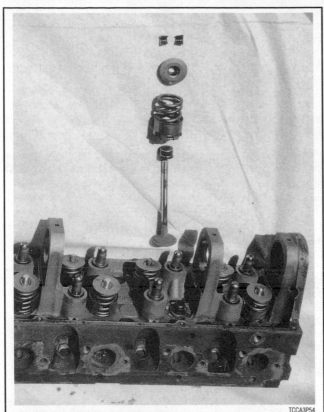

Fig. 152 Exploded view of a valve, seal, spring, retainer and locks from an OHC cylinder head

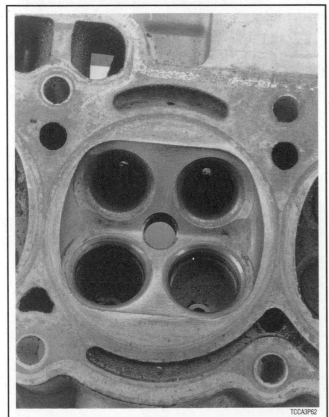

Fig. 153 Example of a multi-valve cylinder head. Note how it has 2 intake and 2 exhaust valve ports

followers and they must be labeled as such. In some cases, the components are identical and could easily be installed incorrectly. DO NOT MIX THEM UP! Determining which is which is very simple; the intake camshaft and components are on the same side of the head as was the intake manifold. Conversely, the exhaust camshaft and components are on the same side of the head as was the exhaust manifold.

CUP TYPE CAMSHAFT FOLLOWERS

◢ See Figures 154, 155 and 156

Most cylinder heads with cup type camshaft followers will have the valve spring, retainer and locks recessed within the follower's bore. You will need a C-clamp style valve spring compressor tool, an OHC spring removal tool (or equivalent) and a small magnet to disassemble the head.

1. If not already removed, remove the camshaft(s) and/or followers. Mark their positions for assembly.
2. Position the cylinder head to allow use of a C-clamp style valve spring compressor tool.

➡It is preferred to position the cylinder head gasket surface facing you with the valve springs facing the opposite direction and the head laying horizontal.

Fig. 154 C-clamp type spring compressor and an OHC spring removal tool (center) for cup type followers

Fig. 155 Most cup type follower cylinder heads retain the camshaft using bolt-on bearing caps

Fig. 156 Position the OHC spring tool in the follower bore, then compress the spring with a C-clamp type tool

Fig. 157 Example of the shaft mounted rocker arms on some OHC heads

Fig. 158 Another example of the rocker arm type OHC head. This model uses a follower under the camshaft

Fig. 159 Before the camshaft can be removed, all of the followers must first be removed . . .

3. With the OHC spring removal adapter tool positioned inside of the follower bore, compress the valve spring using the C-clamp style valve spring compressor.

4. Remove the valve locks. A small magnetic tool or screwdriver will aid in removal.

5. Release the compressor tool and remove the spring assembly.

6. Withdraw the valve from the cylinder head.

7. If equipped, remove the valve seal.

➡Special valve seal removal tools are available. Regular or needle nose type pliers, if used with care, will work just as well. If using ordinary pliers, be sure not to damage the follower bore. The follower and its bore are machined to close tolerances and any damage to the bore will effect this relationship.

8. If equipped, remove the valve spring shim. A small magnetic tool or screwdriver will aid in removal.

9. Repeat Steps 3 through 8 until all of the valves have been removed.

ROCKER ARM TYPE CAMSHAFT FOLLOWERS

▶ **See Figures 157 thru 165**

Most cylinder heads with rocker arm-type camshaft followers are easily disassembled using a standard valve spring compressor. However, certain models may not have enough open space around the spring for the standard tool and may require you to use a C-clamp style compressor tool instead.

1. If not already removed, remove the rocker arms and/or shafts and the camshaft. If applicable, also remove the hydraulic lash adjusters. Mark their positions for assembly.

2. Position the cylinder head to allow access to the valve spring.

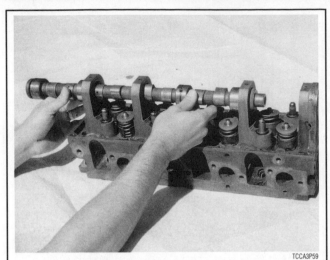

Fig. 160 . . . then the camshaft can be removed by sliding it out (shown), or unbolting a bearing cap (not shown)

3. Use a valve spring compressor tool to relieve the spring tension from the retainer.

➡**Due to engine varnish, the retainer may stick to the valve locks. A gentle tap with a hammer may help to break it loose.**

4. Remove the valve locks from the valve tip and/or retainer. A small magnet may help in removing the small locks.

5. Lift the valve spring, tool and all, off of the valve stem.

6. If equipped, remove the valve seal. If the seal is difficult to remove with the valve in place, try removing the valve first, then the seal. Follow the steps below for valve removal.

7. Position the head to allow access for withdrawing the valve.

➡**Cylinder heads that have seen a lot of miles and/or abuse may have mushroomed the valve lock grove and/or tip, causing difficulty in removal of the valve. If this has happened, use a metal file to carefully remove the high spots around the lock grooves and/or tip. Only file it enough to allow removal.**

8. Remove the valve from the cylinder head.

9. If equipped, remove the valve spring shim. A small magnetic tool or screwdriver will aid in removal.

10. Repeat Steps 3 though 9 until all of the valves have been removed.

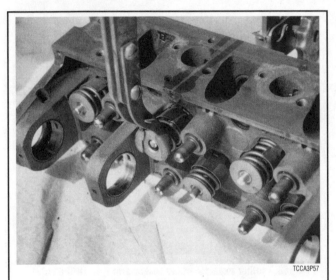

Fig. 161 Compress the valve spring . . .

Fig. 163 Remove the valve spring and retainer from the cylinder head

Fig. 162 . . . then remove the valve locks from the valve stem and spring retainer

Fig. 164 Remove the valve seal from the guide. Some gentle prying or pliers may help to remove stubborn ones

Fig. 165 All aluminum and some cast iron heads will have these valve spring shims. Remove all of them as well

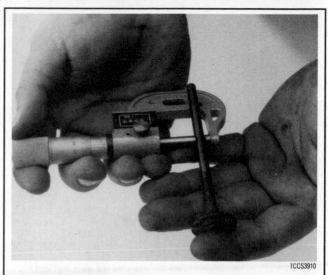

Fig. 167 Use a micrometer to check the valve stem diameter

INSPECTION

Now that all of the cylinder head components are clean, it's time to inspect them for wear and/or damage. To accurately inspect them, you will need some specialized tools:

- A 0–1 inch micrometer for the valves
- A dial indicator or inside diameter gauge for the valve guides
- A spring pressure test gauge

If you do not have access to the proper tools, you may want to bring the components to a shop that does.

Valves

 See Figures 166 and 167

The first thing to inspect are the valve heads. Look closely at the head, margin and face for any cracks, excessive wear or burning. The margin is the best place to look for burning. It should have a squared edge with an even width all around the diameter. When a valve burns, the margin will look melted and the edges rounded. Also inspect the valve head for any signs of tulipping. This will show as a lifting of the edges or dishing in the center of the head and will usually not occur to all of the valves. All of the

heads should look the same, any that seem dished more than others are probably bad. Next, inspect the valve lock grooves and valve tips. Check for any burrs around the lock grooves, especially if you had to file them to remove the valve. Valve tips should appear flat, although slight rounding with high mileage engines is normal. Slightly worn valve tips will need to be machined flat. Last, measure the valve stem diameter with the micrometer. Measure the area that rides within the guide, especially towards the tip where most of the wear occurs. Take several measurements along its length and compare them to each other. Wear should be even along the length with little to no taper. If no minimum diameter is given in the specifications, then the stem should not read more than 0.001 in. (0.025mm) below the specification. Any valves that fail these inspections should be replaced.

Springs, Retainers and Valve Locks

 See Figures 168 and 169

The first thing to check is the most obvious, broken springs. Next check the free length and squareness of each spring. If applicable, insure to distinguish between intake and exhaust springs. Use a ruler and/or carpenters square to measure the length. A carpenters square should be used to check the springs for squareness. If a spring pressure test gauge is available,

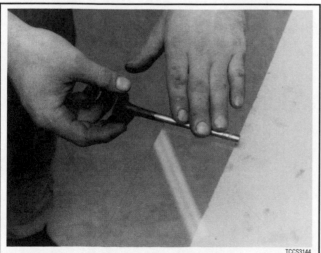

Fig. 166 Valve stems may be rolled on a flat surface to check for bends

Fig. 168 Use a caliper to check the valve spring free-length

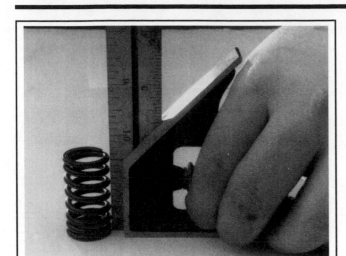

Fig. 169 Check the valve spring for squareness on a flat surface; a carpenter's square can be used

check each springs rating and compare to the specifications chart. Check the readings against the specifications given. Any springs that fail these inspections should be replaced.

The spring retainers rarely need replacing, however they should still be checked as a precaution. Inspect the spring mating surface and the valve lock retention area for any signs of excessive wear. Also check for any signs of cracking. Replace any retainers that are questionable.

Valve locks should be inspected for excessive wear on the outside contact area as well as on the inner notched surface. Any locks which appear worn or broken and its respective valve should be replaced.

Cylinder Head

There are several things to check on the cylinder head: valve guides, seats, cylinder head surface flatness, cracks and physical damage.

VALVE GUIDES

▶ See Figure 170

Now that you know the valves are good, you can use them to check the guides, although a new valve, if available, is preferred. Before you measure anything, look at the guides carefully and inspect them for any cracks,

chips or breakage. Also if the guide is a removable style (as in most aluminum heads), check them for any looseness or evidence of movement. All of the guides should appear to be at the same height from the spring seat. If any seem lower (or higher) from another, the guide has moved. Mount a dial indicator onto the spring side of the cylinder head. Lightly oil the valve stem and insert it into the cylinder head. Position the dial indicator against the valve stem near the tip and zero the gauge. Grasp the valve stem and wiggle towards and away from the dial indicator and observe the readings. Mount the dial indicator 90 degrees from the initial point and zero the gauge and again take a reading. Compare the two readings for a out of round condition. Check the readings against the specifications given. An Inside Diameter (I.D.) gauge designed for valve guides will give you an accurate valve guide bore measurement. If the I.D. gauge is used, compare the readings with the specifications given. Any guides that fail these inspections should be replaced or machined.

VALVE SEATS

A visual inspection of the valve seats should show a slightly worn and pitted surface where the valve face contacts the seat. Inspect the seat carefully for severe pitting or cracks. Also, a seat that is badly worn will be recessed into the cylinder head. A severely worn or recessed seat may need to be replaced. All cracked seats must be replaced. A seat concentricity gauge, if available, should be used to check the seat run-out. If run-out exceeds specifications the seat must be machined (if no specification is given use 0.002 in. or 0.051mm).

CYLINDER HEAD SURFACE FLATNESS

▶ See Figures 171 and 172

After you have cleaned the gasket surface of the cylinder head of any old gasket material, check the head for flatness.

Place a straightedge across the gasket surface. Using feeler gauges, determine the clearance at the center of the straightedge and across the cylinder head at several points. Check along the centerline and diagonally on the head surface. If the warpage exceeds 0.003 in. (0.076mm) within a 6.0 in. (15.2cm) span, or 0.006 in. (0.152mm) over the total length of the head, the cylinder head must be resurfaced. After resurfacing the heads of a V-type engine, the intake manifold flange surface should be checked, and if necessary, milled proportionally to allow for the change in its mounting position.

CRACKS AND PHYSICAL DAMAGE

Generally, cracks are limited to the combustion chamber, however, it is not uncommon for the head to crack in a spark plug hole, port, outside of the head or in the valve spring/rocker arm area. The first area to inspect is always the hottest: the exhaust seat/port area.

Fig. 170 A dial gauge may be used to check valve stem-to-guide clearance; read the gauge while moving the valve stem

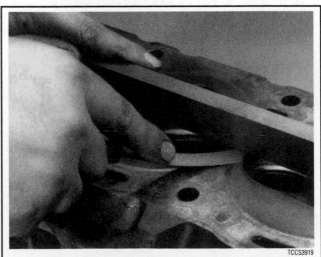

Fig. 171 Check the head for flatness across the center of the head surface using a straightedge and feeler gauge

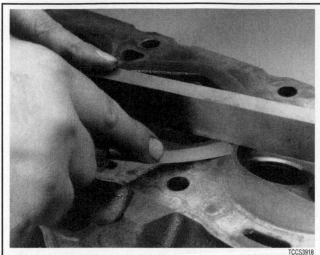

Fig. 172 Checks should also be made along both diagonals of the head surface

A visual inspection should be performed, but just because you don't see a crack does not mean it is not there. Some more reliable methods for inspecting for cracks include Magnaflux®, a magnetic process or Zyglo®, a dye penetrant. Magnaflux® is used only on ferrous metal (cast iron) heads. Zyglo® uses a spray on fluorescent mixture along with a black light to reveal the cracks. It is strongly recommended to have your cylinder head checked professionally for cracks, especially if the engine was known to have overheated and/or leaked or consumed coolant. Contact a local shop for availability and pricing of these services.

Physical damage is usually very evident. For example, a broken mounting ear from dropping the head or a bent or broken stud and/or bolt. All of these defects should be fixed or, if unrepairable, the head should be replaced.

Camshaft and Followers

Inspect the camshaft(s) and followers as described earlier in this section.

REFINISHING & REPAIRING

Many of the procedures given for refinishing and repairing the cylinder head components must be performed by a machine shop. Certain steps, if the inspected part is not worn, can be performed yourself inexpensively. However, you spent a lot of time and effort so far, why risk trying to save a couple bucks if you might have to do it all over again?

Valves

Any valves that were not replaced should be refaced and the tips ground flat. Unless you have access to a valve grinding machine, this should be done by a machine shop. If the valves are in extremely good condition, as well as the valve seats and guides, they may be lapped in without performing machine work.

It is a recommended practice to lap the valves even after machine work has been performed and/or new valves have been purchased. This insures a positive seal between the valve and seat.

LAPPING THE VALVES

➥**Before lapping the valves to the seats, read the rest of the cylinder head section to insure that any related parts are in acceptable enough condition to continue.**

➥**Before any valve seat machining and/or lapping can be performed, the guides must be within factory recommended specifications.**

1. Invert the cylinder head.
2. Lightly lubricate the valve stems and insert them into the cylinder head in their numbered order.
3. Raise the valve from the seat and apply a small amount of fine lapping compound to the seat.
4. Moisten the suction head of a hand-lapping tool and attach it to the head of the valve.
5. Rotate the tool between the palms of both hands, changing the position of the valve on the valve seat and lifting the tool often to prevent grooving.
6. Lap the valve until a smooth, polished circle is evident on the valve and seat.
7. Remove the tool and the valve. Wipe away all traces of the grinding compound and store the valve to maintain its lapped location.

✳✳ WARNING

Do not get the valves out of order after they have been lapped. They must be put back with the same valve seat they were lapped with.

Springs, Retainers and Valve Locks

There is no repair or refinishing possible with the springs, retainers and valve locks. If they are found to be worn or defective, they must be replaced with new (or known good) parts.

Cylinder Head

Most refinishing procedures dealing with the cylinder head must be performed by a machine shop. Read the sections below and review your inspection data to determine whether or not machining is necessary.

VALVE GUIDES

➥**If any machining or replacements are made to the valve guides, the seats must be machined.**

Unless the valve guides need machining or replacing, the only service to perform is to thoroughly clean them of any dirt or oil residue.

There are only two types of valve guides used on automobile engines: the replaceable-type (all aluminum heads) and the cast-in integral-type (most cast iron heads). There are four recommended methods for repairing worn guides.
- Knurling
- Inserts
- Reaming oversize
- Replacing

Knurling is a process in which metal is displaced and raised, thereby reducing clearance, giving a true center, and providing oil control. It is the least expensive way of repairing the valve guides. However, it is not necessarily the best, and in some cases, a knurled valve guide will not stand up for more than a short time. It requires a special knurlizer and precision reaming tools to obtain proper clearances. It would not be cost effective to purchase these tools, unless you plan on rebuilding several of the same cylinder head.

Installing a guide insert involves machining the guide to accept a bronze insert. One style is the coil-type which is installed into a threaded guide. Another is the thin-walled insert where the guide is reamed oversize to accept a split-sleeve insert. After the insert is installed, a special tool is then run through the guide to expand the insert, locking it to the guide. The insert is then reamed to the standard size for proper valve clearance.

Reaming for oversize valves restores normal clearances and provides a true valve seat. Most cast-in type guides can be reamed to accept an valve with an oversize stem. The cost factor for this can become quite high as you will need to purchase the reamer and new, oversize stem valves for all guides which were reamed. Oversizes are generally 0.003 to 0.030 in. (0.076 to 0.762mm), with 0.015 in. (0.381mm) being the most common.

To replace cast-in type valve guides, they must be drilled out, then reamed to accept replacement guides. This must be done on a fixture which will allow centering and leveling off of the original valve seat or guide, otherwise a serious guide-to-seat misalignment may occur making it impossible to properly machine the seat.

Replaceable-type guides are pressed into the cylinder head. A hammer and a stepped drift or punch may be used to install and remove the guides. Before removing the guides, measure the protrusion on the spring side of the head and record it for installation. Use the stepped drift to hammer out the old guide from the combustion chamber side of the head. When installing, determine whether or not the guide also seals a water jacket in the head, and if it does, use the recommended sealing agent. If there is no water jacket, grease the valve guide and its bore. Use the stepped drift, and hammer the new guide into the cylinder head from the spring side of the cylinder head. A stack of washers the same thickness as the measured protrusion may help the installation process.

VALVE SEATS

➡**Before any valve seat machining can be performed, the guides must be within factory recommended specifications.**

➡**If any machining or replacements were made to the valve guides, the seats must be machined.**

If the seats are in good condition, the valves can be lapped to the seats, and the cylinder head assembled. See the valves section for instructions on lapping.

If the valve seats are worn, cracked or damaged, they must be serviced by a machine shop. The valve seat must be perfectly centered to the valve guide, which requires very accurate machining.

CYLINDER HEAD SURFACE

If the cylinder head is warped, it must be machined flat. If the warpage is extremely severe, the head may need to be replaced. In some instances, it may be possible to straighten a warped head enough to allow machining. In either case, contact a professional machine shop for service.

➡**Any OHC cylinder head that shows excessive warpage should have the camshaft bearing journals align bored after the cylinder head has been resurfaced.**

❊❊ WARNING

Failure to align bore the camshaft bearing journals could result in severe engine damage including but not limited to: valve and piston damage, connecting rod damage, camshaft and/or crankshaft breakage.

CRACKS AND PHYSICAL DAMAGE

Certain cracks can be repaired in both cast iron and aluminum heads. For cast iron, a tapered threaded insert is installed along the length of the crack. Aluminum can also use the tapered inserts, however welding is the preferred method. Some physical damage can be repaired through brazing or welding. Contact a machine shop to get expert advice for your particular dilemma.

ASSEMBLY

OHC Engines

◆ **See Figure 173**

The first step for any assembly job is to have a clean area in which to work. Next, thoroughly clean all of the parts and components that are to be assembled. Finally, place all of the components onto a suitable work space and, if necessary, arrange the parts to their respective positions.

CUP TYPE CAMSHAFT FOLLOWERS

To install the springs, retainers and valve locks on heads which have these components recessed into the camshaft follower's bore, you will need

TCCA3P64

Fig. 173 Once assembled, check the valve clearance and correct as needed

a small screwdriver-type tool, some clean white grease and a lot of patience. You will also need the C-clamp style spring compressor and the OHC tool used to disassemble the head.

1. Lightly lubricate the valve stems and insert all of the valves into the cylinder head. If possible, maintain their original locations.
2. If equipped, install any valve spring shims which were removed.
3. If equipped, install the new valve seals, keeping the following in mind:
   • If the valve seal presses over the guide, lightly lubricate the outer guide surfaces.
   • If the seal is an O-ring type, it is installed just after compressing the spring but before the valve locks.
4. Place the valve spring and retainer over the stem.
5. Position the spring compressor and the OHC tool, then compress the spring.
6. Using a small screwdriver as a spatula, fill the valve stem side of the lock with white grease. Use the excess grease on the screwdriver to fasten the lock to the driver.
7. Carefully install the valve lock, which is stuck to the end of the screwdriver, to the valve stem then press on it with the screwdriver until the grease squeezes out. The valve lock should now be stuck to the stem.
8. Repeat Steps 6 and 7 for the remaining valve lock.
9. Relieve the spring pressure slowly and insure that neither valve lock becomes dislodged by the retainer.
10. Remove the spring compressor tool.
11. Repeat Steps 2 through 10 until all of the springs have been installed.
12. Install the followers, camshaft(s) and any other components that were removed for disassembly.

ROCKER ARM TYPE CAMSHAFT FOLLOWERS

1. Lightly lubricate the valve stems and insert all of the valves into the cylinder head. If possible, maintain their original locations.
2. If equipped, install any valve spring shims which were removed.
3. If equipped, install the new valve seals, keeping the following in mind:
   • If the valve seal presses over the guide, lightly lubricate the outer guide surfaces.
   • If the seal is an O-ring type, it is installed just after compressing the spring but before the valve locks.
4. Place the valve spring and retainer over the stem.
5. Position the spring compressor tool and compress the spring.
6. Assemble the valve locks to the stem.
7. Relieve the spring pressure slowly and insure that neither valve lock becomes dislodged by the retainer.
8. Remove the spring compressor tool.

9. Repeat Steps 2 through 8 until all of the springs have been installed.

10. Install the camshaft(s), rockers, shafts and any other components that were removed for disassembly.

Engine Block

GENERAL INFORMATION

A thorough overhaul or rebuild of an engine block would include replacing the pistons, rings, bearings, timing belt/chain assembly and oil pump. For OHV engines also include a new camshaft and lifters. The block would then have the cylinders bored and honed oversize (or if using removable cylinder sleeves, new sleeves installed) and the crankshaft would be cut undersize to provide new wearing surfaces and perfect clearances. However, your particular engine may not have everything worn out. What if only the piston rings have worn out and the clearances on everything else are still within factory specifications? Well, you could just replace the rings and put it back together, but this would be a very rare example. Chances are, if one component in your engine is worn, other components are sure to follow, and soon. At the very least, you should always replace the rings, bearings and oil pump. This is what is commonly called a "freshen up".

Cylinder Ridge Removal

Because the top piston ring does not travel to the very top of the cylinder, a ridge is built up between the end of the travel and the top of the cylinder bore.

Pushing the piston and connecting rod assembly past the ridge can be difficult, and damage to the piston ring lands could occur. If the ridge is not removed before installing a new piston or not removed at all, piston ring breakage and piston damage may occur.

➡ **It is always recommended that you remove any cylinder ridges before removing the piston and connecting rod assemblies. If you know that new pistons are going to be installed and the engine block will be bored oversize, you may be able to forego this step. However, some ridges may actually prevent the assemblies from being removed, necessitating its removal.**

There are several different types of ridge reamers on the market, none of which are inexpensive. Unless a great deal of engine rebuilding is anticipated, borrow or rent a reamer.

1. Turn the crankshaft until the piston is at the bottom of its travel.

2. Cover the head of the piston with a rag.

3. Follow the tool manufacturers instructions and cut away the ridge, exercising extreme care to avoid cutting too deeply.

4. Remove the ridge reamer, the rag and as many of the cuttings as possible. Continue until all of the cylinder ridges have been removed.

DISASSEMBLY

▶ **See Figures 174 and 175**

The engine disassembly instructions following assume that you have the engine mounted on an engine stand. If not, it is easiest to disassemble the engine on a bench or the floor with it resting on the bellhousing or transmission mounting surface. You must be able to access the connecting rod fasteners and turn the crankshaft during disassembly. Also, all engine covers (timing, front, side, oil pan, whatever) should have already been removed. Engines which are seized or locked up may not be able to be completely disassembled, and a core (salvage yard) engine should be purchased.

OHC Engines

If not done during the cylinder head removal, remove the timing chain/belt and/or gear/sprocket assembly. Remove the oil pick-up and pump assembly and, if necessary, the pump drive. If equipped, remove any balance or auxiliary shafts. If necessary, remove the cylinder ridge from the top of the bore. See the cylinder ridge removal procedure earlier in this section.

All Engines

Rotate the engine so that the crankshaft is exposed. Use a number punch or scribe and mark each connecting rod with its respective cylinder number. The cylinder closest to the front of the engine is always number 1. However, depending on the engine placement, the front of the engine could either be the flywheel or damper/pulley end. Generally the front of the engine faces the front of the vehicle. Use a number punch or scribe and also mark the main bearing caps from front to rear with the front most cap being number 1 (if there are five caps, mark them 1 through 5, front to rear).

TCCS3803

Fig. 174 Place rubber hose over the connecting rod studs to protect the crankshaft and cylinder bores from damage

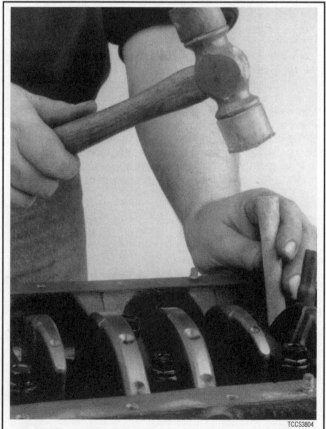

TCCS3804

Fig. 175 Carefully tap the piston out of the bore using a wooden dowel

✳✳✳ WARNING

Take special care when pushing the connecting rod up from the crankshaft because the sharp threads of the rod bolts/studs will score the crankshaft journal. Insure that special plastic caps are installed over them, or cut two pieces of rubber hose to do the same.

Again, rotate the engine, this time to position the number one cylinder bore (head surface) up. Turn the crankshaft until the number one piston is at the bottom of its travel, this should allow the maximum access to its connecting rod. Remove the number one connecting rods fasteners and cap and place two lengths of rubber hose over the rod bolts/studs to protect the crankshaft from damage. Using a sturdy wooden dowel and a hammer, push the connecting rod up about 1 in. (25mm) from the crankshaft and remove the upper bearing insert. Continue pushing or tapping the connecting rod up until the piston rings are out of the cylinder bore. Remove the piston and rod by hand, put the upper half of the bearing insert back into the rod, install the cap with its bearing insert installed, and hand-tighten the cap fasteners. If the parts are kept in order in this manner, they will not get lost and you will be able to tell which bearings came form what cylinder if any problems are discovered and diagnosis is necessary. Remove all the other piston assemblies in the same manner. On V-style engines, remove all of the pistons from one bank, then reposition the engine with the other cylinder bank head surface up, and remove that banks piston assemblies.

The only remaining component in the engine block should now be the crankshaft. Loosen the main bearing caps evenly until the fasteners can be turned by hand, then remove them and the caps. Remove the crankshaft from the engine block. Thoroughly clean all of the components.

INSPECTION

Now that the engine block and all of its components are clean, it's time to inspect them for wear and/or damage. To accurately inspect them, you will need some specialized tools:
- Two or three separate micrometers to measure the pistons and crankshaft journals
- A dial indicator
- Telescoping gauges for the cylinder bores
- A rod alignment fixture to check for bent connecting rods

If you do not have access to the proper tools, you may want to bring the components to a shop that does.

Generally, you shouldn't expect cracks in the engine block or its components unless it was known to leak, consume or mix engine fluids, it was severely overheated, or there was evidence of bad bearings and/or crankshaft damage. A visual inspection should be performed on all of the components, but just because you don't see a crack does not mean it is not there. Some more reliable methods for inspecting for cracks include Magnaflux®, a magnetic process or Zyglo®, a dye penetrant. Magnaflux® is used only on ferrous metal (cast iron). Zyglo® uses a spray on fluorescent mixture along with a black light to reveal the cracks. It is strongly recommended to have your engine block checked professionally for cracks, especially if the engine was known to have overheated and/or leaked or consumed coolant. Contact a local shop for availability and pricing of these services.

Engine Block

ENGINE BLOCK BEARING ALIGNMENT

Remove the main bearing caps and, if still installed, the main bearing inserts. Inspect all of the main bearing saddles and caps for damage, burrs or high spots. If damage is found, and it is caused from a spun main bearing, the block will need to be align-bored or, if severe enough, replacement. Any burrs or high spots should be carefully removed with a metal file.

Place a straightedge on the bearing saddles, in the engine block, along the centerline of the crankshaft. If any clearance exists between the straightedge and the saddles, the block must be align-bored.

Align-boring consists of machining the main bearing saddles and caps by means of a flycutter that runs through the bearing saddles.

DECK FLATNESS

The top of the engine block where the cylinder head mounts is called the deck. Insure that the deck surface is clean of dirt, carbon deposits and old gasket material. Place a straightedge across the surface of the deck along its centerline and, using feeler gauges, check the clearance along several points. Repeat the checking procedure with the straightedge placed along both diagonals of the deck surface. If the reading exceeds 0.003 in. (0.076mm) within a 6.0 in. (15.2cm) span, or 0.006 in. (0.152mm) over the total length of the deck, it must be machined.

CYLINDER BORES

▶ See Figure 176

The cylinder bores house the pistons and are slightly larger than the pistons themselves. A common piston-to-bore clearance is 0.0015–0.0025 in. (0.0381mm–0.0635mm). Inspect and measure the cylinder bores. The bore should be checked for out-of-roundness, taper and size. The results of this inspection will determine whether the cylinder can be used in its existing size and condition, or a rebore to the next oversize is required (or in the case of removable sleeves, have replacements installed).

The amount of cylinder wall wear is always greater at the top of the cylinder than at the bottom. This wear is known as taper. Any cylinder that has a taper of 0.0012 in. (0.305mm) or more, must be rebored. Measurements are taken at a number of positions in each cylinder: at the top, middle and bottom and at two points at each position; that is, at a point 90 degrees from the crankshaft centerline, as well as a point parallel to the crankshaft centerline. The measurements are made with either a special dial indicator or a telescopic gauge and micrometer. If the necessary precision tools to check the bore are not available, take the block to a machine shop and have them mike it. Also if you don't have the tools to check the cylinder bores, chances are you will not have the necessary devices to check the pistons, connecting rods and crankshaft. Take these components with you and save yourself an extra trip.

For our procedures, we will use a telescopic gauge and a micrometer. You will need one of each, with a measuring range which covers your cylinder bore size.

1. Position the telescopic gauge in the cylinder bore, loosen the gauges lock and allow it to expand.

➥ **Your first two readings will be at the top of the cylinder bore, then proceed to the middle and finally the bottom, making a total of six measurements.**

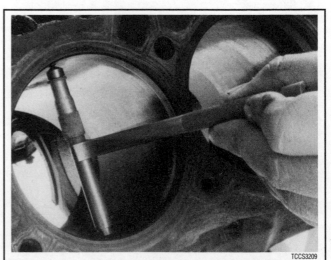

TCCS3209

Fig. 176 Use a telescoping gauge to measure the cylinder bore diameter—take several readings within the same bore

2. Hold the gauge square in the bore, 90 degrees from the crankshaft centerline, and gently tighten the lock. Tilt the gauge back to remove it from the bore.

3. Measure the gauge with the micrometer and record the reading.

4. Again, hold the gauge square in the bore, this time parallel to the crankshaft centerline, and gently tighten the lock. Again, you will tilt the gauge back to remove it from the bore.

5. Measure the gauge with the micrometer and record this reading. The difference between these two readings is the out-of-round measurement of the cylinder.

6. Repeat steps 1 through 5, each time going to the next lower position, until you reach the bottom of the cylinder. Then go to the next cylinder, and continue until all of the cylinders have been measured.

The difference between these measurements will tell you all about the wear in your cylinders. The measurements which were taken 90 degrees from the crankshaft centerline will always reflect the most wear. That is because at this position is where the engine power presses the piston against the cylinder bore the hardest. This is known as thrust wear. Take your top, 90 degree measurement and compare it to your bottom, 90 degree measurement. The difference between them is the taper. When you measure your pistons, you will compare these readings to your piston sizes and determine piston-to-wall clearance.

Crankshaft

Inspect the crankshaft for visible signs of wear or damage. All of the journals should be perfectly round and smooth. Slight scores are normal for a used crankshaft, but you should hardly feel them with your fingernail. When measuring the crankshaft with a micrometer, you will take readings at the front and rear of each journal, then turn the micrometer 90 degrees and take two more readings, front and rear. The difference between the front-to-rear readings is the journal taper and the first-to-90 degree reading is the out-of-round measurement. Generally, there should be no taper or out-of-roundness found, however, up to 0.0005 in. (0.0127mm) for either can be overlooked. Also, the readings should fall within the factory specifications for journal diameters.

If the crankshaft journals fall within specifications, it is recommended that it be polished before being returned to service. Polishing the crankshaft insures that any minor burrs or high spots are smoothed, thereby reducing the chance of scoring the new bearings.

Pistons and Connecting Rods

PISTON

▶ See Figure 177

The piston should be visually inspected for any signs of cracking or burning (caused by hot spots or detonation), and scuffing or excessive wear on the skirts. The wristpin attaches the piston to the connecting rod. The piston should move freely on the wrist pin, both sliding and pivoting. Grasp the connecting rod securely, or mount it in a vise, and try to rock the piston back and forth along the centerline of the wristpin. There should not be any excessive play evident between the piston and the pin. If there are C-clips retaining the pin in the piston then you have wrist pin bushings in the rods. There should not be any excessive play between the wrist pin and the rod bushing. Normal clearance for the wrist pin is approx. 0.001–0.002 in. (0.025mm–0.051mm).

Use a micrometer and measure the diameter of the piston, perpendicular to the wrist pin, on the skirt. Compare the reading to its original cylinder measurement obtained earlier. The difference between the two readings is the piston-to-wall clearance. If the clearance is within specifications, the piston may be used as is. If the piston is out of specification, but the bore is not, you will need a new piston. If both are out of specification, you will need the cylinder rebored and oversize pistons installed. Generally if two or more pistons/bores are out of specification, it is best to rebore the entire block and purchase a complete set of oversize pistons.

TCCS3210

Fig. 177 Measure the piston's outer diameter, perpendicular to the wrist pin, with a micrometer

CONNECTING ROD

You should have the connecting rod checked for straightness at a machine shop. If the connecting rod is bent, it will unevenly wear the bearing and piston, as well as place greater stress on these components. Any bent or twisted connecting rods must be replaced. If the rods are straight and the wrist pin clearance is within specifications, then only the bearing end of the rod need be checked. Place the connecting rod into a vice, with the bearing inserts in place, install the cap to the rod and torque the fasteners to specifications. Use a telescoping gauge and carefully measure the inside diameter of the bearings. Compare this reading to the rods original crankshaft journal diameter measurement. The difference is the oil clearance. If the oil clearance is not within specifications, install new bearings in the rod and take another measurement. If the clearance is still out of specifications, and the crankshaft is not, the rod will need to be reconditioned by a machine shop.

➡You can also use Plastigage® to check the bearing clearances. The assembling section has complete instructions on its use.

Camshaft

Inspect the camshaft and lifters/followers as described earlier in this section.

Bearings

All of the engine bearings should be visually inspected for wear and/or damage. The bearing should look evenly worn all around with no deep scores or pits. If the bearing is severely worn, scored, pitted or heat blued, then the bearing, and the components that use it, should be brought to a machine shop for inspection. Full-circle bearings (used on most camshafts, auxiliary shafts, balance shafts, etc.) require specialized tools for removal and installation, and should be brought to a machine shop for service.

Oil Pump

➡The oil pump is responsible for providing constant lubrication to the whole engine and so it is recommended that a new oil pump be installed when rebuilding the engine.

Completely disassemble the oil pump and thoroughly clean all of the components. Inspect the oil pump gears and housing for wear and/or damage. Insure that the pressure relief valve operates properly and there is no binding or sticking due to varnish or debris. If all of the parts are in proper working condition, lubricate the gears and relief valve, and assemble the pump.

REFINISHING

▶ **See Figure 178**

Almost all engine block refinishing must be performed by a machine shop. If the cylinders are not to be rebored, then the cylinder glaze can be removed with a ball hone. When removing cylinder glaze with a ball hone, use a light or penetrating type oil to lubricate the hone. Do not allow the hone to run dry as this may cause excessive scoring of the cylinder bores and wear on the hone. If new pistons are required, they will need to be installed to the connecting rods. This should be performed by a machine shop as the pistons must be installed in the correct relationship to the rod or engine damage can occur.

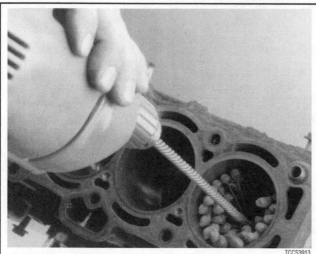

Fig. 178 Use a ball type cylinder hone to remove any glaze and provide a new surface for seating the piston rings

Pistons and Connecting Rods

▶ **See Figure 179**

Only pistons with the wrist pin retained by C-clips are serviceable by the home-mechanic. Press fit pistons require special presses and/or heaters to remove/install the connecting rod and should only be performed by a machine shop.

Fig. 179 Most pistons are marked to indicate positioning in the engine (usually a mark means the side facing the front)

All pistons will have a mark indicating the direction to the front of the engine and the must be installed into the engine in that manner. Usually it is a notch or arrow on the top of the piston, or it may be the letter F cast or stamped into the piston.

ASSEMBLY

Before you begin assembling the engine, first give yourself a clean, dirt free work area. Next, clean every engine component again. The key to a good assembly is cleanliness.

Mount the engine block into the engine stand and wash it one last time using water and detergent (dishwashing detergent works well). While washing it, scrub the cylinder bores with a soft bristle brush and thoroughly clean all of the oil passages. Completely dry the engine and spray the entire assembly down with an anti-rust solution such as WD-40® or similar product. Take a clean lint-free rag and wipe up any excess anti-rust solution from the bores, bearing saddles, etc. Repeat the final cleaning process on the crankshaft. Replace any freeze or oil galley plugs which were removed during disassembly.

Crankshaft

▶ **See Figures 180, 181, 182 and 183**

1. Remove the main bearing inserts from the block and bearing caps.
2. If the crankshaft main bearing journals have been refinished to a definite undersize, install the correct undersize bearing. Be sure that the bearing inserts and bearing bores are clean. Foreign material under inserts will distort bearing and cause failure.
3. Place the upper main bearing inserts in bores with tang in slot.

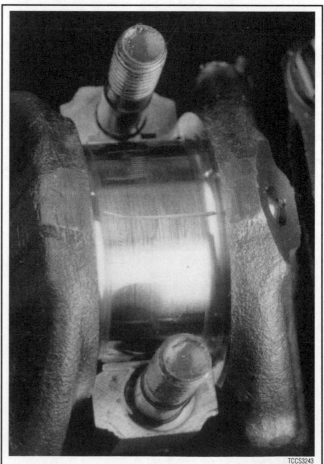

Fig. 180 Apply a strip of gauging material to the bearing journal, then install and torque the cap

➡ **The oil holes in the bearing inserts must be aligned with the oil holes in the cylinder block.**

4. Install the lower main bearing inserts in bearing caps.
5. Clean the mating surfaces of block and rear main bearing cap.
6. Carefully lower the crankshaft into place. Be careful not to damage bearing surfaces.
7. Check the clearance of each main bearing by using the following procedure:

a. Place a piece of Plastigage® or its equivalent, on bearing surface across full width of bearing cap and about ¼ in. off center.

b. Install cap and tighten bolts to specifications. Do not turn crankshaft while Plastigage® is in place.

c. Remove the cap. Using the supplied Plastigage® scale, check width of Plastigage® at widest point to get maximum clearance. Difference between readings is taper of journal.

d. If clearance exceeds specified limits, try a 0.001 in. or 0.002 in. undersize bearing in combination with the standard bearing. Bearing clearance must be within specified limits. If standard and 0.002 in. undersize bearing does not bring clearance within desired limits, refinish crankshaft journal, then install undersize bearings.

8. Install the rear main seal.

Fig. 181 After the cap is removed again, use the scale supplied with the gauging material to check the clearance

Fig. 182 A dial gauge may be used to check crankshaft end-play

Fig. 183 Carefully pry the crankshaft back and forth while reading the dial gauge for end-play

9. After the bearings have been fitted, apply a light coat of engine oil to the journals and bearings. Install the rear main bearing cap. Install all bearing caps except the thrust bearing cap. Be sure that main bearing caps are installed in original locations. Tighten the bearing cap bolts to specifications.
10. Install the thrust bearing cap with bolts finger-tight.
11. Pry the crankshaft forward against the thrust surface of upper half of bearing.
12. Hold the crankshaft forward and pry the thrust bearing cap to the rear. This aligns the thrust surfaces of both halves of the bearing.
13. Retain the forward pressure on the crankshaft. Tighten the cap bolts to specifications.
14. Measure the crankshaft end-play as follows:

a. Mount a dial gauge to the engine block and position the tip of the gauge to read from the crankshaft end.

b. Carefully pry the crankshaft toward the rear of the engine and hold it there while you zero the gauge.

c. Carefully pry the crankshaft toward the front of the engine and read the gauge.

d. Confirm that the reading is within specifications. If not, install a new thrust bearing and repeat the procedure. If the reading is still out of specifications with a new bearing, have a machine shop inspect the thrust surfaces of the crankshaft, and if possible, repair it.

15. Rotate the crankshaft so as to position the first rod journal to the bottom of its stroke.

Pistons and Connecting Rods

▶ **See Figures 184, 185, 186 and 187**

1. Before installing the piston/connecting rod assembly, oil the pistons, piston rings and the cylinder walls with light engine oil. Install connecting rod bolt protectors or rubber hose onto the connecting rod bolts/studs. Also perform the following:

a. Select the proper ring set for the size cylinder bore.

b. Position the ring in the bore in which it is going to be used.

c. Push the ring down into the bore area where normal ring wear is not encountered.

d. Use the head of the piston to position the ring in the bore so that the ring is square with the cylinder wall. Use caution to avoid damage to the ring or cylinder bore.

e. Measure the gap between the ends of the ring with a feeler gauge. Ring gap in a worn cylinder is normally greater than specification. If the ring gap is greater than the specified limits, try an oversize ring set.

f. Check the ring side clearance of the compression rings with a feeler gauge inserted between the ring and its lower land according to specification. The gauge should slide freely around the entire ring circumference without binding. Any wear that occurs will form a step at the inner portion of the lower land. If the lower lands have high steps, the piston should be replaced.

2. Unless new pistons are installed, be sure to install the pistons in the cylinders from which they were removed. The numbers on the connecting rod and bearing cap must be on the same side when installed in the cylinder bore. If a connecting rod is ever transposed from one engine or cylinder to another, new bearings should be fitted and the connecting rod should be numbered to correspond with the new cylinder number. The notch on the piston head goes toward the front of the engine.

3. Install all of the rod bearing inserts into the rods and caps.

4. Install the rings to the pistons. Install the oil control ring first, then the second compression ring and finally the top compression ring. Use a piston ring expander tool to aid in installation and to help reduce the chance of breakage.

5. Make sure the ring gaps are properly spaced around the circumference of the piston. Fit a piston ring compressor around the piston and slide the piston and connecting rod assembly down into the cylinder bore, pushing it in with the wooden hammer handle. Push the piston down until it is only slightly below the top of the cylinder bore. Guide the connecting rod onto the crankshaft bearing journal carefully, to avoid damaging the crankshaft.

6. Check the bearing clearance of all the rod bearings, fitting them to the crankshaft bearing journals. Follow the procedure in the crankshaft installation above.

7. After the bearings have been fitted, apply a light coating of assembly oil to the journals and bearings.

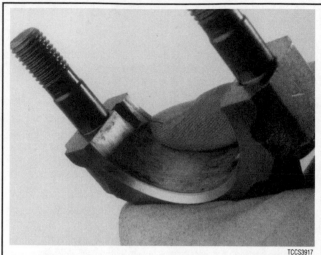

Fig. 185 The notch on the side of the bearing cap matches the tang on the bearing insert

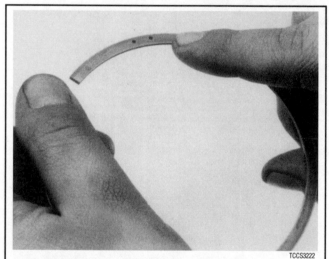

Fig. 186 Most rings are marked to show which side of the ring should face up when installed to the piston

Fig. 184 Checking the piston ring-to-ring groove side clearance using the ring and a feeler gauge

Fig. 187 Install the piston and rod assembly into the block using a ring compressor and the handle of a hammer

8. Turn the crankshaft until the appropriate bearing journal is at the bottom of its stroke, then push the piston assembly all the way down until the connecting rod bearing seats on the crankshaft journal. Be careful not to allow the bearing cap screws to strike the crankshaft bearing journals and damage them.

9. After the piston and connecting rod assemblies have been installed, check the connecting rod side clearance on each crankshaft journal.

10. Prime and install the oil pump and the oil pump intake tube.

Cylinder Head

1. Install the cylinder head using new gaskets.
2. Install the timing sprockets/gears and the belt/chain assemblies.

Engine Covers and Components

Install the timing cover(s) and oil pan. Refer to your notes and drawings made prior to disassembly and install all of the components that were removed. Install the engine into the vehicle.

Engine Start-up and Break-in

STARTING THE ENGINE

Now that the engine is installed and every wire and hose is properly connected, go back and double check that all coolant and vacuum hoses are connected. Check that you oil drain plug is installed and properly tightened. If not already done, install a new oil filter onto the engine. Fill the crankcase with the proper amount and grade of engine oil. Fill the cooling system with a 50/50 mixture of coolant/water.

1. Connect the vehicle battery.
2. Start the engine. Keep your eye on your oil pressure indicator; if it does not indicate oil pressure within 10 seconds of starting, turn the vehicle off.

✳✳ WARNING

Damage to the engine can result if it is allowed to run with no oil pressure. Check the engine oil level to make sure that it is full. Check for any leaks and if found, repair the leaks before continuing. If there is still no indication of oil pressure, you may need to prime the system.

3. Confirm that there are no fluid leaks (oil or other).
4. Allow the engine to reach normal operating temperature (the upper radiator hose will be hot to the touch).
5. If necessary, set the ignition timing.
6. Install any remaining components such as the air cleaner (if removed for ignition timing) or body panels which were removed.

BREAKING IT IN

Make the first miles on the new engine, easy ones. Vary the speed but do not accelerate hard. Most importantly, do not lug the engine, and avoid sustained high speeds until at least 100 miles. Check the engine oil and coolant levels frequently. Expect the engine to use a little oil until the rings seat. Change the oil and filter at 500 miles, 1500 miles, then every 3000 miles past that.

KEEP IT MAINTAINED

Now that you have just gone through all of that hard work, keep yourself from doing it all over again by thoroughly maintaining it. Not that you may not have maintained it before, heck you could have had one to two hundred thousand miles on it before doing this. However, you may have bought the vehicle used, and the previous owner did not keep up on maintenance. Which is why you just went through all of that hard work. See?

TORQUE SPECIFICATIONS

Component	Ft. lbs.	Nm
Engine		
With an automatic transaxle		
Engine mount through bolt	39-47	53-64
Flywheel-to-torque converter nuts	25-36	34-49
Engine rear plate bolt	61-87 inch lbs.	7-10
Transaxle case-to-block front bracket bolts	27-38	37-52
Muffler pipe bracket bolts	28-41	38-56
Rear transaxle insulator nuts	21-34	28-46
Front transaxle insulator nuts	27-38	37-52
Power steering pump-to-engine bolts	27-40	36-54
Wheel hub bolt	65-87	88-118
With an manual transaxle		
Transaxle case-to-cylinder block front bracket bolts	27-38	37-52
Muffler pipe bracket bolts	28-41	38-56
Engine mount through bolt	39-47	53-64
Rear transaxle insulator nuts	21-34	28-46
Front transaxle insulator nuts	27-38	37-52
Power steering pump-to-engine bolts	27-40	36-54
Wheel hub bolt	65-87	88-118
Rocker Arm (Valve) Cover		
Valve cover retainers	44-80 inch lbs.	5-9
Rocker arms/Shafts		
Rocker arm bolts	16-21	22-28
Thermostat		
Thermostat housing retainers	14-19	19-26
Upper Intake Manifold		
Upper intake manifold-to-lower intake manifold bolts	14-20	19-26
Upper intake manifold support bolts	22-34	31-46
Lower Intake Manifold		
Intake manifold-to-cylinder head bolts	14-20	19-26
Exhaust Manifold		
Exhaust manifold nuts and bolts	12-17	16-23
Manifold shield bolts	12-17	16-23
Radiator		
Radiator support bracket bolts	71-89 inch lbs.	8-10
Engine Fan		
Fan assembly bolts	71-97 inch lbs.	8-11
Engine Fan Motor		
Fan blade nut	0.35-0.53 inch lbs.	0.04-0.06
Water Pump		
Water pump bolts	14-19	19-26
Inlet connector bolts	14-22	19-30
Cylinder Head		
Cylinder head bolts		
First pass	35-40	50-60
Second pass	56-60	75-81

89723C01

TORQUE SPECIFICATIONS

Component	Ft. lbs.	Nm
Oil Pan		
Oil pan retainers	69-78 inch lbs.	8-9
Oil pan drain plug	22-30	29-41
Oil Pump		
Oil pump bolts	14-19	19-25
Screen cover tube retainers	71-97 inch lbs.	8-11
Crankshaft Pulleys		
Crankshaft pulley bolt	80-85	108-118
Retaining washer bolts	109-152 inch lbs.	12-17
Timing Belt Cover and Belt		
Tensioner bolt	14-19	19-26
Front cover retainers	71-97 inch lbs.	8-11
Sprockets		
Camshaft sprocket bolt	36-45	49-61
Camshaft		
Camshaft thrust plate bolt	71-88 inch lbs.	8-10
Crankshaft Rear Cover		
Flywheel reinforcing plate retainers	71-97 inch lbs.	8-11
Flywheel		
Flywheel retaining bolts	71-76	96-103

89723C02

USING A VACUUM GAUGE

White needle = steady needle   *Dark needle = drifting needle*

The vacuum gauge is one of the most useful and easy-to-use diagnostic tools. It is inexpensive, easy to hook up, and provides valuable information about the condition of your engine.

Indication: Normal engine in good condition

Gauge reading: Steady, from 17–22 in./Hg.

Indication: Sticking valve or ignition miss

Gauge reading: Needle fluctuates from 15–20 in./Hg. at idle

Indication: Late ignition or valve timing, low compression, stuck throttle valve, leaking carburetor or manifold gasket.

Gauge reading: Low (15–20 in./Hg.) but steady

Indication: Improper carburetor adjustment, or minor intake leak at carburetor or manifold

NOTE: Bad fuel injector O-rings may also cause this reading.

Gauge reading: Drifting needle

Indication: Weak valve springs, worn valve stem guides, or leaky cylinder head gasket (vibrating excessively at all speeds).

NOTE: A plugged catalytic converter may also cause this reading.

Gauge reading: Needle fluctuates as engine speed increases

Indication: Burnt valve or improper valve clearance. The needle will drop when the defective valve operates.

Gauge reading: Steady needle, but drops regularly

Indication: Choked muffler or obstruction in system. Speed up the engine. Choked muffler will exhibit a slow drop of vacuum to zero.

Gauge reading: Gradual drop in reading at idle

Indication: Worn valve guides

Gauge reading: Needle vibrates excessively at idle, but steadies as engine speed increases

TCCS3C01

Troubleshooting Engine Mechanical Problems

Problem	Cause	Solution
External oil leaks	• Cylinder head cover RTV sealant broken or improperly seated	• Replace sealant; inspect cylinder head cover sealant flange and cylinder head sealant surface for distortion and cracks
	• Oil filler cap leaking or missing	• Replace cap
	• Oil filter gasket broken or improperly seated	• Replace oil filter
	• Oil pan side gasket broken, improperly seated or opening in RTV sealant	• Replace gasket or repair opening in sealant; inspect oil pan gasket flange for distortion
	• Oil pan front oil seal broken or improperly seated	• Replace seal; inspect timing case cover and oil pan seal flange for distortion
	• Oil pan rear oil seal broken or improperly seated	• Replace seal; inspect oil pan rear oil seal flange; inspect rear main bearing cap for cracks, plugged oil return channels, or distortion in seal groove
	• Timing case cover oil seal broken or improperly seated	• Replace seal
	• Excess oil pressure because of restricted PCV valve	• Replace PCV valve
	• Oil pan drain plug loose or has stripped threads	• Repair as necessary and tighten
	• Rear oil gallery plug loose	• Use appropriate sealant on gallery plug and tighten
	• Rear camshaft plug loose or improperly seated	• Seat camshaft plug or replace and seal, as necessary
Excessive oil consumption	• Oil level too high	• Drain oil to specified level
	• Oil with wrong viscosity being used	• Replace with specified oil
	• PCV valve stuck closed	• Replace PCV valve
	• Valve stem oil deflectors (or seals) are damaged, missing, or incorrect type	• Replace valve stem oil deflectors
	• Valve stems or valve guides worn	• Measure stem-to-guide clearance and repair as necessary
	• Poorly fitted or missing valve cover baffles	• Replace valve cover
	• Piston rings broken or missing	• Replace broken or missing rings
	• Scuffed piston	• Replace piston
	• Incorrect piston ring gap	• Measure ring gap, repair as necessary
	• Piston rings sticking or excessively loose in grooves	• Measure ring side clearance, repair as necessary
	• Compression rings installed upside down	• Repair as necessary
	• Cylinder walls worn, scored, or glazed	• Repair as necessary

TCCS3C02

Troubleshooting Engine Mechanical Problems

Problem	Cause	Solution
Excessive oil consumption (cont.)	• Piston ring gaps not properly staggered	• Repair as necessary
	• Excessive main or connecting rod bearing clearance	• Measure bearing clearance, repair as necessary
No oil pressure	• Low oil level	• Add oil to correct level
	• Oil pressure gauge, warning lamp or sending unit inaccurate	• Replace oil pressure gauge or warning lamp
	• Oil pump malfunction	• Replace oil pump
	• Oil pressure relief valve sticking	• Remove and inspect oil pressure relief valve assembly
	• Oil passages on pressure side of pump obstructed	• Inspect oil passages for obstruction
	• Oil pickup screen or tube obstructed	• Inspect oil pickup for obstruction
	• Loose oil inlet tube	• Tighten or seal inlet tube
Low oil pressure	• Low oil level	• Add oil to correct level
	• Inaccurate gauge, warning lamp or sending unit	• Replace oil pressure gauge or warning lamp
	• Oil excessively thin because of dilution, poor quality, or improper grade	• Drain and refill crankcase with recommended oil
	• Excessive oil temperature	• Correct cause of overheating engine
	• Oil pressure relief spring weak or sticking	• Remove and inspect oil pressure relief valve assembly
	• Oil inlet tube and screen assembly has restriction or air leak	• Remove and inspect oil inlet tube and screen assembly. (Fill inlet tube with lacquer thinner to locate leaks.)
	• Excessive oil pump clearance	• Measure clearances
	• Excessive main, rod, or camshaft bearing clearance	• Measure bearing clearances, repair as necessary
High oil pressure	• Improper oil viscosity	• Drain and refill crankcase with correct viscosity oil
	• Oil pressure gauge or sending unit inaccurate	• Replace oil pressure gauge
	• Oil pressure relief valve sticking closed	• Remove and inspect oil pressure relief valve assembly
Main bearing noise	• Insufficient oil supply	• Inspect for low oil level and low oil pressure
	• Main bearing clearance excessive	• Measure main bearing clearance, repair as necessary
	• Bearing insert missing	• Replace missing insert
	• Crankshaft end-play excessive	• Measure end-play, repair as necessary
	• Improperly tightened main bearing cap bolts	• Tighten bolts with specified torque
	• Loose flywheel or drive plate	• Tighten flywheel or drive plate attaching bolts
	• Loose or damaged vibration damper	• Repair as necessary

TCCS3C03

Troubleshooting Engine Mechanical Problems

Problem	Cause	Solution
Connecting rod bearing noise	• Insufficient oil supply	• Inspect for low oil level and low oil pressure
	• Carbon build-up on piston	• Remove carbon from piston crown
	• Bearing clearance excessive or bearing missing	• Measure clearance, repair as necessary
	• Crankshaft connecting rod journal out-of-round	• Measure journal dimensions, repair or replace as necessary
	• Misaligned connecting rod or cap	• Repair as necessary
	• Connecting rod bolts tightened improperly	• Tighten bolts with specified torque
Piston noise	• Piston-to-cylinder wall clearance excessive (scuffed piston)	• Measure clearance and examine piston
	• Cylinder walls excessively tapered or out-of-round	• Measure cylinder wall dimensions, rebore cylinder
	• Piston ring broken	• Replace all rings on piston
	• Loose or seized piston pin	• Measure piston-to-pin clearance, repair as necessary
	• Connecting rods misaligned	• Measure rod alignment, straighten or replace
	• Piston ring side clearance excessively loose or tight	• Measure ring side clearance, repair as necessary
	• Carbon build-up on piston is excessive	• Remove carbon from piston
Valve actuating component noise	• Insufficient oil supply	• Check for: (a) Low oil level (b) Low oil pressure (c) Wrong hydraulic tappets (d) Restricted oil gallery (e) Excessive tappet to bore clearance
	• Rocker arms or pivots worn	• Replace worn rocker arms or pivots
	• Foreign objects or chips in hydraulic tappets	• Clean tappets
	• Excessive tappet leak-down	• Replace valve tappet
	• Tappet face worn	• Replace tappet; inspect corresponding cam lobe for wear
	• Broken or cocked valve springs	• Properly seat cocked springs; replace broken springs
	• Stem-to-guide clearance excessive	• Measure stem-to-guide clearance, repair as required
	• Valve bent	• Replace valve
	• Loose rocker arms	• Check and repair as necessary
	• Valve seat runout excessive	• Regrind valve seat/valves
	• Missing valve lock	• Install valve lock
	• Excessive engine oil	• Correct oil level

TCCS3C04

Troubleshooting Engine Performance

Problem	Cause	Solution
Hard starting (engine cranks normally)	• Faulty engine control system component	• Repair or replace as necessary
	• Faulty fuel pump	• Replace fuel pump
	• Faulty fuel system component	• Repair or replace as necessary
	• Faulty ignition coil	• Test and replace as necessary
	• Improper spark plug gap	• Adjust gap
	• Incorrect ignition timing	• Adjust timing
	• Incorrect valve timing	• Check valve timing; repair as necessary
Rough idle or stalling	• Incorrect curb or fast idle speed	• Adjust curb or fast idle speed (If possible)
	• Incorrect ignition timing	• Adjust timing to specification
	• Improper feedback system operation	• Refer to Chapter 4
	• Faulty EGR valve operation	• Test EGR system and replace as necessary
	• Faulty PCV valve air flow	• Test PCV valve and replace as necessary
	• Faulty TAC vacuum motor or valve	• Repair as necessary
	• Air leak into manifold vacuum	• Inspect manifold vacuum connections and repair as necessary
	• Faulty distributor rotor or cap	• Replace rotor or cap (Distributor systems only)
	• Improperly seated valves	• Test cylinder compression, repair as necessary
	• Incorrect ignition wiring	• Inspect wiring and correct as necessary
	• Faulty ignition coil	• Test coil and replace as necessary
	• Restricted air vent or idle passages	• Clean passages
	• Restricted air cleaner	• Clean or replace air cleaner filter element
Faulty low-speed operation	• Restricted idle air vents and passages	• Clean air vents and passages
	• Restricted air cleaner	• Clean or replace air cleaner filter element
	• Faulty spark plugs	• Clean or replace spark plugs
	• Dirty, corroded, or loose ignition secondary circuit wire connections	• Clean or tighten secondary circuit wire connections
	• Improper feedback system operation	• Refer to Chapter 4
	• Faulty ignition coil high voltage wire	• Replace ignition coil high voltage wire (Distributor systems only)
	• Faulty distributor cap	• Replace cap (Distributor systems only)
Faulty acceleration	• Incorrect ignition timing	• Adjust timing
	• Faulty fuel system component	• Repair or replace as necessary
	• Faulty spark plug(s)	• Clean or replace spark plug(s)
	• Improperly seated valves	• Test cylinder compression, repair as necessary
	• Faulty ignition coil	• Test coil and replace as necessary

TCCS3C05

Troubleshooting Engine Performance

Problem	Cause	Solution
Faulty acceleration (cont.)	• Improper feedback system operation	• Refer to Chapter 4
Faulty high speed operation	• Incorrect ignition timing • Faulty advance mechanism	• Adjust timing (if possible) • Check advance mechanism and repair as necessary (Distributor systems only)
	• Low fuel pump volume • Wrong spark plug air gap or wrong plug • Partially restricted exhaust manifold, exhaust pipe, catalytic converter, muffler, or tailpipe • Restricted vacuum passages • Restricted air cleaner	• Replace fuel pump • Adjust air gap or install correct plug • Eliminate restriction • Clean passages • Cleaner or replace filter element as necessary
	• Faulty distributor rotor or cap	• Replace rotor or cap (Distributor systems only)
	• Faulty ignition coil • Improperly seated valve(s)	• Test coil and replace as necessary • Test cylinder compression, repair as necessary
	• Faulty valve spring(s)	• Inspect and test valve spring tension, replace as necessary
	• Incorrect valve timing	• Check valve timing and repair as necessary
	• Intake manifold restricted	• Remove restriction or replace manifold
	• Worn distributor shaft	• Replace shaft (Distributor systems only)
	• Improper feedback system operation	• Refer to Chapter 4
Misfire at all speeds	• Faulty spark plug(s) • Faulty spark plug wire(s) • Faulty distributor cap or rotor	• Clean or relace spark plug(s) • Replace as necessary • Replace cap or rotor (Distributor systems only)
	• Faulty ignition coil • Primary ignition circuit shorted or open intermittently • Improperly seated valve(s)	• Test coil and replace as necessary • Troubleshoot primary circuit and repair as necessary • Test cylinder compression, repair as necessary
	• Faulty hydraulic tappet(s) • Improper feedback system operation • Faulty valve spring(s)	• Clean or replace tappet(s) • Refer to Chapter 4 • Inspect and test valve spring tension, repair as necessary
	• Worn camshaft lobes • Air leak into manifold	• Replace camshaft • Check manifold vacuum and repair as necessary
	• Fuel pump volume or pressure low • Blown cylinder head gasket • Intake or exhaust manifold passage(s) restricted	• Replace fuel pump • Replace gasket • Pass chain through passage(s) and repair as necessary
Power not up to normal	• Incorrect ignition timing • Faulty distributor rotor	• Adjust timing • Replace rotor (Distributor systems only)

Troubleshooting Engine Performance

Problem	Cause	Solution
Power not up to normal (cont.)	• Incorrect spark plug gap	• Adjust gap
	• Faulty fuel pump	• Replace fuel pump
	• Faulty fuel pump	• Replace fuel pump
	• Incorrect valve timing	• Check valve timing and repair as necessary
	• Faulty ignition coil	• Test coil and replace as necessary
	• Faulty ignition wires	• Test wires and replace as necessary
	• Improperly seated valves	• Test cylinder compression and repair as necessary
	• Blown cylinder head gasket	• Replace gasket
	• Leaking piston rings	• Test compression and repair as necessary
	• Improper feedback system operation	• Refer to Chapter 4
Intake backfire	• Improper ignition timing	• Adjust timing
	• Defective EGR component	• Repair as necessary
	• Defective TAC vacuum motor or valve	• Repair as necessary
Exhaust backfire	• Air leak into manifold vacuum	• Check manifold vacuum and repair as necessary
	• Faulty air injection diverter valve	• Test diverter valve and replace as necessary
	• Exhaust leak	• Locate and eliminate leak
Ping or spark knock	• Incorrect ignition timing	• Adjust timing
	• Distributor advance malfunction	• Inspect advance mechanism and repair as necessary (Distributor systems only)
	• Excessive combustion chamber deposits	• Remove with combustion chamber cleaner
	• Air leak into manifold vacuum	• Check manifold vacuum and repair as necessary
	• Excessively high compression	• Test compression and repair as necessary
	• Fuel octane rating excessively low	• Try alternate fuel source
	• Sharp edges in combustion chamber	• Grind smooth
	• EGR valve not functioning properly	• Test EGR system and replace as necessary
Surging (at cruising to top speeds)	• Low fuel pump pressure or volume	• Replace fuel pump
	• Improper PCV valve air flow	• Test PCV valve and replace as necessary
	• Air leak into manifold vacuum	• Check manifold vacuum and repair as necessary
	• Incorrect spark advance	• Test and replace as necessary
	• Restricted fuel filter	• Replace fuel filter
	• Restricted air cleaner	• Clean or replace air cleaner filter element
	• EGR valve not functioning properly	• Test EGR system and replace as necessary
	• Improper feedback system operation	• Refer to Chapter 4

TCCS3C07

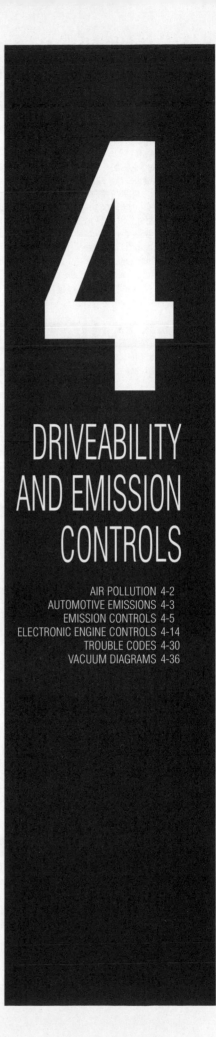

4

DRIVEABILITY AND EMISSION CONTROLS

AIR POLLUTION

The earth's atmosphere, at or near sea level, consists approximately of 78 percent nitrogen, 21 percent oxygen and 1 percent other gases. If it were possible to remain in this state, 100 percent clean air would result. However, many varied sources allow other gases and particulates to mix with the clean air, causing our atmosphere to become unclean or polluted.

Some of these pollutants are visible while others are invisible, with each having the capability of causing distress to the eyes, ears, throat, skin and respiratory system. Should these pollutants become concentrated in a specific area and under certain conditions, death could result due to the displacement or chemical change of the oxygen content in the air. These pollutants can also cause great damage to the environment and to the many man made objects that are exposed to the elements.

To better understand the causes of air pollution, the pollutants can be categorized into 3 separate types, natural, industrial and automotive.

Natural Pollutants

Natural pollution has been present on earth since before man appeared and continues to be a factor when discussing air pollution, although it causes only a small percentage of the overall pollution problem. It is the direct result of decaying organic matter, wind born smoke and particulates from such natural events as plain and forest fires (ignited by heat or lightning), volcanic ash, sand and dust which can spread over a large area of the countryside.

Such a phenomenon of natural pollution has been seen in the form of volcanic eruptions, with the resulting plume of smoke, steam and volcanic ash blotting out the sun's rays as it spreads and rises higher into the atmosphere. As it travels into the atmosphere the upper air currents catch and carry the smoke and ash, while condensing the steam back into water vapor. As the water vapor, smoke and ash travel on their journey, the smoke dissipates into the atmosphere while the ash and moisture settle back to earth in a trail hundreds of miles long. In some cases, lives are lost and millions of dollars of property damage result.

Industrial Pollutants

Industrial pollution is caused primarily by industrial processes, the burning of coal, oil and natural gas, which in turn produce smoke and fumes. Because the burning fuels contain large amounts of sulfur, the principal ingredients of smoke and fumes are sulfur dioxide and particulate matter. This type of pollutant occurs most severely during still, damp and cool weather, such as at night. Even in its less severe form, this pollutant is not confined to just cities. Because of air movements, the pollutants move for miles over the surrounding countryside, leaving in its path a barren and unhealthy environment for all living things.

Working with Federal, State and Local mandated regulations and by carefully monitoring emissions, big business has greatly reduced the amount of pollutant introduced from its industrial sources, striving to obtain an acceptable level. Because of the mandated industrial emission clean up, many land areas and streams in and around the cities that were formerly barren of vegetation and life, have now begun to move back in the direction of nature's intended balance.

Automotive Pollutants

The third major source of air pollution is automotive emissions. The emissions from the internal combustion engines were not an appreciable problem years ago because of the small number of registered vehicles and the nation's small highway system. However, during the early 1950's, the trend of the American people was to move from the cities to the surrounding suburbs. This caused an immediate problem in transportation because the majority of suburbs were not afforded mass transit conveniences. This lack of transportation created an attractive market for the automobile manufacturers, which resulted in a dramatic increase in the number of vehicles produced and sold, along with a marked increase in highway construction

between cities and the suburbs. Multi-vehicle families emerged with a growing emphasis placed on an individual vehicle per family member. As the increase in vehicle ownership and usage occurred, so did pollutant levels in and around the cities, as suburbanites drove daily to their businesses and employment, returning at the end of the day to their homes in the suburbs.

It was noted that a smoke and fog type haze was being formed and at times, remained in suspension over the cities, taking time to dissipate. At first this "smog," derived from the words "smoke" and "fog," was thought to result from industrial pollution but it was determined that automobile emissions shared the blame. It was discovered that when normal automobile emissions were exposed to sunlight for a period of time, complex chemical reactions would take place.

It is now known that smog is a photo chemical layer which develops when certain oxides of nitrogen (NOx) and unburned hydrocarbons (HC) from automobile emissions are exposed to sunlight. Pollution was more severe when smog would become stagnant over an area in which a warm layer of air settled over the top of the cooler air mass, trapping and holding the cooler mass at ground level. The trapped cooler air would keep the emissions from being dispersed and diluted through normal air flows. This type of air stagnation was given the name "Temperature Inversion."

TEMPERATURE INVERSION

In normal weather situations, surface air is warmed by heat radiating from the earth's surface and the sun's rays. This causes it to rise upward, into the atmosphere. Upon rising it will cool through a convection type heat exchange with the cooler upper air. As warm air rises, the surface pollutants are carried upward and dissipated into the atmosphere.

When a temperature inversion occurs, we find the higher air is no longer cooler, but is warmer than the surface air, causing the cooler surface air to become trapped. This warm air blanket can extend from above ground level to a few hundred or even a few thousand feet into the air. As the surface air is trapped, so are the pollutants, causing a severe smog condition. Should this stagnant air mass extend to a few thousand feet high, enough air movement with the inversion takes place to allow the smog layer to rise above ground level but the pollutants still cannot dissipate. This inversion can remain for days over an area, with the smog level only rising or lowering from ground level to a few hundred feet high. Meanwhile, the pollutant levels increase, causing eye irritation, respiratory problems, reduced visibility, plant damage and in some cases, even disease.

This inversion phenomenon was first noted in the Los Angeles, California area. The city lies in terrain resembling a basin and with certain weather conditions, a cold air mass is held in the basin while a warmer air mass covers it like a lid.

Because this type of condition was first documented as prevalent in the Los Angeles area, this type of trapped pollution was named Los Angeles Smog, although it occurs in other areas where a large concentration of automobiles are used and the air remains stagnant for any length of time.

HEAT TRANSFER

Consider the internal combustion engine as a machine in which raw materials must be placed so a finished product comes out. As in any machine operation, a certain amount of wasted material is formed. When we relate this to the internal combustion engine, we find that through the input of air and fuel, we obtain power during the combustion process to drive the vehicle. The by-product or waste of this power is, in part, heat and exhaust gases with which we must dispose.

The heat from the combustion process can rise to over 4000°F (2204°C). The dissipation of this heat is controlled by a ram air effect, the use of cooling fans to cause air flow and a liquid coolant solution surrounding the combustion area to transfer the heat of combustion through the cylinder walls and into the coolant. The coolant is then directed to a thin-finned, multi-tubed radiator, from which the excess heat is transferred to the atmosphere by 1 of the 3 heat transfer methods, conduction, convection or radiation.

The cooling of the combustion area is an important part in the control of exhaust emissions. To understand the behavior of the combustion and transfer of its heat, consider the air/fuel charge. It is ignited and the flame front burns progressively across the combustion chamber until the burning charge reaches the cylinder walls. Some of the fuel in contact with the walls is not hot enough to burn, thereby snuffing out or quenching the combustion process. This leaves unburned fuel in the combustion chamber. This unburned fuel is then forced out of the cylinder and into the exhaust system, along with the exhaust gases.

Many attempts have been made to minimize the amount of unburned fuel in the combustion chambers due to quenching, by increasing the coolant temperature and lessening the contact area of the coolant around the combustion area. However, design limitations within the combustion chambers prevent the complete burning of the air/fuel charge, so a certain amount of the unburned fuel is still expelled into the exhaust system, regardless of modifications to the engine.

AUTOMOTIVE EMISSIONS

Before emission controls were mandated on internal combustion engines, other sources of engine pollutants were discovered along with the exhaust emissions. It was determined that engine combustion exhaust produced approximately 60 percent of the total emission pollutants, fuel evaporation from the fuel tank and carburetor vents produced 20 percent, with the final 20 percent being produced through the crankcase as a by-product of the combustion process.

Exhaust Gases

The exhaust gases emitted into the atmosphere are a combination of burned and unburned fuel. To understand the exhaust emission and its composition, we must review some basic chemistry.

When the air/fuel mixture is introduced into the engine, we are mixing air, composed of nitrogen (78 percent), oxygen (21 percent) and other gases (1 percent) with the fuel, which is 100 percent hydrocarbons (HC), in a semi-controlled ratio. As the combustion process is accomplished, power is produced to move the vehicle while the heat of combustion is transferred to the cooling system. The exhaust gases are then composed of nitrogen, a diatomic gas (N_2), the same as was introduced in the engine, carbon dioxide (CO_2), the same gas that is used in beverage carbonation, and water vapor (H_2O). The nitrogen (N_2), for the most part, passes through the engine unchanged, while the oxygen (O_2) reacts (burns) with the hydrocarbons (HC) and produces the carbon dioxide (CO_2) and the water vapors (H_2O). If this chemical process would be the only process to take place, the exhaust emissions would be harmless. However, during the combustion process, other compounds are formed which are considered dangerous. These pollutants are hydrocarbons (HC), carbon monoxide (CO), oxides of nitrogen (NOx) oxides of sulfur (SOx) and engine particulates.

HYDROCARBONS

Hydrocarbons (HC) are essentially fuel which was not burned during the combustion process or which has escaped into the atmosphere through fuel evaporation. The main sources of incomplete combustion are rich air/fuel mixtures, low engine temperatures and improper spark timing. The main sources of hydrocarbon emission through fuel evaporation on most vehicles used to be the vehicle's fuel tank and carburetor float bowl.

To reduce combustion hydrocarbon emission, engine modifications were made to minimize dead space and surface area in the combustion chamber. In addition, the air/fuel mixture was made more lean through the improved control which feedback carburetion and fuel injection offers and by the addition of external controls to aid in further combustion of the hydrocarbons outside the engine. Two such methods were the addition of air injection systems, to inject fresh air into the exhaust manifolds and the installation of catalytic converters, units that are able to burn traces of hydrocarbons without affecting the internal combustion process or fuel economy.

To control hydrocarbon emissions through fuel evaporation, modifications were made to the fuel tank to allow storage of the fuel vapors during periods of engine shut-down. Modifications were also made to the air intake system so that at specific times during engine operation, these vapors may be purged and burned by blending them with the air/fuel mixture.

CARBON MONOXIDE

Carbon monoxide is formed when not enough oxygen is present during the combustion process to convert carbon (C) to carbon dioxide (CO_2). An increase in the carbon monoxide (CO) emission is normally accompanied by an increase in the hydrocarbon (HC) emission because of the lack of oxygen to completely burn all of the fuel mixture.

Carbon monoxide (CO) also increases the rate at which the photo chemical smog is formed by speeding up the conversion of nitric oxide (NO) to nitrogen dioxide (NO_2). To accomplish this, carbon monoxide (CO) combines with oxygen (O_2) and nitric oxide (NO) to produce carbon dioxide (CO_2) and nitrogen dioxide (NO_2). ($CO + O_2 + NO = CO_2 + NO_2$).

The dangers of carbon monoxide, which is an odorless and colorless toxic gas are many. When carbon monoxide is inhaled into the lungs and passed into the blood stream, oxygen is replaced by the carbon monoxide in the red blood cells, causing a reduction in the amount of oxygen supplied to the many parts of the body. This lack of oxygen causes headaches, lack of coordination, reduced mental alertness and, should the carbon monoxide concentration be high enough, death could result.

NITROGEN

Normally, nitrogen is an inert gas. When heated to approximately 2500°F (1371°C) through the combustion process, this gas becomes active and causes an increase in the nitric oxide (NO) emission.

Oxides of nitrogen (NOx) are composed of approximately 97–98 percent nitric oxide (NO). Nitric oxide is a colorless gas but when it is passed into the atmosphere, it combines with oxygen and forms nitrogen dioxide (NO_2). The nitrogen dioxide then combines with chemically active hydrocarbons (HC) and when in the presence of sunlight, causes the formation of photochemical smog.

Ozone

To further complicate matters, some of the nitrogen dioxide (NO_2) is broken apart by the sunlight to form nitric oxide and oxygen. ($NO_2 +$ sunlight $= NO + O$). This single atom of oxygen then combines with diatomic (meaning 2 atoms) oxygen (O_2) to form ozone (O_3). Ozone is one of the smells associated with smog. It has a pungent and offensive odor, irritates the eyes and lung tissues, affects the growth of plant life and causes rapid deterioration of rubber products. Ozone can be formed by sunlight as well as electrical discharge into the air.

The most common discharge area on the automobile engine is the secondary ignition electrical system, especially when inferior quality spark plug cables are used. As the surge of high voltage is routed through the secondary cable, the circuit builds up an electrical field around the wire, which acts upon the oxygen in the surrounding air to form the ozone. The faint glow along the cable with the engine running that may be visible on a dark night, is called the "corona discharge." It is the result of the electrical field passing from a high along the cable, to a low in the surrounding air, which forms the ozone gas. The combination of corona and ozone has been a major cause of cable deterioration. Recently, different and better quality insulating materials have lengthened the life of the electrical cables.

Although ozone at ground level can be harmful, ozone is beneficial to the earth's inhabitants. By having a concentrated ozone layer called the "ozonosphere," between 10 and 20 miles (16–32 km) up in the atmosphere, much of the ultra violet radiation from the sun's rays are absorbed and screened. If this ozone layer were not present, much of the earth's surface would be burned, dried and unfit for human life.

OXIDES OF SULFUR

Oxides of sulfur (SOx) were initially ignored in the exhaust system emissions, since the sulfur content of gasoline as a fuel is less than $\frac{1}{10}$ of 1 percent. Because of this small amount, it was felt that it contributed very little to the overall pollution problem. However, because of the difficulty in solving the sulfur emissions in industrial pollution's and the introduction of catalytic converter to the automobile exhaust systems, a change was mandated. The automobile exhaust system, when equipped with a catalytic converter, changes the sulfur dioxide (SO_2) into sulfur trioxide (SO_3).

When this combines with water vapors (H_2O), a sulfuric acid mist (H_2SO_4) is formed and is a very difficult pollutant to handle since it is extremely corrosive. This sulfuric acid mist that is formed, is the same mist that rises from the vents of an automobile battery when an active chemical reaction takes place within the battery cells.

When a large concentration of vehicles equipped with catalytic converters are operating in an area, this acid mist may rise and be distributed over a large ground area causing land, plant, crop, paint and building damage.

PARTICULATE MATTER

A certain amount of particulate matter is present in the burning of any fuel, with carbon constituting the largest percentage of the particulates. In gasoline, the remaining particulates are the burned remains of the various other compounds used in its manufacture. When a gasoline engine is in good internal condition, the particulate emissions are low but as the engine wears internally, the particulate emissions increase. By visually inspecting the tail pipe emissions, a determination can be made as to where an engine defect may exist. An engine with light gray or blue smoke emitting from the tail pipe normally indicates an increase in the oil consumption through burning due to internal engine wear. Black smoke would indicate a defective fuel delivery system, causing the engine to operate in a rich mode. Regardless of the color of the smoke, the internal part of the engine or the fuel delivery system should be repaired to prevent excess particulate emissions.

Diesel and turbine engines emit a darkened plume of smoke from the exhaust system because of the type of fuel used. Emission control regulations are mandated for this type of emission and more stringent measures are being used to prevent excess emission of the particulate matter. Electronic components are being introduced to control the injection of the fuel at precisely the proper time of piston travel, to achieve the optimum in fuel ignition and fuel usage. Other particulate after-burning components are being tested to achieve a cleaner emission.

Good grades of engine lubricating oils should be used, which meet the manufacturer's specification. Cut-rate oils can contribute to the particulate emission problem because of their low flash or ignition temperature point. Such oils burn prematurely during the combustion process causing emission of particulate matter.

The cooling system is an important factor in the reduction of particulate matter. The optimum combustion will occur, with the cooling system operating at a temperature specified by the manufacturer. The cooling system must be maintained in the same manner as the engine oiling system, as each system is required to perform properly in order for the engine to operate efficiently for a long time.

Crankcase Emissions

Crankcase emissions are made up of water, acids, unburned fuel, oil fumes and particulates. These emissions are classified as hydrocarbons (HC) and are formed by the small amount of unburned, compressed air/fuel mixture entering the crankcase from the combustion area (between the cylinder walls and piston rings) during the compression and power strokes. The head of the compression and combustion help to form the remaining crankcase emissions.

Since the first engines, crankcase emissions were allowed into the atmosphere through a road draft tube, mounted on the lower side of the engine block. Fresh air came in through an open oil filler cap or breather. The air passed through the crankcase mixing with blow-by gases. The motion of the vehicle and the air blowing past the open end of the road draft tube caused a low pressure area (vacuum) at the end of the tube. Crankcase emissions were simply drawn out of the road draft tube into the air.

To control the crankcase emission, the road draft tube was deleted. A hose and/or tubing was routed from the crankcase to the intake manifold so the blow-by emission could be burned with the air/fuel mixture. However, it was found that intake manifold vacuum, used to draw the crankcase emissions into the manifold, would vary in strength at the wrong time and not allow the proper emission flow. A regulating valve was needed to control the flow of air through the crankcase.

Testing, showed the removal of the blow-by gases from the crankcase as quickly as possible, was most important to the longevity of the engine. Should large accumulations of blow-by gases remain and condense, dilution of the engine oil would occur to form water, soots, resins, acids and lead salts, resulting in the formation of sludge and varnishes. This condensation of the blow-by gases occurs more frequently on vehicles used in numerous starting and stopping conditions, excessive idling and when the engine is not allowed to attain normal operating temperature through short runs.

Evaporative Emissions

Gasoline fuel is a major source of pollution, before and after it is burned in the automobile engine. From the time the fuel is refined, stored, pumped and transported, again stored until it is pumped into the fuel tank of the vehicle, the gasoline gives off unburned hydrocarbons (HC) into the atmosphere. Through the redesign of storage areas and venting systems, the pollution factor was diminished, but not eliminated, from the refinery standpoint. However, the automobile still remained the primary source of vaporized, unburned hydrocarbon (HC) emissions.

Fuel pumped from an underground storage tank is cool but when exposed to a warmer ambient temperature, will expand. Before controls were mandated, an owner might fill the fuel tank with fuel from an underground storage tank and park the vehicle for some time in warm area, such as a parking lot. As the fuel would warm, it would expand and should no provisions or area be provided for the expansion, the fuel would spill out of the filler neck and onto the ground, causing hydrocarbon (HC) pollution and creating a severe fire hazard. To correct this condition, the vehicle manufacturers added overflow plumbing and/or gasoline tanks with built in expansion areas or domes.

However, this did not control the fuel vapor emission from the fuel tank. It was determined that most of the fuel evaporation occurred when the vehicle was stationary and the engine not operating. Most vehicles carry 5–25 gallons (19–95 liters) of gasoline. Should a large concentration of vehicles be parked in one area, such as a large parking lot, excessive fuel vapor emissions would take place, increasing as the temperature increases.

To prevent the vapor emission from escaping into the atmosphere, the fuel systems were designed to trap the vapors while the vehicle is stationary, by sealing the system from the atmosphere. A storage system is used to collect and hold the fuel vapors from the carburetor (if equipped) and the fuel tank when the engine is not operating. When the engine is started, the storage system is then purged of the fuel vapors, which are drawn into the engine and burned with the air/fuel mixture.

EMISSION CONTROLS

Positive Crankcase Ventilation (PCV) System

OPERATION

The Positive Crankcase Ventilation (PCV) System vents harmful blow-by gases from the crankcase into the upper intake manifold, so that they can be burned along with the air/fuel mixture. The PCV valve limits the fresh air intake to suit engine demand and prevents combustion from backfiring into the crankcase.

The PCV valve is operated by engine vacuum. As the engine operates, blow-by gases are drawn into the intake manifold for burning. When the engine is at idle, the valve is fully open and a large amount of blow-by gases are burned. As the engine speed increases, the valve closes, allowing fewer blow-by gases to enter the intake manifold.

TESTING

▶ **See Figure 1**

1. Remove the PCV valve from the valve cover grommet.
2. Shake the PCV valve.
   a. If the valve rattles when shaken, reinstall it and proceed to Step 3.
   b. If the valve does not rattle, it is sticking and must be replaced.
3. Start the engine and allow it to reach normal operating temperature.
4. Check the PCV valve for vacuum by placing your finger over the end of the valve.
   a. If vacuum exists, proceed to Step 5.
   b. If vacuum does not exist, check for loose hose connections, vacuum leaks or blockage. Correct as necessary.
5. Disconnect the fresh air intake hose from the air inlet tube (connects the air cleaner housing to the throttle body).
6. Place a stiff piece of paper over the hose end and wait one minute.
   a. If vacuum holds the paper in place, the system is OK; reconnect the hose.
   b. If the paper is not held in place, check for loose hose connections, vacuum leaks or blockage. Correct as necessary.

Fig. 1 Check the PCV valve for vacuum at idle by placing your finger over the end of the valve

REMOVAL & INSTALLATION

For removal and installation of the PCV valve, refer to the procedure in Section 1.

Evaporative Emission Controls

OPERATION

▶ **See Figures 2 and 3**

Evaporative Emission (EVAP) Canister

▶ **See Figure 4**

The fuel vapors from the fuel tank are stored in the fuel vapor canister until the vehicle is operated, at which time the vapors will purge from the canister into the engine for consumption. The fuel vapor canister contains activated carbon, which absorbs the fuel vapor. The canister is located in the engine compartment or along the frame rail.

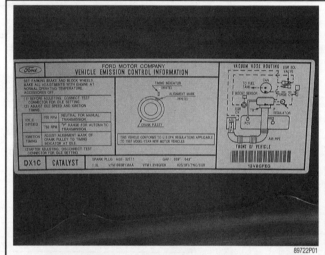

Fig. 2 The Vehicle Emission Control Information (VECI) label is located under the hood

EVAP Canister Purge (CANP) Valve

▶ **See Figure 5**

The evaporative emission canister purge valve (solenoid) is in-line with the canister and controls the flow of fuel vapors leaving the canister. The canister purge valve is normally closed when the engine is not operating. When the engine is **OFF**, vapors from the fuel tank flow into the canister. When the engine is turned **ON**, the valve opens and purges the vapors into the intake manifold to be burned.

The canister purge valve is controlled by the Powertrain Control Module (PCM), which actuates the solenoid based on information received by various sensors.

Pressure and Vacuum Relief System

EVAPORATIVE EMISSION SEPARATOR

The two-door model is the only one equipped with the evaporative emission separator. The separator is attached to the evaporative emission valve. The separator prevents liquid fuel from flooding the EVAP canister when the fuel in the fuel tank splashes.

FUEL TANK FILLER CAP

The filler cap is sealed with a built-in pressure-vacuum relief valve. Fuel system vacuum relief is provided after negative 0.25 psi (1.7 kPa) and pressure relief above 2 psi (14 kPa). Under normal conditions, the filler cap acts

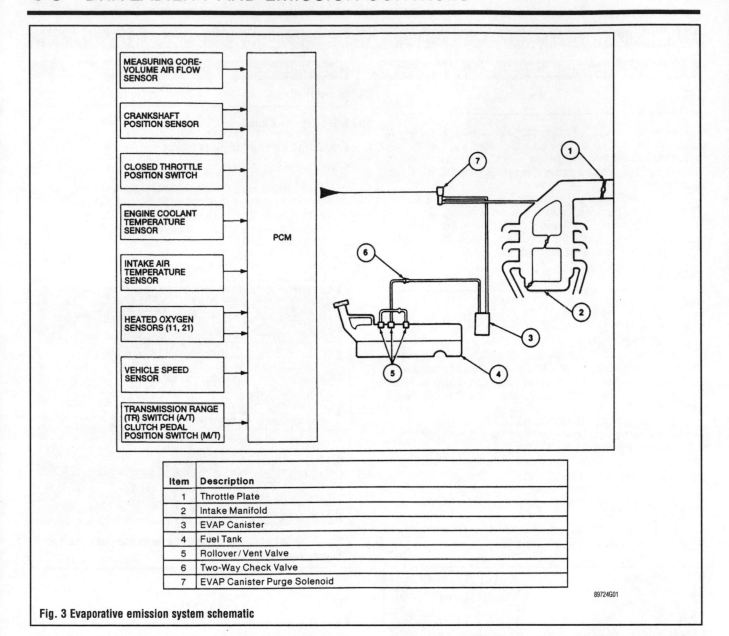

Item	Description
1	Throttle Plate
2	Intake Manifold
3	EVAP Canister
4	Fuel Tank
5	Rollover / Vent Valve
6	Two-Way Check Valve
7	EVAP Canister Purge Solenoid

89724G01

Fig. 3 Evaporative emission system schematic

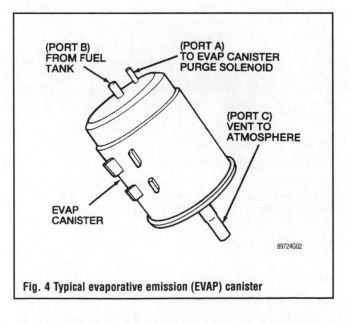

89724G02

Fig. 4 Typical evaporative emission (EVAP) canister

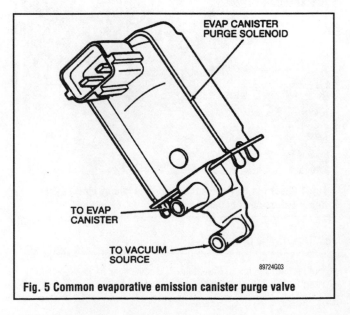

89724G03

Fig. 5 Common evaporative emission canister purge valve

as a check valve, which allows air to enter the tank as the fuel is used, while preventing vapors from escaping through the tank.

Evaporative Emission Valve

▶ See Figures 6 and 7

The evaporative emission valve uses a small orifice and shutoff valve to allow fuel vapor, and not liquid, to enter into the fuel evaporation pipe and EVAP canister. The valve is mounted on the fuel tank in a rubber grommet.

The fuel vapors from the tank are vented through the orifice in the top of the tank. The vapors are transmitted to the EVAP canister by a single vapor tube. A spring loaded poppet valve provides pressure relief ahead of the orifice to the EVAP canister. The poppet valve opens gradually and vents vapors to the atmosphere through a second vapor tube.

Two-Way Check Valve

▶ See Figure 8

The two-way check valve is located behind the left quarter trim panel on two-door models and under the rear seat cushion and cover on four-door models.

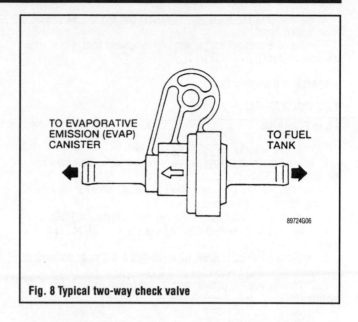

Fig. 8 Typical two-way check valve

The valve allows air to pass in or out of the fuel tank to equalize the pressure inside the tank. This prevents the fuel tank from a heat build-up or cool-down collapse.

COMPONENT TESTING

Evaporative Emission (EVAP) Canister

Generally, the only testing done to the canister is a visual inspection. Look over the canister and replace it with a new one if there is any evidence of cracks or other damage. Check the lines for cracks or wear and blockage.

Two-Way Check Valve

▶ See Figure 9

1. Inspect the valve and its connections for pinching, blockage, looseness or any other damage.
2. Remove the valve and connect a vacuum tester such as 014-R1058 or equivalent to port **A** of the valve.
3. Apply 1.01 in. Hg (3.4 kPa) of vacuum to port **A**.
4. The valve should open and not hold vacuum.
5. Connect the vacuum tester to port **B** of the valve.

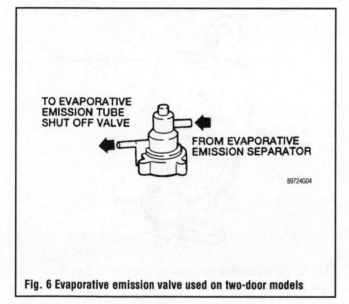

Fig. 6 Evaporative emission valve used on two-door models

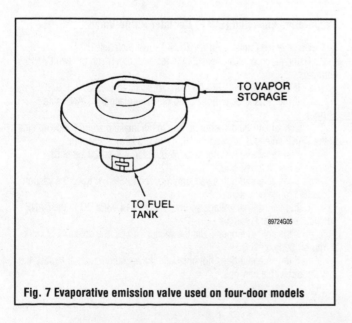

Fig. 7 Evaporative emission valve used on four-door models

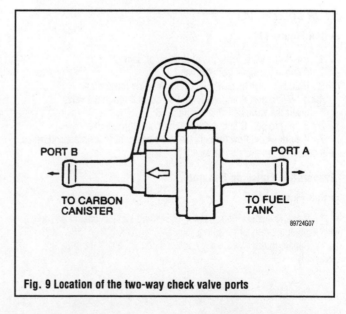

Fig. 9 Location of the two-way check valve ports

6. Apply 1.73 in. Hg (5.8 kPa) of vacuum to port **B** and make sure the valve remains open.

7. If the valve does not open when performing these tests, it is defective and must be replaced.

Evaporative Emission Valve

TWO-DOOR MODEL

▶ See Figure 10

1. Check the valve for leakage or signs of damage.
2. Remove the valve and connect the a vacuum tester to the valve as illustrated for TEST 1.
3. Hold the valve vertically and blow into port **A**. Verify that the valve opens at 1.0 psi (6.8 kPa) maximum.
4. Connect the vacuum tester to the valve as illustrated for TEST 2.
5. Blow into port **B**. Verify that the valve opens at 0.7 psi (4.9 kPa) maximum.
6. Hold the valve upside down, blow into port **A** and verify that pressure is held.
7. If the valve fails any of these tests, it is defective and must be replaced.

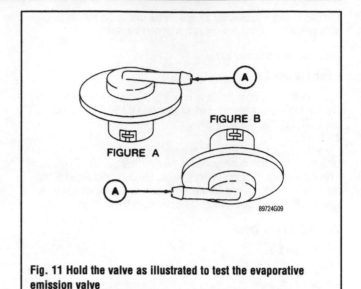

Fig. 11 Hold the valve as illustrated to test the evaporative emission valve

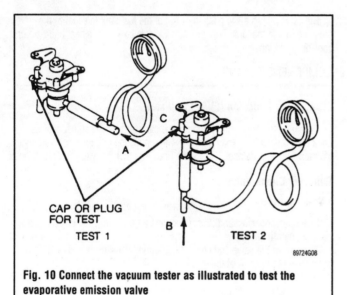

Fig. 10 Connect the vacuum tester as illustrated to test the evaporative emission valve

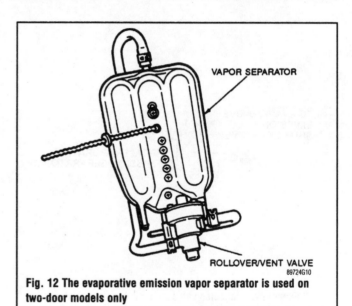

Fig. 12 The evaporative emission vapor separator is used on two-door models only

FOUR-DOOR MODEL

▶ See Figure 11

1. Check the valve for signs of leakage or damage.
2. Remove the valve from the car.
3. Hold the valve as shown in figure **A** of the illustration.
4. Blow into port **A** and verify that air flows through the valve.
5. Invert the valve as shown in figure **B**.
6. Blow into port **B** and verify that air flows through the valve.
7. If air does not flow through the valve when these tests are performed, it is defective and must be replaced.

Evaporative Emission Separator

▶ See Figure 12

1. Visually inspect the separator, hoses and connections for damage, blockage, looseness or pinching.
2. Repair and/or replace any damaged component of the separator assembly.

Evaporative Emission (EVAP) Canister Purge Valve

1. Remove the Canister Purge (CANP) valve (solenoid).
2. Using an ohmmeter, measure the resistance between the two CANP terminals.
   a. If the resistance is 30–90 ohms, proceed to Step 3.
   b. If the resistance is not 30–90 ohms, replace the CANP solenoid.
3. Attach a hand-held vacuum pump to the intake manifold vacuum side of the CANP solenoid, then apply 16 in. Hg (53 kPa) of vacuum.
   a. If the solenoid will not hold vacuum for at least 20 seconds, replace it with a new one.
   b. If the solenoid holds vacuum, proceed to Step 4. Keep the vacuum applied to the solenoid.
4. Using an external voltage source, apply 9–14 volts DC to the CANP solenoid electrical terminals.
   a. If the solenoid opens and the vacuum drops, the solenoid is working properly.
   b. If the solenoid does not open and the vacuum remains, replace the solenoid with a new one.

REMOVAL & INSTALLATION

Evaporative Emission (EVAP) Canister

♦ See Figure 13

1. Tag and disconnect the hoses from the canister.
2. Slide the canister up and out to disengage it from the bracket.
3. Remove the canister from the engine compartment.
4. Installation is the reverse of removal.

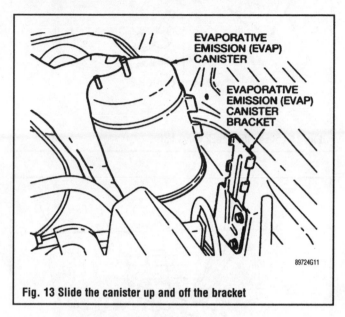

Fig. 13 Slide the canister up and off the bracket

Evaporative Emission Separator

TWO-DOOR MODELS

♦ See Figures 14 and 15

1. Remove the left quarter trim panel.
2. Loosen the separator bracket bolts.
3. Remove the bracket and the separator from the quarter panel.
4. Loosen the separator-to-bracket bolts and disengage the separator from the bracket.

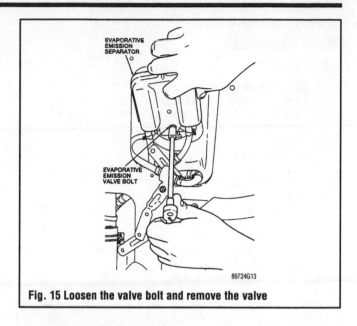

Fig. 15 Loosen the valve bolt and remove the valve

5. Loosen the evaporative emission valve bolt from the separator and remove the valve.
6. Disconnect the separator from the hoses.
To install:
7. Connect the hoses to the separator.
8. Install the valve and tighten the evaporative emission valve bolt.
9. Connect the separator to the bracket and tighten the bolts.
10. Install the bracket and separator on the trim panel and tighten the bracket bolts.
11. Install the left quarter trim panel.

EVAP Canister Purge (CANP) Valve

♦ See Figure 16

The purge valve is located to the right of the intake manifold, near the fuel rail.

1. Disconnect the negative battery cable.
2. Disengage the electrical connection from the purge valve.
3. Tag and disconnect the emission hoses from the purge valve and remove the valve.
4. Installation is the reverse of removal.

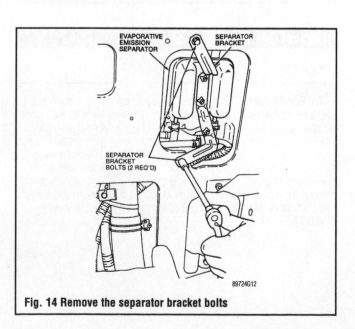

Fig. 14 Remove the separator bracket bolts

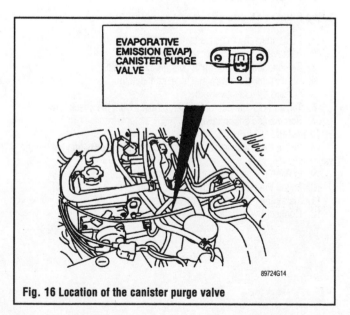

Fig. 16 Location of the canister purge valve

Two-Way Check Valve

TWO-DOOR MODELS

♦ **See Figure 17**

1. Remove the left quarter trim panel.
2. Loosen the separator bracket bolts.
3. Remove the bracket and the separator from the quarter panel.
4. Loosen the separator-to-bracket bolts and disengage the separator from the bracket.
5. Loosen the check valve bolt.
6. Tag and disconnect the emission hoses from the check valve.
7. Remove the check valve from the engine compartment.

To install:

8. Install the check valve, connect the emission hoses and tighten the valve bolt.
9. Connect the separator to the bracket and tighten the bolts.
10. Install the bracket and separator on the quarter panel and tighten the bracket bolts.
11. Install the left quarter trim panel.

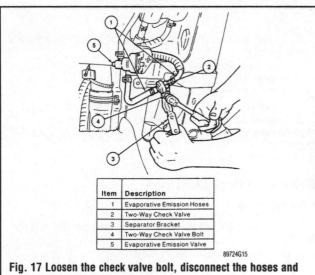

Item	Description
1	Evaporative Emission Hoses
2	Two-Way Check Valve
3	Separator Bracket
4	Two-Way Check Valve Bolt
5	Evaporative Emission Valve

89724G15

Fig. 17 Loosen the check valve bolt, disconnect the hoses and remove the valve—two-door models

FOUR-DOOR MODELS

♦ **See Figures 18 and 19**

1. Disconnect the negative battery cable.
2. Remove the rear seat cushion and cover.
3. Remove the rear floor pan opening cover plate.
4. Unplug the fuel pump electrical connection.
5. Loosen the check valve bolt.
6. Tag and disconnect the emission hoses from the check valve.
7. Remove the check valve.

To install:

8. Install the check valve, connect the emission hoses and tighten the valve bolt.
9. Engage the fuel pump electrical connection.
10. Install the rear floor pan opening cover plate.
11. Install the rear seat cushion and cover.
12. Connect the negative battery cable.

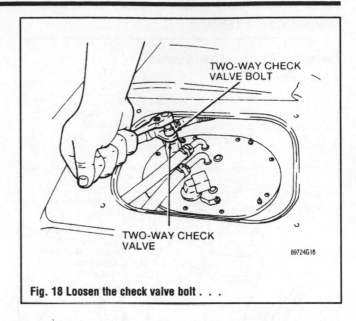

Fig. 18 Loosen the check valve bolt . . .

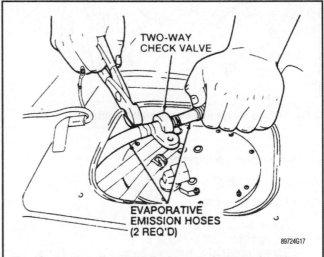

Fig. 19 . . . then disconnect the hoses and remove the valve—four-door models

Exhaust Gas Recirculation System

OPERATION

The Exhaust Gas Recirculation (EGR) system recirculates exhaust gas to the intake manifold to be burned. This process lowers the combustion temperatures and greatly reduces the formation of oxides of nitrogen (NOx). The EGR valve is vacuum actuated, and the amount of gas reintroduced and timing of the cycle varies by calibration. The timing and volume are controlled by the Powertrain Control Module (PCM), which also controls the EGR solenoid vacuum valve. When energized, the manifold vacuum outlet fitting and cap allow exhaust gas to be circulated in the engine and burned. The EGR system does not operate when the system is cold, to improve driveability.

COMPONENT TESTING

Before performing any test on the EGR system components, make sure the hoses are not kinked or damaged, and that no electrical connection is loose, corroded or damaged.

Exhaust Gas Recirculation (EGR) Valve

▶ See Figure 20

1. Start the car and let the engine reach normal operating temperature.
2. Turn the engine **OFF** and connect a vacuum tester (pump) to the EGR valve vacuum source port.
3. Turn the engine **ON** and idle the engine.
4. Apply at least 2.59 in. Hg (8.67 kPa) of vacuum; if the engine idles rough or stalls, the EGR valve is functioning properly.
5. If the engine does not idle rough, replace the EGR valve.

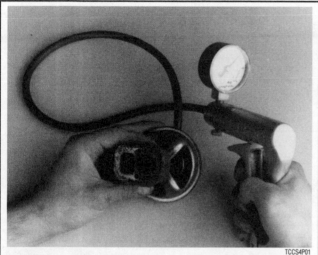

Fig. 20 Some EGR valves may be tested by using a vacuum pump and watching for diaphragm movement

EGR Valve Position (EVP) Sensor

▶ See Figures 21, 22 and 23

1. Turn the ignition **OFF**.
2. Use a high impedance Digital Volt Ohmmeter (DVOM) to backprobe the EVP and SIG RTN wires.

➡ **The procedures that call for backprobing can be performed using test wires with a third terminal. These wires can be purchased at your local auto parts store.**

3. Connect a vacuum pump to the EGR valve vacuum port.
4. Turn the ignition **ON**.
5. At 0 in. Hg of vacuum (no vacuum applied), the voltage reading should be approximately 0.8 volts.
6. Apply 5.9 in. Hg (20 kPa) of vacuum; the voltage reading should now be approximately 5.0 volts.
7. If the voltage readings are not as specified at the 0 and 5.9 in. Hg vacuum readings, replace the EVP sensor.

EGR Control Solenoid

▶ See Figure 24

1. Turn the ignition **OFF**.
2. Unplug the control solenoid's electrical connection.
3. Tag and disconnect the vacuum hoses.
4. Attach a hose to port **A** (refer to the accompanying illustration) and blow into it. While blowing, check that air does not flow through port **B**.

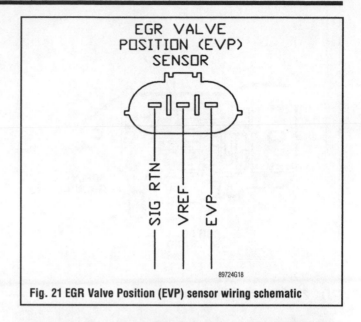

Fig. 21 EGR Valve Position (EVP) sensor wiring schematic

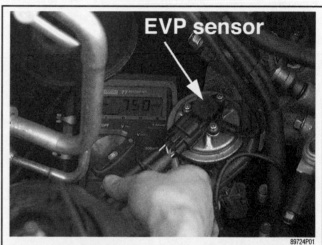

Fig. 22 When testing the EVP sensor, with the ignition ON and no vacuum present, the voltage reading should be around 0.8 volts

Fig. 23 After applying 5.9 in. Hg of vacuum, the voltage reading should be approximately 5.0 volts

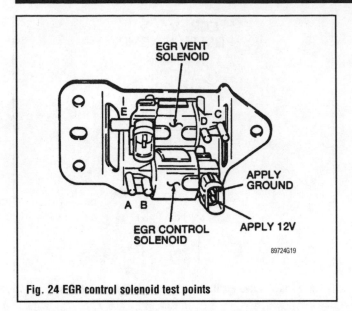

Fig. 24 EGR control solenoid test points

5. Apply 12 volts and ground the control solenoid as illustrated.

6. Again, blow through a hose attached to port **A** and check that air does flow through port **B**.

7. If the solenoid fails either of these tests, it must be replaced.

EGR Vent Solenoid

▶ **See Figure 25**

1. Turn the ignition **OFF**.
2. Unplug the control solenoid's electrical connection.
3. Tag and disconnect the vacuum hoses.
4. Block port **D** (refer to the accompanying illustration).
5. Blow through port **C** and verify that air flows through port **E**.
6. Apply 12 volts and ground the vent solenoid as illustrated.
7. Blow through port **C** and verify that air does not flow through port **E**.
8. If the solenoid fails either of these tests, it must be replaced.

EGR Boost Sensor

1. Turn the key **OFF**.
2. Disengage the EGR boost pressure hose from sensor.
3. Connect a vacuum pump to the EGR boost sensor.
4. Turn the key to the **ON** position.

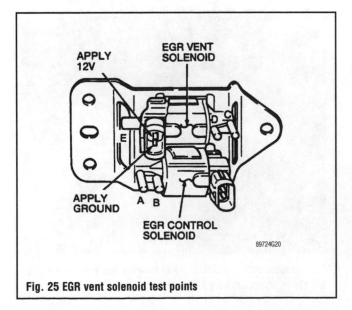

Fig. 25 EGR vent solenoid test points

5. Use a Digital Volt Ohmmeter (DVOM) to measure the voltage between the EGRB and SIG RTN terminals.

6. Apply 4.4 in. Hg (15 kPa) of vacuum to the sensor and observe the voltage reading, which should be approximately 0.3 volts.

7. Apply 31 in. Hg (105 kPa) of vacuum to the sensor and observe the voltage reading, which should be approximately 4.8 volts.

8. If the voltages are not within specification, the sensor is defective and must be replaced.

EGR Boost Solenoid

▶ **See Figures 26 and 27**

1. Turn the ignition **OFF**.
2. Disengage the solenoid electrical connection.
3. Tag and disconnect the hoses from the solenoid.
4. Blow air into ports **A** and **B**.
5. If air does (or does not) pass through as illustrated, replace the solenoid.
6. If the air flow results all comply with the first chart, continue with the test.
7. With the key still in the **OFF** position and the electrical connection still disengaged, remove the solenoid from the vehicle.

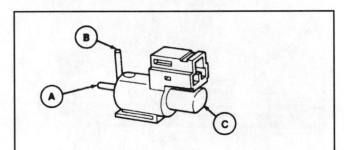

Ports	Air Flow
A —> B	NO
A —> C	NO
B —> C	YES

Fig. 26 Blow through ports A and B, while checking for air flow from ports B and C; compare your findings to the chart to see if the boost solenoid is working properly

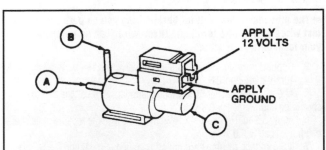

Ports	Air Flow
A —> B	YES
A —> C	NO
B —> C	NO

Fig. 27 Apply 12 volts to the solenoid and again blow through ports A and B; refer to the chart to see if the boost solenoid is functioning properly

8. Use jumper wires to apply 12 volts to the solenoid and blow through ports **A** and **B**.

9. If air does (or does not) pass through as illustrated, replace the solenoid.

REMOVAL & INSTALLATION

EGR Valve

▶ See Figures 28, 29, 30 and 31

1. Disconnect the negative battery cable.
2. Tag and disengage the EGR valve electrical connection and vacuum hoses.
3. Loosen the two EGR valve retaining bolts.
4. Remove the valve and gasket. Discard the old gasket.

To install:

5. Clean the EGR valve mounting surface with a scraper to remove any old gasket material residue.
6. Position a new gasket with the EGR valve.
7. Install and tighten the valve retaining bolts.
8. Engage the electrical connection and vacuum hoses.
9. Connect the negative battery cable.

Fig. 30 Unbolt the EGR valve retainers

Fig. 28 Unplug the EGR Valve Position (EVP) sensor electrical connection

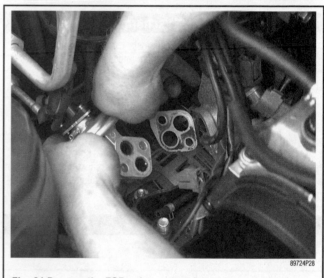

Fig. 31 Remove the EGR valve and gasket

EGR Control Solenoid

The EGR control solenoid cannot be serviced separately. If the EGR control solenoid is defective, replace the EGR solenoid assembly.

EGR Vent Solenoid

The EGR vent solenoid cannot be serviced separately. If the EGR vent solenoid is defective, replace the EGR solenoid assembly.

EGR Solenoid Assembly

1. Disconnect the negative battery cable.

➡Mark the location of the vacuum hoses before their removal, as this will aid installation.

2. Remove the EGR boost sensor from the bracket and set it to one side.
3. Disengage the electrical connections and vacuum hoses from the EGR vent and control solenoids.
4. Loosen the EGR solenoid assembly nuts and remove the solenoid.

To install:

5. Install the solenoid and tighten the nuts.

Fig. 29 Tag and disconnect all hoses from the valve

6. Engage the vacuum and electrical connections to the EGR vent and control solenoids.

7. Connect the boost sensor to the bracket.

8. Connect the negative battery cable.

EGR Valve Position (EVP) Sensor

1. The EGR valve position sensor is an integral part of the EGR valve. If the valve position sensor requires service, replace the EGR valve.

ELECTRONIC ENGINE CONTROLS

✳✳ WARNING

Electronic modules are very sensitive to Electrostatic Discharge (ESD). If modules are exposed to such charges, they may be damaged. Many vehicles and/or their electronic components display a label informing you that such components can be damaged by ESD; even components without warning labels may be damaged. To avoid possible damage to any of these components, follow the steps outlined below in Handling Electrostatic Discharge Sensitive Parts.

Handling Electrostatic Discharge Sensitive Parts

1. Body movement produces an electrostatic charge. To discharge personal static electricity, touch a ground point (metal) on the vehicle. This should be performed any time you:
   - Slide across the vehicle seat
   - Sit down or get up
   - Do any walking

2. Do not touch any exposed terminals on components or connectors with your fingers or any tools.

3. Never use jumper wires, ground a terminal on a component, or use test equipment on any component or terminal, unless instructed to do so in a diagnostic or testing procedure. When using test equipment, always connect the ground lead first.

Powertrain Control Module

OPERATION

➡ **The models covered by this manual employ the fourth and fifth generation Electronic Engine Control systems, commonly designated EEC-IV and EEC-V, to manage fuel, ignition and emissions on vehicle engines.**

Typically, the EEC-IV systems were used on 1994–95 models and the EEC-V systems were used on 1996–97 models.

The Powertrain Control Module (PCM) detects engine operating and driving conditions, along with the exhaust gas oxygen content. Various switches, sensors and components provide the PCM with information that allows it to control the air/fuel ratio (mixture). The PCM can also control some evaporative emission, ignition and deceleration systems.

The PCM is located underneath the left-hand side of the instrument panel.

REMOVAL & INSTALLATION

1. Disconnect the negative battery cable.

2. Loosen the three Powertrain Control Module (PCM) nuts.

3. If equipped, move the anti-lock brake control module aside, then pull the PCM down until you can gain access to the electrical connectors.

4. Grasp the PCM electrical connectors and unplug them from the back of the unit.

5. Remove the PCM from under the instrument panel.

EGR Boost Sensor

1. Disconnect the negative battery cable.

2. Disengage the sensor's electrical connection and vacuum hose.

3. Remove the sensor from the bracket.

4. Installation is the reverse of removal.

To install:

6. Engage the PCM electrical connectors to the rear of the unit.

7. Place the PCM and, if equipped, the anti-lock control module into position.

8. Install and tighten the PCM retaining nuts.

9. Connect the negative battery cable, start the car and check for proper operation.

Oxygen Sensor

OPERATION

An Oxygen Sensor (O2S) is used on all engines, and is mounted in the exhaust manifold. The sensor protrudes into the exhaust stream and monitors the oxygen content of the exhaust gases. The difference between the oxygen content of the exhaust gases and that of the outside air generates a voltage signal to the PCM. The PCM monitors this voltage and, depending upon the value of the signal received, issues a command to adjust for a rich or lean condition.

TESTING

▶ **See Figures 32, 33 and 34**

1. Perform a visual inspection of the oxygen sensor as follows:

   a. Remove the sensor from the exhaust manifold.

   b. If the sensor tip has a black/sooty deposit, this may indicate a rich fuel mixture.

   c. If the sensor tip has a white, gritty deposit, this may indicate an internal coolant leak.

   d. If the sensor tip has a brown deposit, this could indicate oil consumption.

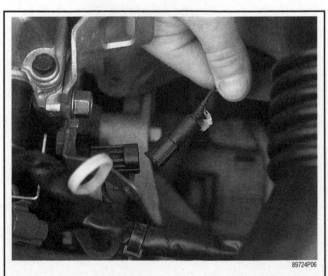

89724P06

Fig. 32 Unplug the oxygen sensor's electrical connection

→All these contaminants can destroy the sensor; if the problem is not repaired, the new sensor will also be damaged.

2. Reinstall the sensor, but do not engage its electrical connection.

3. Connect jumper wires from the sensor connector to the wiring harness. This permits the engine to operate normally while you check the sensor.

✳✳ WARNING

Never disengage any sensor while the ignition is ON.

4. Start the engine and allow it to reach normal operating temperature. This will take around ten minutes.

5. Connect the positive lead of a high impedance Digital Volt Ohmmeter (DVOM) to the sensor signal wire and the negative lead to a good known engine ground, such as the battery negative terminal.

6. The voltage reading should fluctuate as the sensor detects varying levels of oxygen in the exhaust stream.

7. If the sensor voltage does not fluctuate, the sensor may be defective, or the fuel mixture could be extremely out of range.

8. If the sensor reads above 550 millivolts constantly, the fuel mixture may be too lean, or you could have an exhaust leak near the sensor.

Fig. 33 Connect jumper wires to the oxygen sensor and harness; this will allow you to probe the sensor without damaging it

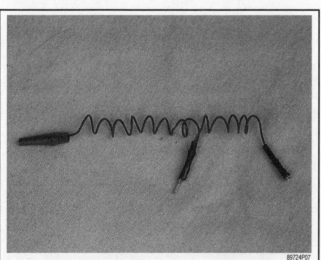

Fig. 34 Jumper wires that will make sensor testing easier and safer (for the sensor) are available from your local auto parts store

9. Under normal conditions, the sensor should fluctuate high and low. Prior to condemning the sensor, try forcing the system to have a rich fuel mixture by restricting the air intake, or lean by removing a vacuum line. If this causes the sensor to respond, look for problems in other areas of the system.

REMOVAL & INSTALLATION

1. Disconnect the negative battery cable.

2. Remove the air cleaner intake tube.

3. Disengage the oxygen sensor electrical connection, then remove the upstream wire from the hanger.

4. Loosen the exhaust manifold heat shield bolts and remove the shield.

5. Unscrew the oxygen sensor from the exhaust manifold.

To install:

6. Apply anti-seize compound to the oxygen sensor threads.

7. Screw the sensor into the threads in the exhaust manifold, then tighten it 22–36 ft. lbs. (29–49 Nm).

8. Install the heat shield and tighten the retainers to 12–17 ft. lbs. (16–23 Nm).

9. Connect the sensor wire to the hanger and engage the electrical connection.

10. Install the air cleaner intake tube.

11. Connect the negative battery cable.

Heated Oxygen Sensor

OPERATION

A Heated Oxygen Sensor (HO2S) is mounted on the muffler inlet pipe, just below the three-way catalytic converter. The sensor monitors the oxygen content in the three-way catalytic converter and then transmits this information to the Powertrain Control Module (PCM). The PCM then adjusts the air/fuel ratio to provide a rich (more fuel) or lean (less fuel) condition.

TESTING

▶ **See Figures 35 and 36**

1. Perform a visual inspection of the heated oxygen sensor as follows:
   a. Disconnect the electrical lead, then remove the sensor from the exhaust system.

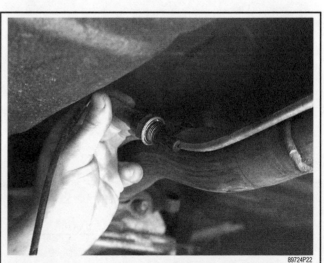

Fig. 35 Check the tip of the heated oxygen oxygen sensor for contamination

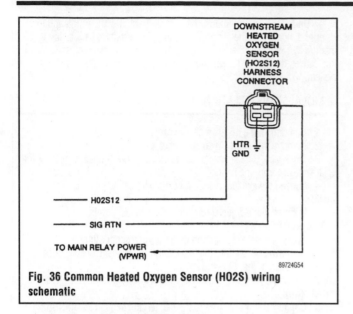

Fig. 36 Common Heated Oxygen Sensor (HO2S) wiring schematic

b. If the sensor tip has a black/sooty deposit, this may indicate a rich fuel mixture.

c. If the sensor tip has a white, gritty deposit, this may indicate an internal coolant leak.

d. If the sensor tip has a brown deposit, this could indicate oil consumption.

➡All these contaminants can destroy the sensor; if the problem is not repaired, the new sensor will also be damaged.

2. Reinstall the heated oxygen sensor, but do not connect its electrical lead.

3. Measure resistance between the PWR and GND (heater) terminals of the sensor. If the reading is about 6 ohms at 68°F (20°C) the sensor's heater element is okay. Connect the sensor's electrical lead.

4. With the heated oxygen sensor connected and the engine running, measure voltage with a DVOM by backprobing the **SIG RTN** wire of the HO2S connector. The voltage readings at idle should stay below 1.0 volts. When the speed is increased or decreased, the voltage should fluctuate between 0 and 1.0 volts; if so, the sensor is okay.

REMOVAL & INSTALLATION

▶ **See Figures 37, 38 and 39**

1. Disconnect the negative battery cable.
2. Raise the car and support it with safety stands.
3. Unplug the Heated Oxygen Sensor (HO2S) electrical connection.
4. Disengage the wiring from the retaining clips.
5. Use oxygen sensor wrench T94P-9472-A, or equivalent open end wrench, to remove the sensor.

To install:

6. Apply anti-seize compound to the oxygen sensor threads.
7. Use oxygen sensor wrench T94P-9472-A or equivalent to install the sensor.
8. Engage the sensor electrical connection and the wiring to the clips.
9. Lower the car and connect the negative battery cable.

Idle Air Control Bypass Air Valve

OPERATION

The Idle Air Control Bypass Air (IAC BPA) valve consists of an idle air control valve and a bypass air valve.

The bypass air valve functions during cold engine conditions to increase engine idle speed. It consists of a thermowax bead and a valve.

Fig. 37 Unplug the heated oxygen sensor's electrical connection

Fig. 38 Disengage the wiring from the retaining clips

Fig. 39 Use an open end wrench to remove the oxygen sensor

Engine coolant is directed around the thermowax, which opens and closes the valve. During cold engine operation below 140°F (60°C), the thermowax is contracted enough to allow the valve to open. As the coolant heats, the thermowax begins to expand. When the coolant reaches temperatures above 140°F (60°C), the thermowax expands and closes the valve.

The valve controls the amount of throttle valve bypass, which ensures a smooth idle under all engine operating conditions.

1. When the engine is cold, air flows through the valve during all modes of engine operation, to maintain the factory set idle speed.

TESTING

▶ **See Figures 40, 41 and 42**

1. To check the Idle Air Control (IAC) valve resistance, unplug the IAC valve connector.

2. Connect a high impedance Digital Volt Ohmmeter (DVOM) to the terminals.

3. Measure the resistance.

4. The resistance should be 7.7–9.3 ohms.

5. If the resistance does not meet specification, replace the IAC BPA assembly.

Fig. 40 Unplug the IAC valve electrical connector

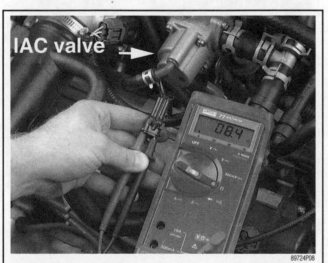

Fig. 41 Connect an ohmmeter to the IAC valve; the resistance should be 7.7–9.3 ohms

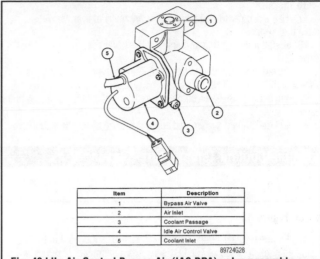

Item	Description
1	Bypass Air Valve
2	Air Inlet
3	Coolant Passage
4	Idle Air Control Valve
5	Coolant Inlet

Fig. 42 Idle Air Control Bypass Air (IAC BPA) valve assembly components

6. To check the BPA valve function, remove the BPA valve from the engine.

7. Wait until the valve reaches room temperature. When the valve is cold, blow through the air inlet and verify that air flows freely through the valve.

8. Heat the valve with a hair dryer; the air valve should move out and block the passage.

9. If the valve does not function as specified, replace the IAC BPA assembly.

10. To test the solenoid, connect a scan tool to the Data Link Connector (DLC).

11. Turn the key **ON** and enter the simulation test.

12. Access the IACV Parameter Identification (PID) and turn the dial to cycle at 75 degrees.

13. Listen for the IAC solenoid to click when using the simulation test.

14. If the solenoid clicks it is working properly.

REMOVAL & INSTALLATION

1. Disconnect the negative battery cable.

✳ CAUTION

Never open, service or drain the radiator or cooling system when hot; serious burns can occur from the steam and hot coolant. Also, when draining engine coolant, keep in mind that cats and dogs are attracted to ethylene glycol antifreeze and could drink any that is left in an uncovered container or in puddles on the ground. This will prove fatal in sufficient quantities. Always drain coolant into a sealable container. Coolant should be reused unless it is contaminated or is several years old.

2. Drain the coolant until it is at a level below the Idle Air Control Bypass Air (IAC BPA) valve.

➡**The lower coolant line should be disconnected after the valve is separated from the upper intake manifold.**

3. Tag and disconnect the upper coolant hose from the valve.

4. Unplug the valve's electrical connector, then loosen the two nuts and two bolts attaching the valve to the upper intake manifold.

5. Pull the valve from the manifold and disconnect the lower coolant line from the valve.

6. Remove the valve and gasket from the engine.

To install:

7. Use a scraper to clean any old gasket material from the valve mounting surface.

8. Install a new gasket and connect the lower coolant line to the valve.

9. Install the valve and its retainers. Tighten the nuts and bolts to 71–88 inch lbs. (8–10 Nm).

10. Engage the valve's electrical connection and the coolant hoses to the valve.

11. Fill the cooling system and connect the negative battery cable.

Engine Coolant Temperature Sensor

OPERATION

▶ **See Figure 43**

The Engine Coolant Temperature (ECT) sensor is mounted in the intake manifold coolant passage. The ECT sensor is a thermistor (a device which changes resistance as temperature changes). This sensor detects the temperature of engine coolant and provides a corresponding signal to the Powertrain Control Module (PCM).

TESTING

1994–95 Models

▶ **See Figure 44**

1. Disengage the engine coolant temperature sensor's electrical connection.

2. Attach jumper wires to the sensor's terminals.

➡ **Do not attach to the wiring harness connector, since the sensor's resistance, rather than voltage, will be measured.**

3. Connect a Digital Volt Ohmmeter (DVOM), set to the kilohms scale, to the jumper wires.

4. Measure the resistance with the engine **OFF** and cool, and also with the engine warmed up. Compare the temperature and resistance values obtained with those in the chart.

Coolant Temperature °C (°F)	ECT Sensor Resistance (kohms)
-20 (-4)	14.6 - 17.8
20 (68)	2.2 - 2.7
80 (176)	0.25 - 0.35

89724G29

Fig. 44 ECT sensor temperature versus resistance chart—OBD-I systems

5. Remove the jumper wires.

6. Replace the sensor if any readings are incorrect.

1996–97 Models

▶ **See Figures 45 and 46**

1. Disengage the engine coolant temperature sensor's electrical connection.

2. Attach jumper wires from the sensor terminals to the wiring harness connector. This permits the engine to operate normally while you check the sensor.

3. Connect a Digital Volt Ohmmeter (DVOM) between the jumper wires.

4. Measure the voltage with the engine **OFF** and cool, and also with the engine running and warmed up. Compare the temperature and voltage values obtained with those in the chart.

5. Remove the jumper wires.

6. Replace the sensor if any readings are incorrect.

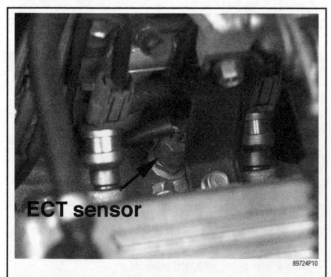

Fig. 43 Location of the ECT sensor

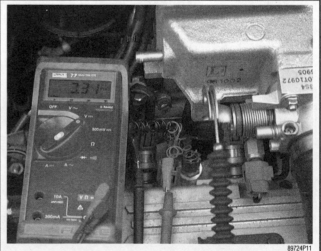

Fig. 45 Use jumper wires to backprobe the ECT sensor terminals and measure the voltage with a DVOM—OBD-II models

| Temperature | | Voltage* |
°F	°C	Volts
-4	-20	4.7
32	0	3.4
68	20	2.5
104	40	2.0
140	60	1.2
176	80	0.7
194	90	0.45
203	95	0.33
212	100	0.2

89724G30

Fig. 46 ECT and IAT sensors' temperature versus voltage chart—OBD-II systems

REMOVAL & INSTALLATION

✷✷ CAUTION

Never open, service or drain the radiator or cooling system when hot; serious burns can occur from the steam and hot coolant. Also, when draining engine coolant, keep in mind that cats and dogs are attracted to ethylene glycol antifreeze and could drink any that is left in an uncovered container or in puddles on the ground. This will prove fatal in sufficient quantities. Always drain coolant into a sealable container. Coolant should be reused unless it is contaminated or is several years old.

1. Disconnect the negative battery cable.
2. Drain the coolant until below the level of the Engine Coolant Temperature (ECT) sensor.
3. Loosen the upper intake manifold bracket retaining bolts and remove the bracket.
4. Detach the wiring connection from the sensor.
5. Using a ratchet and a deep well socket, remove the coolant temperature sensor.
6. Remove the washer from the sensor and discard it.

To install:

7. Install a new washer and the ECT sensor. Tighten the sensor to 19–21 ft. lbs. (25–29 Nm).
8. Install the upper intake manifold bracket and tighten the retainers to 14–19 ft. lbs. (19–26 Nm).
9. Attach the sensor's wiring connector.
10. Connect the negative battery cable.
11. Fill the engine cooling system with a 50/50 coolant and water mixture.
12. Start the engine and top off the cooling system.

Intake Air Temperature Sensor

OPERATION

The Intake Air Temperature (IAT) sensor is a thermistor that changes its resistance in response to the intake air temperature. This sensor is mounted on the upper side of the upper engine air cleaner, where it senses the intake air temperature, then sends this information to the Powertrain Control Module (PCM). The PCM uses this information to calculate the correct amount of fuel injection.

TESTING

1994–95 Models

▶ **See Figure 47**

1. Disengage the intake air temperature sensor's electrical connection.
2. Attach jumper wires to the sensor's terminals.

➡**Do not attach to the wiring harness connector, since the sensor's resistance, rather than voltage, will be measured.**

3. Connect a Digital Volt Ohmmeter (DVOM), set to the kilohms scale, to the jumper wires.
4. Measure the resistance with the engine **OFF** and cool, and also with the engine warmed up. Compare the temperature and resistance values obtained with those in the chart.
5. Remove the jumper wires.
6. Replace the sensor if any readings are incorrect.

Temperature °C (°F)	Resistance (kohms)
0 (32)	72.1 - 79.4
13 (55)	54.3 - 58.6
25 (77)	29.7 - 36.3
43 (110)	17.9 - 19.3
85 (185)	3.3 - 3.7

89724G31

Fig. 47 IAT sensor temperature versus resistance chart—OBD-I systems

1996–97 Models

▶ **See Figures 46 and 48**

1. Disengage the Intake Air Temperature (IAT) sensor electrical connection.
2. Connect jumper wires from the sensor terminal to the wiring harness connector. This permits the engine to operate normally while you check the sensor.
3. Connect a Digital Volt Ohmmeter (DVOM) between the jumper wires.
4. Measure the voltage with the engine **OFF** and cool, and also with the engine running and warmed up. Compare the temperature versus voltage values obtained with those in the chart.
5. Remove the jumper wires.
6. Replace the sensor if any readings are incorrect.

REMOVAL & INSTALLATION

1. Disconnect the negative battery cable.
2. Unplug the Mass Air Flow (MAF) sensor electrical connection.
3. Unplug the Intake Air Temperature (IAT) sensor electrical connection.
4. Use a wrench to remove the IAT sensor from its mounting.

To install:

5. Install the sensor and tighten it to 71–97 inch lbs. (8–11 Nm).
6. Connect the IAT sensor electrical connection.
7. Connect the MAF sensor electrical connection.
8. Connect the negative battery cable.

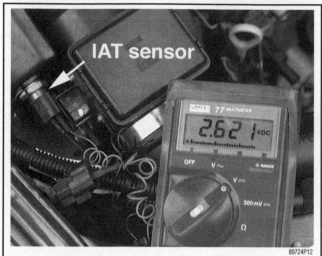

Fig. 48 Use jumper wires to backprobe the IAT sensor terminals and measure the voltage with a DVOM—OBD-II models

Mass Air Flow Sensor

OPERATION

The Mass Air Flow (MAF) sensor detects the intake air quantity and converts the measurement to a voltage reading by way of a heated resistor. The voltage signal is sent to the Powertrain Control Module (PCM) which, in turn, determines such things as fuel injection quantities and engine speed.

TESTING

▶ **See Figures 49, 50 and 51**

1. Make sure the ignition is **OFF**.
2. Connect jumper wires from the sensor terminal to the wiring harness connector. This permits the engine to operate normally while you check the sensor.
3. Connect a Digital Volt Ohmmeter (DVOM) between the jumper wires.
4. Check for voltage at the MAF sensor connections. On OBD-I systems, test terminals MAF and SIG RTN. On OBD-II systems, check MAF and GND. Refer to the wiring illustrations.

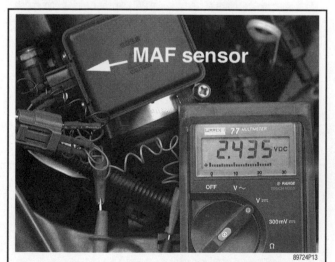

Fig. 49 Measuring the voltage of the MAF sensor using jumper wires and a DVOM

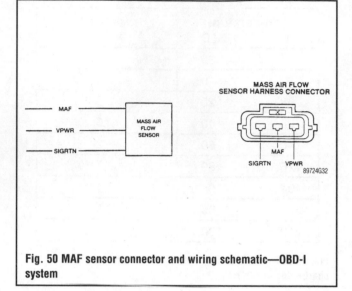

Fig. 50 MAF sensor connector and wiring schematic—OBD-I system

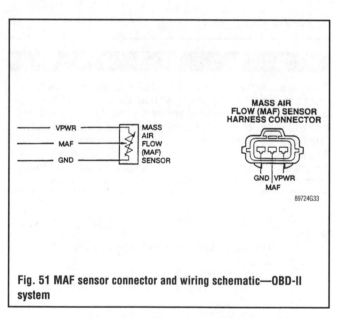

Fig. 51 MAF sensor connector and wiring schematic—OBD-II system

5. Turn the ignition switch to the **ON** position, but do not start the engine. The voltage should be 1.0–1.5 volts.
6. Start the engine, then check the voltage, which should be 1.5–5.0 volts.
7. If the voltage readings do not meet specifications, replace the sensor.
8. Remove the jumper wires.

REMOVAL & INSTALLATION

1. Disconnect the negative battery cable.
2. Unplug the Mass Air Flow (MAF) sensor electrical connector.
3. Unplug the Intake Air Temperature (IAT) sensor electrical connection.
4. Loosen the clamp attaching the air cleaner-to-intake manifold tube to the MAF sensor, and remove the tube from the sensor.
5. Disconnect the vacuum hose and remove the upper engine air cleaner.
6. Loosen the MAF sensor bolts and remove the sensor.

To install:

7. Install the MAF sensor and tighten the retaining bolts to 71–88 inch lbs. (8–10 Nm).

8. Install the upper engine air cleaner and connect the vacuum hose.

9. Connect the air cleaner-to-intake manifold tube to the MAF sensor and tighten the clamp.

10. Connect the IAT sensor electrical connection.

11. Connect the MAF sensor electrical connection.

12. Connect the negative battery cable.

Barometric Pressure Sensor

OPERATION

The Barometric Pressure (BARO) sensor is located inside the Powertrain Control Module (PCM). The BARO sensor provides the PCM with atmospheric pressure information.

TESTING

OBD-I System

1. Connect a scan tool to the Data Link Connector (DLC).

2. Operate the scan tool and check for trouble codes.

3. If code 14 is present, clear the codes and repeat the scan tool test.

4. If code 14 is still present, the Barometric Pressure (BARO) sensor is defective and the Powertrain Control Module (PCM) must be replaced.

REMOVAL & INSTALLATION

The Barometric Pressure (BARO) sensor is an integral part of the Powertrain Control Module (PCM) and is not serviceable separately. If the sensor is defective, the PCM must be replaced.

Throttle Position Sensor

OPERATION

The Throttle Position (TP) sensor is a variable resistor type sensor. The sensor is mounted on the left-hand side of the throttle body, and detects the angle which the throttle valve has been opened. The sensor then relays this information to the Powertrain Control Module (PCM) which, after analyzing the data, regulates the air/fuel mixture.

TESTING

▶ See Figures 52 thru 58

1. Backprobe the TP terminal at the TP sensor connector, with the positive lead of a Digital Volt Ohmmeter (DVOM).

2. Backprobe the SIG RTN terminal with the negative lead.

3. Have an assistant turn the ignition key **ON**, then depress the accelerator pedal (or manually rotate the throttle lever) so that the throttle lever attains ¼ open, ½ open, ¾ open and wide-open positions.

4. Observe the voltmeter at each of these positions and note the voltage displayed. Compare your readings with the figures in the accompanying charts.

5. If the TP sensor readings match the values in the chart, the sensor is working properly. If, however, the TP sensor readings are not as specified, continue with the test procedure.

6. Turn the ignition switch **OFF**.

7. Unplug the TP sensor electrical connector, then attach the positive lead of the DVOM to the VREF terminal of the wiring harness connector.

8. Turn the ignition switch **ON** and observe the voltage reading on the DVOM; it should be between 4.5 and 5.5 volts DC.

9. If the VREF voltage is within specifications, and the TP voltage readings do not agree with the values displayed in the chart, replace the TP sensor.

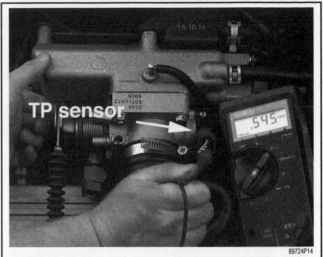

Fig. 52 Backprobe the TP sensor terminals with a DVOM, move the throttle lever and observe the voltage reading

Fig. 53 Move the throttle lever through different opening positions and note the voltage readings

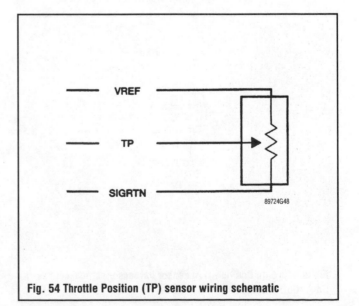

Fig. 54 Throttle Position (TP) sensor wiring schematic

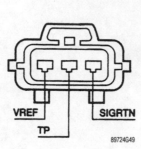

Fig. 55 Throttle Position (TP) sensor harness electrical connection—OBD-I systems

GRAPH DATA VALUES

Throttle Position	Volts
1/4	0.5
HALF	2.75
3/4	3.88
FULL	5.0

89724G50

Fig. 56 Throttle position sensor voltage chart—OBD-I systems

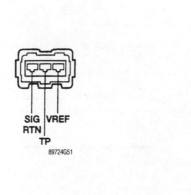

Fig. 57 Throttle Position (TP) sensor harness electrical connection—OBD-II systems

Throttle Position	Voltage (Volts)
0	0.5
1/4	1.3
Half	2.2
3/4	2.9
Full	3.7

89724G52

Fig. 58 Throttle position sensor voltage chart—OBD-II systems

REMOVAL & INSTALLATION

▶ **See Figures 59, 60 and 61**

1. Disconnect the negative battery cable.
2. If installing the old sensor again, matchmark its location in relation to the throttle body assembly.
3. Unplug the Throttle Position (TP) sensor electrical connection.
4. Loosen the TP sensor retaining screws and remove the sensor.
To install:
5. Install the TP sensor and its retaining screws. Tighten the screws to 14.2–20.3 inch lbs. (1.6–2.3 Nm).
6. Engage the sensor's electrical connection.
7. Connect the negative battery cable.

ADJUSTMENT

1. Unplug the Throttle Position (TP) sensor's electrical connection.
2. Connect a high impedance Digital Volt Ohmmeter (DVOM) between terminals **A** and **B** of the TP sensor.
3. Turn the throttle lever to the Wide Open Throttle (WOT) position and check the resistance. The reading should be about 5 ohms.

Fig. 59 If installing the old sensor again, matchmark the TPS and throttle body assembly

Fig. 60 Remove the TP sensor retainers . . .

Fig. 61 . . . and remove the sensor from the throttle body

4. Turn the throttle lever to the fully closed position and check the resistance. The reading should be below 1 ohm.

5. If the readings do not meet the specifications, perform the following adjustment:

    a. Loosen, but do not remove, the TP sensor retaining screws.

    b. With the throttle lever in the fully closed position, turn the sensor until the resistance reading on the DVOM is below 1 ohm.

    c. Turn the throttle lever to the Wide Open Throttle (WOT) position; the resistance reading on the DVOM should be about 5 ohms.

6. If the specification cannot be achieved, the throttle body must be replaced.

7. Tighten the TP sensor retainers to specification and engage the electrical connections.

Camshaft Position Sensor

OPERATION

On OBD-I systems, the Camshaft Position (CMP) sensor detects the No.1 cylinder when it reaches Top Dead Center (TDC) and signals the Powertrain Control Module (PCM) to control fuel injection.

On OBD-II systems, there are two Camshaft Position Sensors. One CMP detects the No.1 cylinder when it reaches Top Dead Center (TDC) and signals the Powertrain Control Module (PCM) to control fuel injection. The other CMP signals the PCM when the camshaft turns a quarter of a revolution.

TESTING

OBD-I System

▶ **See Figure 62**

1. Turn the ignition switch **OFF**.

2. Set a DVOM to a low DC voltage range (under 20 volts).

3. Backprobe the ground terminal of the distributor connector with the negative lead.

4. Backprobe the VPWR terminal of the distributor connector with the positive lead.

5. Turn the ignition switch to the **ON** position. The DVOM should read battery voltage. If not, check the wiring to the ECM.

6. Turn the ignition switch to the **OFF** position.

7. Backprobe the CMP terminal of the distributor connector with the positive lead.

8. Turn the ignition switch to the **ON** position.

9. Bump the starter to rotate the engine, but do not start the engine.

10. As the vanes of the distributor rotor pass through the Hall effect sensor, the voltage should switch back and forth between 5 volts and less than 1 volt.

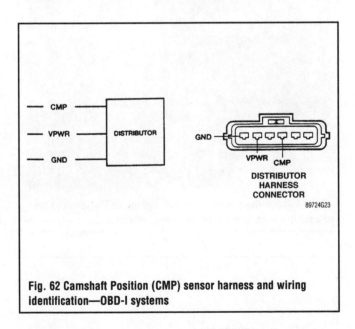

Fig. 62 Camshaft Position (CMP) sensor harness and wiring identification—OBD-I systems

OBD-II System

▶ **See Figures 63, 64 and 65**

1. Turn the ignition switch **OFF**.

2. Set a DVOM to a low DC voltage range (under 20 volts).

3. Backprobe the ground terminal of the distributor connector with the negative lead.

4. Backprobe the VPWR terminal of the distributor connector with the positive lead.

5. Turn the ignition switch to the **ON** position. The DVOM should read battery voltage. If not, check the wiring to the ECM.

6. Turn the ignition switch to the **OFF** position.

7. Backprobe the CMP1 terminal of the distributor connector with the positive lead.

8. Turn the ignition switch to the **ON** position.

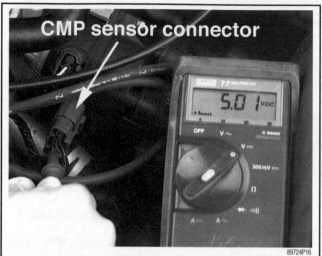

Fig. 63 Backprobe the GND and the CMP 1 and CMP 2 terminals with a DVOM, and observe the readings

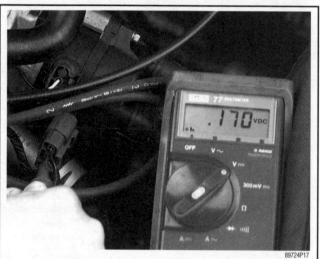

Fig. 64 The voltage readings should change as the vanes in the distributor pass through the Hall effect sensor

9. Bump the starter to rotate the engine, but do not start the engine.
10. As the vanes in the distributor pass through the Hall effect sensor, the voltage should switch back and forth between 5 volts and less than 1 volt.
11. Perform the same test on the CMP 2 terminal.
12. If the voltage doesn't vary, check that the distributor is rotating. If the distributor is rotating, the CMP sensor may be defective.

REMOVAL & INSTALLATION

The Camshaft Position (CMP) sensor is an integral part of the distributor assembly. If the CMP sensor is defective, the entire distributor assembly must be replaced.

Crankshaft Position Sensor

The Crankshaft Position (CKP) sensor is located in the distributor assembly on 1994–95 models, and on the lower front of the oil pump on 1996–97 models.

OPERATION

The Crankshaft Position (CKP) sensor relays engine speed and crankshaft position to the Powertrain Control Module (PCM).

TESTING

OBD-I System

▶ **See Figure 66**

1. Turn the ignition switch **OFF**.
2. Using a Digital Volt Ohmmeter (DVOM), backprobe the CKP1 terminal of the CKP sensor connector with the DVOM's positive lead. Attach the DVOM's negative lead to a good engine ground.
3. While an assistant bumps over the engine with the starter motor (using the ignition switch), observe the voltage displayed on the DVOM.
4. The CKP sensor voltage should fluctuate between approximately 0 and 5 volts. If the CKP sensor performs as specified, it is functioning properly. If, however, the voltage is not as specified, continue with the test procedure.
5. Turn the ignition switch **OFF**.
6. Disengage the wiring harness connector from the distributor, then attach the positive lead of the DVOM to the VPWR terminal on the wiring harness connector. Attach the negative lead to a good ground.

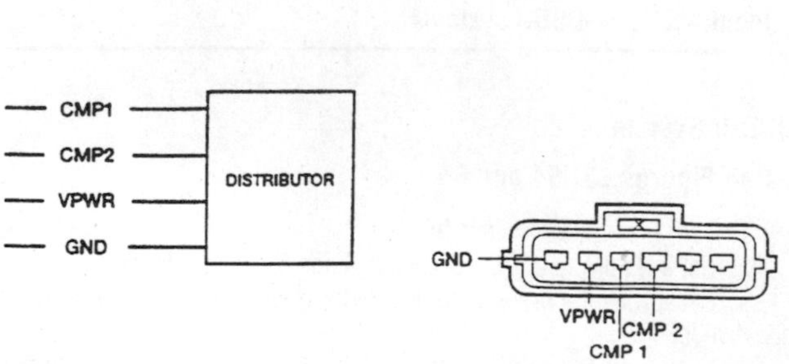

Fig. 65 Camshaft Position (CMP) sensor harness and wiring identification—OBD-II systems

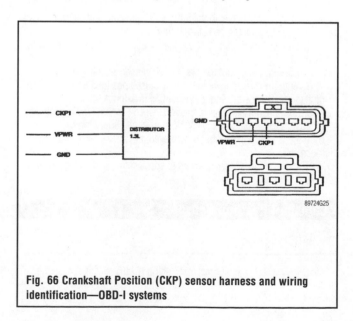

Fig. 66 Crankshaft Position (CKP) sensor harness and wiring identification—OBD-I systems

7. Turn the ignition key **ON** and observe the voltage displayed on the DVOM. The voltage should be greater than 10 volts. If not, the CKP sensor is not receiving the proper voltage from the PCM; the problem lies elsewhere in the electrical system.

8. If the VPWR voltage is satisfactory and the CKP output is not as specified, replace the CKP sensor.

OBD-II System

▶ **See Figures 67 and 68**

➡ **To perform this test accurately, the ambient air temperature should be 68°F (20°C).**

1. Turn the ignition switch **OFF**.
2. Unplug the CKP electrical connection.
3. Using a Digital Volt Ohmmeter (DVOM) set to read resistance, probe the CKP (+) terminal of the CKP sensor connector with the DVOM's positive lead. Attach the DVOM's negative lead to a good engine ground. Note the reading.
4. Backprobe the CKP + terminal of the CKP (-) sensor connector with the DVOM's positive lead in the same manner and note the resistance reading.
5. The resistance should be 520–580 ohms at 68°F (20°C). If readings are not as specified, replace the CKP sensor.

REMOVAL & INSTALLATION

1994–95 Models

The Crankshaft Position (CKP) sensor is located in the distributor assembly. If the sensor is found to be defective, the entire distributor assembly must be replaced.

1996–97 Models

▶ **See Figure 69**

1. Disconnect the negative battery cable.
2. Unplug the Crankshaft Position (CKP) sensor electrical connection.
3. Unfasten the sensor retainers and remove the sensor.

To install:
4. Install the sensor and tighten its retainers.
5. Engage the sensor electrical connection.
6. Connect the negative battery cable.

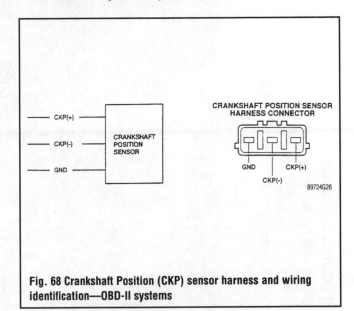

Fig. 68 Crankshaft Position (CKP) sensor harness and wiring identification—OBD-II systems

Fig. 67 Backprobe the CKP sensor connector with the DVOM and note the readings

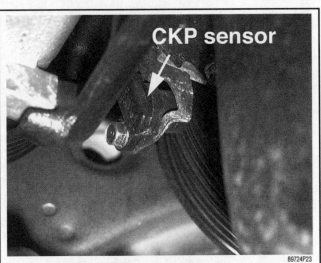

Fig. 69 Location of the Crankshaft Position (CKP) sensor— 1996–97 models

COMPONENT LOCATIONS

ELECTRONIC ENGINE CONTROL COMPONENT LOCATIONS (LATE MODEL)

1. EGR Valve Position (EVP) sensor
2. Throttle Position sensor (TPS)
3. Idle Air Control (IAC) valve
4. Camshaft Position (CMP) sensor (inside distributor)
5. Crankshaft Position (CKP) sensor (on lower front of oil pump)
6. Mass Air Flow (MAF) sensor
7. Intake Air Temperature (IAT) sensor
8. EGR Boost sensor
9. Engine Coolant Temperature (ECT) sensor
10. Idle switch

89724P32

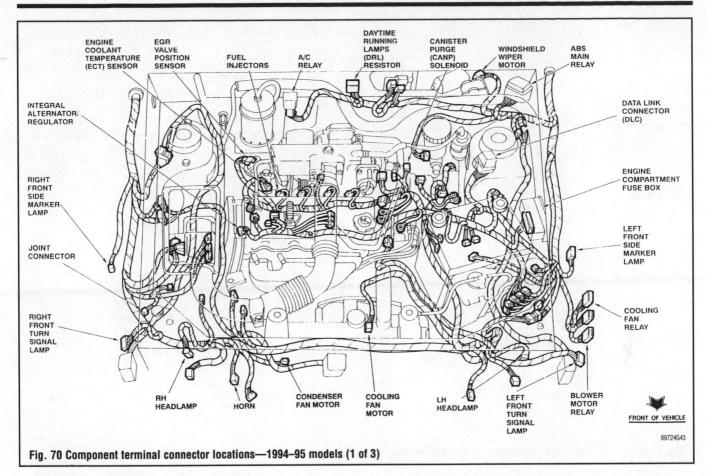

Fig. 70 Component terminal connector locations—1994–95 models (1 of 3)

89724G43

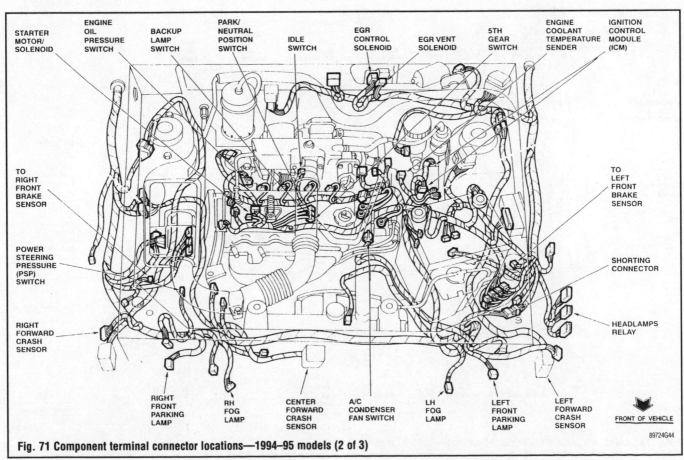

Fig. 71 Component terminal connector locations—1994–95 models (2 of 3)

89724G44

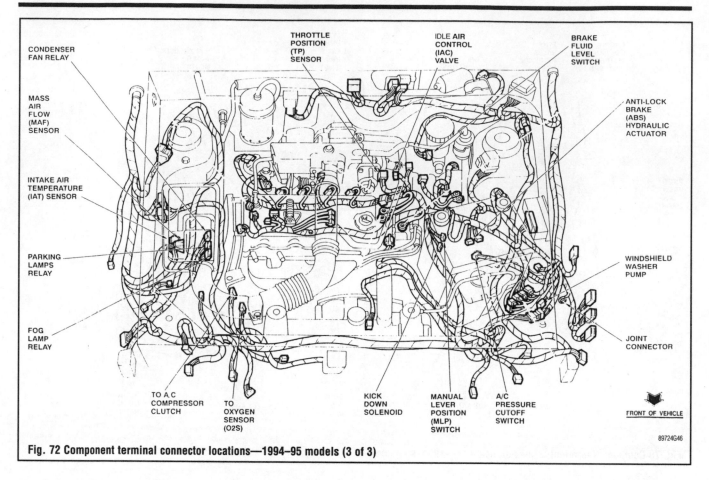

Fig. 72 Component terminal connector locations—1994–95 models (3 of 3)

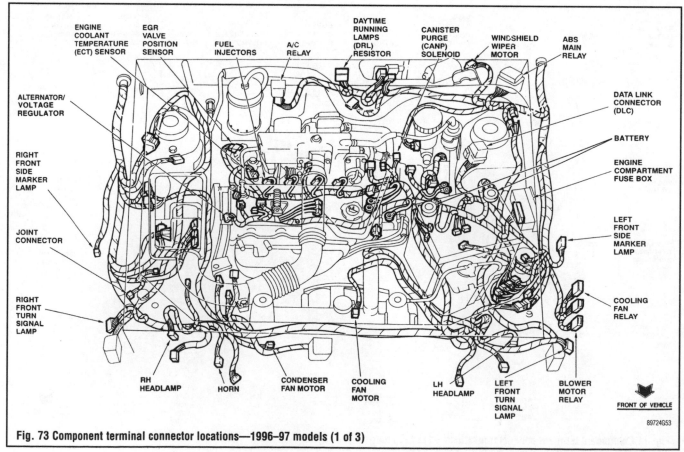

Fig. 73 Component terminal connector locations—1996–97 models (1 of 3)

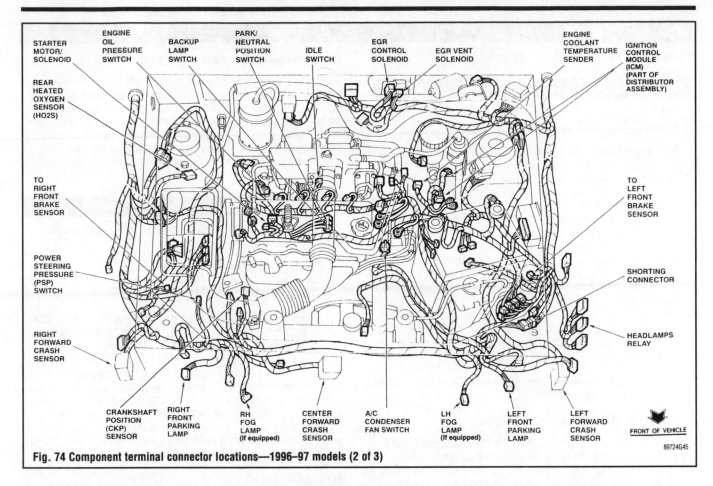

Fig. 74 Component terminal connector locations—1996–97 models (2 of 3)

89724G45

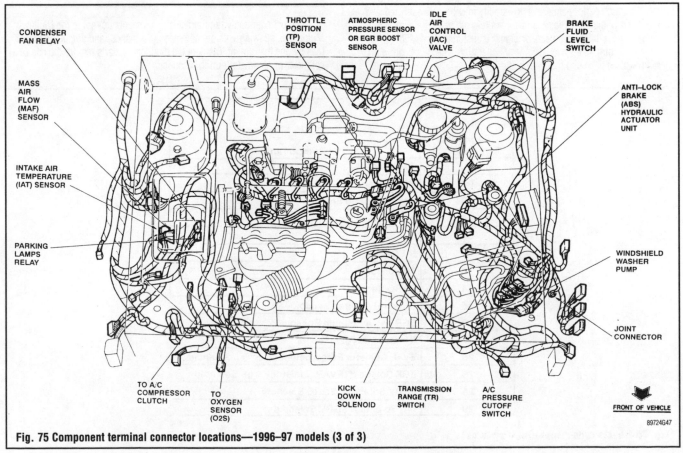

Fig. 75 Component terminal connector locations—1996–97 models (3 of 3)

89724G47

TROUBLE CODES

▶ See Figures 76, 77 and 78

EEC-IV Systems

GENERAL INFORMATION

One part of the Powertrain Control Module (PCM) is devoted to monitoring both input and output functions within the system. This ability forms the core of the self-diagnostic system. If a problem is detected within a circuit, the controller will recognize the fault, assign it an identification code, and store the code in a memory section. Depending on the year and model, the fault code(s) may be represented by two or three-digit numbers. The stored code(s) may be retrieved during diagnosis.

While the EEC-IV system is capable of recognizing many internal faults, certain faults will not be recognized. Because the computer system sees only electrical signals, it cannot sense or react to mechanical or vacuum faults affecting engine operation. Some of these faults may affect another component which will set a code. For example, the PCM monitors the output signal to the fuel injectors, but cannot detect a partially clogged injector. As long as the output driver responds correctly, the computer will read the system as functioning correctly. However, the improper flow of fuel may result in a lean mixture. This would, in turn, be detected by the oxygen sensor and be noticed as a constantly lean signal by the PCM. Once the signal falls outside the pre-programmed limits, the engine control assembly would notice the fault and set an identification code.

Failure Mode Effects Management (FMEM)

The PCM contains back-up programs which allow the engine to operate if a sensor signal is lost. If a sensor input is seen to be out of range—either high or low—the FMEM program is used. The processor substitutes a fixed value for the missing sensor signal. The engine will continue to operate, although performance and driveability may be noticeably reduced. This function of the controller is sometimes referred to as the limp-in or fail-safe mode. If the missing sensor signal is restored, the FMEM system immediately returns the system to normal operation. The dashboard warning lamp will be lit when FMEM is in effect.

Hardware Limited Operation Strategy (HLOS)

This mode is only used if the fault is too extreme for the FMEM circuit to handle. In this mode, the processor has ceased all computation and control; the entire system is run on fixed values. The vehicle may be operated, but performance and driveability will be greatly reduced. The fixed or default settings provide minimal calibration, allowing the vehicle to be carefully driven in for service. The dashboard warning lamp will be lit when HLOS is engaged. Codes cannot be read while the system is operating in this mode.

Data Link Connector

The Data Link Connector (DLC) is located on the left-hand side of the engine compartment.

HAND-HELD SCAN TOOLS

▶ See Figure 79

Although stored codes may be read through the flashing of the CHECK ENGINE or SERVICE ENGINE SOON lamp, the use of hand-held scan tools such as Ford's Self-Test Automatic Readout (STAR) tester or the second generation SUPER STAR II tester, or their equivalent, is highly recommended. There are many manufacturers of these tools; the purchaser must be certain that the tool is proper for the intended use.

The scan tool allows any stored faults to be read from the engine controller memory. Use of the scan tool provides additional data during troubleshooting, but does not eliminate the use of the charts. The scan tool makes collecting information easier, but the data must be correctly interpreted by an operator familiar with the system.

ELECTRICAL TOOLS

The most commonly required electrical diagnostic tool is the Digital Multimeter, allowing voltage, ohmmage (resistance) and amperage to be read by one instrument. Many of the diagnostic charts require the use of a voltmeter or ohmmeter during diagnosis.

Diagnostic Trouble Code	Component
03	CMP Sensor
04	CKP Sensor
06	Vehicle Speed Sensor
08	Air Flow Sensor
09	ECT Sensor
10	IAT Sensor
12	TP Sensor
14	BARO Sensor
15	(Heated) Oxygen Sensor
16	EGR Valve Position Sensor
17	(Heated) Oxygen Sensor
25	EVAP Canister Purge Solenoid / FPRC Solenoid
26	EGR Solenoid / EVAP Canister Purge Solenoid
28	EGRV Solenoid / EGRC Solenoid
29	IAC Solenoid / EGRV Solenoid

89724G40

Fig. 76 Trouble code chart—OBD-I systems

DIAGNOSTIC TROUBLE CODE (DTC) PINPOINT TEST CHART

DTC	Component Fault Description
P0100	Measuring core-volume air flow (MC-VAF) or mass air flow (MAF) sensor circuit malfunction
P0110	Intake air temperature (IAT) circuit malfunction
P0115	Engine coolant temperature (ECT) sensor circuit malfunction
P0120	Throttle position (TP) sensor circuit malfunction
P0125	Insufficient coolant temperature for closed loop control
P0130	Oxygen sensor (O2S) circuit malfunction
P0134	Heated oxygen sensor (HO2S 11) circuit no activity detected (Bank 1 Sensor 1) (1.3L uses O2S)
P0135	HO2S heater circuit malfunction (Bank 1 Sensor 1)
P0140	Heated oxygen sensor (HO2S12) circuit no activity detected
P0150	HO2S circuit malfunction (Bank 2 Sensor 1)
P0154	HO2S circuit no activity detected (Bank 2 Sensor 1)
P0155	HO2S heater circuit malfunction (Bank 2 Sensor 1)
P0160	HO2S circuit malfunction (Bank 2 Sensor 2)
P0170	Fuel trim malfunction (Bank 1)
P0173	Fuel trim malfunction (Bank 2)
P0300[1]	Random/multiple cylinder misfire detected
P0301[1]	Cylinder #1 misfire detected
P0302[1]	Cylinder #2 misfire detected
P0303[1]	Cylinder #3 misfire detected
P0304[1]	Cylinder #4 misfire detected
P0335	Crankshaft position (CKP) sensor circuit malfunction
P0340	Camshaft position (CMP) sensor circuit malfunction
P0400	Exhaust gas recirculation (EGR) flow malfunction
P0420	Catalyst system efficiency below threshold (Bank # 1)
P0430	Catalyst system efficiency below threshold (Bank #2)
P0440	Evaporative emission control system malfunction
P0443	Evaporative emission control system purge control valve circuit malfunction
P0470	EGR boost sensor
P0500	Vehicle speed sensor (VSS) malfunction
P0505	Idle control system malfunction
P0510	Closed throttle position switch malfunction (idle switch)
P0703	Brake on/off (BOO) switch
P0705	Transmission range (TR) sensor circuit malfunction
P0710	Transmission fluid temperature (TFT) sensor circuit malfunction
P0731	Incorrect gear 1 ratio

89724G41

Fig. 77 Trouble code chart—OBD-II systems

DIAGNOSTIC TROUBLE CODE (DTC) PINPOINT TEST CHART (Cont'd)

DTC	Component Fault Description
P0732	Incorrect gear 2 ratio
P0733	Incorrect gear 3 ratio
P0734	Incorrect gear 4 ratio
P0740	Torque converter clutch (TCC) circuit malfunction
P0745	Pressure control solenoid malfunction
P0750	Shift solenoid # 1 (SS1) malfunction
P0755	Shift solenoid #2 (SS2) malfunction
P0760	Shift solenoid #3 (SS3) malfunction
P1000	OBD II readiness function code
P1170	RHO2S voltage fixed
P1173	HO2S (front LH) inversion
P1173	RHO2S voltage fixed
P1195[2]	Barometric (BARO) pressure sensor circuit malfunction (signal is from EGR boost sensor)
P1196	Starter switch circuit malfunction
P1250	Fuel pressure regulator control (FPRC) solenoid malfunction
P1345	Cylinder discrimination signal (from CMP Sensor)
P1402	EGR valve position sensor
P1485	EGR control (EGRC) solenoid
P1486	EGR control (EGRV) solenoid
P1487	EGR check solenoid
P1521	Variable resonance induction system (VRIS) solenoid # 1 malfunction
P1522	VRIS solenoid #2
P1523	High speed inlet air (HSIA) solenoid malfunction
P1609	PCM internal circuit malfunction
P1709	Throttle position (TP) sensor malfunction
P1720	Vehicle speed sensor (VSS) circuit malfunction
P1743	Torque converter clutch control (TCCC) solenoid malfunction
P1744	Torque converter clutch (TCC) solenoid malfunction
P1765	3-2 timing solenoid malfunction
P1792	Idle (IDL) switch (closed throttle position switch) malfunction
P1794	Loss of battery voltage input
P1795	EGR boost sensor malfunction
P1797	Clutch pedal position (CPP) switch or neutral switch circuit malfunction

89724G42

1 There are two severity levels of misfire faults recognized by the PCM. The first is a catalyst damaging misfire which will cause the PCM to flash the MIL rapidly. The second is a misfire which will cause exhaust emissions to exceed standards. This fault will cause the PCM to constantly illuminate the MIL and store a DTC.

2 DTC P1195 will not set if the ambient temperature is lower than 10°C.

Fig. 78 Trouble code chart—OBD-II systems (cont.)

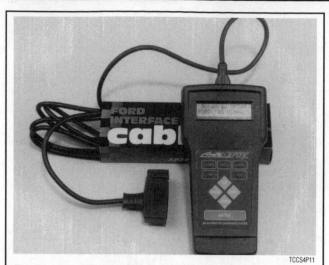

TCCS4P11

Fig. 79 Inexpensive scan tools, such as this Auto Xray®, are available to interface with your Ford vehicle

The multimeter must be a high impedance unit, with 10 megohms of impedance in the voltmeter. This type of meter will not place an additional load on the circuit it is testing; this is extremely important in low voltage circuits. The multimeter must be of high quality in all respects. It should be handled carefully and protected from impact or damage. Replace the batteries frequently in the unit.

Additionally, an analog (needle type) voltmeter may be used to read stored fault codes if the STAR tester is not available. The codes are transmitted as visible needle sweeps on the face of the instrument.

Many diagnostic procedures will be easier to perform with the use of jumper wires. Since direct testing of the harness connectors at the terminals or by backprobing could damage the wiring and/or terminals, exercise extreme caution if such a practice is necessary.

Other necessary tools include a quality tachometer with inductive (clip-on) pickup, a fuel pressure gauge with system adapters, and a vacuum gauge with an auxiliary source of vacuum.

Reading Codes

Diagnosis of a driveability problem requires attention to detail and following the diagnostic procedures in the correct order. Resist the temptation to begin extensive testing before completing the preliminary diagnostic steps. The preliminary or visual inspection must be completed in detail before diagnosis begins. In many cases, this will shorten diagnostic time and often cure the problem without electronic testing.

VISUAL INSPECTION

This is possibly the most critical step of diagnosis. A detailed examination of all connectors, wiring and vacuum hoses can often lead to a repair without further diagnosis. Performance of this step relies on the skill of the technician performing it; a careful inspector will check the undersides of hoses as well as the integrity of hard-to-reach hoses blocked by the air cleaner or other components. Wiring should be checked carefully for any sign of strain, burning, crimping or terminal pull-out from a connector.

Checking connectors at components or in harnesses is required; usually, pushing them together will reveal a loose fit. Pay particular attention to ground circuits, making sure they are not loose or corroded. Remember to inspect connectors and hose fittings at components not mounted on the engine, such as the evaporative canister or relays mounted on the fender aprons. Any component or wiring in the vicinity of a fluid leak or spillage should be given extra attention during inspection.

Additionally, inspect maintenance items such as belt condition and tension, battery charge and condition and the radiator cap carefully. Any of these very simple items may affect the system enough to set a fault.

ELECTRONIC TESTING

If a code was set before a problem self-corrected (such as a momentarily loose connector), the code will be erased if the problem does not reoccur within 80 warm-up cycles. Codes will be output and displayed as numbers on the hand-held scan tool, such as 23. If the codes are being read on an analog voltmeter, the needle sweeps indicate the code digits. code 23 will appear as two needle pulses (sweeps) then, after a 1.6 second pause, the needle will pulse (sweep) three times.

Key On Engine Off (KOEO) Test

▶ **See Figures 80, 81 and 82**

1. Connect the scan tool to the self-test connectors. Make certain the test button is unlatched or up.
2. Start the engine and run it until normal operating temperature is reached.
3. Turn the engine **OFF** for 10 seconds.
4. Activate the test button on the STAR tester.
5. Turn the ignition switch **ON** but do not start the engine.
6. The KOEO codes will be transmitted. Six to nine seconds after the last KOEO code, a single separator pulse will be transmitted. Six to nine

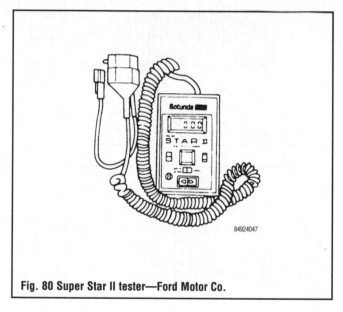

84924047

Fig. 80 Super Star II tester—Ford Motor Co.

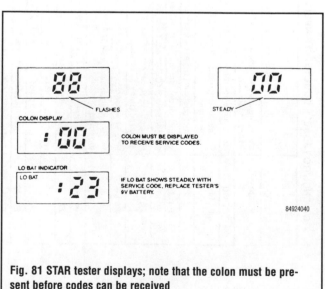

84924040

Fig. 81 STAR tester displays; note that the colon must be present before codes can be received

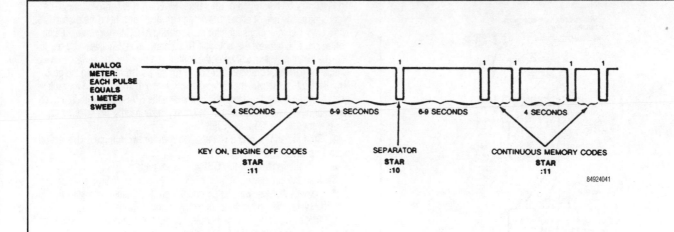

Fig. 82 Code transmission during KOEO test. Note that the continuous memory codes are transmitted after a pause and a separator pulse

seconds after this pulse, the codes from the Continuous Memory will be transmitted.

7. Record all service codes displayed. Do not depress the throttle on gasoline engines during the test.

Key On Engine Running (KOER) Test

▶ See Figures 80, 81 and 83

1. Make certain the self-test button is released or de-activated on the STAR tester.

2. Start the engine and run it at 2000 rpm for two minutes. This action warms up the oxygen sensor.

3. Turn the ignition switch **OFF** for 10 seconds.

4. Activate or latch the self-test button on the scan tool.

5. Start the engine. The engine identification code will be transmitted. This is a single digit number representing ½ the number of cylinders in a gasoline engine. On the STAR tester, this number may appear with a zero, such as 20 = 2. The code is used to confirm that the correct processor is installed and that the self-test has begun.

6. If the vehicle is equipped with a Brake On/Off (BOO) switch, the brake pedal must be depressed and released after the ID code is transmitted.

7. If the vehicle is equipped with a Power Steering Pressure Switch (PSPS), the steering wheel must be turned at least ½ turn and released within 2 seconds after the engine ID code is transmitted.

8. Certain Ford vehicles will display a Dynamic Response code 6–20 seconds after the engine ID code. This will appear as one pulse on a meter or as a 10 on the STAR tester. When this code appears, briefly take the engine to wide open throttle. This allows the system to test the throttle position, MAF and MAP sensors.

9. All relevant codes will be displayed and should be recorded. Remember that the codes refer only to faults present during this test cycle. Codes stored in Continuous Memory are not displayed in this test mode.

10. Do not depress the throttle during testing unless a dynamic response code is displayed.

Reading Codes With Analog Voltmeter

▶ See Figures 84 and 85

In the absence of a scan tool, an analog voltmeter may be used to retrieve stored fault codes. Set the meter range to read DC 0–15 volts. Connect the (+) lead of the meter to the battery positive terminal and connect the (–) lead of the meter to the self-test output pin of the diagnostic connector.

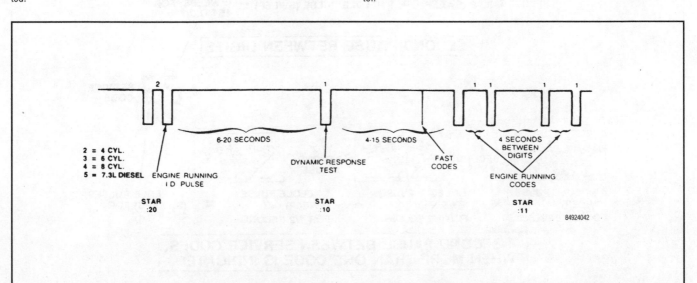

Fig. 83 Code transmission during KOER testing begins with the engine identification pulse and may include a dynamic response prompt

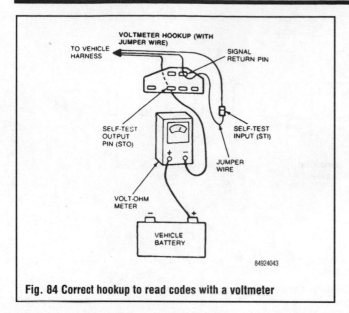

Fig. 84 Correct hookup to read codes with a voltmeter

Follow the directions given previously for performing the KOEO and KOER tests. To activate the tests, use a jumper wire to connect the signal return pin on the diagnostic connector to the self-test input connector. The self-test input line is the separate wire and connector with or near the diagnostic connector.

The codes will be transmitted as groups of needle sweeps. This method may be used to read either 2 or 3-digit codes. The Continuous Memory codes are separated from the KOEO codes by 6 seconds, a single sweep and another 6 second delay.

Other Test Modes

CONTINUOUS MONITOR OR WIGGLE TEST

Once entered, this mode allows the operator to attempt to recreate intermittent faults by wiggling or tapping components, wiring or connectors.

The test may be performed during either KOEO or KOER procedures. The test requires the use of either an analog voltmeter or a hand-held scan tool.

To enter the continuous monitor mode during KOEO testing, turn the ignition switch ON. Activate the test, wait 10 seconds, then deactivate and reactivate the test; the system will enter the continuous monitor mode. Tap, move or wiggle the harness, component or connector suspected of causing the problem; if a fault is detected, the code will store in the memory. When the fault occurs, the dash warning lamp will illuminate, the STAR tester will light a red indicator (and possibly beep) and the analog meter needle will sweep once.

To enter this mode in the KOER test:

1. Start the engine and run it at 2000 rpm for two minutes. This action warms up the oxygen sensor.

2. Turn the ignition switch **OFF** for 10 seconds.

3. Start the engine.

4. Activate the test, wait 10 seconds, then deactivate and reactivate the test; the system will enter the continuous monitor mode.

5. Tap, move or wiggle the harness, component or connector suspected of causing the problem; If a fault is detected, the code will store in the memory.

6. When the fault occurs, the dash warning lamp will illuminate, the STAR tester will light a red indicator (and possibly beep) and the analog meter needle will sweep once.

OUTPUT STATE CHECK

This testing mode allows the operator to energize and de-energize most of the outputs controlled by the EEC-IV system. Many of the outputs may be checked at the component by listening for a click or feeling the item move or engage by a hand placed on the case. To enter this check:

1. Enter the KOEO test mode.

2. When all codes have been transmitted, depress the accelerator all the way to the floor and release it.

3. The output actuators are now all ON. Depressing the throttle pedal to the floor again switches the all the actuator outputs OFF.

4. This test may be performed as often as necessary, switching between ON and OFF by depressing the throttle.

5. Exit the test by turning the ignition switch **OFF**, disconnecting the jumper at the diagnostic connector or releasing the test button on the scan tool.

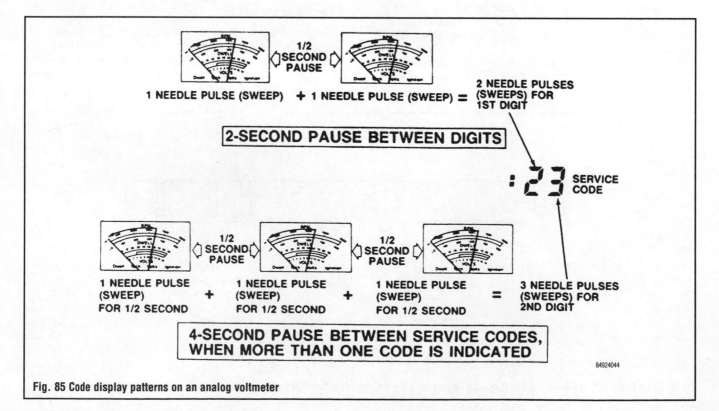

Fig. 85 Code display patterns on an analog voltmeter

Clearing Codes

CONTINUOUS MEMORY CODES

If using a scan tool, use the Clear code command on the tool menu.

If you do not have a scan tool, disconnect the negative battery cable and depress the brake pedal 5–10 times. Reconnect the cable and recheck the system for codes to ensure they have all been erased.

KEEP ALIVE MEMORY

The Keep Alive Memory (KAM) contains the adaptive factors used by the processor to compensate for component tolerances and wear. It should not be routinely cleared during diagnosis. If an emissions related part is replaced during repair, the KAM must be cleared. Failure to clear the KAM may cause severe driveability problems since the correction factor for the old component will be applied to the new component.

To clear the Keep Alive Memory, disconnect the negative battery cable for at least 5 minutes. After the memory is cleared and the battery reconnected, the vehicle must be driven at least 10 miles (16 km) so that the processor may relearn the needed correction factors. The distance to be driven depends on the engine and vehicle, but all drives should include steady-throttle cruise on open roads. Certain driveability problems may be noted during the drive because the adaptive factors are not yet functioning.

EEC-V Systems

GENERAL INFORMATION

The Powertrain Control Module (PCM) is given responsibility for the operation of the emission control devices, cooling fans, ignition and advance and, in some cases, automatic transaxle functions. Because the EEC-V system oversees both the ignition timing and the fuel injector operation, a precise air/fuel ratio will be maintained under all operating conditions. The PCM is a microprocessor or small computer which receives electrical inputs from several sensors, switches and relays on and around the engine.

Based on combinations of these inputs, the PCM controls outputs to various devices concerned with engine operation and emissions. The control module relies on the signals to form a correct picture of current vehicle operation. If any of the input signals is incorrect, the PCM reacts to what ever picture is painted for it. For example, if the coolant temperature sensor is inaccurate and reads too low, the PCM may see a picture of the engine never warming up. Consequently, the engine settings will be maintained as if the engine were cold. Because so many inputs can affect one output, correct diagnostic procedures are essential on these systems.

One part of the PCM is devoted to monitoring both input and output functions within the system. This ability forms the core of the self-diagnostic system. If a problem is detected within a circuit, the control module will recognize the fault, assign it an Diagnostic Trouble Code (DTC), and store the code in memory. The stored code(s) may be retrieved during diagnosis.

While the EEC-V system is capable of recognizing many internal faults, certain faults will not be recognized. Because the control module sees only electrical signals, it cannot sense or react to mechanical or vacuum faults affecting engine operation. Some of these faults may affect another component which will set a code. For example, the PCM monitors the output signal to the fuel injectors, but cannot detect a partially clogged injector. As long as the output driver responds correctly, the computer will read the system as functioning correctly. However, the improper flow of fuel may result in a lean mixture. This would, in turn, be detected by the oxygen sensor and noticed as a constantly lean signal by the PCM. Once the signal falls outside the pre-programmed limits, the control module would notice the fault and set an trouble code.

Additionally, the EEC-V system employs adaptive fuel logic. This process is used to compensate for normal wear and variability within the fuel system. Once the engine enters steady-state operation, the control module watches the oxygen sensor signal for a bias or tendency to run slightly rich or lean. If such a bias is detected, the adaptive logic corrects the fuel delivery to bring the air/fuel mixture towards a centered or 14.7:1 ratio. This compensating shift is stored in a non-volatile memory which is retained by battery power even with the ignition switched OFF. The correction factor is then available the next time the vehicle is operated.

MALFUNCTION INDICATOR LAMP (MIL)

The Malfunction Indicator Lamp (MIL) is located on the instrument panel. The lamp is connected to the control unit and will alert the driver to certain malfunctions within the EEC-V system. When the lamp is illuminated, the PCM has detected a fault and stored an DTC in memory.

The light will stay illuminated as long as the fault is present. Should the fault self-correct, the MIL will extinguish but the stored code will remain in memory.

Under normal operating conditions, the MIL should illuminate briefly when the ignition key is turned ON. This is commonly known as a bulb check. As soon as the PCM receives a signal that the engine is cranking, the lamp should extinguish. The lamp should remain extinguished during the normal operating cycle.

Data Link Connector

▶ See Figures 86 and 87

One Data Link Connector (DLC) is located on the left-hand side of the engine compartment, and a second DLC is located at the lower center of the instrument panel.

The DLC is rectangular in design and capable of allowing access to numerous terminals. The connector has keying features that allow easy connection. The test equipment and the DLC have a latching feature to ensure a good mated connection.

ELECTRICAL TOOLS

The most commonly required electrical diagnostic tool is the Digital Multimeter, allowing voltage, ohmmage (resistance) and amperage to be read by one instrument. Many of the diagnostic charts require the use of a volt or ohmmeter during diagnosis.

The multimeter must be a high impedance unit, with 10 megohms of impedance in the voltmeter. This type of meter will not place an additional load on the circuit it is testing; this is extremely important in low voltage circuits. The multimeter must be of high quality in all respects. It should be handled carefully and protected from impact or damage. Replace the batteries frequently in the unit.

Fig. 86 One DLC is located on the left-hand side of the engine compartment

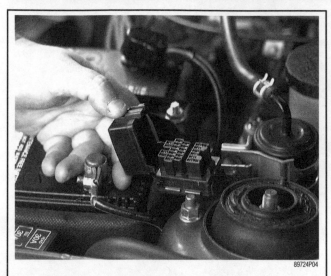

Fig. 87 Remove the cover to gain access to the DLC pins

Fig. 88 When using a scan tool, make sure to follow all of the manufacturer's instructions carefully to ensure proper diagnosis

Reading Codes

 See Figure 88

The EEC-V equipped engines utilize On Board Diagnostic II (OBD-II) DTC's, which are alpha-numeric (they use letters and numbers). The letters in the OBD-II DTC's make it highly difficult to convey the codes through the use of anything but a scan tool. Therefore, to read the codes on these vehicles it is necessary to utilize an OBD-II compatible scan tool.

Since each manufacturer's scan tool is different, please follow the manufacturer's instructions for connecting the tool and obtaining code information.

Clearing Codes

CONTINUOUS MEMORY CODES

These codes are retained in memory for 40 warm-up cycles. To clear the codes for the purposes of testing or confirming repair, perform the code reading procedure. When the fault codes begin to be displayed, de-activate the test by either disconnecting the jumper wire (meter, MIL or message center) or releasing the test button on the hand scanner. Stopping the test during code transmission will erase the Continuous Memory. Do not disconnect the negative battery cable to clear these codes; the Keep Alive memory will be cleared and a new code, 19, will be stored for loss of PCM power.

KEEP ALIVE MEMORY

The Keep Alive Memory (KAM) contains the adaptive factors used by the processor to compensate for component tolerances and wear. It should not be routinely cleared during diagnosis. If an emissions related part is replaced during repair, the KAM must be cleared. Failure to clear the KAM may cause severe driveability problems since the correction factor for the old component will be applied to the new component.

To clear the Keep Alive Memory, disconnect the negative battery cable for at least 5 minutes. After the memory is cleared and the battery reconnected, the vehicle must be driven at least 10 miles so that the processor may relearn the needed correction factors. The distance to be driven depends on the engine and vehicle, but all drives should include steady-throttle cruise on open roads. Certain driveability problems may be noted during the drive because the adaptive factors are not yet functioning.

VACUUM DIAGRAMS

Following are vacuum diagrams for most of the engine and emissions package combinations covered by this manual. Because vacuum circuits will vary based on various engine and vehicle options, always refer first to the vehicle emission control information label, if present. Should the label be missing, or should the vehicle be equipped with a different engine from the vehicle's original equipment, refer to the diagrams below for the same or similar configuration.

If you wish to obtain a replacement emissions label, most manufacturers make the labels available for purchase. The labels can usually be ordered from a local dealer.

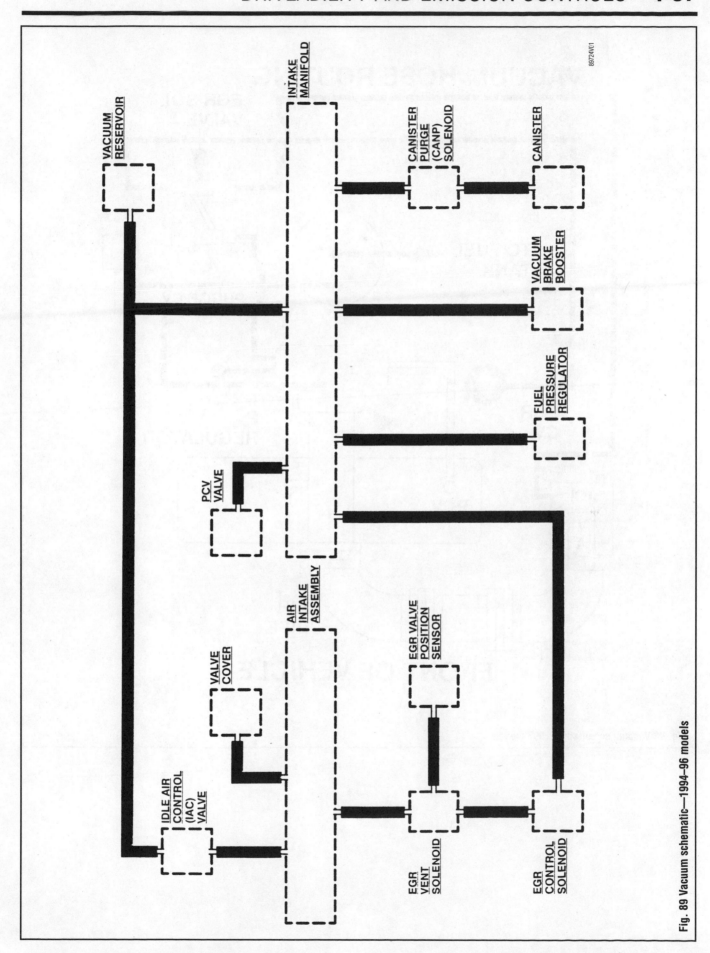

Fig. 89 Vacuum schematic—1994—96 models

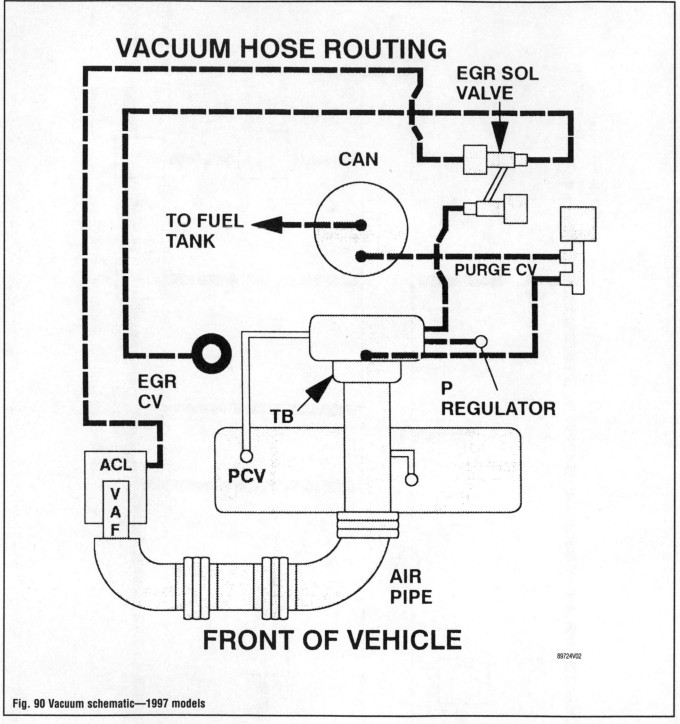

VACUUM HOSE ROUTING

EGR SOL VALVE

CAN

TO FUEL TANK

PURGE CV

EGR CV

TB

P REGULATOR

ACL

V A F

PCV

AIR PIPE

FRONT OF VEHICLE

89724V02

Fig. 90 Vacuum schematic—1997 models

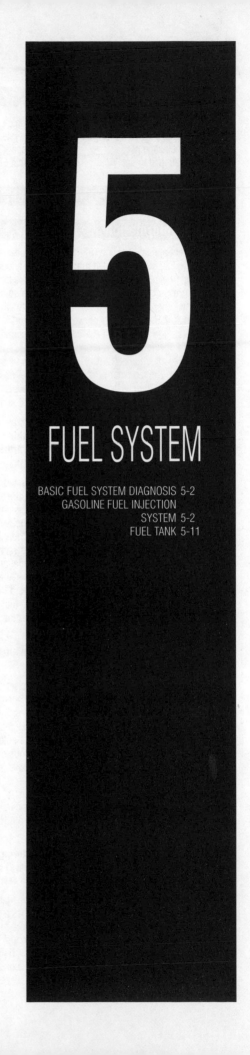

5

FUEL SYSTEM

BASIC FUEL SYSTEM DIAGNOSIS

When there is a problem starting or driving a vehicle, two of the most important checks involve the ignition and the fuel systems. The questions most mechanics attempt to answer first, "is there spark?" and "is there fuel?" will often lead to solving most basic problems. For ignition system diagnosis and TESTING, please refer to the information on engine electrical components and ignition systems found earlier in this manual. If the ignition system checks out (there is spark), then you must determine if the fuel system is operating properly (is there fuel?).

GASOLINE FUEL INJECTION SYSTEM

General Information

The Sequential Fuel Injection (SFI) system includes a high pressure, inline electric fuel pump mounted in the fuel tank, a fuel supply manifold, a throttle body (meters the incoming air charge for the correct mixture with the fuel), a pressure regulator, fuel filters, and both solid and flexible fuel lines. The fuel supply manifold includes 4 electronically-controlled fuel injectors, each mounted directly above an intake port in the lower intake manifold. Each injector fires once every other crankshaft revolution, in sequence with the engine firing order.

The fuel pressure regulator maintains a constant pressure drop across the injector nozzles. The regulator is attached to the fuel injection supply manifold downstream of the injectors. Any excess fuel supplied by the fuel pump passes through the regulator and is returned to the fuel tank via a return line.

➡**The pressure regulator maintains fuel pressure at 30–38 psi (206–262 kPa) under normal operating conditions. At idle or high manifold vacuum condition, fuel pressure is further reduced to approximately 30 psi (206 kPa).**

The fuel pressure regulator is a diaphragm-operated relief valve, in which one side of the diaphragm senses fuel pressure and the other side senses manifold vacuum. Normal fuel pressure is established by a spring preload applied to the diaphragm. Control of the fuel system is maintained through the Powertrain Control Module (PCM), although electrical power is routed through the fuel pump relay and an inertia switch. The fuel pump relay is normally located behind the instrument panel at the left-hand cowl panel and the inertia switch is located behind the left-hand luggage compartment side cover. The inline fuel pump is mounted in the fuel tank.

The inertia switch opens the power circuit to the fuel pump in the event of a collision or roll over. Once tripped, the switch must be reset manually by pushing the reset button on the assembly.

➡**Check that the inertia switch is reset before diagnosing power supply problems to the fuel pump.**

Fuel injectors used with the SFI system are an electro-mechanical (solenoid) type, designed to meter and atomize fuel delivered to the intake ports of the engine. The injectors are mounted in the lower intake manifold and positioned so that their spray nozzles direct the fuel charge to the back face of the intake valves. The injector body consists of a solenoid-actuated pintle and needle-valve assembly. The control unit sends an electrical impulse that activates the solenoid, causing the pintle to move inward off the seat and allow the fuel to flow. The amount of fuel delivered is controlled by the length of time the injector is energized (pulse width), since the fuel flow orifice is fixed and the fuel pressure drop across the injector tip is constant. Correct atomization is achieved by contouring the pintle at the point where the fuel enters the pintle chamber.

➡**Exercise care when handling fuel injectors during service. Be careful not to lose the pintle cap and always replace O-rings to assure a tight seal. Never apply direct battery voltage to test a fuel injector.**

The injectors receive high-pressure fuel from the fuel supply manifold (fuel rail) assembly. The complete assembly includes a tubular rail, fuel injector connectors, mounting flange for the pressure regulator, and mounting attachments to locate the manifold and provide fuel injector retainers.

The fuel supply manifold is normally removed with the fuel injectors and pressure regulator attached. Fuel injector electrical connectors are plastic and have locking tabs that must be released when disconnecting the wiring harness.

FUEL SYSTEM SERVICE PRECAUTIONS

Safety is the most important factor when performing not only fuel system maintenance, but any type of maintenance. Failure to conduct maintenance and repairs in a safe manner may result in serious personal injury or death. Work on a vehicle's fuel system components can be accomplished safely and effectively by adhering to the following rules and guidelines.

• To avoid the possibility of fire and personal injury, always disconnect the negative battery cable unless the repair or test procedure requires that battery voltage be applied.

• Always relieve fuel system pressure prior to disconnecting any fuel system component (injector, fuel rail, pressure regulator, etc.) fitting or fuel line connection. Exercise extreme caution whenever relieving fuel system pressure to avoid exposing skin, face and eyes to fuel spray. Please be advised that fuel under pressure may penetrate the skin or any part of the body that it contacts.

• Always place a shop towel or cloth around the fitting or connection prior to loosening to absorb any excess fuel due to spillage. Ensure that all fuel spillage is quickly remove from engine surfaces. Ensure that all fuel-soaked cloths or towels are deposited into a flame-proof waste container with a lid.

• Always keep a dry chemical (Class B) fire extinguisher near the work area.

• Do not allow fuel spray or fuel vapors to come into contact with a spark or open flame.

• Always use a second wrench when loosening or tightening fuel line connection fittings. This will prevent unnecessary stress and torsion to the fuel piping. Always adhere to the proper torque specifications.

• Always replace worn fuel fitting O-rings with new ones. Do not substitute fuel hose where rigid pipe is installed.

Relieving Fuel System Pressure

◗ **See Figure 1**

❋❋ WARNING

Fuel lines can remain pressurized for a long period of time after the engine has been turned off. Always relieve the fuel system pressure before performing any service on the fuel system.

1. Remove the fuel tank filler cap.
2. Unplug the fuel pump relay electrical connection which is located behind the left-hand side of the instrument panel.
3. Turn the engine **ON** and let it idle normally.
4. The engine will stall, when it does, turn the ignition key **OFF** and engage the fuel pump relay electrical connection.
5. The fuel system pressure has now been relieved and will remain so until the engine is turned **ON**.

Inertia Switch

GENERAL INFORMATION

◗ **See Figures 2 and 3**

This switch shuts off the fuel pump in the event of a collision. Once the switch has been tripped, it must be reset manually in order to start the engine.

The inertia switch is located behind the left-hand luggage compartment side cover.

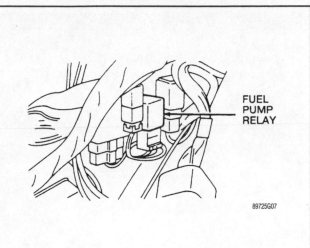

Fig. 1 The fuel pump relay electrical connection is located behind the left-hand side of the instrument panel

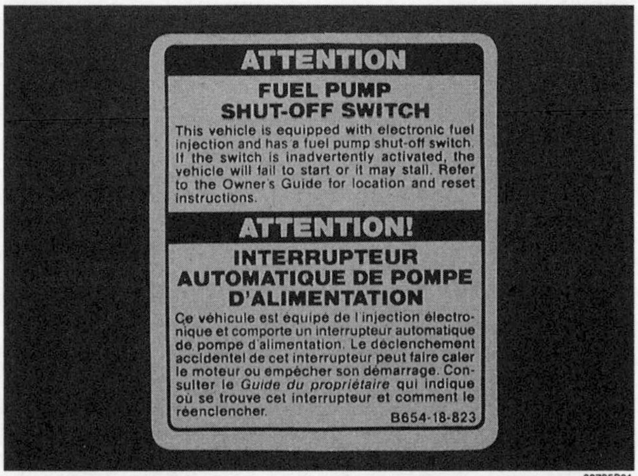

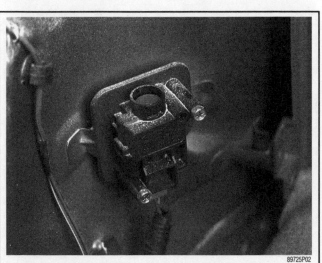

Fig. 2 The fuel pump shut-off (inertia) switch label is located under the hood. Refer to this manual or your owner's manual for the resetting procedure

Fig. 3 The inertia switch is located behind the left-hand luggage compartment side cover

RESETTING THE SWITCH

♦ See Figures 4 and 5

1. Turn the ignition switch **OFF**.

2. Ensure that there is no fuel leaking in the engine compartment, along any of the lines or at the tank. There should be no odor of fuel as well.

3. Remove the inertia switch cover on the left side of the luggage compartment to gain access to the switch.

4. If no leakage and/or odor is apparent, reset the switch by pushing the reset button on the switch.

5. Cycle the ignition switch from the **ON** to **OFF** positions several times, allowing five seconds at each position, to build fuel pressure within the system.

6. Again, check the fuel system for leaks. There should be no odor of fuel as well.

7. If there is no leakage and/or odor of fuel, it is safe to operate the vehicle. However, it is recommended that the entire system be checked by a professional, especially if the vehicle was in an accident severe enough to trip the inertia switch.

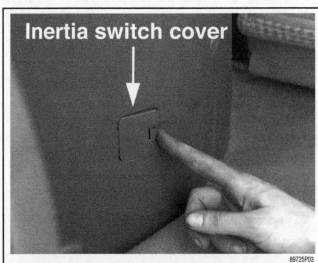

Fig. 4 Remove the inertia switch cover on the left side of the luggage compartment to gain access to the switch

Fig. 5 Push the button to reset the inertia switch

REMOVAL & INSTALLATION

1. Disconnect the negative battery cable.
2. Remove the cover from the left side of the luggage compartment.
3. Unplug the inertia switch electrical connection.
4. Loosen the two switch retaining screws and remove the switch.

To install:

5. Install the switch and tighten the retaining screws.
6. Engage the switch electrical connection.
7. Install the cover to the left side of the luggage compartment.
8. Connect the negative battery cable.

Fuel Pump

REMOVAL & INSTALLATION

▶ See Figures 6 thru 13

✳✳ CAUTION

Observe all applicable safety precautions when working around fuel. Whenever servicing the fuel system, always work in a well ventilated area. Do not allow fuel spray or vapors to come in contact with a spark or open flame. Keep a dry chemical fire extinguisher near the work area. Always keep fuel in a container specifically designed for fuel storage; also, always properly seal fuel containers to avoid the possibility of fire or explosion.

1. Properly relieve the fuel system pressure.
2. Disconnect the negative battery cable.
3. Remove the rear seat cushion and cover.
4. Loosen the three upper and three lower luggage compartment floor covering hold-down pins, and fold the cover forward until the fuel pump assembly access plate can be seen.
5. Loosen the access plate retaining screws, disengage the ground lead and remove the access plate.
6. Disengage the fuel pump electrical connection.
7. On four-door models, loosen the fuel vapor shut-off valve bolt and remove the evaporative emission tube shut-off valve from the bracket on the fuel pump housing.
8. Loosen the fuel pump hose clamp(s) and disconnect the hose(s) from the fuel pump housing.
9. Loosen the retaining screws and lift the fuel pump assembly from the tank.

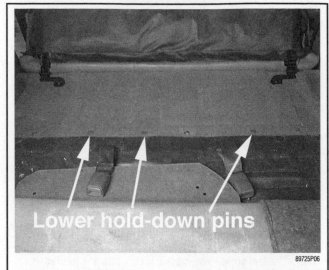

Fig. 7 . . . and loosen the lower covering's hold-down pins

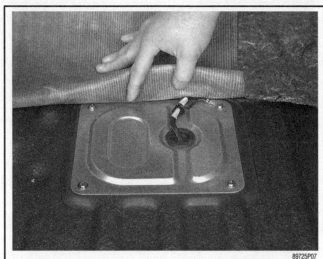

Fig. 8 Roll back the lower floor covering to find the fuel pump assembly's access cover

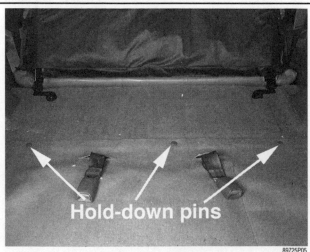

Fig. 6 Loosen the upper floor covering's hold-down pins, then roll back the covering . . .

Fig. 9 Loosen the retaining screws, disengage the electrical connection and remove the access plate

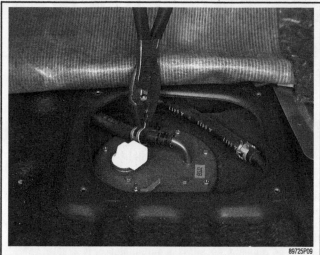

Fig. 10 Use pliers to disengage the fuel pump hose clamp, then disconnect the hose from the pump housing

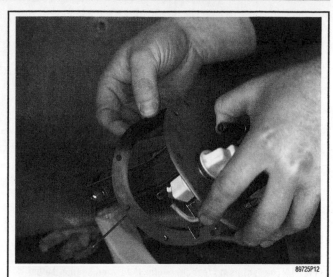

Fig. 13 If necessary, remove the pump assembly gasket

Fig. 11 Use a Phillips head screwdriver to loosen the pump assembly retaining screws . . .

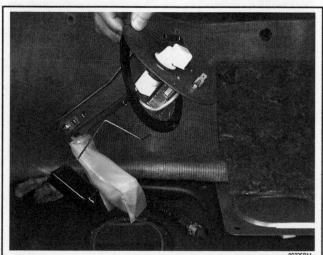

Fig. 12 . . . then lift the pump assembly up and out of the fuel tank

10. If necessary, remove the pump assembly gasket.

11. Unplug the fuel level sensor electrical connection.

12. Remove the fuel level sensor nuts and washers.

13. Remove the fuel level sensor.

14. Loosen the fuel pump screw, then remove the fuel pump grommet and bracket from the bottom of the pump.

15. Remove the fuel tank sender filter bracket, sender filter and sender filter retainer from the pump.

16. Unplug the fuel pump electrical connection.

17. Loosen the clamp and remove the pump from the housing.

To install:

18. Position the pump on the housing and tighten the clamp.

19. Engage the pump electrical connection.

20. Install the fuel tank sender, filter, sender filter retainer and filter bracket.

21. Install the fuel pump bracket and grommet, then tighten the pump screw.

22. Position the fuel level sensor on the pump assembly housing, install the washers and tighten the retaining nuts.

23. Engage the sensor electrical connection.

24. If removed, install a new pump assembly gasket.

25. Install the pump assembly in the tank and tighten the retaining screws.

26. Connect the fuel pump hoses and tighten the clamps.

27. On four-door models, place the evaporative emission tube shut-off valve on the fuel valve assembly and tighten the fuel vapor shut-off valve bolt.

28. Engage the fuel pump electrical connection.

29. Connect the negative battery cable.

30. Start the engine and check for fuel leaks at the fuel line connections.

31. Connect the ground lead, install the access plate and tighten the retaining screws.

32. Fold the luggage compartment floor cover over the access plate and install the hold-down pins.

33. Install the seat cushion and cover.

TESTING

◆ See Figure 14

※※ **CAUTION**

Observe all applicable safety precautions when working around fuel. Whenever servicing the fuel system, always work in a well ventilated area. Do not allow fuel spray or vapors to come

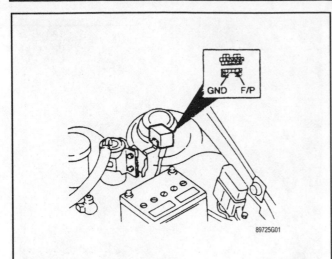

Fig. 14 The fuel pump test connector is located beside the battery

in contact with a spark or open flame. Keep a dry chemical fire extinguisher near the work area. Always keep fuel in a container specifically designed for fuel storage; also, always properly seal fuel containers to avoid the possibility of fire or explosion.

1. Properly relieve the fuel system pressure.
2. Connect Rotunda fuel pressure testing kit 134-R0087 or its equivalent with a Multi-port Fuel Injection (MFI) test adapter D87C-9974-A in the fuel line between the fuel rails, with its main valve open and its drain valve closed.
3. Using a jumper wire, connect the fuel pump test terminal to ground. Refer to the accompanying illustration.
4. Turn the key **ON**. The fuel pressure should be 38–46 psi (265–320 kPa).
5. If the pump pressure reads within specifications, the pump is fully operational; if not, continue with the test.

➡Check that the inertia switch is reset before diagnosing power supply problems to the fuel pump.

6. Turn the ignition key **OFF** and remove the pump relay.
7. Turn the ignition key **ON**.
8. Using a high impedance Digital Volt Ohmmeter (DVOM), measure the voltage in the yellow wire with the black stripe at the relay connector. The voltage should be 10–14 volts. If not, check the wire(s) for damage.
9. Turn the ignition key **OFF** and unplug the fuel pump electrical connection at the pump.
10. Using a jumper wire, connect the fuel pump test terminal to ground. Refer to the accompanying illustration.
11. Turn the ignition key **ON**.
12. Using a high impedance Digital Volt Ohmmeter (DVOM), measure the voltage in the green wire with the yellow stripe at the pump's vehicle harness connector. The voltage should be 10–14 volts. If not, check the wire(s) for damage.
13. Turn the ignition key **OFF**.
14. Measure the resistance between the green wire and ground. If the resistance is less than 5 ohms and the pump has passed all the other electrical tests, replace the pump.

Throttle Body

REMOVAL & INSTALLATION

▶ See Figures 15 thru 21

1. Disconnect the negative battery cable.
2. Drain and recycle the engine coolant.

✸✸ CAUTION

Never open, service or drain the radiator or cooling system when hot; serious burns can occur from the steam and hot coolant. Also, when draining engine coolant, keep in mind that cats and dogs are attracted to ethylene glycol antifreeze and could drink any that is left in an uncovered container or in puddles on the ground. This will prove fatal in sufficient quantities. Always drain coolant into a sealable container. Coolant should be reused unless it is contaminated or is several years old.

Fig. 15 Location of the idle switch

Fig. 16 Unplug the throttle position sensor electrical connections

3. Remove the air cleaner inlet tube, then disconnect the accelerator cable from the throttle lever.

4. Unplug the idle switch and Throttle Position (TP) sensor electrical connections.

5. Loosen the throttle body nut and the three retaining bolts. Slide the throttle body off the stud on the upper intake manifold.

6. If necessary, maneuver the throttle body so that you can gain access to the coolant hoses.

7. Tag the hoses, tilt the throttle body back and disconnect the coolant hoses.

8. Remove the throttle body and gasket from the engine. Discard the gasket.

To install:

9. Clean the throttle body mounting surfaces with a scraper until all the old gasket material is removed.

10. Position a new gasket and install the throttle body.

11. Connect the coolant hoses to the throttle body and finger-tighten the retaining nut and bolts.

12. Use a torque wrench to tighten the nut and bolts to 14–19 ft. lbs. (19–25 Nm).

13. Engage the TP sensor and idle switch electrical connections.

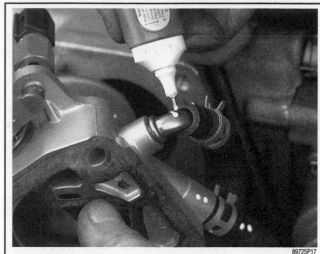

Fig. 19 Mark the coolant hoses that are connected to the throttle body

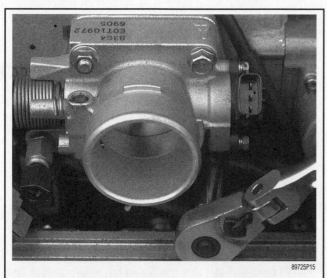

Fig. 17 Unfasten the throttle body assembly retaining fasteners

Fig. 20 Compress the hose clamps with pliers and slide them back, then disconnect the hoses

Fig. 18 Slide the throttle body off the stud on the upper intake manifold

Fig. 21 Remove the throttle body gasket and replace it with a new one

14. Connect the accelerator cable to the throttle lever and install the air cleaner inlet tube.
15. Replenish the cooling system and connect the negative battery cable.
16. Turn the ignition key from **ACC** to **ON** several times without starting the engine and check for fuel leaks.
17. Start the car and check for fuel and coolant leaks in and around the throttle body.

Fuel Injectors

REMOVAL & INSTALLATION

▶ **See Figures 22 thru 30**

✳✳ CAUTION

Observe all applicable safety precautions when working around fuel. Whenever servicing the fuel system, always work in a well ventilated area. Do not allow fuel spray or vapors to come in contact with a spark or open flame. Keep a dry chemical fire extinguisher near the work area. Always keep fuel in a container specifically designed for fuel storage; also, always properly seal fuel containers to avoid the possibility of fire or explosion.

1. Properly relieve the fuel system pressure.
2. Disconnect the negative battery cable.
3. Remove the upper intake manifold.
4. Tag, disconnect and plug the fuel lines.
5. Unplug the fuel injector electrical connections.
6. Loosen the fuel supply manifold (fuel rail) retaining bolts.

➡**Make sure that the insulators do not get lost when removing the fuel injection supply manifold (rail).**

7. Remove the fuel injection supply manifold (fuel rail) and the insulators. The injectors will come off with the manifold.

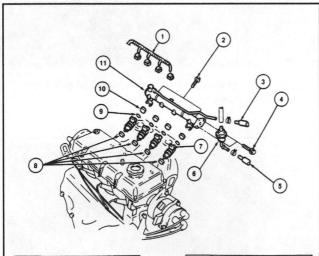

Item	Description
1	Fuel Charging Wiring
2	Fuel Injection Supply Manifold Bolts (2 Req'd)
3	Fuel Tube Hose
4	Fuel Pressure Regulator Bolts (2 Req'd)
5	Fuel Hose
6	Fuel Pressure Regulator
7	Fuel Injector

Item	Description
8	Fuel Injector O-Rings
9	O-Rings
10	Fuel Injector Insulators
11	Fuel Injection Supply Manifold

89725G05

Fig. 22 Exploded view of the fuel injectors and supply manifold assembly

8. Remove the injectors from the fuel rail.
9. Remove and discard the fuel injector O-rings and the insulators.

To install:

➡**Always use new O-rings and insulators on the injectors when installing them.**

10. Install new O-rings and insulators on the fuel injectors.
11. Engage the injectors to the fuel supply rail.

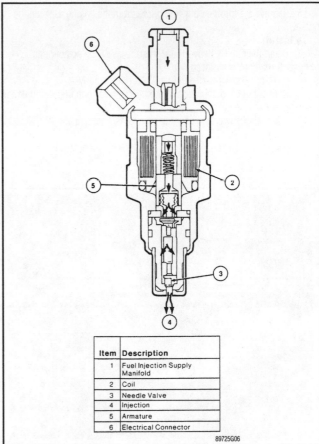

Item	Description
1	Fuel Injection Supply Manifold
2	Coil
3	Needle Valve
4	Injection
5	Armature
6	Electrical Connector

89725G06

Fig. 23 Cross-sectional view of a typical fuel injector used in the SFI system

89725P24

Fig. 24 Unplug the fuel injector electrical connections

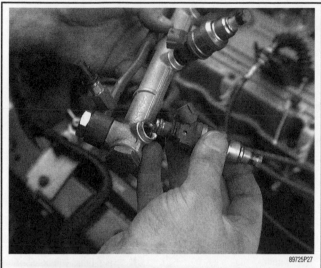

Fig. 25 Remove the injectors from the fuel rail

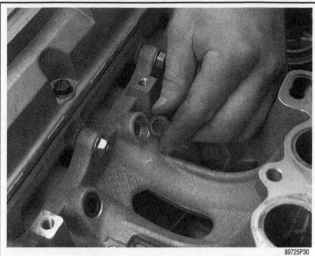

Fig. 28 Remove and discard the lower O-rings from the lower intake manifold

Fig. 26 Remove and discard the upper O-ring . . .

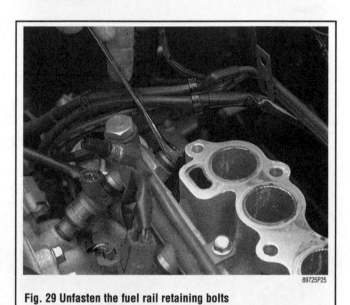

Fig. 29 Unfasten the fuel rail retaining bolts

Fig. 27 . . . and insulator from each fuel injector

Fig. 30 Remove the fuel rail and injectors as an assembly

12. Guide the injectors into their bores while installing the fuel supply manifold (rail) assembly.

13. Install the supply manifold retaining bolts and tighten them to 14–17 ft. lbs. (19–23 Nm).

14. Engage the injector electrical connections.

15. Connect the fuel lines and install the upper intake manifold.

16. Connect the negative battery cable.

17. Turn the ignition key from **ACC** to **ON** several times without starting the engine and check for fuel leaks.

TESTING

▶ **See Figure 31**

➡**Do not connect a test light to the injector harness, as this may cause damage to the Powertrain Control Module (PCM).**

1. Disconnect the engine wiring harness from the fuel injector.

➡**This may require removing the upper intake manifold or other engine components.**

2. Measure the resistance of the injector by probing one terminal with the positive lead and the other injector terminal with the negative lead of an ohmmeter.

3. The resistance should be 12–16 ohms at 68°F (20°C).

4. If resistance is not within specification, the fuel injector may be faulty.

5. If resistance is within specification, install a noid light and check for injector pulse from the PCM while cranking the engine.

6. If injector pulse is present, check for proper fuel pressure.

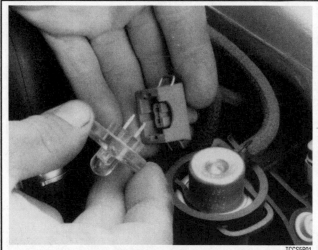

TCCS5P01

Fig. 31 A noid light can be attached to the fuel injector harness in order to test for injector pulse

Fuel Supply Manifold

REMOVAL & INSTALLATION

▶ **See Figures 22, 29 and 30**

❊❊ **CAUTION**

Observe all applicable safety precautions when working around fuel. Whenever servicing the fuel system, always work in a well ventilated area. Do not allow fuel spray or vapors to come in contact with a spark or open flame. Keep a dry chemical fire extinguisher near the work area. Always keep fuel in a container specifically designed for fuel storage; also, always properly seal fuel containers to avoid the possibility of fire or explosion.

1. Properly relieve the fuel system pressure.

2. Disconnect the negative battery cable.

3. Remove the upper intake manifold.

4. Tag, disconnect and plug the fuel lines.

5. Unplug the fuel injector electrical connections.

6. Loosen the fuel supply manifold (fuel rail) retaining bolts.

➡**Make sure that the insulators do not get lost when removing the fuel supply manifold.**

7. Remove the fuel supply manifold and the insulators. The injectors will come off with the manifold.

To install:

8. Guide the injectors into their bores while installing the fuel supply manifold assembly.

9. Install the supply manifold retaining bolts and tighten them to 14–17 ft. lbs. (19–23 Nm).

10. Engage the injector electrical connections.

11. Connect the fuel lines and install the upper intake manifold.

12. Connect the negative battery cable.

13. Turn the ignition key from **ACC** to **ON** several times without starting the engine and check for fuel leaks.

Fuel Pressure Regulator

REMOVAL & INSTALLATION

▶ **See Figures 32, 33, 34, 35 and 36**

1. Properly relieve the fuel system pressure.

2. Disconnect the negative battery cable.

3. Disconnect the vacuum supply hose from the top of the fuel pressure regulator.

4. Tag, disconnect and plug the fuel line.

5. Loosen the two pressure regulator mounting bolts and remove the pressure regulator.

6. Remove and discard the pressure regulator O-ring seal.

To install:

7. Install a new O-ring seal and place the pressure regulator in position.

8. Install the pressure regulator mounting bolts and tighten them to 71–97 inch lbs. (8–11 Nm).

9. Engage the fuel line and the pressure regulator vacuum hose.

10. Connect the negative battery cable.

11. Turn the ignition key from **ACC** to **ON** several times without starting the engine and check for fuel leaks.

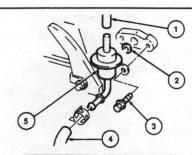

Item	Description
1	Vacuum Supply Hose
2	O-Ring Seal
3	Fuel Pressure Regulator Bolt (2 Req'd)
4	Fuel Hose
5	Fuel Pressure Regulator

89725G08

Fig. 32 Exploded view of the fuel pressure regulator mounting

Fig. 33 Disconnect the fuel line from the pressure regulator

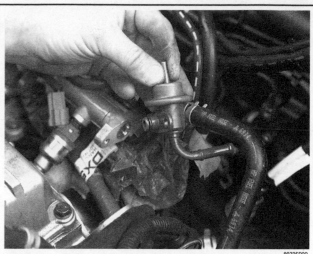

Fig. 35 . . . and remove the pressure regulator from the fuel rail

Fig. 34 Unbolt the fuel pressure regulator retainers . . .

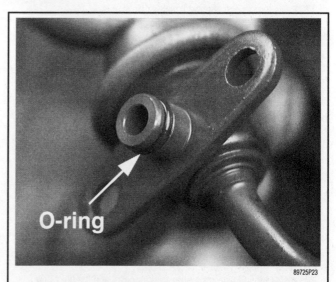

Fig. 36 Replace the pressure regulator O-ring with a new one

FUEL TANK

Tank Assembly

REMOVAL & INSTALLATION

Two-Door Models

▶ See Figure 37

❊❊ CAUTION

Observe all applicable safety precautions when working around fuel. Whenever servicing the fuel system, always work in a well ventilated area. Do not allow fuel spray or vapors to come in contact with a spark or open flame. Keep a dry chemical fire extinguisher near the work area. Always keep fuel in a container specifically designed for fuel storage; also, always properly seal fuel containers to avoid the possibility of fire or explosion.

1. Properly relieve the fuel system pressure.
2. Disconnect the negative battery cable.
3. Remove the left-hand quarter trim panel.
4. Loosen the three luggage compartment floor cover hold-down pins and fold the cover forward until the fuel pump assembly access plate can be seen.
5. Loosen the access plate retaining screws, lift the access plate and disengage the sending unit electrical connection.
6. Disconnect the fuel supply line from the sending unit and plug the line to avoid contamination.
7. Disconnect the fuel return line from the top of the fuel tank.
8. Loosen the inner rear floor filler cover bolts (6) and the inner rear floor filler cover nuts (2).
9. Remove the inner floor and disconnect the fuel tank-to-filler pipe hose and the three fuel vapor hoses from the tank.
10. Loosen the hose clamp and disconnect the fuel tank-to-filler pipe hose from the tank.
11. Disconnect the overflow hose from the tank.

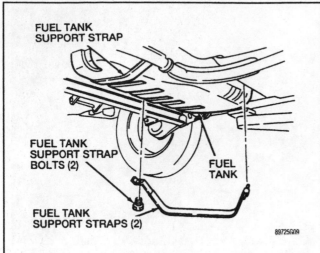

Fig. 37 Unfasten the fuel tank retaining strap bolts and remove the straps

12. Raise the car and support it with safety stands.

13. Use a pair of pliers to squeeze and compress the vapor hose clamp and disconnect the hose from the fuel evaporation pipe.

14. Loosen the tank support strap bolts and remove the straps.

15. Loosen the fuel tank bolts (4), move the tank towards the left and remove it from the car.

To install:

16. Slide the tank into position, then install the retaining straps and bolts. Tighten the bolts to 13–19 ft. lbs. (18–26 Nm).

17. Connect the vapor hose to the evaporation pipe.

18. Remove the safety stands and lower the car.

19. Connect the fuel vapor and overflow hoses to the tank.

20. Connect the filler pipe, return line and supply lines.

21. Add fuel to the tank and visually inspect for leaks.

22. Connect the negative battery cable.

23. Start the car and check for fuel leaks.

24. Install the inner rear floor cover and the retaining bolts. Tighten the bolts and cover nuts to 8–16 ft. lbs. (10–23 Nm).

25. Engage the fuel sending unit electrical connection and install the access plate. Tighten the access plate screws.

26. Install the luggage compartment floor cover and the hold-down pins.

27. Install the left-hand quarter trim panel.

28. Install the rear seat cushion and cover.

Four-Door Models

♦ See Figure 37

☼☼ CAUTION

Observe all applicable safety precautions when working around fuel. Whenever servicing the fuel system, always work in a well ventilated area. Do not allow fuel spray or vapors to come in contact with a spark or open flame. Keep a dry chemical fire extinguisher near the work area. Always keep fuel in a container specifically designed for fuel storage; also, always properly seal fuel containers to avoid the possibility of fire or explosion.

1. Properly relieve the fuel system pressure.

2. Disconnect the negative battery cable.

3. Remove the left-hand quarter trim panel.

4. Loosen the three luggage compartment floor cover hold-down pins and fold the cover forward until the fuel pump assembly access plate can be seen.

5. Loosen the access plate retaining screws, lift the access plate and disengage the sending unit electrical connection.

6. Disconnect the fuel supply line from the sending unit and plug the line to avoid contamination.

7. Disconnect the fuel return line from the top of the fuel tank.

8. Raise the car and support it with safety stands.

9. Position a jack beneath the fuel tank.

10. Loosen the two screw type clamps and remove the tank-to-filler pipe hose and the overflow hose.

11. Loosen the tank support strap bolts and remove the straps.

12. Push the brake hose clip through the bracket on the tank and position the parking brake cable and conduit aside.

➡**Make sure the tank-to-filler pipe hose and the parking brake cable are positioned in such a way as not to interfere with tank removal.**

13. Lower the tank and remove it from the car.

To install:

14. Place the tank on the jack, position the parking brake cable and conduit, then engage the brake hose clip to the bracket.

15. Raise the tank into position, install the support straps and bolts. Tighten the bolts to 33–44 ft. lbs. (44–60 Nm).

16. Remove the safety stands and lower the car.

17. Connect the tank-to-filler pipe hose, the overflow hose and overflow pipe on the tank. Tighten all clamps.

18. Connect the fuel return and supply lines.

19. Add fuel to the tank and visually inspect for leaks.

20. Connect the negative battery cable.

21. Start the car and check for fuel leaks.

22. Engage the fuel sending unit electrical connection and install the access plate. Tighten the access plate screws.

23. Install the luggage compartment floor cover and the hold-down pins.

24. Install the left-hand quarter trim panel.

25. Install the rear seat cushion and cover.

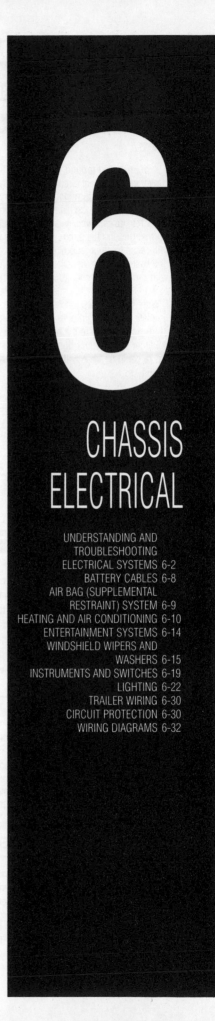

6

CHASSIS
ELECTRICAL

UNDERSTANDING AND TROUBLESHOOTING ELECTRICAL SYSTEMS

Basic Electrical Theory

♦ **See Figure 1**

For any 12 volt, negative ground, electrical system to operate, the electricity must travel in a complete circuit. This simply means that current (power) from the positive (+) terminal of the battery must eventually return to the negative (-) terminal of the battery. Along the way, this current will travel through wires, fuses, switches and components. If, for any reason, the flow of current through the circuit is interrupted, the component fed by that circuit will cease to function properly.

Perhaps the easiest way to visualize a circuit is to think of connecting a light bulb (with two wires attached to it) to the battery—one wire attached to the negative (-) terminal of the battery and the other wire to the positive (+) terminal. With the two wires touching the battery terminals, the circuit would be complete and the light bulb would illuminate. Electricity would follow a path from the battery to the bulb and back to the battery. It's easy to see that with longer wires on our light bulb, it could be mounted anywhere. Further, one wire could be fitted with a switch so that the light could be turned on and off.

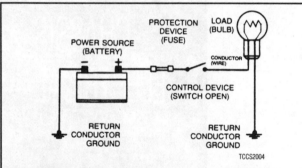

Fig. 1 This example illustrates a simple circuit. When the switch is closed, power from the positive (+) battery terminal flows through the fuse and the switch, and then to the light bulb. The light illuminates and the circuit is completed through the ground wire back to the negative (-) battery terminal. In reality, the two ground points shown in the illustration are attached to the metal frame of the vehicle, which completes the circuit back to the battery

The normal automotive circuit differs from this simple example in two ways. First, instead of having a return wire from the bulb to the battery, the current travels through the frame of the vehicle. Since the negative (-) battery cable is attached to the frame (made of electrically conductive metal), the frame of the vehicle can serve as a ground wire to complete the circuit. Secondly, most automotive circuits contain multiple components which receive power from a single circuit. This lessens the amount of wire needed to power components on the vehicle.

HOW DOES ELECTRICITY WORK: THE WATER ANALOGY

Electricity is the flow of electrons—the subatomic particles that constitute the outer shell of an atom. Electrons spin in an orbit around the center core of an atom. The center core is comprised of protons (positive charge) and neutrons (neutral charge). Electrons have a negative charge and balance out the positive charge of the protons. When an outside force causes the number of electrons to unbalance the charge of the protons, the electrons

will split off the atom and look for another atom to balance out. If this imbalance is kept up, electrons will continue to move and an electrical flow will exist.

Many people have been taught electrical theory using an analogy with water. In a comparison with water flowing through a pipe, the electrons would be the water and the wire is the pipe.

The flow of electricity can be measured much like the flow of water through a pipe. The unit of measurement used is amperes, frequently abbreviated as amps (a). You can compare amperage to the volume of water flowing through a pipe. When connected to a circuit, an ammeter will measure the actual amount of current flowing through the circuit. When relatively few electrons flow through a circuit, the amperage is low. When many electrons flow, the amperage is high.

Water pressure is measured in units such as pounds per square inch (psi); The electrical pressure is measured in units called volts (v). When a voltmeter is connected to a circuit, it is measuring the electrical pressure.

The actual flow of electricity depends not only on voltage and amperage, but also on the resistance of the circuit. The higher the resistance, the higher the force necessary to push the current through the circuit. The standard unit for measuring resistance is an ohm (Ω) Resistance in a circuit varies depending on the amount and type of components used in the circuit. The main factors which determine resistance are:

• Material—some materials have more resistance than others. Those with high resistance are said to be insulators. Rubber materials (or rubber-like plastics) are some of the most common insulators used in vehicles as they have a very high resistance to electricity. Very low resistance materials are said to be conductors. Copper wire is among the best conductors. Silver is actually a superior conductor to copper and is used in some relay contacts, but its high cost prohibits its use as common wiring. Most automotive wiring is made of copper.

• Size—the larger the wire size being used, the less resistance the wire will have. This is why components which use large amounts of electricity usually have large wires supplying current to them.

• Length—for a given thickness of wire, the longer the wire, the greater the resistance. The shorter the wire, the less the resistance. When determining the proper wire for a circuit, both size and length must be considered to design a circuit that can handle the current needs of the component.

• Temperature—with many materials, the higher the temperature, the greater the resistance (positive temperature coefficient). Some materials exhibt the opposite trait of lower resistance with higher temperatures (negative temperature coefficient). These principles are used in many of the sensors on the engine.

OHM'S LAW

There is a direct relationship between current, voltage and resistance. The relationship between current, voltage and resistance can be summed up by a statement known as Ohm's law.

Voltage (E) is equal to amperage (I) times resistance (R): $E = I \times R$

Other forms of the formula are $R = E/I$ and $I = E/R$

In each of these formulas, E is the voltage in volts, I is the current in amps and R is the resistance in ohms. The basic point to remember is that as the resistance of a circuit goes up, the amount of current that flows in the circuit will go down, if voltage remains the same.

The amount of work that the electricity can perform is expressed as power. The unit of power is the watt (w). The relationship between power, voltage and current is expressed as:

Power (w) is equal to amperage (I) times voltage (E): $W = I \times E$

This is only true for direct current (DC) circuits; The alternating current formula is a tad different, but since the electrical circuits in most vehicles are DC type, we need not get into AC circuit theory.

Electrical Components

POWER SOURCE

Power is supplied to the vehicle by two devices: The battery and the alternator. The battery supplies electrical power during starting or during periods when the current demand of the vehicle's electrical system exceeds the output capacity of the alternator. The alternator supplies electrical current when the engine is running. Just not does the alternator supply the current needs of the vehicle, but it recharges the battery.

The Battery

In most modern vehicles, the battery is a lead/acid electrochemical device consisting of six 2 volt subsections (cells) connected in series, so that the unit is capable of producing approximately 12 volts of electrical pressure. Each subsection consists of a series of positive and negative plates held a short distance apart in a solution of sulfuric acid and water.

The two types of plates are of dissimilar metals. This sets up a chemical reaction, and it is this reaction which produces current flow from the battery when its positive and negative terminals are connected to an electrical load. The power removed from the battery is replaced by the alternator, restoring the battery to its original chemical state.

The Alternator

On some vehicles there isn't an alternator, but a generator. The difference is that an alternator supplies alternating current which is then changed to direct current for use on the vehicle, while a generator produces direct current. Alternators tend to be more efficient and that is why they are used.

Alternators and generators are devices that consist of coils of wires wound together making big electromagnets. One group of coils spins within another set and the interaction of the magnetic fields causes a current to flow. This current is then drawn off the coils and fed into the vehicles electrical system.

GROUND

Two types of grounds are used in automotive electric circuits. Direct ground components are grounded to the frame through their mounting points. All other components use some sort of ground wire which is attached to the frame or chassis of the vehicle. The electrical current runs through the chassis of the vehicle and returns to the battery through the ground (-) cable; if you look, you'll see that the battery ground cable connects between the battery and the frame or chassis of the vehicle.

➥**It should be noted that a good percentage of electrical problems can be traced to bad grounds.**

PROTECTIVE DEVICES

▶ **See Figure 2**

It is possible for large surges of current to pass through the electrical system of your vehicle. If this surge of current were to reach the load in the circuit, the surge could burn it out or severely damage it. It can also overload the wiring, causing the harness to get hot and melt the insulation. To prevent this, fuses, circuit breakers and/or fusible links are connected into the supply wires of the electrical system. These items are nothing more than a built-in weak spot in the system. When an abnormal amount of current flows through the system, these protective devices work as follows to protect the circuit:

• Fuse—when an excessive electrical current passes through a fuse, the fuse "blows" (the conductor melts) and opens the circuit, preventing the passage of current.

• Circuit Breaker—a circuit breaker is basically a self-repairing fuse. It will open the circuit in the same fashion as a fuse, but when the surge subsides, the circuit breaker can be reset and does not need replacement.

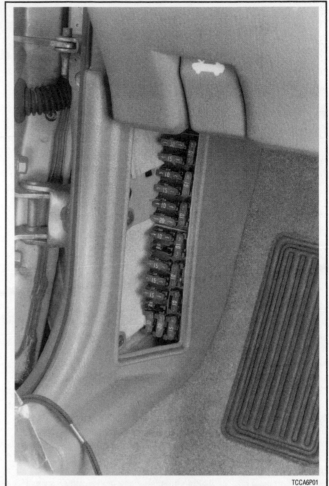

TCCA6P01

Fig. 2 Most vehicles use one or more fuse panels. This one is located on the driver's side kick panel

• Fusible Link—a fusible link (fuse link or main link) is a short length of special, high temperature insulated wire that acts as a fuse. When an excessive electrical current passes through a fusible link, the thin gauge wire inside the link melts, creating an intentional open to protect the circuit. To repair the circuit, the link must be replaced. Some newer type fusible links are housed in plug-in modules, which are simply replaced like a fuse, while older type fusible links must be cut and spliced if they melt. Since this link is very early in the electrical path, it's the first place to look if nothing on the vehicle works, yet the battery seems to be charged and is properly connected.

> ☀ **CAUTION**
>
> **Always replace fuses, circuit breakers and fusible links with identically rated components. Under no circumstances should a component of higher or lower amperage rating be substituted.**

SWITCHES & RELAYS

▶ **See Figures 3 and 4**

Switches are used in electrical circuits to control the passage of current. The most common use is to open and close circuits between the battery and the various electric devices in the system. Switches are rated according to the amount of amperage they can handle. If a sufficient amperage rated switch is not used in a circuit, the switch could overload and cause damage.

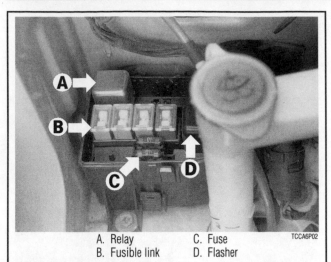

A. Relay   C. Fuse
B. Fusible link   D. Flasher

TCCA6P02

Fig. 3 The underhood fuse and relay panel usually contains fuses, relays, flashers and fusible links

Some electrical components which require a large amount of current to operate use a special switch called a relay. Since these circuits carry a large amount of current, the thickness of the wire in the circuit is also greater. If this large wire were connected from the load to the control switch, the switch would have to carry the high amperage load and the fairing or dash would be twice as large to accommodate the increased size of the wiring harness. To prevent these problems, a relay is used.

Relays are composed of a coil and a set of contacts. When the coil has a current passed though it, a magnetic field is formed and this field causes the contacts to move together, completing the circuit. Most relays are normally open, preventing current from passing through the circuit, but they can take any electrical form depending on the job they are intended to do. Relays can be considered "remote control switches." They allow a smaller current to operate devices that require higher amperages. When a small current operates the coil, a larger current is allowed to pass by the contacts. Some common circuits which may use relays are the horn, headlights, starter, electric fuel pump and other high draw ciruits.

LOAD

Every electrical circuit must include a "load" (something to use the electricity coming from the source). Without this load, the battery would attempt to deliver its entire power supply from one pole to another. This is called a

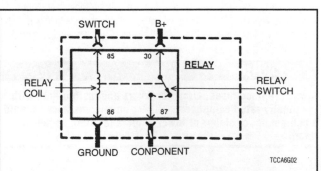

TCCA6G02

Fig. 4 Relays are composed of a coil and a switch. These two components are linked together so that when one operates, the other operates at the same time. The large wires in the circuit are connected from the battery to one side of the relay switch (B+) and from the opposite side of the relay switch to the load (component). Smaller wires are connected from the relay coil to the control switch for the circuit and from the opposite side of the relay coil to ground

"short circuit." All this electricity would take a short cut to ground and cause a great amount of damage to other components in the circuit by developing a tremendous amount of heat. This condition could develop sufficient heat to melt the insulation on all the surrounding wires and reduce a multiple wire cable to a lump of plastic and copper.

WIRING & HARNESSES

The average vehicle contains meters and meters of wiring, with hundreds of individual connections. To protect the many wires from damage and to keep them from becoming a confusing tangle, they are organized into bundles, enclosed in plastic or taped together and called wiring harnesses. Different harnesses serve different parts of the vehicle. Individual wires are color coded to help trace them through a harness where sections are hidden from view.

Automotive wiring or circuit conductors can be either single strand wire, multi-strand wire or printed circuitry. Single strand wire has a solid metal core and is usually used inside such components as alternators, motors, relays and other devices. Multi-strand wire has a core made of many small strands of wire twisted together into a single conductor. Most of the wiring in an automotive electrical system is made up of multi-strand wire, either as a single conductor or grouped together in a harness. All wiring is color coded on the insulator, either as a solid color or as a colored wire with an identification stripe. A printed circuit is a thin film of copper or other conductor that is printed on an insulator backing. Occasionally, a printed circuit is sandwiched between two sheets of plastic for more protection and flexibility. A complete printed circuit, consisting of conductors, insulating material and connectors for lamps or other components is called a printed circuit board. Printed circuitry is used in place of individual wires or harnesses in places where space is limited, such as behind instrument panels.

Since automotive electrical systems are very sensitive to changes in resistance, the selection of properly sized wires is critical when systems are repaired. A loose or corroded connection or a replacement wire that is too small for the circuit will add extra resistance and an additional voltage drop to the circuit.

The wire gauge number is an expression of the cross-section area of the conductor. Vehicles from countries that use the metric system will typically describe the wire size as its cross-sectional area in square millimeters. In this method, the larger the wire, the greater the number. Another common system for expressing wire size is the American Wire Gauge (AWG) system. As gauge number increases, area decreases and the wire becomes smaller. An 18 gauge wire is smaller than a 4 gauge wire. A wire with a higher gauge number will carry less current than a wire with a lower gauge number. Gauge wire size refers to the size of the strands of the conductor, not the size of the complete wire with insulator. It is possible, therefore, to have two wires of the same gauge with different diameters because one may have thicker insulation than the other.

It is essential to understand how a circuit works before trying to figure out why it doesn't. An electrical schematic shows the electrical current paths when a circuit is operating properly. Schematics break the entire electrical system down into individual circuits. In a schematic, usually no attempt is made to represent wiring and components as they physically appear on the vehicle; switches and other components are shown as simply as possible. Face views of harness connectors show the cavity or terminal locations in all multi-pin connectors to help locate test points.

CONNECTORS

▶ **See Figures 5 and 6**

Three types of connectors are commonly used in automotive applications—weatherproof, molded and hard shell.

• Weatherproof—these connectors are most commonly used where the connector is exposed to the elements. Terminals are protected against moisture and dirt by sealing rings which provide a weathertight seal. All repairs require the use of a special terminal and the tool required to service it. Unlike standard blade type terminals, these weatherproof terminals cannot be straightened once they are bent. Make certain that the connectors are properly seated and all of the sealing rings are in place when connecting leads.

TCCA6P03

Fig. 5 Hard shell (left) and weatherproof (right) connectors have replaceable terminals

• Molded—these connectors require complete replacement of the connector if found to be defective. This means splicing a new connector assembly into the harness. All splices should be soldered to insure proper contact. Use care when probing the connections or replacing terminals in them, as it is possible to create a short circuit between opposite terminals. If this happens to the wrong terminal pair, it is possible to damage certain components. Always use jumper wires between connectors for circuit checking and NEVER probe through weatherproof seals.

• Hard Shell—unlike molded connectors, the terminal contacts in hard-shell connectors can be replaced. Replacement usually involves the use of a special terminal removal tool that depresses the locking tangs (barbs) on the connector terminal and allows the connector to be removed from the rear of the shell. The connector shell should be replaced if it shows any evidence of burning, melting, cracks, or breaks. Replace individual terminals that are burnt, corroded, distorted or loose.

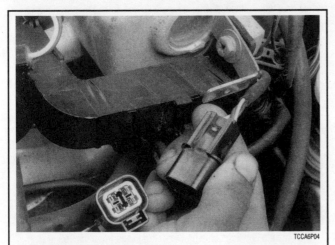

TCCA6P04

Fig. 6 Weatherproof connectors are most commonly used in the engine compartment or where the connector is exposed to the elements

Test Equipment

Pinpointing the exact cause of trouble in an electrical circuit is most times accomplished by the use of special test equipment. The following describes different types of commonly used test equipment and briefly explains how to use them in diagnosis. In addition to the information covered below, the tool manufacturer's instructions booklet (provided with the tester) should be read and clearly understood before attempting any test procedures.

JUMPER WIRES

✳ CAUTION

Never use jumper wires made from a thinner gauge wire than the circuit being tested. If the jumper wire is of too small a gauge, it may overheat and possibly melt. Never use jumpers to bypass high resistance loads in a circuit. Bypassing resistances, in effect, creates a short circuit. This may, in turn, cause damage and fire. Jumper wires should only be used to bypass lengths of wire or to simulate switches.

Jumper wires are simple, yet extremely valuable, pieces of test equipment. They are basically test wires which are used to bypass sections of a circuit. Although jumper wires can be purchased, they are usually fabricated from lengths of standard automotive wire and whatever type of connector (alligator clip, spade connector or pin connector) that is required for the particular application being tested. In cramped, hard-to-reach areas, it is advisable to have insulated boots over the jumper wire terminals in order to prevent accidental grounding. It is also advisable to include a standard automotive fuse in any jumper wire. This is commonly referred to as a "fused jumper". By inserting an in-line fuse holder between a set of test leads, a fused jumper wire can be used for bypassing open circuits. Use a 5 amp fuse to provide protection against voltage spikes.

Jumper wires are used primarily to locate open electrical circuits, on either the ground (-) side of the circuit or on the power (+) side. If an electrical component fails to operate, connect the jumper wire between the component and a good ground. If the component operates only with the jumper installed, the ground circuit is open. If the ground circuit is good, but the component does not operate, the circuit between the power feed and component may be open. By moving the jumper wire successively back from the component toward the power source, you can isolate the area of the circuit where the open is located. When the component stops functioning, or the power is cut off, the open is in the segment of wire between the jumper and the point previously tested.

You can sometimes connect the jumper wire directly from the battery to the "hot" terminal of the component, but first make sure the component uses 12 volts in operation. Some electrical components, such as fuel injectors or sensors, are designed to operate on about 4 to 5 volts, and running 12 volts directly to these components will cause damage.

TEST LIGHTS

◆ See Figure 7

The test light is used to check circuits and components while electrical current is flowing through them. It is used for voltage and ground tests. To use a 12 volt test light, connect the ground clip to a good ground and probe wherever necessary with the pick. The test light will illuminate when voltage is detected. This does not necessarily mean that 12 volts (or any particular amount of voltage) is present; it only means that some voltage is present. It is advisable before using the test light to touch its ground clip and probe across the battery posts or terminals to make sure the light is operating properly.

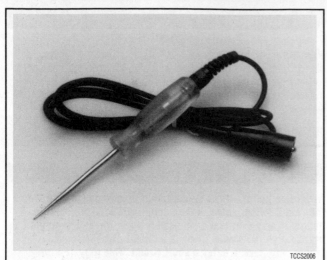

TCCS2006

Fig. 7 A 12 volt test light is used to detect the presence of voltage in a circuit

✳✳ WARNING

Do not use a test light to probe electronic ignition, spark plug or coil wires. Never use a pick-type test light to probe wiring on computer controlled systems unless specifically instructed to do so. Any wire insulation that is pierced by the test light probe should be taped and sealed with silicone after testing.

Like the jumper wire, the 12 volt test light is used to isolate opens in circuits. But, whereas the jumper wire is used to bypass the open to operate the load, the 12 volt test light is used to locate the presence of voltage in a circuit. If the test light illuminates, there is power up to that point in the circuit; if the test light does not illuminate, there is an open circuit (no power). Move the test light in successive steps back toward the power source until the light in the handle illuminates. The open is between the probe and a point which was previously probed.

The self-powered test light is similar in design to the 12 volt test light, but contains a 1.5 volt penlight battery in the handle. It is most often used in place of a multimeter to check for open or short circuits when power is isolated from the circuit (continuity test).

The battery in a self-powered test light does not provide much current. A weak battery may not provide enough power to illuminate the test light even when a complete circuit is made (especially if there is high resistance in the circuit). Always make sure that the test battery is strong. To check the battery, briefly touch the ground clip to the probe; if the light glows brightly, the battery is strong enough for testing.

➡**A self-powered test light should not be used on any computer controlled system or component. The small amount of electricity transmitted by the test light is enough to damage many electronic automotive components.**

MULTIMETERS

Multimeters are an extremely useful tool for troubleshooting electrical problems. They can be purchased in either analog or digital form and have a price range to suit any budget. A multimeter is a voltmeter, ammeter and ohmmeter (along with other features) combined into one instrument. It is often used when testing solid state circuits because of its high input impedance (usually 10 megaohms or more). A brief description of the multimeter main test functions follows:

• Voltmeter—the voltmeter is used to measure voltage at any point in a circuit, or to measure the voltage drop across any part of a circuit. Voltmeters usually have various scales and a selector switch to allow the reading of different voltage ranges. The voltmeter has a positive and a negative lead. To avoid damage to the meter, always connect the negative lead to the negative (-) side of the circuit (to ground or nearest the ground side of the circuit) and connect the positive lead to the positive (+) side of the circuit (to the power source or the nearest power source). Note that the negative voltmeter lead will always be black and that the positive voltmeter will always be some color other than black (usually red).

• Ohmmeter—the ohmmeter is designed to read resistance (measured in ohms) in a circuit or component. Most ohmmeters will have a selector switch which permits the measurement of different ranges of resistance (usually the selector switch allows the multiplication of the meter reading by 10, 100, 1,000 and 10,000). Some ohmmeters are "auto-ranging" which means the meter itself will determine which scale to use. Since the meters are powered by an internal battery, the ohmmeter can be used like a self-powered test light. When the ohmmeter is connected, current from the ohmmeter flows through the circuit or component being tested. Since the ohmmeter's internal resistance and voltage are known values, the amount of current flow through the meter depends on the resistance of the circuit or component being tested. The ohmmeter can also be used to perform a continuity test for suspected open circuits. In using the meter for making continuity checks, do not be concerned with the actual resistance readings. Zero resistance, or any ohm reading, indicates continuity in the circuit. Infinite resistance indicates an opening in the circuit. A high resistance reading where there should be none indicates a problem in the circuit. Checks for short circuits are made in the same manner as checks for open circuits, except that the circuit must be isolated from both power and normal ground. Infinite resistance indicates no continuity, while zero resistance indicates a dead short.

✳✳ WARNING

Never use an ohmmeter to check the resistance of a component or wire while there is voltage applied to the circuit.

• Ammeter—an ammeter measures the amount of current flowing through a circuit in units called amperes or amps. At normal operating voltage, most circuits have a characteristic amount of amperes, called "current draw" which can be measured using an ammeter. By referring to a specified current draw rating, then measuring the amperes and comparing the two values, one can determine what is happening within the circuit to aid in diagnosis. An open circuit, for example, will not allow any current to flow, so the ammeter reading will be zero. A damaged component or circuit will have an increased current draw, so the reading will be high. The ammeter is always connected in series with the circuit being tested. All of the current that normally flows through the circuit must also flow through the ammeter; if there is any other path for the current to follow, the ammeter reading will not be accurate. The ammeter itself has very little resistance to current flow and, therefore, will not affect the circuit, but it will measure current draw only when the circuit is closed and electricity is flowing. Excessive current draw can blow fuses and drain the battery, while a reduced current draw can cause motors to run slowly, lights to dim and other components to not operate properly.

Troubleshooting Electrical Systems

When diagnosing a specific problem, organized troubleshooting is a must. The complexity of a modern automotive vehicle demands that you approach any problem in a logical, organized manner. There are certain troubleshooting techniques, however, which are standard:

• Establish when the problem occurs. Does the problem appear only under certain conditions? Were there any noises, odors or other unusual symptoms?

Isolate the problem area. To do this, make some simple tests and observations, then eliminate the systems that are working properly. Check for obvious problems, such as broken wires and loose or dirty connections. Always check the obvious before assuming something complicated is the cause.

• Test for problems systematically to determine the cause once the problem area is isolated. Are all the components functioning properly? Is there power going to electrical switches and motors. Performing careful, systematic checks will often turn up most causes on the first inspection, without wasting time checking components that have little or no relationship to the problem.

• Test all repairs after the work is done to make sure that the problem is fixed. Some causes can be traced to more than one component, so a careful verification of repair work is important in order to pick up additional malfunctions that may cause a problem to reappear or a different problem to arise. A blown fuse, for example, is a simple problem that may require more than another fuse to repair. If you don't look for a problem that caused a fuse to blow, a shorted wire (for example) may go undetected.

Experience has shown that most problems tend to be the result of a fairly simple and obvious cause, such as loose or corroded connectors, bad grounds or damaged wire insulation which causes a short. This makes careful visual inspection of components during testing essential to quick and accurate troubleshooting.

Testing

OPEN CIRCUITS

▶ **See Figure 8**

This test already assumes the existance of an open in the circuit and it is used to help locate the open portion.

1. Isolate the circuit from power and ground.
2. Connect the self-powered test light or ohmmeter ground clip to the ground side of the circuit and probe sections of the circuit sequentially.
3. If the light is out or there is infinite resistance, the open is between the probe and the circuit ground.
4. If the light is on or the meter shows continuity, the open is bewtween the probe and the end of the circuit toward the power source.

SHORT CIRCUITS

➡ **Never use a self-powered test light to perform checks for opens or shorts when power is applied to the circuit under test. The test light can be damaged by outside power.**

1. Isolate the circuit from power and ground.

2. Connect the self-powered test light or ohmmeter ground clip to a good ground and probe any easy-to-reach point in the circuit.
3. If the light comes on or there is continuity, there is a short somewhere in the circuit.
4. To isolate the short, probe a test point at either end of the isolated circuit (the light should be on or the meter should indicate continuity).
5. Leave the test light probe engaged and sequentially open connectors or switches, remove parts, etc. until the light goes out or continuity is broken.
6. When the light goes out, the short is between the last two circuit components which were opened.

VOLTAGE

This test determines voltage available from the battery and should be the first step in any electrical troubleshooting procedure after visual inspection. Many electrical problems, especially on computer controlled systems, can be caused by a low state of charge in the battery. Excessive corrosion at the battery cable terminals can cause poor contact that will prevent proper charging and full battery current flow.

1. Set the voltmeter selector switch to the 20V position.
2. Connect the multimeter negative lead to the battery's negative (-) post or terminal and the positive lead to the battery's positive (+) post or terminal.
3. Turn the ignition switch **ON** to provide a load.
4. A well charged battery should register over 12 volts. If the meter reads below 11.5 volts, the battery power may be insufficient to operate the electrical system properly.

VOLTAGE DROP

▶ **See Figure 9**

When current flows through a load, the voltage beyond the load drops. This voltage drop is due to the resistance created by the load and also by small resistances created by corrosion at the connectors and damaged insulation on the wires. The maximum allowable voltage drop under load is critical, especially if there is more than one load in the circuit, since all voltage drops are cumulative.

1. Set the voltmeter selector switch to the 20 volt position.
2. Connect the multimeter negative lead to a good ground.
3. Operate the circuit and check the voltage prior to the first component (load).
4. There should be little or no voltage drop in the circuit prior to the first component. If a voltage drop exists, the wire or connectors in the circuit are suspect.

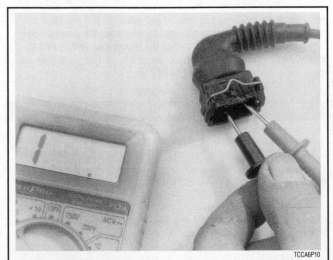

Fig. 8 The infinite reading on this multimeter (1 .) indicates that the circuit is open

Fig. 9 This voltage drop test revealed high resistance (low voltage) in the circuit

5. While operating the first component in the circuit, probe the ground side of the component with the positive meter lead and observe the voltage readings. A small voltage drop should be noticed. This voltage drop is caused by the resistance of the component.

6. Repeat the test for each component (load) down the circuit.

7. If a large voltage drop is noticed, the preceding component, wire or connector is suspect.

RESISTANCE

♦ **See Figures 10 and 11**

✳✳ WARNING

Never use an ohmmeter with power applied to the circuit. The ohmmeter is designed to operate on its own power supply. The normal 12 volt electrical system voltage could damage the meter!

1. Isolate the circuit from the vehicle's power source.

2. Ensure that the ignition key is **OFF** when disconnecting any components or the battery.

3. Where necessary, also isolate at least one side of the circuit to be checked, in order to avoid reading parallel resistances. Parallel circuit resistances will always give a lower reading than the actual resistance of either of the branches.

4. Connect the meter leads to both sides of the circuit (wire or component) and read the actual measured ohms on the meter scale. Make sure the selector switch is set to the proper ohm scale for the circuit being tested, to avoid misreading the ohmmeter test value.

TCCA6P08

Fig. 10 Checking the resistance of a coolant temperature sensor with an ohmmeter. Reading is 1.04 kilohms

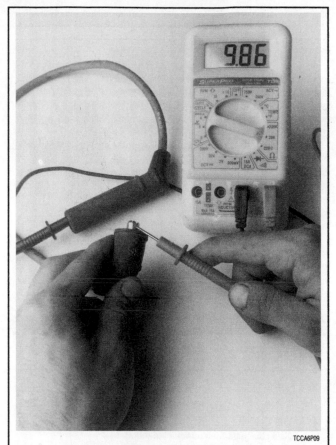

TCCA6P09

Fig. 11 Spark plug wires can be checked for excessive resistance using an ohmmeter

Wire and Connector Repair

Almost anyone can replace damaged wires, as long as the proper tools and parts are available. Wire and terminals are available to fit almost any need. Even the specialized weatherproof, molded and hard shell connectors are now available from aftermarket suppliers.

Be sure the ends of all the wires are fitted with the proper terminal hardware and connectors. Wrapping a wire around a stud is never a permanent solution and will only cause trouble later. Replace wires one at a time to avoid confusion. Always route wires exactly the same as the factory.

➡**If connector repair is necessary, only attempt it if you have the proper tools. Weatherproof and hard shell connectors require special tools to release the pins inside the connector. Attempting to repair these connectors with conventional hand tools will damage them.**

BATTERY CABLES

Disconnecting the Cables

When working on any electrical component on the vehicle, it is always a good idea to disconnect the negative (-) battery cable. This will prevent potential damage to many sensitive electrical components such as the Powertrain Control Module (PCM), radio, alternator, etc.

➡**Any time you disengage the battery cables, it is recommended that you disconnect the negative (-) battery cable first. This will prevent your accidentally grounding the positive (+) terminal to the body of the vehicle when disconnecting it, thereby preventing damage to the above mentioned components.**

Before you disconnect the cable(s), first turn the ignition to the **OFF** position. This will prevent a draw on the battery which could cause arcing (electricity trying to ground itself to the body of a vehicle, just like a spark plug jumping the gap) and, of course, damaging some components such as the alternator diodes.

When the battery cable(s) are reconnected (negative cable last), be sure to check that your lights, windshield wipers and other electrically operated safety components are all working correctly. If your vehicle contains an Electronically Tuned Radio (ETR), don't forget to also reset your radio stations. Ditto for the clock.

AIR BAG (SUPPLEMENTAL RESTRAINT) SYSTEM

General Information

▶ **See Figures 12, 13 and 14**

The Supplemental Restraint System (SRS) is designed to work in conjunction with the standard three-point safety belts to reduce injury in a head-on collision.

❊❊❊ CAUTION

The SRS can actually cause physical injury or death if the safety belts are not used, or if the manufacturer's warnings are not followed. The manufacturer's warnings can be found in your owner's manual or, in some cases, on your sun visors.

The SRS is comprised of the following components:
- Driver's side air bag module
- Passenger's side air bag module
- Radiator primary crash center air bag sensor and bracket
- Center cowl safing rear air bag sensor and bracket

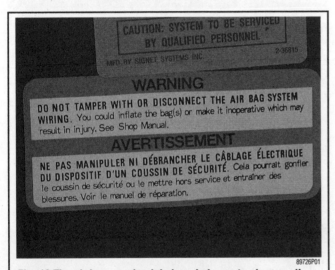

Fig. 12 The air bag warning label reminds you to observe all service precautions when working on the vehicle

Fig. 13 Location of the radiator primary crash center air bag sensor

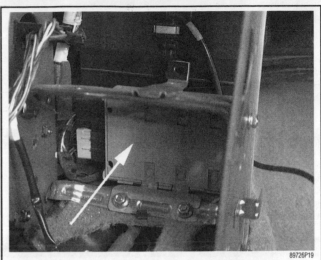

Fig. 14 The air bag diagnostic monitor is located behind the shift console

- Left and right-hand fender primary crash front air bag sensor and brackets
- Air bag diagnostic monitor computer
- Air bag warning indicator
- Tone generator (internal to the air bag diagnostic monitor)
- Electrical wiring

The sensors in the car are designed to detect a severe frontal impact. When at least one of the primary crash sensors and the center cowl safing rear air bag sensor close at the same time, electric current flows to the inflator and ignites the chemicals.

The chemicals burn rapidly in the metal container. This burning produces nitrogen gas and small amounts of dust; both the gas and dust are cooled and filtered during the air bag(s) inflation.

The air bag(s) split the trim covers open while inflating. The air bag(s) then rapidly unfold and inflate in front of the driver and, if so equipped, front seat passenger.

After the air bag(s) have inflated, the gas escapes through holes in the bag(s) as they deflate.

SERVICE PRECAUTIONS

Whenever working around, or on, the air bag supplemental restraint system, ALWAYS adhere to the following warnings and cautions:
- Always wear safety glasses when servicing an air bag vehicle and when handling an air bag module.
- Carry a live air bag module with the bag and trim cover facing away from your body, so that an accidental deployment of the air bag will pose only a small chance of personal injury.
- Place an air bag module on a table or other flat surface with the bag and trim cover pointing up.
- Wear gloves, a dust mask and safety glasses whenever handling a deployed air bag module. The air bag surface may contain traces of sodium hydroxide, a by-product of the gas that inflates the air bag and which can cause skin irritation.
- Be sure to wash your hands with mild soap and water after handling a deployed air bag.
- All air bag modules with discolored or damaged cover trim must be replaced, not repainted.
- All component replacement and wiring service must wait until the negative and positive battery cables have been disconnected from the battery for a minimum of one minute.
- NEVER probe the air bag electrical terminals. Doing so could result in air bag deployment, which can cause serious physical injury.

• If the vehicle is involved in a "fender-bender" which results in a damaged front bumper or grille, have the air bag sensors inspected by a qualified automotive technician to ensure that they were not damaged.

• If, at any time, the air bag light indicates that the computer has noted a problem, have your vehicle's SRS serviced immediately by a qualified automotive technician. A faulty SRS can cause severe physical injury or death.

DISARMING THE SYSTEM

> ※※ **CAUTION**
>
> **If you are disarming the system with the intent of testing it, do not! The SRS is a sensitive, complex system and should only be tested or serviced by a qualified automotive technician. Also, specific tools are needed for SRS testing.**

1. Disconnect the negative battery cable from the battery.
2. Disconnect the positive battery cable from the battery.
3. Wait at least one minute. This time is required for the back-up power supply in the air bag diagnostic monitor to completely drain. The system is now disarmed.

ARMING THE SYSTEM

1. Connect the positive battery cable.
2. Connect the negative battery cable.
3. Stand outside the vehicle and carefully turn the ignition to the **RUN** position. Be sure that no part of your body is in front of the air bag module on the steering wheel, to prevent injury in case of an accidental air bag deployment.
4. Ensure that the air bag indicator light turns off after approximately 6 seconds. If the light does not illuminate at all, does not turn off, or starts to flash, have the system tested by a qualified automotive technician. If the light does turn off after 6 seconds and does not flash, the SRS is working properly.

HEATING AND AIR CONDITIONING

Blower Motor

REMOVAL & INSTALLATION

▶ **See Figure 15**

1. Disconnect the negative battery cable.
2. Loosen the two top blower motor housing nuts.

➡**The left-hand lower nut attaches the blower motor housing and the A/C evaporator case to the chassis.**

3. Loosen the left-hand lower nut and slide the housing out from behind the evaporator case.
4. Disengage the motor's electrical connection.
5. Loosen the three blower motor retaining screws and remove the motor.
To install:
6. Install the blower motor and tighten the retaining screws.
7. Engage the motor's electrical connection.
8. Slide the housing into position and tighten all the retaining nuts.
9. Connect the negative battery cable.

Blower Motor Relay

REMOVAL & INSTALLATION

▶ **See Figure 15**

The blower motor resistor is mounted above the blower motor, in the motor housing.
1. Disconnect the negative battery cable.
2. Unplug the blower motor resistor electrical connection.
3. Loosen the resistor retaining screws and remove the resistor assembly.
To install:
4. Install the resistor and tighten the retaining screws.
5. Engage the resistor's electrical connection.
6. Connect the negative battery cable.

Heater Core

REMOVAL & INSTALLATION

▶ **See Figures 16, 17, 18 and 19**

1. Disconnect the negative battery cable.

> ※※ **CAUTION**
>
> **Never open, service or drain the radiator or cooling system when hot; serious burns can occur from the steam and hot coolant. Also, when draining engine coolant, keep in mind that cats and dogs are attracted to ethylene glycol antifreeze and could drink any that is left in an uncovered container or in puddles on the ground. This will prove fatal in sufficient quantities. Always drain coolant into a sealable container. Coolant should be reused unless it is contaminated or is several years old.**

2. Drain and recycle the engine coolant.
3. Remove the instrument panel.
4. Tag and disconnect the inlet and outlet heater water hoses in the engine compartment.
5. Tag and disengage the wiring harness and antenna lead from the bracket on the front of the heater core case.
6. Loosen the A/C evaporator register duct-to-heater core case retaining screw.
7. Loosen the two nuts from the upper and lower right side of the case.

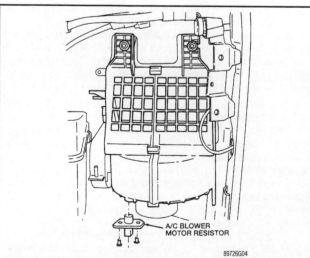

89726G04

Fig. 15 The blower motor and resistor are located under the right-hand side of the instrument panel

Fig. 16 Tag and disconnect the inlet and outlet heater hoses in the engine compartment

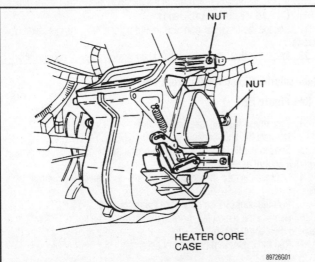

Fig. 17 Remove the nuts from the upper and lower right side of the heater core case

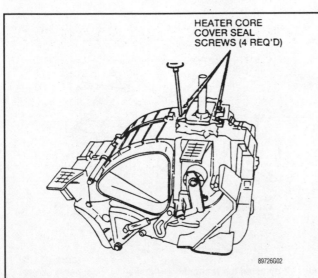

Fig. 18 Remove the heater core cover seal screws and seal . . .

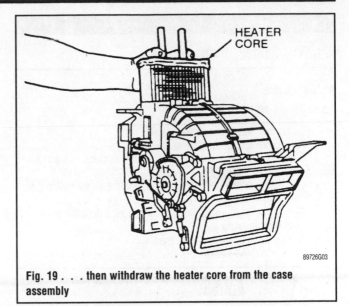

Fig. 19 . . . then withdraw the heater core from the case assembly

8. Loosen the nut on the lower left side, and disengage the case from the windshield defroster nozzle connectors.

9. Loosen the heater core cover seal retaining screws, then remove the seal.

10. Remove the heater core from the case.

To install:

11. Insert the heater core into its case.

12. Install the seal and tighten the retaining screws.

➡**Make sure the windshield defroster nozzle connectors and the A/C evaporator register duct are properly seated on the heater core case before installing the case.**

13. Install the heater core case and tighten the retaining nuts.

14. Tighten the A/C evaporator register duct-to-heater core case retaining screw.

15. Engage the antenna and wiring harness to the bracket on the front of the case.

16. Install the instrument panel.

17. Connect the inlet and outlet heater hoses.

18. Fill the cooling system to its proper level with the proper mixture of coolant.

19. Connect the negative battery cable.

20. Start the engine, let it idle until it reaches normal operating temperature, and check for cooling system leaks.

Air Conditioning Components

REMOVAL & INSTALLATION

Repair or service of air conditioning components is not covered by this manual, because of the risk of personal injury or death, and because of the legal ramifications of servicing these components without the proper EPA certification and experience. Cost, personal injury or death, environmental damage, and legal considerations (such as the fact that it is a federal crime to vent refrigerant into the atmosphere), dictate that the A/C components on your vehicle should be serviced only by a Motor Vehicle Air Conditioning (MVAC) trained, and EPA certified automotive technician.

➡**If your vehicle's A/C system uses R-12 refrigerant and is in need of recharging, the A/C system can be converted over to R-134a refrigerant (less environmentally harmful and expensive). Refer to Section 1 for additional information on your vehicle's A/C system.**

Control Cables

REMOVAL & INSTALLATION

Air Flow Cable

▶ See Figure 20

1. Disconnect the negative battery cable.
2. Remove the shift console panel.
3. Loosen the three screws and disengage the electrical connection from the control assembly.
4. Depress the tabs on the air door shafts and detach the control cable ends.
5. Remove the air flow control cable clip attaching the cable to the underside of the control assembly.
6. Pull the cable from the control lever.

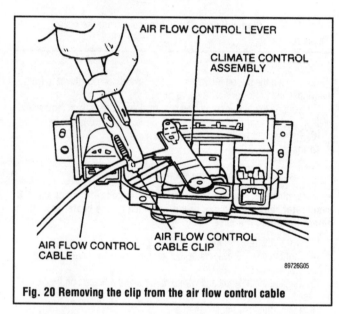

Fig. 20 Removing the clip from the air flow control cable

To install:

7. Engage the cable to the control lever.
8. Install the air flow control cable clip attaching the cable to the underside of the control assembly.
9. Install the control cable ends.
10. Engage the electrical connection and tighten the control assembly screws.
11. Install the shift console panel and connect the negative battery cable.

Temperature Control Cable

▶ See Figure 21

1. Disconnect the negative battery cable.
2. Remove the shift console panel.
3. Loosen the three screws and disengage the electrical connection from the control assembly.
4. Depress the tabs on the air door shafts and detach the control cable ends.
5. Pull the control assembly from the dashboard.
6. Remove the temperature control cable clip attaching the cable to the control assembly.
7. Pull the cable from the control assembly.

To install:

8. Connect the cable to the control assembly.
9. Install the temperature control cable clip attaching the cable to the control assembly.

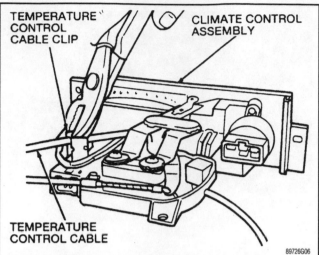

Fig. 21 Removing the clip that attaches the temperature control cable to the control assembly

10. Install the control assembly in the dashboard.
11. Connect the control cable ends.
12. Engage the electrical connection and tighten the control assembly screws.
13. Install the shift console panel and connect the negative battery cable.

Recirculation/Fresh Air Control Cable

▶ See Figure 22

1. Disconnect the negative battery cable.
2. Remove the shift console panel.
3. Loosen the three screws and disengage the electrical connection from the control assembly.
4. Depress the tabs on the air door shafts and detach the control cable ends.
5. Pull the control assembly from the dashboard.
6. Remove the recirculation/fresh air control cable screw attaching the cable to the control assembly.
7. Pull the cable from the control assembly.

To install:

8. Connect the cable to the control assembly.
9. Install the recirculation/fresh air control cable screw attaching the cable to the control assembly.

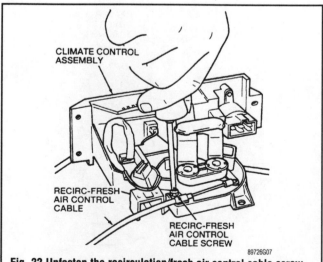

Fig. 22 Unfasten the recirculation/fresh air control cable screw attaching the cable to the control assembly

10. Install the control assembly in the dashboard.
11. Connect the control cable ends.
12. Engage the electrical connection and tighten the control assembly screws.
13. Install the shift console panel and connect the negative battery cable.

ADJUSTMENT

Air Flow Cable

▶ **See Figure 23**

1. Move the air flow selector lever to the panel position.
2. Release the cable clip.
3. While holding down the air flow selector control lever against its stop, secure the selector cable with the clip.

Temperature Control Cable

▶ **See Figure 24**

1. Move the temperature control lever to the full HOT position.
2. Connect the control cable to the temperature control door.
3. Set the door to the HOT position and clamp the control cable into place.
4. Make sure the control lever moves its full stroke (range of motion).

Recirculation/Fresh Air Control Cable

▶ **See Figure 25**

1. Loosen the glove compartment door screws and remove the door.
2. Disengage the cable clip and move the recirculation/fresh air control lever to the FRESH position.
3. While holding the control lever in the FRESH position, secure the recirculation/fresh air control cable with the clip.
4. Install the glove compartment door and tighten the retaining screws.

Control Panel

REMOVAL & INSTALLATION

▶ **See Figures 26, 27 and 28**

1. Disconnect the negative battery cable.
2. Remove the shift console panel.

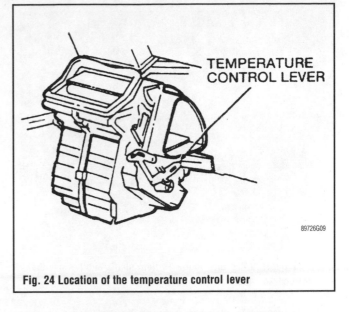

Fig. 24 Location of the temperature control lever

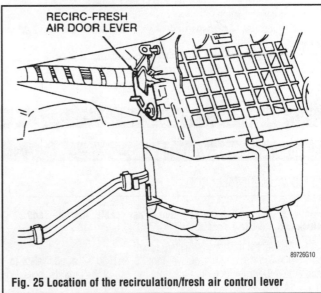

Fig. 25 Location of the recirculation/fresh air control lever

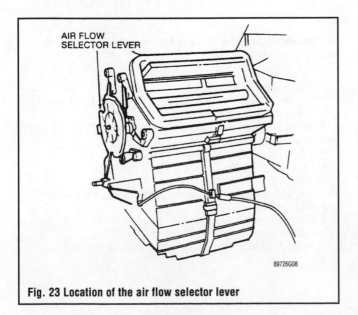

Fig. 23 Location of the air flow selector lever

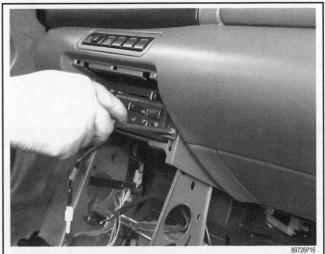

Fig. 26 Loosen the control panel retaining screws using a Phillips head screwdriver

Fig. 27 Depress the tabs on the air door shafts and remove the control cable ends

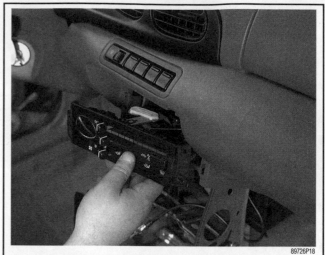

Fig. 28 Pull the control panel out, disengage the cables and electrical connections, then remove the panel

3. Loosen the three screws and disengage the electrical connections from the control assembly.

4. Depress the tabs on the air door shafts and detach the control cable ends.

5. Pull the control panel assembly from the dashboard.

6. Detach the cables from the control assembly.

To install:

7. Install the control panel assembly in the dashboard.

8. Connect the control cable ends.

9. Engage the electrical connection and tighten the control assembly screws.

10. Install the shift console panel and connect the negative battery cable.

ENTERTAINMENT SYSTEMS

Radio/Tape Player/CD Player

REMOVAL & INSTALLATION

➡**After disconnecting the negative battery cable, the radio and clock will have to be reset.**

1. Disconnect the negative battery cable.

2. Use two-piece radio removal tool T87P-19061-A or equivalent to slide the radio from its mounting, until the rear of the radio is accessible.

3. Disengage the antenna and electrical connectors from the rear of the radio.

4. Remove the radio from the instrument panel.

To install:

5. Engage the radio antenna and electrical connections.

6. Slide the radio into its mounting in the instrument panel until it is properly engaged.

7. Connect the negative battery cable.

8. Check for proper radio operation. Reset the station settings and the clock.

Speakers

REMOVAL & INSTALLATION

Front

➡**After disconnecting the negative battery cable, the radio and clock will have to be reset.**

1. Disconnect the negative battery cable.

2. Remove the front door trim panel.

3. Loosen the speaker retaining screws, then pull the speaker assembly from the door until access to the rear of the speaker is possible.

4. Disengage the speaker electrical connection and remove the speaker.

To install:

5. Engage the speaker electrical connection and position the speaker on the door.

6. Tighten the speaker retaining screws and install the door trim panel.

7. Connect the negative battery cable.

8. Turn the radio **ON** and check for proper speaker operation.

Rear

➡**After disconnecting the negative battery cable, the radio and clock will have to be reset.**

1. Disconnect the negative battery cable.

2. Remove the package tray panel.

3. On two-door models, remove the package tray upper trim support screws (3) and the push pins (2).

4. On four-door models, remove the cover, push pins (4) and the package tray upper trim panel screws (2).

5. Lift up the package tray upper trim panel support.

6. On four-door models, loosen the speaker rear strap screw and remove the strap.

7. Unplug the speaker electrical connection and loosen the speaker retaining screws.

8. Remove the speaker assembly.

To install:

9. Install the speaker, tighten the retaining screws and engage the electrical connection.

➡On two-door models, make sure the speaker strap is secured in its original position by one of the package tray upper trim panel support screws.

10. On four-door models, install the strap and tighten the speaker rear strap screw.

11. Lower the package tray upper trim panel support.

12. On four-door models, install the package tray upper trim panel screws, push pins and cover.

13. On two-door models, install the push pins, and the package tray upper trim support screws.

14. Install the package tray panel.

WINDSHIELD WIPERS AND WASHERS

Windshield Wiper Blade and Arm

REMOVAL & INSTALLATION

Wiper Arm

▶ **See Figures 29, 30, 31, 32 and 33**

1. Remove the wiper arm cover to access the retaining nut.
2. Loosen the retaining nut, then gently pry on the wiper arm to separate it from the splines on the wiper arm shaft.
3. Remove the wiper arm from the car.

To install:
4. Turn the ignition switch **ON**.

➡**The ON/OFF cycling of the wiper motor will locate the wiper mounting arm and shaft in the park position.**

5. Turn the wiper motor **ON** and allow it to cycle several times, then turn the motor **OFF**.
6. Turn the ignition switch **OFF**.
7. Install the wiper arm and nut onto the shaft, then tighten the retaining nut to 12–14 ft. lbs. (16–20 Nm).
8. Check the operation and, if necessary, adjust the park position.
9. Install the wiper arm cover.

Fig. 29 Remove the cover to gain access to the wiper arm retaining nut

Fig. 31 Loosen the wiper arm retaining nut

Fig. 30 Matchmark the shaft and arm location; this will help with alignment during installation

Fig. 32 If the wiper arm is firmly attached to the shaft, disengage it with a small puller . . .

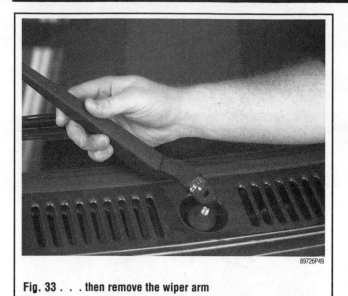

Fig. 33 . . . then remove the wiper arm

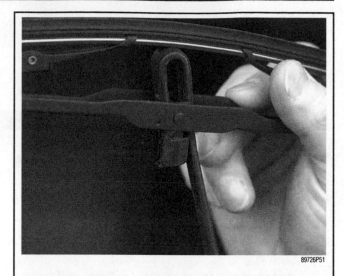

Fig. 35 Disengage the hooked end of the arm from the blade . . .

Wiper Blade

▶ See Figures 34, 35 and 36

1. Rotate the wiper blade until it is perpendicular with the wiper arm.

2. Use a small prytool to depress the tab and release the hooked end of the wiper arm from the wiper blade holder.

3. Disconnect the hooked end of the wiper arm by pulling down on the wiper blade frame.

4. Separate the wiper blade from the wiper arm.

To install:

5. Attach the wiper blade to the arm.

6. Engage the hooked end of the arm to the blade holder, making sure the tab engages.

7. Place the blade in its normal position. Turn the wiper motor **ON** and check for proper wiper operation.

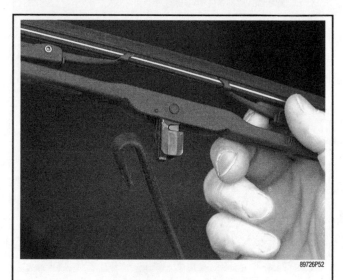

Fig. 36 . . . and separate the blade from the arm

ADJUSTMENT

Park Position

▶ See Figure 37

1. Remove the wiper arm.

2. Turn the wiper motor **ON** and allow the wiper mounting arm and pivot shaft to cycle three or four times, then turn the motor **OFF**.

3. Place the wiper arm on the pivot shaft with the tip of the wiper blade 1.12–1.28 in. (28–32mm) above the edge of the cowl top panel.

➡Make sure the wiper arm and blade assembly is aligned with the wiper arm shaft so that the wiper shaft splines are fully seated.

4. Install the wiper arm.

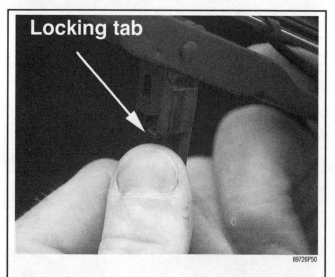

Locking tab

Fig. 34 Disengage the wiper blade locking tab

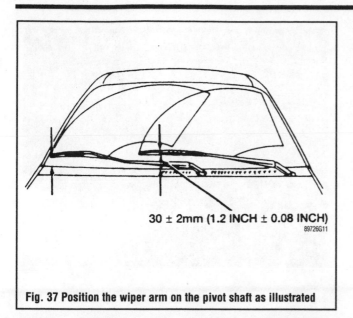

Fig. 37 Position the wiper arm on the pivot shaft as illustrated

30 ± 2mm (1.2 INCH ± 0.08 INCH)

89726G11

Wiper Motor

REMOVAL & INSTALLATION

▶ **See Figures 38 thru 46**

1. Disconnect the negative battery cable.
2. Unplug the wiper motor electrical connection.
3. Loosen the Exhaust Gas Recirculation (EGR) solenoid vacuum valve bracket nuts and slide the intake manifold vacuum outlet fitting and cap off the access plate.
4. Remove the access panel nuts and the wiper motor bolts.
5. Pull the wiper motor and access panel assembly away from the bulkhead.
6. Detach the wiper linkage pivot from the motor output arm, then separate the motor from the access panel.

To install:

➡ **Make sure the ground wire is fastened with the top left wiper motor bolt.**

7. Attach the wiper motor to the access panel and the motor output arm to the wiper linkage.

Fig. 38 Unplug the wiper motor electrical connection

89726P53

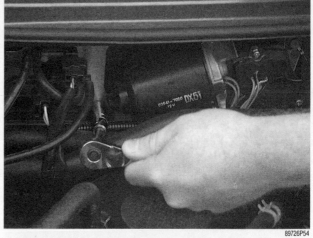

Fig. 39 Loosen the Exhaust Gas Recirculation (EGR) solenoid vacuum valve bracket nuts

89726P54

Fig. 40 Remove the Exhaust Gas Recirculation (EGR) solenoid vacuum valve bracket assembly

89726P55

Fig. 41 Loosen the access panel nuts and the wiper motor bolts

89726P56

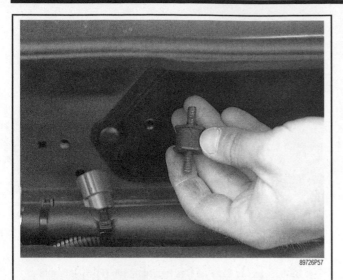

Fig. 42 Remove the rubber insulators from the access panel

Fig. 43 Use a prytool to separate the wiper linkage pivot from the motor output arm

Fig. 44 Remove the motor and access panel assembly from the engine compartment

Fig. 45 Location of the wiper motor output arm

Fig. 46 The wiper linkage pivot is located behind the access panel and below the cowl panel

8. Install the wiper motor bolts and tighten them to 62–88 inch lbs. (7–10 Nm).

9. Install and tighten the access panel nuts.

10. Install the intake manifold vacuum fitting on the access panel and tighten the EGR solenoid vacuum valve bracket nuts.

11. Engage the wiper motor electrical connection.

12. Connect the negative battery cable.

Windshield Washer Pump

REMOVAL & INSTALLATION

1. Disconnect the negative battery cable.

2. Loosen the filler neck bolt and remove the filler neck from the windshield washer reservoir.

3. Raise the car, support it with safety stands and remove the left front wheel.

4. Remove the front fender splash shield and the front splash shield.

5. Loosen the reservoir retaining bolts and lift the reservoir up until access to the electrical connector and hose is possible.

6. Disengage the electrical connector and hose, then remove the reservoir.

7. Use a prytool to remove the washer pump, being careful not to damage the reservoir.

8. Remove the seal from the reservoir.

To install:

9. Inspect the seal for damage or deterioration. If necessary, install a new seal.

10. When the seal is in place, push the washer pump into position until it is firmly seated.

11. Engage the electrical connection and hose, and place the reservoir in position.

12. When the reservoir is in position, tighten the retaining bolts.

13. Install the front splash shield and front fender splash shield.

14. Install the wheel, remove the safety stands and lower the car.

15. Install the filler neck and tighten its retaining bolt.

16. Connect the negative battery cable.

INSTRUMENTS AND SWITCHES

Instrument Cluster

REMOVAL & INSTALLATION

▶ **See Figures 47 thru 56**

1. Disconnect the negative battery cable.

2. Loosen the instrument panel finish panel screws and remove the panel insert.

3. Use a prytool to pry the finish panel away from the instrument panel.

4. Disconnect the speedometer cable at the transaxle.

5. Loosen the instrument cluster retaining screws.

6. Slide the cluster away from the instrument panel until you can gain access to the rear of the cluster.

7. Reach behind the cluster, press the speedometer cable locktab and detach the cable.

8. Depress the locktabs on the instrument cluster electrical connections and disengage them from the cluster.

9. Remove the instrument cluster.

To install:

10. Engage the instrument cluster electrical connectors and speedometer cable, making sure the tabs lock properly.

11. Position the cluster in its mounting on the instrument panel and tighten the retaining screws.

Fig. 48 Remove the lower finish panel from the instrument panel

12. Connect the speedometer cable at the transaxle and install the instrument panel's finish panel.

13. Install the panel insert and tighten the finish panel retaining screws.

14. Connect the negative battery cable.

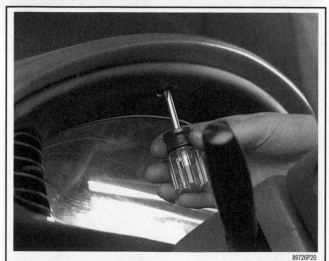

Fig. 47 Loosen the instrument panel finish panel screws and remove the panel insert

Fig. 49 Remove the instrument cluster trim panel

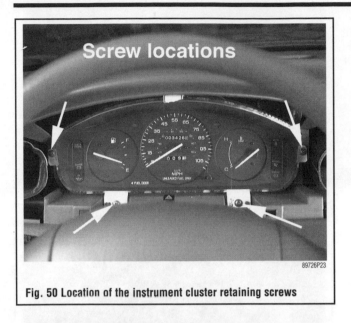

Fig. 50 Location of the instrument cluster retaining screws

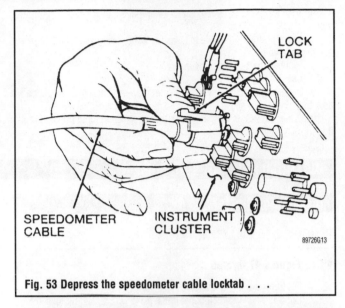

Fig. 53 Depress the speedometer cable locktab . . .

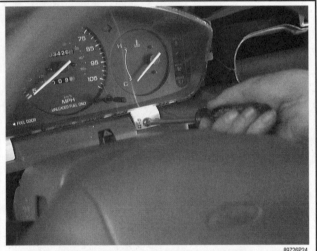

Fig. 51 Use a Phillips head screwdriver to loosen the cluster retaining screws

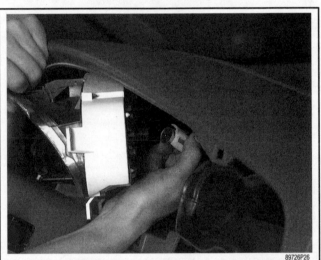

Fig. 54 . . . then disengage the speedometer cable, and slide out the instrument cluster

Fig. 52 Disconnect the speedometer cable at the transaxle

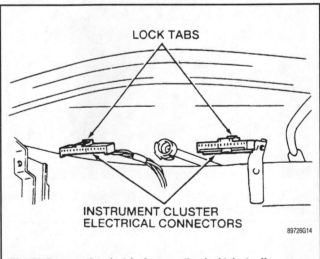

Fig. 55 Depress the electrical connection locktabs to disengage them from the cluster . . .

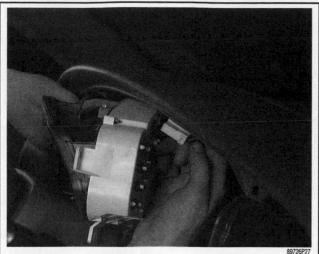

Fig. 56 . . . and detach the electrical connections from the instrument cluster

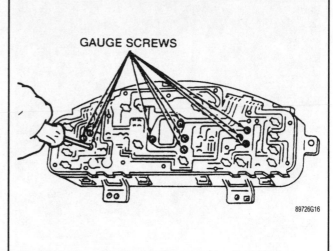

Fig. 58 Location of the instrument cluster's gauge retaining screws

Gauges

REMOVAL & INSTALLATION

Fuel Gauge

▶ See Figures 57, 58, 59, 60 and 61

1. Remove the instrument cluster.
2. Press down on the locktabs and remove the cluster main lens.
3. Loosen the fuel gauge retaining screws (3) from the cluster back plate, then remove the gauge.
   To install:
4. Install the gauge and tighten the retaining screws.

5. Install the cluster main lens, making sure the tabs lock into place.
6. Install the instrument cluster.

Engine Coolant Temperature Gauge

▶ See Figures 57, 58, 59,60 and 61

1. Remove the instrument cluster.
2. Press down on the locktabs and remove the cluster main lens.
3. Loosen the engine coolant temperature gauge retaining screws (3) from the cluster back plate, then remove the gauge.
   To install:
4. Install the gauge and tighten the retaining screws.
5. Install the cluster main lens, making sure the tabs lock into place.
6. Install the instrument cluster.

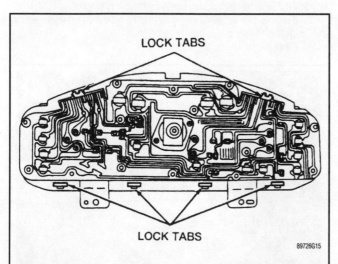

Fig. 57 Depress the main lens locking tabs to separate the lens from the cluster

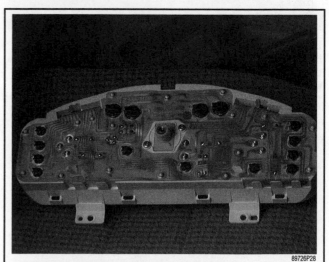

Fig. 59 The cluster bulbs and gauge retaining screws can be accessed at the back plate

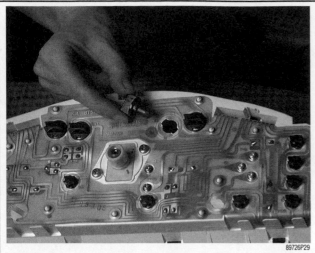

Fig. 60 To remove a gauge bulb, locate the socket assembly at the cluster back plate and twist to remove it . . .

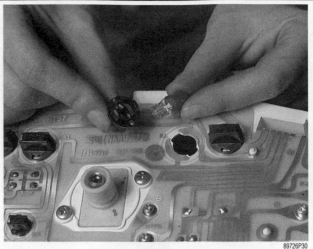

Fig. 61 . . . then grasp the bulb and pull it straight out of its socket

Speedometer/Odometer

▶ **See Figures 57, 58, 59, 60 and 61**

➡ **The mileage on a replacement odometer cannot be reset. If a replacement is used, a sticker recording the vehicle's actual mileage at the time of replacement must be attached to the door jamb.**

1. Remove the instrument cluster.

2. Press down on the locktabs and remove the cluster main lens.
3. Loosen the speedometer/odometer gauge retaining screws (4) from the cluster back plate, then remove the gauge.

To install:
4. Install the gauge and tighten the retaining screws.
5. Install the cluster main lens, making sure the tabs lock into place.
6. Install the instrument cluster.

LIGHTING

Headlights

REMOVAL & INSTALLATION

▶ **See Figures 62 thru 68**

✳ WARNING

Do not touch the glass bulb with your fingers; hold the bulb by its base only. Oil from your fingers can severely shorten the life of the bulb. If necessary, wipe off any dirt or oil from the bulb with rubbing alcohol before completing installation.

1. Open the vehicle's hood and secure it in an upright position.
2. If necessary for access on the passenger's side, remove the air cleaner and air cleaner-to-intake manifold tube.
3. If necessary for access on the driver's side, remove the windshield washer fluid reservoir by sliding it up and off its mounting bracket.
4. Remove the front parking light bulb. This will make removing the headlight bulb assembly easier.
5. Turn the dust boot retaining ring counterclockwise to remove it. Remove the dust boot.
6. Disengage the headlight bulb's electrical connection.
7. After the dust boot has been removed, unlatch the spring clip that retains the bulb, and pivot it clear of the bulb.
8. Pull the bulb straight back and out of the housing. Do not rotate the bulb while removing it.

To install:
9. Align the tabs on the bulb with the slots in the lens housing and install the bulb.
10. Engage the bulb retaining clip over the bulb and install the dust boot.

11. Install the dust boot retaining ring and turn it clockwise to engage it.
12. Secure the bulb's electrical connection.
13. Install the front parking light bulb.
14. Turn the headlights **ON** and check for proper bulb operation.
15. If removed for access on the driver's side, install the windshield washer fluid reservoir by sliding it onto its mounting bracket.
16. If removed for access on the passenger's side, install the air cleaner and air cleaner-to-intake manifold tube.
17. Close the hood.

Fig. 62 Remove the windshield washer fluid reservoir by sliding it up and off its mounting bracket

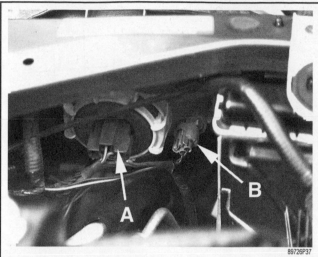

Fig. 63 Location of the headlight bulb (A) and parking light bulb (B) electrical connectors

Fig. 66 . . . and remove the dust boot

Fig. 64 Turn the dust boot retaining ring counterclockwise and remove it

Fig. 67 Unlatch the spring clip that retains the bulb and pivot it clear of the bulb

Fig. 65 Unplug the bulb's electrical connection . . .

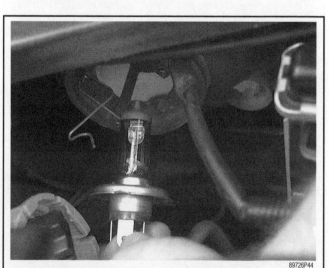

Fig. 68 Grasp the base of the bulb and withdraw the bulb from the lens assembly

AIMING THE HEADLIGHTS

▶ **See Figures 69, 70 and 71**

The headlights must be properly aimed to provide the best, safest road illumination. The lights should be checked for proper aim and adjusted as necessary. Certain state and local authorities have requirements for headlight aiming; these should be checked before adjustment is made.

✳✳ CAUTION

About once a year, when the headlights are replaced or any time front end work is performed on your vehicle, the headlight should be accurately aimed by a reputable repair shop using the proper equipment. Headlights not properly aimed can make it virtually impossible to see and may blind other drivers on the road, possibly causing an accident. Note that the following procedure is a temporary fix, until you can take your vehicle to a repair shop for a proper adjustment.

Headlight adjustment may be temporarily made using a wall, as described below, or on the rear of another vehicle. When adjusted, the lights should not glare in oncoming car or truck windshields, nor should they illuminate the passenger compartment of vehicles driving in front of you. These adjustments are rough and should always be fine tuned by a repair shop which is equipped with headlight aiming tools. Improper adjustments may be both dangerous and illegal.

For most of the vehicles covered by this manual, horizontal and vertical aiming of each headlamp unit is provided by two adjusting screws which move the retaining ring and adjusting plate against the tension of a coil spring. There is no adjustment for focus; this is done during headlight manufacturing.

➥**Because the composite headlight assembly is bolted into position, no adjustment should be necessary or possible. Some applications, however, may be bolted to an adjuster plate or may be retained by adjusting screws. If so, follow this procedure when adjusting the lights, BUT always have the adjustment checked by a reputable shop.**

Before removing the headlight bulb or disturbing the headlamp in any way, note the current settings in order to ease headlight adjustment upon reassembly. If the high or low beam setting of the old lamp still works, this can be done using the wall of a garage or a building:

1. Park the vehicle on a level surface, with the fuel tank about ½ full and with the vehicle empty of all extra cargo (unless normally carried). The vehicle should be facing a wall which is no less than 6 feet (1.8m) high and 12 feet (3.7m) wide. The front of the vehicle should be about 25 feet (7.7m) from the wall.

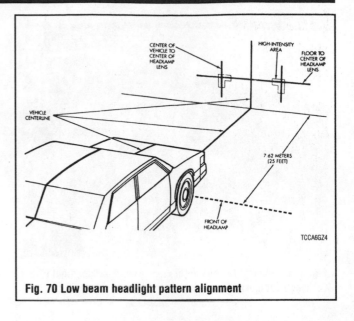

Fig. 70 Low beam headlight pattern alignment

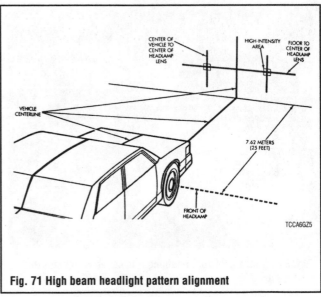

Fig. 71 High beam headlight pattern alignment

2. If aiming is to be performed outdoors, it is advisable to wait until dusk in order to properly see the headlight beams on the wall. If done in a garage, darken the area around the wall as much as possible by closing shades or hanging cloth over the windows.

3. Turn the headlights **ON** and mark the wall at the center of each light's low beam, then switch on the brights and mark the center of each light's high beam. A short length of masking tape which is visible from the front of the vehicle may be used. Although marking all four positions is advisable, marking one position from each light should be sufficient.

4. If neither beam on one side is working, and if another like-sized vehicle is available, park the second one in the exact spot where the vehicle was and mark the beams using the same-side light. Then, switch the vehicles so the one to be aimed is back in the original spot. It must be parked no closer to or farther away from the wall than the second vehicle.

5. Perform any necessary repairs, but make sure the vehicle is not moved, or is returned to the exact spot from which the lights were marked. Turn the headlights **ON** and adjust the beams to match the marks on the wall.

6. Have the headlight adjustment checked as soon as possible by a reputable repair shop.

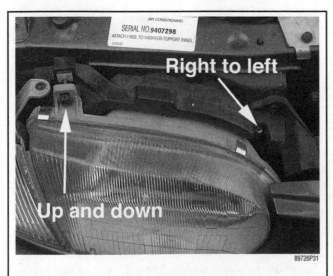

Fig. 69 Location of the headlamp adjusting screws

Signal and Marker Lights

REMOVAL & INSTALLATION

Front Parking Lamp Bulb

▶ See Figures 72 and 73

1. Rotate the parking lamp exterior bulb socket counterclockwise and remove it from the headlamp.
2. Grasp the bulb and pull it from the socket.
3. Installation is the reverse of removal.

Rear Parking, Brake and Turn Signal Bulbs

▶ See Figures 74, 75, 76 and 77

1. Disconnect the negative battery cable.
2. Raise the liftgate and loosen the lamp assembly retaining screws.
3. Press the lamp assembly towards the outside of the vehicle to disengage it from the body.

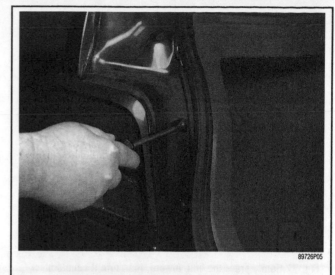

Fig. 74 Loosen the lens retaining screws

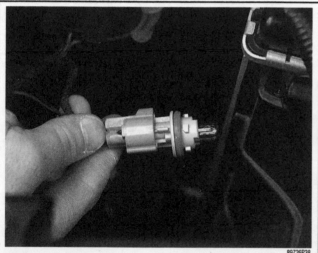

Fig. 72 Turn the parking lamp socket counterclockwise to disengage it from the lens

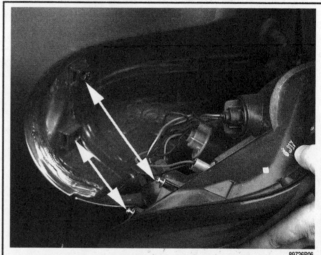

Fig. 75 Press the lamp assembly toward the outside of the vehicle to disengage the retaining pins from their brackets

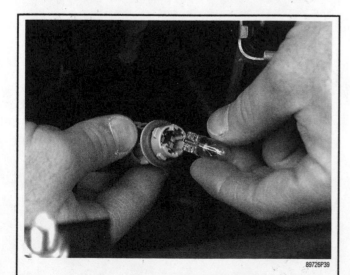

Fig. 73 Grasp the bulb and pull it straight from its socket

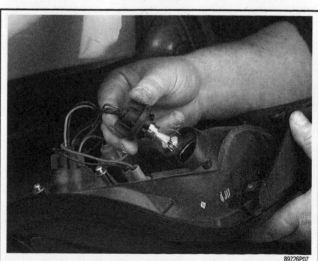

Fig. 76 Turn the bulb socket assembly to unlock the retaining tabs and remove it from the lens

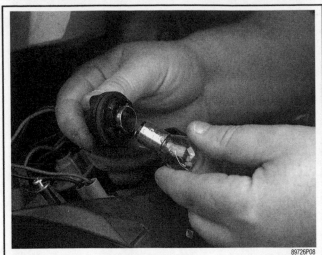

Fig. 77 Gently press the bulb inward, then turn it counterclock-wise and remove it from the socket

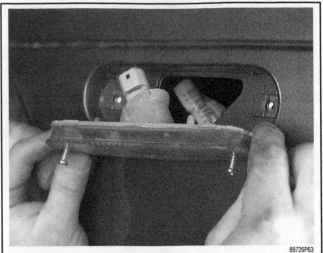

Fig. 79 Pull the lens outward until you can access the bulb socket

4. Pull the lamp assembly away from the body until access to the bulb sockets is possible.

5. Twist the socket(s) approximately ¼ turn counterclockwise to disen-gage from the lamp assembly.

6. Depress the bulb(s) and twist approximately ⅛ turn counterclockwise to remove from the socket(s).

To install:

7. Install the bulb(s) in the socket(s) and connect the socket(s) to the lamp assembly.

8. Place the lamp assembly in position and tighten the assembly retain-ing screws.

9. Connect the negative battery cable.

Front Side Marker Lamp Bulb

◈ See Figures 78, 79, 80 and 81

1. Loosen the lens retaining screws.
2. Slide the lens forward until you can access the bulb socket.
3. Rotate the socket assembly counterclockwise and remove it from the lamp housing.
4. Grasp the bulb and pull it from the socket.

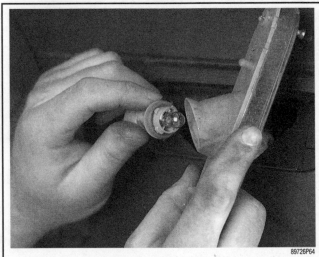

Fig. 80 Rotate the socket assembly counterclockwise and remove it from the lamp housing

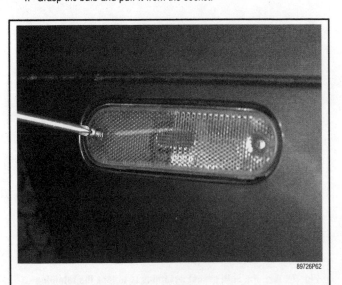

Fig. 78 Loosen the lens retaining screws

Fig. 81 Grasp the bulb and pull it straight from its socket

To install:

5. Install the bulb in the socket.

6. Position the bulb and socket assembly in the housing and turn it clockwise to engage it.

7. Tighten the lens retaining screws.

8. Check for proper lamp operation.

Front Turn Signal Lamp Bulb

▶ **See Figures 82, 83, 84 and 85**

1. Disconnect the negative battery cable.

2. Loosen the turn signal lamp assembly screw.

3. Gently pull the lamp assembly away from the car body until access to the bulb socket is possible.

4. Turn the socket counterclockwise to disengage it from the lamp assembly.

5. Gently push the bulb in and turn it, then remove the bulb from the socket.

To install:

6. Properly line up the bulb's pins with the socket, then install the bulb. Gently depress the bulb, then twist it approximately ⅛ turn clockwise until it is fully engaged.

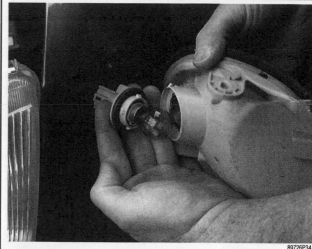

Fig. 84 Turn the socket counterclockwise to disengage it from the lamp assembly

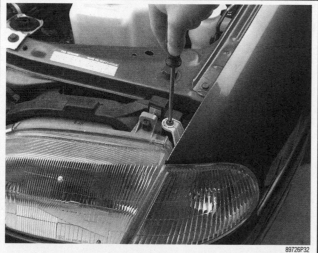

Fig. 82 Use a Phillips head screwdriver to loosen the turn signal lamp assembly screw

Fig. 85 Gently push the bulb in and twist it approximately ⅛ turn counterclockwise, then remove it from the socket

7. Position the socket in the lamp housing and turn it clockwise to engage.

8. Place the lens assembly back into position and tighten the retaining screw.

9. Connect the negative battery cable.

License Plate Lamp Bulb

▶ **See Figures 86, 87, 88 and 89**

1. Disconnect the negative battery cable.

2. Open the liftgate and loosen the license plate lamp lens retaining screws.

3. Remove the lens from the lamp housing.

4. Remove the bulb from the housing.

To install:

5. Push the bulb into its socket in the housing.

6. Position the lens, then install the lamp assembly and tighten the retaining screws.

7. Close the liftgate and connect the negative battery cable.

8. Check for proper bulb operation.

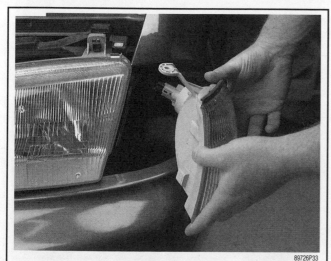

Fig. 83 Pull the lamp assembly away from the car body to access the bulb socket

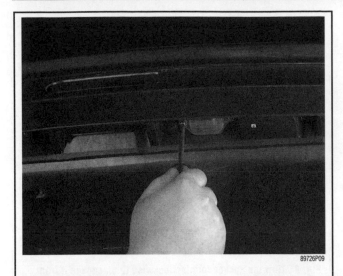

Fig. 86 Loosen the license plate lamp retaining screws

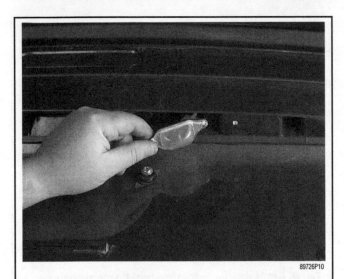

Fig. 87 Pull the lamp assembly down for easier access

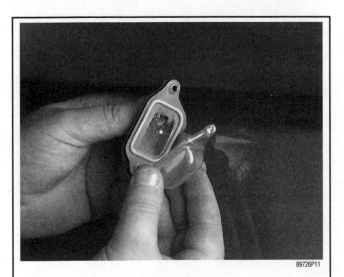

Fig. 88 Separate the lens from the lamp housing . . .

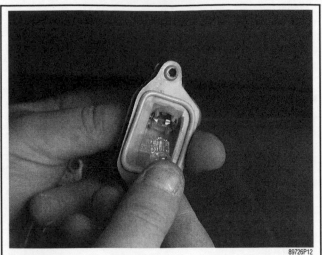

Fig. 89 . . . then grasp the bulb and pull it from the housing assembly

High Mount Brake Lamp Bulb

▶ See Figures 90, 91 and 92

1. Disconnect the negative battery cable.
2. Raise the liftgate and remove the liftgate trim panel.
3. Rotate the bulb socket assembly counterclockwise and remove it from the lamp housing.
4. Pull the bulb from the socket.

➡It is not necessary to disengage the lamp's electrical connection.

To install:
5. Push the bulb into the socket.
6. Insert the bulb and socket assembly in the lens housing, then turn the socket clockwise to engage it.
7. Install the liftgate trim panel and close the liftgate.
8. Connect the negative battery cable and check for proper bulb operation.

Dome Lamp Bulb

1. Disconnect the negative battery cable.
2. Remove the dome lamp lens.
3. Remove the bulb from the socket.

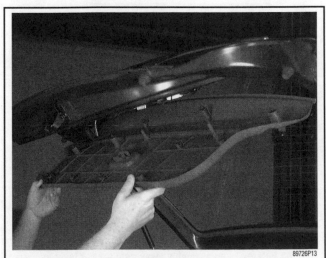

Fig. 90 Remove the liftgate trim panel by VERY CAREFULLY unsnapping the retaining pins

Fig. 91 Twist the socket assembly counterclockwise to disengage the tabs, and withdraw it from the lens

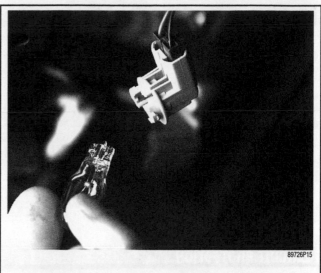

Fig. 92 Grasp the bulb and pull it straight from its socket

To install:
4. Install the bulb in the socket.
5. Install the lamp lens, making sure it is fully engaged.
6. Connect the negative battery cable and check for proper bulb operation.

Luggage Compartment Lamp Lens

1. Disconnect the negative battery cable.

2. Use a small prytool to carefully remove the lamp lens.
3. Remove the bulb from the socket.
To install:
4. Install the bulb in the socket.
5. Install the lens, making sure it is fully engaged.
6. Connect the negative battery cable and check for proper bulb operation.

Light Bulb Specifications

FRONT

	Function	Wattage	SAE trade number
1	Headlamps	60/55	E7GZ-13N021-A
2	Front turn signal lamps	27	1156
3	Side marker lamps	5	194

REAR

	Function	Wattage	SAE trade number
1	Rear turn signal lamps	27	1156
2	Brakelamps and tail lamps	27	1157
3	Back-up lamps	27	1156
4	License plate lamps	5	168
5	Luggage compartment lamp	5	E7GZ-13466-D
6	High-mount brakelamp	27	921
7	Rear side marker lamp	3.4	194

INTERIOR

Function	Wattage	SAE trade number
Interior courtesy lamp	10	E7GZ-13466-H

89726C01

TRAILER WIRING

Wiring the vehicle for towing is fairly easy. There are a number of good wiring kits available and these should be used, rather than trying to design your own.

All trailers will need brake lights and turn signals as well as tail lights and side marker lights. Most areas require extra marker lights for overwide trailers. Also, most areas have recently required back-up lights for trailers, and most trailer manufacturers have been building trailers with back-up lights for several years.

Additionally, some Class I, most Class II and just about all Class III trailers will have electric brakes. Add to this number an accessories wire, to operate trailer internal equipment or to charge the trailer's battery, and you can have as many as seven wires in the harness.

Determine the equipment on your trailer and buy the wiring kit necessary. The kit will contain all the wires needed, plus a plug adapter set which includes the female plug, mounted on the bumper or hitch, and the male plug, wired into, or plugged into the trailer harness.

When installing the kit, follow the manufacturer's instructions. The color coding of the wires is usually standard throughout the industry. One point to note: some domestic vehicles, and most imported vehicles, have separate turn signals. On most domestic vehicles, the brake lights and rear turn signals operate with the same bulb. For those vehicles without separate turn signals, you can purchase an isolation unit so that the brake lights won't blink whenever the turn signals are operated. The isolation units are simple and quick to install.

One, final point, the best kits are those with a spring loaded cover on the vehicle mounted socket. This cover prevents dirt and moisture from corroding the terminals. Never let the vehicle socket hang loosely; always mount it securely to the bumper or hitch.

CIRCUIT PROTECTION

Fuses

REPLACEMENT

Fuses are used in your car to protect the electrical system from overloading. If any electrical component in your car is not working, the first thing you should check is the fuse before testing the component itself.

➡**If a particular fuse repeatedly requires replacement, check other portions of the affected circuit for a defective component or damaged wiring.**

The Aspire is equipped with a main fuse block under the hood and a conventional fuse panel mounted in the instrument panel, behind a cover.

Main Fuse Block

▶ **See Figures 93, 94, 95 and 96**

1. Disconnect the negative battery cable.
2. Unfasten the locking clips on each end, then lift off the fuse block cover.
3. Pull the fuse from the block.

Fig. 94 To remove a fuse, simply remove the cover . . .

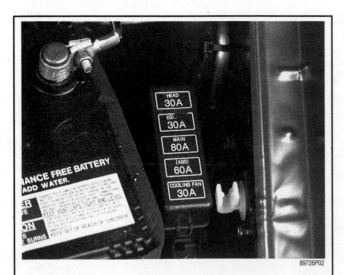

Fig. 93 The main fuse panel is located under the hood

Fig. 95 . . . then grasp the fuse and pull it from the panel

Fuse Location	Fuse Name	Fuse Rating	Protected Component
1	COOLING FAN	30 amp	Cooling fan motor, Condenser fan motor, Magnetic clutch
2	ABS	60 amp	Anti-lock Braking System
3	MAIN	80 amp	Air bag diagnostic monitor, Anti-lock Brake System control unit, Anti-lock Brake System relay, Audio system, Backup lamp, Brake system unit, Blower motor relay, Cargo lamp, Central processing unit, Cigarette lighter, Cooling fan relay, Daytime Running Lamps relay, Flasher unit, Front side marker lamp, Front wiper and washer, Hazard lamp, Horn, Ignition coil, Illumination (A/C switch, Panel, Rear defroster switch, upshift indicator), Instrument cluster warning lights (air bag readiness, anti-lock brake system, brake system, charging, check engine, fuel, oil pressure, rear defroster, safety belt, tachometer), Interior lamp, License plate lamp, Powertrain control module, Rear defroster, Rear defroster relay, Rear wiper and washer, Tail lamp, Tail lamp relay, Turn signal lamp, Stop lamp

89726G18

Fig. 96 Fuse locations and specifications within the main fuse block

To install:

4. Push the replacement fuse into the fuse block. Be sure to replace a defective fuse with one of equal amperage.

5. Install the fuse block cover and secure the clips on both sides.

6. Connect the negative battery cable.

Coventional Fuse Panel

♦ See Figure 97

1. Locate the fuse panel and remove the cover.

2. Locate the position of the fuse you want to check using the accompanying illustration.

3. Use the fuse puller located on the inside of the fuse panel cover to remove the fuse.

4. Look through the side of the fuse to see if the metal wire inside is separated. If it is, replace the fuse.

To install:

5. Replace the fuse with one of equal amperage. Refer to the accompanying chart.

6. Press the fuse into its original location.

7. Place the fuse puller back on the inside of the fuse panel cover and reinstall the cover.

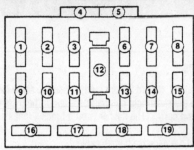

Fuse Location	Fuse Name	Fuse Rating	Protected Component
1	ENGINE	10 amp	Air bag system, Anti-lock Brake System, Anti-lock Brake System relay, Blower motor relay, Cooling fan relay, Ignition main relay
2	METER	15 amp	Back-up lamps, Central processing unit, Flasher unit, Instrument cluster warning lights (Air bag readiness, anti-lock brake, brake system, charging, check engine, oil pressure, safety belt, rear defroster, upshift), Instrument cluster gauges (fuel, shift-lock actuator, tachometer, turn signal indicator), Turn signals lamps, Rear defroster relay
3	DEFOG	20 amp	Rear window defroster
4	—	20 amp	Spare fuse
5	—	15 amp	Spare fuse
6	—	—	—
7	F. FOG	15 amp	Front fog lamps
8	—	—	—
9	—	—	—
10	WIPER	20 amp	A/C switch, A/C relay, Blower motor unit relay, Condenser fan motor, Daytime running lamps system, Front windshield wipers and washer
11	—	—	—
12	BLOWER	30 amp Circuit Breaker	Climate control blower motor
13	HAZARD	15 amp	Hazard warning flashers
14	STOP	15 amp	Anti-lock Brake System unit, Brakelamps, Cargo lamp, Horn
15	TAIL	15 amp	Front side marker lamps, Instrument panel illumination, License plate lamps, Parking lamps, Tail lamps, Turn signal lamp
16	CIGAR	15 amp	Audio system, Cigarette lighter
17	—	—	—
18	—	—	—
19	ROOM	10 amp	Audio system, Back-up lamps, Central processing unit, Interior courtesy lamp, Powertrain control module

89726G19

Fig. 97 Fuse locations and specifications within the conventional fuse block

Flashers

REPLACEMENT

▶ **See Figure 98**

The turn signal and hazard flasher circuits use the same flasher unit. The unit is located in the passenger compartment under the instrument panel in the upper left-hand corner. The flasher is on a bracket that also holds the horn relay.

1. Disconnect the negative battery cable.
2. Disengage the flasher's electrical connection and remove the flasher unit.
3. Installation is the reverse of removal.

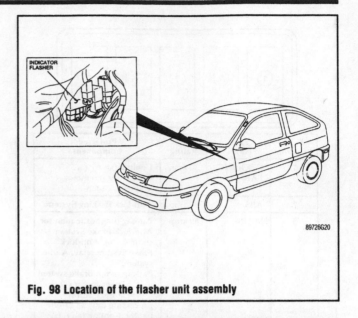

Fig. 98 Location of the flasher unit assembly

WIRING DIAGRAMS

INDEX OF WIRING DIAGRAMS

89726W01

SAMPLE DIAGRAM: HOW TO READ & INTERPRET WIRING DIAGRAMS

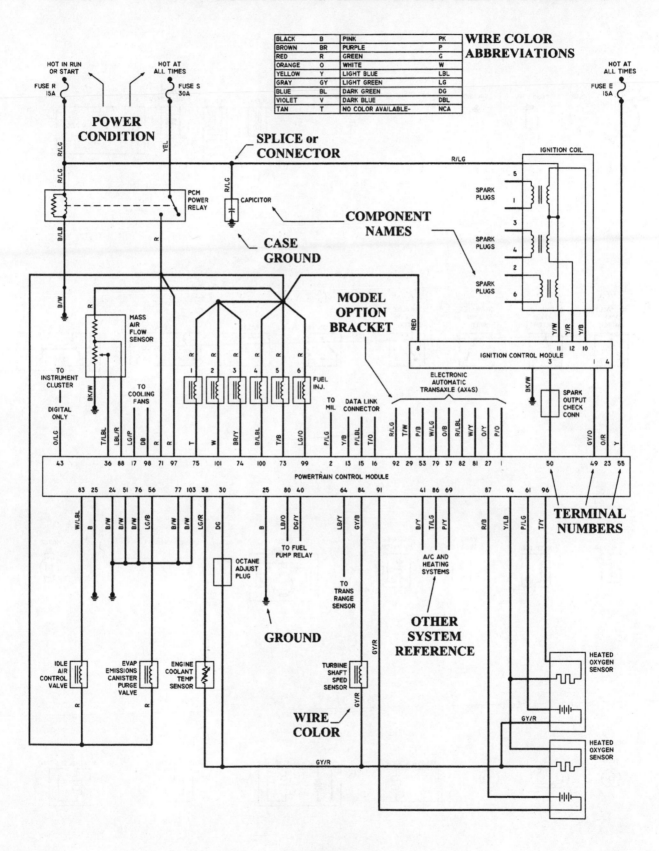

DIAGRAM 1

TCCA6W01

WIRING DIAGRAM SYMBOLS

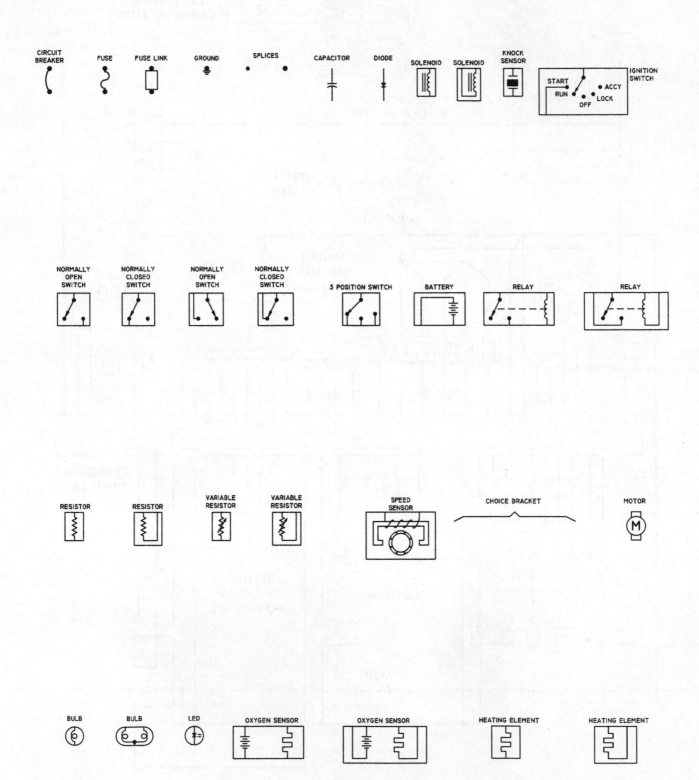

DIAGRAM 2

TCCA6W02

1994-95 ENGINE SCHEMATIC

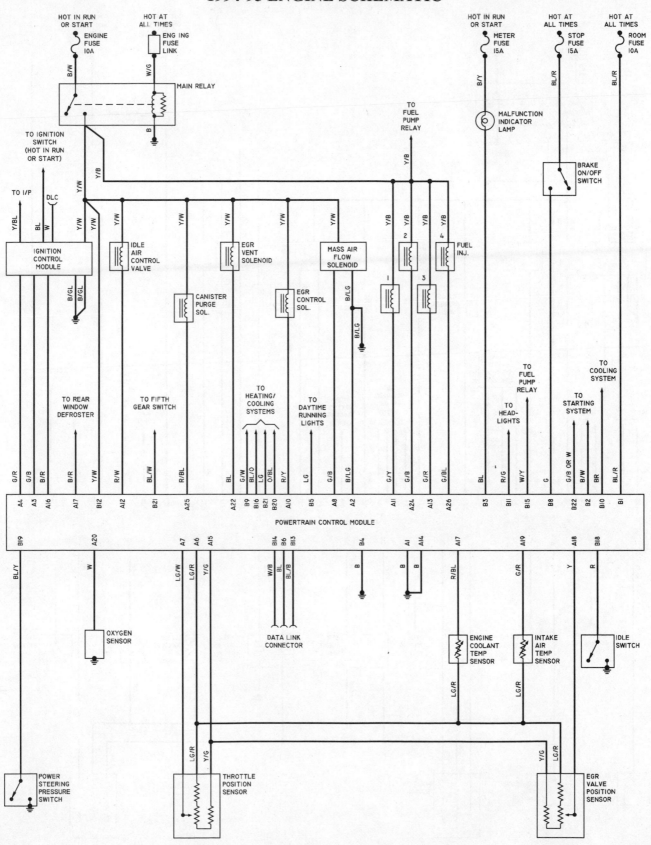

DIAGRAM 3

1996-97 ENGINE SCHEMATIC

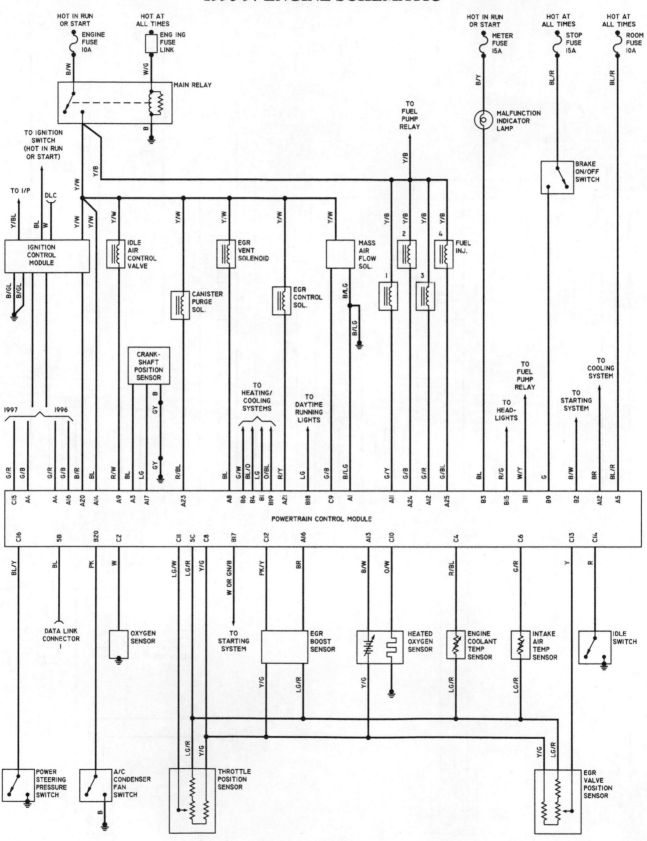

DIAGRAM 4

89726E02

1994-97 CHASSIS SCHEMATICS

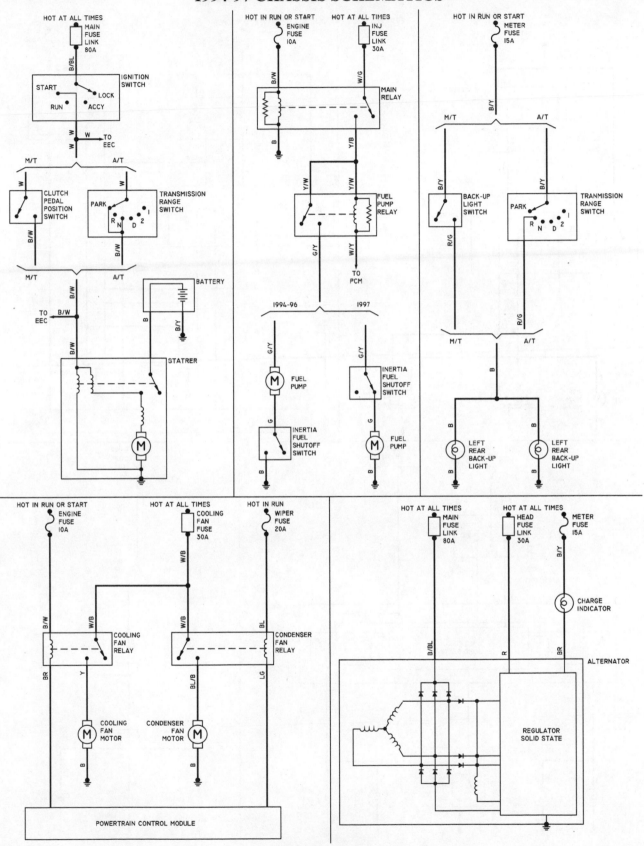

DIAGRAM 5

89726B01

1994-97 CHASSIS SCHEMATICS

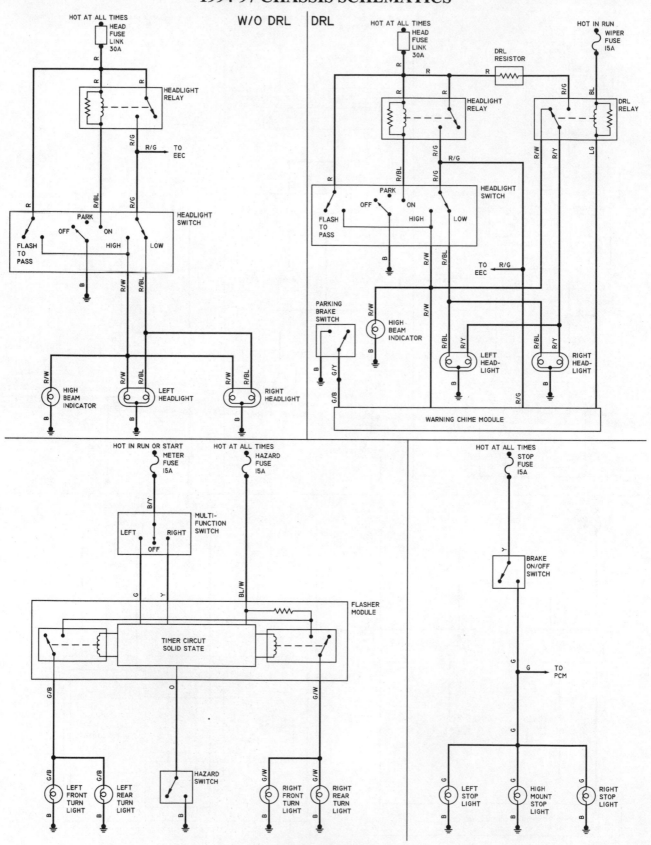

DIAGRAM 6

89726B02

1994-97 CHASSIS SCHEMATICS

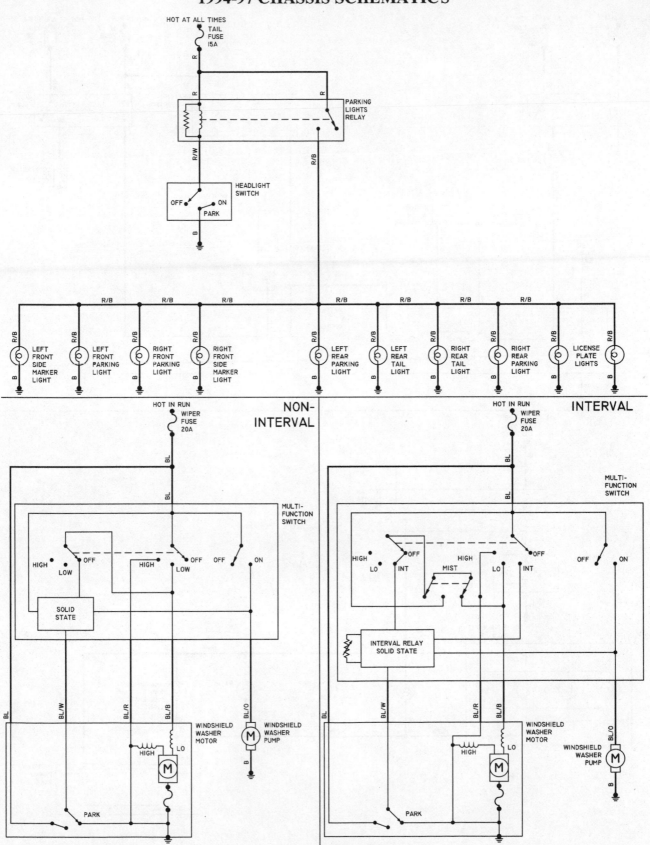

DIAGRAM 7

89726B03

1994-97 CHASSIS SCHEMATICS

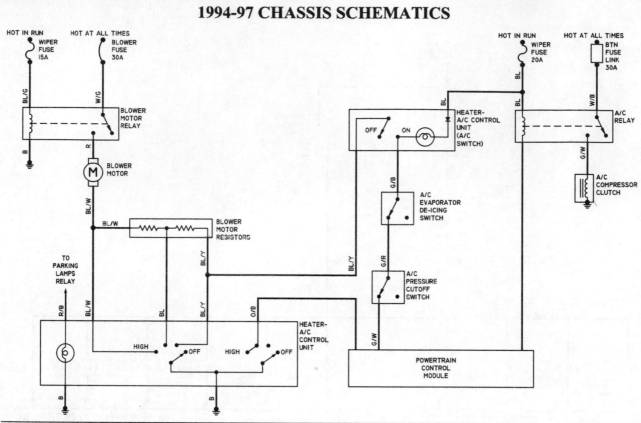

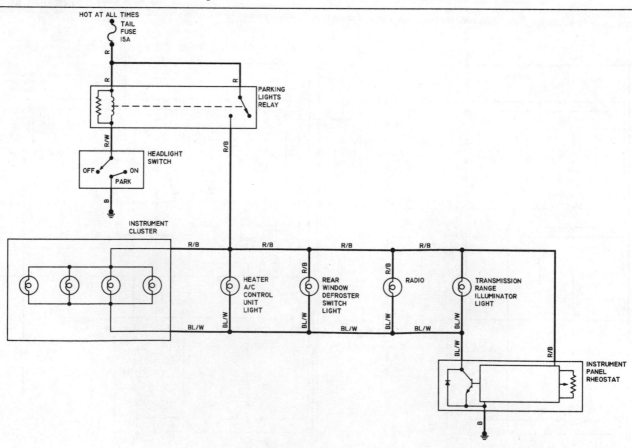

DIAGRAM 8

89726B04

7
DRIVE TRAIN

MANUAL TRANSAXLE

Understanding the Manual Transaxle

Because of the way an internal combustion engine breathes, it can produce torque, or twisting force, only within a narrow speed range. Most modern, overhead valve pushrod engines must turn at about 2500 rpm to produce their peak torque. By 4500 rpm they are producing so little torque that continued increases in engine speed produce no power increases. The torque peak on overhead camshaft engines is generally much higher, but much narrower.

The manual transaxle and clutch are employed to vary the relationship between engine speed and the speed of the wheels so that adequate engine power can be produced under all circumstances. The clutch allows engine torque to be applied to the transaxle input shaft gradually, due to mechanical slippage. Consequently, the vehicle may be started smoothly from a full stop. The transaxle changes the ratio between the rotating speeds of the engine and the wheels by the use of gears. The gear ratios allow full engine power to be applied to the wheels during acceleration at low speeds and at highway/passing speeds.

In a front wheel drive transaxle, power is usually transmitted from the input shaft to a mainshaft or output shaft located slightly beneath and to the side of the input shaft. The gears of the mainshaft mesh with gears on the input shaft, allowing power to be carried from one to the other. All forward gears are in constant mesh and are free from rotating with the shaft unless the synchronizer and clutch are engaged. Shifting from one gear to the next causes one of the gears to be freed from rotating with the shaft and locks another to it. Gears are locked and unlocked by internal dog clutches which slide between the center of the gear and the shaft. The forward gears employ synchronizers; these are friction members which smoothly bring gear and shaft to the same speed before the toothed dog clutches are engaged.

Back-up Light Switch

REMOVAL & INSTALLATION

♦ See Figure 1

1. Disconnect the negative battery cable.
2. Disengage the back-up lamp switch electrical connections.
3. Raise the car and support it with safety stands.
4. Use an open end wrench to remove the switch from the transaxle case.

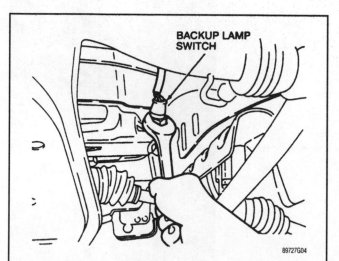

Fig. 1 Use an open end wrench to remove the back-up light switch

To install:
5. Apply pipe sealant with Teflon® D8AZ-19554-A or equivalent to the threads of the switch.
6. Install the switch and tighten it to 15–21 ft. lbs. (20–29 Nm).
7. Lower the car and fasten the switch's electrical connections.
8. Connect the negative battery cable.

Park/Neutral Position Switch

REMOVAL & INSTALLATION

♦ See Figure 2

➥On vehicles equipped with a manual transaxle, the Park/Neutral Position (PNP) switch signals the Powertrain Control Module (PCM) to control idle speed when the transaxle is shifted into NEUTRAL, and activates back-up lights when the transaxle is in REVERSE. The PNP switch is not adjustable.

1. Disconnect the negative battery cable.
2. Unplug the PNP switch electrical connector.
3. Raise and safely support the vehicle.
4. Using an open end wrench, remove the PNP switch from the flywheel housing.

To install:
5. Apply pipe sealant with Teflon® D8AZ-19554-A or equivalent to the threads of the switch.
6. Install the PNP switch to the flywheel housing and tighten to 15–21 ft. lbs. (20–29 Nm).
7. Lower the vehicle.
8. Fasten the PNP switch's electrical connector.
9. Connect the negative battery cable.

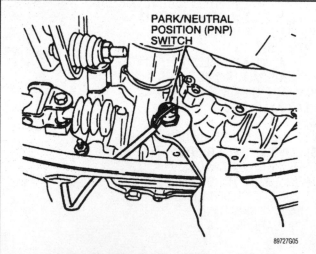

Fig. 2 Loosen the Park/Neutral Position (PNP) switch with an open end wrench

Starter Clutch Pedal Position Switch

REMOVAL & INSTALLATION

♦ See Figure 3

1. Disconnect the negative battery cable.
2. Disengage the Starter Clutch Pedal Position (SCPP) switch's electrical connection.

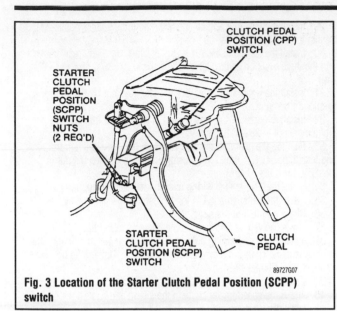

Fig. 3 Location of the Starter Clutch Pedal Position (SCPP) switch

3. Loosen the two switch retaining nuts and remove the switch.
4. Installation is the reverse of removal.

ADJUSTMENT

If the car does not start with the clutch pedal depressed, adjustment of the switch may be necessary.
1. Loosen the switch nuts slightly.
2. Adjust the switch position slightly, depress the clutch pedal and start the car.
3. If the car does not start, keep adjusting the switch until it does and then tighten the retaining nuts.

Clutch Pedal Position Switch

REMOVAL & INSTALLATION

▶ **See Figure 4**

1. Disengage the Clutch Pedal Position (CPP) switch's electrical connection.
2. Loosen the switch locknut and unscrew the switch from the bracket.

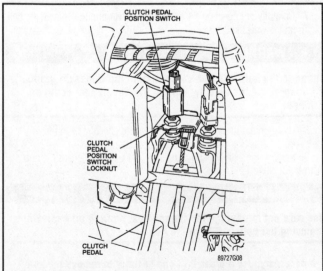

Fig. 4 Location of the Clutch Pedal Position (CPP) switch

To install:
3. Install the switch in the bracket and engage the electrical connection.
4. Adjust the pedal height.
5. Tighten the switch locknut to 124–159 inch lbs. (14–18 Nm).

Differential Oil Seal

REMOVAL & INSTALLATION

▶ **See Figure 5**

1. Raise the car and support it with safety stands.
2. Remove the front wheel halfshaft and CV-joint assembly.
3. Use a prytool to remove the seal(s).
To install:
4. Use seal replacer T87C-77000-H or equivalent to install the seal(s).
5. Install the front wheel halfshaft and CV-joint assembly.
6. Remove the safety stands and lower the car.

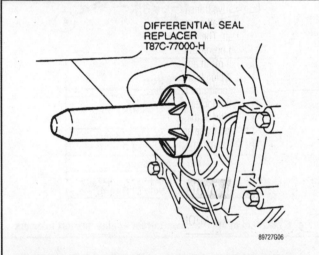

Fig. 5 Use an appropriate tool such as T87C-77000-H or equivalent to install the differential oil seal

Manual Transaxle Assembly

REMOVAL & INSTALLATION

▶ **See Figure 6**

1. Disconnect the negative battery cable.
2. Disengage the two back-up light switch wiring connectors.
3. Disengage the Park/Neutral Position (PNP) switch wiring connector.
4. Remove the clutch cable adjusting nut and disengage the cable from the release lever. Pull the clutch release cable through the cable bracket.
5. Remove the engine compartment wiring harness ground strap from the transaxle.
6. Remove the starter motor.
7. Loosen the speedometer cable retainer and disconnect the speedometer cable.
8. Remove the two bolts from the top of the clutch housing.
9. Install a three bar engine support tool D88L-6000-A, or equivalent. Properly secure the engine to the engine support tool.
10. Raise and safely support the vehicle.
11. Disengage the halfshafts from the differential side gears.
12. Install differential side gear plug tool T87C-7025-C or equivalent, to prevent the side gears from moving.

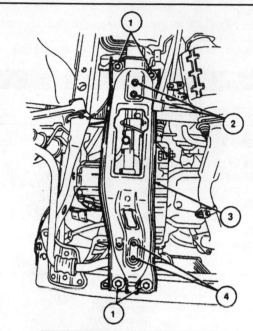

Item	Description
1	Rear Engine Support Rebound Insulator Bolt (4 Req'd)
2	Rear Transaxle Support Insulator Nuts (2 Req'd)
3	Rear Engine Support
4	Front Transaxle Support Insulator Nuts (2 Req'd)

89727G09

Fig. 6 Location of the transaxle-to-rear engine support retainers

13. Remove the nut and bolt attaching the shift rod to the input shaft.

14. Remove the gearshift stabilizer bar nut, lockwasher and flat washer, then remove the bar from the control rod-to-support bar stud.

15. Loosen the three transaxle-to-engine retaining bolts from the transaxle case rear bracket and remove the bracket.

16. Loosen the three transaxle-to-engine retaining bolts from the transaxle case front bracket and remove the bracket.

17. Loosen the two rear and front transaxle support insulator nuts from the rear engine support.

18. Loosen the four rear engine support rebound insulator bolts and remove the rear engine support.

19. Position a suitable transmission jack under the transaxle and secure it with a safety chain or strap.

20. Loosen the four flywheel reinforcing plate bolts.

21. Loosen the two remaining transaxle-to-engine block retaining bolts.

22. Carefully separate the transaxle from the engine and lower the transaxle from the vehicle.

To Install:

23. Raise the transaxle into position and seat it against the rear of the engine.

24. Install the four flywheel reinforcing plate bolts and tighten to 62–86 inch lbs. (7–10 Nm).

25. Install four lower transaxle retaining bolts and tighten to 47–66 ft. lbs. (64–89 Nm).

26. Remove the transmission jack.

27. Position the rear engine support. Install the two rear transaxle support insulator nuts and tighten them to 21–34 ft. lbs. (28–46 Nm).

28. Install the two front transaxle support insulator nuts and tighten to 32–38 ft. lbs. (43–52 Nm).

29. Install the four rear engine support rebound insulator bolts and tighten to 47–66 ft. lbs. (64–89 Nm).

30. Install the transaxle case-to-cylinder block front and rear brackets and the three bolts on each. Tighten the bolts to 27–38 ft. lbs. (37–52 Nm).

31. Install the washer and the gearshift stabilizer bar on the control rod-to-support bar stud.

32. Install the washer, lockwasher and gearshift stabilizer bar nut. Tighten the nut to 28–38 ft. lbs. (38–52 Nm).

33. Position the gearshift rod and clevis on the main shift control shaft and install the selector shift rod adjustment sleeve. Tighten the nut to 12–17 ft. lbs. (16–23 Nm).

34. Route the PNP switch wiring over the rear engine support.

35. Install the halfshaft and CV-joint assemblies.

36. Check and fill the transaxle, if needed.

37. Lower the vehicle and remove the engine support bar.

38. Install the two retaining bolts at the top of the clutch housing. The top bolt is installed through the heater pipe bracket. Tighten the bolts to 47–66 ft. lbs. (64–89 Nm).

39. Connect the ground strap to the transaxle case.

40. Attach the speedometer cable to the sleeve and hand-tighten.

41. Install the starter motor.

42. Engage the PNP and back-up light switch wiring connectors.

43. Connect the clutch cable to the release lever and adjust the clutch pedal free-play.

44. Connect the negative battery cable.

45. Road test the vehicle and check for proper transaxle operation.

Halfshafts

REMOVAL & INSTALLATION

♦ **See Figures 7, 8, 9, 10 and 11**

1. Raise the car and support it with safety stands.

2. Drain the transmission fluid from the transaxle.

3. Remove the front wheels.

4. Use a small cape chisel to carefully raise the staked portion of the front axle wheel hub retainer.

5. Have an assistant apply the brakes, then loosen, but do not remove, the front axle wheel hub retainer.

6. Loosen the front suspension lower arm ball joint nut and bolt.

✳ WARNING

Be careful not to damage the ball joint dust boot.

7. Carefully pry down on the suspension lower arm to separate the ball joint from the wheel knuckle.

✳ WARNING

Separate the halfshaft and CV-joint from the transaxle gradually. If it is removed too quickly, the differential oil seal could be damaged.

8. Use a prybar to separate the halfshaft and CV-joint from the transaxle.

9. Remove the axle wheel hub retainer and washer. Discard the hub retainer.

✳ WARNING

Use care not to damage the inner wheel bearing oil seal while removing the halfshaft from the hub.

➡ **If necessary, use a brass drift and hammer to remove the halfshaft from the hub.**

Fig. 7 Use a small cape chisel to carefully raise the staked portion of the wheel retaining nut . . .

Fig. 8 . . . then use a socket to loosen the nut

Fig. 9 After detaching the lower arm ball joint, separate the halfshaft from the hub. Use care not to damage the inner wheel bearing oil seal

Fig. 10 Use a prytool to separate the halfshaft/CV-joint assembly from the transaxle . . .

Fig. 11 . . . and remove the halfshaft assembly from the car

10. Separate the halfshaft from the hub.

11. Use a prytool to remove the halfshaft bearing retainer from the CV-joint. Discard the bearing retainer circlip.

12. Install plugs in the differential to prevent leaks.

To install:

13. Inspect the differential oil seals and inner wheel bearing seals for damage prior to installation. Replace them if they are defective.

➡The original halfshaft bearing retaining circlip must not be reused.

14. Install a new circlip on the CV-joint. Lubricate the joint with grease.

15. Remove the differential plugs.

❉❉ **WARNING**

Install the CV-joint carefully so that you do not damage the differential oil seal.

16. Install the inboard end of the halfshaft into the differential side gear.

❋❋ WARNING

Install the halfshaft carefully so that you do not damage the inner wheel bearing oil seal.

17. Install the outboard end of the halfshaft into the wheel hub.
18. Install the wheel hub washer and a new retainer onto the halfshaft and tighten by hand.
19. Raise the lower control arm and connect the ball joint. Take care not to damage the ball joint dust boot. Install the clamp nut and bolt, and tighten the nut to 32–40 ft. lbs. (43–54 Nm).
20. Have an assistant apply the brakes. Tighten the wheel hub retainer to 116–174 ft. lbs. (157–235 Nm). Stake the nut using a suitable tool.

➡Do not stake the locking tab with a pointed tool. Make sure the locking tab is depressed at least 0.16 in. (4mm) into the retainer's slot to ensure proper locking capability.

21. Install the wheel and tire assembly. Tighten the lug bolts to 65–87 ft. lbs. (88–118 Nm).
22. Install and tighten the transaxle drain plug.
23. Refill the transaxle with transmission fluid.
24. Lower the vehicle.
25. Road test the vehicle and check for transaxle leaks and proper operation.

CV-JOINTS OVERHAUL

▸ See Figures 12 thru 25

➡On all halfshafts, the outboard CV-joint (Birfield-type) is permanently fitted onto the halfshaft and cannot be removed. To replace the outboard CV-joint boot, the inner CV-joint (Tri-pot-type) must first be removed. If a boot has failed due to age or wear, all boots should be replaced at the same time.

1. Raise and safely support the vehicle.
2. Remove the halfshaft from the vehicle and support the assembly in a vise with protective or soft jaws.
3. Remove the large boot clamp from the inboard CV-joint and roll the boot back over the shaft.
4. Matchmark the outer race, halfshaft and Tri-pot bearing for reassembly using paint or marker. Do not use a punch or chisel.
5. Remove the wire ring bearing retainer from inside the outer race/housing and remove the outer race.
6. Matchmark the Tri-pot bearing and halfshaft. Remove the bearing snapring, then remove the bearing from the halfshaft. It may be necessary to drive the bearing off the shaft with a brass drift.

Fig. 13 Removing the outer band from the CV-boot

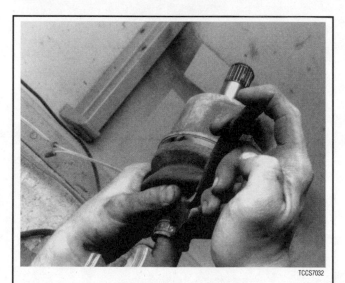

Fig. 14 Removing the inner band from the CV-boot

Fig. 12 Check the CV-boot for wear

Fig. 15 Removing the CV-boot from the joint housing

Fig. 16 Clean the CV-joint housing prior to removing the boot

Fig. 19 Inspecting the CV-joint housing

Fig. 17 Removing the CV-joint housing assembly

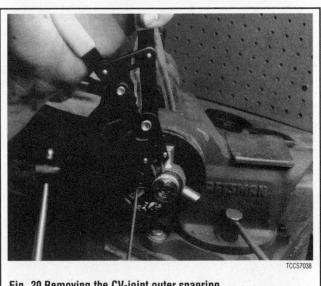

Fig. 20 Removing the CV-joint outer snapring

Fig. 18 Removing the CV-joint

Fig. 21 Checking the CV-joint snapring for wear

Fig. 22 CV-joint snapring (typical)

Fig. 23 Removing the CV-joint assembly

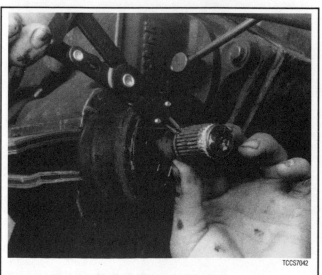

Fig. 24 Removing the CV-joint inner snapring

7. Remove the small clamp and the inboard CV-joint boot from the halfshaft.

➡**Test the CV-joint grease for contamination by rubbing a small amount between 2 fingers. If a gritty feeling is present, the grease is contaminated and the CV-joint must be disassembled and thoroughly cleaned and inspected before adding new grease.**

8. To remove the outboard CV-joint boot, remove the dynamic damper if applicable (right-hand halfshaft only), then remove the boot clamps and slide the boot off of the shaft from the inboard side. If the outboard boot is to be reused, wrap tape around the shaft splines to protect the boot during removal.

9. On vehicles equipped with ABS brakes, the wheel speed sensor can be driven off the outboard CV-joint with a hammer and chisel if the joint is to be replaced.

➡**Do not remove the anti-lock sensor ring if it does not need to be replaced. If the sensor ring must be removed, replace with a new sensor ring.**

To install:

10. If not already installed, wrap smooth electrical tape around the halfshaft spline to protect and ease the installation of the CV-joint boot(s). Slide the clamps and the outboard boot onto the shaft.

11. Before positioning the boot over the CV-joint, pack the CV-joint and boot with grease. Be sure to use all of the grease in the pouch supplied with the boot kit.

12. Fit the boot into place on the CV-joint, making sure it is fully seated in the grooves in the shaft and outer race. Insert a suitable tool between the boot and the outer bearing race to allow trapped air to escape from the boot.

13. Install the boot clamps, wrapping them around the boots in the opposite direction of normal (forward) halfshaft rotation. Pull the clamps tight with a suitable tool and bend the locking tabs to secure in position.

14. After installing the outboard CV-joint boot, if applicable, install the dynamic damper onto the halfshaft at a distance of 18.99–19.27 in. (482.5–489.5mm) from the outboard end of the halfshaft. Measure this distance with the outboard CV-joint fully pushed onto the halfshaft.

➡**The dynamic damper is only used on the right-hand halfshaft assembly.**

15. Fit the inboard CV-joint boot and clamps onto the halfshaft. Remove the tape from the halfshaft splines.

16. Install the Tri-pot assembly on the halfshaft with the matchmarks aligned. Install the Tri-pot retaining ring.

17. Fill the CV-joint outer race with 3.5 oz. (100g) of high temperature CV-joint grease. Install the outer race over the Tri-pot joint with the matchmarks aligned and install the wire ring bearing retainer.

Fig. 25 Installing the CV-joint assembly (typical)

18. Fit the boot into place on the CV-joint, making sure it is fully seated in the grooves in the shaft and outer race. The distance between the CV-joint boot clamp grooves will measure about 3.5 in. (90mm).

19. Insert a suitable tool between the boot and the outer bearing race to allow trapped air to escape from the boot.

20. Install the boot clamps, wrapping them around the boots in the opposite direction of normal (forward) halfshaft rotation. Pull the clamps tight with a suitable tool and bend the locking tabs to secure in position.

21. Work the CV-joint through its full range of travel at various angles. The joint should flex, extend and compress smoothly. Wipe away any excess grease.

22. If necessary, carefully drive or press the wheel speed sensor onto the CV-joint.

23. Install the halfshaft into the vehicle.

24. Lower the vehicle.

25. Check the transaxle fluid level, and add fluid if required.

26. Road test and check for proper operation of the halfshaft assemblies.

CLUTCH

Understanding the Clutch

※※ CAUTION

The clutch driven disc may contain asbestos, which has been determined to be a cancer causing agent. Never clean clutch surfaces with compressed air! Avoid inhaling any dust from any clutch surface! When cleaning clutch surfaces, use a commercially available brake cleaning fluid.

The purpose of the clutch is to disconnect and connect engine power at the transaxle. A vehicle at rest requires a lot of engine torque to get all that weight moving. An internal combustion engine does not develop a high starting torque (unlike steam engines) so it must be allowed to operate without any load until it builds up enough torque to move the vehicle. Torque increases with engine rpm. The clutch allows the engine to build up torque by physically disconnecting the engine from the transaxle, relieving the engine of any load or resistance.

The transfer of engine power to the transaxle (the load) must be smooth and gradual; if it weren't, drive line components would wear out or break quickly. This gradual power transfer is made possible by gradually releasing the clutch pedal. The clutch disc and pressure plate are the connecting link between the engine and transaxle. When the clutch pedal is released, the disc and plate contact each other (the clutch is engaged) physically joining the engine and transaxle. When the pedal is pushed inward, the disc and plate separate (the clutch is disengaged) disconnecting the engine from the transaxle.

Most clutches utilize a single plate, dry friction disc with a diaphragm-style spring pressure plate. The clutch disc has a splined hub which attaches the disc to the input shaft. The disc has friction material where it contacts the flywheel and pressure plate. Torsion springs on the disc help absorb engine torque pulses. The pressure plate applies pressure to the clutch disc, holding it tight against the surface of the flywheel. The clutch operating mechanism consists of a release bearing, fork and cylinder assembly.

The release fork and actuating linkage transfer pedal motion to the release bearing. In the engaged position (pedal released) the diaphragm spring holds the pressure plate against the clutch disc, so engine torque is transmitted to the input shaft. When the clutch pedal is depressed, the release bearing pushes the diaphragm spring center toward the flywheel. The diaphragm spring pivots the fulcrum, relieving the load on the pressure plate. Steel spring straps riveted to the clutch cover lift the pressure plate from the clutch disc, disengaging the engine drive from the transaxle and enabling the gears to be changed.

The clutch is operating properly if:

1. It will stall the engine when released with the vehicle held stationary.

2. The shift lever can be moved freely between 1st and reverse gears when the vehicle is stationary and the clutch disengaged.

Driven Disc and Pressure Plate

REMOVAL & INSTALLATION

▶ See Figures 26 thru 41

1. Disconnect the negative battery cable.
2. Raise and safely support the vehicle.
3. Remove the transaxle assembly.

➡**During the removal procedure, do not allow oil or grease to come in contact with the clutch disc facing if the disc is to be reused. Handle the disc with clean rags wrapped around the edges and do not touch the disc facing. Even a small amount of dirt or grease may cause the clutch to grab or slip.**

4. If the pressure plate is to be reused, paint or scribe alignment marks on the pressure plate and flywheel for assembly reference.

5. Install an appropriate locking tool to prevent the flywheel from turning.

6. Install a clutch aligning tool to prevent the clutch plate from dropping when the retaining bolts are removed.

7. Loosen the 6 pressure plate retaining bolts in an alternate pattern, one turn at a time; this will relieve the pressure plate spring tension evenly and prevent distortion of the pressure plate.

8. Remove the pressure plate and clutch disc once the retaining bolts are loosened.

TCCS7142

Fig. 26 Typical clutch alignment tool—note how the splines match the transaxle's input shaft

Fig. 27 Loosen and remove the clutch and pressure plate bolts evenly, a little at a time . . .

Fig. 28 . . . then carefully remove the clutch and pressure plate assembly from the flywheel

Fig. 29 Check across the flywheel surface, it should be flat

Fig. 30 If necessary, lock the flywheel in place and remove the retaining bolts . . .

Fig. 31 . . . then remove the flywheel from the crankshaft in order to replace it or have it machined

9. Inspect all clutch components including the clutch release fork and release bearing, and replace as required.

10. Inspect the flywheel for scoring, cracks and heat checks. Resurface or replace the flywheel, as necessary.

11. Inspect the pilot bearing for damage. Make sure the bearing turns easily. If replacement is necessary, remove the flywheel and the pilot bearing.

To install:

12. If necessary, install a new pilot bearing using a suitable installation tool. Use only a driver tool that contacts the bearing outer race. A driver tool that contacts the inner race or the bearing area will damage the bearing.

13. If the flywheel was removed, clean the sealant from the flywheel retaining bolts. Coat the bolt threads with a suitable sealer compound.

14. Make sure the crankshaft flange and the back of the flywheel are clean. Position the flywheel on the crankshaft and install the 6 retaining bolts. Tighten the bolts to 71–76 ft. lbs. (96–103 Nm).

15. Position the clutch disc on the flywheel and install a clutch alignment tool to hold the disc in place.

➡️When installing the clutch disc, make sure the disc dampener springs are facing away from the flywheel. A new disc will be stamped FLYWHEEL to indicate the correct installation position.

Fig. 32 Upon installation, it is usually a good idea to apply a threadlocking compound to the flywheel bolts

Fig. 35 Install a clutch alignment arbor, to align the clutch assembly during installation

Fig. 33 Check the pressure plate for excessive wear

Fig. 36 Clutch plate installed with the arbor in place

Fig. 34 Be sure that the flywheel surface is clean, before installing the clutch

Fig. 37 Clutch plate and pressure plate installed with the alignment arbor in place

Fig. 38 Pressure plate-to-flywheel bolt holes should align

Fig. 39 You may want to use a threadlocking compound on the clutch assembly bolts

Fig. 40 Install the clutch assembly bolts and tighten in steps, using an X pattern

Fig. 41 Be sure to use a torque wrench to tighten all bolts

16. Align the reference marks, if present, and position the pressure plate on the flywheel, then install the retaining bolts. Tighten the bolts evenly, in an alternate pattern, to 13–20 ft. lbs. (18–26 Nm). The bolts must be tightened in this manner to prevent distortion of the pressure plate.

17. Remove the clutch alignment tool.

18. Clean the clutch disc splines on the input shaft with a dry rag and coat the spline surfaces with a light film of clutch grease.

19. Install the transaxle.

20. Lower the vehicle.

21. Connect the negative battery cable.

22. Adjust the clutch pedal free-play.

23. Road test the car and check for proper clutch operation.

ADJUSTMENTS

Clutch Pedal Height

▶ See Figure 42

1. Disconnect the clutch cable at the release lever.

2. Move the carpet and padding aside so that it will not influence the measurement.

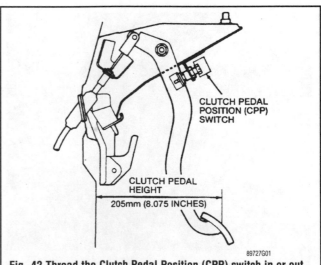

Fig. 42 Thread the Clutch Pedal Position (CPP) switch in or out to adjust clutch pedal height

3. Measure the distance from the upper center of the pedal to the bulkhead. The pedal height should be 8.075 in. (205mm). If the height is not as specified, continue with the adjustment.

4. Inspect the pedal mounting, for damaged, worn or missing parts. Repair as necessary and continue with the adjustments.

➡**The Clutch Pedal Position (CPP) switch also serves as the pedal stop.**

5. Loosen the CPP switch locknut and thread the switch in or out until the pedal is at the specified height. Tighten the locknut to 10–13 ft. lbs. (14–18 Nm).

6. Connect the clutch cable to the release lever and adjust clutch free-play.

7. Recheck the pedal height. If connecting the clutch cable affected pedal height, check the cable for binding or damage. Repair as necessary.

Clutch Free-Play

♦ **See Figures 43 and 44**

1. Move the clutch pedal back and forth, and measure the amount of travel (free-play).

2. The free-play should be 0.35–0.59 in.(9–15mm). If the measurement is not as specified, continue with the adjustments.

3. Pull back on the clutch release lever and measure the clearance between the lever and the clutch cable connecting link. Thread the adjuster in or out until the measurement between the connecting link and lever is 0.06–0.10 in. (1.5–2.5mm).

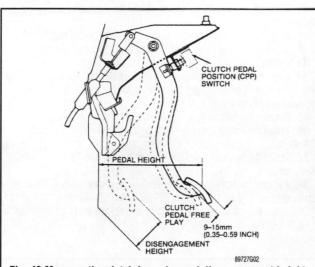

Fig. 43 Measure the clutch free-play and disengagement height at the points illustrated

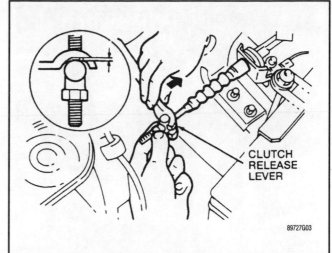

Fig. 44 Pull back on the clutch release lever and measure the clearance between the lever and the clutch cable connecting link

4. Check the free-play again and make sure the measurement is as specified. If not, check the clutch release components for damage or binding.

5. After the adjustment, measure the clutch disengagement height. It should be a minimum of 2.92 in. (74mm) when disengaged.

Clutch Cable

REMOVAL & INSTALLATION

1. Remove the clutch cable adjusting nut and disengage the cable from the release lever. Pull the clutch release cable through the cable bracket.

2. Remove the cable mounting clip that attaches the cable case to the support bracket.

3. Pull upwards on the cable and disengage it from the pedal.

4. If necessary, loosen the cable bracket bolts and remove the bracket.

5. Guide the cable through the hole in the bulkhead and remove it from the car.

To install:

6. Install the cable and guide it through the hole in the bulkhead.

7. If removed, install the cable bracket and tighten the bolts.

8. Engage the cable to the pedal and install the clip that connects the cable case to the bracket.

9. Insert the cable through the bracket, and engage it to the release lever.

10. Adjust the clutch pedal free-play.

AUTOMATIC TRANSAXLE

Understanding the Automatic Transaxle

The automatic transaxle allows engine torque and power to be transmitted to the front wheels within a narrow range of engine operating speeds. It will allow the engine to turn fast enough to produce plenty of power and torque at very low speeds, while keeping it at a sensible rpm at high vehicle speeds (and it does this job without driver assistance). The transaxle uses a light fluid as the medium for the transmission of power. This fluid also works in the operation of various hydraulic control circuits and as a lubricant. Because the transaxle fluid performs all of these functions, trouble within the unit can easily travel from one part to another. For this reason, and because of the complexity and unusual operating principles of the transaxle, a very sound understanding of the basic principles of operation will simplify troubleshooting.

Park/Neutral Position Switch

REMOVAL & INSTALLATION

♦ **See Figure 45**

➡**On vehicles equipped with an automatic transaxle, the Park/Neutral Position (PNP) switch allows the engine to start only with the transaxle in PARK or NEUTRAL, activates back-up lights with the transaxle in REVERSE, and signals gear position to the Powertrain Control Module (PCM) for engine idle control. The PNP switch is not adjustable.**

Fig. 45 The Park/Neutral Position (PNP) switch is located on the automatic transaxle case

1. Disconnect the negative battery cable.
2. Disengage the PNP switch electrical connector.
3. Place a drain pan under the transaxle to catch any lost transaxle fluid.
4. Using an extension and a crow's foot wrench, remove the PNP switch from the front left-hand side of the transaxle.

To install:

5. Apply silicone sealer E1FZ-19562-A or equivalent to the threads of the PNP switch.
6. Install the PNP switch into the transaxle case and tighten to 14–19 ft. lbs. (19–26 Nm).
7. Engage the PNP switch electrical connector.
8. Connect the negative battery cable.
9. Check the PNP switch operation. Make sure that the engine will only crank in the **PARK** or **NEUTRAL** positions, and that the back-up lights operate when the transaxle is in the **REVERSE** position.

Automatic Transaxle Assembly

REMOVAL & INSTALLATION

▶ See Figure 46

1. Disconnect the negative battery cable.
2. Remove the manual control lever nut and arm from inside the engine compartment.
3. Remove the shift cable and bracket from the transaxle.
4. Disconnect the speedometer cable from the transaxle.
5. Disengage the transaxle electrical connectors, located next to the governor.
6. Loosen the ground strap retaining bolt and disconnect the ground strap from the transaxle.
7. Tag and disconnect the transaxle vacuum hose and vent hose, located below the distributor cap.
8. Remove the coolant pipe retaining bracket, located below the distributor cap.
9. Remove the 2 upper bell housing bolts.
10. Support the engine using engine support bar tool 014-00750 or equivalent.
11. Raise and safely support the vehicle.
12. Remove the front wheel and tire assemblies.
13. Remove the starter motor.
14. Drain the transaxle fluid.
15. Remove the front fender splash shield.
16. Remove the front stabilizer bar.

17. Remove the lower arm clamp bolts and nuts. Pull the lower arms downward, separating the lower arms from the knuckles.

➡**Use care not to damage the ball joint dust boots.**

18. Remove the tie rod end cotter pin and nut. Disconnect the tie rod end from the knuckle.
19. Remove the halfshafts. Install differential plug tool T87C-7025-C or equivalent between the differential side gears to prevent side gear movement.
20. Remove the front and rear transaxle support insulator nuts.
21. Remove the four rear engine support rebound insulator bolts and the transaxle support crossmember.
22. Loosen the front transaxle support insulator through-bolt and nut. Remove the front transaxle support insulator.
23. Remove the four front transaxle support bracket bolts and the front transaxle support bracket.
24. Unfasten the two rear transaxle support bracket bolts, then remove the rear transaxle support bracket and transaxle insulator.
25. Remove the intake manifold support.
26. Loosen the three transaxle-to-engine bolts and remove the transaxle case rear bracket.
27. Loosen the three transaxle-to-engine bolts from the transaxle case-to-cylinder block front bracket and remove the bracket.
28. Remove the flywheel cover bolts and cover.
29. Using a wrench, rotate the crankshaft pulley bolt clockwise to gain access to 4 torque converter-to-flywheel nuts and remove all the nuts.
30. Make alignment marks between the oil cooler tubes and hoses. Disconnect and plug the oil cooler lines.
31. Position a transmission jack under the transaxle and secure with a chain or strap.
32. Remove the remaining engine-to-transaxle retaining bolts.
33. Carefully separate and lower the transaxle from the vehicle.

To install:

34. Raise the transaxle into position and install two engine-to-transaxle bolts. Make sure that the torque converter is in alignment with the flywheel. Tighten the bolts to 47–66 ft. lbs. (64–89 Nm).
35. Remove the transaxle jack and install the starter motor.
36. Install the torque converter bolts and tighten them to 26–36 ft. lbs. (34–49 Nm).
37. Install the flywheel cover and tighten the bolts to 71–97 inch lbs. (8–11 Nm).
38. Position the front transaxle-to-engine support and install the three retaining bolts. Tighten the bolts to 27–38 ft. lbs. (37–52 Nm).
39. Install the intake manifold support and tighten the bolts to 27–38 ft. lbs. (37–52 Nm).

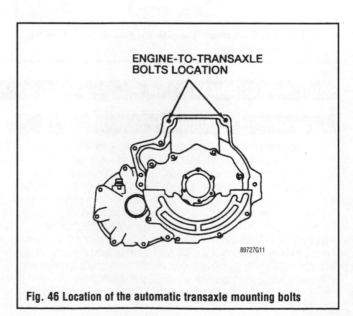

ENGINE-TO-TRANSAXLE BOLTS LOCATION

Fig. 46 Location of the automatic transaxle mounting bolts

40. Install the transaxle case rear bracket and three retaining bolts. Tighten the bolts to 27–38 ft. lbs. (37–52 Nm).

41. Install the front transaxle support insulator bracket and four retaining bolts. Tighten the bolts to 28–37 ft. lbs. (38–51 Nm).

42. Install the front transaxle support bracket, along with the through-bolt and nut. Do not tighten the through-bolt and nut until the rear engine support is installed.

43. Position the transaxle support crossmember and install the rear engine support rebound insulator bolts. Tighten the insulator bolts to 47–66 ft. lbs. (64–89 Nm).

44. Tighten the front transaxle support bracket through-bolt and nut to 69–83 ft. lbs. (93–113 Nm).

45. Install the two front transaxle support insulator nuts and tighten to 32–38 ft. lbs. (43–52 Nm).

46. Install the two rear transaxle support insulator nuts and tighten to 21–34 ft. lbs. (28–46 Nm).

47. Remove the differential plugs and install the halfshafts.

48. Align the marks made on the oil cooler lines and install. Install the hose clamps.

49. Connect the tie rod ends to the steering knuckles and tighten the attaching nuts to 26–30 ft. lbs. (35–40 Nm). Install new cotter pins.

50. Attach the lower arm ball joints to the knuckles. Tighten the lower arm clamp bolt to 40–50 ft. lbs. (54–68 Nm).

51. Install the front stabilizer bar. Tighten the retaining nuts to 43–52 ft. lbs. (43–52 Nm).

52. Install the front fender splash shield and tighten the bolts to 65–95 inch lbs. (8–10 Nm).

53. Install the front wheel and tire assemblies. Tighten the lug bolts to 65–87 ft. lbs. (88–118 Nm).

54. Lower the vehicle and remove the engine support tool.

55. Attach the shift cable and bracket to the transaxle. Install the manual control lever arm on the manual control lever. Install the retaining nut and tighten to 34–47 ft. lbs. (44–64 Nm).

➡**Do not use any type of power wrench to tighten the nut. Damage to the transaxle may result.**

56. Install the coolant pipe retaining bracket, located below the distributor.

57. Connect the vacuum hose and vent hose, located below the distributor cap.

58. Engage the transaxle electrical connectors, located next to the governor.

59. Connect the ground wire to the transaxle and tighten the bolt to 65–95 inch lbs. (8–10 Nm).

60. Connect the speedometer cable.

61. Connect the negative battery cable.

62. Fill the transaxle with the specified fluid to the proper level.

➡**Make sure that the gearshift lever position aligns exactly with the manual control lever position before starting the engine.**

63. Start the engine. Check for leaks and proper fluid level.

64. Road test the vehicle and check for proper operation.

ADJUSTMENTS

Shift Control Cable

▶ **See Figure 47**

1. Disconnect the negative battery cable.

2. Remove the shift console panel and place the gearshift lever in the **PARK** position.

3. Loosen the gearshift lever knob retaining screws and remove the knob.

➡**Make sure the detent spring roller is in the PARK detent.**

4. Loosen the transmission control selector dial bezel screws and remove the bezel.

5. Loosen the shift cable and bracket bolts.

6. Adjust the shift cable and bracket at the lever and move it to the desired position.

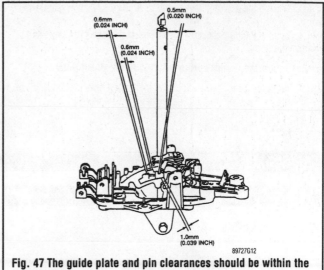

Fig. 47 The guide plate and pin clearances should be within the specifications shown

7. Check the shift cable and bracket for proper adjustment at the lever and at the lever trunnion on the transaxle.

8. Lightly press the selector cam and make sure the guide plate and pin clearances are within the specifications shown in the accompanying illustration.

9. Check that the guide plate and pin clearances are also within the specifications shown when in the **NEUTRAL** position.

10. Tighten the shift cable and bracket bolts to 71–97 inch lbs. (8–11 Nm).

11. Make sure the lever operates properly.

12. Route the control selector indicator lamp wires through the bezel clips.

13. Insert the lamp housing and turn it counterclockwise to secure it.

14. Install the control selector dial bezel and tighten its retaining screws.

15. Install the knob and tighten the screws.

16. Install the shift console panel.

17. Connect the negative battery cable.

Transmission Control Selector Dial Bezel

▶ **See Figure 48**

1. Disconnect the negative battery cable.

2. Remove the shift console panel and place the gearshift lever in the **PARK** position.

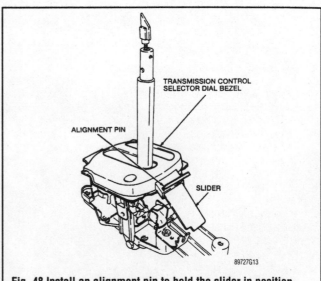

Fig. 48 Install an alignment pin to hold the slider in position

3. Loosen the gearshift lever knob retaining screws and remove the knob.

4. Loosen the transmission control selector dial bezel screws and remove the bezel.

➡**Make sure the detent spring roller is in the PARK detent.**

5. Align the holes in the slider and the control selector dial bezel, then install an alignment pin to hold the slider in this position.

6. Place the bezel in position and tighten the bezel screws.

7. Remove the alignment pin.

8. Install the knob and tighten the screws.
9. Install the shift console panel.
10. Connect the negative battery cable.

Halfshafts

Removal, installation and overhaul of the halfshafts on automatic transaxle equipped models is the same as for models equipped with manual transaxles. Refer to the Manual Transaxle portion of this section for Halfshaft procedures.

REAR AXLE

Wheel Spindle

REMOVAL & INSTALLATION

▶ **See Figure 49**

1. Raise and safely support the rear of the vehicle securely on jackstands.
2. Loosen the lug bolts/nuts on the appropriate rear wheel.
3. Block the front wheels, then raise and safely support the rear of the vehicle on jackstands.
4. Remove the rear wheel.
5. Remove the brake drum.
6. If equipped with ABS, loosen the anti-lock sensor bolt and remove the sensor.
7. Place a hydraulic jack under the axle torsion beam and raise the jack until the tension is removed from the rear strut.
8. Loosen the strut, lower the hydraulic jack and disengage the strut.

➡**The hex heads on the outboard of the brake backing plate appear to be rear wheel spindle nuts. Do not attempt to remove the studs. The spindle nuts are located on the inboard side of the axle torsion beam bars.**

9. Loosen the spindle nuts, support the backing plate with wire and remove the spindle.

To install:
10. Place the backing plate in position and install the spindle.
11. Install the spindle nuts and tighten them to 31–45 ft. lbs. (43–61 Nm).
12. Pull down on the axle torsion beam and engage the strut.
13. Place a hydraulic jack under the axle torsion beam and raise the jack until the strut's bolt hole is aligned. Install the bolt and tighten it to 50–60 ft. lbs. (68–81 Nm).

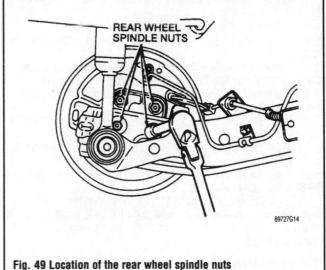

Fig. 49 Location of the rear wheel spindle nuts

14. Remove the hydraulic jack.
15. If removed, install the rear brake anti-lock sensor and bolt. Tighten the bolt to 12–16 ft. lbs. (16–23 Nm).
16. Install the brake drum.
17. Install the rear wheel and hand-tighten the lug bolts/nuts.
18. Lower the rear of the vehicle.
19. Tighten the lug bolts/nuts on the rear wheels to 65–87 ft. lbs. (88–118 Nm).

TORQUE SPECIFICATIONS

System	Component	Ft. Lbs.	Nm
Manual Transaxle			
	Back-up light switch	15-21	20-29
	Park/Neutral position switch	15-21	20-29
	Clutch pedal position switch locknut	124-159 inch lbs.	14-18
	Flywheel reinforcing plate bolts	62-86 inch lbs.	7-10
	Lower transaxle bolts	47-66	64-89
	Rear transaxle support insulator nuts	21-34	28-46
	Front transaxle support insulator nuts	32-38	43-52
	Rear engine support rebound insulator bolts	47-66	64-89
	Transaxle front and rear bracket bolts	27-38	37-52
	Gearshift stabilizer bar nut	28-38	38-52
Clutch			
	Flywheel retaining bolts	71-76	96-103
	Pressure plate bolts	13-20	18-26
Automatic Transaxle			
	Park/Neutral position switch	14-19	19-26
	Engine-to-transaxle bolts	47-66	64-89
	Torque converter bolts	26-36	34-49
	Flywheel cover bolts	71-97 inch lbs.	8-11
	Front transaxle-to-engine support bolts	27-38	37-52
	Intake manifold bolts	27-38	37-52
	Transaxle case rear bracket bolts	27-38	37-52
	Front transaxle support insulator bracket bolts	28-37	38-51
	Engine support rebound insulator bolts	47-66	64-89
	Front transaxle support bracket through-bolt and nut	69-83	93-113
	Front transaxle support insulator nuts	32-38	43-52
	Rear transaxle support insulator nuts	21-34	28-46
	Tie rod end-to-steering knuckle attaching nuts	26-30	35-40
	Lower arm clamp bolt	40-50	54-68
	Front stabilizer bar nuts	43-52	58-70
	Front fender splash shield bolts	65-95 inch lbs.	8-10
	Manual control lever nut	34-47	44-64
	Ground wire-to-transaxle bolt	65-95 inch lbs.	8-10
Rear axle			
	Wheel spindle nuts	31-45	43-61
	Shock absorber bolt		
	Rear brake anti-lock sensor bolt	12-16	16-23
Halfshafts			
	Wheel hub retainer	116-174	157-235
	Wheel lug bolts	65-87	88-118

89727C01

Troubleshooting Basic Clutch Problems

Problem	Cause
Excessive clutch noise	Throwout bearing noises are more audible at the lower end of pedal travel. The usual causes are: • Riding the clutch • Too little pedal free-play • Lack of bearing lubrication A bad clutch shaft pilot bearing will make a high pitched squeal, when the clutch is disengaged and the transmission is in gear or within the first 2″ of pedal travel. The bearing must be replaced. Noise from the clutch linkage is a clicking or snapping that can be heard or felt as the pedal is moved completely up or down. This usually requires lubrication. Transmitted engine noises are amplified by the clutch housing and heard in the passenger compartment. They are usually the result of insufficient pedal free-play and can be changed by manipulating the clutch pedal.
Clutch slips (the car does not move as it should when the clutch is engaged)	This is usually most noticeable when pulling away from a standing start. A severe test is to start the engine, apply the brakes, shift into high gear and SLOWLY release the clutch pedal. A healthy clutch will stall the engine. If it slips it may be due to: • A worn pressure plate or clutch plate • Oil soaked clutch plate • Insufficient pedal free-play
Clutch drags or fails to release	The clutch disc and some transmission gears spin briefly after clutch disengagement. Under normal conditions in average temperatures, 3 seconds is maximum spin-time. Failure to release properly can be caused by: • Too light transmission lubricant or low lubricant level • Improperly adjusted clutch linkage
Low clutch life	Low clutch life is usually a result of poor driving habits or heavy duty use. Riding the clutch, pulling heavy loads, holding the car on a grade with the clutch instead of the brakes and rapid clutch engagement all contribute to low clutch life.

TCCA7C01

Transmission Fluid Indications

The appearance and odor of the transmission fluid can give valuable clues to the overall condition of the transmission. Always note the appearance of the fluid when you check the fluid level or change the fluid. Rub a small amount of fluid between your fingers to feel for grit and smell the fluid on the dipstick.

If the fluid appears:	It indicates:
Clear and red colored	• Normal operation
Discolored (extremely dark red or brownish) or smells burned	• Band or clutch pack failure, usually caused by an overheated transmission. Hauling very heavy loads with insufficient power or failure to change the fluid, often result in overheating. Do not confuse this appearance with newer fluids that have a darker red color and a strong odor (though not a burned odor).
Foamy or aerated (light in color and full of bubbles)	• The level is too high (gear train is churning oil) • An internal air leak (air is mixing with the fluid). Have the transmission checked professionally.
Solid residue in the fluid	• Defective bands, clutch pack or bearings. Bits of band material or metal abrasives are clinging to the dipstick. Have the transmission checked professionally.
Varnish coating on the dipstick	• The transmission fluid is overheating

TCCA7C02

8

SUSPENSION AND STEERING

WHEELS

Wheels

REMOVAL & INSTALLATION

◆ **See Figures 1 thru 7**

1. Park the vehicle on a level surface.
2. Remove the jack, tire iron and, if necessary, the spare tire from their storage compartments.
3. Check the owner's manual or refer to Section 1 of this manual for the jacking points on your vehicle. Then, place the jack in the proper position.
4. If equipped with lug nut trim caps, remove them by either unscrewing or pulling them off the lug nuts, as appropriate. Consult the owner's manual, if necessary.

5. If equipped with a wheel cover or hub cap, insert the tapered end of the tire iron in the groove and pry off the cover.
6. Apply the parking brake and block the diagonally opposite wheel with a wheel chock or two.

➡**Wheel chocks may be purchased at your local auto parts store, or a block of wood cut into wedges may be used. If possible, keep one or two of the chocks in your tire storage compartment, in case any of the tires has to be removed on the side of the road.**

7. If equipped with an automatic transaxle, place the selector lever in **P** or Park; with a manual transmission/transaxle, place the shifter in Reverse.
8. With the tires still on the ground, use the tire iron/wrench to break the lug bolts/nuts loose.

TCCA8P00

Fig. 1 Place the jack at the proper lifting point on your vehicle

TCCA8P02

Fig. 3 With the vehicle still on the ground, break the lug bolts/nuts loose using the wrench end of the tire iron

TCCA8P01

Fig. 2 Before jacking the vehicle, block the diagonally opposite wheel with one or, preferably, two chocks

TCCA8P03

Fig. 4 After the lug bolts/nuts have been loosened, raise the vehicle using the jack until the tire is clear of the ground

Fig. 5 Remove the lug nuts from the studs. (Lug bolts are removable in a similar manner)

Fig. 6 Remove the wheel and tire assembly from the vehicle

➡If a nut is stuck, never use heat to loosen it or damage to the wheel and bearings may occur. If the nuts are seized, one or two heavy hammer blows directly on the end of the bolt usually loosens the rust. Be careful, as continued pounding will likely damage the brake drum or rotor.

9. Using the jack, raise the vehicle until the tire is clear of the ground. Support the vehicle safely using jackstands.

10. Remove the lug bolts/nuts, then remove the tire and wheel assembly.

To install:

11. Make sure the wheel and hub mating surfaces, as well as the wheel lug studs, are clean and free of all foreign material. Always remove rust from the wheel mounting surface and the brake rotor or drum. Failure to do so may cause the lug bolts/nuts to loosen in service.

12. Install the tire and wheel assembly and hand-tighten the lug bolts/nuts.

13. Using the tire wrench, tighten all the lug bolts/nuts, in a crisscross pattern, until they are snug.

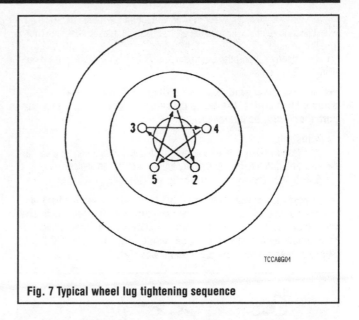

Fig. 7 Typical wheel lug tightening sequence

14. Raise the vehicle and withdraw the jackstand, then lower the vehicle.

15. Using a torque wrench, tighten the lug bolts/nuts in a crisscross pattern to 65–87 ft. lbs. (88–118 Nm). Check your owner's manual or refer to Section 1 of this manual for the proper tightening sequence.

✳✳ WARNING

Do not overtighten the lug bolts/nuts, as this may cause the wheel studs to stretch or the brake disc (rotor) to warp.

16. If so equipped, install the wheel cover or hub cap. Make sure the valve stem protrudes through the proper opening before tapping the wheel cover into position.

17. If equipped, install the lug nut trim caps by pushing them or screwing them on, as applicable.

18. Remove the jack from under the vehicle, and place the jack and tire iron/wrench in their storage compartments. Remove the wheel chock(s).

19. If you have removed a flat or damaged tire, place it in the storage compartment of the vehicle and take it to your local repair station to have it fixed or replaced as soon as possible.

INSPECTION

Inspect the tires for lacerations, puncture marks, nails and other sharp objects. Repair or replace as necessary. Also check the tires for treadwear and air pressure as outlined in Check the wheel assemblies for dents, cracks, rust and metal fatigue. Repair or replace as necessary.

Wheel Lug Studs

REMOVAL & INSTALLATION

With Disc Brakes

♦ **See Figures 8, 9 and 10**

1. Raise and support the appropriate end of the vehicle safely using jackstands, then remove the wheel.

2. Remove the brake pads and caliper. Support the caliper aside using wire or a coat hanger. For details, please refer to Section 9 of this manual.

3. Remove the outer wheel bearing and lift off the rotor. For details on wheel bearing removal, installation and adjustment, please refer to Section 1 of this manual.

4. Properly support the rotor using press bars, then drive the stud out using an arbor press.

➡**If a press is not available, CAREFULLY drive the old stud out using a blunt drift. MAKE SURE the rotor is properly and evenly supported or it may be damaged.**

To install:

5. Clean the stud hole with a wire brush and start the new stud with a hammer and drift pin. Do not use any lubricant or thread sealer.

6. Finish installing the stud with the press.

➡**If a press is not available, start the lug stud through the bore in the hub, then position about 4 flat washers over the stud and thread the lug nut. Hold the hub/rotor while tightening the lug nut, and the stud should be drawn into position. MAKE SURE THE STUD IS FULLY SEATED, then remove the lug nut and washers.**

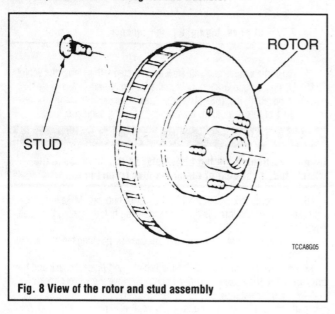

Fig. 8 View of the rotor and stud assembly

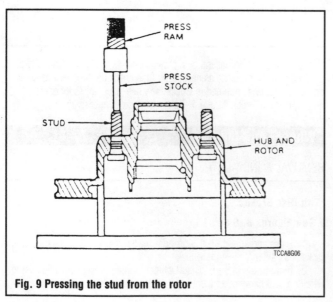

Fig. 9 Pressing the stud from the rotor

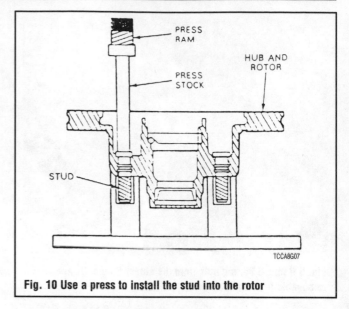

Fig. 10 Use a press to install the stud into the rotor

7. Install the rotor and adjust the wheel bearings.

8. Install the brake caliper and pads.

9. Install the wheel, then remove the jackstands and carefully lower the vehicle.

10. Tighten the lug bolts/nuts to the proper torque.

With Drum Brakes

◆ **See Figures 11, 12 and 13**

1. Raise the vehicle and safely support it with jackstands, then remove the wheel.

2. Remove the brake drum.

3. If necessary to provide clearance, remove the brake shoes, as outlined in Section 9 of this manual.

4. Using a large C-clamp and socket, press the stud from the axle flange.

5. Coat the serrated part of the stud with liquid soap and place it into the hole.

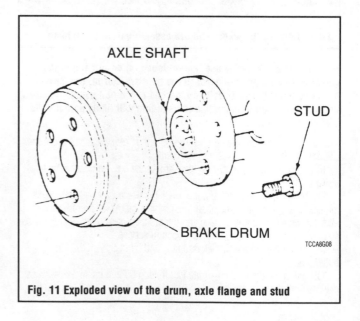

Fig. 11 Exploded view of the drum, axle flange and stud

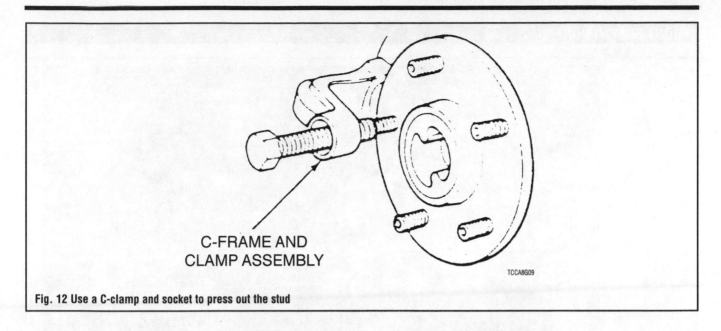

Fig. 12 Use a C-clamp and socket to press out the stud

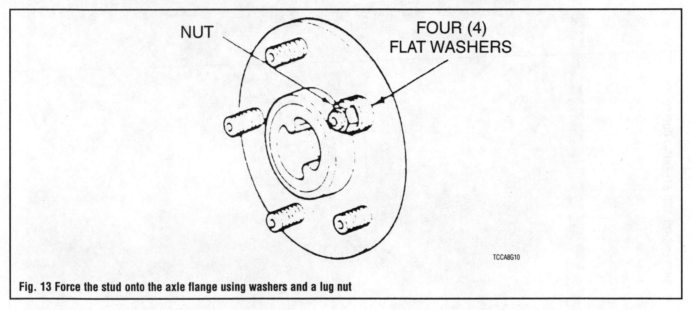

Fig. 13 Force the stud onto the axle flange using washers and a lug nut

To install:

6. Position about 4 flat washers over the stud and thread the lug nut. Hold the flange while tightening the lug nut, and the stud should be drawn into position. MAKE SURE THE STUD IS FULLY SEATED, then remove the lug nut and washers.

7. If applicable, install the brake shoes.
8. Install the brake drum.
9. Install the wheel, then remove the jackstands and carefully lower the vehicle.
10. Tighten the lug bolts/nuts to the proper torque.

FRONT SUSPENSION

FRONT SUSPENSION AND STEERING COMPONENT LOCATIONS

1. Sway bar bracket
2. Sway bar
3. MacPherson strut assembly
4. Ball joint
5. Lower control arm
6. Drive axle and CV-joint
7. Steering rack
8. Tie rod

MacPherson Struts

REMOVAL & INSTALLATION

▶ **See Figures 14, 15, 16, 17 and 18**

1. Raise and safely support the vehicle.
2. Remove the wheel and tire assembly.
3. Remove the brake line clip from the shock absorber lower mounting bracket and disengage the brake line.
4. Remove the two nuts and bolts securing the shock absorber lower bracket to the steering knuckle.
5. Working in the engine compartment, remove the two nuts securing the shock absorber mounting block in the shock absorber tower.
6. Disengage the shock absorber lower bracket from the steering knuckle and lower the shock absorber clear of the wheel well.

To install:

7. Place the shock absorber assembly with spacer plate in the shock absorber tower with the white alignment mark facing outward.
8. Install the two upper mounting block stud nuts and tighten to 34–46 ft. lbs. (46–63 Nm).

Fig. 16 . . . then remove the bolts

Fig. 14 Remove the brake line clip from the shock absorber lower mounting bracket and disengage the brake line

Fig. 17 Working in the engine compartment, loosen the nuts securing the shock absorber mounting block in the tower . . .

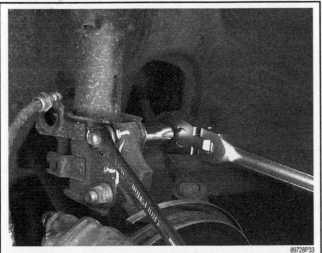

Fig. 15 Using a box end wrench to hold the nut, loosen the strut bracket bolts . . .

Fig. 18 . . . then lower the strut assembly from the car

9. Engage the steering knuckle in the shock absorber tower lower bracket, install the two retaining bolts and nuts, and tighten them to 69–86 ft. lbs. (93–117 Nm).

10. Position the brake line into the shock absorber lower mounting bracket cutout and install the retaining clip.

11. Install the wheel and tire assembly.

12. Lower the vehicle.

13. Check the front wheel alignment, and adjust as necessary.

14. Road test the vehicle and check for proper operation.

OVERHAUL

▶ **See Figures 19 thru 25**

1. Pry out the mounting block cap and remove the shock absorber upper nut and lockwasher.

2. Secure the shock absorber mounting bracket in a vise.

3. Hold the shock bushing with a prytool to prevent it from turning, then turn the shock absorber piston rod nut one revolution to loosen.

4. Attach spring compressor tool 164-R3571 or equivalent, and compress the coil spring.

5. Remove the shock absorber mounting bracket and spring insulator.

6. Remove the washer, bearing seal and bearing from the shock absorber piston rod.

7. Remove the upper spring seat, seat insulator and coil spring. Slide the jounce bumper/shield off the shock absorber.

➡**If replacing the spring, release the spring compressor progressively to prevent spring arching. Open the compressor jaws wide enough to grip the new spring in the same position and tighten the compressor screws progressively, compressing the spring until the shock absorber can be assembled without interference.**

To assemble:

8. Check the condition of the jounce bumper and spring seat insulator and replace, as necessary.

9. Make sure the bearing operates smoothly.

10. Check the spring for uniform coil spacing, as well as for nicks or burrs.

11. Slide the jounce bumper/shield onto the shock absorber rod and over the body.

12. Install the compressed spring, upper spring seat insulator and upper seat, positioning the spring ends against the steps in the seats.

13. Install the bearing, seal and washer on the shock absorber rod.

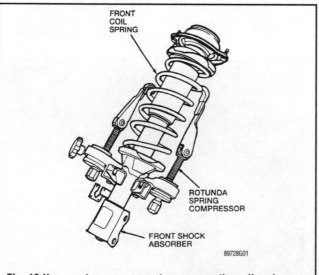

Fig. 19 Use a spring compressor to compress the coil spring

14. Install the shock absorber mounting bracket with the white alignment spot on the same side of the shock absorber as the steering knuckle mounting bracket.

15. Install the spacer plate. Install the lockwasher and nut and tighten to 40–50 ft. lbs. (54–67 Nm).

16. Release and remove the spring compressor.

Fig. 20 Hold the shock bushing stationary with a prytool, and turn the shock absorber piston rod nut one revolution

Fig. 21 With the strut assembly mounted in a vise, compress the spring with a suitable compressor tool

Fig. 22 Remove the nut and insulator plate

Fig. 23 Remove the washer and spring seat from the strut assembly

Fig. 24 Remove the insulator and coil spring assembly

Fig. 25 Remove the jounce bumper/shield from the shock absorber

Lower Ball Joint

INSPECTION

1. Raise the front of the car until the wheel and tire assembly are clear of the ground.
2. Support the suspension lower arm until there is no load on the shock absorber.
3. Try to rock the wheel top-to-bottom; if any wobble is felt, look for movement between the lower arm and the wheel knuckle.
4. If the ball joint appears to be tight, check and adjust the front wheel bearing, then repeat the wobble test.
5. If any movement is present, this would probably indicate ball joint wear and the ball joint should be replaced.
6. If wear is present, check the tie rod end. The lower arm and stabilizer bar should also be checked.

REMOVAL & INSTALLATION

The lower ball joint is an integral component of the lower control arm. If the lower ball joint is defective, the entire lower control arm must be replaced.

Sway Bar

REMOVAL & INSTALLATION

▶ See Figure 26

1. Raise and safely support the vehicle.
2. Remove the four stabilizer bar (sway bar) bracket nuts and two stabilizer bar brackets.
3. Remove the split bushings from the stabilizer bar. Replace deteriorated or worn bushings as required.
4. Remove the cotter pins and front stabilizer bar retaining nuts at the lower control arms and remove the rear washers and bushings. Discard the cotter pins.
5. Pull the stabilizer bar forward to disengage it from the lower control arms.
6. Remove the front bushings and washers. Replace deteriorated or worn bushings as required.
   To install:
7. Install the control arm bushing washers on the ends of the stabilizer bar and install the control arm front bushings.

Fig. 26 Loosen the sway bar bracket nuts and remove the brackets

Fig. 28 Loosen the lower control arm-to-chassis bolt . . .

8. Support the stabilizer bar by hand and insert the ends of the bar into the lower control arms.

9. Install the rear control arm bushings and washers with the retaining nuts. Make the retaining nuts finger-tight.

10. Install the two split bushings on the stabilizer bar with the split side forward and position them next to the white alignment marks on the bar.

11. Install the two stabilizer bar brackets. Tighten the four bracket retaining nuts to 40–50 ft. lbs. (54–68 Nm).

12. Tighten the front stabilizer bar retaining nuts to 47–57 ft. lbs. (64–77 Nm) and install new cotter pins.

13. Lower the vehicle.

Lower Control Arm

REMOVAL & INSTALLATION

♦ See Figures 27 thru 35

➡The ball joint is an integral component of the lower control arm and cannot be serviced separately.

1. Raise and safely support the vehicle.
2. Remove the front wheel and tire assembly.

Fig. 29 . . . and remove the bolt

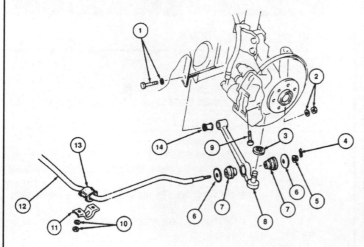

Item	Description
1	Front Suspension Lower Arm-to-Chassis Bolt and Washer
2	Front Suspension Lower Arm Ball Joint Washer and Nut
3	Front Suspension Lower Arm Ball Joint Dust Boot
4	Cotter Pin
5	Front Stabilizer Bar Nut
6	Front Stabilizer Bar Washers (2 Req'd)
7	Front Stabilizer Bar Bushings (2 Req'd)
8	Front Suspension Lower Arm

Item	Description
9	Front Suspension Lower Arm Ball Joint Bolt
10	Stabilizer Bar Bracket Washers and Nuts (2 Req'd)
11	Stabilizer Bar Bracket
12	Front Stabilizer Bar
13	Lower Suspension Arm Stabilizer Bar Insulator
14	Front Suspension Lower Arm Mounting Bolt Bushing

Fig. 27 Exploded view of the lower control arm assembly

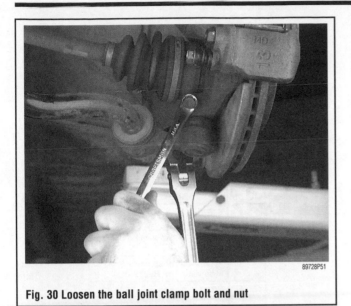

Fig. 30 Loosen the ball joint clamp bolt and nut

Fig. 31 Separate the ball joint stud from the steering knuckle

Fig. 32 Remove the cotter pin from the stabilizer bar

Fig. 33 Remove the stabilizer bar bushing nut and washer

Fig. 34 Remove the outer bushing and the lower control arm

Fig. 35 Remove the inner bushing and washer

3. Loosen the lower control arm-to-chassis bolt and washer at the frame bracket.

4. Remove the ball joint clamp bolt and nut from the steering knuckle assembly.

5. Remove the cotter pin and stabilizer bar bushing nut from the rear of the control arm.

6. Remove the rear bushing washer and bushing. Discard the cotter pin.

7. Lower the control arm, prying the ball joint stud out of the steering knuckle if necessary.

8. Disengage and remove the control arm from the stabilizer bar end and remove from the vehicle.

9. If the lower control arm is to be reused, inspect the control arm bushings for damage or excessive wear. Verify that the ball joint swivels freely, but is not loose.

10. Replace the lower control arm as required.

To install:

11. Position the front bushing washer and bushing onto the stabilizer bar end. Engage the lower control arm with the stabilizer bar.

12. Raise the control arm inner end into the pivot bracket on the frame and start the pivot bolt to hold the control arm in place. Do not completely tighten the bolt at this time.

13. Engage the control arm ball joint stud with the clamp bore in the steering knuckle, and install the clamp bolt and nut. Do not tighten yet.

14. Install the stabilizer bar rear bushing and washer onto the stabilizer bar end with the retaining nut. Tighten the retaining nut to 47–57 ft. lbs. (64–77 Nm). Install a new cotter pin.

15. Tighten the lower arm-to-chassis bolt at the frame bracket to 32–40 ft. lbs. (43–54 Nm).

16. Hold the clamp bolt stationary and tighten the clamp nut to 32–40 ft. lbs. (43–54 Nm).

17. Install the wheel and tire assembly.

18. Check the front wheel alignment.

CONTROL ARM BUSHING REPLACEMENT

▶ **See Figure 36**

1. Remove the lower control arm.

2. Use C-frame tool T74P-3044-A1, bushing tool T81P-5493-B and receiver cup tool T88C-5493-E, or equivalents, to remove the bushing from the control arm.

To install:

3. Center the new bushing in the center of the control arm eye and install using the same tools.

4. Install the lower control arm.

Wheel Hub and Knuckle

REMOVAL & INSTALLATION

▶ **See Figures 37, 38 and 39**

1. With the vehicle sitting on all 4 wheels, use a small chisel to straighten the staked edge of the wheel hub retaining nut. Take care not to damage the halfshaft threads.

2. Remove and discard the wheel hub retaining nut.

3. Raise and safely support the vehicle.

4. Remove the wheel.

5. Remove the retaining clip securing the brake hose to the strut.

6. If equipped, remove the front brake anti-lock sensor.

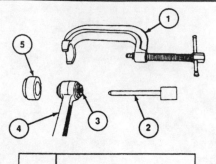

Item	Description
1	C-Frame and Clamp Assembly
2	Lower Control Arm Bushing Tool
3	Front Suspension Lower Arm Mounting Bolt Bushing
4	Front Suspension Lower Arm
5	Receiver Adapter

89728G03

Fig. 36 Use the appropriate tools to remove or install the control arm bushing

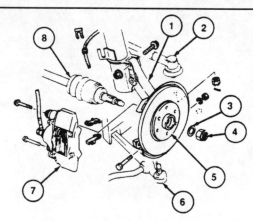

Item	Description
1	Front Wheel Knuckle
2	Tie Rod End
3	Front Axle Wheel Hub Retainer Washer
4	Front Axle Wheel Hub Retainer
5	Front Disc Brake Rotor
6	Front Suspension Lower Arm Ball Joint
7	Disc Brake Caliper
8	Front Wheel Driveshaft and Joint

89728G04

Fig. 37 Exploded view of the wheel hub and knuckle assembly

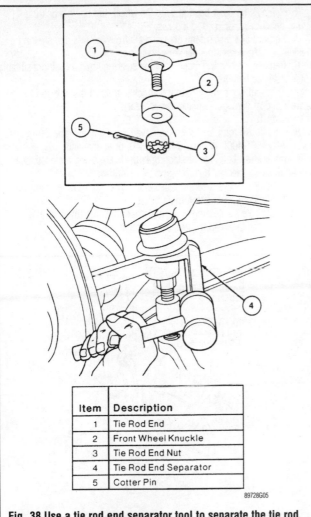

Item	Description
1	Tie Rod End
2	Front Wheel Knuckle
3	Tie Rod End Nut
4	Tie Rod End Separator
5	Cotter Pin

89728G05

Fig. 38 Use a tie rod end separator tool to separate the tie rod end from the steering knuckle arm

7. Remove the cotter pin and tie rod end attaching nut. Discard the cotter pin and set the nut aside. Inspect the nut for damage, and replace if necessary.

8. Using a tie rod end separator tool T85M-3395-A or equivalent, separate the tie rod end from the steering knuckle arm.

9. Without disconnecting the brake hose, remove the brake caliper attaching bolts and lift the caliper assembly from the steering knuckle. Support the caliper by a length of wire attached to the strut. Do not allow the caliper to hang by the brake hose.

10. Loosen the screws and remove the brake rotor.

11. Remove the clamp bolt and nut at the point where the lower control arm ball joint connects to the steering knuckle.

12. With a medium prybar, release the lower ball joint from the steering knuckle by prying downward on the lower control arm.

13. Loosen the two bolts that position the steering knuckle between the strut bracket flanges.

14. Slide the knuckle/hub assembly from the end of the halfshaft. If necessary, use a wheel puller to press the shaft out of the hub and remove from the vehicle.

15. If necessary, use a chisel to separate the disc brake rotor shield from the knuckle/hub assembly. Discard the shield.

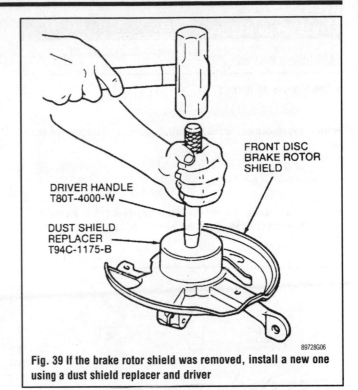

FRONT DISC
BRAKE ROTOR
SHIELD

DRIVER HANDLE
T80T-4000-W

DUST SHIELD
REPLACER
T94C-1175-B

89728G06

Fig. 39 If the brake rotor shield was removed, install a new one using a dust shield replacer and driver

To install:

16. If the brake rotor shield was removed, install a new one using installation tools T80T-4000-W and T94C-1175-B, or equivalents.

17. Clean the halfshaft spline end and lubricate with a coating of wheel bearing grease. Apply a thin film of clean SAE 30 weight oil to the steering knuckle/hub assembly up to the point where the uppermost arm of the steering knuckle seats into the strut bracket. Guide the steering knuckle/hub assembly onto the halfshaft and the strut.

18. Install the strut-to-steering knuckle bolts and attaching nuts. Tighten the nuts to 69–86 ft. lbs. (93–117 Nm).

19. Position the lower control arm ball joint in the steering knuckle. Install the lower control arm pinch bolt and attaching nut. Tighten the nut to 32–40 ft. lbs. (43–54 Nm).

20. Install the brake rotor.

21. Position the caliper on the steering knuckle and install the attaching bolts. Tighten the bolts to 29–36 ft. lbs. (39–49 Nm).

22. Position the caliper hose in the strut routing bracket and install the retaining clip.

23. If equipped, install the brake anti-lock sensor.

24. Install a new wheel hub retaining nut and tighten by hand.

25. Connect the tie rod end to the steering knuckle and install the attaching nut. Tighten the attaching nut to 22–33 ft. lbs. (29–44 Nm).

26. Install a new cotter pin through the nut and ball stud. If the openings in the nut and the hole in the ball stud are not aligned, tighten the nut to the point of alignment. Never loosen the nut.

27. Install the wheel and tire assembly.

28. Tighten the wheel hub retaining nut to 116–174 ft. lbs. (157–235 Nm). After installation, the wheel hub assembly must rotate freely by hand. Stake the halfshaft attaching nut into the shaft groove.

➥**Do not use a pointed tool to stake the nut. If the nut cracks even slightly during staking, replace it with another new one.**

29. Check the front wheel alignment.

30. Road test the vehicle and check for proper operation.

Front Wheel Bearings

REMOVAL & INSTALLATION

♦ **See Figures 40 thru 45**

1. Remove the front wheel and hub assembly.

➡**Shield replacement is not a requirement for normal bearing service.**

2. Using puller tool T87C-1104-A and hub/bearing remover adapter T92C-1104-AH, or equivalents, separate the hub from the knuckle.

3. Remove the outer bearing retainer washer.

➡**The outer bearing retainer washer is pre-selected to yield the correct bearing preload. Save the washer for use during assembly.**

4. Remove the outer bearing from the wheel hub using a bearing pulling attachment, driver and a press.

5. Remove and discard the grease seals from the hub and steering knuckle bore. Remove the inner wheel bearing.

6. Remove the bearing races from the steering knuckle using a suitable puller and slide hammer.

7. Thoroughly clean the hub and knuckle. Inspect the hub and knuckle for wear and/or damage. Replace as necessary.

To install:

8. If the brake rotor shield was removed, install a new one using installation tools T80T-4000-W and T94C-1175-B, or equivalents.

9. If the wheel bearings or steering knuckle are being replaced, bearing preload must be checked before assembly as follows:

   a. Install the outer bearing races in the steering knuckle using suitable bearing cup installation tools.

   b. Lubricate the bearing races and bearing with a thin film of clean grease. Install the bearings in the steering knuckle.

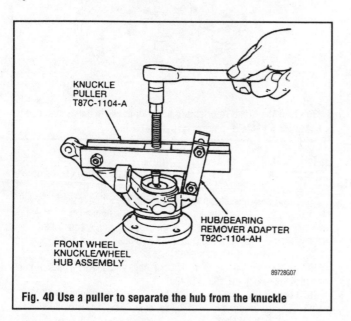

Fig. 40 Use a puller to separate the hub from the knuckle

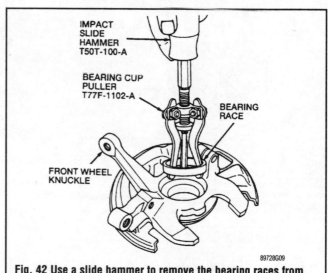

Fig. 42 Use a slide hammer to remove the bearing races from the steering knuckle

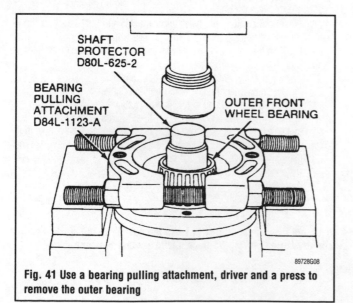

Fig. 41 Use a bearing pulling attachment, driver and a press to remove the outer bearing

Stamped mark	Thickness
1	6.285 mm (0.2474 inch)
2	6.325 mm (0.2490 inch)
3	6.365 mm (0.2506 inch)
4	6.405 mm (0.2522 inch)
5	6.445 mm (0.2538 inch)
6	6.485 mm (0.2554 inch)
7	6.525 mm (0.2570 inch)
8	6.565 mm (0.2586 inch)
9	6.605 mm (0.2602 inch)
10	6.645 mm (0.2618 inch)
11	6.685 mm (0.2634 inch)
12	6.725 mm (0.2650 inch)
13	6.765 mm (0.2666 inch)
14	6.805 mm (0.2682 inch)
15	6.845 mm (0.2698 inch)
16	6.885 mm (0.2714 inch)
17	6.925 mm (0.2730 inch)
18	6.965 mm (0.2746 inch)
19	7.005 mm (0.2762 inch)
20	7.045 mm (0.2778 inch)
21	7.085 mm (0.2794 inch)

Fig. 43 Outer bearing retainer washer thickness chart

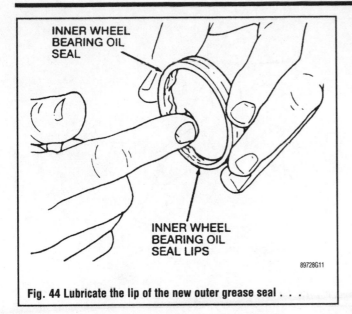

Fig. 44 Lubricate the lip of the new outer grease seal . . .

INNER WHEEL BEARING OIL SEAL

INNER WHEEL BEARING OIL SEAL LIPS

89728G11

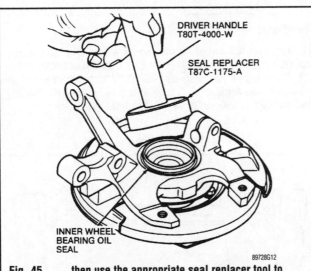

Fig. 45 . . . then use the appropriate seal replacer tool to install it

DRIVER HANDLE T80T-4000-W

SEAL REPLACER T87C-1175-A

INNER WHEEL BEARING OIL SEAL

89728G12

c. Install spacer selection tool T87C-1104-B or equivalent, and clamp the bolt head in a vise.

d. Tighten the center bolt in increments to 36, 72, 108 and 145 ft. lbs. (49, 98, 147 and 196 Nm). After tightening the center bolt to a specified increment, seat the bearings by rotating the steering knuckle.

e. Remove the tool/steering knuckle from the vise. Remount the assembly in the vise, clamping it where the strut mounts.

f. Measure the amount of torque required to rotate the spacer selector tool, using an inch pound torque wrench. The torque wrench reading must be taken just as the tool starts to rotate.

g. If the torque wrench indicates 2.2–10.4 inch lbs. (0.25–1.80 Nm), the outer bearing retainer washer is the correct thickness. If the torque wrench indicates less than 2.2 inch lbs. (0.25 Nm), a thinner outer bearing retainer washer must be installed. If the torque wrench indicates more than 10.4 inch lbs. (1.8 Nm), a thicker outer bearing retainer washer must be installed.

h. Each outer bearing retainer washer has a numerical code that identifies its thickness, which is stamped onto the outer diameter of the washer. The numbers range from 1 to 21, with 1 being the thinnest washer. If the number stamped on the washer is not legible, measure the washer with a micrometer and compare it to the thickness chart to determine the number.

i. Changing the outer bearing retainer washer thickness by 1 number, either higher or lower, will change the bearing preload by 1.7–3.5 inch lbs. (0.2–0.4 Nm).

10. Pack the bearings and the hub area with a suitable high temperature wheel bearing grease. Place the inner wheel bearing into the steering knuckle bore.

11. Lubricate the lip of the new inner grease seal with the bearing grease. Form the lubricant into a strip, concentrated along the edges of the seal lip. Install the bore, using a suitable installation tool.

12. Place the original outer bearing retainer washer, or the outer bearing retainer washer selected from the front wheel bearing adjustment procedure, in the steering knuckle bore. Position the outer wheel bearing in the steering knuckle bore.

13. Lubricate the lip of the new outer grease seal with the bearing grease. Form the lubricant into a strip, concentrated along the edges of the seal lip. Install the outer seal into the bore, using a suitable installation tool.

14. Position the hub in the steering knuckle bore and press it into position using a suitable driver.

15. Install the steering knuckle/hub assembly.

Wheel Alignment

If the tires are worn unevenly, if the vehicle is not stable on the highway or if the handling seems uneven in spirited driving, the wheel alignment should be checked. If an alignment problem is suspected, first check for improper tire inflation and other possible causes. These can be worn suspension or steering components, accident damage or even unmatched tires. If any worn or damaged components are found, they must be replaced before the wheels can be properly aligned. Wheel alignment requires very expensive equipment and involves minute adjustments which must be accurate; it should only be performed by a trained technician. Take your vehicle to a properly equipped shop.

Following is a description of the alignment angles which are adjustable on most vehicles and how they affect vehicle handling. Although these angles can apply to both the front and rear wheels, usually only the front suspension is adjustable.

CASTER

▶ **See Figure 46**

Looking at a vehicle from the side, caster angle describes the steering axis rather than a wheel angle. The steering knuckle is attached to a control arm or strut at the top and a control arm at the bottom. The wheel pivots around the line between these points to steer the vehicle. When the upper point is tilted back, this is described as positive caster. Having a positive caster tends to make the wheels self-centering, increasing directional stability. Excessive positive caster makes the wheels hard to steer, while an uneven caster will cause a pull to one side. Overloading the vehicle or sagging rear springs will affect caster, as will raising the rear of the vehicle. If the rear of the vehicle is lower than normal, the caster becomes more positive.

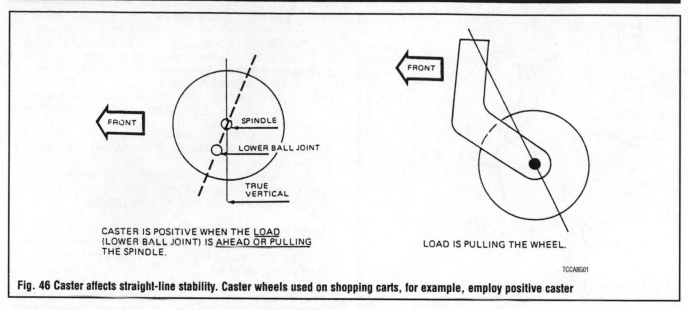

CASTER IS POSITIVE WHEN THE <u>LOAD</u> (LOWER BALL JOINT) IS <u>AHEAD OR PULLING</u> THE SPINDLE.

LOAD IS PULLING THE WHEEL.

TCCA8G01

Fig. 46 Caster affects straight-line stability. Caster wheels used on shopping carts, for example, employ positive caster

CAMBER

▶ **See Figure 47**

Looking from the front of the vehicle, camber is the inward or outward tilt of the top of wheels. When the tops of the wheels are tilted in, this is negative camber; if they are tilted out, it is positive. In a turn, a slight amount of negative camber helps maximize contact of the tire with the road. However, too much negative camber compromises straight-line stability, increases bump steer and torque steer.

TOE

▶ **See Figure 48**

Looking down at the wheels from above the vehicle, toe angle is the distance between the front of the wheels, relative to the distance between the back of the wheels. If the wheels are closer at the front, they are said to be toed-in or to have negative toe. A small amount of negative toe enhances directional stability and provides a smoother ride on the highway.

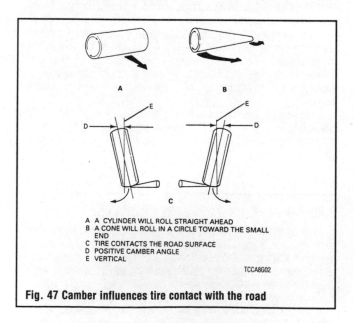

A A CYLINDER WILL ROLL STRAIGHT AHEAD
B A CONE WILL ROLL IN A CIRCLE TOWARD THE SMALL END
C TIRE CONTACTS THE ROAD SURFACE
D POSITIVE CAMBER ANGLE
E VERTICAL

TCCA8G02

Fig. 47 Camber influences tire contact with the road

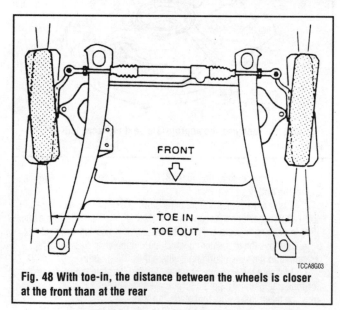

FRONT

TOE IN
TOE OUT

TCCA8G03

Fig. 48 With toe-in, the distance between the wheels is closer at the front than at the rear

REAR SUSPENSION

REAR SUSPENSION COMPONENT LOCATIONS

1. MacPherson strut assembly
2. Axle torsion beam
3. Torsion bar bracket

MacPherson Struts

REMOVAL & INSTALLATION

▶ See Figures 49 thru 61

❉ WARNING

Do not attempt to remove both left and right spring and strut assemblies at the same time. Do one side at a time to prevent damage to the rear suspension.

1. From the cargo compartment, remove the side cover.
2. If necessary for more access, remove the quarter trim panel as follows:
   a. Remove the luggage compartment cover.
   b. Remove the rear seat.
   c. Remove the screws and pushpins from the package tray. Unfasten the radio speaker electrical connector.
   d. Remove the rear safety belt anchor bolt.
   e. Remove the push pins and the luggage compartment side cover.
   f. Remove the rear door scuff plate.
   g. Pull the seaming welt away from the quarter trim panel and remove the panel.
3. Remove the strut cap, jam nut and flanged nut from the strut rod and remove the bushing washer and upper bushing.
4. Raise and safely support the vehicle.

➡**Raising the vehicle will release any tension left on the coil spring.**

5. Remove the rear wheel and tire assembly.
6. Remove the lower strut mounting bolt from the torsion beam.
7. Remove the strut assembly from the vehicle, and separate it from the spring and seat insulator.

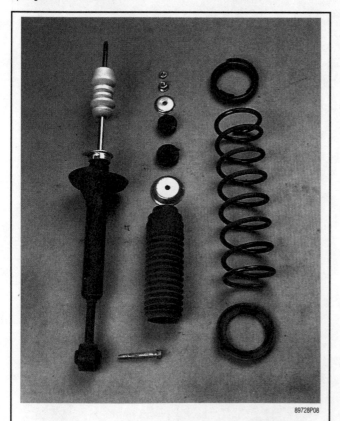

Fig. 49 Exploded view of the rear shock absorber and spring assembly components

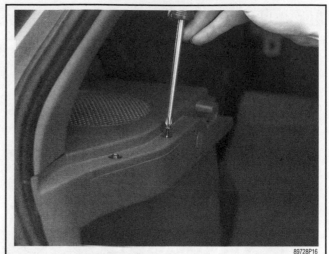

Fig. 50 Loosen the speaker cover screws . . .

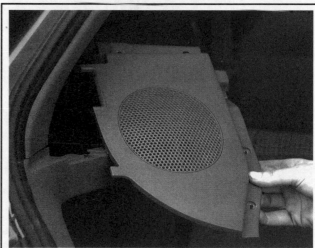

Fig. 51 . . . and remove the speaker cover

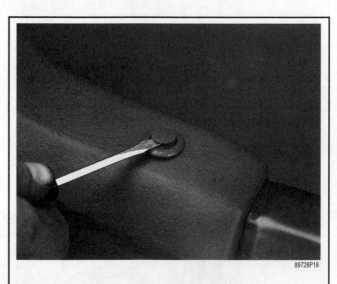

Fig. 52 Use a prytool to loosen the trim panel clips . . .

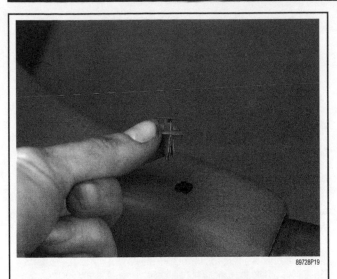

Fig. 53 . . . and remove the clips from the trim panel

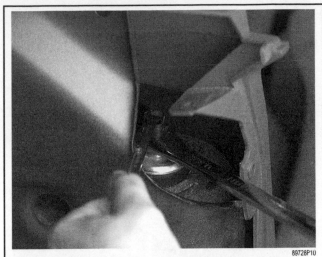

Fig. 56 Holding the end of the strut stud with an open end wrench, loosen the flanged nut with a box end wrench

Fig. 54 Remove the trim panel and set it aside

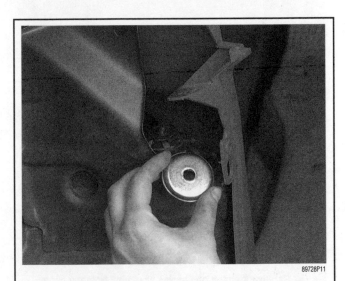

Fig. 57 Remove the bushing washer from the strut

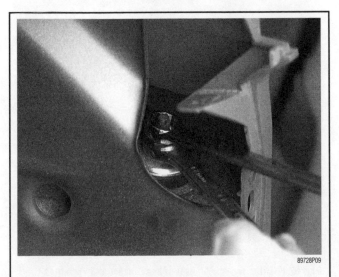

Fig. 55 Using two box end wrenches, loosen the jam nut

Fig. 58 Loosen the lower strut mounting bolt . . .

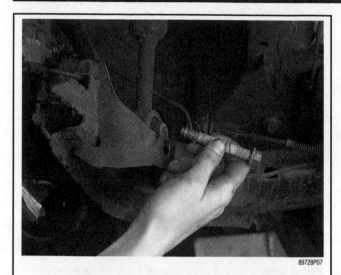

Fig. 59 . . . and remove the bolt from the torsion beam

Fig. 60 Remove the strut and spring assembly from the car as one unit

Fig. 61 Make sure the end of the coil seats against the step in the strut spring seat insulator when installing the strut

8. Inspect the condition of the spring, spring seat insulator and strut. Replace any damaged or deteriorated components, as required.

To install:

9. If the upper spring seat insulator is being replaced, install the new insulator on the spring's upper end, seating the end of the coil against the step in the insulator. Position the spring on the strut, making sure the end of the coil seats against the step in the strut spring seat.

10. Guide the strut into the upper strut mounting hole through the wheel well.

11. Align the strut lower end with the mounting hole in the torsion beam. Start the mounting bolt in by hand to hold the strut in position.

12. Install the wheel and tire assembly. Tighten the lug bolts to 65–87 ft. lbs. (88–118 Nm).

13. Lower the vehicle.

➡**Make sure that the coil spring is positioned properly on the spring seat insulator.**

14. From the cargo compartment, install the rod upper end bushing, bushing washer and flanged nut. Tighten the flanged nut to 12–18 ft. lbs. (16–24 Nm). Hold the flanged nut stationary and tighten the locknut.

15. Install the jam nut and the strut cap.

16. Install the side cover in the cargo compartment.

17. If removed, install the quarter trim panel.

18. Raise and safely support the vehicle.

19. Tighten the lower strut mounting bolt to 50–60 ft. lbs. (68–81 Nm).

20. Lower the vehicle.

21. Check the rear wheel alignment.

OVERHAUL

◗ **See Figures 62 and 63**

1. Remove the rear spring and shock absorber.

2. Separate the shock absorber from the spring anti-squeak insert.

3. Remove the lower bushing and dust boot seat from the shock absorber rod.

4. Slide the dust boot off the shock absorber.

To install:

5. Slide the shock absorber dust boot onto the shock absorber.

6. Install the dust boot seat and lower bushing.

7. If the spring anti-squeak insert is being replaced, install the new insert on the spring upper end, seating the end of the spring against the step in the spring insert.

8. Install the spring on the shock absorber, making sure the end of spring seats against the step in the seat.

9. Install the rear spring and shock absorber.

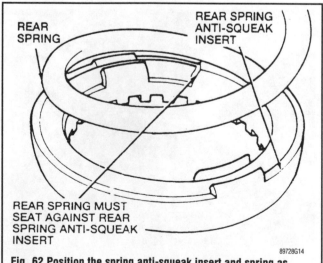

Fig. 62 Position the spring anti-squeak insert and spring as illustrated

Fig. 63 Install the lower bushing with the correct side facing up

Axle Torsion Beam

REMOVAL & INSTALLATION

♦ **See Figure 64**

1. Raise and support the car with safety stands.
2. Remove the wheel and tire assemblies.
3. Remove the rear wheel spindles.
4. Disconnect the rear wheel brake hoses.
5. Disconnect the front parking brake cable and conduit clevises at the brake backing plates.
6. Remove the front parking brake cable and conduit from the axle torsion beam.
7. Remove the drum brakes.
8. Remove the brake adjusting hole covers and pull the wheel speed sensors through the backing plate.
9. Remove the backing plate and assemblies.
10. Loosen the axle torsion beam retaining nuts.
11. Loosen the torsion bar retaining nuts from the brackets and remove the torsion beam.

➡ If the torsion beam brackets are not to be replaced, leave them on the car. The brackets' mounting holes are slotted and, if removed, require alignment when the torsion beam is installed.

To install:

12. Inspect the torsion beam bushings; if defective, replace them.
13. If installing a new torsion beam, install the beam bushings.
14. Install the bushing flange washers and place the beam into position on the brackets.
15. Align the bolts and finger-tighten the retaining nuts and bolts.
16. Install the brake backing plates.
17. Re-route and install the wheel speed sensor.
18. Install the wheel spindles, the parking brake cables and conduit.
19. Connect the rear wheel brake hoses.
20. Install the wheel and tire assemblies, and lower the car onto the ground.
21. Tighten the torsion beam nuts to 69–86 ft. lbs. (93–117 Nm).
22. Check the rear suspension alignment as follows:
    a. Locate and mark the center of the underbody at a point of equal distance from the inner and upper right and left axle torsion beam bolts.
    b. From this point, measure the distance to the centers of both the right and left shock absorber bolts.
    c. If these measurements are not within 0.2 inches (5mm) of each other, shift the torsion beam brackets side-to-side until the suspension alignment is within specification.
23. When the alignment is correct, tighten the upper axle beam bolts to 40–50 ft. lbs. (54–68 Nm) and the lower bolts to 69–86 ft. lbs. (93–117 Nm).
24. Bleed the brake system and test drive the car.

Axle Torsion Beam Bushings

REMOVAL & INSTALLATION

♦ **See Figure 65**

1. Raise and support the car with safety stands.
2. Remove the wheel and tire assemblies.
3. Remove the right rear wheel brake hose bracket and disconnect the hoses.
4. Disconnect the left brake hose clip, then disengage the hose at the body crossmember.
5. Loosen the axle torsion beam retaining nuts.
6. Loosen the torsion bar retaining nuts from the brackets.
7. Swing the beam arms downward until they are clear of the brackets.

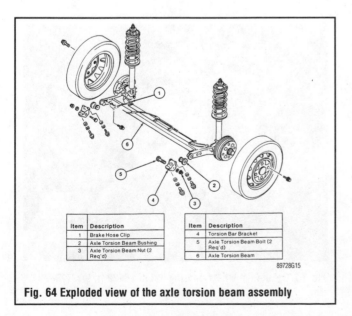

Item	Description	Item	Description
1	Brake Hose Clip	4	Torsion Bar Bracket
2	Axle Torsion Beam Bushing	5	Axle Torsion Beam Bolt (2 Req'd)
3	Axle Torsion Beam Nut (2 Req'd)	6	Axle Torsion Beam

Fig. 64 Exploded view of the axle torsion beam assembly

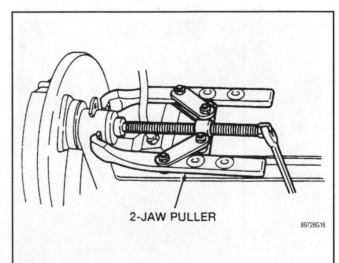

2-JAW PULLER

Fig. 65 Use a two-jawed puller to press the beam bushings out of the arms

8. Block the beam in the disengaged position with a piece of wood so that the bushings are accessible.

9. Use a two-jawed puller to press the beam bushings out of the arms from the inside.

To install:

➡**To distinguish between the right and left beam bushings, observe the F and R marks molded on the bushing face. These should be right side up when the F is towards the front of the car.**

10. Lubricate the bushing with soapy water to ease installation.

11. Position the bushing on the outboard sides of the beam with the marks parallel to the arm axis.

12. Press the bushings into place from the outboard side with a two-jawed puller.

13. Remove the piece of wood and install the bushing flange washers on the outboard faces of the bushings, then raise the beam arms into the brackets until the pivot bolt holes align.

14. Tighten the torsion beam retaining bolts.

15. Connect the brake hoses and engage the clips.

16. Install the wheel and tire assemblies and lower the car onto the ground.

17. Tighten the beam nuts to 69–86 ft. lbs. (93–117 Nm).

18. Bleed the brake system.

Rear Wheel Bearings

REMOVAL & INSTALLATION

◆ **See Figure 66**

1. Make sure the parking brake is fully released.
2. Raise and safely support the vehicle.
3. Remove the wheel and tire assembly.
4. Remove the hub grease cap.
5. Remove the cotter pin, nut cover and nut. Discard the cotter pin.
6. Pull the brake drum bearings and hub assembly away from the spindle shaft. Take care not to damage the spindle shaft threads.
7. Remove the outer wheel bearing assembly and washer.
8. With a small roll-head prybar, or equivalent, remove the bearing grease seal from the bearing hub. Discard the seal, regardless of condition.
9. Remove the inner wheel bearing assembly from the bearing hub. If the bearings are to be reused, identify and tag each bearing for installation reference.
10. Thoroughly clean the wheel bearings and hub using suitable solvent and allow to dry. Inspect the bearings and bearing races for scoring, pitting, wear or other damage, and replace as necessary.

➡**If replacing the bearings, the bearing races must also be replaced.**

11. Remove the bearing races from the hub using a brass drift.

To install:

12. If replacing the bearing races, install new races in the hub using suitable installation tools.

13. Pack the bearings and the drum hub area with high temperature wheel bearing grease. Do not fill the entire hub with grease.

14. Position the inner bearing in the hub. Install and seat a new grease seal with a suitable driving tool. Lubricate the lip of the seal with wheel bearing grease.

15. Position the brake drum and hub assembly on the spindle. Keep the hub centered during positioning to prevent damage to the new grease seal and the spindle threads.

16. Install the outer wheel bearing, washer and nut.

17. Adjust the bearing preload.

18. Install the wheel bearing nut cover and a new cotter pin.

19. Install the hub grease cap.

20. Install the wheel and tire assembly.

21. Check and adjust the brakes as required.

22. Check for proper brake operation.

ADJUSTMENT

◆ **See Figures 67 and 68**

1. Make sure the parking brake is fully released.
2. Raise and safely support the vehicle.
3. Remove the wheel and tire assembly.
4. Remove the grease cap.
5. Rotate the brake drum to make sure there is no brake drag.
6. Remove the cotter pin, wheel bearing nut cover. Discard the cotter pin.
7. To seat the bearings, tighten the wheel bearing nut to 18–22 ft. lbs. (25–29 Nm). Rotate the brake drum by hand while tightening the nut.
8. Loosen the wheel bearing nut until it can be turned by hand.
9. Before the bearing preload can be set, the amount of seal drag must be measured and added to the required preload.
10. To measure the seal drag, proceed as follows:
   a. Install a lug bolt and rotate the brake drum until the stud is in the 12 o'clock position.
   b. Place an inch pound torque wrench onto the bolt to measure the amount of force required to rotate the brake drum.
   c. Pull the torque wrench and record the torque reading when rotation begins.

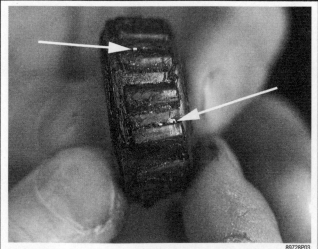

Fig. 66 Inspect the wheel bearing assembly for signs of damage, as indicated by the arrows

Fig. 67 Tighten the wheel bearing nut to 18–22 ft. lbs. (25–29 Nm)

Fig. 68 A large socket and hammer can be used to install the grease cap

11. Add the oil seal drag value obtained in Step 9 to the specified value of 0.6–1.9 lbs. (2.6–8.5 N). This is the standard bearing preload.

12. Loosely tighten the bearing nut and rotate the brake drum until the nut and wheel are at the 12 o'clock position.

13. Position an inch lb. torque wrench onto the nut and measure the amount of pull required to rotate the drum.

14. Tighten the wheel bearing nut until the torque shown is within the range calculated previously.

15. Turn the wheel bearing nut slowly to adjust to the standard bearing preload.

16. Install the nut retaining cap and a new cotter pin.

17. Install the grease cap and the wheel and tire assembly.

18. Lower the car.

19. Road test the car and check for proper operation.

STEERING

Steering Wheel

REMOVAL & INSTALLATION

▶ See Figures 69 thru 78

✳✳ CAUTION

Some models covered by this manual may be equipped with a Supplemental Restraint System (SRS), which uses an air bag. Whenever working near any of the SRS components, such as the impact sensors, air bag module, steering column or instrument panel, disable the SRS, as described in Section 6.

1. Position the front wheels in the straight-ahead position.

2. Disconnect the negative battery cable.

3. Wait one minute before proceeding further. This is the time required for the backup power supply in the air bag diagnostic monitor to deplete its stored energy.

4. Loosen the four driver side air bag module bolts and remove the module.

5. Disengage the two electrical connectors by depressing the catches while pulling.

✳✳ CAUTION

When carrying a live air bag, make sure the bag and trim cover are pointed away from the body. In the unlikely event of an accidental deployment, the bag will then deploy with minimal chance of injury. When placing a live air bag on a bench or other surface, always face the bag and trim cover up, away from the surface. This will reduce the motion of the module if it is accidentally deployed.

6. Set the air bag module aside with the trim cover face up.

7. Matchmark the steering wheel and steering column shaft for assembly reference.

8. Remove the steering wheel nut.

9. Using a steering wheel puller tool, remove the steering wheel. Do not hit the steering column with a hammer.

10. Route the wiring harness through the steering wheel as it is lifted off the steering column shaft.

11. Place tape across the air bag clockspring to prevent the contact from rotating.

To install:

12. If the air bag sliding contact has been accidentally rotated, proceed as follows:

a. Unfasten the steering column shroud screws, then separate and remove the shroud.

✳✳ WARNING

Do not rotate the air bag sliding contact more than 2½ turns in either direction to avoid damaging the air bag sliding contact.

b. Turn the air bag sliding contact clockwise to lock it, then back it off 2¾ turns.

c. Align the arrows on the air bag sliding contact and the air bag sliding contact housing.

d. Install the shroud and secure with the screws.

13. Position the steering wheel onto the steering column shaft and align the matchmarks. Tighten the nut to 29–36 ft. lbs. (39–49 Nm).

Fig. 69 From the rear of the steering wheel, loosen the four driver side air bag module bolts

Fig. 70 Gently lift the module off the steering wheel enough to gain access to the electrical connections at the rear

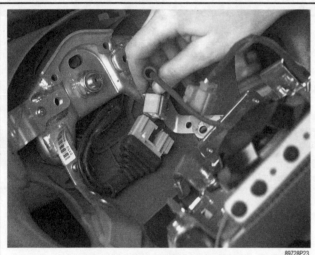

Fig. 71 Tilt the module slightly back and disengage the electrical connections while depressing their catches

Fig. 72 Matchmark the steering wheel nut and the steering column shaft to ease wheel alignment during installation

Fig. 73 Remove the steering wheel retaining nut, then attach a suitable steering wheel puller . . .

Fig. 74 . . . and tighten the puller's threaded rod to separate the steering wheel from the shaft

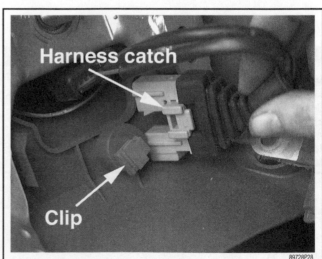

Fig. 75 Disengage the wiring harness from the clip on the steering wheel . . .

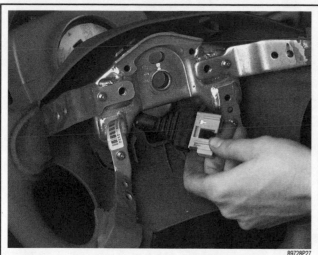

Fig. 76 . . . and route the wiring harness through the steering wheel as it is lifted off the steering column shaft

Fig. 77 Pay attention to the orientation of the arrow on the clockspring

Fig. 78 The clockspring may have installation instructions printed on it; read them carefully

14. Engage the 2 electrical connectors, position the air bag module, and install the four bolts.

15. Tighten the bolts to 36–53 inch lbs. (4–6 Nm.).

16. Connect the negative battery cable.

17. Confirm operational status of the air bag system by turning the ignition switch to the **RUN** position while watching the air bag warning indicator. The air bag diagnostic monitor will illuminate the warning indicator for approximately 6 seconds and then turn it off, indicating that the air bag warning indicator is functional. If the air bag warning indicator does not illuminate, stays on steady, or flashes, a fault has been detected by the air bag diagnostic monitor.

Turn Signal (Combination) Switch

REMOVAL & INSTALLATION

◗ **See Figures 79 and 80**

✳✳ CAUTION

Some models covered by this manual may be equipped with a Supplemental Restraint System (SRS), which uses an air bag. Whenever working near any of the SRS components, such as the impact sensors, air bag module, steering column or instrument panel, disable the SRS, as described in Section 6.

1. Disconnect the negative battery cable.

2. Before proceeding further, wait one minute for the air bag backup power supply to deplete its stored energy.

3. Remove the steering wheel.

4. Remove the three steering column shroud screws.

5. Separate the upper and lower portions of the steering column shroud.

6. Remove the shroud from the steering column.

7. Apply two strips of tape across the air bag sliding contact to prevent accidental rotation.

8. Remove the three air bag sliding contact screws and pull the air bag sliding contact off the steering column.

9. Remove the air bag sliding contact ground wire screw.

10. Disengage the air bag sliding contact electrical connector.

11. Remove the air bag sliding contact.

12. Loosen the three combination switch retaining screws.

13. Disengage the combination switch electrical connectors.

14. Slide the combination switch off the steering column.

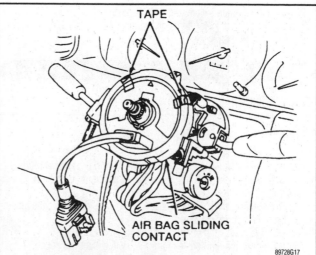

Fig. 79 Apply two strips of tape across the air bag sliding contact to prevent accidental rotation

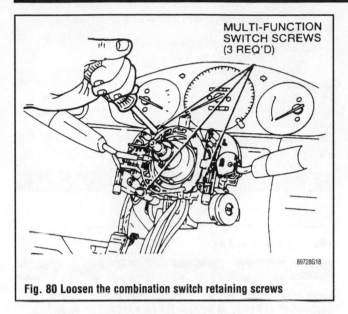

Fig. 80 Loosen the combination switch retaining screws

To install:

15. Slide the combination switch onto the steering column.
16. Engage the combination switch electrical connectors.
17. Install and tighten the three combination switch retaining screws.
18. Engage the air bag sliding contact electrical connector.
19. Install and tighten the air bag sliding contact ground wire screw.
20. Place the air bag sliding contact onto the steering column and tighten the three retaining screws to 18–26 inch lbs. (2–3 Nm).
21. Remove the 2 strips of tape from the air bag sliding contact.

➟**If the air bag sliding contact has been accidentally rotated, the air bag sliding contact alignment must be adjusted.**

22. If required, adjust the air bag sliding contact as follows:
    a. Center the front wheels to the straight-ahead position.
    b. Turn the air bag sliding contact clockwise to its locked position and then back it off 2¾ turns.
    c. Align the arrows on the air bag sliding contact and the air bag sliding contact housing.
23. Place the steering column shroud onto the steering column.
24. Install and tighten the three steering column shroud screws.
25. Install the steering wheel.
26. Connect the negative battery cable.
27. Check all functions of the combination switch for proper operation.
28. Turn the ignition switch to the **RUN** position and visually check that the air bag warning indicator lights on the dashboard momentarily to verify operation of the air bag system.

Ignition Switch

REMOVAL & INSTALLATION

▶ **See Figure 81**

1. Disconnect the negative battery cable.
2. Remove the three screws retaining the steering column shroud.
3. Separate and remove the upper and lower steering column shrouds.
4. Remove the ignition switch attaching screw and separate the ignition switch from the steering column.
5. Disengage the ignition switch electrical connector.
6. Disengage the ignition key reminder switch electrical connector.
7. If necessary, remove the ignition key reminder switch screws and the ignition key reminder switch.

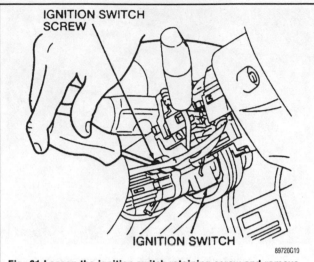

Fig. 81 Loosen the ignition switch retaining screw and remove the switch

To install:

8. If removed, position the ignition key reminder switch and install the two ignition key reminder switch screws.
9. Engage the ignition key reminder switch electrical connector.
10. Engage the ignition switch electrical connector.
11. Position the ignition switch in the lock cylinder housing and install with the attaching screw.
12. Install the upper and lower steering column shrouds.
13. Connect the negative battery cable.
14. Check the ignition switch operation.

Steering Linkage

REMOVAL & INSTALLATION

Tie Rod Ends

▶ **See Figures 82 thru 87**

1. Raise and safely support the vehicle.
2. Remove the wheel and tire assembly.
3. Remove the cotter pin from the tie rod end stud. Discard the cotter pin.

Fig. 82 Remove the cotter pin from the nut

Fig. 83 Use a suitable puller to disengage the tie rod end from the steering knuckle

4. Disengage the tie rod end from the steering knuckle using tie rod end remover tool T85M-3395-A or equivalent.

5. Remove the nut and examine it for damage, and replace as required.

6. Separate the tie rod end from the steering knuckle.

7. With paint or a suitable marker, mark the tie rod end, jam nut and tie rod spindle to ease assembly without changing the toe setting.

8. Loosen the jam nut and unscrew the tie rod end, counting the number of turns required for removal. Replace the tie rod end as required.

➡**If a new tie rod end is being installed, place the old and new ends side-by-side and place alignment marks on the new end that match as closely as possible to those on the old end. The existing jam nut may not seat in exactly the same position on the new tie rod end and the toe setting may have to be checked and/or readjusted as a precaution.**

To install:

9. When replacing a tie rod end, install a new dust boot over the stud with a suitable adapter. A ¾ in. socket will accomplish the task simply and effectively.

10. Thread the jam nut and tie rod end onto the tie rod and align the index marks made during the removal procedure.

Fig. 84 Remove the nut and separate the tie rod end from the steering knuckle

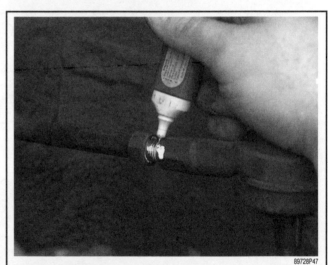

Fig. 86 With paint or a suitable marker, mark the tie rod threads. This will aid in installation and alignment

Fig. 85 Loosen the jam nut using one wrench as a backup and another to loosen the nut

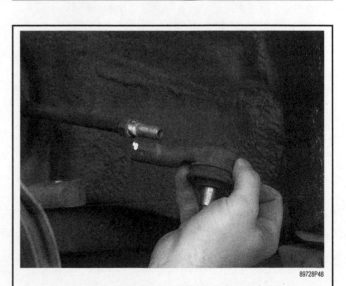

Fig. 87 Unscrew the tie rod end and remove it from the tie rod

11. If installing a new tie rod end, match the position of the old one as closely as possible.

12. Install the tie rod end into the knuckle and tighten the jam nut to 25–36 ft. lbs. (34–50 Nm). If the cotter pin's keyway does not align with the stud bore, tighten (do not loosen) the nut until the castellations align with the pin bore. Install a new cotter pin.

13. Tighten the tie rod end nut to 31–42 ft. lbs. (42–57 Nm).

14. Install the wheel and tire assembly.

15. Lower the vehicle.

16. Check the toe setting.

17. Road test the vehicle and check for proper operation.

Manual Rack and Pinion

REMOVAL & INSTALLATION

♦ **See Figures 88 and 89**

1. Disconnect the negative battery cable.

2. Matchmark the steering column lower universal joint and steering rack pinion for assembly reference. Remove the steering column and intermediate shaft assembly from the vehicle.

3. Remove the floor set plate bolts and the floor set plate.

4. Cut the plastic tie wrap securing the steering column boot to the steering rack.

5. Raise and safely support the vehicle.

6. Remove the front wheel and tire assemblies.

7. Using a suitable puller, separate both tie rod ends from the steering knuckles.

8. Remove the catalytic converter.

9. Remove the plastic splash shield from the right inner fender.

10. Remove the two steering rack mounting bolts and lower the steering rack until it is free of the steering column boot.

11. Slide the rack to the right, through the inner fender opening until the left tie rod is clear of the left inner fender, then lower the left end until the steering rack assembly can be withdrawn from the left side of the vehicle.

➡**While maneuvering the tie rod boots in and out of the inner fender openings, guide the steering rack assembly carefully to avoid cutting or nicking the boots.**

12. Remove the steering column intermediate shaft coupling bolt and the coupling from the steering rack.

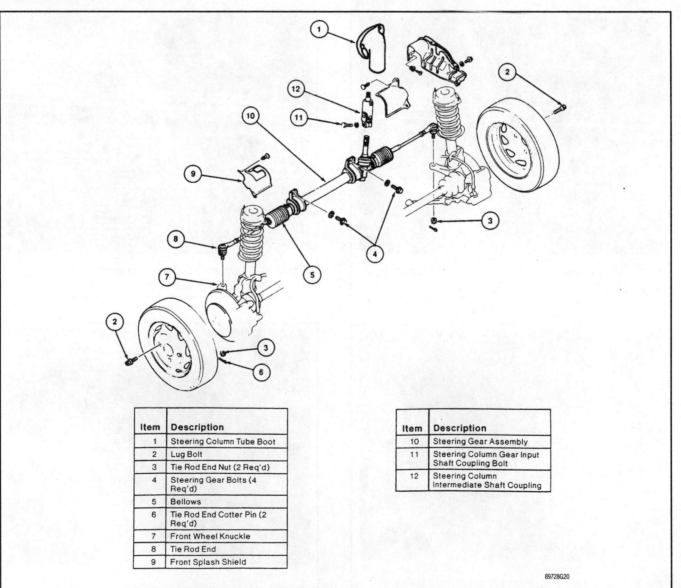

Item	Description
1	Steering Column Tube Boot
2	Lug Bolt
3	Tie Rod End Nut (2 Req'd)
4	Steering Gear Bolts (4 Req'd)
5	Bellows
6	Tie Rod End Cotter Pin (2 Req'd)
7	Front Wheel Knuckle
8	Tie Rod End
9	Front Splash Shield

Item	Description
10	Steering Gear Assembly
11	Steering Column Gear Input Shaft Coupling Bolt
12	Steering Column Intermediate Shaft Coupling

89728G20

Fig. 88 Exploded view of the manual steering gear and related components

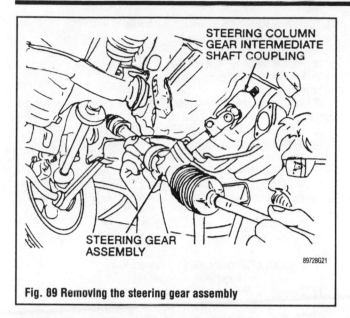

Fig. 89 Removing the steering gear assembly

To install:

13. Install the steering column intermediate shaft coupling and retaining bolts to the steering rack and tighten to 13–20 ft. lbs. (18–26 Nm).

14. Position the steering rack by starting the right side tie rod end through the right inner fender opening far enough to insert the left end of the steering gear assembly into the left front fender opening. Adjust the positioning of the steering rack to the left, being careful not to snag the bellows.

15. Align the intermediate shaft coupling with the steering column boot. Raise the steering rack fully into position.

16. Install the left steering rack mounting bolt, followed by the right steering rack mounting bolt. Tighten the bolts to 27–38 ft. lbs. (37–52 Nm).

17. Connect the tie rod ends to the steering knuckles. Install and tighten the tie rod end nuts to 31–42 ft. lbs. (42–57 Nm). Install new cotter pins.

18. Attach the right side splash shield on the right inner fender panel.

19. Install the catalytic converter.

20. Install the tire and wheel assemblies.

21. Secure the steering column boot to the steering rack housing with a new tie wrap.

22. Install the floor set plate and bolts.

23. Align the matchmarks made on the steering column lower universal joint and the steering rack pinion shaft. Install the steering column when the proper alignment is achieved.

24. Connect the negative battery cable.

25. Check the front end alignment.

26. Road test the vehicle and check for proper steering rack operation.

Power Rack and Pinion

REMOVAL & INSTALLATION

♦ **See Figure 90**

1. Disconnect the negative battery cable.
2. Remove the steering column tube boot retainer and pry up the boot.
3. Remove the steering column gear input shaft coupling bolt.
4. Raise and safely support the vehicle.

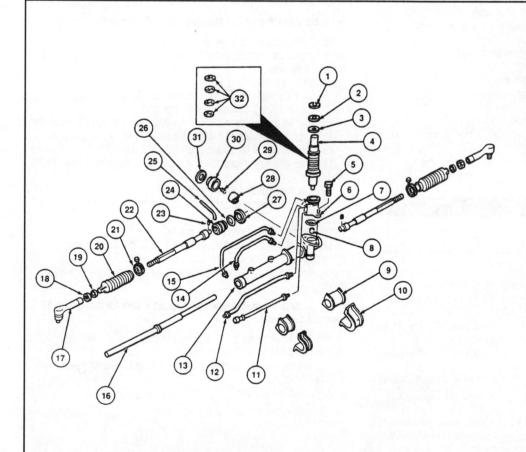

Item	Description
1	Steering Gear Pinion Snap Ring
2	Steering Gear Actuator Housing Oil Seal
3	Steering Gear Worm Thrust Bearing
4	Power Steering Gear Input Shaft and Control
5	Power Steering Gear Actuator Housing Bolt
6	Power Steering Gear Actuator Housing
7	Power Steering Gear Valve Body Housing Gasket
8	Power Steering Gear Shaft and Control Lower Bearing
9	Steering Gear Insulator
10	Steering Gear Mounting Bracket
11	Power Steering Return Hose
12	Power Steering Pressure Hose
13	Steering Gear Housing
14	Power Steering Right Turn Pressure Hose
15	Power Steering Left Turn Pressure Hose
16	Steering Gear Sector Shaft
17	Tie Rod End
18	Tie Rod End Jam Nut
19	Bellows Clip
20	Bellows
21	Bellow Wires
22	Front Wheel Spindle Tie Rod
23	Lockpin
24	Steering Gear Housing Sector Shaft Bushing
25	Retaining Wire
26	O-Ring
27	Seal
28	Support Yoke
29	Spring
30	Yoke Plug
31	Yoke Locking Nut
32	Teflon® Seals

Fig. 90 Exploded view of the power steering gear assembly

5. Remove the front tire and wheel assemblies.

6. Remove the power steering hose bracket. Disconnect and plug the high pressure and return lines.

7. Remove the tie rod end cotter pins and nuts. Using the proper tool, separate both tie rod ends from the steering knuckles. Discard the cotter pins.

8. Remove the front fender splash shields.

➡ **Lowering the exhaust system will ease access to the steering gear.**

9. Remove the three exhaust inlet pipe nuts and two bracket bolts.

10. Remove the muffler inlet pipe hanger posts from the exhaust hanger insulators.

11. Place alignment marks on the right tie rod end to ease installation. Loosen the jam nut and remove the right tie rod end.

12. Remove the steering rack mounting bolts and lower the steering rack until it is free of the steering column boot. Slide the rack to the left and pull the right tie rod through the fender opening. Remove the steering gear by sliding it to the right.

To install:

13. Position the steering rack in its mounting location.

14. With an assistant lifting the steering gear, align the intermediate shaft with the universal joint and install the coupling bolt, but do not tighten.

15. Install the four steering rack bracket bolts and tighten to 27–38 ft. lbs. (37–52 Nm).

16. Tighten the input shaft coupling bolt to 13–20 ft. lbs. (18–26 Nm).

17. Unplug and connect the high pressure and return lines, and install the power steering hose bracket.

18. Install the muffler inlet pipe hanger posts onto the exhaust hanger insulators.

19. Raise the exhaust system and install the three exhaust inlet pipe nuts. Tighten the nuts to 28–38 ft. lbs. (38–53 Nm).

20. Install the two exhaust inlet pipe bracket bolts.

21. Install the right tie rod end and attach the tie rod ends to the steering knuckles.

22. Install the tie rod end nuts and tighten them to 31–42 ft. lbs. (42–57 Nm). Install new cotter pins.

23. Install the small front fender splash shield.

24. Install the front wheel and tire assemblies.

25. Lower the vehicle.

26. Connect the negative battery cable.

27. Add power steering fluid and allow any air to bleed from the power steering system. Check for leaks.

28. Adjust the toe setting by performing a front end alignment.

29. Road test the vehicle and check for proper operation.

Power Steering Pump

REMOVAL & INSTALLATION

1. Disconnect the negative battery cable.

2. Remove the air cleaner intake tube and engine air cleaner.

3. Disengage the electrical connector from the Power Steering Pressure (PSP) switch.

4. Disconnect and plug the reservoir hose at the power steering pump.

5. Loosen the power steering pressure hose nut and retainer bracket bolt, and remove the hose from the power steering pump. Plug the pressure hose.

6. Loosen the power steering pump adjustment locknut and adjustment bolt.

7. Remove the two power steering pump support bolts.

8. Remove the accessory drive belt.

9. Remove the tensioner bolt.

10. Remove the power steering pump through-bolt and nut.

11. Remove the power steering pump.

To install:

12. Position the power steering pump and install the two power steering pump support bolts. Tighten the bolts to 22–29 ft. lbs. (29–39 Nm).

13. Loosely install the power steering pump through-bolt and nut.

14. Install the accessory drive belt.

15. Loosely install the tensioner bolt.

16. Adjust the accessory drive belt tension.

17. Unplug and connect the power steering pressure hose to the power steering pump and tighten the pressure hose nut to 12–17 ft. lbs. (16–23 Nm).

18. Connect the pressure hose to its retainer bracket.

19. Remove the plug and connect the reservoir hose to the power steering pump.

20. Engage the PSP switch electrical connector.

21. Install the air cleaner intake tube and engine air cleaner.

22. Connect the negative battery cable.

23. Add power steering fluid and properly bleed the system.

24. Check for proper pump operation, making sure there are no leaks.

BLEEDING

1. Place the front wheels in a straight-ahead position. Do not turn the steering wheel during the initial fill.

2. Add power steering fluid to the FULL mark on the reservoir cap dipstick.

3. Disengage the distributor electrical connectors.

4. Crank the engine for 5–10 seconds.

➡ **Do not allow the power steering reservoir to run dry.**

5. Refill the power steering reservoir after cranking.

6. Repeat the cranking procedure until the fluid level in the reservoir remains constant.

7. Attach the distributor electrical connectors.

8. Start the engine and allow it to idle for several minutes.

9. Turn the steering wheel lock-to-lock several times.

10. Turn off the engine and check the fluid level. Add fluid if necessary.

11. If noise or aeration is present, the system must be purged of air.

12. Make sure that the power steering reservoir is full.

13. Raise and safely support the vehicle so that the front wheels are off the ground.

14. Turn the ignition key to the **ON** position.

15. Turn the steering wheel lock-to-lock several times with the engine not running.

16. Recheck the fluid and add if needed.

17. Repeat the previous two steps until the fluid level stabilizes.

18. Start the engine and let it idle.

19. Turn the steering wheel lock-to-lock several times with the engine running.

➡ **Do not hold the steering wheel against a stop for more than 10 seconds at a time.**

20. Verify that the fluid is not foamy and that the fluid level has not dropped. Repeat the air bleed procedure as necessary.

21. The fluid level should be between the **L** and **H** marks on the reservoir cap dipstick.

22. Lower the vehicle.

TORQUE SPECIFICATIONS

System	Component	Ft. Lbs.	Nm
Wheels			
	Lug nuts	65-87	88-118
Front suspension			
	MacPherson Struts		
	Upper mounting block stud nuts	34-46	46-63
	Front spring and shock absorber bolts and nuts	69-86	93-117
	Sway Bar		
	Bracket retaining nuts	40-50	54-68
	Stabilizer bar retaining nuts	47-57	64-77
	Lower Control Arm		
	Stabilizer bar nut	47-57	64-77
	Lower arm-to-chassis bolt	32-40	43-54
	Ball joint nut	32-40	43-54
	Wheel Hub and Knuckle		
	Strut-to-steering knuckle bolts and nuts	69-86	93-117
	Lower control arm pinch bolt and nut	32-40	43-54
	Caliper bolts	29-36	39-49
	Tie rod end nut	22-33	29-44
	Wheel hub retaining nut	116-174	157-235
Rear Suspension			
	MacPherson struts		
	Shock absorber flanged nut	12-18	16-24
	Lower strut mounting bolt	50-60	68-81
	Axle Torsion Beam		
	Torsion beam nuts	69-86	93-117
	Upper axle beam bolts	40-50	54-68
	Axle beam lower bolts	69-86	93-117
	Rear Wheel Bearings		
	Wheel bearing nut	18-22	25-29
Steering			
	Steering Wheel		
	Steering wheel nut	29-36	39-49
	Air bag module	36-53 inch lbs.	4-6
	Turn Signal (Combination Switch)		
	Air bag sliding contact screws	18-26 inch lbs.	2-3
	Steering Linkage		
	Tie Rod Ends		
	Tie rod end jam nut	25-36	34-50
	Tie rod end nut	31-42	42-57
	Manual Rack and Pinion		
	Steering column intermediate shaft coupling and retaining bolts	13-20	18-26
	Steering rack mounting bolts	27-38	37-52
	Tie rod end nuts	31-42	42-57
	Power Rack and Pinion		
	Steering rack bracket bolts	27-37	37-52
	Input shaft coupling bolt	13-20	18-26
	Exhaust inlet pipe nuts	28-38	38-53
	Tie rod end nuts	31-42	42-57
	Power Steering Pump		
	Power steering pump support bolts	22-29	29-39
	Power steering pressure hose nut	12-17	16-23

89728C01

Troubleshooting Basic Steering and Suspension Problems

Problem	Cause	Solution
Hard steering (steering wheel is hard to turn)	• Low or uneven tire pressure • Loose power steering pump drive belt • Low or incorrect power steering fluid • Incorrect front end alignment • Defective power steering pump • Bent or poorly lubricated front end parts	• Inflate tires to correct pressure • Adjust belt • Add fluid as necessary • Have front end alignment checked/adjusted • Check pump • Lubricate and/or replace defective parts
Loose steering (too much play in the steering wheel)	• Loose wheel bearings • Loose or worn steering linkage • Faulty shocks • Worn ball joints	• Adjust wheel bearings • Replace worn parts • Replace shocks • Replace ball joints
Car veers or wanders (car pulls to one side with hands off the steering wheel)	• Incorrect tire pressure • Improper front end alignment • Loose wheel bearings • Loose or bent front end components • Faulty shocks	• Inflate tires to correct pressure • Have front end alignment checked/adjusted • Adjust wheel bearings • Replace worn components • Replace shocks
Wheel oscillation or vibration transmitted through steering wheel	• Improper tire pressures • Tires out of balance • Loose wheel bearings • Improper front end alignment • Worn or bent front end components	• Inflate tires to correct pressure • Have tires balanced • Adjust wheel bearings • Have front end alignment checked/adjusted • Replace worn parts
Uneven tire wear	• Incorrect tire pressure • Front end out of alignment • Tires out of balance	• Inflate tires to correct pressure • Have front end alignment checked/adjusted • Have tires balanced

TCCA8C01

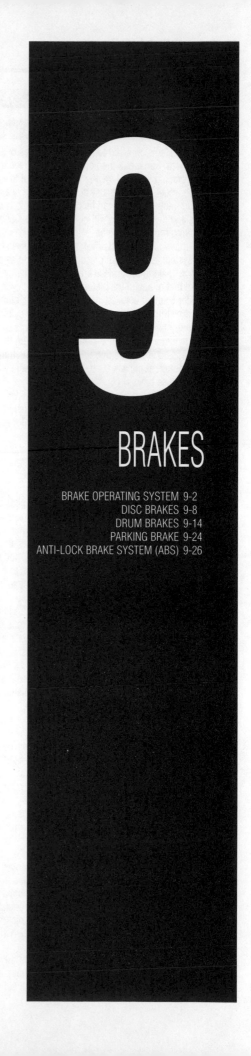

9

BRAKES

BRAKE OPERATING SYSTEM

Basic Operating Principles

Hydraulic systems are used to actuate the brakes of all modern automobiles. The system transports the power required to force the frictional surfaces of the braking system together from the pedal to the individual brake units at each wheel. A hydraulic system is used for two reasons:

First, fluid under pressure can be carried to all parts of an automobile by small pipes and flexible hoses without taking up a significant amount of room or posing routing problems.

Second, a great mechanical advantage can be given to the brake pedal end of the system, and the foot pressure required to actuate the brakes can be reduced by making the surface area of the master cylinder pistons smaller than that of any of the pistons in the wheel cylinders or calipers.

The master cylinder consists of a fluid reservoir, along with a double cylinder and piston assembly. Double type master cylinders are designed to separate the front and rear braking systems hydraulically in case of a leak. The master cylinder coverts mechanical motion from the pedal into hydraulic pressure within the lines. This pressure is translated back into mechanical motion at the wheels by either the wheel cylinder (drum brakes) or the caliper (disc brakes).

Steel lines carry the brake fluid to a point on the vehicle's frame near each of the vehicle's wheels. The fluid is then carried to the calipers and wheel cylinders by flexible tubes in order to allow for suspension and steering movements.

In drum brake systems, each wheel cylinder contains two pistons, one at either end, which push outward in opposite directions and force the brake shoe into contact with the drum.

In disc brake systems, the cylinders are part of the calipers. At least one cylinder in each caliper is used to force the brake pads against the disc.

All pistons employ some type of seal, usually made of rubber, to minimize fluid leakage. A rubber dust boot seals the outer end of the cylinder against dust and dirt. The boot fits around the outer end of the piston on disc brake calipers, and around the brake actuating rod on wheel cylinders.

The hydraulic system operates as follows: When at rest, the entire system, from the piston(s) in the master cylinder to those in the wheel cylinders or calipers, is full of brake fluid. Upon application of the brake pedal, fluid trapped in front of the master cylinder piston(s) is forced through the lines to the wheel cylinders. Here, it forces the pistons outward, in the case of drum brakes, and inward toward the disc, in the case of disc brakes. The motion of the pistons is opposed by return springs mounted outside the cylinders in drum brakes, and by spring seals, in disc brakes.

Upon release of the brake pedal, a spring located inside the master cylinder immediately returns the master cylinder pistons to the normal position. The pistons contain check valves and the master cylinder has compensating ports drilled in it. These are uncovered as the pistons reach their normal position. The piston check valves allow fluid to flow toward the wheel cylinders or calipers as the pistons withdraw. Then, as the return springs force the brake pads or shoes into the released position, the excess fluid returns to the reservoir through the compensating ports. It is during the time the pedal is in the released position that any fluid that has leaked out of the system will be replaced through the compensating ports.

Dual circuit master cylinders employ two pistons, located one behind the other, in the same cylinder. The primary piston is actuated directly by mechanical linkage from the brake pedal through the power booster. The secondary piston is actuated by fluid trapped between the two pistons. If a leak develops in front of the secondary piston, it moves forward until it bottoms against the front of the master cylinder, and the fluid trapped between the pistons will operate the rear brakes. If the rear brakes develop a leak, the primary piston will move forward until direct contact with the secondary piston takes place, and it will force the secondary piston to actuate the front brakes. In either case, the brake pedal moves farther when the brakes are applied, and less braking power is available.

All dual circuit systems use a switch to warn the driver when only half of the brake system is operational. This switch is usually located in a valve body which is mounted on the firewall or the frame below the master cylin-der. A hydraulic piston receives pressure from both circuits, with each circuit's pressure being applied to one end of the piston. When the pressures are in balance, the piston remains stationary. When one circuit has a leak, however, the greater pressure in that circuit during application of the brakes will push the piston to one side, closing the switch and activating the brake warning light.

In disc brake systems, this valve body also contains a metering valve and, in some cases, a proportioning valve. The metering valve keeps pressure from traveling to the disc brakes on the front wheels until the brake shoes on the rear wheels have contacted the drums, ensuring that the front brakes will never be used alone. The proportioning valve controls the pressure to the rear brakes to lessen the chance of rear wheel lock-up during very hard braking.

Warning lights may be tested by depressing the brake pedal and holding it while opening one of the wheel cylinder bleeder screws. If this does not cause the light to go on, substitute a new lamp, make continuity checks and, finally, replace the switch as necessary.

The hydraulic system may be checked for leaks by applying pressure to the pedal gradually and steadily. If the pedal sinks very slowly to the floor, the system has a leak. This is not to be confused with a springy or spongy feel due to the compression of air within the lines. If the system leaks, there will be a gradual change in the position of the pedal with a constant pressure.

Check for leaks along all lines and at wheel cylinders. If no external leaks are apparent, the problem is inside the master cylinder.

DISC BRAKES

Instead of the traditional expanding brakes that press outward against a circular drum, disc brake systems utilize a disc (rotor) with brake pads positioned on either side of it. An easily-seen analogy is the hand brake arrangement on a bicycle. The pads squeeze onto the rim of the bike wheel, slowing its motion. Automobile disc brakes use the identical principle, but apply the braking effort to a separate disc instead of the wheel.

The disc (rotor) is a casting, usually equipped with cooling fins between the two braking surfaces. This enables air to circulate between the braking surfaces, making them less sensitive to heat buildup and more resistant to fade. Dirt and water do not drastically affect braking action, since contaminants are thrown off by the centrifugal action of the rotor or scraped off by the pads. Also, the equal clamping action of the two brake pads tends to ensure uniform, straight line stops. Disc brakes are inherently self-adjusting. There are three general types of disc brake:

1. Fixed caliper
2. Floating caliper
3. Sliding caliper

The fixed caliper design uses two pistons mounted on either side of the rotor (in each side of the caliper). The caliper is mounted rigidly and does not move.

The sliding and floating designs are quite similar. In fact, these two types are often lumped together. In both designs, the pad on the inside of the rotor is moved into contact with the rotor by hydraulic force. The caliper, which is not held in a fixed position, moves slightly, bringing the outside pad into contact with the rotor. There are various methods of attaching floating calipers. Some pivot at the bottom or top, and some slide on mounting bolts. In any event, the end result is the same.

DRUM BRAKES

Drum brakes employ two brake shoes mounted on a stationary backing plate. These shoes are positioned inside a circular drum which rotates with the wheel assembly. The shoes are held in place by springs. This allows them to move toward the drums (when they are applied), while keeping the linings and drums in alignment. The shoes are actuated by a wheel cylinder which is mounted at the top of the backing plate. When the brakes are applied, hydraulic pressure forces the wheel cylinder's actuating links outward. Since these links bear directly against the top of the brake shoes, the tops of the shoes are then forced against the inner side of the drum. This action forces the bottoms of the two shoes to contact the brake drum by rotating the entire assembly slightly (known as servo action). When pressure within the wheel cylinder is relaxed, return springs pull the shoes back away from the drum.

Most modern drum brakes are designed to self-adjust themselves during application when the vehicle is moving in reverse. This motion causes both shoes to rotate very slightly with the drum, rocking an adjusting lever, thereby causing rotation of the adjusting screw. Some drum brake systems are designed to self-adjust during application whenever the brakes are applied. This on-board adjustment system reduces the need for maintenance adjustments and keeps both the brake function and pedal feel satisfactory.

POWER BOOSTERS

Virtually all modern vehicles use a vacuum assisted power brake system to multiply the braking force and reduce pedal effort. Since vacuum is always available when the engine is operating, the system is simple and efficient. A vacuum diaphragm is located on the front of the master cylinder and assists the driver in applying the brakes, reducing both the effort and travel he must put into moving the brake pedal.

The vacuum diaphragm housing is normally connected to the intake manifold by a vacuum hose. A check valve is placed at the point where the hose enters the diaphragm housing, so that during periods of low manifold vacuum, braking assist will not be lost.

Depressing the brake pedal closes off the vacuum source and allows atmospheric pressure to enter on one side of the diaphragm. This causes the master cylinder pistons to move and apply the brakes. When the brake pedal is released, vacuum is applied to both sides of the diaphragm and springs return the diaphragm and master cylinder pistons to the released position.

If the vacuum supply fails, the brake pedal rod will contact the end of the master cylinder actuator rod and the system will apply the brakes without any power assistance. The driver will notice that much higher pedal effort is needed to stop the car and that the pedal feels harder than usual.

Vacuum Leak Test

1. Operate the engine at idle without touching the brake pedal for at least one minute.
2. Turn **OFF** the engine and wait one minute.
3. Test for the presence of assist vacuum by depressing the brake pedal and releasing it several times. If vacuum is present in the system, light application will produce less and less pedal travel. If there is no vacuum, air is leaking into the system.

System Operation Test

1. With the engine **OFF**, pump the brake pedal until the supply vacuum is entirely gone.
2. Put light, steady pressure on the brake pedal.
3. Start the engine and let it idle. If the system is operating correctly, the brake pedal should fall toward the floor if the constant pressure is maintained.

Power brake systems may be tested for hydraulic leaks just as ordinary systems are tested.

Brake On/Off (BOO) Switch

REMOVAL & INSTALLATION

1. Disengage the brake on/off switch electrical connection.
2. Loosen the nuts and remove the switch from the bracket.
3. Remove the nuts from the switch.
To install:
4. Install the nuts on the switch.
5. Install the switch and tighten the retaining nuts.
6. Engage the switch's electrical connection.

ADJUSTMENT

▶ **See Figure 1**

1. Disengage the brake on/off switch electrical connection.
2. Loosen the switch nuts.
3. Connect a high impedance digital ohmmeter (or multimeter set on the resistance scale), across the switch terminals.
4. Position the switch until the meter indicates continuity.
5. Carefully move the switch toward the brake pedal until the meter indicates the switch is open (infinite resistance).
6. Rotate the switch towards the pedal one half turn and tighten the switch retaining nuts.

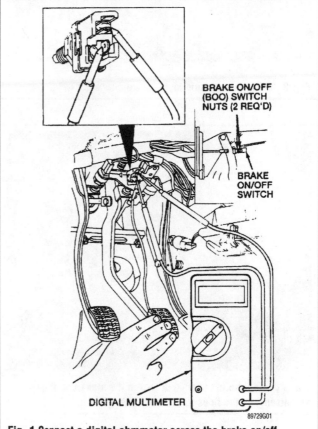

BRAKE ON/OFF (BOO) SWITCH NUTS (2 REQ'D)

BRAKE ON/OFF SWITCH

DIGITAL MULTIMETER

89729G01

Fig. 1 Connect a digital ohmmeter across the brake on/off switch terminals as illustrated

Master Cylinder

REMOVAL & INSTALLATION

▶ **See Figures 2, 3, 4 and 5**

1. Disconnect the negative battery cable.
2. Disengage the low fluid level sensor connector.
3. Disengage the lines from the master cylinder connections. Cap the brake lines and plug the master cylinder ports.
4. Loosen the two master cylinder retaining nuts and washers.
5. Remove the master cylinder from the vehicle.
To install:
6. If a new master cylinder is being installed, check the pushrod length adjustment as follows:
   a. Position master cylinder gauge T87C-2500-A or equivalent on the end of the master cylinder, loosen the setscrew and push the gauge plunger against the bottom of the primary piston.

Fig. 2 Unplug the low fluid level sensor connector

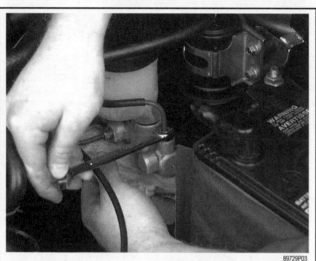

Fig. 3 Use a flare nut wrench to loosen the brake line fittings and disengage the lines from the master cylinder

Fig. 4 Loosen the master cylinder-to-power booster retaining nuts . . .

Fig. 5 . . . then remove the master cylinder from the engine compartment

   b. While holding the gauge in position, tighten the setscrew.

   c. Invert the master cylinder gauge and place it over the brake booster pushrod.

   d. If the clearance is not zero, loosen the pushrod locknut and adjust the pushrod.

➡ **Proper pushrod length adjustment is critical. If the pushrod length is too long, the brakes will drag. If the pushrod length is too short, the brake pedal will be low.**

✳✳ WARNING

Clean, high quality brake fluid is essential to the safe and proper operation of the brake system. You should always buy the highest quality brake fluid that is available. If the brake fluid becomes contaminated, drain and flush the system, then refill the master cylinder with new fluid. Never reuse any brake fluid. Any brake fluid that is removed from the system should be discarded. Also, do not allow any brake fluid to come in contact with a painted surface; it will damage the paint.

  7. Before installation, bench bleed a new master cylinder as follows:

   a. Mount the new master cylinder in a suitable holding fixture. Be careful not to damage the housing.

   b. Fit short lengths of brake lines to the master cylinder ports, so that they are directed into the master cylinder reservoir and submerged by brake fluid.

   c. Fill the master cylinder reservoir with clean DOT 3 or equivalent brake fluid.

   d. Using a suitable tool inserted into the booster pushrod cavity, push the master cylinder piston in slowly and allow it to return.

   e. Repeat the procedure until clear fluid only (no bubbles) is expelled into the master cylinder reservoir.

   f. Remove the short brake lines and plug the outlet ports. Remove the master cylinder from the holding fixture.

  8. Position the master cylinder and install the attaching washers and nuts. Tighten the nuts to 7–12 ft. lbs. (10–16 Nm).

  9. Connect the brake lines to the master cylinder ports and tighten.

  10. Have an assistant push down on the brake pedal.

  11. When the pedal is all the way down, crack open the brake line fittings at the master cylinder, one at a time, to expel any remaining air at the master cylinder.

  12. With the pedal still down, tighten the brake line fitting, then allow the brake pedal to return.

  13. Repeat until all air is expelled. Final-tighten the brake line fittings to 10–15 ft. lbs. (13–21 Nm).

14. Bleed the brake system.
15. Connect the low fluid level sensor.
16. Make sure the master cylinder reservoir is full.
17. Connect the negative battery cable.
18. Check for leaks and proper brake operation.

Power Brake Booster

REMOVAL & INSTALLATION

1. Remove the master cylinder.
2. Disconnect the vacuum hose from the booster.
3. From inside the car, remove the cotter pin that secures the clevis pin.
4. Remove the clevis pin from the clevis.
5. Have an assistant support the booster and loosen the booster-to-bulkhead retaining nuts.
6. Remove the booster from the engine compartment.
To install:
7. Install the booster and tighten its retaining nuts to 14–19 ft. lbs. (19–26 Nm).
8. Lubricate the clevis pin with white lithium grease and install it to the clevis.
9. Install a new cotter pin and connect the vacuum hose to the booster.
10. Install the master cylinder and bleed the brake system.

Brake Pressure Control Valve

▶ See Figure 6

The brake pressure control valve is used in the hydraulic brake system to balance front-to-rear brake application. The valve reduces hydraulic pressure to the rear wheel cylinders to prevent rear wheel lock-up.

The valve is not repairable and must be replaced if defective.

The valve is located in the engine compartment on the firewall, below and to the right of the power brake booster.

Fig. 6 The brake pressure control valve is located on the firewall, below and to the right of the power booster

REMOVAL & INSTALLATION

▶ See Figure 7

✳✳ CAUTION

Brake fluid contains polyglycol ethers and polyglycols. Avoid contact with the eyes and wash your hands thoroughly after han-

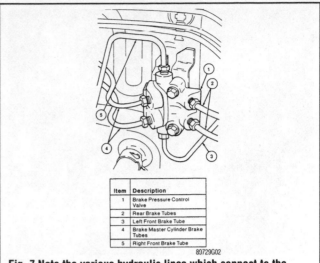

Item	Description
1	Brake Pressure Control Valve
2	Rear Brake Tubes
3	Left Front Brake Tube
4	Brake Master Cylinder Brake Tubes
5	Right Front Brake Tube

89729G02

Fig. 7 Note the various hydraulic lines which connect to the brake pressure control valve

dling brake fluid. If you do get brake fluid in your eyes, flush your eyes with clean, running water for 15 minutes. If eye irritation persists, or if you have taken brake fluid internally, IMMEDIATELY seek medical assistance.

1. Use a line wrench to loosen the brake pressure control valve's hydraulic lines.
2. Loosen the valve retaining bolts and remove the valve.
To install:
3. Install the valve and tighten the retaining bolts.
4. Connect the brake lines to the valve and, using a line wrench, tighten the flare nuts to 10–15 ft. lbs. (13–21 Nm).
5. Bleed the brake system.

Brake Hoses and Lines

Metal lines and rubber brake hoses should be checked frequently for leaks and external damage. Metal lines are particularly prone to crushing and kinking under the vehicle. Any such deformation can restrict the proper flow of fluid and, therefore, impair braking at the wheels. Rubber hoses should be checked for cracking or scraping; such damage can create a weak spot in the hose and it could fail under pressure.

Any time the lines are removed or disconnected, extreme cleanliness must be observed. Clean all joints and connections before disassembly (use a stiff bristle brush and clean brake fluid); be sure to plug the lines and ports as soon as they are opened. New lines and hoses should be flushed clean with brake fluid before installation to remove any contamination.

REMOVAL & INSTALLATION

▶ See Figures 8 thru 13

1. Disconnect the negative battery cable.
2. Raise and safely support the vehicle on jackstands.
3. Remove any wheel and tire assemblies necessary for access to the particular line you are removing.
4. Thoroughly clean the surrounding area at the joints to be disconnected.
5. Place a suitable catch pan under the joint to be disconnected.
6. Using two wrenches (one to hold the joint and one to turn the fitting), disconnect the hose or line to be replaced.
7. Disconnect the other end of the line or hose, moving the drain pan if necessary. Always use a back-up wrench to avoid damaging the fitting.
8. Disconnect any retaining clips or brackets holding the line and remove the line from the vehicle.

Fig. 8 View of the rear left side brake hose and lines

Fig. 9 View of the rear right side brake hose and lines

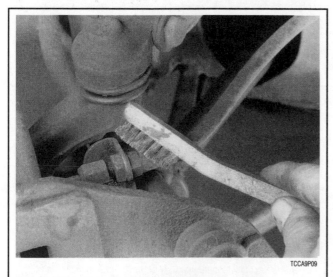

Fig. 10 Use a brush to clean the fittings of any debris

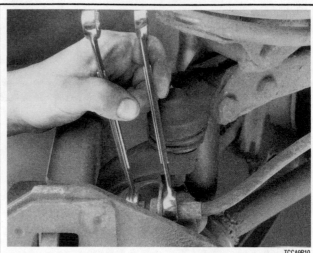

Fig. 11 Use two wrenches to loosen the fitting. If available, use flare nut type wrenches

Fig. 12 Any gaskets/crush washers should be replaced with new ones during installation

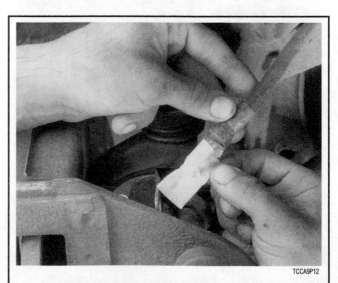

Fig. 13 Tape or plug the line to prevent contamination

➡If the brake system is to remain open for more time than it takes to swap lines, tape or plug each open line to keep contaminants out and fluid in.

To install:

9. Install the new line or hose, starting with the end farthest from the master cylinder. Connect the other end, then confirm that both fittings are correctly threaded and turn smoothly using finger pressure. Make sure the new line will not rub against any other part. Brake lines must be at least ½ in. (13mm) from the steering column and other moving parts. Any protective shielding or insulators must be reinstalled in the original location.

✳✳ WARNING

Make sure the hose is NOT kinked or touching any part of the frame or suspension after installation. These conditions may cause the hose to fail prematurely.

10. Using two wrenches as before, tighten each fitting.
11. Install any retaining clips or brackets on the lines.
12. If removed, install the wheel and tire assemblies, then carefully lower the vehicle to the ground.
13. Refill the brake master cylinder reservoir with clean, fresh brake fluid, meeting DOT 3 specifications. Properly bleed the brake system.
14. Connect the negative battery cable.

Bleeding the Brake System

▶ **See Figures 14, 15 and 16**

✳✳ CAUTION

Brake fluid contains polyglycol ethers and polyglycols. Avoid contact with the eyes and wash your hands thoroughly after handling brake fluid. If you do get brake fluid in your eyes, flush your eyes with clean, running water for 15 minutes. If eye irritation persists, or if you have taken brake fluid internally, IMMEDIATELY seek medical assistance.

The brake hydraulic circuits form a split diagonal hydraulic system. Brake lines for the left front and right rear wheels form one circuit, while those for the right front and left rear wheels form the other circuit. When bleeding one of these circuits, bleed the rear wheel first and then the front wheel at the opposite corner.

Fig. 15 Connect one end of a hose to the screw and place the other end in a clear container of brake fluid. Use a wrench to open and close the screw as needed

➡Do not allow the master cylinder to run dry during the bleeding procedure. Only use fresh DOT 3 or equivalent brake fluid from a closed container.

✳✳ WARNING

Clean, high quality brake fluid is essential to the safe and proper operation of the brake system. You should always buy the highest quality brake fluid that is available. If the brake fluid becomes contaminated, drain and flush the system, then refill the master cylinder with new fluid. Never reuse any brake fluid. Any brake fluid that is removed from the system should be discarded. Also, do not allow any brake fluid to come in contact with a painted surface; it will damage the paint.

1. Clean all dirt from the master cylinder filler cap.
2. Fill the master cylinder with DOT 3 brake fluid.
3. If the master cylinder is known or suspected to contain air, it must be bled before the wheel cylinders or caliper. Bleed the master cylinder as follows:

    a. Loosen the front line fitting and have an assistant push the brake pedal slowly through its full range of travel.

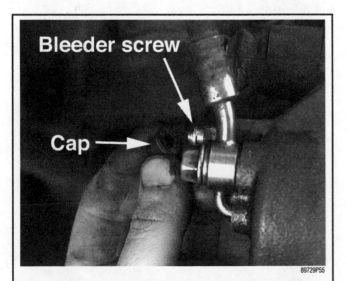

Fig. 14 Remove the front disc brake caliper bleeder screw cap

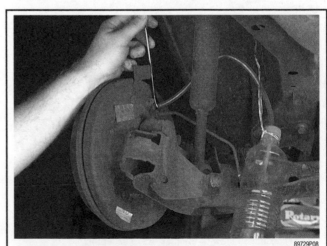

Fig. 16 Connect one end of a plastic hose to the rear wheel cylinder bleeder screw and submerge the other end in a container of clean brake fluid

b. While the assistant holds the pedal down, tighten the brake line fitting. After the line fitting is tightened, the assistant may release the brake pedal.

c. Repeat the procedure on the rear brake line.

d. Repeat the entire process several times to make sure all air has been removed from the master cylinder.

4. Remove the bleeder screw cap from the appropriate rear wheel cylinder. Position a flare nut wrench on the bleeder fitting.

5. Attach a rubber hose to the bleeder fitting. The hose must fit snugly around the bleeder fitting.

6. Submerge the other end of the hose in a clear container partially filled with brake fluid.

7. Loosen the bleeder fitting approximately ¾ turn. Have an assistant push the brake pedal slowly through its full range of travel and hold it there. Close the bleeder fitting, then have the assistant release the brake pedal.

8. Repeat the procedure until air bubbles no longer appear at the submerged end of the bleeder hose.

9. When the fluid entering the bottle is completely free of bubbles, tighten the bleeder screw, remove the hose and install the bleeder screw cap.

✳✳ WARNING

Clean, high quality brake fluid is essential to the safe and proper operation of the brake system. You should always buy the highest quality brake fluid that is available. If the brake fluid becomes contaminated, drain and flush the system, then refill the master cylinder with new fluid. Never reuse any brake fluid. Any brake fluid that is removed from the system should be discarded. Also, do not allow any brake fluid to come in contact with a painted surface; it will damage the paint.

10. Bleed the front caliper located diagonally to the wheel cylinder just completed.

11. Check the master cylinder fluid level, and add fluid if necessary.

12. Bleed the other diagonal circuit in the same manner.

13. Check the pedal feel. If the pedal is still spongy, repeat the bleeding procedure.

14. Road test the vehicle and check for proper brake system operation.

DISC BRAKES

▶ See Figure 17

✳✳ CAUTION

Older brake pads or shoes may contain asbestos, which has been determined to be a cancer causing agent. Never clean the brake surfaces with compressed air! Avoid inhaling any dust from any brake surface! When cleaning brake surfaces, use a commercially available brake cleaning fluid.

Brake Pads

REMOVAL & INSTALLATION

▶ See Figures 18 thru 24

1. Remove brake fluid from the master cylinder reservoir to lower the level by approximately ⅓, preventing brake fluid overflow when the caliper piston is pressed back into its bore.

2. Raise and safely support the vehicle.

3. Remove the tire and wheel assembly.

4. Use the proper brake tool or a C-clamp to move the caliper piston into its bore approximately ⅛ in. (3mm) to allow removal of the disc brake pads.

➡ Do not use a screwdriver or similar tool to pry the piston away from the rotor.

5. Disengage the anti-rattle clip from the brake caliper locating pins. Remove the clip.

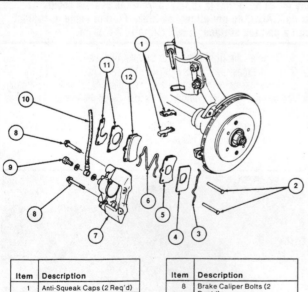

Item	Description
1	Anti-Squeak Caps (2 Req'd)
2	Disc Brake Caliper Locating Pins (2 Req'd)
3	Disc Brake Pad Anti-Rattle Clip
4	Brake Pad Shim
5	Brake Shoe and Lining
6	M-Shaped Anti-Rattle Spring
7	Disc Brake Caliper, Front

Item	Description
8	Brake Caliper Bolts (2 Req'd)
9	Banjo Bolt
10	Front Brake Hose
11	Brake Pad Shims
12	Brake Shoe and Lining

89729G03

Fig. 17 Exploded view of the disc brake assembly

89729P41

Fig. 18 Disengage the anti-rattle clip . . .

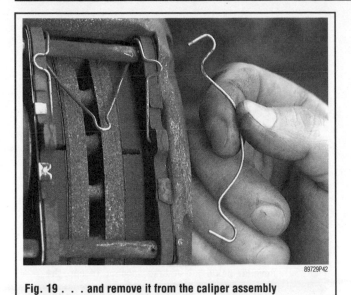

Fig. 19 . . . and remove it from the caliper assembly

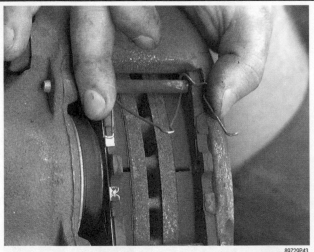

Fig. 20 Squeeze the sides of the M-shaped anti-rattle spring to disengage it from the caliper

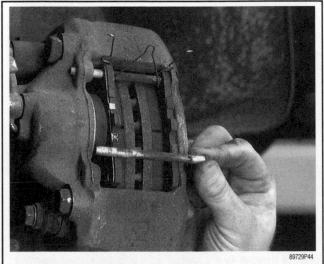

Fig. 21 Remove the bottom caliper locating pin

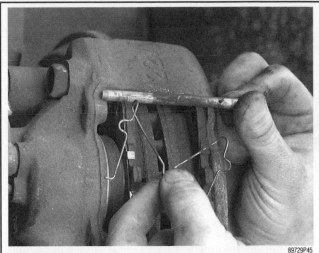

Fig. 22 Remove the top locating pin and the M-shaped anti-rattle spring

Fig. 23 Remove the brake pads from the opening in the rear of the caliper

Shim

Fig. 24 Remove, but do not discard, the shims found behind the brake pads

6. Remove the two disc brake caliper locating pins and the M-shaped anti-rattle spring.

7. Remove the brake pads and shims. Do not discard the shims found behind the brake pads.

To install:

8. Use a C-clamp and one of the old brake pads to push the caliper piston back into the caliper bore. Do not push directly against the caliper piston, or damage to the piston may result.

9. Apply suitable grease, normally supplied with the brake pad set, to both surfaces of the inner shim and to the back of the brake pads. Be careful not to get grease on the friction surface of the brake pads.

10. Install the brake pads, making sure the shims are properly positioned.

11. Install the two disc brake caliper locating pins and the M-shaped anti-rattle spring.

12. Install the disc brake pad anti-rattle clip.

13. Install the wheel and tire assembly. Tighten the lug nuts/bolts to 65–87 ft. lbs. (88–118 Nm).

14. Lower the vehicle.

15. Apply the brake pedal several times to seat the pads, before moving the vehicle. Check the brake fluid level in the master cylinder, and add fluid as necessary.

16. Check for proper brake operation.

INSPECTION

Inspect the brake pads for wear using a ruler or Vernier caliper. The maximum thickness is 0.39 in. (10mm) and the minimum thickness allowable is 0.08 in. (2mm). If the lining is thinner than specification or there is evidence of the lining being contaminated by brake fluid or oil, replace all brake pad assemblies (a complete axle set).

Brake Caliper

REMOVAL & INSTALLATION

▶ See Figures 25, 26, 27, 28 and 29

1. Raise and safely support the vehicle.
2. Remove the wheel and tire assembly.
3. Remove the brake pads.
4. Remove the banjo bolt securing the brake hose to the caliper and plug the hose end. Discard and replace the two copper sealing washers.
5. Remove the two caliper retaining bolts.
6. Remove the caliper and the anti-squeak caps from the vehicle.

Fig. 26 Remove the banjo bolt and the washers. Discard the washers and replace them with new ones

Fig. 27 Loosen the caliper mounting bolts

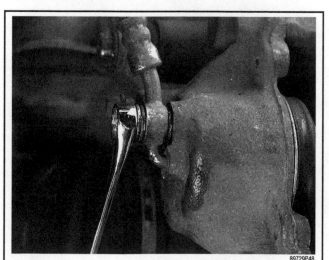

Fig. 25 Loosen the banjo bolt securing the brake hose to the caliper

Fig. 28 Remove the anti-squeak caps from the caliper mounting bosses . . .

Fig. 29 . . . then remove the caliper assembly from the steering knuckle

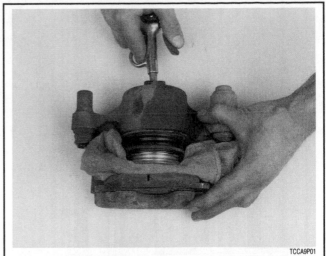

Fig. 30 For some types of calipers, use compressed air to drive the piston out of the caliper, but make sure to keep your fingers clear

To install:

7. Install the anti-squeak caps.

8. Position the caliper on the steering knuckle and install the two caliper retaining bolts. Tighten the caliper retaining bolts to 29–36 ft. lbs. (39–49 Nm).

9. Connect the brake hose to the caliper using the banjo bolt and two new copper sealing washers. Tighten the banjo bolt to 16–22 ft. lbs. (22–29 Nm).

10. Install the brake pads and bleed the brake system.

11. Install the wheel and tire assembly.

12. Lower the vehicle.

13. Apply the brake pedal several times to position the brake pads, before attempting to move the vehicle.

14. Check for proper brake operation.

OVERHAUL

♦ **See Figures 30 thru 37**

➡Some vehicles may be equipped dual piston calipers. The procedure to overhaul the caliper is essentially the same with the exception of multiple pistons, O-rings and dust boots.

1. Remove the caliper from the vehicle and place on a clean workbench.

❋❋ CAUTION

NEVER place your fingers in front of the pistons in an attempt to catch or protect the pistons when applying compressed air. This could result in personal injury!

➡Depending upon the vehicle, there are two different ways to remove the piston from the caliper. Refer to the brake pad replacement procedure to make sure you have the correct procedure for your vehicle.

2. The first method is as follows:

a. Stuff a shop towel or a block of wood into the caliper to catch the piston.

b. Remove the caliper piston by applying compressed air into the caliper inlet hole. Inspect the piston for scoring, nicks, corrosion and/or worn or damaged chrome plating. The piston must be replaced if any of these conditions are found.

3. For the second method, you must rotate the piston to retract it from the caliper.

Fig. 31 Withdraw the piston from the caliper bore

Fig. 32 On some vehicles, you must remove the anti-rattle clip

Fig. 33 Use a prytool to carefully pry around the edge of the boot . . .

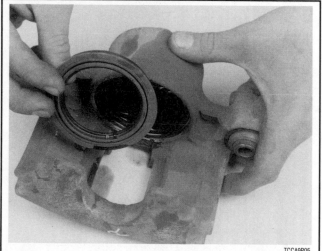

Fig. 34 . . . then remove the boot from the caliper housing, taking care not to score or damage the bore

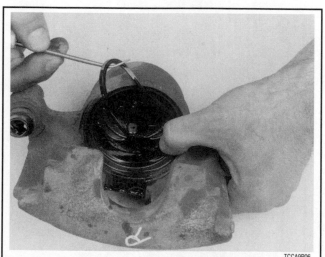

Fig. 35 Use extreme caution when removing the piston seal; DO NOT scratch the caliper bore

4. If equipped, remove the anti-rattle clip.

5. Use a prytool to remove the caliper boot, being careful not to scratch the housing bore.

6. Remove the piston seals from the groove in the caliper bore.

7. Carefully loosen the brake bleeder valve cap and valve from the caliper housing.

8. Inspect the caliper bores, pistons and mounting threads for scoring or excessive wear.

9. Use crocus cloth to polish out light corrosion from the piston and bore.

10. Clean all parts with denatured alcohol and dry with compressed air.

To assemble:

11. Lubricate and install the bleeder valve and cap.

12. Install the new seals into the caliper bore grooves, making sure they are not twisted.

13. Lubricate the piston bore.

14. Install the pistons and boots into the bores of the caliper and push to the bottom of the bores.

15. Use a suitable driving tool to seat the boots in the housing.

16. Install the caliper in the vehicle.

17. Install the wheel and tire assembly, then carefully lower the vehicle.

18. Properly bleed the brake system.

Fig. 36 Use the proper size driving tool and a mallet to properly seal the boots in the caliper housing

Fig. 37 There are tools, such as this Mighty-Vac, available to assist in proper brake system bleeding

Brake Disc (Rotor)

REMOVAL & INSTALLATION

♦ **See Figures 38 and 39**

1. Raise and safely support the vehicle.
2. Remove the tire and wheel assembly.
3. Remove the disc brake pads and shims.
4. Remove the caliper.

Fig. 38 Unfasten the rotor retaining screws . . .

Fig. 39 . . . and remove the rotor from the hub

➥**Do not allow the caliper to hang by the brake hose. Support the caliper by a length of wire attached to the strut.**

5. Loosen the two front disc brake rotor retaining screws and remove the rotor from the vehicle.

To install:

6. Position the disc brake rotor to the wheel hub, then install the two retaining screws and tighten them securely.
7. Install the brake caliper.
8. Install the disc brake pads and shims.
9. Install the tire and wheel assembly.
10. Lower the vehicle.
11. Apply the brake pedal several times to seat the pads, before moving the vehicle.
12. Check the brake fluid level in the master cylinder and add fluid as necessary.
13. Check for proper brake operation.

INSPECTION

♦ **See Figure 40**

1. Using a brake rotor micrometer or Vernier caliper, measure the rotor thickness in several places around the rotor.
2. On models with an automatic transaxle, the minimum thickness is 0.78 in. (20mm). On models equipped with a manual transaxle, the minimum thickness is 0.63 in. (16mm).
3. If the rotor thickness is less than the minimum, replace the rotor.
4. Mount a magnetic base dial indicator to the strut member and zero the indicator stylus on the face of the rotor. Rotate the rotor 360 degrees (one revolution) by hand and record the run-out.
5. The run-out should be a maximum of 0.004 in. (0.1mm). If run-out exceeds the limit, replace the rotor.

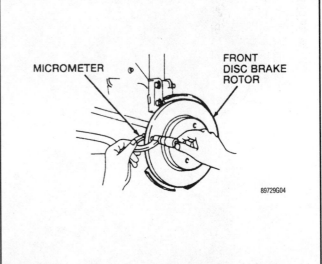

Fig. 40 Using a micrometer to measure the rotor thickness

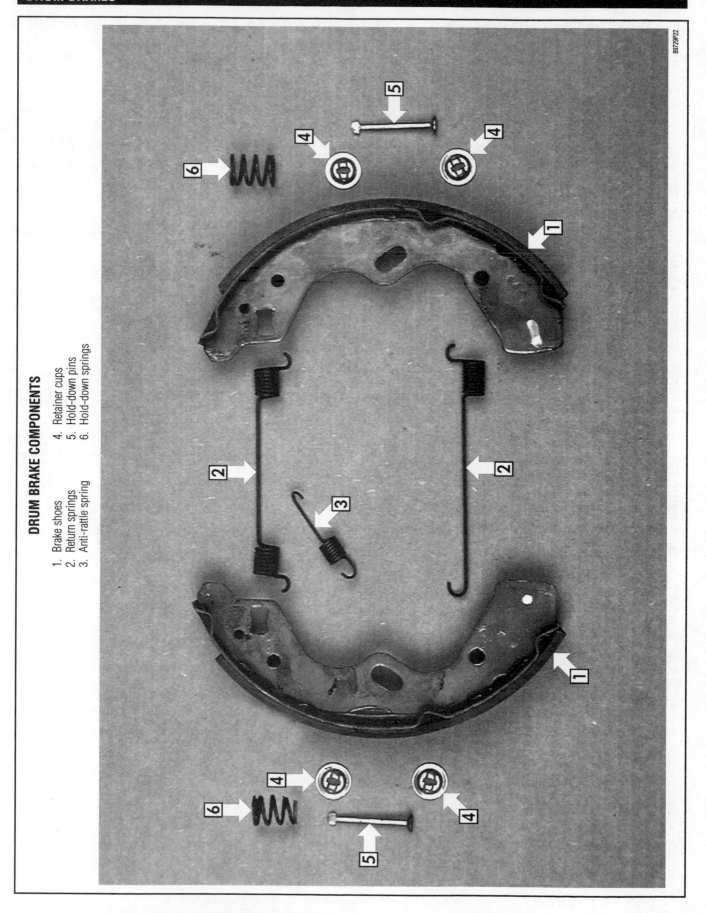

DRUM BRAKE COMPONENTS

1. Brake shoes
2. Return springs
3. Anti-rattle spring
4. Retainer cups
5. Hold-down pins
6. Hold-down springs

CAUTION

Older brake pads or shoes may contain asbestos, which has been determined to be a cancer causing agent. Never clean the brake surfaces with compressed air! Avoid inhaling any dust from any brake surface! When cleaning brake surfaces, use a commercially available brake cleaning fluid.

Brake Drums

REMOVAL & INSTALLATION

◆ See Figures 41 thru 47

1. Raise and safely support the vehicle.
2. Remove the tire and wheel assembly.
3. Remove the hub grease cap.
4. Remove the cotter pin and wheel bearing nut cover. Discard the cotter pin.
5. Remove the wheel bearing locknut.

Fig. 43 . . . then remove the bearing nut cover

Fig. 41 Use a prytool to remove the hub grease cap

Fig. 44 Remove the wheel bearing locknut . . .

Fig. 42 Use needlenosed pliers to remove the cotter pin . . .

Fig. 45 . . . and the washer assembly

Fig. 46 Slide the drum outward, then push it back in. This will allow you to grasp the bearing and remove it

Fig. 47 Grasp the drum and remove it from the spindle

➡A left-hand threaded locknut is used on the vehicle's right rear wheel spindle. Turn this locknut clockwise to loosen.

6. Remove the washer and the bearing assembly.

7. Remove the brake drum.

8. If the brake drum is to be machined or replaced, remove the inner wheel bearing and grease seal.

To install:

9. If removed, install the inner wheel bearing and a new grease seal.

10. Make sure the bearings and hub contain an adequate amount of clean wheel bearing grease.

11. Adjust the distance between the brake shoes to match the inner diameter of the brake drum, if the brake drum has been machined or replaced.

12. Position the brake drum on the spindle. Keep the drum centered on the spindle to prevent damage to the grease seal and spindle threads.

13. Install the outer wheel bearing, washer and wheel bearing locknut.

14. Properly adjust the wheel bearing preload.

15. Install the wheel bearing nut cover and a new cotter pin.

16. Install the tire and wheel assembly. Tighten the lug nuts/bolts to 65–87 ft. lbs. (88–118 Nm).

17. Lower the vehicle.

18. Check the brake system for proper operation.

INSPECTION

▶ **See Figures 48 and 49**

1. Inspect the inside surface of the drum for scratches and uneven or abnormal wear.

2. Resurface the drum if the damage is minor, and replace the drum if the damage is excessive.

3. Measure the inside diameter of the drum with a brake drum micrometer.

✳✳ CAUTION

Make sure to check the drum-to-shoe contact after repairing or replacing the drum.

4. If the drum diameter exceeds 7.93 in. (201.5mm), replace the drum.

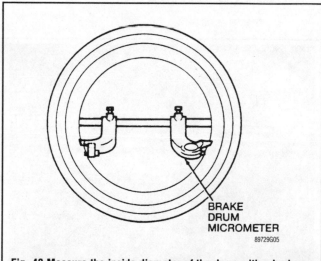

Fig. 48 Measure the inside diameter of the drum with a brake drum micrometer

Fig. 49 The brake drum maximum diameter is stamped on the drum

Brake Shoes

REMOVAL & INSTALLATION

◆ **See Figures 50 thru 63**

1. Raise and safely support the vehicle.
2. Remove the wheel and tire assembly.
3. Remove the brake drum.
4. Remove the brake shoe retracting springs and the anti-rattle spring.
5. Using an appropriate tool, depress and twist the retainer cups ¼ turn, and carefully remove them, along with the brake shoe hold-down springs and pins.
6. Pull the brake shoes away from the backing plate and remove.
7. If necessary, remove the parking brake levers by disengaging the cables and loosening the retainers.

To install:

8. Clean the brake backing plate.
9. Lubricate the backing plate's brake shoe contact areas with a suitable high temperature grease.

89729P17

Fig. 51 Use needlenose pliers to disengage the upper . . .

89729P38

Fig. 50 View of the assembled rear drum brakes

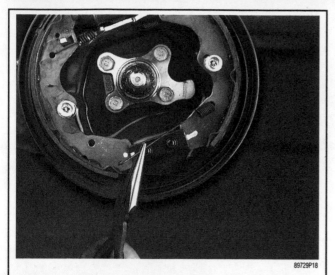

Fig. 52 . . . and the lower return springs

Fig. 53 Also use needlenose pliers to remove the anti-rattle spring

Fig. 54 Remove the hold-down springs, pins and retainer cups

Fig. 55 Remove the brake shoes from the backing plate

Fig. 56 If necessary, remove the self-adjuster/brake operating lever by disengaging the parking brake cable and loosening the retainer

➡Synthetic brake caliper grease also works well for drum brake shoe installation.

10. Install the brake shoe upper retracting spring on the primary (front) brake shoe. Position the primary brake shoe on the backing plate and install the hold-down pin, spring and retainer cup. Using an appropriate tool, depress the cup and rotate it ¼ turn to lock it in place.

11. Connect the upper retracting spring to the secondary (rear) brake shoe and position the shoe against the backing plate.

12. Install the secondary brake shoe hold-down pin, spring and retainer cup.

13. Install the anti-rattle spring and the lower brake shoe retracting spring.

➡The self-adjuster is part of the rear brake operating lever.

14. Set the self-adjuster to the fully released position. Place a suitable tool against the adjuster cam and push it to the released position.

15. Install the brake drum and properly adjust the wheel bearing pre-load.

16. Install the wheel and tire assembly and lower the vehicle.

17. Push the brake pedal several times to set the self-adjuster.

18. Check the brake system for proper operation.

Fig. 57 Clean the dirt from the brake backing plate with a shop rag

Fig. 58 Lubricate the backing plate's shoe contact areas with a suitable high temperature grease

Fig. 59 If the brake operating lever is removed, clean the backing plate's shoe contact area with a rag . . .

Fig. 60 . . . then lubricate the contact area with a suitable high temperature grease

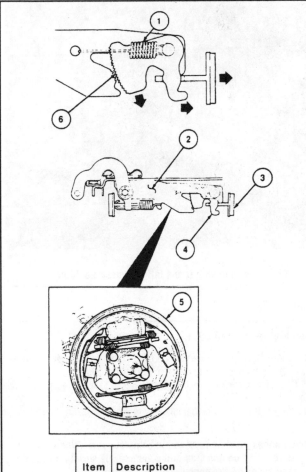

Item	Description
1	Spring
2	Rear Brake Operating Lever
3	Brake Shoe and Lining
4	Self Adjuster Cam
5	Brake Backing Plate
6	Self Adjuster Cam Teeth

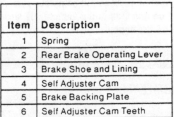

Fig. 61 Rear brake operating lever and self-adjuster assembly

Fig. 62 Place a suitable tool against the adjuster cam . . .

Fig. 63 . . . and push it to the fully released position

INSPECTION

▶ **See Figures 64 and 65**

1. Check the brake shoe linings for peeling, cracks or extremely uneven wear.
2. Use a Vernier caliper to measure the lining thickness.
3. If the lining thickness is less than 0.04 in. (1.0mm), replace the brake shoes.
4. If there is evidence of the lining being contaminated by brake fluid or oil, replace the shoes.

➡ **Brake shoes must be replaced in complete sets. When replacement is required on one side of the vehicle, be sure to also replace the brake shoes on the opposite side.**

Wheel Cylinders

REMOVAL & INSTALLATION

▶ **See Figures 66 thru 72**

1. Raise and safely support the vehicle.
2. Remove the wheel and tire assembly.

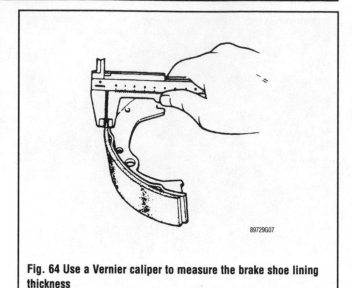

Fig. 64 Use a Vernier caliper to measure the brake shoe lining thickness

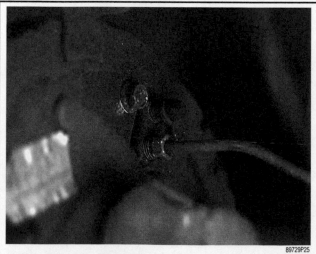

Fig. 65 A small ruler can also be used to measure the brake shoe lining thickness

Fig. 66 View of the wheel cylinder retainers, bleeder screw and brake line fitting

➡A left-hand threaded locknut is used on the vehicle's right rear wheel spindle. Turn this locknut clockwise to loosen.

3. Remove the brake drum.
4. Remove the brake shoes.
5. Clean the dirt from the back of the wheel cylinder and fittings using a clean shop towel.
6. Remove the bleeder screw to allow better access to the brake line's flare nut fitting.
7. Unscrew the brake line fitting with a flare nut wrench. Slide the nut away from the wheel cylinder.
8. Loosen the two wheel cylinder retaining bolts and remove the wheel cylinder from the backing plate.
9. Plug the brake line to prevent contamination.

To install:

10. Position the wheel cylinder onto the backing plate.
and hand start the brake line flare nut.
11. Install the 2 retaining bolts and tighten them to 7–9 ft. lbs. (10–13 Nm).
12. Connect the brake line and tighten the fitting to 10–15 ft. lbs. (13–21 Nm).
13. Install the rear brake shoes.

Fig. 69 Use a flare nut wrench to loosen the brake line fitting

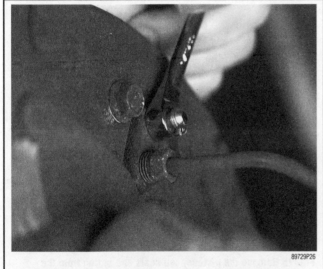

Fig. 67 Use a box end wrench to loosen the bleeder screw . . .

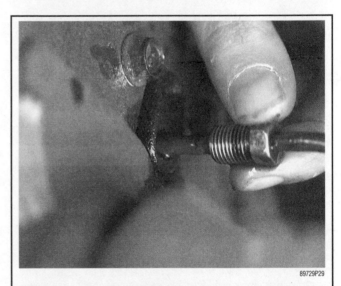

Fig. 70 Slide the flare nut fitting away from the wheel cylinder

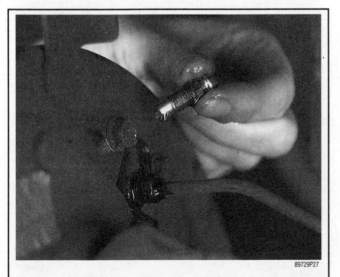

Fig. 68 . . . and remove it from the rear of the wheel cylinder

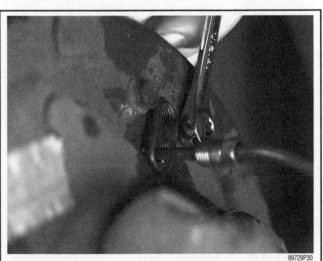

Fig. 71 Use a 10mm box end wrench to loosen the wheel cylinder retaining nuts

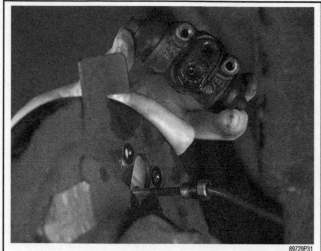

Fig. 72 Hold the brake line so that it will not kink and remove the wheel cylinder

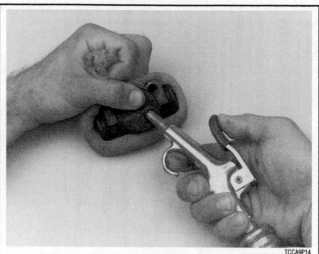

Fig. 74 Compressed air can be used to remove the pistons and seals

14. Install the brake drum and adjust the wheel bearing preload. Insert a new cotter pin.
15. Install the wheel and tire assembly.
16. Lower the vehicle.
17. Bleed the brake system and adjust the rear brakes as required.
18. Check the brake system for leaks and proper operation.

OVERHAUL

▶ **See Figures 73 thru 82**

Wheel cylinder overhaul kits may be available, but often at little or no savings over a reconditioned wheel cylinder. It often makes sense with these components to substitute a new or reconditioned part instead of attempting an overhaul.

If no replacement is available, or you would prefer to overhaul your wheel cylinders, the following procedure may be used. When rebuilding and installing wheel cylinders, avoid getting any contaminants into the system. Always use clean, new, high quality brake fluid. If dirty or improper fluid has been used, it will be necessary to drain the entire system, flush the system with proper brake fluid, replace all rubber components, then refill and bleed the system.

Fig. 75 Remove the pistons, cup seals and spring from the cylinder

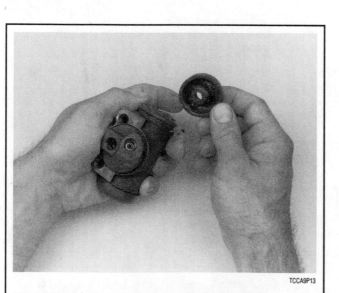

Fig. 73 Remove the outer boots from the wheel cylinder

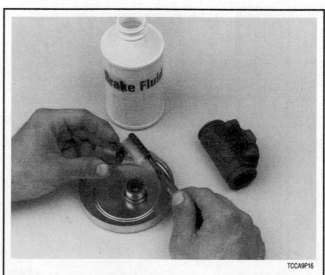

Fig. 76 Use brake fluid and a soft brush to clean the pistons . . .

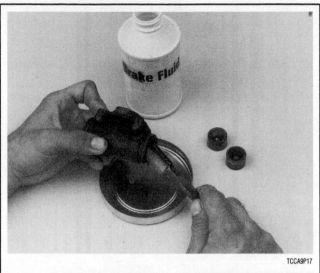

Fig. 77 . . . and the bore of the wheel cylinder

TCCA9P17

1. Remove the wheel cylinder from the vehicle and place on a clean workbench.

2. First remove and discard the old rubber boots, then withdraw the pistons. Piston cylinders are equipped with seals and a spring assembly, all located behind the pistons in the cylinder bore.

3. Remove the remaining inner components, seals and spring assembly. Compressed air may be useful in removing these components. If no compressed air is available, be VERY careful not to score the wheel cylinder bore when removing parts from it. Discard all components for which replacements were supplied in the rebuild kit.

4. Wash the cylinder and metal parts in denatured alcohol or clean brake fluid.

✳✳ WARNING

Never use a mineral-based solvent such as gasoline, kerosene or paint thinner for cleaning purposes. These solvents will swell rubber components and quickly deteriorate them.

5. Allow the parts to air dry or use compressed air. Do not use rags for cleaning, since lint will remain in the cylinder bore.

Fig. 78 Once cleaned and inspected, the wheel cylinder is ready for assembly

TCCA9P18

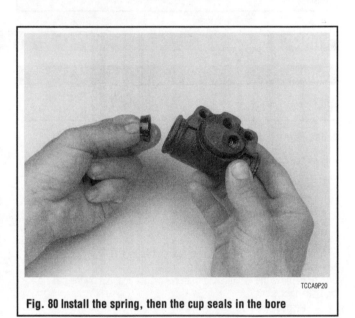

Fig. 80 Install the spring, then the cup seals in the bore

TCCA9P20

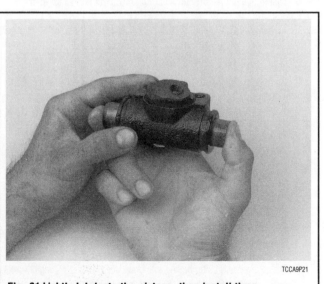

Fig. 79 Lubricate the cup seals with clean brake fluid

TCCA9P19

Fig. 81 Lightly lubricate the pistons, then install them

TCCA9P21

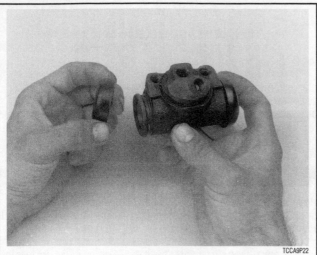

TCCA9P22

Fig. 82 The boots can now be installed over the wheel cylinder ends

6. Inspect the piston and replace it if it shows scratches.
7. Lubricate the cylinder bore and seals using clean brake fluid.
8. Position the spring assembly.
9. Install the inner seals, then the pistons.
10. Insert new boots into the counterbores by hand. Do not lubricate the boots.
11. Install the wheel cylinder.

PARKING BRAKE

Cable

REMOVAL & INSTALLATION

▶ **See Figures 83 and 84**

1. Disconnect the negative battery cable.
2. Remove the parking brake console as follows:
   a. Slide both front seats all the way forward.
   b. Remove the ashtray receptacle from the console by lifting the cover and pulling straight up.
   c. Remove the screw located below the ashtray receptacle.
   d. Apply the parking brake control.
   e. Remove the parking brake access cover.
   f. Remove the parking brake console.
3. Remove the locking clip from the adjustment nut on the parking brake control.
4. Remove the nut.
5. Disengage the parking brake switch electrical connector from the switch and bracket.
6. Loosen the two parking brake control retaining bolts and the parking brake control.
7. Remove the attaching screws and parking brake console mounting bracket.
8. Remove the bolts attaching the lower half of the rear seat hinge to the floor pan.
9. Fold the rear seat forward and remove the bolts attaching the upper half of the rear seat hinge to the floor pan.
10. Remove the rear seat.
11. Remove the rear carpet push retainers and carefully pull the carpeting forward to expose the parking brake cable cover.
12. Remove the two parking brake cable cover screws and remove the cable cover.
13. Raise and safely support the vehicle.
14. Remove the rear wheel and tire assemblies.
15. Remove the two cotter pins and clevis pins attaching the parking brake cable ends to the rear brake levers.
16. Unfasten the parking brake cable retaining clips.
17. Disengage the parking brake routing sleeves from the routing brackets.

18. Remove the nut and bolt attaching the parking brake routing bracket to the fuel tank.
19. Remove the parking brake cable equalizer attaching bolts.
20. Withdraw the lever end of the cable through the body opening and remove from the vehicle.

To install:

21. Position the lever end of the cable through the body opening.
22. Position the cable routing bracket on the fuel tank and install the attaching bolt and nut.
23. Make sure the cable seal is properly positioned in the floor pan.
24. Position the cable equalizer and install the attaching bolts. Make sure the equalizer spacers are in position before tightening the attaching bolts.
25. Route the cable ends through the body brackets and install the retaining clips.
26. Seat the cable sleeves in the routing brackets.
27. Attach the cable ends to the brake levers using the clevis pins and new cotter pins.
28. Install the rear wheel and tire assemblies.
29. Lower the vehicle.
30. Route the end of the cable through the parking brake lever.
31. Position the parking brake cable cover and secure with the attaching screws.
32. Position the carpet and install the luggage compartment floor cover hold-down pins.
33. Install the rear seat cushion and cover.
34. Position the console mounting bracket and install the retaining screws.
35. Position the parking brake control and install the two retaining bolts. Tighten the bolts to 14–19 ft. lbs. (19–26 Nm).
36. Engage the parking brake switch electrical connector to the switch and bracket.
37. With the end of the parking brake cable properly routed at the parking brake control, install the adjustment nut.
38. Adjust the parking brake cable.
39. Install the locking clip to the adjustment nut.
40. Install the console as follows:
   a. Install the parking brake access cover.
   b. Apply the parking brake control.
   c. Install the retaining screw below the ashtray receptacle.

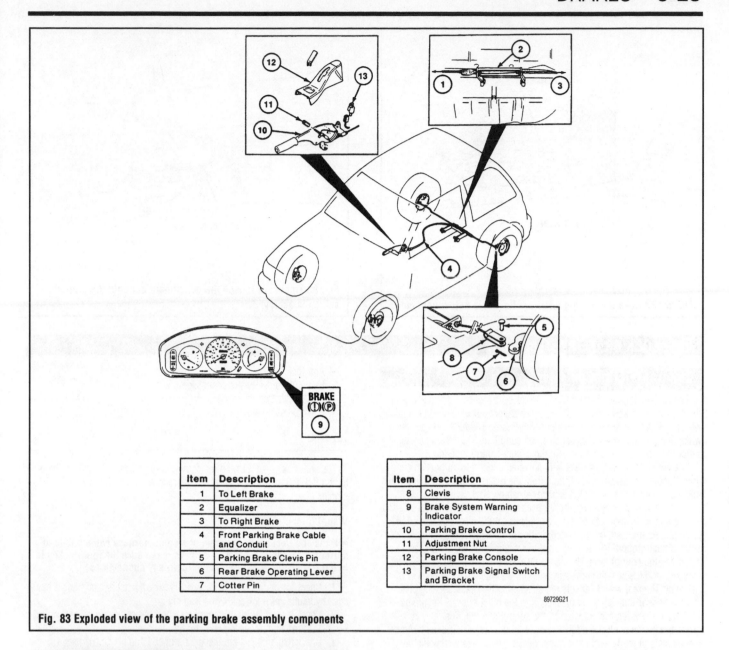

Item	Description
1	To Left Brake
2	Equalizer
3	To Right Brake
4	Front Parking Brake Cable and Conduit
5	Parking Brake Clevis Pin
6	Rear Brake Operating Lever
7	Cotter Pin

Item	Description
8	Clevis
9	Brake System Warning Indicator
10	Parking Brake Control
11	Adjustment Nut
12	Parking Brake Console
13	Parking Brake Signal Switch and Bracket

89729G21

Fig. 83 Exploded view of the parking brake assembly components

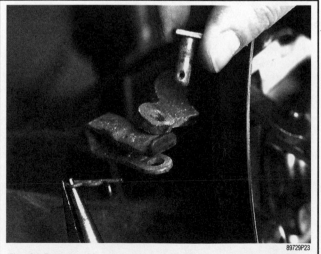

89729P23

Fig. 84 Remove the cotter pin and clevis pin, then disconnect the cable end from the brake operating lever

   d. Install the ashtray receptacle. Reposition both seats.

41. Connect the negative battery cable.

42. Road test the vehicle and verify proper operation of the parking brake system.

ADJUSTMENT

▶ **See Figures 85 and 86**

1. Make sure the parking brake is fully released.
2. Remove the parking brake console access cover.
3. Remove the locking clip from the cable adjustment nut.
4. Raise and safely support the vehicle.
5. Make sure the rear wheels turn freely.
6. Tighten the cable adjuster nut until there is a slight brake drag when the rear wheels are rotated.
7. Back off on the adjustment nut until the brake drag disappears.
8. Check the operation of the parking brake. The rear brakes should be fully applied when the brake lever is pulled upward 11–16 notches.
9. Install the locking clip onto the cable adjustment nut.
10. Install the parking brake console access cover.

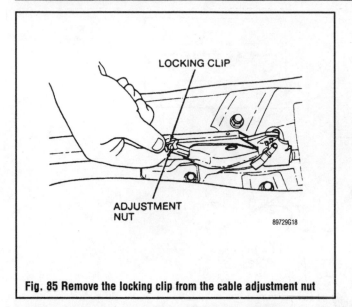

Fig. 85 Remove the locking clip from the cable adjustment nut

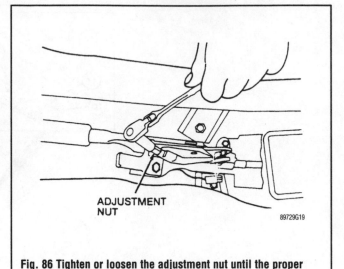

Fig. 86 Tighten or loosen the adjustment nut until the proper setting is achieved

ANTI-LOCK BRAKE SYSTEM (ABS)

General Information

The Anti-lock Brake System (ABS) functions by releasing and applying fluid pressure to either the front disc brake calipers or the rear drum brake wheel cylinders during certain braking conditions. The ABS only actuates when one or more wheels approach a slip condition. The ABS automatically senses the slip and activates the fluid pressure control function.

The anti-lock actuator assembly is not used under normal braking conditions. Under normal conditions, fluid from the master cylinder enters the two inlet ports located on top of the actuator assembly. The fluid then flows through the normally open solenoid valves to each respective wheel location.

The anti-lock wheel speed sensors operate on the magnetic induction principle. As the teeth on the sensor indicator rotate past the stationary sensor, a signal proportional to the speed of rotation is generated and sent via a cable to the control module. The front sensors are attached to the wheel knuckles and the sensor indicators are pressed onto the outer ends of the halfshaft. The rear wheel sensors are attached to the brake backing plate and the sensor indicators are pressed onto the inner hubs of the drums.

The anti-lock relay is actuated by the control module. The relay is grounded by the control module to power up the system. The control module consists of the fail-safe and motor relays. The fail-safe relay inhibits solenoid operation and turns the anti-lock brake warning indicator on and off. The motor relay controls pump and motor operation.

The ABS system is operated and monitored by a control module. The module receives readings from the two rear and two front wheel speed sensors and uses this information to compare wheel speeds. Once the control module senses wheel lock-up under a severe braking condition, it signals the anti-lock actuator assembly, which closes the flow control valve of the affected circuit. This regulates the fluid entering the circuit, thus preventing wheel lock-up. When the control module senses that the wheel is decelerating, it sends a signal to open the flow control valve, thus reducing any pressure between the control valve and the affected brake actuator. The fluid is then returned to the master cylinder.

Anti-lock Brake System (ABS) Components

♦ See Figure 87

The ABS system is comprised of the following components:
- Power brake booster
- Front and rear wheel speed sensors and indicators
- Anti-lock brake control module
- Data Link Connector (DLC)
- Anti-lock relay
- Hydraulic anti-lock actuator assembly
- Master cylinder
- Brake pressure control valve

TESTING

The anti-lock brake warning indicator is illuminated when the engine is turned **ON**. If the light fails to go out, there may be a problem with the ABS system.

Visual Check

➡It may be necessary to disengage some harness connections to perform a through inspection. Always make sure the ignition key is in the OFF position before disengaging any connections.

1. Check for a low brake fluid level, damaged sensors, leaks and a damaged hydraulic anti-lock actuator assembly.
2. Check the ABS wiring harness for improper connections, bent or broken pins, corrosion, loose wires and improper routing.
3. Check that all fuses are installed properly and are not damaged.
4. Check the control module for physical damage.

Scan Tool Test

1. Apply the parking brake and place the transaxle in **PARK** (automatic transaxle) or **NEUTRAL** (manual transaxle).
2. Block both drive wheels.
3. Turn off all electrical loads such as the radio, lamps, heater blower, A/C system, etc.
4. With the key **OFF**, connect the scan tool to the Data Link Connector (DLC), located in the engine compartment.
5. Follow the tool manufacturer's instructions on the hook-up and use of the tool.

Analog Volt/Ohmmeter Test

♦ See Figure 88

1. Turn the key **OFF**.
2. Connect a jumper wire at the Data Link Connector (DLC) between terminals GND and TBS.
3. Connect an analog volt/ohmmeter between the Failure Brake System (FBS) terminal and a good engine ground.

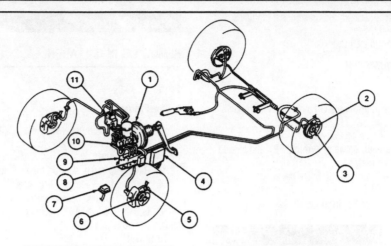

Item	Description	Item	Description
1	Power Brake Booster	6	Front Brake Anti-Lock Sensor Indicator
2	Rear Brake Anti-Lock Sensor	7	Data Link Connector (DLC)
3	Rear Brake Anti-Lock Sensor Indicator (Pressed Onto Brake Drum)	8	Anti-Lock Relay
4	Anti-Lock Brake Control Module	9	Hydraulic Anti-Lock Actuator Assembly
5	Front Brake Anti-Lock Sensor	10	Brake Master Cylinder
		11	Brake Pressure Control Valve

89729G08

Fig. 87 Location of the ABS system components

89729G09

Fig. 88 Install a jumper wire at the DLC between terminals GND and TBS, then connect an analog meter between terminal FBS and a good engine ground

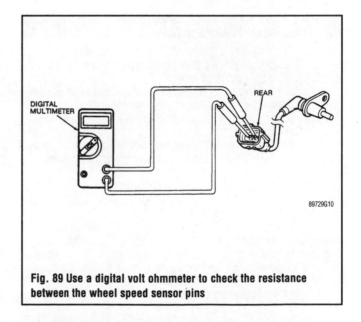

89729G10

Fig. 89 Use a digital volt ohmmeter to check the resistance between the wheel speed sensor pins

4. Set the meter to read from 0 to 20 volts DC.

The trouble code will represent itself on the analog volt/ohmmeter as a needle sweep or pulse. If, for example, a code 51 is present, the needle will sweep or pulse across the meter five times, pause for a very short time, then sweep or pulse once. After all the codes have been retrieved, the meter will begin to repeat the codes.

Digital Volt/Ohmmeter Test (For Wheel Speed Sensors)

♦ **See Figure 89**

1. Disengage the sensor electrical connection.

2. Use a Digital Volt Ohmmeter (DVOM) to measure the resistance between the following pins on the connector for each sensor:

- Left front sensor: white and red wires
- Right front sensor: yellow and orange wires
- Left rear sensor: yellow with green stripe and yellow with blue stripe wires
- Right rear sensor: green and blue wires
3. If the resistance is not 1600–2000 ohms, replace the sensor.

Clearing Codes

USING A SCAN TOOL

1. With the key **ON** and the scan tool connected to the Data Link Connector (DLC), follow the tool manufacturer's instructions and begin to retrieve the trouble codes.

2. After the first code is repeated, depress the brake pedal ten times (once per second) and turn the key **OFF**.

3. Disconnect the scan tool from the DLC.

USING AN ANALOG VOLT/OHMMETER

▶ **See Figure 88**

1. Connect a jumper wire between terminals GND and TBS of the Data Link Connector (DLC).

2. Turn the key to the **ON** position.

3. Connect an analog volt/ohmmeter between terminal FBS and a good engine ground to retrieve the trouble codes.

4. After the first code is repeated, depress the brake pedal ten times (once per second) and turn the key **OFF**.

5. Disconnect the jumper wire and meter from the DLC.

ABS Trouble Codes

The following is a list of the ABS system trouble codes:
- Code 11: Right-hand front anti-lock sensor (wheel speed sensor) or sensor indicator
- Code 12. Left-hand front anti-lock sensor (wheel speed sensor) or sensor indicator
- Code 13: Right-hand rear anti-lock sensor (wheel speed sensor) or sensor indicator
- Code 14: Left-hand rear anti-lock sensor (wheel speed sensor) or sensor indicator
- Code 15: Front and rear anti-lock sensor (wheel speed sensor)
- Code 22: Solenoid valve or actuator assembly
- Code 51: Fail-safe relay
- Code 53: Motor relay or motor
- Code 61: Control module

ABS System Service Precautions

1. Certain components within the ABS system are not intended to be serviced or repaired individually. Only those components with removal and installation procedures should be serviced.

2. Do not use rubber hoses or other parts not specified for an ABS system. When using repair kits, replace all parts included in the kit. Partial or incorrect repair may lead to functional problems and require the replacement of other components.

3. Lubricate rubber parts with clean, fresh brake fluid to ease assembly. Do not use lubricated shop air to clean parts; damage to rubber components may result.

4. Use only DOT 3 brake fluid from an unopened container.

5. If any hydraulic component or line is removed or replaced, it may be necessary to bleed the entire system.

6. A clean repair area is essential. Always clean the reservoir and cap thoroughly before removing the cap. The slightest amount of dirt in the fluid may plug an orifice and impair the system's function. Perform repairs only after components have been thoroughly cleaned: use only denatured alcohol to clean components. Do not allow ABS components to come in contact with any substance containing mineral oil; this includes used shop rags.

7. The Anti-Lock Control Unit (ALCU) is a microprocessor similar to other computer units in the vehicle. Ensure that the ignition switch is **OFF** before removing or installing controller harnesses. Avoid static electricity discharge at or near the controller.

8. If any arc welding is to be done on the vehicle, the ALCU connectors should be disconnected before welding operations begin.

Speed Sensors

REMOVAL & INSTALLATION

Front

▶ **See Figure 90**

1. Disconnect the negative battery cable.

2. Disengage the front anti-lock sensor electrical connector and remove the grommet.

3. Raise and safely support the vehicle.

4. Remove the wheel and tire assembly.

5. Remove the two sensor wiring harness support bolts.

6. Loosen the two bolts retaining the wheel sensor and remove the sensor from the knuckle.

To install:

7. Position the wheel sensor in the knuckle and install the two retaining bolts. Tighten the bolts to 12–16 ft. lbs. (16–23 Nm).

8. Install the two sensor wiring harness support bolts.

9. Install the wheel and tire assembly.

10. Push the rubber grommet into place and engage the electrical connector.

11. Connect the negative battery cable.

12. Check out the ABS system by turning the ignition key to the **KEY ON, ENGINE OFF (KOEO)** position while watching the ABS warning indicator. When the ABS system is operating properly, the indicator will illuminate while in the **KOEO** position, and will go out after the engine has started with a delay of up to 60 seconds.

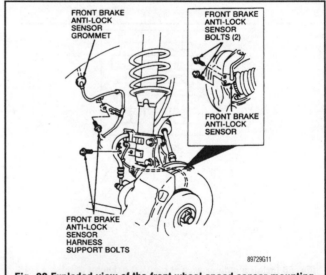

FRONT BRAKE ANTI-LOCK SENSOR GROMMET

FRONT BRAKE ANTI-LOCK SENSOR BOLTS (2)

FRONT BRAKE ANTI-LOCK SENSOR

FRONT BRAKE ANTI-LOCK SENSOR HARNESS SUPPORT BOLTS

89729G11

Fig. 90 Exploded view of the front wheel speed sensor mounting

Rear

▶ **See Figure 91**

1. Disconnect the negative battery cable.

2. Remove the quarter trim panel as follows:
   a. Remove the luggage compartment cover.

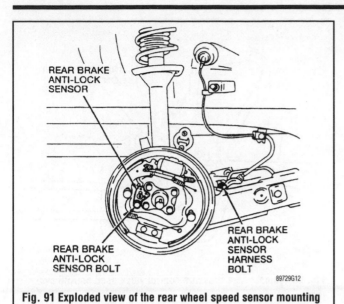

REAR BRAKE
ANTI-LOCK
SENSOR

REAR BRAKE
ANTI-LOCK
SENSOR BOLT

REAR BRAKE
ANTI-LOCK
SENSOR
HARNESS
BOLT

89729G12

Fig. 91 Exploded view of the rear wheel speed sensor mounting

b. Remove the rear seat.

c. Remove the screws and push pins from the package tray. Detach the radio speaker electrical connector.

d. Remove the rear safety belt anchor bolt.

e. Remove the push pins and the luggage compartment side cover.

f. Remove the rear door scuff cover.

g. Pull the seaming welt away from the quarter trim panel and remove the panel.

3. Disengage the rear brake sensor electrical connector.

4. Pry out the rubber grommet.

5. Raise and safely support the vehicle.

6. Remove the wheel and tire assembly.

7. Remove the hub grease cap, cotter pin and wheel bearing nut cover.

8. Remove the wheel bearing nut and washer. Remove the brake drum and bearings as an assembly.

9. Remove the four sensor harness bolts.

10. From the backing plate, remove the sensor retaining bolt and remove the speed sensor from the backing plate.

To install:

11. Position the speed sensor wiring through the backing plate and through the wheel well grommet hole.

12. Install the sensor and retaining bolt and tighten the bolt to 12–16 ft. lbs. (16–23 Nm).

13. Install the four sensor harness bolts.

14. Install the brake drum and bearings, wheel bearing washer and nut. Adjust the wheel bearing preload to specifications.

15. Install the nut cover with a new cotter pin, then attach the hub grease cap.

16. Install the wheel and tire assembly and lower the vehicle.

17. Push the grommet in place and engage the sensor electrical connector.

18. Install the quarter trim panel as follows:

a. Position the quarter trim panel and seaming welt.

b. Install the rear door scuff plate.

c. Install the luggage compartment side cover using the push pins.

d. Install the rear safety belt and anchor pin. Tighten the anchor bolt to 28–58 ft. lbs. (38–78 Nm).

e. Fasten the speaker electrical connector.

f. Install the push pins in the package tray.

g. Install the rear seat.

h. Install the luggage compartment cover.

19. Connect the negative battery cable.

20. Check out the ABS system by turning the ignition key to the **KEY ON, ENGINE OFF (KOEO)** position while watching the ABS warning indicator. When the ABS system is operating properly, the indicator will illuminate while in the **KOEO** position, and will go out after the engine has started with a delay of up to 60 seconds.

Anti-lock Actuator Assembly

REMOVAL & INSTALLATION

♦ See Figure 92

1. Disconnect the battery cables (negative cable first).

2. Remove the battery from the engine compartment.

3. Disengage the two actuator assembly electrical connections from the bracket.

4. Disengage the actuator assembly electrical connector.

➡**Make a note of the brake line routing, as this will help during installation.**

❋❋ WARNING

Clean, high quality brake fluid is essential to the safe and proper operation of the brake system. You should always buy the highest quality brake fluid that is available. If the brake fluid becomes contaminated, drain and flush the system, then refill the master cylinder with new fluid. Never reuse any brake fluid. Any brake fluid that is removed from the system should be discarded. Also, do not allow any brake fluid to come in contact with a painted surface; it will damage the paint.

5. Use a line wrench to loosen the brake line flare nuts and disconnect the lines from the actuator.

6. Loosen the actuator retaining nuts and remove the actuator.

To install:

7. Install the actuator and tighten its retaining nuts to 14–16 ft. lbs. (19–22 Nm).

8. Connect the brake lines to the actuator and use a flare nut wrench to tighten the fittings to 10–15 ft. lbs. (13–21 Nm).

9. Engage the actuator assembly and bracket electrical connections.

10. Install the battery and connect the battery cables (positive cable first).

11. Bleed the brake system.

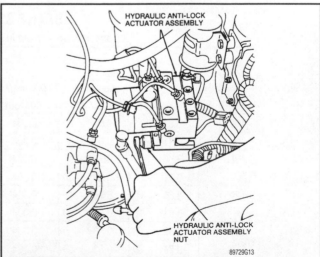

HYDRAULIC ANTI-LOCK
ACTUATOR ASSEMBLY

HYDRAULIC ANTI-LOCK
ACTUATOR ASSEMBLY
NUT

89729G13

Fig. 92 Detach the electrical connections and brake lines before loosening the actuator mounting bolts

Brake Pressure Control Valve

REMOVAL & INSTALLATION

▶ See Figure 93

1. Use a flare nut wrench to loosen the brake line fittings and disconnect the lines from the control valve.
2. Loosen the bolts and remove the valve.

To install:

3. Install the valve and tighten the bolts.
4. Connect the brake lines to the valve and use a flare nut wrench to tighten the fittings.

Control Module

REMOVAL & INSTALLATION

▶ See Figure 94

The control module is located behind the left-hand side of the instrument panel.

1. Disconnect the negative battery cable.
2. Disengage the control module electrical connection.
3. Loosen the two module retaining nuts and remove the module.

To install:

4. Install the module and tighten the nuts to 14–18 ft. lbs. (19–25 Nm).
5. Engage the module's electrical connection.
6. Connect the negative battery cable.

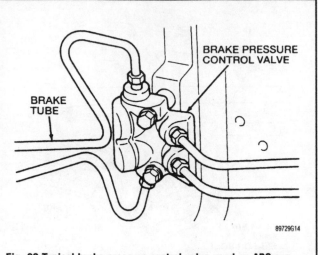

Fig. 93 Typical brake pressure control valve used on ABS systems

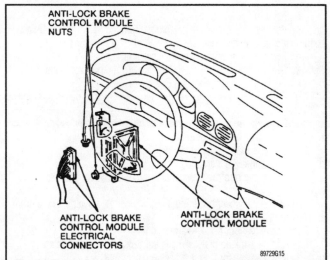

Fig. 94 The ABS control module is mounted behind the left-hand side of the instrument panel

BRAKE SPECIFICATIONS
All specifications given in inches unless otherwise indicated

Year	Brake Disc				Maximum Run-out	Brake Drum Diameter		Minimum Lining Thickness	
	Original Thickness		Maximum Refinish			Original Inside Diameter	Max. Wear Limit	Front	Rear
1994	0.86	①	0.78	①	0.004	7.87	7.93	0.08	0.040
	0.71	②	0.63	②	0.004	7.87	7.93	0.08	0.040
1995	0.86	①	0.78	①	0.004	7.87	7.93	0.08	0.040
	0.71	②	0.63	②	0.004	7.87	7.93	0.08	0.040
1996	0.86	①	0.78	①	0.004	7.87	7.93	0.08	0.040
	0.71	②	0.63	②	0.004	7.87	7.93	0.08	0.040
1997	0.86	①	0.78	①	0.004	7.87	7.93	0.08	0.040
	0.71	②	0.63	②	0.004	7.87	7.93	0.08	0.040

① Automatic Transaxle

② Manual Transaxle

89729C01

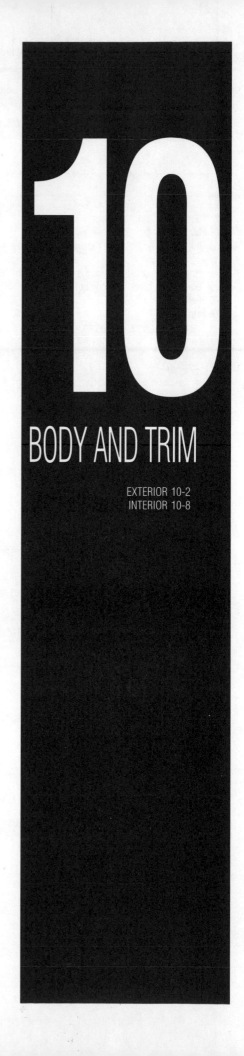

10
BODY AND TRIM

EXTERIOR

Doors

REMOVAL & INSTALLATION

Front

1. Remove the door trim panel and hinge pin.
2. Matchmark the hinge-to-body location.
3. If necessary, disengage the speaker wires and any electrical connections.
4. Have an assistant support the door.
5. Loosen the hinge-to-body bolts and nuts.
6. Remove the door.

To install:

7. Install the door and align the hinges with the marks made prior to removal.
8. Install the hinge-to-body bolts and nuts. Tighten them to 13–21 ft. lbs. (17–29 Nm).
9. Install the hinge pin and trim panel.
10. If necessary, adjust the door alignment.

Rear

1. Remove the hinge pin.
2. Matchmark the hinge-to-body location.
3. If necessary, disengage the speaker wires and any electrical connections.
4. Have an assistant support the door.
5. Loosen the hinge-to-body bolts and nuts.
6. Remove the door.

To install:

7. Install the door and align the hinges with the marks made prior to removal.
8. Install the hinge-to-body bolts and nuts. Tighten them to 13–21 ft. lbs. (17–29 Nm).
9. Install the hinge pin.
10. If necessary, adjust the door alignment.

ADJUSTMENT

1. Check the door-to-body clearance.
2. If the clearance is uneven, loosen the hinge-to-body bolts and nuts, and adjust the door.
3. When the door is properly aligned, tighten the nuts and bolts to specification.
4. If there is excessive door play or door-to-body clearance when the door is closed, adjust the striker.
5. Loosen the striker retainers and move the striker to the desired position.
6. Tighten the striker retainers to 13–19 ft. lbs. (18–26 Nm).

Hood

REMOVAL & INSTALLATION

▶ **See Figures 1, 2 and 3**

1. Open the vehicle's hood and secure it in an upright position.
2. Disconnect any hoses or wires from the hood.
3. Matchmark the hinge-to-hood location.
4. Have an assistant support the hood, then loosen the hinge-to-hood bolts.
5. Remove the hood from the car.

Fig. 1 Disconnect any hoses or wires such as the windshield washer hose

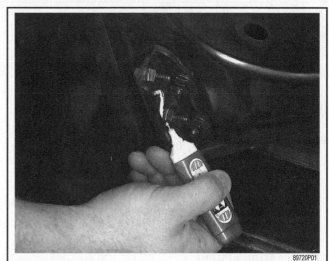

Fig. 2 Matchmark the hinge-to-hood location before removal; this will aid during installation

To install:

6. Install the hood and align the hinge-to-hood marks made prior to removal.
7. Install the retaining bolts and tighten them to 14–19 ft. lbs. (19–25 Nm).
8. Engage the wires and hoses, if removed.
9. Close the hood to make sure it latches properly, and adjust the alignment if necessary.

ADJUSTMENT

▶ **See Figure 4**

1. Check that the hood can be closed easily and that there is no looseness in the hinges. Replace the hinges if they cannot be tightened.
2. Measure the hood clearance; it should not exceed 0.12–0.20 inch (3–5mm) at the points shown in the accompanying illustration.
3. If the clearance is incorrect, loosen the hinge-to-hood bolts and adjust the hood until the clearance is as specified.
4. Tighten the hinge-to-hood bolts to 14–19 ft. lbs. (19–25 Nm).

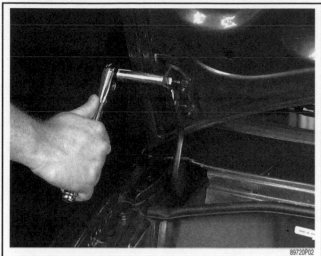

Fig. 3 Loosen the hinge retaining bolts and, with the aid of an assistant, remove the hood

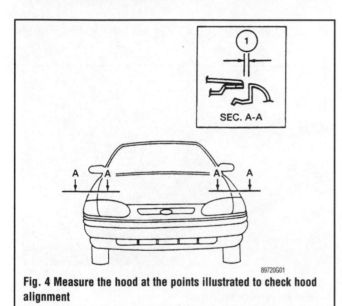

SEC. A-A

Fig. 4 Measure the hood at the points illustrated to check hood alignment

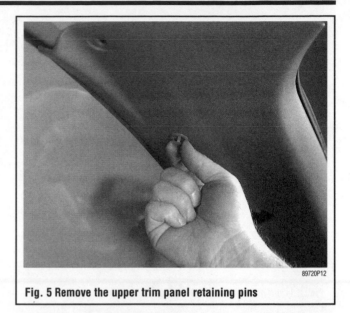

Fig. 5 Remove the upper trim panel retaining pins

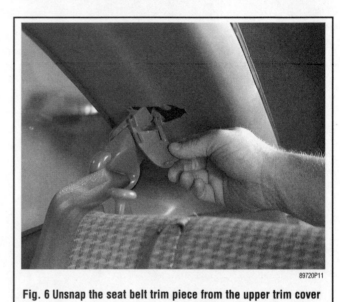

Fig. 6 Unsnap the seat belt trim piece from the upper trim cover

Liftgate

REMOVAL & INSTALLATION

♦ **See Figures 5 thru 13**

1. Disconnect the negative battery cable.
2. Open the liftgate and support it with a suitable prop, such as a broom handle. It is a good idea to have an assistant support the liftgate as well.
3. Remove the right-hand luggage compartment side cover.
4. Remove the quarter trim panel and upper trim panel.
5. Disengage the electrical connector and pull the wiring harness through the C-pillar.
6. Remove the access plug and grommet, and detach the washer hose.
7. Loosen the hydraulic lift bolts.
8. Unfasten the lift ball joint and remove the lift.
9. Have an assistant support the door.
10. Mark the hinge-to-liftgate location.
11. Loosen the hinge-to-liftgate nuts and, with the aid of an assistant, remove the liftgate.

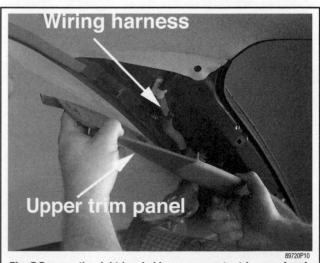

Wiring harness

Upper trim panel

Fig. 7 Remove the right-hand side cover, quarter trim panel and upper trim panel to gain access to the liftgate wiring harness

Fig. 8 Loosen the hydraulic lift hinge retaining bolts . . .

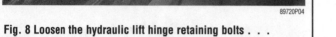

Fig. 9 . . . and separate the hinge from the body

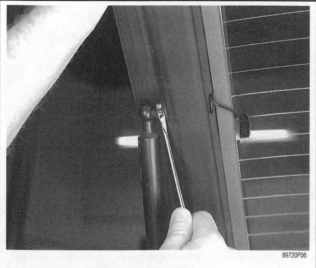

Fig. 10 Unfasten the hydraulic lift ball joint . . .

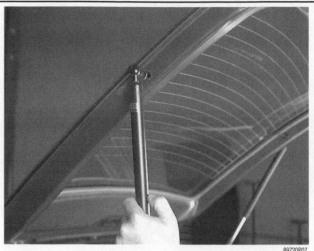

Fig. 11 . . . then remove the hydraulic lift assembly from the liftgate

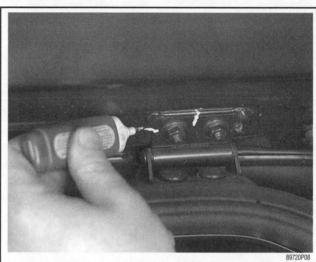

Fig. 12 Matchmark the hinge-to-liftgate location. This will aid in alignment during installation

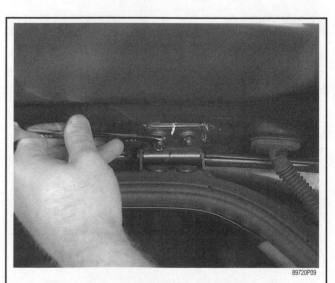

Fig. 13 Loosen the hinge-to-liftgate retaining bolts

To install:

12. Install the liftgate and align the hinges with the marks made prior to removal.

13. Install the hinge-to-liftgate nuts and tighten them to 7–9 ft. lbs. (9–12 Nm).

14. Install the hydraulic lift and engage the ball joint. Tighten the lift bolts to 14–18 ft. lbs. (19–25 Nm).

15. Connect the washer hose and install the access plug and grommet.

16. Route the wiring harness through the C-pillar and engage the electrical connector.

17. Install the trim panels and side cover.

18. Connect the negative battery cable.

19. Adjust the liftgate alignment as necessary.

ADJUSTMENT

1. Make sure the liftgate can be closed easily and that there is no looseness in the hinges. If the hinges cannot be tightened, they must be replaced.

2. If there is excessive play when the liftgate is closed, adjust the latch striker.

3. Loosen the latch striker bolts and adjust the striker as necessary.

4. Tighten the latch striker bolts to 71–97 inch lbs. (8–11 Nm).

5. If the liftgate-to-body clearance is excessive or uneven, loosen the hinge-to-liftgate nuts and adjust the liftgate as necessary. Tighten the nuts to 7–9 ft. lbs. (9–12 Nm).

Grille

REMOVAL & INSTALLATION

Except SE Models

1994–96 MODELS

1. Loosen the grille retaining screws.
2. Remove the grille retaining clips.
3. Remove the grille.
4. Installation is the reverse of removal.

1997 MODELS

▶ **See Figures 14, 15 and 16**

1. Open the vehicle's hood and secure it in an upright position.
2. Loosen the right-hand front turn signal lamp retaining screw.

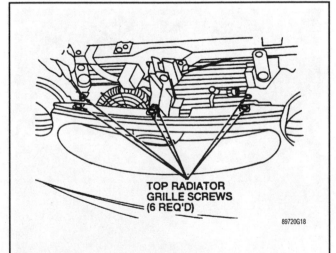

Fig. 14 Remove the six retaining screws from the top of the grille

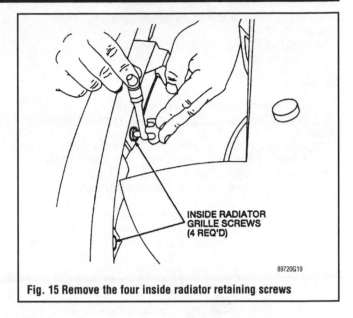

Fig. 15 Remove the four inside radiator retaining screws

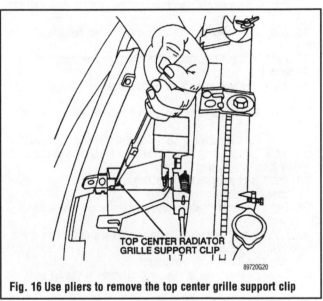

Fig. 16 Use pliers to remove the top center grille support clip

3. Pull the lamp away from the body and remove the bulb socket by turning it counterclockwise.

4. After the lamp and socket have been separated, set the lamp assembly aside.

5. Loosen the six retaining screws from the top of the grille.

6. Tag and disengage the headlamp bulb and parking lamp bulb electrical connections.

7. Loosen the headlamp housing mounting screws and remove the headlamp assembly.

8. Loosen the four screws at the back of the grille.

9. Use pliers to remove the top center grille support clip.

10. Slide the grille to the right and remove it from the vehicle.

To install:

11. Install the grille by sliding it from right-to-left into position.

12. Install the center grille support clip.

13. Install and tighten the four screws at the back of the grille.

14. Install the headlamp assembly and tighten the retaining screws.

15. Engage the headlamp bulb and parking lamp bulb electrical connections.

16. Install and tighten the six retaining screws at the top of the grille.

17. Engage the socket assembly to the turn signal lamp by turning it clockwise.

18. Install the lamp and tighten the retaining screw.

19. Close the hood.

SE Models

1. Disconnect the negative battery cable.

2. Remove the headlamps and loosen the two upper bumper-to-body screws.

3. Raise the front of the car and support it with safety stands.

4. Remove the front wheels and move the front fender splash shields until access to the lower front bumper-to-body screws is possible.

5. Loosen the bumper-to-body screws and the front valance panel screws.

6. Disengage the side marker lamp electrical connections.

7. If equipped, disengage the fog lamp electrical connections.

8. Loosen the lower front bumper-to-body nuts. Remove the bumper and cover.

9. Place the bumper on a clean, covered work surface.

10. Loosen the license plate mounting bracket bolts and remove the bracket.

11. Loosen the side marker lamp screws and remove the lamps.

12. Remove the bumper cover plastic fasteners and the cover retaining screws.

13. Separate the cover from the bumper and loosen the grille retaining screws.

14. Remove the grille, guiding it off the bumper cover tabs.

To install:

15. Engage the grille to the bumper and tighten the retaining screws.

16. Install the bumper cover and fasten the screws and plastic retainers.

17. Install the side marker lamps and tighten the retaining screws.

18. Install the bumper on the car and tighten the bumper-to-body nuts to 24–34 ft. lbs. (31–46 Nm).

19. Install and tighten the license plate mounting bracket.

20. Engage the electrical connections.

21. Tighten the lower front bumper-to-body nuts to 24–34 ft. lbs. (31–46 Nm).

22. Install and tighten the valance panel screws, then place the splash shields in their original positions.

23. Install the wheels and lower the car.

24. Install the headlamps and tighten the bumper-to-body retainers to 24–34 ft. lbs. (31–46 Nm).

25. Connect the negative battery cable.

Outside Mirrors

REMOVAL & INSTALLATION

▶ **See Figures 17 thru 22**

1. Remove the rubber boot from the rear view mirror remote control knob.

2. Loosen the control knob retaining screw and remove the knob.

3. Use a prytool to gently pry the mirror inside mounting hole cover loose and remove the cover.

4. Hold the mirror and unfasten the mirror retaining screws. Remove the mirror from the door.

To install:

5. Install the mirror and tighten the retaining screws.

6. Install the control knob and tighten the retaining screw.

7. Install the cover making sure it fits snugly into position.

8. Install the rubber boot on the remote control knob.

Fig. 17 Remove the rubber boot from the rear view mirror remote control knob

Fig. 18 Loosen the control knob retaining screw . . .

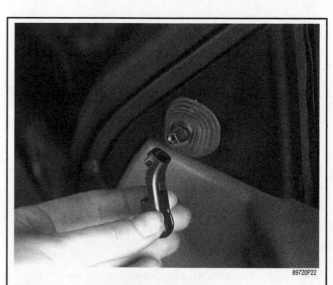

Fig. 19 . . . and remove the control knob

Fig. 20 Remove the mirror's inside mounting hole cover with a prytool

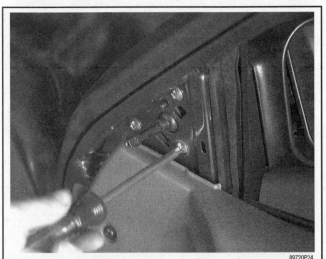

Fig. 21 While holding the mirror, loosen the mirror retaining screws . . .

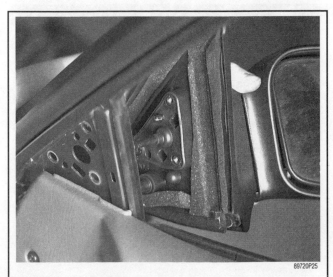

Fig. 22 . . . and remove the mirror from the door

Antenna

REMOVAL & INSTALLATION

♦ **See Figures 23 and 24**

1. Remove the instrument cluster and unhook the antenna from the wiring harness retainer, located at the rear of the cluster.
2. Remove the radio and disconnect the antenna lead from the heater and wiring harness retainer.
3. Loosen the antenna base-to-body retaining screws.
4. Pull the antenna, base, insulating tube and antenna lead up until access to the lead is possible.
5. Cut the old lead near the base.
6. Tape the new lead to the old lead, as this will help pull the new lead through the car.

To install:

7. While pulling on the old lead, insert the lead and insulating tube down through the body pillar.
8. Once the base is in position, tighten its retaining screws. Make sure the drain tube end fits into the drain hole.

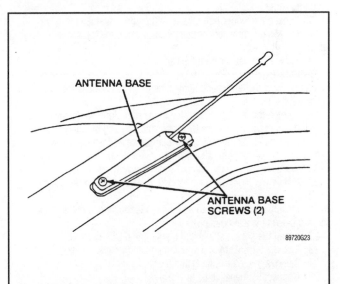

Fig. 23 Remove the antenna base-to-body retaining screws

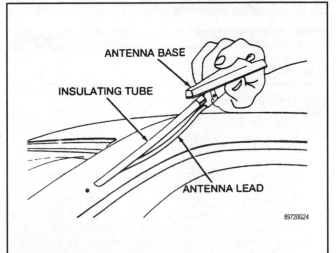

Fig. 24 Pull the antenna, base, insulating tube and antenna lead up until access to the lead is possible

9. Connect the lead to the wiring harness retainer on the heater, and route it behind the instrument cluster.

10. Remove the old lead, then install the radio and instrument cluster.

Fender

REMOVAL & INSTALLATION

♦ **See Figures 25 and 26**

1. Disconnect the negative battery cable.
2. Raise the front of the car and support it with safety stands.
3. Remove the front wheels.
4. Loosen the front stone guard screws and remove the guard.
5. Loosen the splash shield screws and remove the shield.
6. Loosen the three front fender bolts, one nut and one screw from inside the wheel housing.
7. Loosen the fender bolt located at the bottom of the fender.
8. Lower the car and remove the front turn signal lamp.
9. If equipped, remove the upper bumper cover-to-body screws.
10. If equipped, remove the two headlamp opening molding screws from the fender.
11. Loosen the fender bolt located in the turn signal lamp cavity.
12. Loosen the three fender bolts located along the top of the fender.
13. Remove the fender from the car.

To install:

14. Position the fender and tighten the three fender bolts located along the top of the fender.
15. Tighten the fender bolt located in the turn signal lamp cavity.
16. If equipped, tighten the two headlamp opening molding screws.
17. If equipped, tighten the upper bumper cover-to-body screws.
18. Install the front turn signal lamp.
19. Raise the front of the car and support it with safety stands.
20. Install and tighten the fender bolt located at the bottom of the fender.
21. Install and tighten the three front fender bolts, one nut and one screw inside the wheel housing.
22. Install the splash shield and tighten the retaining screws.
23. Install the front stone guard and tighten the retaining screws.
24. Remove the safety stands and lower the car.
25. Connect the negative battery cable.

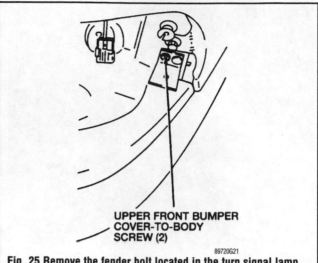

UPPER FRONT BUMPER COVER-TO-BODY SCREW (2)

89720G21

Fig. 25 Remove the fender bolt located in the turn signal lamp cavity

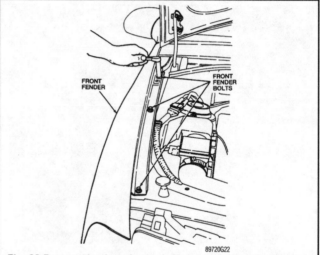

FRONT FENDER

FRONT FENDER BOLTS

89720G22

Fig. 26 Remove the three fender bolts located along the top of the fender

INTERIOR

Instrument Panel and Pad

REMOVAL & INSTALLATION

♦ **See Figures 27 thru 36**

1. Disable the air bag system.
2. Remove the driver's side air bag module as follows:
   a. Loosen the air bag module retainers from the back side of the steering wheel.
   b. Disengage the air bag/horn electrical connection and remove the air bag from the steering wheel.
3. Remove the steering wheel.
4. Remove the steering column as follows:
   a. Remove the multi-function switch and the ignition switch.
   b. Loosen the lower column shaft lower bolt.
   c. Loosen the lower column bracket nuts.
   d. Loosen the two upper column bracket bolts.
   e. To ensure correct alignment, matchmark the juncture of the column intermediate shaft coupling and the lower column shaft.
   f. Remove the steering column.
5. Remove the instrument cluster.
6. Remove the fuse panel cover, loosen the fuse panel screws and push the panel forward, but do not remove it.
7. Remove the parking brake console and the shift console.
8. Remove the air bag diagnostic monitor as follows:
   a. If not already done, remove the shift console panel.
   b. Disengage the two air bag diagnostic monitor electrical connections.
   c. Loosen the monitor retaining nuts and slide the monitor from its mounting bracket.
9. Remove the climate control panel assembly.
10. Open the glove compartment door, loosen the compartment retaining screws and remove the glove compartment.
11. Remove the passenger side air bag as follows:
   a. Loosen the air bag module bolts.

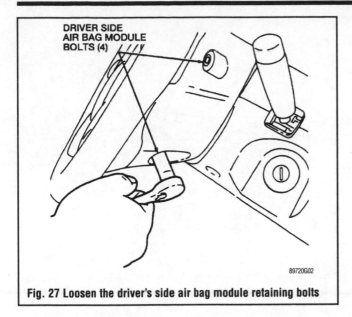

Fig. 27 Loosen the driver's side air bag module retaining bolts

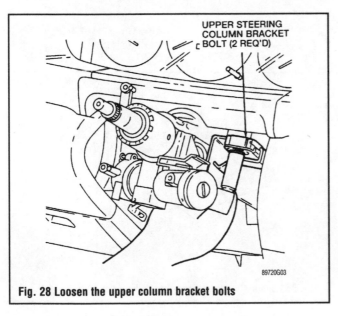

Fig. 28 Loosen the upper column bracket bolts

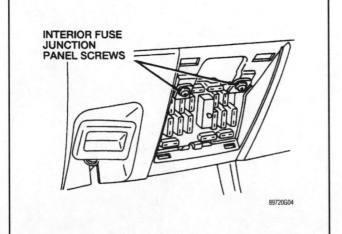

Fig. 29 Loosen the fuse panel screws and push the panel forward, but do not remove it

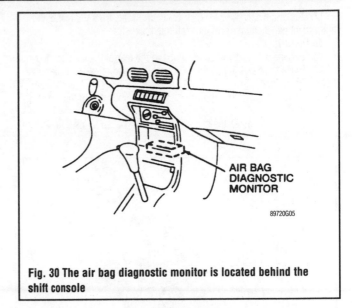

Fig. 30 The air bag diagnostic monitor is located behind the shift console

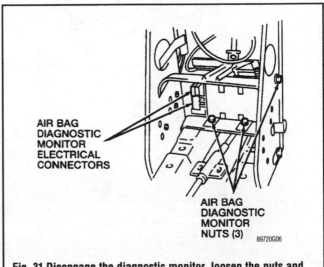

Fig. 31 Disengage the diagnostic monitor, loosen the nuts and remove the monitor

➡Do not pull the wiring when handling the module.

☼ CAUTION

Always carry the module with the deployment doors facing away from the body.

    b. Remove the module by pushing on the module from inside the instrument panel.
    c. Press the orange tab and unplug the orange connector.
    d. Press the blue tab and unplug the blue connector.
    e. Disengage the white ground electrical connection and remove the module.
  12. Remove the instrument panel control opening cover and loosen the tapping screw, which is located in the center of the panel.
  13. Loosen the panel lower mounting bolts.
  14. Remove the panel side covers and loosen the side bolts.
  15. Loosen the hood release handle locknut and lower the handle until it is out of the way.
  16. Slide the instrument panel towards you until access to the back of it is possible.

17. Tag and disengage the electrical connections from the rear of the instrument panel and remove the instrument panel.

To install:

18. Engage the electrical connections to the rear of the instrument panel.

19. Place the panel in position, connect the hood release handle and tighten its locknut.

20. Loosely tighten the tapping screw which is located in the center of the panel.

21. Install and tighten the panel side bolts to 14–18 ft. lbs. (19–25 Nm).

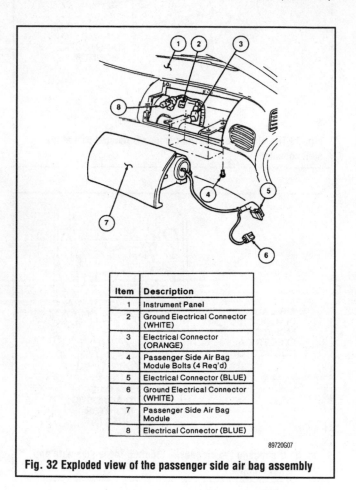

Item	Description
1	Instrument Panel
2	Ground Electrical Connector (WHITE)
3	Electrical Connector (ORANGE)
4	Passenger Side Air Bag Module Bolts (4 Req'd)
5	Electrical Connector (BLUE)
6	Ground Electrical Connector (WHITE)
7	Passenger Side Air Bag Module
8	Electrical Connector (BLUE)

89720G07

Fig. 32 Exploded view of the passenger side air bag assembly

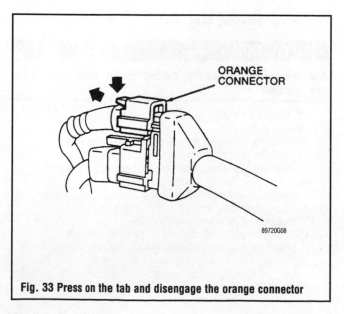

Fig. 33 Press on the tab and disengage the orange connector

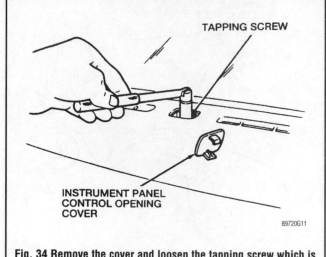

89720G11

Fig. 34 Remove the cover and loosen the tapping screw which is located in the center of the panel

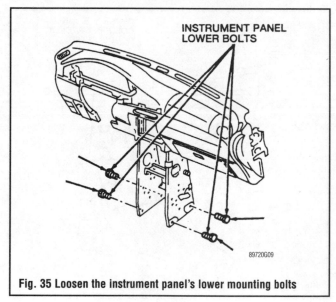

89720G09

Fig. 35 Loosen the instrument panel's lower mounting bolts

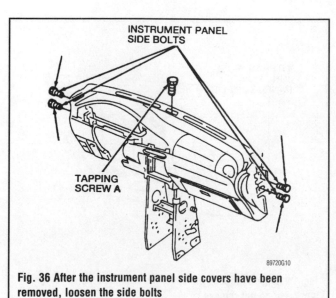

89720G10

Fig. 36 After the instrument panel side covers have been removed, loosen the side bolts

22. Tighten the tapping screw located in the center of the panel to 71–97 inch lbs. (8–11 Nm).
23. Install the panel side covers.
24. Install and tighten the panel lower bolts to 14–18 ft. lbs. (19–25 Nm).
25. Install the passenger side air bag module as follows:
  a. Engage the module's electrical connections.
  b. Position the module in the panel, then install and tighten the module retaining bolts to 80–91 inch lbs. (9–12 Nm).
26. Install the glove compartment and tighten its retaining screws.
27. Install the climate control panel assembly.
28. Install the air bag diagnostic monitor as follows:
  a. Slide the monitor onto its bracket and tighten the retaining nuts.
  b. Engage the electrical connections and install the shift console panel.
29. Install the shift console, parking brake console and instrument cluster.
30. Install the steering column as follows:
  a. Install the steering column and align the marks made on the juncture of the column intermediate shaft coupling and the lower column shaft.
  b. Install and tighten the upper column bracket bolts to 13–20 ft. lbs. (18–26 Nm).
  c. Install and tighten the lower column bracket nuts to 13–20 ft. lbs. (18–26 Nm).
  d. Install and tighten the lower column shaft lower bolt to 12–17 ft. lbs. (16–23 Nm).
  e. Install the ignition switch and multi-function switch.
31. Install the steering wheel.
32. Install the driver's side air bag module as follows:
  a. Install the module and engage its electrical connections.
  b. Install the module retaining bolts at the back of the steering wheel and tighten them to 80–115 inch lbs. (9–13 Nm).
33. Connect the negative battery cable.

Parking Brake Console

REMOVAL & INSTALLATION

▶ See Figures 37, 38 and 39

1. Remove the storage bin from the parking brake console panel by pulling it straight up.
2. Loosen the parking brake console screw, which is located in the storage bin opening.
3. Apply the parking brake and remove the parking brake access cover.

Fig. 37 Pull the storage bin straight up to remove it from the parking brake console

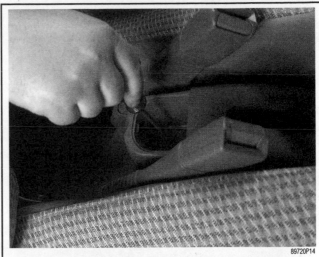

Fig. 38 Use a Phillips head screwdriver to loosen the parking brake console screw, located in the storage bin opening

Fig. 39 Lift up the rear of the console and gently disengage the retaining pins at the front. Remove the console

4. Remove the console.
To install:
5. Install the console and the access cover.
6. Release the brake and tighten the console screw.
7. Install the storage bin by pushing it down until it is fully seated.

Shift Console

REMOVAL & INSTALLATION

▶ See Figures 40, 41, 42, 43 and 44

1. Remove the parking brake console.
2. Remove the gear shift knob or handle.
3. Loosen the two console panel screws and two panel fasteners.
4. Remove the console and disengage any electrical connections.
To install:
5. Engage any electrical connections and install the shift console.
6. Tighten the panel screws and engage the fasteners.
7. Install the gear shift knob or handle.
8. Install the parking brake console.

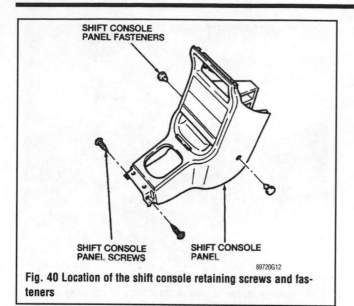

Fig. 40 Location of the shift console retaining screws and fasteners

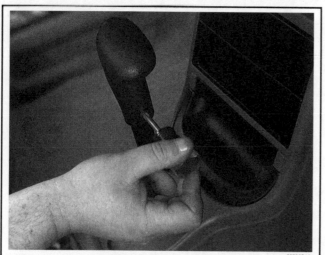

Fig. 41 Loosen the two gear shift knob retaining screws (front and side) and remove the knob

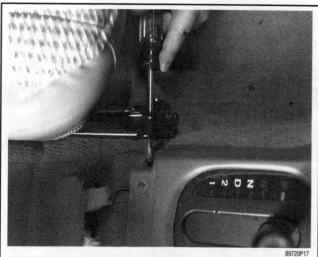

Fig. 42 Loosen the two console panel screws (access to the screws is possible through a slot in the seat rail)

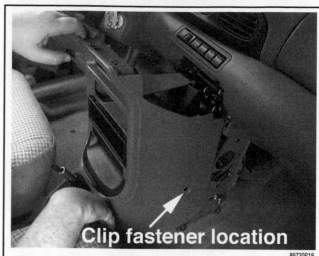

Fig. 43 Disengage the two clip fasteners (one on each side) and slide the console back

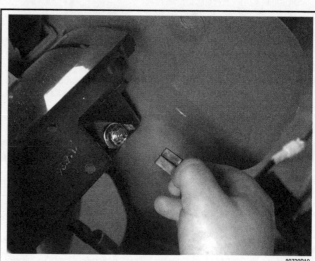

Fig. 44 Disengage all the electrical connections at the rear and remove the console

Door Panels

REMOVAL & INSTALLATION

Front and Rear

◆ See Figures 45 thru 53

1. Use a shop towel to disengage the regulator handle snapring and remove the handle.
2. Loosen the door handle trim piece screw and, if applicable, the inside door pull screw.
3. On four-door models, when removing the front door panel, loosen the two trim panel screws.
4. On two-door models, loosen the two trim panel screws, remove the trim plug and loosen the panel screw at the rear.
5. Pull the panel away from the door to disengage the retaining clips, turn the panel on an angle and move it so that the handle passes through the opening.
6. Remove the trim panel.

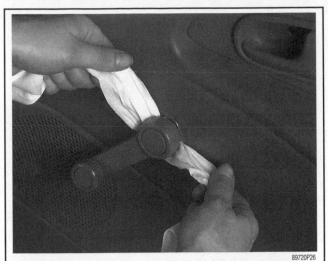

Fig. 45 A shop towel can be used to disengage the regulator handle snapring

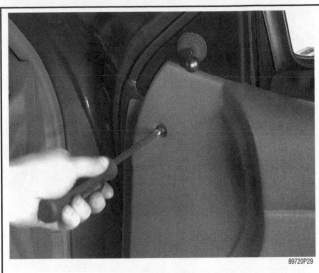

Fig. 48 Loosen the trim panel upper . . .

Fig. 46 Loosen the handle trim piece screw

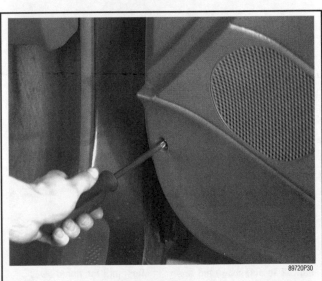

Fig. 49 . . . and lower retaining screws

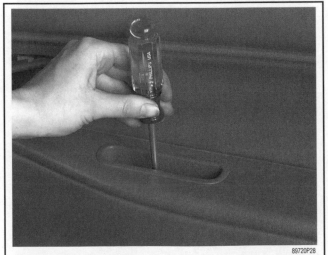

Fig. 47 Loosen the screw inside the armrest handle, if applicable

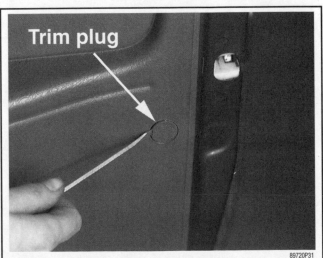

Trim plug

Fig. 50 On two-door models, remove the trim plug to access the screw beneath the plug . . .

Fig. 51 . . . then remove the screw

89720P32

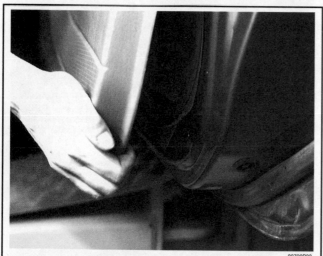

Fig. 52 To disengage the retaining clips, pull the panel away from the door

89720P33

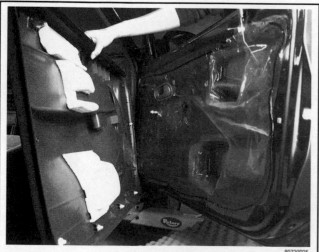

Fig. 53 Pull the handle through the opening in the panel and remove the panel

89720P35

To install:

7. Make sure all the panel retainers are present and in the correct position.

8. Guide the handle through the opening and place the panel into position.

9. Press the panel retainers until they are firmly engaged.

10. On two-door models, tighten the panel screws and install the trim plug.

11. On four-door models, when installing the front door panel, tighten the two trim panel screws.

12. Install and tighten the door handle screw and, if applicable, the inside door pull screw.

13. Install the door handle and snapring, making sure the snapring is fully engaged.

Liftgate

1. Disconnect the negative battery cable.
2. Use a prytool to carefully separate the panel from the door.
3. Disengage the luggage compartment lamp electrical connection.
4. Remove the trim panel.

To install:

5. Install the trim panel and engage the electrical connection.
6. Press on the panel fasteners until they are fully engaged and the panel is firmly attached to the liftgate.
7. Connect the negative battery cable.

Door Locks

REMOVAL & INSTALLATION

Front Door

▶ **See Figure 54**

1. Remove the front door trim panel and watershield.
2. Remove the lock cylinder retainer.
3. Disconnect the door latch rod retainer and disengage the latch connecting rod.
4. Remove the lock cylinder.

To install:

5. Install the lock cylinder.
6. Engage the latch connecting rod and rod retainer.
7. Install the lock cylinder retainer.
8. Install the watershield and trim panel.

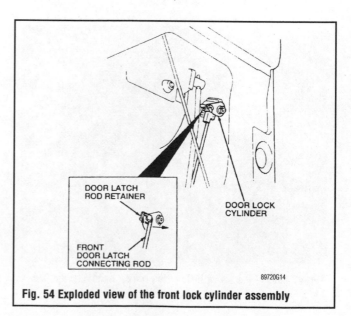

DOOR LATCH ROD RETAINER

DOOR LOCK CYLINDER

FRONT DOOR LATCH CONNECTING ROD

89720G14

Fig. 54 Exploded view of the front lock cylinder assembly

Liftgate

▶ **See Figure 55**

1. Remove the liftgate trim panel.
2. Disconnect the latch rod retainer and disengage the latch connecting rod.
3. Remove the lock cylinder retaining clip.
4. Remove the lock cylinder.

To install:

5. Install the lock cylinder and engage the retaining clip.
6. Engage the latch connecting rod and retainer.
7. Install the trim panel.

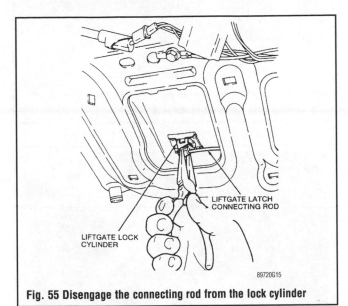

LIFTGATE LATCH
CONNECTING ROD

LIFTGATE LOCK
CYLINDER

89720G15

Fig. 55 Disengage the connecting rod from the lock cylinder

Door Glass and Regulator

REMOVAL & INSTALLATION

Front Door

▶ **See Figure 56**

1. Remove the door trim panel and watershield.
2. Lower the window and position the regulator so that access to the glass-to-regulator bolts is possible, then loosen the bolts.
3. Remove the glass through the top of the door.
4. Loosen the five regulator retaining nuts and one bolt.
5. Remove the regulator through the access hole in the door.

To install:

6. Install the regulator and retainers. Tighten the nuts to 7–9 ft. lbs. (9–13 Nm) and the bolt to 6–8 ft. lbs. (8–11 Nm).
7. Install the glass and tighten the glass-to-regulator bolts to 6–8 ft. lbs. (8–11 Nm).
8. Install the watershield and trim panel.

Rear Door

1. Remove the door trim panel and watershield.
2. Loosen the bottom glass run retainer and division bar screw.
3. Lower the window glass and pull out the weatherstrip to expose the door glass run retainer and division bar screw.
4. Loosen the screw and remove the door glass run retainer and division bar.
5. Lower the window and position the regulator so that access to the glass-to-regulator bolts is possible, then loosen the bolts.

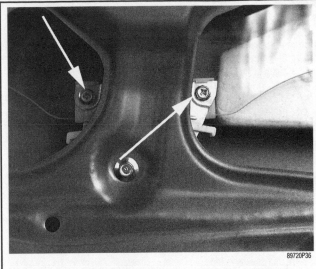

89720P36

Fig. 56 Location of the glass-to-regulator retaining bolts

6. Remove the glass through the top of the door with a rotating motion, so that the rear edge points up.
7. Remove the regulator through the access hole in the door.

To install:

8. Install the regulator and retainers. Tighten the nuts to 7–9 ft. lbs. (9–13 Nm) and the bolt to 6–8 ft. lbs. (8–11 Nm).
9. Install the glass and tighten the glass-to-regulator bolts to 6–8 ft. lbs. (8–11 Nm).
10. Install the door glass run retainer and division bar, and tighten its retaining screws.
11. Make sure the weatherstrip is properly installed.
12. Install the watershield and trim panel.

Windshield and Fixed Glass

REMOVAL & INSTALLATION

If your windshield, or other fixed window, is cracked or chipped, you may decide to replace it with a new one yourself. However, there are two main reasons why replacement windshields and other window glass should be installed only by a professional automotive glass technician: safety and cost.

The most important reason a professional should install automotive glass is for safety. The glass in the vehicle, especially the windshield, is designed with safety in mind in case of a collision. The windshield is specially manufactured from two panes of specially-tempered glass with a thin layer of transparent plastic between them. This construction allows the glass to "give" in the event that a part of your body hits the windshield during the collision, and prevents the glass from shattering, which could cause lacerations, blinding and other harm to passengers of the vehicle. The other fixed windows are designed to be tempered so that if they break during a collision, they shatter in such a way that there are no large pointed glass pieces. The professional automotive glass technician knows how to install the glass in a vehicle so that it will function optimally during a collision. Without the proper experience, knowledge and tools, installing a piece of automotive glass yourself could lead to additional harm if an accident should ever occur.

Cost is also a factor when deciding to install automotive glass yourself. Performing this could cost you much more than a professional may charge for the same job. Since the windshield is designed to break under stress, an often life saving characteristic, windshields tend to break VERY easily when an inexperienced person attempts to install one. Do-it-yourselfers buying two, three or even four windshields from a salvage yard because they have broken them during installation are common stories. Also, since the automotive glass is designed to prevent the outside elements from entering your vehicle, improper installation can lead to water and air leaks. Annoying whining noises at highway speeds from air leaks or inside body panel rusting from water leaks can add to your stress level and subtract from your wallet. After buying two or three windshields, installing them and ending up with a leak that produces a noise while driving and water damage during rainstorms, the cost of having a professional do it correctly the first time may be much more alluring. We here at Chilton, therefore, advise that you have a professional automotive glass technician service any broken glass on your vehicle.

WINDSHIELD CHIP REPAIR

▶ **See Figures 57 thru 71**

➡**Check with your state and local authorities on the laws for state safety inspection. Some states or municipalities may not allow chip repair as a viable option for correcting stone damage to your windshield.**

Although severely cracked or damaged windshields must be replaced, there is something that you can do to prolong or even prevent the need for

Fig. 59 Remove the center from the adhesive disc and peel off the backing from one side of the disc . . .

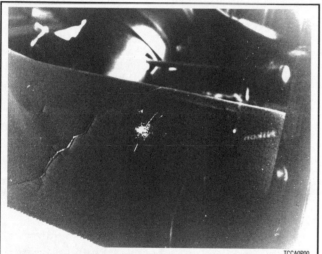

Fig. 57 Small chips on your windshield can be fixed with an aftermarket repair kit, such as the one from Loctite®

Fig. 60 . . . then press it on the windshield so that the chip is centered in the hole

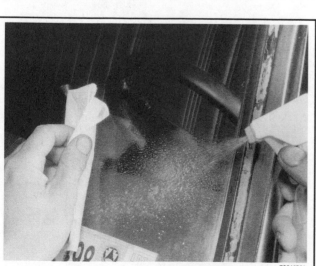

Fig. 58 To repair a chip, clean the windshield with glass cleaner and dry it completely

Fig. 61 Be sure that the tab points upward on the windshield

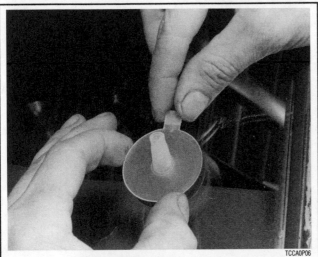

Fig. 62 Peel the backing off the exposed side of the adhesive disc . . .

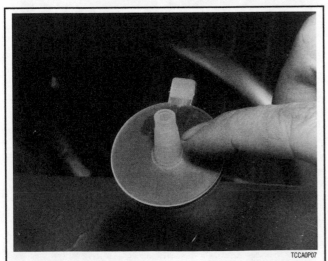

Fig. 63 . . . then position the plastic pedestal on the adhesive disc, ensuring that the tabs are aligned

Fig. 64 Press the pedestal firmly on the adhesive disc to create an adequate seal . . .

replacement of a chipped windshield. There are many companies which offer windshield chip repair products, such as Loctite's® Bullseye™ windshield repair kit. These kits usually consist of a syringe, pedestal and a sealing adhesive. The syringe is mounted on the pedestal and is used to

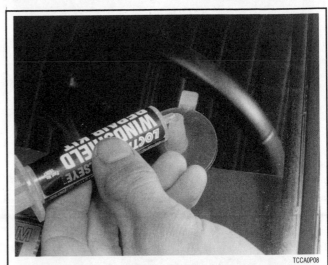

Fig. 65 . . . then install the applicator syringe nipple in the pedestal's hole

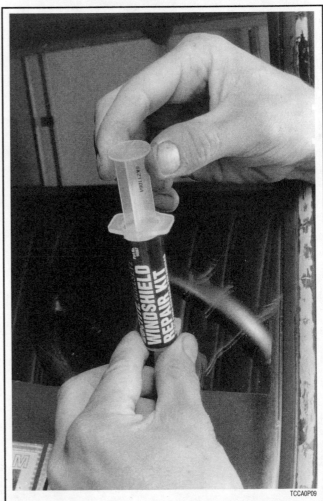

Fig. 66 Hold the syringe with one hand while pulling the plunger back with the other hand

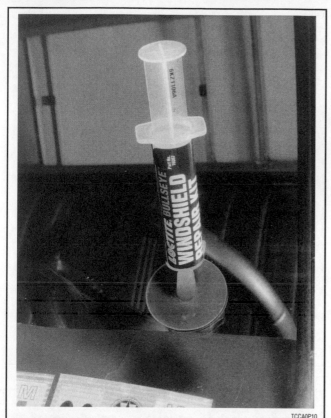

Fig. 67 After applying the solution, allow the entire assembly to sit until it has set completely

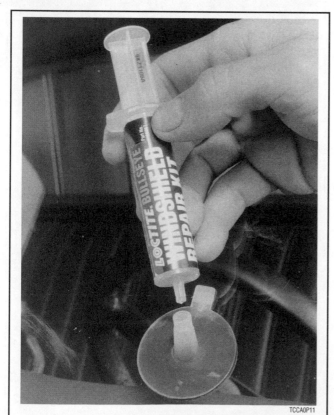

Fig. 68 After the solution has set, remove the syringe from the pedestal . . .

create a vacuum which pulls the plastic layer against the glass. This helps make the chip transparent. The adhesive is then injected which seals the chip and helps to prevent further stress cracks from developing. Refer to the sequence of photos to get a general idea of what windshield chip repair involves.

➡Always follow the specific manufacturer's instructions.

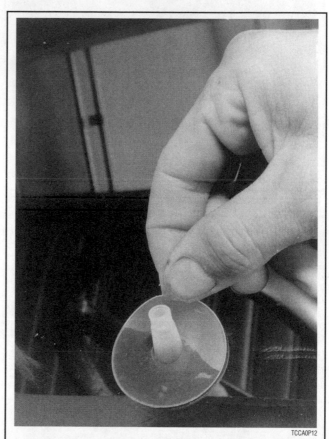

Fig. 69 . . . then peel the pedestal off of the adhesive disc . . .

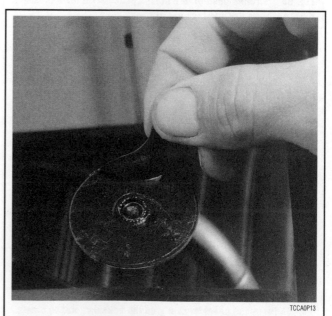

Fig. 70 . . . and peel the adhesive disc off of the windshield

Fig. 71 The chip will still be slightly visible, but it should be filled with the hardened solution

Inside Rear View Mirror

REPLACEMENT

1. Use a prytool to gently pry the cap from the mirror.
2. Loosen the mirror bracket screws and remove the mirror.
3. Installation is the reverse of removal.

ADJUSTMENT

1. If the mirror will not stay in its desired position, remove the mirror from its mounting.
2. Tighten the adjusting screw, located on the back of the mirror, until the mirror will stay in the desired position.
3. Install the mirror and make sure it will remain at the proper position.

Seats

REMOVAL & INSTALLATION

Front

1. Loosen the four seat cushion frame and spring bolts.
2. Carefully remove the seat and track assembly from the car.
To install:

➡Before installing the seat and track assembly, make sure the seat back latch and, if applicable, slide lock knob (on the two-door model's passenger seat) move freely and are not damaged.

3. Apply multi-purpose grease to all moving parts and install the seat in the car.

➡If installing the passenger seat, tighten the right-hand seat frame spring bolt on the track last.

4. Install the seat frame and spring bolts, and tighten to 28–38 ft. lbs. (38–51 Nm).

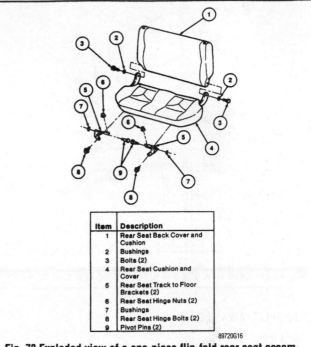

Item	Description
1	Rear Seat Back Cover and Cushion
2	Bushings
3	Bolts (2)
4	Rear Seat Cushion and Cover
5	Rear Seat Track to Floor Brackets (2)
6	Rear Seat Hinge Nuts (2)
7	Bushings
8	Rear Seat Hinge Bolts (2)
9	Pivot Pins (2)

Fig. 72 Exploded view of a one-piece flip-fold rear seat assembly

Rear

ONE-PIECE FLIP-FOLD

◆ See Figure 72

1. Loosen the rear seat hinge bolts from the front of the seat cushion and cover.
2. Flip the seat back cover and cushion forward, and loosen the hinge nuts from the car's floor.
3. Remove the seat assembly from the car.
To install:
4. Install the seat assembly and tighten the hinge nuts to 28–38 ft. lbs. (38–51 Nm).
5. Flip the seat back cover and cushion rearward, install the seat hinge bolts and tighten them to 28–38 ft. lbs. (38–51 Nm).

ONE-PIECE FOLDING

◆ See Figure 73

1. Fold the rear seat cover and cushion forward.
2. Remove the seat back-to-floor bolts and the seat back-to-floor bracket that attaches each side of the cover and cushion to the floor.
3. Fold the seat back cover forward and carefully push the back cover inward, disengaging the back cover from the pivot stud on each seat back-to-floor bracket.
4. Loosen the seat cushion bolts and remove the seat.
To install:
5. Install the seat and tighten the bolts to 28–38 ft. lbs. (38–51 Nm).
6. Engage the seat back cover to the pivot stud on each seat back-to-floor bracket and fold the seat rearward.
7. Install the seat back-to-floor brackets and bolts. Tighten the bolts to 28–38 ft. lbs. (38–51 Nm).
8. Fold the rear seat cover and cushion rearward.

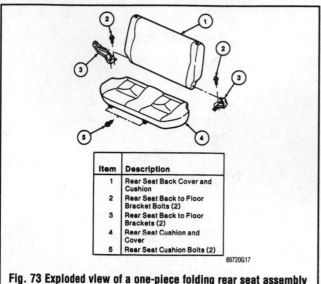

Item	Description
1	Rear Seat Back Cover and Cushion
2	Rear Seat Back to Floor Bracket Bolts (2)
3	Rear Seat Back to Floor Brackets (2)
4	Rear Seat Cushion and Cover
5	Rear Seat Cushion Bolts (2)

89720G17

Fig. 73 Exploded view of a one-piece folding rear seat assembly

50/50 SPLIT FLIP-FOLD

◆ See Figure 74

1. Remove the rear seat hinge bolts from the front of the seat cushion and cover.

2. Remove the hinge nuts from the studs on the car's floor.
3. Remove the seat assembly from the car.
To install:
4. Install the seat assembly. Tighten the seat retaining hinge nuts and bolts to 28–38 ft. lbs. (38–51 Nm).

50/50 SPLIT FOLD

◆ See Figure 75

1. Fold the rear seat back cover and cushion forward.
2. Remove the seat back-to-floor bolts and the seat back-to-floor bracket that attaches each side of the cover and cushion to the floor.
3. Remove the center hinge bolts, washers and hinge.
4. Fold the seat back cover forward and carefully push the back cover inward, disengaging the back cover from the pivot stud on each seat back-to-floor bracket.
5. Loosen the rear seat cushion bolts and remove the seat.
To install:
6. Install the seat and tighten the bolts to 28–38 ft. lbs. (38–51 Nm).
7. Engage the seat back cover to the pivot stud on each seat back-to-floor bracket and fold the seat rearward.
8. Install the center hinge, washers and bolts. Tighten the bolts to 28–38 ft. lbs. (38–51 Nm).
9. Install the seat back-to-floor brackets and bolts. Tighten the bolts to 28–38 ft. lbs. (38–51 Nm).
10. Fold the seat cover and cushion rearward.

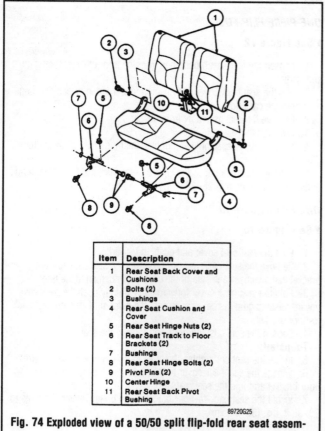

Item	Description
1	Rear Seat Back Cover and Cushions
2	Bolts (2)
3	Bushings
4	Rear Seat Cushion and Cover
5	Rear Seat Hinge Nuts (2)
6	Rear Seat Track to Floor Brackets (2)
7	Bushings
8	Rear Seat Hinge Bolts (2)
9	Pivot Pins (2)
10	Center Hinge
11	Rear Seat Back Pivot Bushing

89720G25

Fig. 74 Exploded view of a 50/50 split flip-fold rear seat assembly

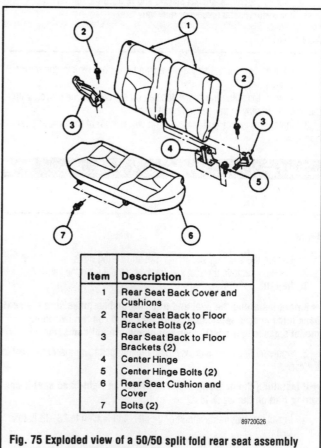

Item	Description
1	Rear Seat Back Cover and Cushions
2	Rear Seat Back to Floor Bracket Bolts (2)
3	Rear Seat Back to Floor Brackets (2)
4	Center Hinge
5	Center Hinge Bolts (2)
6	Rear Seat Cushion and Cover
7	Bolts (2)

89720G26

Fig. 75 Exploded view of a 50/50 split fold rear seat assembly

TORQUE SPECIFICATIONS

System	Component	Ft. Lbs.	Nm
Exterior			
Doors			
	Hinge-to-body bolts and nuts	13-21	17-29
	Striker retainers	13-19	18-26
Hood			
	Hinge-to-hood bolts	14-19	19-25
Liftgate			
	Hinge-to-liftgate nuts	7-9	9-12
	Hydraulic lift bolts	14-18	19-25
	Latch striker bolts	71-97 inch lbs.	8-11
Interior			
Instrument Panel and Pad			
	Panel side bolts	14-18	19-25
	Tapping screw	71-97 inch lbs.	8-11
	Panel lower bolts	14-18	19-25
	Air Bag module	80-91 inch lbs.	9-12
	Steering column upper bracket bolts	13-20	18-26
	Steering column lower bracket nuts	13-20	18-26
	Steering column lower shaft lower bolt	12-17	16-23
	Drivers side air bag module bolts	80-115 inch lbs.	9-13
Door Glass and Regulator			
	Regulator retaining nuts	7-9	9-13
	Regulator retaining bolt	6-8	8-11
	Glass-to-regulator bolts	6-8	8-11
Seats			
	Seat retaining bolts	28-38	38-51

89720C01

How to Remove Stains from Fabric Interior

For rest results, spots and stains should be removed as soon as possible. Never use gasoline, lacquer thinner, acetone, nail polish remover or bleach. Use a 3′ x 3″ piece of cheesecloth. Squeeze most of the liquid from the fabric and wipe the stained fabric from the outside of the stain toward the center with a lifting motion. Turn the cheesecloth as soon as one side becomes soiled. When using water to remove a stain, be sure to wash the entire section after the spot has been removed to avoid water stains. Encrusted spots can be broken up with a dull knife and vacuumed before removing the stain.

Type of Stain	How to Remove It
Surface spots	Brush the spots out with a small hand brush or use a commercial preparation such as K2R to lift the stain.
Mildew	Clean around the mildew with warm suds. Rinse in cold water and soak the mildew area in a solution of 1 part table salt and 2 parts water. Wash with upholstery cleaner.
Water stains	Water stains in fabric materials can be removed with a solution made from 1 cup of table salt dissolved in 1 quart of water. Vigorously scrub the solution into the stain and rinse with clear water. Water stains in nylon or other synthetic fabrics should be removed with a commercial type spot remover.
Chewing gum, tar, crayons, shoe polish (greasy stains)	Do not use a cleaner that will soften gum or tar. Harden the deposit with an ice cube and scrape away as much as possible with a dull knife. Moisten the remainder with cleaning fluid and scrub clean.
Ice cream, candy	Most candy has a sugar base and can be removed with a cloth wrung out in warm water. Oily candy, after cleaning with warm water, should be cleaned with upholstery cleaner. Rinse with warm water and clean the remainder with cleaning fluid.
Wine, alcohol, egg, milk, soft drink (non-greasy stains)	Do not use soap. Scrub the stain with a cloth wrung out in warm water. Remove the remainder with cleaning fluid.
Grease, oil, lipstick, butter and related stains	Use a spot remover to avoid leaving a ring. Work from the outisde of the stain to the center and dry with a clean cloth when the spot is gone.
Headliners (cloth)	Mix a solution of warm water and foam upholstery cleaner to give thick suds. Use only foam—liquid may streak or spot. Clean the entire headliner in one operation using a circular motion with a natural sponge.
Headliner (vinyl)	Use a vinyl cleaner with a sponge and wipe clean with a dry cloth.
Seats and door panels	Mix 1 pint upholstery cleaner in 1 gallon of water. Do not soak the fabric around the buttons.
Leather or vinyl fabric	Use a multi-purpose cleaner full strength and a stiff brush. Let stand 2 minutes and scrub thoroughly. Wipe with a clean, soft rag.
Nylon or synthetic fabrics	For normal stains, use the same procedures you would for washing cloth upholstery. If the fabric is extremely dirty, use a multi-purpose cleaner full strength with a stiff scrub brush. Scrub thoroughly in all directions and wipe with a cotton towel or soft rag.

TCCA0C01

GLOSSARY

AIR/FUEL RATIO: The ratio of air-to-gasoline by weight in the fuel mixture drawn into the engine.

AIR INJECTION: One method of reducing harmful exhaust emissions by injecting air into each of the exhaust ports of an engine. The fresh air entering the hot exhaust manifold causes any remaining fuel to be burned before it can exit the tailpipe.

ALTERNATOR: A device used for converting mechanical energy into electrical energy.

AMMETER: An instrument, calibrated in amperes, used to measure the flow of an electrical current in a circuit. Ammeters are always connected in series with the circuit being tested.

AMPERE: The rate of flow of electrical current present when one volt of electrical pressure is applied against one ohm of electrical resistance.

ANALOG COMPUTER: Any microprocessor that uses similar (analogous) electrical signals to make its calculations.

ARMATURE: A laminated, soft iron core wrapped by a wire that converts electrical energy to mechanical energy as in a motor or relay. When rotated in a magnetic field, it changes mechanical energy into electrical energy as in a generator.

ATMOSPHERIC PRESSURE: The pressure on the Earth's surface caused by the weight of the air in the atmosphere. At sea level, this pressure is 14.7 psi at 32°F (101 kPa at 0°C).

ATOMIZATION: The breaking down of a liquid into a fine mist that can be suspended in air.

AXIAL PLAY: Movement parallel to a shaft or bearing bore.

BACKFIRE: The sudden combustion of gases in the intake or exhaust system that results in a loud explosion.

BACKLASH: The clearance or play between two parts, such as meshed gears.

BACKPRESSURE: Restrictions in the exhaust system that slow the exit of exhaust gases from the combustion chamber.

BAKELITE: A heat resistant, plastic insulator material commonly used in printed circuit boards and transistorized components.

BALL BEARING: A bearing made up of hardened inner and outer races between which hardened steel balls roll.

BALLAST RESISTOR: A resistor in the primary ignition circuit that lowers voltage after the engine is started to reduce wear on ignition components.

BEARING: A friction reducing, supportive device usually located between a stationary part and a moving part.

BIMETAL TEMPERATURE SENSOR: Any sensor or switch made of two dissimilar types of metal that bend when heated or cooled due to the different expansion rates of the alloys. These types of sensors usually function as an on/off switch.

BLOWBY: Combustion gases, composed of water vapor and unburned fuel, that leak past the piston rings into the crankcase during normal engine operation. These gases are removed by the PCV system to prevent the buildup of harmful acids in the crankcase.

BRAKE PAD: A brake shoe and lining assembly used with disc brakes.

BRAKE SHOE: The backing for the brake lining. The term is, however, usually applied to the assembly of the brake backing and lining.

BUSHING: A liner, usually removable, for a bearing; an anti-friction liner used in place of a bearing.

CALIPER: A hydraulically activated device in a disc brake system, which is mounted straddling the brake rotor (disc). The caliper contains at least one piston and two brake pads. Hydraulic pressure on the piston(s) forces the pads against the rotor.

CAMSHAFT: A shaft in the engine on which are the lobes (cams) which operate the valves. The camshaft is driven by the crankshaft, via a belt, chain or gears, at one half the crankshaft speed.

CAPACITOR: A device which stores an electrical charge.

CARBON MONOXIDE (CO): A colorless, odorless gas given off as a normal byproduct of combustion. It is poisonous and extremely dangerous in confined areas, building up slowly to toxic levels without warning if adequate ventilation is not available.

CARBURETOR: A device, usually mounted on the intake manifold of an engine, which mixes the air and fuel in the proper proportion to allow even combustion.

CATALYTIC CONVERTER: A device installed in the exhaust system, like a muffler, that converts harmful byproducts of combustion into carbon dioxide and water vapor by means of a heat-producing chemical reaction.

CENTRIFUGAL ADVANCE: A mechanical method of advancing the spark timing by using flyweights in the distributor that react to centrifugal force generated by the distributor shaft rotation.

CHECK VALVE: Any one-way valve installed to permit the flow of air, fuel or vacuum in one direction only.

CHOKE: A device, usually a moveable valve, placed in the intake path of a carburetor to restrict the flow of air.

CIRCUIT: Any unbroken path through which an electrical current can flow. Also used to describe fuel flow in some instances.

CIRCUIT BREAKER: A switch which protects an electrical circuit from overload by opening the circuit when the current flow exceeds a predetermined level. Some circuit breakers must be reset manually, while most reset automatically.

COIL (IGNITION): A transformer in the ignition circuit which steps up the voltage provided to the spark plugs.

COMBINATION MANIFOLD: An assembly which includes both the intake and exhaust manifolds in one casting.

COMBINATION VALVE: A device used in some fuel systems that routes fuel vapors to a charcoal storage canister instead of venting them into the atmosphere. The valve relieves fuel tank pressure and allows fresh air into the tank as the fuel level drops to prevent a vapor lock situation.

COMPRESSION RATIO: The comparison of the total volume of the cylinder and combustion chamber with the piston at BDC and the piston at TDC.

CONDENSER: 1. An electrical device which acts to store an electrical charge, preventing voltage surges. 2. A radiator-like device in the air conditioning system in which refrigerant gas condenses into a liquid, giving off heat.

CONDUCTOR: Any material through which an electrical current can be transmitted easily.

CONTINUITY: Continuous or complete circuit. Can be checked with an ohmmeter.

COUNTERSHAFT: An intermediate shaft which is rotated by a mainshaft and transmits, in turn, that rotation to a working part.

CRANKCASE: The lower part of an engine in which the crankshaft and related parts operate.

CRANKSHAFT: The main driving shaft of an engine which receives reciprocating motion from the pistons and converts it to rotary motion.

CYLINDER: In an engine, the round hole in the engine block in which the piston(s) ride.

CYLINDER BLOCK: The main structural member of an engine in which is found the cylinders, crankshaft and other principal parts.

CYLINDER HEAD: The detachable portion of the engine, usually fastened to the top of the cylinder block and containing all or most of the combustion chambers. On overhead valve engines, it contains the valves and their operating parts. On overhead cam engines, it contains the camshaft as well.

DEAD CENTER: The extreme top or bottom of the piston stroke.

DETONATION: An unwanted explosion of the air/fuel mixture in the combustion chamber caused by excess heat and compression, advanced timing, or an overly lean mixture. Also referred to as "ping".

DIAPHRAGM: A thin, flexible wall separating two cavities, such as in a vacuum advance unit.

DIESELING: A condition in which hot spots in the combustion chamber cause the engine to run on after the key is turned off.

DIFFERENTIAL: A geared assembly which allows the transmission of motion between drive axles, giving one axle the ability to turn faster than the other.

DIODE: An electrical device that will allow current to flow in one direction only.

DISC BRAKE: A hydraulic braking assembly consisting of a brake disc, or rotor, mounted on an axle, and a caliper assembly containing, usually two brake pads which are activated by hydraulic pressure. The pads are forced against the sides of the disc, creating friction which slows the vehicle.

DISTRIBUTOR: A mechanically driven device on an engine which is responsible for electrically firing the spark plug at a predetermined point of the piston stroke.

DOWEL PIN: A pin, inserted in mating holes in two different parts allowing those parts to maintain a fixed relationship.

DRUM BRAKE: A braking system which consists of two brake shoes and one or two wheel cylinders, mounted on a fixed backing plate, and a brake drum, mounted on an axle, which revolves around the assembly.

DWELL: The rate, measured in degrees of shaft rotation, at which an electrical circuit cycles on and off.

ELECTRONIC CONTROL UNIT (ECU): Ignition module, module, amplifier or igniter. See Module for definition.

ELECTRONIC IGNITION: A system in which the timing and firing of the spark plugs is controlled by an electronic control unit, usually called a module. These systems have no points or condenser.

END-PLAY: The measured amount of axial movement in a shaft.

ENGINE: A device that converts heat into mechanical energy.

EXHAUST MANIFOLD: A set of cast passages or pipes which conduct exhaust gases from the engine.

FEELER GAUGE: A blade, usually metal, or precisely predetermined thickness, used to measure the clearance between two parts.

FIRING ORDER: The order in which combustion occurs in the cylinders of an engine. Also the order in which spark is distributed to the plugs by the distributor.

FLOODING: The presence of too much fuel in the intake manifold and combustion chamber which prevents the air/fuel mixture from firing, thereby causing a no-start situation.

FLYWHEEL: A disc shaped part bolted to the rear end of the crankshaft. Around the outer perimeter is affixed the ring gear. The starter drive engages the ring gear, turning the flywheel, which rotates the crankshaft, imparting the initial starting motion to the engine.

FOOT POUND (ft. lbs. or sometimes, ft.lb.): The amount of energy or work needed to raise an item weighing one pound, a distance of one foot.

FUSE: A protective device in a circuit which prevents circuit overload by breaking the circuit when a specific amperage is present. The device is constructed around a strip or wire of a lower amperage rating than the circuit it is designed to protect. When an amperage higher than that stamped on the fuse is present in the circuit, the strip or wire melts, opening the circuit.

GEAR RATIO: The ratio between the number of teeth on meshing gears.

GENERATOR: A device which converts mechanical energy into electrical energy.

HEAT RANGE: The measure of a spark plug's ability to dissipate heat from its firing end. The higher the heat range, the hotter the plug fires.

HUB: The center part of a wheel or gear.

HYDROCARBON (HC): Any chemical compound made up of hydrogen and carbon. A major pollutant formed by the engine as a byproduct of combustion.

HYDROMETER: An instrument used to measure the specific gravity of a solution.

INCH POUND (inch lbs.; sometimes in.lb. or in. lbs.): One twelfth of a foot pound.

INDUCTION: A means of transferring electrical energy in the form of a magnetic field. Principle used in the ignition coil to increase voltage.

INJECTOR: A device which receives metered fuel under relatively low pressure and is activated to inject the fuel into the engine under relatively high pressure at a predetermined time.

INPUT SHAFT: The shaft to which torque is applied, usually carrying the driving gear or gears.

INTAKE MANIFOLD: A casting of passages or pipes used to conduct air or a fuel/air mixture to the cylinders.

JOURNAL: The bearing surface within which a shaft operates.

KEY: A small block usually fitted in a notch between a shaft and a hub to prevent slippage of the two parts.

MANIFOLD: A casting of passages or set of pipes which connect the cylinders to an inlet or outlet source.

MANIFOLD VACUUM: Low pressure in an engine intake manifold formed just below the throttle plates. Manifold vacuum is highest at idle and drops under acceleration.

MASTER CYLINDER: The primary fluid pressurizing device in a hydraulic system. In automotive use, it is found in brake and hydraulic clutch systems and is pedal activated, either directly or, in a power brake system, through the power booster.

MODULE: Electronic control unit, amplifier or igniter of solid state or integrated design which controls the current flow in the ignition primary circuit based on input from the pick-up coil. When the module opens the primary circuit, high secondary voltage is induced in the coil.

NEEDLE BEARING: A bearing which consists of a number (usually a large number) of long, thin rollers.

OHM: (Ω) The unit used to measure the resistance of conductor-to-electrical flow. One ohm is the amount of resistance that limits current flow to one ampere in a circuit with one volt of pressure.

OHMMETER: An instrument used for measuring the resistance, in ohms, in an electrical circuit.

OUTPUT SHAFT: The shaft which transmits torque from a device, such as a transmission.

OVERDRIVE: A gear assembly which produces more shaft revolutions than that transmitted to it.

OVERHEAD CAMSHAFT (OHC): An engine configuration in which the camshaft is mounted on top of the cylinder head and operates the valve either directly or by means of rocker arms.

OVERHEAD VALVE (OHV): An engine configuration in which all of the valves are located in the cylinder head and the camshaft is located in the cylinder block. The camshaft operates the valves via lifters and pushrods.

OXIDES OF NITROGEN (NOx): Chemical compounds of nitrogen produced as a byproduct of combustion. They combine with hydrocarbons to produce smog.

OXYGEN SENSOR: Use with the feedback system to sense the presence of oxygen in the exhaust gas and signal the computer which can reference the voltage signal to an air/fuel ratio.

PINION: The smaller of two meshing gears.

PISTON RING: An open-ended ring with fits into a groove on the outer diameter of the piston. Its chief function is to form a seal between the piston and cylinder wall. Most automotive pistons have three rings: two for compression sealing; one for oil sealing.

PRELOAD: A predetermined load placed on a bearing during assembly or by adjustment.

PRIMARY CIRCUIT: the low voltage side of the ignition system which consists of the ignition switch, ballast resistor or resistance wire, bypass, coil, electronic control unit and pick-up coil as well as the connecting wires and harnesses.

PRESS FIT: The mating of two parts under pressure, due to the inner diameter of one being smaller than the outer diameter of the other, or vice versa; an interference fit.

RACE: The surface on the inner or outer ring of a bearing on which the balls, needles or rollers move.

REGULATOR: A device which maintains the amperage and/or voltage levels of a circuit at predetermined values.

RELAY: A switch which automatically opens and/or closes a circuit.

RESISTANCE: The opposition to the flow of current through a circuit or electrical device, and is measured in ohms. Resistance is equal to the voltage divided by the amperage.

RESISTOR: A device, usually made of wire, which offers a preset amount of resistance in an electrical circuit.

RING GEAR: The name given to a ring-shaped gear attached to a differential case, or affixed to a flywheel or as part of a planetary gear set.

ROLLER BEARING: A bearing made up of hardened inner and outer races between which hardened steel rollers move.

ROTOR: 1. The disc-shaped part of a disc brake assembly, upon which the brake pads bear; also called, brake disc. 2. The device mounted atop the distributor shaft, which passes current to the distributor cap tower contacts.

SECONDARY CIRCUIT: The high voltage side of the ignition system, usually above 20,000 volts. The secondary includes the ignition coil, coil wire, distributor cap and rotor, spark plug wires and spark plugs.

SENDING UNIT: A mechanical, electrical, hydraulic or electro-magnetic device which transmits information to a gauge.

SENSOR: Any device designed to measure engine operating conditions or ambient pressures and temperatures. Usually electronic in nature and designed to send a voltage signal to an on-board computer, some sensors may operate as a simple on/off switch or they may provide a variable voltage signal (like a potentiometer) as conditions or measured parameters change.

SHIM: Spacers of precise, predetermined thickness used between parts to establish a proper working relationship.

SLAVE CYLINDER: In automotive use, a device in the hydraulic clutch system which is activated by hydraulic force, disengaging the clutch.

SOLENOID: A coil used to produce a magnetic field, the effect of which is to produce work.

SPARK PLUG: A device screwed into the combustion chamber of a spark ignition engine. The basic construction is a conductive core inside of a ceramic insulator, mounted in an outer conductive base. An electrical charge from the spark plug wire travels along the conductive core and jumps a preset air gap to a grounding point or points at the end of the conductive base. The resultant spark ignites the fuel/air mixture in the combustion chamber.

SPLINES: Ridges machined or cast onto the outer diameter of a shaft or inner diameter of a bore to enable parts to mate without rotation.

TACHOMETER: A device used to measure the rotary speed of an engine, shaft, gear, etc., usually in rotations per minute.

THERMOSTAT: A valve, located in the cooling system of an engine, which is closed when cold and opens gradually in response to engine heating, controlling the temperature of the coolant and rate of coolant flow.

TOP DEAD CENTER (TDC): The point at which the piston reaches the top of its travel on the compression stroke.

TORQUE: The twisting force applied to an object.

TORQUE CONVERTER: A turbine used to transmit power from a driving member to a driven member via hydraulic action, providing changes in drive ratio and torque. In automotive use, it links the driveplate at the rear of the engine to the automatic transmission.

TRANSDUCER: A device used to change a force into an electrical signal.

TRANSISTOR: A semi-conductor component which can be actuated by a small voltage to perform an electrical switching function.

TUNE-UP: A regular maintenance function, usually associated with the replacement and adjustment of parts and components in the electrical and fuel systems of a vehicle for the purpose of attaining optimum performance.

TURBOCHARGER: An exhaust driven pump which compresses intake air and forces it into the combustion chambers at higher than atmospheric pressures. The increased air pressure allows more fuel to be burned and results in increased horsepower being produced.

VACUUM ADVANCE: A device which advances the ignition timing in response to increased engine vacuum.

VACUUM GAUGE: An instrument used to measure the presence of vacuum in a chamber.

VALVE: A device which control the pressure, direction of flow or rate of flow of a liquid or gas.

VALVE CLEARANCE: The measured gap between the end of the valve stem and the rocker arm, cam lobe or follower that activates the valve.

VISCOSITY: The rating of a liquid's internal resistance to flow.

VOLTMETER: An instrument used for measuring electrical force in units called volts. Voltmeters are always connected parallel with the circuit being tested.

WHEEL CYLINDER: Found in the automotive drum brake assembly, it is a device, actuated by hydraulic pressure, which, through internal pistons, pushes the brake shoes outward against the drums.

MASTER
INDEX